WORK IN AMERICA

WORK IN AMERICA

An Encyclopedia of History, Policy, and Society

VOLUME 1: A–M

Edited by
Carl E. Van Horn and Herbert A. Schaffner

Foreword by
Ray Marshall, former U.S. Secretary of Labor

A B C CLIO

Santa Barbara, California   Denver, Colorado   Oxford, England

Library of Congress Cataloging-in-Publication Data

Work in America: an encyclopedia of history, policy, and society /
edited by Carl E. Van Horn and Herbert A. Schaffner; foreword by Ray Marshall.

p. cm.

Includes bibliographical references and index.

ISBN 1-57607-676-8 (2 v. : hardcover : alk. paper) 1-57607-677-6 (e-book)

1. Work—United States—Encyclopedias. 2. Working class—United States—Encyclopedias. 3. Labor policy—United States—Encyclopedias. 4. Labor market—United States—Encyclopedias. 5. Industrial relations—United States—Encyclopedias. I. Van Horn, Carl E. II. Schaffner, Herbert A., 1959–

HD8066.W637 2003
331'.0973'03—dc22

2003018708

07 06 05 04 03 10 9 8 7 6 5 4 3 2 1

This book is also available on the World Wide Web as an e-book. Visit abc-clio.com for details.

ABC-CLIO, Inc.
130 Cremona Drive, P.O. Box 1911
Santa Barbara, California 93116-1911
This book is printed on acid-free paper.

Manufactured in the United States of America.

ADVISORY BOARD

CONTENTS

Work in America

VOLUME ONE, A–M

VOLUME TWO, N–Z

CONTRIBUTORS AND THEIR ENTRIES

Steven E. Abraham
School of Business, State University of New York at Oswego
Oswego, New York
Employee Retirement Income Security Act
Equal Employment Opportunity Commission
Equal Pay Act
Glass Ceiling
Job Security
Layoffs
Pensions
Sexual Harassment
Workers Compensation

Vivyan C. Adair
Department of Women's Studies, Hamilton College
Clinton, New York
Asian Americans and Work
Great Depression
Living Wage
Medicaid
Wage and Income Gaps
Women and Work
Work First
Work in Literature
Working Class

Nikol G. Alexander-Floyd
Black Studies, Center for Interdisciplinary Studies, Virginia Polytechnic and State University
Blacksburg, Virginia
Pell Grants

Natalie Ammarell
Human Service Systems
Chapel Hill, North Carolina
American Association of Retired Persons
Comprehensive Employment and Training Act
Employment and Training Administration
Job Training Partnership Act

Roland Anglin
New Jersey Public Policy Research Institute, Rutgers, The State University of New Jersey
New Brunswick, New Jersey
African Americans and Work

Derek Barker
Department of Political Science, Rutgers, The State University of New Jersey
New Brunswick, New Jersey
Justice for Janitors
Knights of Labor

Bob Batchelor
Independent Scholar
San Rafael, California
The Dot-com Revolution
E-commerce

William J. Bauer Jr.
Department of History, University of Oklahoma
Norman, Oklahoma
Cowboys
Homestead Strike
Ironworkers
Native Americans and Work

Chris Benner
Department of Geography, Pennsylvania State University
University Park, Pennsylvania
Careers
Contingent and Temporary Workers
Lifelong Learning
New Economy
Professionals
Silicon Valley

Paget Berger
John J. Heldrich Center for Workforce Development, Rutgers, The State University of New Jersey
New Brunswick, New Jersey
Corporate Consolidation and Reengineering
Total Quality Management

Mythreyi Bhargavan
American College of Radiology
Reston, Virginia
Health Insurance
Job Benefits
Nurses and Doctors

Monica Bielski
Department of Labor and Employment Studies, Rutgers, The State University of New Jersey
New Brunswick, New Jersey
Domestic Partner Benefits
Gays at Work
Rosie the Riveter

Joseph Blasi
School of Management and Labor Relations, Rutgers, The State University of New Jersey
New Brunswick, New Jersey
Employee Stock Ownership

Timothy G. Borden
Independent Scholar
Toledo, Ohio
Automotive Industry
Ford, Henry
General Motors
Hawthorne Plant Experiments
Manufacturing Jobs
Reuther, Walter
Rust Belt
United Auto Workers

Susan Roth Breitzer
Department of History, University of Iowa
Iowa City, Iowa
Child Labor
Civilian Conservation Corps
Garment/Textile Industries
Greenspan, Alan
Haymarket Square Incident
Immigrants and Work
Lowell Strike
New Deal
Piecework
Randolph, Phillip A.
Servants and Maids
Teaching
Tenure, Academic

Nina Brown
Department of Anthropology, University of California–Santa Barbara
Santa Barbara, California
Postindustrial Workforce

John W. Budd
Industrial Relations Center, University of Minnesota
Minneapolis, Minnesota
Collective Bargaining
Fair Labor Standards Act
International Labor Organization
Railway Labor Act
Right to Work
Strikes
National Labor Relations Act
Worksharing

Brenda Choresi Carter
American Studies Program, Yale University
New Haven, Connecticut
White Collar

Debra L. Casey
Division of Social and Behavioral Sciences, Pennsylvania State University, Abington College
Abington, Pennsylvania
Federal Unemployment Tax and Insurance System
Humphrey-Hawkins Act
Prevailing Wage Laws
Terkel, Studs
Whyte, William

Jennifer M. Cleary
John J. Heldrich Center for Workforce Development, Rutgers, The State University of New Jersey
New Brunswick, New Jersey
Green Cards
Job Placement and Recruitment Firms

N.C. Christopher Couch
Department of Comparative Literature, University of Massachusetts, Amherst
Amherst, Massachusetts
Work in Visual Arts

Sandra L. Dahlberg
Department of English, University of Houston
Houston, Texas
Affirmative Action
Day Laborers
Lewis, Sinclair
Minimum Wage
On-the-Job Training
Sinclair, Upton
Steinbeck, John
Work in Literature

James I. Deutsch
George Washington University
Washington, DC
Veterans

Victor G. Devinatz
Department of Management and Quantitative Methods, College of Business, Illinois State University
Normal, Illinois
Communism in the U.S. Trade Union Movement
Industrial Workers of the World
Meany, George

K. A. Dixon
John J. Heldrich Center for Workforce Development, Rutgers, The State University of New Jersey
New Brunswick, New Jersey
Americans with Disabilities Act
Dilbert
Disability and Work
Estate Tax
Food Service Industry
Severance Pay
Swing Shift
Time Cards
Vacations

Clifford B. Donn
Department of Industrial Relations and Human Resource Management, Le Moyne College
Syracuse, New York
Maritime Trades and Work

Ariana Funaro
Independent Scholar
Somerset, New Jersey
Elder Care
Immigration Reform and Control Act
Summer Jobs

Karin A. Garver
New Jersey Department of Education
Trenton, New Jersey
Education Reform and the Workforce
Guilds
Job Skills
Labor Force
Labor Market
Profit Sharing
Recesssion

Sharon Gormley
ACCESS Project, Hamilton College
Clinton, New York
Asian Americans and Work
Women and Work

Richard A. Greenwald
Humanities Department, U.S. Merchant Marine Academy
Kings Point, New York
Perkins, Francis
Roosevelt, Eleanor
Roosevelt, Franklin
Sweatshops

Sarah B. Gyarfas
John J. Heldrich Center for Workforce Development, Rutgers, The State University of New Jersey
New Brunswick, New Jersey
Communications Workers of America
Council of Economic Advisers
Dos Passos, John
Earnings and Education
Industrial Engineering
Whitman, Walt
Works Progress Administration

D. A. Hamlin
Department of English, Rutgers, The State University of New Jersey
New Brunswick, New Jersey
International Business Machines

Lawrence F. Hanley
Department of English, The City College of The City University of New York
New York, New York
Blue Collar
Work in Television

Joyce A. Hanson
Department of History, California State University–San Bernardino
San Bernardino, California
African American Women and Work
Triangle Shirtwaist Fire

Jennifer Harrison
The College of William and Mary
Williamsburg, Virginia
Civil Service
E-learning
Literacy
National Education Association

Leela Hebbar
John J. Heldrich Center for Workforce Development, Rutgers, The State University of New Jersey
New Brunswick, New Jersey
Apprenticeship

Caroline Heldman
Department of Political Science, Whittier College
Whittier, California
Secretaries
World Trade Organization

Scott A. Jeffrey
Center for Decision Research, Graduate School of Business, University of Chicago
Chicago, Illinois
Bonuses
High-Performance Workforce

Jesse Keyes
Edward J. Bloustein School of Planning and Public Policy, Rutgers, The State University of New Jersey
New Brunswick, New Jersey
Maquiladora *Zone*
Worker Housing

Julie Kimmel
Philadelphia University
Philadelphia, Pennsylvania
Deming, W. Edwards
Industrial Psychology
Personnel Management
Taylor, Frederick

Steven Koczak Jr.
New York State Senate Research Service
Albany, New York
Part-Time Work
Workday

Douglas Kruse
School of Management and Labor Relations, Rutgers, The State University of New Jersey
New Brunswick, New Jersey
Employee Stock Ownership

Geoffrey Kurtz
Department of Political Science, Rutgers, The State University of New Jersey
New Brunswick, New Jersey
Solidarity

Albert Vetere Lannon
Emeritus, Labor Studies, Laney College
Oakland, California
Drug Testing and Substance Abuse in the Workplace
Sayles, John
Work in Film

Elayne M. Marinos
Independent Scholar
Manalapan, New Jersey
Defined Benefit/Defined Contribution Plans
Manpower, Inc.

Vernon Mogensen
Kingsborough Community College, CUNY
Brooklyn, New York
Ergonomics
Stress and Violence in the Workplace
Workplace Safety

Joshua Moses
Independent Scholar
Jersey City, New Jersey
Capitalism
Occupations and Occupational Trends in the United States
Socialism

Raissa Muhutdinova-Foroughi
Department of Political Science, University of Utah
Salt Lake City, Utah
Democratic Socialism
Federal Reserve Board
Globalization and Workers
Industrial Revolution and Assembly Line Work
Secretary of Labor, U.S.
Social Security Act

Janet Butler Munch
Lehman College of the City University of New York (CUNY)
Bronx, New York
Baldrige Awards
Bureau of Labor Statistics
Mother Jones

Mark Myers
Department of History, West Virginia University
Morgantown, West Virginia
Black Lung Disease
Lewis, John
Scrip

Mitchell Newton-Matza
Department of History and Political Science, University of St. Francis
Joliet, Illinois
Meatpacking Industry
Sherman Antitrust Act

Katie Otis
History Department, University of North Carolina at Chapel Hill
Chapel Hill, North Carolina
Homework
Internships
Older Workers
Retirement

Denise A. Pierson-Balik
John J. Heldrich Center for Workforce Development and Department of Political Science, Rutgers, The State University of New Jersey
New Brunswick, New Jersey
Child Care
Comparable Worth
Family and Medical Leave Act
Mommy Track
Pay Equity
Temporary Assistance for Needy Families
Welfare to Work

Edwin R. Render
Louis D. Brandeis School of Law, University of Louisville
Louisville, Kentucky
Arbitration

Government Organizations

Theories and Systems of the Economy, Management, and Human Capital

Public Policy and Legislation

Arts and Media

Diversity and Discrimination in the Workplace

Home and Family

Education and Workforce Training

Immigration Issues

FOREWORD

This comprehensive work is guided at its core by an in-depth understanding of the essential nature of globalization reshaping virtually every facet of human activity in the United States and around the world. Competition and survival in the new global economy are driven by knowledge and innovation at all levels of the workforce. The student, the worker, the teacher, the scholar, and the entrepreneur: all need to understand how the rules of the global economy are being made—and will be made for years to come. Human potential and ability make the difference. In a book I wrote with Marc Tucker a few years back titled *Thinking for a Living: Education and the Wealth of Nations,* we emphasized that workers at the point of production must be able to think and decide for themselves, and we pointed to the need for national policies that would build ladders of training and skill development from high school through community college and other educational institutions. The lives of U. S. workers and employers, we found, are a constant search for new and relevant skills and insights that provide security and opportunity. Of course workers face personal, social, and institutional barriers to achieving the knowledge that will keep their skills razor-sharp. Governments, employers, worker groups, unions, schools, faith-based organizations, and other institutions all must recognize the "knowledge gaps" faced by workers and find ways within their institutional limits to help bridge those gaps.

Work in America: An Encyclopedia of History, Policy, and Society is a source of the trustworthy knowledge and research that all of us, especially students, require for educational and career achievement. It provides a thoughtful source for plumbing the new realities of our knowledge and innovation-driven global economy. The editors, along with dozens of nationally well-regarded scholars, analysts, and writers, have provided an intellectual blueprint to the realities of our competitive, innovation-driven economy and the implications and effects of these changes upon critical institutions. Every significant area of economic and work life and scholarship is addressed herein. Contributed entries of quality and depth address business and industry, union and labor relations, the importance of education and training, the nature of compensation and benefits, major demographic and social trends, economic principles, law and public policy, government organizations, arts and the media, home and family, and the major systems of thought that have shaped our knowledge of the economy, business management, and human capital. The editors address developing trends of great importance to the future U. S. economy and the individuals who shape policy, including entries on immigration, welfare and the working poor, discrimination and diversity, and the expansion of female participation in the workforce and work-family concerns. The entries were not assigned to advance the interests of narrow ideologies or perspectives but to incorporate the best research and sources from all major points of view. For those who seek further exploration, the lists of recommended further reading and research are treasure troves of the best analysis, writing, and scholarship in every aspect of employment, labor, and economic study. You need no other tool to begin a journey of discovery into the U.S. workforce and the scholars who study it.

It is of little surprise to me that the wise architects of this work are Dr. Carl E. Van Horn and Herb Schaffner of the John J. Heldrich Center for Workforce Development at Rutgers University. The Heldrich Center has become one of the leading academically based centers in the United States for the study and improvement of the U.S. workforce and economy. Its research and applied studies are followed and used by policymakers in state and federal governments as well as in the academy. Its national *Work Trends* surveys of the U.S. workforce have earned wide respect and attention and are invaluable to many researchers. The editors were able to draw upon the center's respected policy and research staff to contribute many significant entries to this work. It is clear from the scope and depth of the work that the Heldrich Center gave this enterprise its full commitment and resources. To everyone who cares to understand this economy and his or her place in it—to all of those who are thinking for a living—I recommend *Work in America* as a faithful and reliable companion.

Ray Marshall

U.S. Secretary of Labor, 1976–1980
Professor Emeritus
Audre and Bernard Rapoport Centennial Chair in Economics and Public Affairs
Chair, National Advisory Committee,
Ray Marshall Center for the Study of Human Resources
University of Texas
March 2003

their skills and workplace autonomy in the early nineteenth century, white workingmen constructed an identity of whiteness to compensate for their feelings of alienation and degradation experienced in the workplace. Through this formulation white workers viewed the African-American population as the "other" and began to treat wealthy white men, their class adversaries, as racial allies. The emergence of "whiteness studies" within U.S. labor history has generated many proponents in support of the whiteness framework (Holt 1994; Lott 1995**(1993 in references)**; Barrett 2001; Nelson 2001) as well as critics (Towers 1998; Arneson(**Arnesen in references.)** 2001; Brody 2001; Reed 2001).

The emergence of African American labor scholarship was rooted in the old labor history, which condemned the racism of white workers, argued that all workers shared common interests, and called for the unity of black and white labor (Trotter 1994). Later works focused on the proletarianization of African American workers in different geographic locations (Trotter 1985, 1990), and the building of African American unions (Harris 1977) or interracial unions (Rachleff 1984; Arneson(**Arnesen in references.)** 1991). Studies also have been conducted demonstrating the interrelationship between the roles of African American workers, interracial unions, and the early civil rights movement (Korstad and Lichtenstein 1988; Halpern 1991; Stein 1991; Honey 1993). Finally, there have been historical works documenting the role of African American labor radicalism (Painter 1979; Naiso 1983; Kelley 1990).

With respect to Latino labor history, Guerin-Gonzales (1994a) discusses in great detail the twentieth-century research in the field, from the earliest studies in the 1920s through the early 1990s. According to Guerin-Gonzales (1994a), much research in this field focuses on farm labor, including well-known studies of Mexican immigrant and Mexican American workers such as the monograph by McWilliams (1939) and two books by Ernesto Galarza (1964, 1970). These latter two works discuss the plight of the farmworkers, which is brought on by the California agriculture industry's discriminatory labor relations practices, and documents the attempts of these workers to organize labor unions from the 1940s through the 1970s.

Many works have been written of the organizing, struggles, and strikes of the United Farm Workers and the leadership role played by Cesar Chavez in the 1960s and the early 1970s (Dunne 1967; Mathiessen 1969; Day 1971; Taylor 1975; Kushner 1975; Levy 1975).

Concerning Asian American labor, Friday (1994a) points out that these workers were virtually ignored in labor scholarship until Jones's (1970) article appeared in *Labor History,* and it was not until 1984 that five more articles in the field had been published in the journal (Ichioka 1980; Masson and Guimary 1981; Takaki 1982; Posadas 1982; Almaguer 1984). Much of the literature related to Asian American labor appears within the context of broader studies of the Asian American experience and is found in a variety of history, ethnohistory, sociological, industrial relations, and economics journals (Friday 1994a). Major books in the field include Kwong (1979), Takaki (1983), Cheng and Bonacich (1984), Kodama-Nishimoto, Nishimoto, and Oshiro (1984), Beechert (1985), Yu (1992), and Friday (1994b).

During World War II, U.S. labor economics began to move away from the purely historical-institutional approach of the Wisconsin School. With a significant expansion in union membership based on the organization of the basic industries (auto, rubber, steel, etc.) by the mid-1940s, labor economists became interested in how collective bargaining affected union wage policies. Books by Dunlop (1944) and Ross (1948) offered alternative theories and dominated discussion of union wage policy throughout the late 1940s and early 1950s. Dunlop (1944) viewed trade union behavior to be best represented by an economic model in which the organization functioned as a market enterprise. In contrast, Ross (1948) theorized the trade union as primarily a political entity that operated within the context of an economic environment.

Throughout the 1950s and early 1960s, a primary interest of labor economists remained how unionism affected wage determination; studies were performed to determine how collective bargaining impacted wage rates in various industries (Rees 1951; Sobotka 1953; Sobel 1954; Rayack 1958; Lurie 1961). During this era, the classic treatment of this subject was Lewis's (1963) book, which labor economists acknowledge as a major impetus toward the development of an analytical and quantitative approach to labor economics.

In addition to these wage determination studies, in the late 1950s and early 1960s, labor economists became interested in the concept of human capital, which is capital embodied in people as opposed to factories, machinery, etc. Pioneering scholars in the development of human capital theory include Mincer (1958), Schultz (1961), and Becker (1964) who examined issues such as the rate of return on investment in formal schooling, on-the-job training, etc. By the mid-1970s, more than 100 studies dealing with human capital theory, including criticisms (Berg 1971; Thurow 1972; Bowles and Gintis 1975), had been published in the labor economic literature.

Although the orientation of U.S. labor history away from the Wisconsin School began approximately during the mid-twentieth century, the postwar decade from approximately 1945 through 1960 represented the peak of U.S. industrial relations research. This fifteen-year period coincided with the peak of union density in the United States (35 percent) and the inception of a major academic journal in the field, *Industrial and Labor Relations Review* (1947). During this era, much industrial relations research was multidisciplinary in nature, with significant contributions coming from scholars in the fields of economics, history, law, psychology, and sociology (Derber et al. 1953; Kornhauser, Dubin, and Ross 1954; Golden and Parker 1955). And at the end of the 1950s, Dunlop's (1958) pathbreaking theoretical work , which provided a general theory of the field, appeared, arguing that the major industrial relations actors were directly impacted by the web of rules that were found in every industrial relations system. Even after this book's publication, scholars argued that industrial relations lacked an integrative theoretical framework (Chamberlain 1960; Aronson 1961; Derber 1964; Heneman 1969; Somers 1969).

In the 1960s, the dominant industrial relations monograph was Walton and McKersie's (1965) classic text. A second major academic journal, *Industrial Relations* (1961), appeared at the start of the decade as did a significant cross-cultural study (Kerr, Dunlop, Harbison, and Myers 1960). This book argued in favor of the "convergence hypothesis," that is, the belief that the industrialization process leads the economic, political, and social systems of nations to converge to a single measure such as an open society, a dramatic decrease in class conflict, and an increasing role for the government in labor market regulation.

Although there were no books that dominated the field in the 1970s, there was increasing growth of U.S. public sector unionism aided by President Kennedy's issuance of Executive Order 10988 in 1962, which gave most public sector employees the right to bargain collectively, and the passage of state laws. The *Journal of Collective Negotiations in the Public Sector* (1972) emerged and began to publish scholarly research on public sector collective bargaining. During the 1980s, three scholarly monographs were written, devoted to theory construction that critically impacted industrial relations (Barbash 1984; Freeman and Medoff 1984; Kochan, Katz, and McKersie 1986). Barbash (1984), writing in the tradition of the Wisconsin School, conceptualized employment relationship problems to be rooted in the conflict between management's emphasis on achieving efficiency and the workers' desire for job security. Freeman and Medoff (1984) developed the exit/voice model of trade unionism in which they argue that voice mechanisms, such as grievance procedures in labor contracts, help increase economic efficiency through reduced employee turnover, increased productivity, and improved managerial behavior. Finally, Kochan, Katz, and McKersie (1986) created a strategic choice framework for analyzing the development and interrelationship of union and nonunion economic sectors. Another theoretical contribution during this decade includes Wheeler's (1985) integrative theory of industrial conflict. In addition, this decade saw the emergence the *Journal of Labor Research* (1980), and the research volume series, *Advances in Industrial and Labor Relations* (1985), which contained numerous scholarly articles on important industrial relations topics.

The 1990s brought a continuing decline in union density. Labor advocates and experts supported a variety of reforms to expand union influence but no new governmental legislation, extending the rights of employees to organize unions or to collectively bargain, was passed during this decade. However, two federal laws, the Americans with Disabilities Act (ADA) and the Family Medical Leave Act (FMLA), were enacted at this time, which expanded the rights of workers as individual employees. The ADA (1991) mandated that employers make reasonable accommodations for disabled workers who were qualified to perform the job, and the FMLA (1993) provided employees with up to twelve weeks of unpaid leave per year to deal with family medical emergencies.

During this time, when individual employment rights were expanding while unions remained on the defensive, academic interest in alternatives to traditional trade unionism and collective bargaining as well as nonunion employment relations appeared on industrial relations scholars' agenda. Jacoby (1997) demonstrated the resilience of the nonunion model of U.S. employment relations and showed how it was able to become the dominant model of employment relations during the last few decades of the twentieth century. At the end of the twentieth century, several scholars outlined alternatives to traditional trade unionism, which provide employees with voice and some form of collective representation (Kaufman 2000; Kaufman and Taras 2000).

With the voluminous research conducted within the new labor history paradigm during the last four decades, Brody (1979), Montgomery (1980), Kazin (1987), and Kimeldorf (1991) have called for a synthesis of the multitude of studies of different groups of workers located in various geographies and industries. In spite of all of the criticisms launched against the Wisconsin School of labor history, the Commons-Perlman framework remains the touchstone for much research, and the only coherent synthesis, in U.S. labor history (Brody 1979; Montgomery 1980; Kazin 1987; Kimeldorf 1991). And although the major U.S. industrial relations journals still carry articles on trade unionism and collective bargaining, Kaufman (1993, 180) calls for industrial relations scholars to return to "cross-disciplinary research, the collection of primary data, interviews with company and union officials, and immersion in the nitty-gritty of institutional details and daily practice." This is the methodology that was used by the Wisconsin School labor scholars in the first few decades of the twentieth century. Thus, in the first decade of the twenty-first century, the Wisconsin School still casts a large shadow over the fields of U.S. labor history and industrial relations.

Victor G. Devinatz

References

Alexander, Robert J. 1981. *The Right Opposition: The Lovestoneites and the International Communist Opposition of the 1930s.* Westport, CT: Greenwood Press.

———. 1991. *International Trotskyism, 1929–1985: A Documented Analysis of the Movement.* Durham, NC: Duke University Press.

Almaguer, Tomas. 1984. "Racial Domination and Class Conflict in Capitalist Agriculture: The Oxnard Sugar Beet Workers' Strike of 1903." *Labor History* 25: 325–350.

Anderson, Karen Tucker. 1982. "Last Hired, First Fired: Black Women Workers during World War II." *Journal of American History* 69: 82–97.

Arnesen, Eric. 1991. *Waterfront Workers of New Orleans: Race, Class, and Politics, 1863–1923.* New York: Oxford University Press.

———. 2001. "Whiteness and the Historian's Imagination." *International Labor and Working-Class History* 60: 3–32.

Aronson, Robert L. 1961. "Research and Writing in Industrial Relations—Are They Intellectually Respectable?" Pp. 19–44 in *Essays on Industrial Relations Research-Problems and Prospects.* Ann Arbor: Institute of Labor and Industrial Relations, University of Michigan and Wayne State University.

Ashworth, John H. 1915. *The Helper and American Trade Unions.* Baltimore: Johns Hopkins University Press.

Barbash, Jack. 1984. *The Elements of Industrial Relations.* Madison: University of Wisconsin Press.

Barnard, John. 1983. *Walter Reuther and the Rise of the Auto Workers.* Boston: Little, Brown.

Barnett, George E. 1926. *Chapters on Machinery and Labor.* Cambridge, MA: Harvard University Press.

Baron, Ava, ed. 1991. *Work Engendered: Toward a New History of American Labor.* Ithaca, NY: Cornell University Press.

Barrett, James R. 1999. *William Z. Foster and the Tragedy of American Radicalism.* Urbana: University of Illinois Press.

———. 2001. "Whiteness Studies: Anything Here for Historians of the Working Class?" *International Labor and Working-Class History* 60: 33–42.

———. 2002. "Revolution and Personal Crisis: William Z. Foster, Personal Narrative, and the Subjective in the History of American Communism." *Labor History* 43: 465–482.

Becker, Gary S. 1964. *Human Capital.* New York: National Bureau of Economic Research.

Beechert, Edward D. 1985. *Working in Hawaii: A Labor History.* Honolulu: University of Hawaii Press.

Benson, Susan Porter. 1986. *Counter Cultures: Saleswomen, Managers, and Customers in American Department Stores, 1890–1940.* Urbana: University of Illinois Press.

Berg, Ivar. 1971. *Education and Jobs: The Great Training Robbery.* Boston: Beacon Press.

Bernstein, Irving. 1960. *The Lean Years: A History of the American Worker, 1920–1933.* Boston: Houghton Mifflin.

———. 1970. *Turbulent Years: A History of the American Worker, 1933–1941.* Boston: Houghton Mifflin.

Bimba, Anthony. 1927. *The History of the American Working Class.* New York: International Publishers.

Blewett, Mary H. 1983. "Work, Gender and the Artisan Tradition in New England Shoemaking, 1780–1860." *Journal of Social History* 17: 221–248.

———. 1988. *Men, Women and Work: Class, Gender and Protest in the New England Shoe Industry, 1830–1920.* Urbana: University of Illinois Press.

Bowles, Samuel, and Herbert Gintis. 1975. "The Problem with Human Capital Theory—A Marxian Critique." *American Economic Review* 65: 74–82.

Braverman, Harry. 1974. *Labor and Monopoly Capital: The Degradation of Work in the Twentieth Century.* New York: Monthly Review Press.

Brody, David. 1960. *Steelworkers in America: The Nonunion Era.* Cambridge, MA: Harvard University Press.

———. 1965. *Labor in Crisis: The Steel Strike of 1919.* Philadelphia: Lippincott.

———. 1979. "The Old Labor History and the New: In Search of An American Working Class." *Labor History* 20: 111–126.

———. 1987. "The Origins of Modern Steel Unionism: The SWOC Era." Pp. 13–29 in *Forging a Union in Steel.* Edited by Paul F. Clark, Peter Gottlieb, and Donald Kennedy. Ithaca, NY: ILR Press.

———. 2001. "Charismatic History: Pros and Cons." *International Labor and Working-Class History* 60: 43–47.

Burawoy, Michael. 1979. *Manufacturing Consent.* Chicago: University of Chicago Press.

———. 1985. *The Politics of Production.* London: Verso.

Chamberlain, Neil. 1960. "Issues for the Future." Pp. 101–109 in *Proceedings of the Thirteenth Annual Meeting, Industrial Relations Research Association.* Madison: IRRA.

Cheng, Lucie, and Edna Bonacich, eds. 1984. *Labor Immigration under Capitalism: Asian Workers in the United States before World War II.* Berkeley: University of California Press.

Clive, Alan. 1979. "Women Workers in World War II: Michigan as a Test Case." *Labor History* 20: 44–72.

Cobble, Dorothy Sue. 1991. *Dishing it Out: Waitresses and their Unions in the Twentieth Century.* Urbana: University of Illinois Press.

Cochran, Bert. 1977. *Labor and Communism: The Struggle That Shaped American Unions.* Princeton, NJ: Princeton University Press.

Commons, John R. et al., eds. 1910–1911. *A Documentary History of American Industrial Society.* 11 vols. Cleveland: Arthur Clark Company.

Commons, John R. et al.1918–1935. *History of Labor in the United States.* 4 vols. New York: Macmillan.

Conlin, Joseph R. 1970. *Bread and Roses Too: Studies of the Wobblies.* Westport, CT: Greenwood Press.

Cooper, Patricia. 1987. *Once a Cigar Maker: Men, Women, and Work Culture in America Cigar Factories, 1900–1919.* Urbana: University of Illinois Press.

Day, Mark. 1971. *Forty Acres: Cesar Chavez and the Farm Workers.* New York: Praeger Publishers.

Derber, Milton. 1964. "Divergent Tendencies in Industrial Relations Research." *Industrial and Labor Relations Review* 17: 598–611.

Derber, Milton et al.1953. *Labor-Management Relations in Illini City.* Champaign: Institute of Labor and Industrial Relations, University of Illinois.

Devinatz, Victor G. 1996a. "The Labor Philosophy of William Z. Foster: From the IWW to the TUEL." *International Social Science Review* 71: 3–13.

———. 1996b. "An Alternative Strategy: Lessons from the UAW Local 6 and the FE, 1946–1952." Pp. 145–160 in *Beyond Survival: Wage Labor in the Late Twentieth Century.* Edited by C. Bina, L. Clements, and C. Davis. Armonk, NY: M. E. Sharpe.

———. 2002. "Reassessing the Historical UAW: Walter Reuther's Affiliation with the Communist Party and Something of its Meaning—A Document of Party Involvement, 1939." *Labour/Le Travail* 49: 223–245.

———. 2003. "Nelson Lichtenstein and the Politics of Reuther Scholarship." *Labour/Le Travail* 51: 171–176.

Dollinger, Sol, and Genora Johnson Dollinger. 2000. *Not Automatic: Women and the Left in the Forging of the Auto Workers' Union.* New York: Monthly Review Press.

Draper, Theodore. 1957. *The Roots of American Communism.* New York: Viking Press.

———. 1960. *American Communism and Soviet Russia.* New York: Viking Press.

Dubofsky, Melvyn. 1968. *When Workers Organize: New York City in the Progressive Era.* Amherst: University of Massachusetts Press.

———. 1969. *We Shall Be All: A History of the Industrial Workers of the World.* Chicago: Quadrangle Books.

Dunlop, John T. 1944. *Wage Determination under Trade Unions.* New York: Augustus M. Kelley.

———. 1958. *Industrial Relations Systems.* New York: Holt.

Dunne, John Gregory. 1967. *Delano, The Story of the California Grape Strike.* New York: Farrar, Straus, and Giroux.

Ely, Richard T. 1886. *The Labor Movement in America.* New York: Thomas Y. Crowell.

Faue, Elizabeth. 1991. *Community of Suffering and Struggle: Women, Men, and the Labor Movement in Minneapolis, 1915–1945.* Chapel Hill: University of North Carolina Press.

———. 1993. "Gender and the Reconstruction of Labor History, An Introduction." *Labor History* 34: 169–177.

Filipelli, Ronald L., and Mark D. McColloch. 1995. *Cold War in the Working Class: The Rise and Decline of the United Electrical Workers.* Albany: State University of New York Press.

Fine, Sidney. 1969. *Sit-Down: The General Motors Strike of 1936–1937.* Ann Arbor: University of Michigan Press.

Fink, Leon. 1993. "Culture's Last Stand? Gender and the Search for Synthesis in American Labor History." *Labor History* 34: 178–189.

Foner, Philip S. 1947. *History of the Labor Movement in the United States.* Vol. 1, *From Colonial Times to the Founding of the American Federation of Labor.* New York: International Publishers.

Affirmative Action

Affirmative action is a federally mandated process intended to ensure that access to employment and promotion is not restricted because of race, religion, gender, or national origin. By 1974 the categories of individuals covered under affirmative action expanded to include employees over forty, disabled individuals, and Vietnam-era veterans. The most common criticism of affirmative action is that it establishes a quota system that privileges the hiring of women and minorities, with too little regard to qualifications. Proponents counter that what affirmative action actually requires is that hiring be nondiscriminatory within a specific pool of qualified applicants. Affirmative action was envisioned as a temporary means to achieve equitable employment opportunities for those who historically faced workplace discrimination. When the workplace replicated the labor pool, the measures could be relaxed or discarded. Affirmative action enjoyed bipartisan political support until the 1980s, as well as the support of business and the public.

Affirmative action emerged from New Deal concepts that tried to end employment practices that openly discriminated against African Americans. Centuries of slavery, segregation, race-based employment restrictions, and Jim Crow laws (which legislated racial segregation in all aspects of society including work, housing, and recreation) had reinforced racial hierarchies in hiring, promotion, and education. The first executive order addressing nondiscrimination was issued by Franklin D. Roosevelt in 1942 and prohibited discrimination in industry supporting the war effort and in the employment practices of the federal government (Eisaguirre 1999, 9). Affirmative action policies initially applied only to federal contractors and governmental agencies in an effort to create a "representative bureaucracy," in the belief that a workforce that represented the demographics of the public would better assess and address the needs of its constituency (Selden and Selden 2001, 4).

Throughout the 1950s and the 1960s, the civil rights movement led by Martin Luther King Jr. gained momentum by exposing the deep-seated racial prejudice evident in laws that reinforced white supremacy. King and the civil rights movement demanded the unrestricted right to vote, an end to segregated schools and public spaces, and the right to equal opportunities in employment and compensation. In response, John F. Kennedy issued Executive Order 10925 in 1961 requiring that federal contractors take "affirmative action" to "hire minorities on government contracts," thus introducing the term and concept of an affirmative rather than a passive effort to end workplace discrimination (Sugrue 2001, 39). This was followed by Executive Order 11114 in 1963 that disallowed employment discrimination of minority workers on government contracts (Sugrue 2001, 39).

During the Johnson administration, the U.S. Congress passed the Civil Rights Act of 1964, which was regarded as a major victory for the civil rights movement and King. Title VII of the Act established the Equal Employment Opportunity Commission (EEOC) to oversee the compliance of affirmative action and nondiscrimination policies for employers with more than fifty employees. Title VII placed more focus on achieving results than did existing law, but it did not clearly define what actions constituted discrimination or spell out what methods should be used to ensure nondiscrimination. Companies were allowed to develop their own approaches for ensuring that affirmative action was implemented. The EEOC offered mediation services to facilitate reconciliation between employees filing complaints and their employers. When employee and employer could not come to an agreement through the EEOC, the employee had the right to sue; some suits were independently initiated by the Department of Justice when a "pattern or practice of discrimination" existed (Skrentny 2001, 3). Because the act did not clearly state how affirmative action would be accomplished or measured, the courts had to decide if the ways employers applied or responded to the law were in keeping with the act's intent and in compliance with the U.S. Constitution.

In 1970, under the Nixon administration, the Office of Federal Contract Compliance (OFCC) issued Order 4 that required all federal contractors to report hiring practices and employment demographics to the federal government. Under Order 4, companies also had to create an affirmative action plan that included stated goals and a timetable for implementing these goals (Kelly and Dobbin 2001, 92). Hiring goals and timetables provide benchmarks by which compliance and success can be determined. Affirmative action goals can include recruitment strategies, hiring or promotional objectives, or assessment procedures. Timetables allow businesses to demonstrate their success or lack thereof in meeting the goals. Subsequent decisions made by the Nixon administration included a 1972 ruling that introduced the concept of "underutilization." This ruling allowed the government to analyze the employment patterns of federal contractors to make sure that specific categories of workers were not underrepresented, or underutilized, at a level greater than the labor pool indicated (Kelly and Dobbin 2001, 92). The Equal Opportunity Employment Act of 1972 permitted the EEOC to file suit against offending companies and required even small companies to comply with affirmative action legislation, thus covering nearly 80 percent of the nation's workforce (Holzer and Neumark 1999, 540). The fear of lawsuits led many companies to establish EEO offices and establish affirmative action plans. In 1978 Jimmy Carter extended the commitment to affirmative action through the Uniform Guidelines on Employee Selection Procedures, which banned explicit business practices that resulted in discrimination on the basis of race, gender, or ethnicity (Tucker 2000, 17). By 1979, two-thirds of top executives supported the government's efforts to increase the representation of women and minorities in the workforce (Dobbin and Sutton 1998, 455).

Bipartisan commitment to affirmative action ended with the election of Ronald Reagan in 1980. Reagan dismantled equal opportunity programs by severely cutting the EEOC budget, thereby ending the ability of government to initiate nondiscrimination litigation. Reagan also appointed federal and Supreme Court justices opposed to affirmative action. In the 1990s the Clinton administration's defense of affirmative action and Clinton's efforts to engage the country in discussions about discrimination kept affirmative action from further legislative reductions. At the beginning of the twenty-first century, the outlook for affirmative action is unclear. There appears to be no political consensus to address it through legislation; increasingly the Supreme Court determines the scope, range, and constitutionality of affirmative action.

The U.S. Supreme Court has had a major and often contradictory influence on affirmative action through its interpretations of Title VII and the Fourteenth Amendment to the U.S. Constitution. Major decisions have addressed which party to the lawsuit has the burden of proof, goals, impact, and equal protection. In *Griggs v. Duke Power Company* (1971), the Court shifted the burden of proof to defendants in employment discrimination cases and ruled that instruments such as employment tests that had a demonstrated "disparate impact" on groups covered by Title VII were illegal. By 1989, in *Wards Cove Packing v. Antonio et al.*, the Court reversed *Griggs* by ruling that "disparate impact" did not in itself indicate intentionally discriminatory practices and reinscribed the statistical data necessary to meet the burden of proof as a comparison between the jobs or workplace in question and the "racial composition of the qualified population in the relevant labor market" (Tucker 2000, 174). In addition, the Court returned the burden of proof to the plaintiff, a decision interpreted widely as a setback for affirmative action because complainants generally lack the resources possessed by corporations.

United States v. Paradise (1987) affirmed lower court rulings that forced Alabama state police to accept hiring mandates because of the severity of the discrimination in that agency. The case began when the National Association for the Advancement of Colored People (NAACP) charged the Alabama Department of Public Safety with intentional employment discrimination because in thirty-seven years, it had hired no black troopers. A federal district court ordered the hiring of one qualified black trooper or support person for each white person until 25 percent of the Alabama Department of Public Safety workforce was black. The Fifth Circuit Court of Appeals held that the hiring mandate did not constitute reverse discrimination against white applicants or subvert the hiring process, even when some of the white applicants had stronger qualifications, because of the need to remedy the entrenched discrimination signified by a previously all-white force.

The Supreme Court's adherence to the concept of "strict scrutiny" of affirmative action laws became increasingly important in court decisions regarding the composition of the labor market. The "strict scrutiny" standard as applied to affirmative action plans finds these plans are constitutional only when discrimination is evidenced by overwhelming statistical disparities. In *Richmond v. Croson* (1989), for instance, the Supreme Court concluded that the evidence did not demonstrate that blacks were economically disenfranchised in Richmond, Virginia. Therefore, the Court held that a minority business enterprise (MBE) set-aside policy that required city contractors to subcontract 30 percent of their work to minority-owned companies was unconstitutional and in violation of the equal protection clause of the Fourteenth Amendment (Tucker 2000, 133). Later, in *Adarand Constructors, Inc. v. Pena* (1995) the Court reinforced strict scrutiny by ruling that a history of discrimination must be a compelling component of MBE programs. In *Adarand,* the Court decided that race alone does not prove that a disadvantage existed requiring remediation through MBEs, in this case ruling that there was no evidence of discrimination against Hispanics. Therefore, when a contract was issued to a Hispanic-owned company under the MBE program, absent decisive data to indicate ongoing discrimination that justified a corrective measure, the award violated the equal protection rights of the white contractor who submitted the lowest bid. The Court concluded that if there is no demonstrated need to remedy statistically verified inequities, MBEs are unconstitutional (Kelly and Dobbin 2001, 101).

Agreements that include hiring goals generate most of the opposition to affirmative action because many people incorrectly perceive goals as hiring quotas that privilege the hiring of less qualified women and minorities over more qualified white males. In actuality, affirmative action is not a quota system; only in extremely egregious circumstances were hiring mandates imposed by the courts (such as *United States v. Paradise*). Affirmative action does not require employers to hire unqualified persons. It has resulted in the increased hiring and promotion of minorities and women, but studies have not confirmed that less qualified minorities and women were hired or promoted as a result (Holzer and Neumark 1999). Affirmative action does, however, work to inhibit hiring habits reinforced by "old boy networks" that disproportionately favor white males (Buford 2002, 173). Even after thirty years of affirmative action, studies show that there still exists an often unconscious tendency on the part of managers to hire individuals of a similar race, gender, and socioeconomic background. This preference has a demonstrably negative effect upon women and minorities with credentials identical to those of white men (Holzer and Neumark 1999, n3 535).

With the viability of federally mandated affirmative action in flux, proponents argue that correctives are still necessary to keep ability-based employment available to women and minorities. Some scholars assert that access to employment and advancement predicated on ability is so central to the American concept of self-worth that work has become a "proxy for citizenship" (Sturm and Guinier 2001, 31). As such, proponents contend that measures need to be in place to ensure that all Americans can find the work necessary for their full participation in the civil processes of this nation. Others contend that many white Americans regard their "whiteness as a property right" and feel besieged by affirmative action that undermines their privilege while ignoring the inherent racism of such concepts (Bell 2001, 46). At the same time, these whiteness privileges compel many white Americans to act against their own self-interest by ignoring the fact that white women are the primary beneficiaries of affirmative action (Bell 2001, 46).

The polarizing debates about the efficacy of affirmative action most commonly occur in the realm of the media and the courts; business and the public react negatively only with regard to perceived hiring quotas. Even with the legal future of affirmative action uncertain, the corporate community remains supportive of efforts to correct underutilization based on race and gender, as well as disability (Buford 2002, 176). Business may have initially reacted to affirmative action with plans designed to avoid litigation, but that quickly changed as business saw affirmative action as an effective way to foster creativity and productivity. A diverse workforce is considered good for business, so although affirmative action per se may be on the decline, commitments to workforce diversity and diversity management continue to be integral to corporate America (Dobbin and Sutton 1998, 455). At the same time, even as the American public rejects hiring quotas, there continues to be overwhelming support for nondiscrimination policies and recruitment programs to ensure equitable job opportunities for all Americans (Holzer and Neumark 1999, 535), efforts that are the essence of affirmative action.

Sandra L. Dahlberg

See also African American Women and Work; African Americans and Work; American Slavery; Americans with Disabilities Act; Asian Americans and Work; Gays at Work; Glass Ceiling; Immigrants and Work; Older Workers; Veterans; Women and Work; Work and Hispanic Americans

References and further reading

Bell, Derrick. 2001. "Love's Labor Lost? Why Racial Fairness Is a Threat to Many White Americans." Pp. 42–48 in *Who's Qualified?* Edited by Lani Guinier and Susan Sturm. Boston: Beacon Press.

Buford, James A., Jr. 2000. "Affirmative Action Benefits the Workplace and Economy." Pp. 29–34 in *Affirmative Action.* Edited by Bryan J. Grapes. San Diego: Greenhaven Press.

———. 2002. "Affirmative Action Promotes Equality." Pp. 171–180 in *Work.* Edited by James Haley. San Diego: Greenhaven Press.

Dobbin, Frank, and Frank R. Sutton. 1998. "The Strength of a Weak State: The Rights Revolution and the Rise of Human Resources Management Divisions." *American Journal of Sociology* 104, no. 2: 441–476.

Eisaguirre, Lynne. 1999. *Affirmative Action: A Reference Handbook.* Santa Barbara: ABC-CLIO.

Holzer, Harry, and David Neumark. 1999. "Are Affirmative Action Hires Less Qualified? Evidence from Employer-Employee Data on New Hires." *Journal of Labor Economics* 17, no. 3: 534–569.

Kelly, Erin, and Frank Dobbin. 2001. "How Affirmative Action Became Diversity Management: Employer Response to Antidiscrimination Law, 1961–1996." Pp. 87–117 in *Color Lines: Affirmative Action, Immigration, and Civil Rights Options for America.* Edited by John David Skrentny. Chicago: University of Chicago Press.

Selden, Sally Coleman, and Frank Selden. 2001. "Rethinking Diversity in Public Organizations for the Twenty-first Century: Moving toward a Multicultural Model." *Administration and Society* 33, no. 3: 303–340.

Skrentny, John David. 2001. "Introduction." Pp. 1–28 in *Color Lines: Affirmative Action, Immigration, and Civil Rights Options for America.* Edited by John David Skrentny. Chicago: University of Chicago Press.

Sturm, Susan, and Lani Guinier. 2001. "The Future of Affirmative Action." Pp. 3–34 in *Who's Qualified?* Edited by Lani Guinier and Susan Sturm. Boston: Beacon Press.

Sugrue, Thomas J. 2001. "Breaking Through: The Troubled Origins of Affirmative Action in the Workplace." Pp. 31–52 in *Color Lines: Affirmative Action, Immigration, and Civil Rights Options for America.* Edited by John David Skrentny. Chicago: University of Chicago Press.

Tucker, Ronnie Bernard. 2000. *Affirmative Action, the Supreme Court, and Political Power in the Old Confederacy.* Lanham, MD: University Press of America.

African American Women and Work

A greater number of African American women work than do white women. African American women work more years in their lifetime than white women; they earn less than white women, and their unemployment rate is higher than that of white women. As one African American woman observed, "There are two kinds of females in this country—colored women and white ladies. Colored women are maids, cooks, taxi drivers, crossing guards, schoolteachers, welfare recipients, bar maids and the only time they become ladies is when they are cleaning ladies" (Lerner 1973, 217). That has been the reality for African American women.

From the time the first African women were enslaved and brought to America, they have been relegated to the lowest rungs of the economic ladder, to agricultural work and domestic service and the unskilled service sector of the economy. Domestic service work has employed the largest number of black women. In the late nineteenth century, virtually every young black girl, except for those from the most affluent families, knew she would be cleaning house for a white family (Hine, 153). Domestics work longer hours for lower wages than any other group of workers. Domestic service workers are also more likely to experience sexual harassment. Although attempts have been made to organize domestic service workers, they have generally been unsuccessful. Difficulties arise because of the individual nature of the work, the intense competition for jobs, and the historical indifference of many labor unions toward unskilled black women workers (Lerner 1973, 231).

Beginning about 1910, African Americans left the segregated South in large numbers, lured to the North partly by promises of industrial work. However, these industrial jobs went primarily to black men. The majority of African American women remained in the domestic service sector. Although domestic wages were higher in the North, a large proportion of black domestic workers still endured the unrelenting control, interference, and complaints of the white woman for whom they worked (Hine, 214).

Despite these adverse working conditions, African American domestic workers were able to change the nature of domestic work. First, whenever possible, they refused to live with their employers, instituting the widespread practice of "day work." Day work left married black women free to return to their families in the evening but, more importantly, reduced the number of hours a domestic worker was on call to her employers. It also allowed working mothers a more open work schedule and gave African American women more flexibility in choosing their jobs (Jones 1985, 165). When other job opportunities presented themselves, African American women pursued them without hesitation.

African American women preferred industrial jobs to domestic service but were excluded from the textile manufacturing mills of the South. Instead, they were relegated to the least desirable and lowest-paying factory work available: processing raw tobacco for cigarettes, cigars, and chewing tobacco. By 1910, up to 8,482 black women worked annually in the tobacco processing industry (Jones 1985, 137). Black women did the work that white male supervisors considered too "dirty" for white women. They sorted tobacco according to grading systems, stripped the leaves of their center stems, hung them to dry, and labeled and packed boxes. The average black woman worked twelve-hour days, five and one-half days each week, for less than nine months each year. Weekly earnings averaged between $6 and $10 for a sixty-hour workweek (Lerner 1973, 257). Because of the seasonal nature of the industry, most earned less than $200 each year. Their wages remained the lowest in the industry and their working conditions the poorest. A Women's Bureau study reported that "stemmers" had to work standing up in hot, humid, poorly lighted workrooms. Women breathed in tobacco dust daily, resulting in debilitating respiratory disease (Janiewski 1986, 139, 150).

World War I opened the doors to better industrial jobs to black women for the first time. A survey of almost 12,000 black women workers conducted by the U.S. Women's Bureau of the U.S. Department of Labor in 1922 found that most black women workers were between sixteen and thirty years old and that many of these women worked in war industry plants assembling ammunitions or making gas masks, airplane wings, nuts, bolts, rivets, screws, rubber tires, tubes, and shoes (U.S. Department of Labor/U.S. Women's Bureau 1922). Others worked in meatpacking plants, glass and garment factories, or railroad yards. These jobs gave black women more personal freedom than domestic service work and paid significantly higher wages. However, these gains were only modest. Relatively few black women found work in manufacturing, and those who did find such employment remained at the lowest rungs of the industrial ladder in terms of wages and working conditions. African American women workers faced hostility in the industrial sector, but they were excluded from clerical and retail work within the white community. Racial prejudice and discrimination dictated the hiring practices of white business owners whose establishments sold retail consumer goods and services to a white clientele. Even black female high school graduates could not find employment to match their educational qualifications. Most were relegated to a lifetime of menial labor. At the end of World War I, 80 percent of black women workers were still employed as maids, cooks, or washerwomen (Jones 1985, 166–167, 178–179).

Because of the attitudes of white employers in the late nineteenth century, talented and educated African American women turned to entrepreneurial activities within the black community. Many built successful businesses while improving their communities. In the twentieth century, other African American women advanced in business in the areas of beauty and fashion. Madame C. J. Walker built her beauty industry manufacturing "hair goods and preparations." As black women took industrial jobs in the cities, demand grew for products that would help them "improve their appearance" in the eyes of white employers, who held common prejudices about skin color and hair texture. Walker's best-selling products were face creams that promised to lighten skin and tonics and pressing oils to straighten hair. Walker began selling her products door-to-door, but increasing demand led her to open a training school to instruct other black women in selling her products. Walker traveled the country giving lectures to promote her business at black religious, fraternal, and civic meetings, as well as internationally in Jamaica, Cuba, Haiti, and Costa Rica, and along the Panama Canal (Hine 1999, 204). Walker became a millionaire and an internationally known black businesswoman, a symbol of black economic independence who used her wealth and prestige to advance black equality. When Walker died, she gave thousands of dollars to black schools, including Mary McLeod Bethune's Daytona Normal and Industrial School (now Bethune-Cookman College) and Tuskegee Institute.

World War II opened new opportunities for African American woman workers, as black women entered the industrial workforce to replace the men who went to war. Although hundreds of thousands of African American women eventually gained jobs in the aircraft industry, shipyards, electrical equipment and machinery factories, ordnance manufacturing, and steel mills and foundries, as well as civilian jobs in the service industries, canneries, transportation, and auto industry, these positions were hard-won because employers were reluctant to hire black women. Despite the obstacles, World War II was the first time black women had access to high-paying industrial jobs. Through these positions, black women gained specialized skills and status in the workforce. Between 1940 and 1944, the percentage of black women in the industrial workforce rose from between 6 and 8 percent to 18 percent. In addition, for the first time, black women had access to virtually all "white" occupations, including clerical and nursing jobs.

As the United States went to war in 1941, organizations such as the National Council of Negro Women (NCNW) concentrated on helping African American women adjust to their new industrial positions. One of the most active NCNW programs during the war years was the "Hold Your Job" program, which sponsored a series of wartime employment clinics. The clinics sought to promote black women's industrial employment through collective planning, organization, and action while simultaneously trying to change employer's attitudes about black women workers. Clinics helped women adjust to the industrial sector by emphasizing worker health, attendance, personal appearance, attitude, efficiency, behavior on the job, and union participation. Workers learned good work habits, such as arriving at work on time; being "particular about their dress, behavior and attitude on the job and in public places"; consciously trying to improve their job performance; and learning how to get along with other people, even in an "unpleasant" situation (Hanson 2003, 183).

The NCNW also recognized that to secure wartime employment gains, black workers would have to embrace unionism. To that end, the "Hold Your Job" program endorsed union membership and supported organized labor in free collective bargaining. The NCNW also sought to strengthen African American women's position in national defense industries by pushing employers to include women in apprenticeship programs. Clinic organizers arranged meetings with employers to discuss workers' problems and resolve them by appealing to the employer's concern for profit. Organizers stressed that an adjusted worker meant a smoothly run shop, less absenteeism, a lower rate of turnover, and increased production. Clinics for employers tried to convince foremen and supervisors to accept black women workers and facilitate their adjustment to the job. The job campaign raised the consciousness of women workers, although it ultimately failed to secure their place in the industrial sector in general (Hanson 2003, 267–269).

During the 1930s and 1940s, African American women became strong union activists in the Congress of Industrial Organizations (CIO). During World War II, the number of black women in the industrial labor force tripled, and black union membership rose from 200,000 to 1.25 million. Nevertheless, black women remained the "last hired, first fired," white women periodically staged "hate-strikes" against black women workers, and segregated unions endured. The passage of the Taft-Hartley Act in 1947 limited union organizing, and in 1949–1950, the CIO acquiesced to anti-Communist hysteria by expelling eleven "suspect" unions, all strongly associated with interracial organizing. House Un-American Activities Committee investigations further eroded union power, and by 1948 most of the progress made by African American women during the war had been reversed. By 1950, 41 percent of black women worked as domestics. Since the 1960s, African American women have unionized workers at southern textile mills and hospitals. In the 1970s and 1980s, black women worked through the Coalition of Black Trade Unionists to address racism in the workplace and in unions, and the Coalition of Labor Union Women fought sexism in unions (Hine 1993, 685–688).

Title VII of the Civil Rights Act of 1964, which outlawed discrimination in hiring based on race, color, religion, sex, or national origin, helped black women approach parity with white women in terms of wages and access to clerical service positions. Between 1960 and 1970, the percentage of black women in clerical work more than tripled in the South and doubled in the North. By 1980, 34 percent of all black women in the workforce were in the areas of technical, sales, and administrative support, compared to 34 percent of all white women (Jones 1985, 302).

Title VII and affirmative action also succeeded in increasing the number of black workers holding jobs in social services at the local, state, and federal government levels. Certainly, black women have benefited by these changes. Yet in 1988, when the magazine *Black Enterprise* published its list of "25 Hottest Black Managers," black women were conspicuously absent. In 1993, when the same magazine published its list of "America's Most Powerful Black Executives," four women made the list. In 1994, twelve black women sat on the boards of directors of Fortune 500 companies. In 1997, Ann M. Fudge was named president of Maxwell House Coffee. By the 1990s, more than 400,000 black women owned their own businesses (Hine 1993, 305–308).

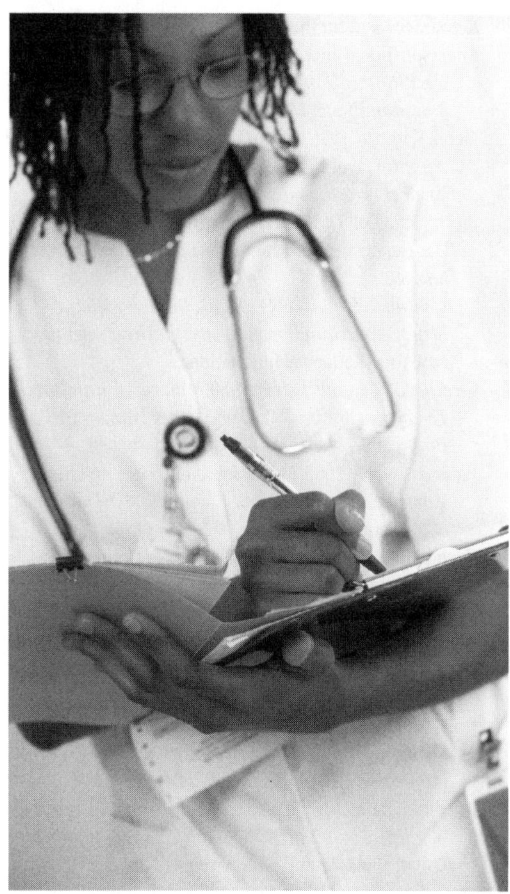

The vast majority of African American women workers have made a transition from servitude to service industries such as health care. (Dex Images/Corbis)

Although the gap in wages and occupations between black and white women workers has narrowed considerably, black women continue to rank lowest in the occupational hierarchy. Today, the number of poorly paid service sector positions held by black women is still high. The vast majority of African American women workers have transitioned from servitude to service work in the health care, fast food, and hotel industries. Rather than poorly paid domestic workers, they now constitute a large percentage of nurses' aids, counter workers, and chambermaids.

Joyce A. Hanson

See also African Americans and Work; American Slavery; Home Economics/Domestic Science; Women and Work; Work and Hispanic Americans

References and further reading

Anderson, Karen Tucker. 1982. "Last Hired, First Fired: Black Women Workers during World War II." *Journal of American History* 69 (June): 82–97.

Blood, Kathryn. 1945. "Negro Women War Workers." U.S. Department of Labor, Women's Bureau Bulletin no. 205.

Brown, Jean Collier. 1938. "The Negro Woman Worker." U.S. Department of Labor, Women's Bureau Bulletin no. 165.

Clark-Lewis, Elizabeth. 1996. *Living In, Living Out: African-American Domestics and the Great Migration.* New York: Kodansha International.

Greenwald, Maurine Wiener. 1980. *Women, War, and Work: The Impact of World War I on Women Workers in the United States.* Westport, CT: Greenwood Press.

Hanson, Joyce A. 2003. *Mary McLeod Bethune and Black Women's Political Activism.* Columbia, MO: University of Missouri Press.

Haynes, Elizabeth Ross. 1923. "Negroes in Domestic Service in the United States." *Journal of Negro History* 8 (October): 384–442.

Hine, Darlene Clark, Elsa Barkley Brown, and Rosalyn Terborg-Penn, eds. 1993. *Black Women in America.* Vol. 1. Bloomington: Indiana University Press.

Hine, Darlene Clark, and Kathleen Thompson. 1999. *A Shining Thread of Hope: The History of Black Women in America.* New York: Broadway Books.

Janiewski, Delores E. 1986. *Sisterhood Denied: Race, Gender, and Class in a New South Community.* Philadelphia: Temple University Press.

Jones, Jacqueline. 1985. *Labor of Love, Labor of Sorrow: Black Women, Work and the Family, from Slavery to the Present.* New York: Vintage Books.

Katzman, David M. 1978. *Seven Days a Week: Women and Domestic Service in Industrializing America.* New York: Oxford University Press.

Kessler-Harris, Alice. 1982. *Out to Work: A History of Wage Earning Women in the United States.* New York: Oxford University Press.

Lerner, Gerda, ed. 1973. *Black Women in White America: A Documentary History.* New York: Vintage Books.

"Negro Women in Industry." 1922. United States Department of Labor, Women's Bureau Bulletin no. 20.

Palmer, Phyllis M. 1989. *Domesticity and Dirt: Housewives and Domestic Servants in the United States.* Philadelphia: Temple University Press.

Shields, Emma L. 1922. "A Half Century in the Tobacco Industry." *Southern Workman* 51 (September): 419–425.

Tilley, Nannie May. 1948. *The Bright-Tobacco Industry, 1860–1929.* Chapel Hill: University of North Carolina Press.

U.S. Department of Labor/U.S. Women's Bureau. 1922. "Industrial Opportunities and Training for Women and Girls." Bulletin 13. Washington, DC: Government Printing Office.

Weaver, Robert C. 1946. *Negro Labor: A National Problem.* New York: Harcourt, Brace.

African Americans and Work

Any discussion of African Americans and work in America must begin with the unalterable fact of slavery. Blacks were first brought to America in 1619. Much like white indentured servants, who worked a period of time for a sponsor, blacks were initially treated as bound servants and were freed when their terms expired. By the 1640s, however, they were being imported and sold as servants for life. In the 1660s and 1670s, statutes in Virginia and Maryland gave slavery its institutional form by mandating servitude for life and a harsh system of discipline called the "black codes." Slavery spread through all the southern colonies.

Slavery was an economic system that needed and used the unpaid labor of blacks to produce agricultural crops such as tobacco, indigo, and rice. The plantation system that developed justified its existence based on racial difference. Blacks were believed to be inferior and so were not accorded the option of indentured servitude. Once established, slavery became a self-perpetuating system that melded economics and a system of human and power relations. Southerners came to regard slavery as essential to their culture, political influence, and economic prosperity.

Although the colonial period saw the creation of a brutal system of unpaid labor for African Americans as a whole, there were pockets of compensated activity. In some instances, southern slave owners allowed skilled slaves to hire themselves out to other plantations, and some owners allowed slaves to keep all or part of the wages. Some slaves were able to save enough from these wages to purchase freedom for themselves and family members.

In the northern colonies, skilled blacks were able to earn a living by plying their trade as artisans. But even in the North, black artisans faced intense competition and reprisal because of their color. In fact, in all the colonies with significant numbers of free black labor (or even slave labor hired out for wages), conflict often occurred with white artisans asserting a privileged position in the labor market.

In 1744, white shipbuilders in Charleston, South Carolina, joined forces to complain that they were reduced to poverty because of black competition. Their protest, supported by white workers in other trades, persuaded the Charleston authorities to enact an ordinance forbidding slave owners to hire out more than two slaves at a time. Such efforts by white workers, although rare, happened throughout the colonial period and set the stage for labor conflict based on race.

The American Revolution, although overtly dedicated to principles of equality and self-determination, did not extend to the institutions of slavery and racial discrimination in the evolving labor market. Slavery and the rights of African Americans posed a dilemma for the framers of the Constitution. Five of the original colonies elected to become free states, but the white laboring classes were less than receptive to the prospect of competition from skilled black workers. The postrevolutionary years saw the beginning of the factory and factory work. No longer could the U.S. economy thrive on small-scale, home-based, artisan manufacturing. Custom work gave way to wholesale order work, and laborers were concentrated in certain expanding industries. In part, this rationalization of industry was due to competition from Britain and the rest of the world. The trend toward factory work also led to the formation of a distinct laboring class. Prior to the revolution, the mode of artisan custom production produced open mobility patterns. Apprentices could move up to take the place of master artisans at some point or open their own shops. The emerging factory system closed this mobility path for the majority of workers. They could not hope to acquire the capital to open a factory shop.

African Americans, like many other workers, started to concentrate in select industries. For example, in the early nineteenth century, African Americans played a dominant role in the caulking trade. Caulking prevented leaking on ships, and so these skills were in great demand.

The Civil War and Beyond

The Civil War brought the open wound of slavery to the forefront. African Americans in the North played a significant role, not only by fighting but by building fortifications and working in factories supporting the Union war effort. As the Civil War progressed, slaves increasingly fled plantations to assist Union troops in many work-related efforts to fight the Civil War. The Civil War in the North further exposed the fissure of race in the workplace. Northern cities saw the occurrence of "draft riots" by immigrants, mostly Irish, who did not want to fight in a war to free those they saw as competition in the labor force.

At the end of the Civil War, former slaves had to adjust to freedom and a new system of labor in the South. Although slavery was abolished, the need to heal the Union saw the plantocracy reestablished under the system of sharecropping. Laws were passed to restrict the mobility of newly freed slaves, forcing them to accept this bad bargain. Essentially, sharecropping created an illusion. The planters rented out land to freed slaves (and later poor whites); if they could not afford rent, the planter took the rent from future earnings from the land. In many cases, the planter became the company store, selling everything from fertilizer to seeds. The economics of sharecropping ensured that the tenant would constantly fall behind. High interest charges, emphasis on production of a single cash crop, and slipshod accounting ran rife throughout the system.

After the Civil War, African Americans continued their efforts to break into the emerging industrial occupations. Although they faced stiff resistance, black workers did not suffer meekly. The record documents many attempts by African Americans to organize themselves into what can only be termed a union. For example, black dockworkers in Pensacola, Florida, organized a Workingman's Association and successfully defended their jobs against Canadian longshoreman brought in by dock owners.

The formation of unions increased during the early Reconstruction period. Black and white workers shared an interest in forming trade unions. Blacks had to form separate union organizations because white unions excluded them. Black unions such as the Colored National Labor Union petitioned the federal government several times (from 1869 on) to uphold basic worker rights and to change the land tenure system in the South after Reconstruction. These entreaties were ignored.

Working conditions did not improve for black workers between the end of Reconstruction in 1877 and the turn of the century. In many industries, white workers demanded and were granted lower pay for black workers. Black and white workers were driven further apart by a series of labor actions in which blacks were used as strikebreakers in the railroad and meatpacking industries.

The twentieth century saw the first of successive waves of black migrants looking for better lives in the North. Many were pushed North both by harsh lives in the South and the increasing mechanization of agriculture, which made their labor redundant. From 1916 to 1930, more than 1 million blacks moved from the South to the North. Historians estimate that 400,000 left the South during the two-year period of 1916–1918 to take advantage of a labor shortage created by World War I. African Americans realized significant gains in industrial employment, especially in the steel, automobile, shipbuilding, and meatpacking industries. Between 1910 and 1920, the number of blacks employed in industry nearly doubled, from 500,000 to 901,000.

The massive movement of people forced the federal government to hear the voice of the African American worker that it had previously ignored. In 1918 a special office called the Office of Negro Economics was instituted to help mobilize black labor for the war. The unions also took notice of the changing demographics and increased their attempts to bridge the divide between black and white workers.

The Great Migration presented an opportunity for African Americans to build new institutions and an expanded vision for life in the United States. The 1920s saw the rise of black nationalism in the movement headed by Marcus Garvey, who encouraged self-reliance and an appreciation of the African continent as the spiritual base and focus of blacks in the United States. A. Phillip Randolph, the most respected labor leader ever to emerge from the African American community, also began his career in the 1920s as an organizing force for black railroad workers and a promoter of racial justice. In 1925, Randolph began his twelve-year fight to gain recognition for the Brotherhood of Sleeping Car Porters by the Pullman Car Company; the American Federation of Labor (AFL), which represented many powerful unions of the era; and the U.S. government. The brotherhood became the AFL's first black affiliate. Other unions, many joining the Congress of Industrial Organizations (CIO), created in 1938, organized semiskilled and unskilled workers in mass production industries with many black workers, such as steel, auto, rubber, and meatpacking.

The Depression and World War II

African American gains in the labor force received a severe setback with the arrival of the Depression. Black workers were the first to be let go and the last to be hired. Desperate for work, many had to take nonunion jobs, limiting the power of unions, while employed blacks faced hostility from unemployed white workers. Union organizing efforts continued through the 1930s, gaining momentum in the latter part of the decade. Despite the attempts by labor unions to incorporate African Americans, they found themselves barred from most of the skilled jobs, and many union affiliates remained segregated.

In an effort to get the economy moving, President Franklin D. Roosevelt created a number of federal agencies many of which were designed to provide temporary work to many Americans. The plight of black labor, though, might not have progressed if not for the coming of World War II. The advance of African Americans in U.S. industry during World War II was the result of the nation's wartime emergency need for workers and soldiers. In 1943 the National War Labor Board issued an order abolishing pay differentials based on race. The executive order became the touchstone for black unions and others arguing for and winning increased respect for African American workers.

Postwar Challenges for Black Workers

The period after World War II saw the best of times for black workers and looming challenges. Another wave of black workers had streamed into urban areas in response to the war effort, and even after the war, the numbers continued to flow into cities. But apart from their value as workers, blacks as citizens were confined to living in the worst neighborhoods. Housing segregation led to the creation of substandard ghettoes where there was differential access to health care, education, and other services that create a strong community. By the1950s, it was obvious that even the full power of the post–World War II economy could not solve the problems brought by racial discrimination that had accrued from the beginning of the republic. In addition, postwar changes to the nature of work, which had been based on labor-intensive manufacturing, displaced many black workers. Blacks came to urban areas looking for a better life, only to have the economy shift to knowledge-intensive work requiring more skills.

African American Labor and the Civil Rights Movement

The 1950s and 1960s saw an alliance between the

civil rights movement and the labor movement. After condemnation of racist practices by African American labor leaders, the newly formed AFL-CIO agreed to support the struggle for civil rights. African American union officials were among the leaders during the Montgomery bus boycott and the 1963 march on Washington. African Americans continued to press their demands for equality within the labor union movement. When redress was not forthcoming, African American civil rights groups sought justice by filing suit under Title VII of the Civil Rights Act of 1964, which prohibits discrimination in employment because of race, color, religion, sex, or national origin.

Organized labor's long refusal to fully incorporate African American workers into the mainstream labor movement led many to feel that their issues would always be ignored. The rise of the black power movement in the late 1960s emboldened certain sectors of black labor to become more strident in their demands. In northern automobile plants, groups of workers formed the League of Revolutionary Black Workers. Beginning with the idea that the issue of black labor was linked to African Americans' broader struggle in a white society committed to racial domination, this group linked organized labor to socialism and black power.

Mainstream organized labor responded to this new militancy by opening leadership positions to more moderate blacks and working with national black organizations. Additionally, in the late 1960s, national black organizations and labor unions worked together to develop several federally funded programs to bring blacks into apprenticeship programs, a key step toward more highly skilled and better-paying jobs.

The gradual incorporation of blacks into high-paying union jobs and the effect of affirmative action in other industries helped to create a significant black middle class in the United States by the end of the twentieth century. Poverty rates for the African American community that hovered around 40 percent in 1965 had been reduced to around 21 percent by 2002 (U.S. Census Bureau 2002). Although poverty is still unacceptably high among African Americans, the United States has made progress, enough so that the prospect of African Americans running Fortune 500 companies is no longer a dream.

Contemporary Challenges

African American participation in the labor force in the postwar period has been tied to the business cycle. With notable exceptions, black unemployment has hovered at twice the national average since the 1940s . Despite government attempts to provide training and to encourage the integration of African Americans into the workforce, a substantial segment of the black community from generation to generation remains unemployed. African Americans are, on average, two and a half times as likely as whites to suffer from unemployment. This gap exists at virtually every educational level.

Figure 1
Black Unemployment Rate 1972–2002

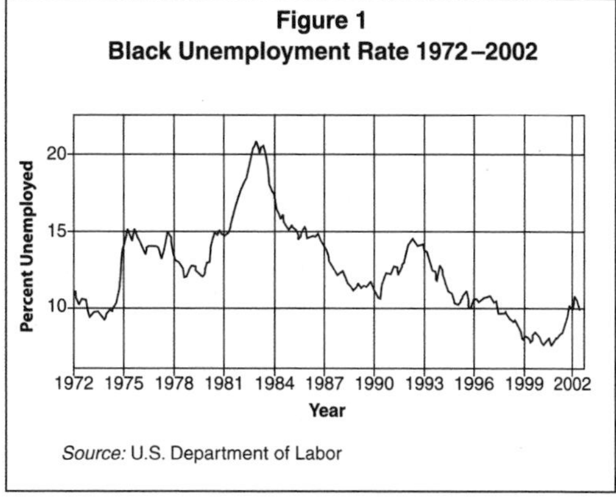

Source: U.S. Department of Labor

Black unemployment reached a thirty-year low of 7.6 percent in 2000. In contrast, the unemployment rate for white Americans was 3.5 percent. In an earlier era, black disadvantage in the labor force was purely a function of racial exclusion. Today, many problems of unemployment have to do with labor force preparation, contact with established formal and informal recruitment (or the lack thereof), and promotion mechanisms. High school dropout rates among black youth and the failure of inner-city schools to prepare graduates for the job market hamper the process of labor force preparation and lead to persistently high rates of unemployment. But this challenge presents an opportunity.

Through the federal Department of Labor, the U.S. government, working with the private sector, has made some inroads into the problems of labor force preparedness. Over the years, many workforce development experiments have been tried with varying levels of success relative to cost such as the Comprehensive Employment and Training Act (1973) and the Job Training Partnership Act (1982).

However, it is clear that for minority workers and youth to gain greater access to jobs and economic opportunities the United States must continue to improve and strengthen its workforce preparedness system.

Roland Anglin

See also Affirmative Action; African American Women and Work; American Slavery; Immigrants and Work; Solidarity; Women and Work

References and further reading

American Social History Project. 1992. *Who Built America? Working People & the Nation's Economy, Politics, Culture & Society.* Vol. 1. New York: Pantheon.

Anderson, Jervis. 1987. *A. Philip Randolph: A Biographical Portrait.* Berkeley: University of California Press.

Baxandall, Rosalyn, and Linda Gordon, eds. 1995. *America's Working Women: A Documentary History, 1600 to the Present.* Rev. ed. New York: W. W. Norton.

Bernhardt, Debra, and Rachel Bernstein. 2000. *Ordinary People, Extraordinary Lives: A Pictorial History of Working People in New York City.* New York: New York University Press.

Brody, David. 1993. *In Labor's Cause: Main Themes on the History of the American Worker.* New York: Oxford University Press.

Craft, Donna, and Terrance W. Peck, eds. 1998. *Profiles of American Labor Unions.* Detroit: Gale Research.

Foner, Philip, and Ronald Lewis, eds. 1989. *Black Workers: A Documentary History from Colonial Times to the Present.* Philadelphia: Temple University Press.

Halpern, Rick, and Roger Horowitz. 1996. *Meatpackers: An Oral History of Black Packinghouse Workers and Their Struggle for Racial and Economic Equality.* Farmington Hills, MI: Twayne Publishers.

Hobsbawm, Eric. 1998. *Uncommon People: Resistance, Rebellion, and Jazz.* New York: The New Press.

Jones, Jacqueline. 1985. *Labor of Love, Labor of Sorrow: Black Women, Work, and the Family from Slavery to the Present.* New York: Random House.

———. 1997. *American Work: Four Centuries of Black and White Labor.* New York: W. W. Norton.

Painter, Nell Irwin. 1993. *The Narrative of Hosea Hudson: The Life and Times of a Black Radical.* Reissue ed. New York: W. W. Norton.

Santino, Jack. 1989. *Miles of Smiles, Years of Struggle: Stories of Black Pullman Porters.* Urbana: University of Illinois Press.

U.S. Census Bureau. 2002. *Historical Poverty Tables.* http://landview.census.gov/hhes/poverty/histpov/hstpov2.html (cited June 17, 2003).

Zieger, Robert H. 1994. *American Workers, American Unions, 1920–1985.* Baltimore: Johns Hopkins University Press.

Zinn, Howard. 1999. *A People's History of the United States, 1492–Present.* Twentieth Anniversary Ed. New York: HarperCollins.

Agricultural Work

The noble yeoman behind his plow is one of the dominant images in U.S. history, yet an examination of agriculture in this country shows that this image is often misleading. In fact, agricultural work and those engaged in it have been diverse. Its history dates back to at least 200 B.C.E. when Native Americans began to domesticate squash, sumpweed (an early seed grass crop), sunflowers, and chenopod (goosefoot). By 1000 C.E., beans, corn, and squash ("the three sisters") had come to dominant food production in what would be the United States. For the most part, agriculture was women's work. Women had the task of clearing and burning the fields. Using wooden hoes and digging sticks, they often planted the three sisters together in earthen hills following a system that allowed the plants to grow in complementary fashion to their full potential. The corn would act as a trellis for the beans and both crops would provide shade for the squash. While older children kept watch for birds, women used stone, bone, or wooden hoes to frequently weed these fields. When fields lost their productivity, many tribes simply moved on and returned to their fields at a later date. In the Great Plains, besides the three sisters, wild plums, tobacco, the prairie turnip, and sunflowers were dominant. In the dry Southwest, women also cultivated cotton in the floodplains. The Hohokam in Arizona built more than 150 miles of canals to irrigate their crops. The Anasazi and Mogollon built walled terraces to conserve water. Because agriculture was seen as women's work, Native American ideals would clash with the cultural biases of the U.S. government and settlers. Native American males refused to participate in agricultural activities, seeing it as an affront to their masculinity. Agents and missionaries perceived this as simple laziness.

When the English first arrived in Virginia in 1607, they did not have much interest in farming. They soon discovered that the real treasure they were looking for came in the form of tobacco. By 1628, they were exporting 553,000 pounds of tobacco to England. Just sixty years later, 18 million pounds were being exported. Given how labor-intensive tobacco raising was, indentured servants were brought in to raise the crop. By 1750, more than half of the immigrants to the American colonies south of New England were indentured servants. Most were required to work four to seven years before they could gain their freedom. Entitled as servants to shelter, medical care, adequate food, and clothing, once free, they were often entitled to "freedom dues," which meant a cash payment or a grant of land at the end of their contract. Although both men and women worked in the fields, women emigrated mainly to serve as domestic servants and household help on plantations and small farms.

As economic conditions improved and the birth rate in England declined, thus making labor in the colonies scarce, tobacco farmers began to turn to another source of labor, African slaves. In August 1619, twenty slaves arrived in Virginia. Although there were 28,000 slaves in the colony by 1700, the African workforce explosion began in the latter half of the eighteenth century. By 1770, approximately 22 percent of the population in the South was African. Of the 459,000 slaves, two-thirds worked in the tobacco fields of the Chesapeake Bay. Most of the rest found themselves in either the rice or indigo fields of South Carolina and Georgia. Because of malaria and yellow fever, slaves almost exclusively inhabited the rice fields. Rice plantations were large, so it was not uncommon for an owner to have a workforce of between 50 to 100 slaves. Other slaves, largely unsupervised, cared for the large cattle herds in the Carolinas.

These slaves generally worked in either the task or the gang system. In the task system, slaves were assigned a certain amount of work for the day, and when they finished their assigned tasks, they could engage in leisure activities or work for themselves. Each slave was responsible for his or her individual work. In the gang system, a group of slaves, supervised by an overseer, engaged in agricultural tasks as a unit. A standard work gang could pick between 150 and 200 pounds of cotton in a day.

In time, the system of slavery hardened, and with the cotton gin's invention in 1793, it exploded across the South. Just seventeen years later, 1 million slaves were working in southern fields. Viewed as instruments of profit, male slaves were bringing between $600 and $700 at the New Orleans market. By 1860, the value of a good field hand increased to $1,800. A slave could produce 3,000 pounds of cotton in a year while costing only about $50 to feed and clothe. Thus, there were enormous profits in maintaining slavery. On the eve of the Civil War, there were 4 million slaves in the South. Most slaves in the upper South worked on cotton and tobacco plantations. Those in the lower South often found themselves working on rice and sugar plantations, where conditions were harsh. A subtle threat used by owners to intimidate slaves in the upper South was the possibility of being sold deeper into the South. Only 10 percent of slaves lived in cities. Fifty percent of slaves were on large plantations of twenty or more bondsmen, and 27 percent of slave owners owned 75 percent of the slaves. Yet, one-quarter of southern families owned at least one slave. Farmers and planters with excess slaves began to hire them out to other families. An elaborate system soon developed regarding these hiring contracts, which generally ran for one year.

After the Civil War, the planters maintained control of the land and former slaves, and poor whites often found themselves part of the sharecropping system. This system enabled freed African Americans to maintain tenancy on a piece of land and pay the landlord a portion of the year's crops. Although rates varied from state to state, tenants often paid the owner one-third to one-half of their crops. More than 75 percent of all farmers in the South were sharecroppers and tenants. Because of living expenses and the low price of cotton, most sharecroppers fell into virtual peonage. Tenants often found themselves owing the furnishing merchants more than they made and had no control over their own lives. Thus, poverty dominated the southern landscape until the New Deal.

Although the average farmer in the South did not own slaves and agricultural slavery never took hold in the North, it would be fair to say that farm labor in these situations was a family affair. Most farmers relied on their children and wives to help with fieldwork. Rural families often had a large number of children out of economic necessity. Child farm labor became so accepted in the United States that most people saw it as healthy and natural. Even in the twentieth century, it was not regulated under the Fair Labor Standards Act of 1938.

There was a division of labor on most farms, with women taking care of the home and children, but women often worked right alongside their husbands during critical times in the crop cycle. They also raised a vegetable garden, raised chickens, sold eggs, made butter, sewed, spun cloth, collected beeswax and feathers, canned fruits and vegetables, and preserved pork—activities necessary to keep the farm economically viable. During the nineteenth century, women often took seasonal jobs in canneries and factories to help make ends meet. They were also the backbone of community and rural social networks.

Northern agricultural work was more diverse than that in the cash-crop South. Farmers grew corn, wheat, barley, other grains, and grasses and raised dairy cattle, beef cattle, swine, sheep, mules, and horses. Tasks on the farm included taking care of the crops and animals as well as providing for most of the family's needs. In the eighteenth century, farms were more self-sufficient in nature than they are today. Roughly 80 percent of the farm's output was geared to home consumption or local markets. As time progressed and a national infrastructure developed, farmers became more specialized.

Given the long hours of work and the variety of tasks to be done, many farmers had hired help. It has been estimated that up to 30 percent of the rural labor force were hired hands. Although few scholars have really examined the lives of these men, they generally lived with the family or in a building nearby and worked with the owner of the farm. Their presence often allowed widows and older farmers to continue their operations. Working as a hired hand enabled young men to save enough money to buy their own farm or wait for their parents to retire. In 1820, wage laborers could earn $9 per month. Thirty years later, they were earning $15 per month. By the late nineteenth century, they became known in some circles as "dollar-a-day men."

At harvest time and other critical moments, neighbors often got together to aid each other. Working together, they were often able to bring in the harvest, which would have been nearly impossible to do on their own. As farm sizes increased in the nineteenth century, young men and nearby city dwellers often hired themselves out for seasonal work as pickers or in threshing crews. Around New York City, vegetable farmers who needed workers began to hire immigrant labor to keep wages low. By the 1860s, grain farmers in the Midwest were hiring itinerant crews with threshing machines to perform the harvest. These large machines were not cost-effective in any other use.

Yet it was in California that large-scale agriculture really developed. By 1886, wheat farmers could cut and thresh between 25 and 35 acres per day. As wheat prices declined, these bonanza wheat farmers began to turn to irrigated fruit and vegetable production, which required a large seasonal labor pool. Growers turned to the large Chinese population in the state for help. By the twentieth century, racism and xenophobia led them to turn to other Asian groups, including the Japanese. By 1920, prejudice against Asian workers led growers to turn to Mexicans and Mexican Americans as a labor source. Ten years later, 80 percent of the fruits and vegetables harvested in California were picked by migrant labor.

By 1945, seventy-eight growers owned roughly 6 million acres of the state. They struggled to maintain control of their labor pool, sometimes through violence. In 1942, under the guise of a wartime emergency, they convinced the federal government to create the bracero program (from the Spanish word for "arm") to bring Mexican workers into California as laborers if an adequate supply of stoop labor (farm workers who handpick produce) could not be found. Growers used this program to keep wages low and replace workers who complained about working conditions. In effect, braceros became federally sanctioned strikebreakers. This program would continue until the presidency of Lyndon Johnson.

Because of the horrible conditions under which they worked, agricultural workers often turned to militant labor unions for assistance. In 1931, the Communist-controlled United Cannery, Agricultural, Packing, and Allied Workers of America fought to improve wages. After World War II, the National Farm and Labor Union (NFLU) joined the cause. Both unions' efforts generally ended in failure, as growers blamed "outside agitators" and hired thugs to break up strikes. The first successful union efforts did not occur until the 1960s, when Cesar Chavez formed the National Farm Workers Association (FWA), which became the United Farm Workers of America in 1967. Chavez's efforts led to growers negotiating concessions in 1970 and a number of legislative concessions later in the decade. Other farm workers' unions, like the American Agriculture Movement (AAM) also began to enjoy success.

The biggest transformation in agricultural labor was the New Deal of the 1930s and 1940s. Roosevelt administration policies and the later promise of wartime jobs led many rural inhabitants to desert the countryside and search for jobs in the city. Technology advances, such as the tractor, com-

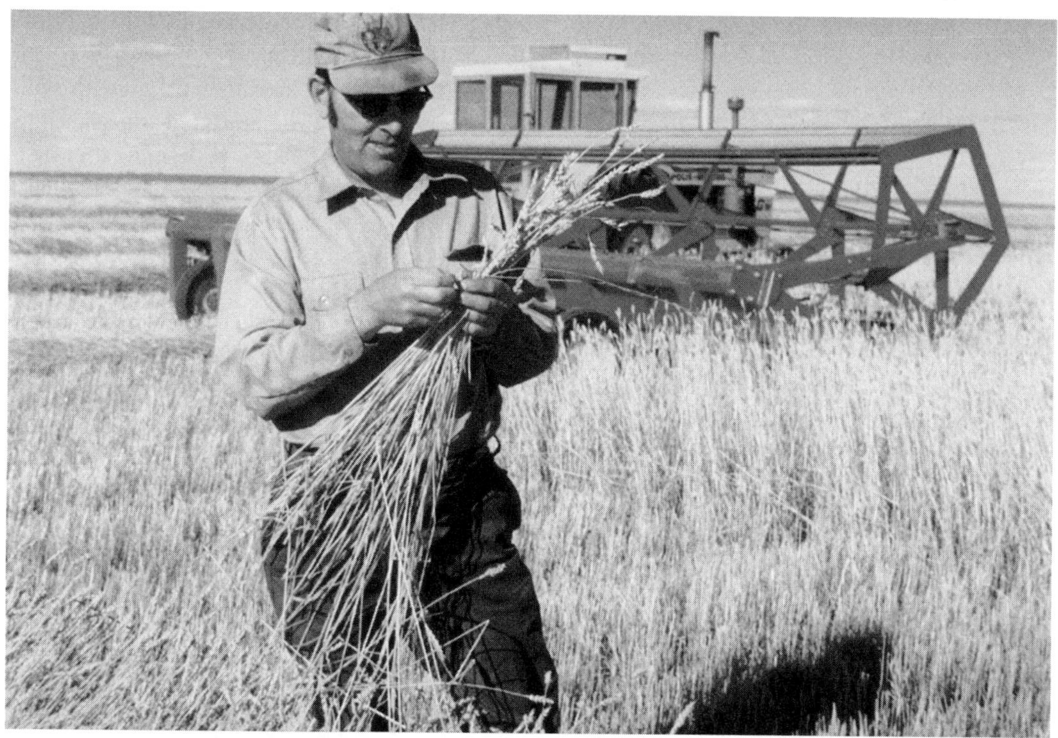

Many farmers find it difficult to make a living from the land and have increasingly looked outside agriculture for jobs. (Corel Corporation)

bine, and cotton picker, lessened the need for a large labor pool. The 8.5 million tenant farmers and sharecroppers basically disappeared. During these years, the rural South's population declined by 20 percent.

At the end of the twentieth century, less than 2 percent of the U.S. population was engaged in agriculture. Land-grant institutions (higher-education institutions that taught agriculture and mechanical arts and were established on land granted by the government) and the Department of Agriculture helped farmers to engage in more scientific agricultural practices and increase the acreage farmed, thus decreasing the need for unskilled labor. With the aid of tractors, farmers were able to increase corn and wheat production by more than 11 million acres in total since World War II. In the South, black farmers virtually vanished from the land. In 1987, only 22,954 African American farmers remained in the United States, of which only 14,954 were full owners of their land. Those involved in agriculture have grown older, especially after the 1980s farm crisis, because the increasing costs of farming inputs such as fertilizers, low crop prices, and heavy indebtedness convinced young people in rural communities to avoid farming as a career.

Farmers who find it difficult to make a living from the land have increasingly looked outside agriculture for jobs. In 1990, 44 percent of farmers received their principal income from nonfarm sources. Farms have grown bigger and become more corporate in structure. The myth of the noble yeoman has increasingly disappeared in the reality of big business farming. Agricultural work has substantially changed since Indian women first domesticated corn.

T. Jason Soderstrum

See also American Slavery; Day Laborers; United Farm Workers

References and further reading

Bogue, Allan G. 1963. *From Prairie to Corn Belt: Farming on the Illinois and Iowa Prairies in the Nineteenth Century.* Chicago: University of Chicago Press.

Cronon, William. 1991. *Nature's Metropolis: Chicago and the Great West.* New York: W. W. Norton.

Daniel, Pete. 1985. *Breaking the Land: The Transformation of Cotton, Tobacco, and Rice Cultures since 1880.* Urbana: University of Illinois Press.

Fite, Gilbert C. 1984a. *American Farmers: The New Minority.* Bloomington: Indiana University Press.

———. 1984b. *Cotton Fields No More: Southern Agriculture, 1865–1980.* Lexington: University of Kentucky Press.

Gates, Paul W. 1960. *The Farmer's Age: Agriculture, 1815–1860.* New York: Holt, Rinehart and Winston.

Hurt, R. Douglas. 1987. *Indian Agriculture in America: Prehistory to the Present.* Lawrence: University of Kansas Press.

———. 1991. *Agricultural Technology in the Twentieth Century.* Manhattan, KS: Sunflower University Press.

———. 1994. *American Agriculture: A Brief History.* Ames: Iowa State University Press.

Russell, Howard S. 1982. *A Long Deep Furrow: Three Centuries of Farming in New England.* Hanover, NH: University Press of New England.

Saloutos, Theodore. 1960. *Farmer Movements in the South, 1865–1933.* Berkeley: University of California Press.

Shover, John L. 1976. *First Majority, Last Minority: The Transformation of Rural Life in America.* DeKalb: Northern Illinois University Press.

Amazon.com

Amazon.com may not have created the concept of "e-tailing" or "e-commerce," but since its inception at the onset of the dot-com age, the Internet-based company has championed the notion that virtually anything can be sold online to the masses. The group's principal activity—and its strength—has been built on selling books, music, DVDs, and videos online for lower prices than consumers can secure by walking into a store. Founded and still managed by CEO Jeff Bezos, one of the highest-profile CEOs of the new economy era, Amazon.com went on to expand its initial product line by serving as an e-commerce distribution channel for small companies to offer consumer electronics, toys, cameras, and most recently, software and computer and video games, tools and hardware, lawn and patio items, kitchen items, and wireless products.

The company's growth, which includes substantial international activities, has helped it create one of the world's most visited Websites. It has also helped to transform the workplace by encouraging companies of all stripes to create online presences to sell and distribute products. The success of these Websites has varied. Some, such as many attached to publications and information outlets, have not yielded expected results. Others, including those for the likes of NutriSystems and Cisco, have registered healthy returns. Regardless of their uneven performance, virtually all companies have established Websites, fostering the overall rush to online shopping. That trend has undermined traditional retail stores, lessening the demand for onsite salespeople while increasing the need for workers with skills related to e-tailing. The impact of Amazon.com's development has helped to undermine the traditional notion of retail employment. Physical contact with the customer is no longer required because high levels of service are now executed via voice and e-mail.

The advent of online shopping, however, didn't protect Amazon.com from the ravages of the dot-com bust that begin in 2000. The crisis saw Amazon.com's stock price fall by more than 80 percent, which, when coupled with cash flow problems and rising debt, led many observers to question whether the world's best-known e-tailer would survive the crisis. "The division that sells books (along with music and video) has been a fabulous growth story," Melanie Warner explained in *Fortune* (2001). Unfortunately, sales in the group's only profitable division began to wane at a time when its moves into the wider product range began to falter. In some cases, the expected growth from the likes of hardware sales didn't pay off at all because it was based on partnerships with weak dot-coms that disappeared entirely under the market's downturn. The ongoing tensions between Amazon.com's management and its workforce were emblematic of labor-management relations during the height of the dot.com era, although Amazon.com continues to be a growing employer. The demands of carrying out Jeff Bezos's vision for a retail revolution often meant extensive overtime for workers, changing performance goals, and numerous deadlines, all while staff were expected to contribute new ideas. In exchange, however, Amazon.com management believes it provides workers with invaluable experience at the world's most visible e-tailer, as well as stock options and other opportunities.

The e-tailer worked through the problems, but not without rethinking much of its business plan. The dot-com bust approach called for Amazon.com to reconsider its partnership and product line without questioning the basic worth of online retailing. The company has struck deals with major brick-and-mortar retailers, such as Target, Circuit City, and Borders, to undertake all or part of their e-commerce operations. The shift aims to tie Amazon to more reliable partners in an effort to drive revenues while leveraging its investments in e-commerce technology and in its underused distribution centers. As a dot-com survivor, Amazon.com positioned itself to take advantage of the renewed interest in e-tailing, championing that process with its accompanying impact on the workforce.

John Salak

See also The Dot-Com Revolution; E-commerce; New Economy; Silicon Valley

References and further reading

Riedman, Patricia. 2002. "Fashion, Food, and Tech Preference of Ad People." Advertising Age. http://www.adage.com (cited September 2).

Shook, David. 2002. "Remapping Amazon's Course." *Business Week,* July 15.

Vogelstein, Fred. 2002. "Amazon's Second Act." *Fortune,* September 2.

Warner, Melanie. 2001. "Can Amazon Be Saved?" *Fortune,* November 26.

American Association of Retired Persons (AARP)

The American Association of Retired Persons (AARP) was founded in 1958 by Ethel Percy Andrus, a retired California educator. This nonprofit organization with a $600 million budget provides information and education, advocacy, opportunities for service, and products to meet the needs and interests of some 35 million members aged fifty and over. The National Retired Teachers Association (NRTA), established in 1947 by Andrus, is a division of AARP for retired educators and school personnel that brings an additional 1.2 million members to the organization.

AARP focuses its energies and resources in four key areas: health and wellness, economic security and work, long-term care and independent living, and personal enrichment. With its large national membership; staffed offices in all fifty states, the District of Columbia, Puerto Rico, and the U.S. Virgin Islands; and a large cadre of volunteer state and chapter leaders and field directors, AARP wields influence that extends deeply into U.S. politics, economy, and society. The association's large budget and growing constituency have enabled it to become a commanding player in national policy debates on issues ranging from ensuring the long-term solvency of Social Security to advocating prescription-drug coverage in Medicare and protecting patient rights in managed care systems and long-term care. AARP reaches out to families and individuals at the state and local levels by connecting them to information and activities that directly affect their lives. AARP helps shape the views of its members through an extensive Website (http://www.aarp.org), three publications (*My Generation, Modern Maturity, Segunda Juventud*), a monthly *Bulletin,* and two radio programs, *Prime Time* and *Mature Focus.*

With one-third of its membership under age sixty and approximately 40 percent still in the workforce, AARP places emphasis on issues, programs, and benefits related to work and economic security. Through a yearly process open to its members, AARP develops *The Policy Book: AARP Policies,* which is available on its Website. According to *The Policy Book: AARP Public Policies 2003,* five principles guide policy development in this arena: (1) a commitment "to expanding employment opportunities, minimizing underemployment and promoting job security for workers of all ages"; (2) freedom from discrimination as "a fundamental right"; (3) protection of workers "from discrimination in hiring, wages, benefits and all other privileges and conditions of employment"; (4) access for all workers to employer and government benefit programs; and (5) provision of special employment-related help for vulnerable populations such as current and former welfare recipients and low-income individuals fifty-five and older.

For thirty years, AARP has operated the Senior Community Service Employment Program (SCSEP) funded by the U.S. Department of Labor. This program offers subsidized part-time employment and job training for lower-income workers aged fifty-five and older who are attempting to make a transition into paid employment. Workers in the program are paid at least the minimum wage and are placed in community nonprofit organizations for twenty hours per week. In 2000, AARP sponsored 102 program sites in thirty-three states and Puerto Rico through SCSEP, providing over 8 million hours of community service. Participants in the program had a 51 percent job placement rate (AARP 2001a).

AARP offers advice and resources to help individuals make career decisions and transitions, run their own businesses, and form work-related partnerships. It provides assistance for all kinds of working people, including retirees looking to begin new careers or become consultants, individuals feeling stuck in their jobs, those who are unemployed, and those simply wishing to change jobs. A small business center with its own Web address (http://www.aarpsmallbiz.com) offers tools and resources to small business owners to help them with taxes, technology, capital development, sales and marketing, and other needs. Special links are included to assist women and Hispanics in their efforts to become successful small business owners.

In conjunction with its support of the one-stop career center concept outlined in the 1998 Workforce Investment Act, AARP advocates at the federal level for employment and training services and funds for older people, displaced homemakers, and other underserved groups. With the workforce aging, AARP is advocating for federal and state job training and employment programs to be more flexible and provide necessary support services (for example, transportation, dependent care) and to encourage older individuals to enter nontraditional jobs. In 1995, NRTA established the Pension Round Table (PRT), which monitors trends in public employee retirement and has developed information on cost-of-living adjustments and on voluntary and employer-sponsored retirement plans. In 2000, AARP joined with other organizations to successfully support passage of legislation to repeal the earnings limit applied to Social Security recipients aged sixty-five through sixty-nine (AARP 2001a). Before, the benefits of persons in this age group were reduced when their salary or wages exceeded a certain level. Now, such individuals can receive full Social Security benefits, regardless of how much they earn in wages or salaries.

A key focus of AARP has been the apparent dilution by the courts of the effects of the Age Discrimination in Employment Act of 1967 (ADEA). AARP is engaged in advocacy for congressional passage of legislation to restore the full power of ADEA and support state measures to prohibit age discrimination in employment. According to the employment section of *The Policy Book: AARP Public Policies 2003,* the organization is targeting age discrimination in a variety of domains related to worker and retirement benefits and health coverage. The "money and work" section of the AARP Website offers resources to help people recognize age discrimination, understand their rights, file charges with the Equal Employment Opportunity Commission (EEOC), and find additional sources of guidance.

In 2001, AARP published *Beyond Fifty: A Report to the Nation on Economic Security,* which contained good news and bad news about the economic status of older Americans. On the positive side, the inflation-adjusted income of individuals fifty and over was found to be 17 percent higher than in 1980, pension income and coverage were up, the poverty rate for persons aged sixty-five and over had dropped to 9.7 percent from 14 percent in 1980, labor force participation was up, and the majority of those over age fifty were feeling confident that they would have enough money to live comfortably in retirement. The bad news included rapidly increasing numbers of older adults without health insurance, the rising costs of health care, a growing wealth gap between high- and low-income Americans, and the extent to which preretirees were found to be economically at risk. The report noted the importance of Social Security as a reliable source of later-life income for U.S. workers while projecting that program solvency is guaranteed for only another thirty-seven years.

Certainly, the stock market debacle and the recession of 2001–2003 swelled the ranks of older Americans facing economic challenges and reaffirmed AARP's recognition that "As a society, there is much still to be done to make the years after 50 more secure and rewarding" (AARP 2001).

Natalie Ammarell

See also Defined Benefit/Defined Contribution Plans; Gold Watch; Pensions; Retirement

References and further reading

AARP. 2001. *Beyond 50: A Report to the Nation on Economic Security.* Washington, DC: AARP, May. http://research.aarp.org/econ/beyond_50_econ.pdf (cited June 18, 2003).

———. 2001a. *Your Choice. Your Voice. Your Attitude. 2000 Annual Report.* Washington, DC: AARP. http://www.aarp.org/ar/2000/graphics/pdfs/ar_full.pdf (cited June 18, 2003).

———. 2003. *The Public Policy Book: AARP Public Policies 2003.* Washington, DC: AARP. http://www.aarp.org/legipoly.html (cited June 18, 2003).

Karoly, Lynn. 1993. "The Trend in Inequality among Families, Individuals, and Workers in the United States." Pp. 19–97 in *Uneven Tides.* Edited by Sheldon Danziger and Peter Gottschalk. New York: Russell Sage.

McCarthy, M., and L. McWhirter. 2000. "Are Employees Missing the Big Picture?" *Benefits Quarterly* 16, no. 1: 26.

Quinn, J. 1999. "Retirement Patterns and Bridge Jobs in the 1990s." *Issue Brief 206.* Employee Benefit Research Institute, Washington, DC. February.

Ryscavage, Paul. 1999. *Income Inequality in America.* Armonk, NY: M. E. Sharpe.

American Federation of Labor and Congress of Industrial Organizations (AFL-CIO)

The American Federation of Labor and Congress of Industrial Organizations (AFL-CIO) is the national umbrella organization representing the interests of U.S. local, state, and national union organizations in legislative, political, and international arenas and providing a unified voice for organized labor and support for its members upon request. About 80 percent of union members in the United States are affiliated with the AFL-CIO, which is governed by an executive council of its president, executive vice president, secretary-treasurer, and about fifty vice presidents, most of them presidents of national unions. The federation acts as a kind of holding company for its affiliated members, which possess a great deal of autonomy but generally share a political and legislative agenda and broad concerns about the importance of matters such as protecting labor laws that ensure union rights. Although union membership has declined dramatically since the 1980s to about 15 percent of the total U.S. workforce, organized labor and its national federation retain enormous legislative, political, and social influence.

Since the Great Depression, the federation has used its voice to advocate for federal laws and regulations that protect and enhance the ability of unions to represent and organize members. It has also struggled to resolve divisions and conflict within its ranks over the federation's priorities and its handling of divisive issues such as employment discrimination and the organizing of immigrant workers. The AFL-CIO provides resources for targeted labor actions or organizing campaigns, giving smaller local and regional unions the resources to confront deep-pocket corporations. The federation has seen its clout and influence rise and ebb over a number of historical cycles since the late nineteenth century; it has not reversed its long decline in membership but nonetheless enjoys political and legislative influence for its members that few organizations can rival.

Formation

The Federation of Organized Trades and Labor Unions in the United States and Canada was formed by a group of organizations representing workers in 1881. This group reorganized as the American Federation of Labor at a Columbus, Ohio, conference in 1886. Opposed to the socialist and political ideals of the Knights of Labor, the AFL established a decentralized organization recognizing the autonomy of each of its member national craft unions. Individual workers were not members of the AFL but only of the affiliated local or national union. From its inception, the AFL emphasized organization of skilled workers into craft unions (composed of those of single occupation, such as painters or electricians), as opposed to industrial unions (in which all the workers in the automobile or steel industry would belong to one union). Samuel Gompers served as president of the new federation every year but one until his death in 1924. Gompers devised the federation structure, requiring that only one union represent each trade and that within each union the national organization should prevail over local chapters. Opposed to the idea of a labor political party, the AFL was a relatively conservative political force within the labor movement of the late nineteenth and early twentieth century. In 1900, the AFL-CIO had about 1 million members.

Expansions during the Great Depression and World War II

When Gompers died in 1924, William Green, a former miners union official, became the new president of the AFL. He would serve until 1952. The stock market crash of 1929 and the advent of the Great Depression would bring overwhelming hardships for many workers, but the policies of President Franklin D. Roosevelt (FDR) unleashed a period of enormous growth in the labor movement. This growth was forged and shaped by an institutional struggle between the largely craft-based union AFL under President Green and the industrial unionism movement led by John L. Lewis under the umbrella of the Committee for Industrial Organization.

John L. Lewis became president of the United Mine Workers of America (UMWA) in 1924 and an AFL vice president in 1930. As the Depression deepened, Lewis became convinced that the survival of organized labor hinged upon organizing the masses of new and often downtrodden workers toiling in the massive factories of the industrial United States. In 1935, Lewis recruited industrial union leaders, including Sidney Hillman of the Clothing Workers, David Dubinsky of the Ladies Garment Workers, Thomas Brown of the Mine and Mill Workers, and

AFL-CIO vice president Linda Chavez-Thompson, the highest-ranking woman in the labor movement, celebrates election results with Richard L. Trumka (right) and AFL-CIO president John Sweeney (left), 1995. (Associated Press)

others to form a Committee for Industrial Organization (CIO) within the AFL, enraging the federation's leadership. Lewis and the CIO were determined to bring into unions vast industrial workforces in steel, autos, rubber, farm equipment, electrical products, and textiles. Backed by the 1935 National Labor Relations Act (Wagner Act), which made collective bargaining a right under the law, CIO organizers recruited millions of new workers between 1935 and 1938. On November 14 of that year, the CIO abandoned negotiations with the AFL, converted itself into the Congress of Industrial Organizations, and conceded that it was a separate labor federation.

The aggressive CIO organizing drives continued through the end of the 1930s, and the competition between the AFL and the CIO also prompted the federation to increase its organizing efforts. The divide between the two organizations was stark and would overshadow the national labor movement for years to come. As described by historian David Kennedy,

> Many of the complacent princelings of the AFL contemplated Lewis's plans for industrial unionism with a distaste that bordered on horror. They recollected the circumstances of the AFL's birth in the turbulent 1880s, when Samuel Gompers had led a handful of craft unionists out of the Knights of Labor. Gompers's express purpose was to protect the economic interests of the "aristocrats" of American labor, like the skilled carpenters, machinists, and steamfitters, by disassociating them from the undifferentiated mass of workers that the Knights had unsuccessfully tried to weld together. . . . The masses of unskilled factory workers whom Lewis now proposed to escort aboard labor's ark conjured visions of a return to the broadly inclusionary, ramshackle organization of the Knights, which most AFL leaders regarded as hopelessly utopian and utterly ineffectual as a guarantor of labor's interests. (Kennedy 1999)

At the center of these events stood the polarizing, dominating, controversial, and influential figure of John L. Lewis. Scornful of the conservative AFL leadership, possessed of a thundering, charismatic oratorical style and an unwavering obsession with converting unionism into a mass social and political movement, Lewis became a figure of controversy and fascination. David Kennedy described Lewis as "dour-visaged, thickly eye-browed, richly maned, his 230-pound bulk always impeccably tailored, Lewis was a man of ursine appearance and volcanic personality, a no-holds-barred advocate for labor and a fearsome adversary" (Kennedy 1999). As the storm clouds of the Depression darkened, Lewis traveled across the nation, denouncing the AFL and big business at open-air rallies of workers, while CIO organizers and workers struck major industries and won a dazzling series of victories. The CIO workers became committed Democratic voters and provided the heart of FDR's electoral coalition for the next eight years.

During these years, critics, politicians, conservatives, and certain union leaders raised accusations and questions about the role of Communists within the CIO. Indeed, many CIO organizers were affiliated with the Communist Party, but for the most part in their work as organizers primarily served the interests of the CIO in recruiting workers into unions. The Communist issue became more serious after Pearl Harbor and U.S. entrance into World War II. The war under FDR's leadership provided an opportunity for union officials at the CIO and the AFL to work closely with the administration in managing the nation's industrial buildup. AFL and CIO leaders participated in FDR's joint industry-labor coalition that led to the establishment of the National War Labor Board (NWLB) by executive order on January 12, 1942. The board would issue rules on wage and price stabilization, arbitrate major union-management disputes, and work to prevent labor unrest.

The system worked well with the exception of a series of mining strikes led by the UMWA and the unpredictable John L. Lewis that many said hampered the war effort. After a firestorm of negative publicity and political pressure, the coal strikes were resolved, but Lewis would never recover from the battering to his public reputation and image. The NWLB issued a hugely influential ruling in 1942 allowing for "maintenance of membership" in union shops. This provision required that all new employees would automatically be enrolled in the workplace union unless they explicitly requested otherwise in their first fifteen days on the job and forced employers to collect union dues and enforce the rule. It guaranteed that millions of new workers would swell union rolls during the war years. By 1944, there were 18,600,000 union workers in the United States.

The CIO continued to grow through the war, although its success was marred by internal dissension; the International Ladies Garment Workers Union (ILGWU) withdrew in 1938, and the UMWA in 1942. The CIO decided in 1948 to bar Communists from holding office in the organization, and in 1949–1950 it expelled eleven of its affiliated unions, which were said to be Communist-dominated. The leadership of both umbrella groups worked together in the late 1940s to support the cause of free and independent trade unions in war-shattered Europe and around the world, including providing support and guidance for a free trade union movement in Germany. In 1946, the AFL refused to join the new World Federation of Trade Unions because of Soviet participation, and by 1949 both the CIO and the AFL had helped forge and then joined the International Confederation of Free Trade Unions (ICFTU). Labor movements from nearly fifty countries attended the founding congress of the ICFTU, which proclaimed as its principles a ban on superpower politics in its organization, protection for the rights of both large and small union movements, and the extension of the organization to all parts of the world.

Merger and the Expansion of the Drive for Civil and Worker Rights

The cooperation of the two federations in the formation of the ICFTU helped build momentum for the idea of a merger of their leadership. The passage of the Taft-Hartley Act in 1947 restricting union activities and allowing states to pass "'right-to-work'" laws, despite the concerted opposition of both federations, combined with labor's concern over the antiunion policies of President Dwight D. Eisenhower's administration, further spurred new considerations for unity among both groups. The death in 1952 of the presidents of both organizations and the appointment of George Meany, known for his intelligence, determination, and integrity, to head the AFL and the charismatic Walter P. Reuther to run the CIO paved the way for a merger in 1955.

The merged organizations held their first convention in 1955, electing Meany unanimously as president, establishing an executive council of AFL and CIO national union presidents, allowing an Industrial Union Department within the federation, and providing for the autonomy of member unions and organizations. The new AFL-CIO embraced 135 national or international unions claiming a total of some 14 million members (Robinson 1981, 183). In the wake of the merger, Meany led an anticorruption drive within the federation, expelling two affiliates, including the Teamsters, for corruption and lobbying Congress for tougher union anticorruption laws. The Labor Management Reporting and Disclosure Act (or Landrum-Griffin) that was passed in Congress and signed by President Eisenhower in 1959 did include the anticorruption and financial disclosure rules that the AFL-CIO supported. But conservative legislators also tacked on a laundry list of antiunion measures that infuriated union leaders. Because the federation viewed the law's "corrupt" union reporting and monitoring requirements as too broad, its anticorruption efforts declined substantially after this event. Although corruption was not widespread, charges and convictions of organized crime participation, embezzlement, and other activities in some unions would hurt the federation's image for decades to come.

AFL-CIO President Meany and other top officials enjoyed strong working relationships with President Kennedy and Labor Secretary Arthur Goldberg. During the 1960s, African American leaders urged organized labor and member unions of the AFL-CIO to provide more black workers with access to full union membership and better-paying jobs. Many union bodies were called to account for keeping their ranks closed for years to minority workers. AFL-CIO president Meany publicly stated his support for the need to address employment discrimination within union ranks and throughout the workforce. Meany and the federation worked closely with the administration on early drafts of equal employment opportunity legislation. It was not until Kennedy's death and the Johnson presidency that these early efforts would culminate in the 1964 Civil Rights Act, banning institutional forms of racial discrimination, and other gains, such as expansions in the value of the federal minimum wage, signed into law in 1966. The AFL-CIO chartered the A. Philip Randolph Institute in 1965 to promote civil rights and full opportunity by educating union members, the public, and government and elected officials about antidiscrimination policies. During the late 1960s and 1970s, the union movement drew national attention with the successful drives of the United Farm Workers (UFW) to organize farm laborers and improve their working conditions. After a two-year strike, wine-grape growers in California reached a collective bargaining agreement with the UFW in 1967.

Turmoil, Decline, and Readjustment

The AFL-CIO and organized labor were caught up in the centripetal forces of the 1960s, as antiwar conflict, racial discrimination, newly liberated social mores, and political assassination strained major U.S. institutions. The federation's leadership maintained its anti-Communist foreign policy, and although he later expressed repeated regret over the position, AFL-CIO President Meany vigorously supported the unpopular Vietnam War. Simmering tensions between Walter Reuther and Meany over the leadership's approach to civil rights, Vietnam, and other positions, as well as internal union politics, eventually erupted in 1968. The United Auto Workers (UAW) and its 1.3 million members withdrew from the AFL-CIO, a difficult blow for the federation to absorb. In 1970, hundreds of flag-waving New York City construction workers, at the prompting of Nixon administration labor officials, attacked a crowd of antiwar demonstrators on Wall Street. The violence received huge play in the national media, stereotyping the hardhats as well as the protesters and tarnishing the image of unions among middle-class citizens for years to come (Early 2000).

After supporting the Democratic presidential candidates since 1956, the AFL-CIO supported neither Nixon nor McGovern in 1972. The federation struggled to work successfully with the Nixon administration but opposed the Nixon wage and price controls, and Meany publicly called for Nixon's resignation during the Watergate affair. The federation could point to the passage of the Occupational Safety and Health Act in 1970 and its creation of a new regulatory agency to protect workers on the job as a positive milestone for which organized labor could claim major credit. In the early 1970s, the federation also created new organizations to diversify its membership and increase its appeal to a broader spectrum of workers. The Coalition of Black Trade Unionists was formed in 1972, the Labor Council for Latin American Advancement in 1973, and the Coalition of Labor Union Women in 1974.

Confined to a wheelchair with arthritis and other health problems, Meany decided not to run for reelection in 1979, and Lane Kirkland, who had been secretary-treasurer for the AFL-CIO, was elected president. Jimmy Carter was in the third year of a difficult presidency that saw few major labor initiatives take root. Union representation declined as the manufacturing sector employment plummeted, although unions continued to make gains representing government workers. Ronald Reagan was elected at a time of high inflation and economic fear. Reagan's handling of a labor controversy and strike involving federal air traffic controllers in the Professional Air Traffic Controllers Organization (PATCO) initiated a strong antiunion climate at the federal level. Most air controllers in the United States at that time were employed by the Federal Aviation Administration (FAA); for years, the controllers fought to be heard by the FAA on the stress and difficulty of their working conditions and what they believed would be improved policies. Their work was absolutely essential to safe air travel and was extremely stressful. With a new contract under discussion, PATCO bargained hard for these improvements. When the parties reached an impasse and the controllers walked out, the Reagan administration launched a crackdown. Controllers were fired and their leaders harassed. The administration attacked them in the media and the courts. Reagan introduced further antilabor policies, including government-sponsored union busting and industry deregulation, labeled organized labor as a special interest, and blamed high inflation rates on workers' "selfish" wage demands.

Reaganomics and other forces, including the rise of offshore manufacturing facilities and the popularity of downsizing and workforce reduction as cost reduction tools among corporate executives, all combined to reduce organized labor's reach into the workplace. By the year 2000, only 13.5 percent of the nation's workforce belonged to unions, down from more than 30 percent in the postwar period (see Figure 2). Since detailed records began to be kept in 1983, the share of unionized wage and salary workers in private industry has declined to 9 percent but has increased slightly in government, where 37 percent of workers are union members (CPS data/BLS analysis 2000, Figure A).

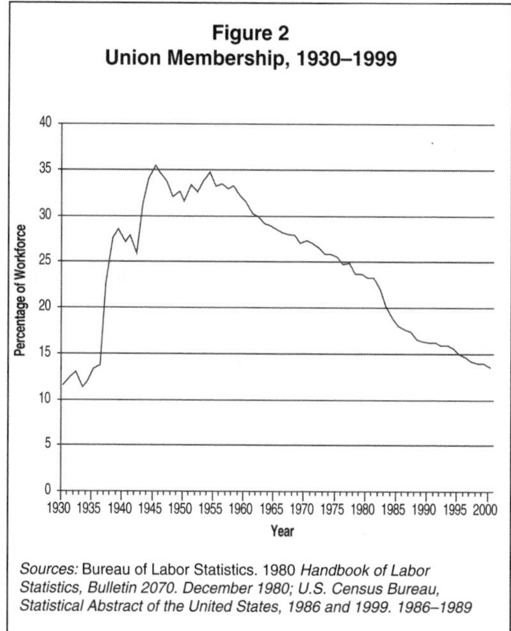

Figure 2
Union Membership, 1930–1999

Sources: Bureau of Labor Statistics. 1980 *Handbook of Labor Statistics, Bulletin 2070. December 1980; U.S. Census Bureau, Statistical Abstract of the United States, 1986 and 1999. 1986–1989*

For the next fifteen years, the AFL-CIO would essentially be playing defense against these forces. The federation sought to organize workers in low-paying service industries and the public sector and to heal its most serious internal wounds. The Teamsters would rejoin the federation in 1998. The AFL-CIO attempted to pass major labor law reforms to remove long-resented obstructions to organizing but fell short. Under Kirkland's leadership, the federation also became deeply engaged in foreign policy, opposing communism and supporting the emergence of new democracies. The federation's financial and operational support for the Polish trade union Solidarity was instrumental in its triumph over the Communist state. The federation improved its standing with the public and burnished its media reputation by prevailing in bitter, difficult, labor actions against the Pittston Coal Company and the Ravenswood Aluminum Corporation. The 1989–1991 Pittston strike and labor action and the 1990–1992 Ravenswood action shared common features. Both actions involved an employer using nonunion replacement workers or facilities to pressure unionized workplaces to accept regressive, substandard working conditions such as working on Sundays, reduced work and retirement benefits at Pittson and excessive overtime and dangerous working conditions in the Ravenswood strike. Both employers made no secret of their determination to roll back union gains, reinforced by what they viewed as antiunion public opinion. In both cases, powerful industrial unions (the United Mine Workers of America and United Steelworkers of America) used integrated campaigns that went far beyond withheld labor. The union campaigns included aggressive public relations, corporate pressure tactics aimed at unnerving the company's board and stakeholders outside the dispute, visible coalitions of political support, and related media efforts that dramatized to union members in the U.S. and around the world that organized labor was facing a life and death struggle in these confrontations. But the federation was still losing strength in the private sector.

The federation devoted growing resources to its political activities, both at the national and state levels. It was buoyed by its success in helping elect the Clinton-Gore ticket in 1992 and Democratic majorities in the U.S. House of Representatives and Senate. Although the federation welcomed what it viewed as long-overdue legislative victories, such as the passage of the Family and Medical Leave Act of 1993, the Clinton administration was careful to keep its distance from some of organized labor's most visible and controversial priorities. Trends associated with the new economy, such as labor mobility, the concentration of manufacturing facilities in certain regions of the country, the rise of Silicon Valley and high-tech firms, and the recruitment of labor from across the globe reduced union appeal. Pressure mounted for the federation to revamp its image, invest in its grassroots networks, and devote more resources to organizing. Kirkland retired under pressure in 1995, and Thomas R. Donahue, the AFL-CIO's secretary-treasurer, was named interim president. John J. Sweeney challenged Donahue for the federation's presidency and won the first contested election for president in the AFL-CIO's history.

Most observers agree that so far, the Sweeney era has marked a genuine departure in policy for the AFL-CIO. The federation devoted new money to organizing and intensified its opposition to employers who harass union organizers or violate labor laws in union or nonunion shops. Labor put together strategies for addressing worker rights in the global economy. The federation expressed its support for providing amnesty for undocumented workers and called for increased enforcement of basic labor laws covering workplace safety, overtime, and other standards, since employers often violate those laws as a way of exploiting illegal aliens. The federation enthusiastically joined the antiglobalization movement, calling attention to the "race to the bottom" dynamic exhibited by large corporations seeking ever-lower-paid and less-protected workforces in nations around the globe.

The prominence and success of the federation's involvement in the Seattle World Trade Organization protests spurred the commitment of the federation to the whole range of global issues, not only trade's impact on manufacturing. The federation is paying more attention to developing countries and increasingly targeting global multinational corporations, demanding that they honor previous commitments to fair global practices and ICFTU codes of conduct. The AFL-CIO now works in close partnership with a range of student, environmental, and developing world organizations.

As part of this new perspective, the federation led the campaign in the U.S. Congress in 2000 and 2001 to deny "most-favored nation" status (that is, a normal trading relationship) to China to provide the United States with more leverage over China's human and worker rights performance and establish labor rights as a precedent for receiving trade benefits from the United States. The federation ultimately lost the legislative battle, but observers generally agree the campaign succeeded in drawing public attention to these issues, building congressional support, and increasing pressure on U.S. government officials to monitor Chinese behavior closely. The federation is also focusing attention on the implications of free trade agreements in the Western Hemisphere. Long after confrontations over organizing unskilled industrial workers during the 1930s nearly destroyed the federation, the AFL-CIO in the twenty-first century seeks to organize new generations of workers within U.S. borders and abroad.

Herbert A. Schaffner

See also Building Trades Unions; Communications Workers of America; Knights of Labor; Meany, George; Randolph, A. Philip; Reuther, Walter; Sweeney, John J.; Teamsters; United Auto Workers; United Farm Workers; United Mine Workers of America

References and further reading

AFL-CIO. 1983. *The Builders: Seventy-five Year History of the Building and Construction Trade Department.* Washington, DC: AFL-CIO.

———. "Labor History Timeline." Adapted from *Democracy at Work: The Union Movement in U.S. History* by James Green. In press. Washington, D.C.: AFL-CIO. http://www.aflcio.org/aboutaflclio/history/history/timeline.cfm (cited June 3, 2003).

Brown, James. 2001. "A Curriculum of United States Labor History for Teachers." Illinois Labor History Society, www.kentlaw.edu/ilhs/curricul.htm (cited November).

Early, Steve. 2000. "Solidarity Sometimes." *The American Prospect,* September 11, p. 52.

Geoghegan, Thomas. 1992. *Which Side Are You On? Trying to be for Labor When It's Flat on Its Back.* New York: Plume/Farrar, Straus & Giroux.

Karatnycky, Adrian. 1999. "Lane Kirkland: A Venerable Labor Leader Who Fought for Freedom." *The American Spectator* (October).

Kennedy, David. 1999. *Freedom from Fear: The American People in Depression and War.* New York: Oxford University Press.

Lichtenstein, Nelson. 2002. "Roll the Union On: Rebuilding the Labor Movement." Pp. 125–127 in *Appeal to Reason: 25 Years in These Times.* Edited by Craig Aaron. New York: Seven Stories Press.

Moberg, David. 2001. "Labor's Critical Condition." *In These Times,* March 5, p. 19.

Robinson, Archie. 1981. *George Meany and His Times.* New York: Simon and Schuster.

Rose, Fred. 2000. *Coalitions across the Class Divide: Lessons from the Labor, Peace, and Environmental Movements.* Ithaca, NY: Cornell University Press.

Schaffner, Herbert A., and Carl E. Van Horn. 2002. *A Nation at Work: The Heldrich Guide to the American Workforce.* New Brunswick, NJ: Rutgers University Press.

American Slavery

The first African slaves in British North America landed in Jamestown, Virginia, in 1619. By the 1660s, the labor of African slaves had become a vital element of the colonial economy. By the time the U.S. Congress outlawed U.S. involvement in the Atlantic slave trade in 1808, nearly 11 million

Africans had been forced to immigrate to the Americas and the Caribbean (Brinkley 1999, 81). Although colonial America was to see the development of a new and distinct African American culture, the labor and social characteristics of this culture varied from region to region. In the low-country rice districts of Georgia and the Carolinas, most slaves worked somewhat independently on large plantations with only a few whites, whereas in the tobacco colonies of Virginia and Maryland, slaves worked in gangs and formed the majority of the population.

Although some slaves became house servants, artisans, or factory workers (city slaves), most worked as field hands on the farms and plantations of the antebellum South. They labored from sunrise to sunset, planting or harvesting cotton or other large cash crops such as tobacco and rice. Most slaves survived on inadequate diets of pork and corn, were poorly clothed in hand-me-downs, and slept in drafty, dirty cabins. In the evenings and on Sundays, the slaves would come to create a culture (which included religion, music, and language) that lessened the pain of slavery. Freedom and resistance were major themes of this culture. This freedom, however, would not come until the ratification of the Thirteenth Amendment in 1865.

Almost from the beginning of European settlement in America, there was a demand for black servants to supplement the continually scarce labor supply. The demand grew rapidly once tobacco cultivation became a staple of the Chesapeake economy.

Slave plantation, 1834. Although some slaves became house servants, artisans, or factory workers (city slaves), most worked as field hands on the farms and plantations of the antebellum South, laboring from sunrise to sunset. (Library of Congress)

African Slave Trade

The movement of Africans across the Atlantic to the Americas was the largest forced migration in world history. Begun by the Portuguese in the fifteenth century, the Atlantic slave trade did not end in the United States until the nineteenth century. Of the tens of thousands of Africans shipped from 1701 to 1808 (the peak period of colonial demand for labor), the majority were delivered to Dutch, French, or British sugar plantations on the Caribbean Islands; one-third went to Portuguese Brazil. North America, however, was always a much less important market for African slaves than were other parts of the New World; 10 percent of the slaves were sent to Spanish America and less than 5 percent to the British North American colonies (Brinkley 1999, 84–85). Around 600,000 men, women, and children, were transported to the British colonies of North America (Faragher et al. 1999, 53).

Portuguese slavers shipped captive men and women from the west coast of Africa to the new European colonies in South America and the Caribbean. Gradually, however, Dutch and French navigators joined the slave trade. A substantial commerce in slaves developed within the Americas, particularly between the Caribbean Islands and the southern colonies of British North America. Because of the need for field workers, male slaves outnumbered female slaves two-to-one. The majority of captured Africans came from every ethnic group in West Africa and were between the ages of fifteen and thirty (Faragher et al. 1999, 53).

The cruel business of slave raiding was forced on the Africans themselves. Ottabah Cugoan, who was sold into slavery in the mid–eighteenth century, wrote, "I must own to the shame of my own countrymen that I was first kidnapped and betrayed by those of my own complexion" (Faragher et al. 1999, 54). African chieftains captured members of enemy tribes in battle, tied them together in long lines or "coffles," and sold them in the thriving slave marts on the African coast. The terrified victims were then packed into the dark, filthy holds of ships for the horrors of the "middle passage," the journey to America. For weeks and sometimes even months, the prisoners remained chained in the bowels of the slave ships. Those who died en route were thrown overboard. Upon arrival in America, slaves were auctioned off to white landowners and transported to their new homes.

The Development of North American Slave Societies

A shortage of laborers plagued English settlers in the American colonies. To attract laborers, the colonists found it necessary to pay wages that would have been considered exorbitant in Europe. The payment of high wages proved inadequate, however, to secure a sufficient number of workers, and in every colony, highly paid free labor was supplemented by forced labor. Like the Spanish to the south, the English forced Indians to work for them. American Indian slavery was most prevalent in South Carolina, where in 1708 the governor estimated that there were 1,400 Indians slaves in a population of 12,580. Indians also served as house servants and occasional laborers in other colonies and were found in New Jersey as late as the middle of the eighteenth century.

American Indian slavery, however, never became a major institution in the English colonies. The close proximity of the wilderness and of friendly tribes made escape relatively easy for American Indian slaves. The absence of a tradition of agricultural work among East Coast American Indian males (women performed the majority of the farming) made them difficult to train as agricultural laborers. Because they were of a "malicious, surly, and revengeful spirit; rude and insolent in their behavior, and very ungovernable," the Massachusetts legislature forbade the importation of Indian slaves in 1712 (Kolchin 1987, 11).

In New England, most of the American Indians present when the Puritans arrived in 1630 died from illness and war during the next half-century. To eliminate the threat of Indian attacks, New England settlers incorporated a policy of eliminating the Indians themselves. Eventually, this policy of elimination proved incompatible with the widespread use of Indians as slaves and created a huge demand for foreign labor.

The institution of black slavery was nearly two centuries old before it became an important system of labor in North America. There were slaves in each of the British colonies during the seventeenth century, but in 1700 they represented only 11 percent of the colonial population. The turning point in the history of the African population in North America came in the mid-1690s when the British Royal African Company's monopoly finally ended. With the trade now opened to English and colonial merchants, prices fell, and the number of Africans arriving in North America rapidly increased. Between 1700 and 1760, the number of Africans in the colonies increased to about 250,000. Although a relatively small number of about 16,000 lived in New England, with slightly more found in the middle colonies, the vast majority lived in the South. By then, the flow of free white labor to the region had all but stopped, and Africans had become securely established as the basis of the southern workforce (Brinkley 1999, 84).

Initially, it was not entirely clear that the status of black laborers in America would be fundamentally different from that of white indentured servants. Some blacks were treated much like white indentured servants and were freed after a fixed term of servitude. A few Africans themselves became landowners, and some owned slaves of their own.

By the early eighteenth century, however, a rigid distinction had become established between black and white. Although masters were contractually obliged to free white servants after a fixed term of service, there was no such obligation to free black workers. The assumption slowly spread that blacks would remain in service permanently. Another incentive for making the status of Africans fixed was that the children of slaves would provide white landowners with an ongoing labor force. At this time, colonial assemblies began to pass "slave codes," limiting the rights of blacks and ensuring almost absolute authority to white masters. One factor alone determined whether a person was subject to the slave codes, and that one factor was color. Unlike the colonial societies of Spanish America, where people of mixed race had a different status than pure Africans, English American law stated that any African ancestry was enough to classify a person as black.

Tobacco

In 1612, Jamestown planter John Rolfe began to experiment in Virginia with a strain of tobacco that local Indians had been growing for years. He eventually produced a high-quality tobacco and found willing buyers in England. Tobacco would evolve to become the single most important commodity produced in North America, accounting for more than one-quarter of all colonial exports.

The expansion of tobacco production could not have taken place without enormous growth in the size of the slave labor force. Tobacco, unlike sugar, did not require large plantations and could be produced successfully on small farms. It was, however, a crop that demanded a great deal of hand labor and close attention and from the beginning of Chesapeake colonization, its cultivation had been the responsibility of indentured servants and slaves. During the seventeenth and into the eighteenth centuries, however, master, servant, and slave worked side by side, with the women and children often joining them in the fields as well.

African workers at this time were presumed to be slaves (they were purchased by slave traders), however, because there were no laws governing slave labor, black hands on tobacco plantations labored according to customary English practices drawn from the Elizabethan Statute of Artificers. As the Chesapeake settlement grew during the seventeenth century, black servants instituted the customary rights of English laborers, so that by midcentury, they seldom worked more than five and a half days a week during the summer and even less in the winter (Berlin 1998, 32). Furthermore, tobacco laborers not only had Sundays off but also half of Saturday and all holidays. English customs required masters to provide their servants with sufficient clothing, food, and shelter and limited the owner's right to discipline his or her workers. Therefore, well into the middle years of the seventeenth century, black slaves enjoyed the benefits given to white servants in the mixed labor force.

Although some slave owners ignored the law to increase productivity, others offered more generous incentives to servants and slaves. Among the benefits was the opportunity to labor independently with the understanding that servants and slaves would feed and clothe themselves. Although laboring to support themselves meant additional work, it provided slaves and servants a way to control a portion of their lives, and in some cases, it offered an opportunity to buy their way out of bondage.

The Lower South

For years after the founding of the colony of South Carolina in 1670, colonists raised cattle with the help of West African slaves experienced in pastoral work. By 1715, rice had become the most significant commodity produced in South Carolina, and like cattle grazing depended on the knowledge of West Africans. Rice cultivation was arduous work, performed knee-deep in the mud of malarial swamps under a fierce sun, surrounded by insects. It was a task so difficult and unhealthy that white laborers generally refused to perform it. Black slaves showed from the beginning a greater resistance than whites to malaria and other local diseases. As a result, planters in South Carolina and Georgia were even more dependent on African slaves. Whites found them so valuable not only because Africans could be made to perform these difficult tasks but also because they were much better at the work than whites. Africans proved more adept at rice cultivation in part because some of them had come from the hot and humid rice-producing regions of West Africa. Some historians have even argued that Africans were responsible for introducing rice cultivation to America in the early seventeenth century.

On the rice plantations of isolated coastal Georgia, enslaved Africans suffered from overwork and numerous physical ailments that resulted from poor diet, inappropriate clothing, and inadequate housing. Mortality rates were exceptionally high, especially for infants. Colonial laws permitted masters to discipline and punish slaves. They were whipped, confined in irons, castrated, or sold away. Nonetheless, Africans struggled to make a home for themselves in this cruel world. Because many of the slaves on the rice coast were familiar with rice cultivation, they had enough bargaining power with their masters to win an acceptance of the work routines used in West Africa. Many rice plantations, therefore, operated according to the task system: once slaves finished their specific jobs, they could use their remaining time to hunt, fish, or tend to family gardens. Masters complained that "tasking" did not produce the same level of profit as the gang labor system of the sugar plantation (where slaves worked from sunup to sundown), but African rice hands refused to work any other way.

In the early 1740s, another important crop began to contribute to the South Carolina economy: indigo. Native to India, the indigo plant produced a deep blue dye important in textile manufacturing. It was discovered that indigo plants could grow on the high ground of South Carolina, which was unsuitable for rice planting, and that its harvest came while the rice was still growing. By the 1770s, both crops were among the most valuable commodities exported from the mainland colonies of North America. Like tobacco, the expansion of rice and indigo production depended on the growth of African slavery. By 1770, there were nearly 90,000 African Americans in the lower South, about 80 percent of the coastal population of South Carolina and Georgia. Before the international slave trade to the United States ended in 1808, at least 100,000 Africans had arrived at Charleston.

Slavery in the Early Spanish Colonies

Slavery was basic to the Spanish colonial labor system, and its character varied with local conditions. One of the most benign forms operated in Florida. In 1699, offering free land to any fugitives who would help defend the colony, the Spanish declared a refuge for escaped slaves from northern English colonies. In New Mexico, the Spanish depended on Indian slavery, and in the sixteenth century, the colonial government sent Pueblo Indian slaves to the mines in Mexico.

Slavery in the North

Slavery was much less important in the colonies north of the Chesapeake and was primarily located in port cities. By 1770, New York and New Jersey were home to some 27,000 African Americans, about 10 percent of the population. Some 3,000 slaves and 100 free blacks, about 17 percent of the population, resided in New York City. The most important center of slavery in the North was Rhode Island. In 1760, in Newport, Rhode Island, African Americans made up about 20 percent of the population because of that city's dominance of the mid-century slave trade.

The vast majority of northern slaves, like northern whites, lived and worked in the countryside. A few were employed in rural industries—iron furnaces, copper and lead mines, salt works, or tanneries—where they worked alongside white indentured servants and hired laborers. Ironmasters, the largest employers of industrial slaves, were also the region's largest slaveholders. In 1727, Pennsylvania iron manufacturers petitioned for a reduction in the tariff on slaves so they could keep their furnaces operating. Although forges and foundries in other colonies similarly relied on slave labor, only a small proportion of the northern slave population worked in industrial labor. Northern society in the eighteenth century, like southern society, was an overwhelmingly agricultural society, and like most rural whites, most rural blacks toiled as agricultural workers. Rural slaves generally lived on farms, not plantations, and frequently worked alongside their owners when they sowed in the spring and reaped in the fall. In slack times, slaves fertilized the land, chopped wood, broke flax, pressed cider, repaired farm buildings, cleared fields, and prepared new land for cultivation. Moving from job to job as work demands changed, slaves found themselves working in the field one day and in the shop the next. Male slaves made horseshoes, tanned leather, made bricks, repaired furniture, and even served as boatmen and wagon drivers. Black women worked as dairy maids as well as domestic servants who cooked, cleaned, and sewed.

Early Colonial Slave Life

It has been said that Africans built the South because slaves made up the overwhelming majority of the labor force that made the plantation colonies successful. As an agricultural people, African men and women were familiar with rural labor and, after arriving in the colonies, became field hands. Even domestic servants worked in the fields when necessary. As plantations grew larger and more extensive in the eighteenth century and crop production expanded, labor became specialized. For example, on large eighteenth-century Virginia plantations, slaves worked as carpenters, coopers, sawyers, blacksmiths, tanners, curriers, shoemakers, spinners, weavers, knitters, and even distillers.

The growing African population and the larger plantations on which many lived and worked together created the climate necessary for the development of African American communities and

African American culture. On small farms, Africans often worked side by side with their owners and, depending on the master, might enjoy living conditions similar to those of other family members. Plantation life was preferred since it offered possibilities for a more autonomous life. Nonetheless, because of continual interaction, many blacks and white southerners came to share a common culture. White masters not only influenced the cultural development of their slaves, but Englishmen and -women in the South were also being Africanized.

Slaves worked in the kitchens of their masters and introduced an African style of cooking into colonial life that had already been influenced by Indian crops. Fried chicken, black-eyed peas, collard greens, and barbecue are just a few such southern perennials introduced by African Americans. African architectural designs featuring high, peaked roofs, and broad, shady porches became part of a distinctive southern style. The West African ironworking tradition was evident throughout the South, especially in the ornate homes of Charleston and New Orleans.

Slavery's Contribution to Economic Growth

Slavery contributed enormously to the economic growth and development of Europe during the colonial era. It was the most dynamic force in the Atlantic economy during the eighteenth century and created many of the conditions for industrialization. But because slave colonists contributed the majority of their resources to developing the plantation system, they benefited little from industrialization.

The most significant economic development in the mid-nineteenth-century South was the transfer of economic power from the upper South (the southern states along the Atlantic coast) to the lower South (the cotton-growing regions of the Southwest). And the primary reason for the shift was the growing dominance of cotton in the southern economy. Much of the upper South in the nineteenth century continued to rely, as it always had, on the cultivation of tobacco. Tobacco not only rapidly exhausted the land on which it grew, but by the 1820s, the market for that crop was extremely unstable.

The southern regions of the coastal South—Georgia, South Carolina, and parts of Florida—continued to rely on the cultivation of rice. Rice, however, required a nine-month growing season and constant irrigation. Sugar growers along the Gulf Coast enjoyed a somewhat profitable market for their crop, but sugar cultivation required intensive, grueling labor and a long growing season. Sugar cultivation, therefore, remained important primarily in southern Louisiana and eastern Texas. Long-staple cotton was another lucrative crop, but, like rice, could only grow in limited areas around the coastal regions of the Southeast. The decline of the tobacco economy in the upper South and the limitations of the sugar, rice, and long-staple cotton economies in the lower South might have forced the South in the nineteenth century to shift its focus toward other, nonagricultural endeavors, had it not been for short-staple cotton. Sea Island, or long-staple cotton, with its long fibers and smooth black seed, was easy to clean but grew only along the Atlantic coast and on the offshore islands of Georgia and South Carolina. The growth of the textile industry in England had created an enormous demand for Southern cotton and Southern planters were finding it impossible to fill these needs with long-staple cotton. Short-staple cotton could grow inland throughout the entire South, but was difficult to process. It contained sticky green seeds that were extremely difficult to remove, and a skilled worker could clean no more than a few pounds a day by hand.

In 1793, Eli Whitney, a tutor on a Georgia plantation, invented a device known as the cotton gin that removed short-staple seeds quickly and efficiently. The cotton gin transformed the life of the South. African American slavery, which was on the decline, expanded and became firmly established in the South. The South, which had grown only 4,000 bales of cotton in 1790, saw production increase to 500,000 bales in 1820. By the time the Civil War broke out in 1861, it was producing over 5 million bales a year.

Life under Slavery

Slaves as a group were much less healthy than southern whites. After 1808, when the importation of slaves became illegal, the proportion of blacks to whites in the nation as a whole declined. In 1820, there was one African American for every four whites; in 1840, one for every five. Slave mothers had large families, but the poverty in which all African Americans lived ensured that few of their children would survive to adulthood. Even those who did survive typically died at a younger age than the average white person. However, according to some historians, the actual material conditions of slavery may have been better than those of many northern factory workers and much better than those of both immigrants and industrial workers in nineteenth-century Europe. The conditions of slaves in the United States were certainly better than those of slaves in the Caribbean and South America, in part because plantations in other parts of the Americas tended to grow crops that required more arduous labor. In the Caribbean, sugar production, in particular, involved extraordinarily backbreaking labor. Working and living conditions in these other slave societies were arduous, and masters at times literally worked their slaves to death. Although growing cotton was difficult work, it was much less debilitating than growing sugar. The United States became the only country in which a slave population actually increased through natural reproduction.

Because of the high cost of slaves, especially in the 1850s, masters did make some effort to preserve the health of their slaves. Slave children were often protected from hard work until early adolescence. Masters believed that doing so would make young slaves more loyal and help them grow into healthier adults. It was not unusual for masters to use hired labor for the most unhealthy and dangerous work. Irish immigrants were employed to clear malarial swamps and to handle cotton bales at the bottom of chutes. If an Irish worker died of disease or an accident, another could be hired for $1 a day. But if a prime field hand died, a master could lose an investment of $1,000 or more. Field slaves, however, were often left to the discipline of the overseers, who had little economic stake in their welfare. Overseers were paid in proportion to the amount of work they could get out of the slaves they supervised.

Types of Slavery

The institution of slavery was established and regulated by law. The slave codes of the southern states forbade slaves to hold property, to be out after dark, or to strike a white person, even in self-defense. The laws contained no provisions to legalize slave marriages or divorces. The codes also contained extremely rigid provisions for defining a person's race. Despite the strict provisions of these laws, there was in reality considerable variety within the slave system. Although some blacks lived in tightly controlled conditions, others enjoyed some flexibility and autonomy.

The relationship between masters and slaves depended in part on the size of the plantation. Most masters possessed few slaves, supervised their workers directly, and often worked closely alongside them. On such farms, blacks and whites developed a form of intimacy unknown on larger plantations. The paternal relationship between master and slave could be warm and friendly or harsh and cruel. In either case, it was a relationship based on the nearly absolute authority of the master and the powerlessness of the slave. African Americans themselves preferred to live on larger plantations, where they had more privacy and the opportunity to develop their own social world and culture.

Although the majority of slave owners were small yeoman farmers, the majority of slaves lived on medium-size or large plantations that had large slave workforces. There the relationship between master and slave was much less intimate. Wealthier planters, too busy to supervise their workforce, hired "overseers" to represent them. Trusted and responsible slaves known as "head drivers," assisted by several "subdrivers," acted as foremen under the supervision of the overseer. Importantly, although plantation production was officially entrusted to overseers and drivers, its pace was effectively in control of the field hands themselves. Although they were denied political and legal rights and the dignity of recognized marriage and family ties, this enslaved labor force exerted subtle control over the power of the masters.

Field Work

About three-quarters of all slaves were field workers. Field hands, both men and women, worked from "can see to can't see" (sunup to sundown) summer and winter and longer at harvest. On most plantations, a bell sounded an hour before sunup, and most slaves were on their way to the field as soon as it was light. The usual pattern of working in groups of twenty to twenty-five originated in African communal systems of agricultural work. Large plantations generally used one of two methods of assigning slave labor. The task system assigned a particular task in the morning. Upon completion of the job, whether clearing an acre of swamp or hoeing an acre of land, the slave was free for the rest of the day. The far more common method was the gang system. Found primarily on cotton, sugar, and tobacco plantations, the gang system divided slaves into groups, and under the direction of a slave driver, they worked for as many hours as the overseer thought reasonable. Cotton growing was hard work: plowing and planting, chopping weeds with a heavy hoe, and picking the ripe cotton from the stiff bolls at the rate of 150 pounds a day. In the rice fields, slaves worked knee-deep in water. On sugar plantations, harvesting the cane and getting it ready for boiling was exceptionally heavy work.

Regardless of the labor method, slaves worked hard. They began performing light tasks as children, and their workdays were always longest and most brutal at harvest time. Slave women worked the hardest. They not only labored all day with the men in the fields but also cooked, cleaned, and took care of the children after returning home at night. Because slave families were often divided, black women found themselves acting as single parents. Therefore, within the slave family, women had special burdens but also special authority.

House Servants

Household servants had a somewhat easier life than field hands. On a small plantation, the slave might do both field work and housework, but on a larger estate, there would generally be a separate domestic staff. Cooks, butlers, housemaids, nursemaids, and coachmen lived close to the master and his family, often eating the leftovers from the family table and in some cases even sleeping in the "big house." Although close ties might develop between blacks and whites living in the same household, more often house servants resented the isolation from their fellow slaves and the lack of privacy that came with living in such close proximity to the master and his family. Minor household accidents and transgressions were more apparent than those made by field hands, and so they were punished more often.

Female house servants were especially vulnerable to sexual abuse by their masters and white overseers. In addition to unwanted sexual attention from white men, female slaves often received vindictive treatment from white women. Punishing their husbands was seldom possible, so white mistresses often inflicted beatings, increased workloads, and used various other forms of torment on female slaves.

Skilled Workers

A small number of slaves were carpenters, weavers, seamstresses, blacksmiths, and mechanics. Solomon Northup, kidnapped into slavery in Washington, D.C., in 1841, spent twelve years of his life as a slave on a Louisiana cotton plantation. During enslavement, Northup had been hired out repeatedly as a carpenter and as a driver of slaves in his owner's sugar mill. Because cooking and domestic work were not considered skilled work, slave men achieved skilled status more often than women. Of the 16,000 lumber workers in the United States, almost all were slaves. Black people also worked as miners; as dockhands and stokers on Mississippi riverboats; and as stevedores loading cotton on the docks of Savannah, New Orleans, and Charleston. The wages of the slaves, because they were their masters' property, belonged to the owner, not to the slave.

Slavery in the City

The extent to which slaves made up the laboring class was most obvious in cities. Because the South failed to attract as much European immigrant labor as the North, southern cities offered both enslaved and free black people opportunities in skilled occupations, such as blacksmithing and carpentering, that free African Americans in the North were denied. Slaves on contract worked in mining and lumbering, and others worked on the docks or on construction sites, drove wagons, and performed other unskilled jobs in cities and towns. Slave women and children worked in textile mills.

The conditions of slavery in the cities differed significantly from those in the countryside. Slaves on isolated plantations had little contact with free blacks and lower-class whites. For the most part, masters maintained direct and effective control. In the city, however, masters often could not supervise their slaves closely and at the same time use them profitably. After regular working hours, many slaves fended for themselves and had opportunities to mingle with free blacks and with whites. After working hours, the line between slavery and freedom became increasingly indistinct.

Rising Tensions

White southerners often referred to slavery as the "peculiar institution," peculiar in the sense that it was distinctive and unique. More than any other single factor, slavery isolated the South from the rest of American society, and as the South became more isolated, so did southerners' commitment to hold on to their peculiar institution.

By the 1850s, assumptions in the North about the proper structure of society centered on the belief in "free soil" and "free labor." An increasing number of northerners came to believe that the existence of slavery was dangerous not because of what it did to blacks but because of what it threatened to do to whites who wanted to control their own labor and to have opportunities to advance. The ideal society was one of small-scale capitalism in which everyone could advance and work as they chose. Northern "free laborites" believed the South was in a conspiracy to extend slavery throughout the growing nation—primarily the growing American West. This "slave power conspiracy," according to many northerners, threatened the future of every white laborer and property owner in the North.

In the South, a very different ideology was emerging—an ideology completely incompatible with the free labor ideology in the North. It emerged out of the hardening of ideas among southerners on the issue and defense of the slave system. And in defending slavery, the South would grow increasingly different from the dynamic, capitalist, free labor system that was gaining strength in the North.

For all its expansion, the South in the nineteenth century experienced much less transformation than the industrial North. The South had begun the century with few important cities and little industry and remained the same sixty years later. In 1800, a plantation system dependent on slave labor had dominated the southern economy, and by 1860, that system, still dominated by great plantations and wealthy landowning planters, had only tightened its grip on the region. As one historian noted, "The South grew, but it did not develop" (Brinkley 1999, 371). The fragile and splintered nature of this slave labor society would soon become apparent when it was subjected to the pressures of civil war.

Karen Utz

See also African American Women and Work; African Americans and Work

References and further reading

Berlin, Ira. 1998. *Many Thousands Gone: The First Two Centuries of Slavery in North America.* Cambridge, MA: Belknap Press of Harvard University Press.

Breen, T. H., Robert A. Divine, George M. Fredrickson, R. Hal Williams. 2002. *America Past and Present,* Vol. 1, *To 1877.* New York: Longman Publisher.

Brinkley, Alan. 1999. *American History: A Survey.* Vol. 1, *To 1877.* New York: McGraw-Hill College Division.

Faragher, John Mack, Mari Jo Buhle, Daniel Czitrom, Susan H. Armitage. 1999. *Out of Many: A History of the American People.* Vol. 1. Upper Saddle River, NJ: Prentice Hall.

Fink, Leon. 1997. *American Labor History.* Washington, DC: American Historical Association.

Finkenbine, Roy. 1997. *Sources of the African-American Past: Primary Sources in American History.* New York: Longman Press.

Kolchnin, Peter. 1987. *Unfree Labor: American Slavery and Russian Serfdom.* Cambridge, MA: Belknap Press of Harvard University Press.

Unger, Irvin. 1999. *The United States: The Questions of Our Past.* New Jersey: Prentice Hall.

American Telephone and Telegraph (AT&T)

Once a stalwart of economic might and brand power, American Telephone and Telegraph (AT&T) is a shadow of its former self thanks to twenty years of constant evolution brought about by regulatory changes, increased competition, and advances in communications technology. "Ma Bell," as it was known, once held the title of the world's largest company. Its century of strength was built on its monopoly position as the carrier of U.S. local and long distance telephone service, as well as its production of telecommunications equipment.

AT&T's strength and position transcended the communications industry. It was once one of a few corporations that set the tone for employers and employees in the United States and the developed world. By the early 1980s, in fact, AT&T employed 1.1 million people and had firmly established itself as a classic "cradle to grave" employer. Joining AT&T was akin to accepting a lifetime position in which skilled and unskilled workers enjoyed job security and, if applicable, career development.

The ground began to change in the early 1980s when mandated divestiture forced AT&T to shed its local telephone operations, creating the seven independent regional Baby Bells. Beyond breaking AT&T's service monopoly, the court-ordered change was designed to open the floodgates to competition in all telecommunications services, including the emerging corporate and data markets. Competition did flood in, at least in the long-distance market. Soon after the breakup, AT&T began to see substantial and growing competition in the long-distance sector from MCI and Sprint and eventually from providers such as WorldCom.

Although it remains the largest provider of long-distance service in the United States, with approximately 60 million customers, the rush of competitors has undercut both AT&T's customer base and, more importantly, its margins. AT&T's long-distance services remain profitable, but the pressure on customers and margins have forced the communications giant to remold itself several times since the 1990s. The first push came with a move into new services, such as wireless (cell phones), data (information transmission via financial service networks and the Internet), and cable television. Eventually, AT&T also sought to remake itself through a corporate reorganization.

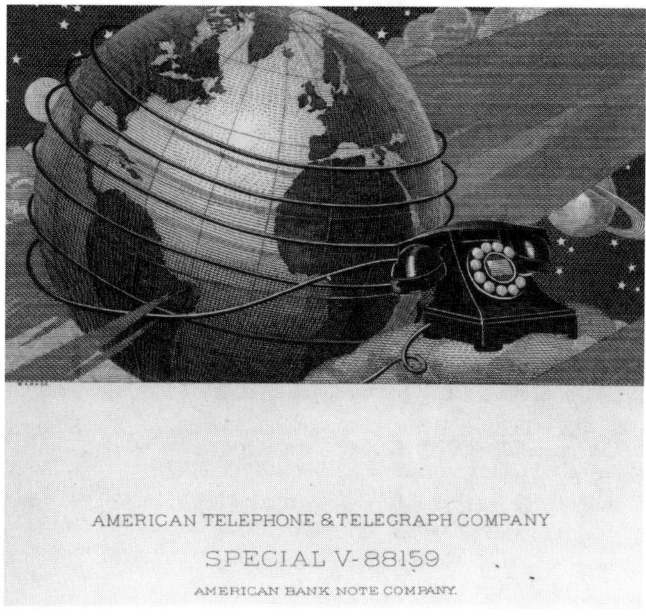

AMERICAN TELEPHONE & TELEGRAPH COMPANY
SPECIAL V-88159
AMERICAN BANK NOTE COMPANY

Advertising used for American Telephone and Telegraph from 1940 to 1949. (Library of Congress)

The importance of the decline and remolding of the telecommunications giant goes beyond AT&T itself and even the communications industry as a whole. The transformation of this American industrial stalwart during the 1990s and early 2000s contributed to the growing awareness that no company or industry was immune to change. In line with this realization came the sometimes painful understanding that both white- and blue-collar workers—even at seemingly rock steady companies—could lose their jobs or have their roles changed to address new market demands. AT&T's unraveling also underscored the precarious nature of all investments. Its share price declined by more than 70 percent in the early 2000s. "This was a stock that every American of voting age thought was safe enough for widows and orphans. That trait had been deregulated away years ago," Geoffrey Colvin wrote in *Fortune* (2002). Perhaps of even more concern was that the major restructuring broke the company into separate or autonomous units without a core simply called AT&T. This change threatened to dilute one of the company's major assets, its enormously valuable brand image.

The cumulative impact of AT&T's troubles and reorganization ultimately cost the company its place among the world's top ten brands as measured by *Business Week*. The decline came despite hundreds of millions of dollars spent on aggressive, youth-oriented ads and new cutting-edge products. The effort failed when it was unable to sell customers on the image of the new AT&T.

The restructuring announced in 2000 split AT&T's wireless, broadband, business, and consumer units into four separate groups. This effort was soon adjusted again when the wireless division was spun off entirely into a separate company with its own stock. The carrier's profitable long-distance service was also spun off into a separate tracking stock. AT&T further altered its portfolio of services when it bought Comcast, the country's third-largest cable television provider, for $72 billion. The cable television services were rolled into AT&T Broadband, with the idea that AT&T might be able to use Comcast's cable connections as a means of providing lucrative local telephone service and high-speed Internet connections to the cable company's subscribers.

AT&T realized few immediate gains from its efforts because none of its newer services—cable, data, business, or local phone service—yielded the kinds of results the company had hoped. The dismal returns, in part, can be attributed to the weak communications market of the early 2000s. Yet for all its operational and branding problems, AT&T actually gained some advantage from the turmoil that enveloped the communications industry, beginning in the late 1990s. The well-publicized problems of competitors such as WorldCom and Qwest helped remind the market that for all its faults, AT&T is still the world's most stable carrier. AT&T leveraged these concerns to draw in and cement interest from major business clients that were unwilling to rely on unstable carriers for their communications needs.

John Salak

See also Communications Workers of America; The Dot-com Revolution; New Economy

References and further reading

Coll, Steve. 1986. *The Deal Of The Century: The Breakup of AT&T.* New York: Atheneum.

Colvin, Geoffrey. 2002. "A History of AT&T, Take 2." *Fortune,* September 2.

Khermouch, Jerry. 2002. "The Best Global Brands." *Business Week,* August 5.

Mehta, Stephanie. 2002a. "Is There Any Way Out of the Telecom Mess?" *Fortune,* July 22.

———. 2002b. "Wireless Carriers Aren't All Talk." *Fortune,* September 16.

Americans with Disabilities Act (ADA) (1990)

In 1990, the U.S. Congress passed and President George H. W. Bush signed the Americans with Disabilities Act (ADA), widely recognized as a landmark civil rights law that has become a major battleground for legal challenges over the rights of people with disabilities to have equal access to facilities, services, technology, public institutions, and employment opportunities. The ADA gives civil rights protections to individuals with disabilities similar to those provided to individuals on the basis of race, color, sex, national origin, age, and religion. It guarantees equal opportunity for individuals with disabilities in public accommodations, employment, transportation, state and local government services, and telecommunications. The ADA enjoys broad support from the public and is viewed generally as a modest success by advocates for people with disabilities, although many believe the law could be strengthened further. Although it is not without controversy, the ADA has prompted the redesign of thousands of public and private facilities so they are accessible to the disabled and is widely credited with helping improve access to services and employment opportunities for people with disabilities. The law is enforced by the U.S. Equal Employment Opportunity Commission (EEOC) and the U.S. Department of Justice.

According to the U.S. Census Bureau, there are approximately 50 million Americans—or 20 percent of the total population—with a disability (U.S. Bureau of the Census 1997, 1). Nearly 25 million people in the United States have a severe disability, and almost 30 million Americans with disabilities are between the ages of fifteen and sixty-four. The average monthly earnings of nondisabled workers between the ages of thirty-five and fifty-four are $2,617, compared to $2,258 for workers with a mild disability and $1,574 for workers with a severe disability (McNeil 2000). Although the ADA and other legislation have spurred enormous progress in providing equal opportunity for people with disabilities, the United States must overcome a long history of discrimination against this community.

For generations, people with disabilities were routinely excluded from the workplace and other areas of public life. Discrimination and discomfort on the part of employers regarding hiring people who were disabled and lack of physical access to the workplace kept many otherwise qualified workers from engaging in meaningful work. In addition, federal laws regarding Social Security income and Medicare prevented many people with disabilities from entering the workplace for fear of losing their health benefits. Today, despite an increased awareness among employers and laws to encourage access, people with disabilities still experience higher levels of unemployment than people without disabilities.

Beginning in the 1960s, the federal government recognized the need for laws to address discrimination against people with disabilities and access to the workplace and other public facilities. One of the first laws passed was the Rehabilitation Act of 1973, which mandated equal treatment of people with disabilities in the federal workplace. The Rehabilitation Act has several key components that require all federal agencies to ensure nondiscrimination and affirmative action in federal employment (Section 501); accessibility in federal buildings (Section 502); affirmative action in employment by federal contractors (Section 503); and affirmative action of recipients of federal funds, including state agencies, housing authorities, educational institutions, private entities, and charitable organizations (Section 504). The Rehabilitation Act made a significant contribution toward making the public sector more accessible to people with disabilities.

Other federal laws affecting people with disabilities include the Individuals with Disabilities Edu-

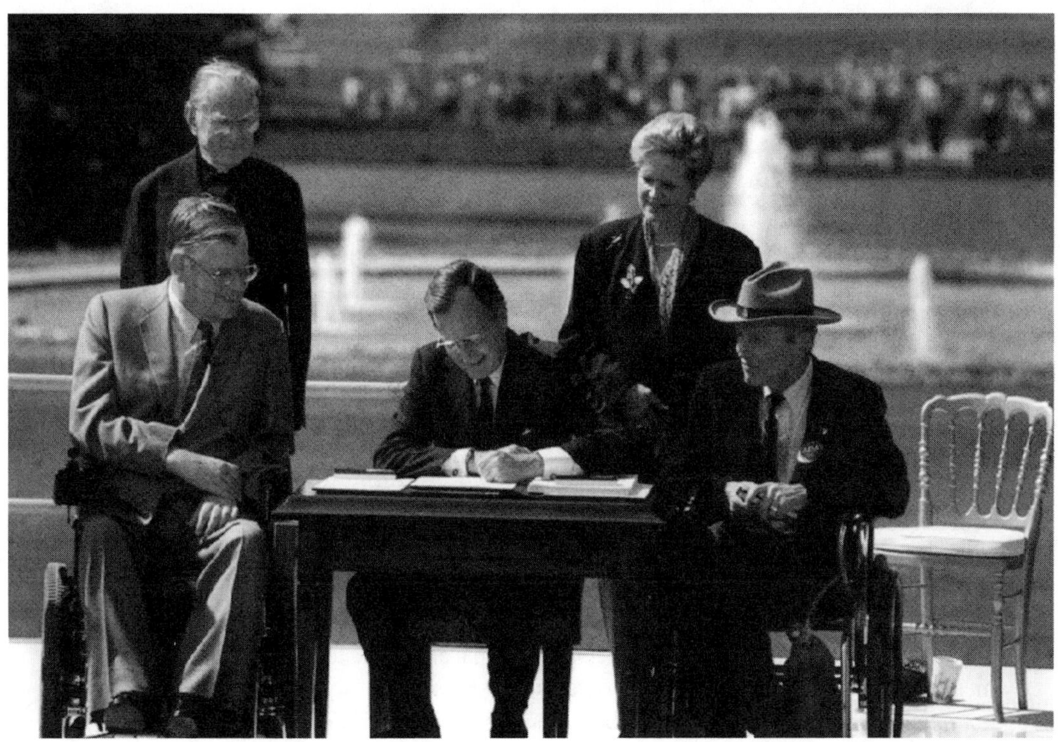

President George H. W. Bush signs into law the Americans with Disabilities Act on the south lawn of the White House, July 26, 1990. (U.S. National Archives)

cation Act of 1975. This law requires school systems to ensure that disabled students have educational opportunities on a par with those provided to nondisabled students. The Fair Housing Act of 1968 prohibits public and private housing agencies from discriminating on the basis of race, color, religion, sex, disability, familial status, and national origin.

To combat the discrimination that people with disabilities continued to face after these laws were enacted, Congress passed the Americans with Disabilities Act. Unlike some of the previous laws targeting disability issues, ADA applies to private employers of fifteen people or more, as well as federal, state, and local governments, employment agencies, and labor unions. The goal of the law is to increase access to all facets of society, including the workplace, transportation, telecommunications, and the public arena for people with disabilities. In addition, it mandates that workers with disabilities have the same job and career opportunities as workers without disabilities. To ensure equal access, the ADA prohibits discrimination against individuals with physical and mental disabilities in employment, housing, education, and access to public services. Under ADA, employers are not allowed to discriminate against qualified workers or job seekers with disabilities in hiring or firing, to inquire about a disability, to limit advancement opportunities or job classifications, to use tests that tend to screen out people with disabilities, or to deny opportunities to anyone in a relationship with a person with disabilities.

Enforcing the ADA

The EEOC reports that since the law took effect, it has collected more than $300 million on behalf of 20,000 people through lawsuits, settlements, mediation, and other enforcement actions. In addition, the agency has helped more than 10,000 individuals settle disputes over training, education, job referrals, union membership, and other issues. A national mediation program begun in 1997 and expanded in 1999 has resolved more than 60 percent of 2,000 ADA charges brought before the commission in about half the time needed for administrative review. The commission has successfully resolved about 90 percent of ADA suits filed in district court either by settlement or favorable court or jury decision (U.S. Equal Employment Opportunity Commission 2000). In the appellate courts, the EEOC has filed nearly 100 amicus curiae (friend of the court) briefs in cases confronting fundamental issues on how the ADA should be applied. Significant cases argued and won by the EEOC include the following:

- In the first lawsuit filed by EEOC under the ADA on June 7, 1993, *EEOC & Charles Wessel v. AIC SecurityInvestigations, Ltd., et al.*, EEOC won a jury verdict finding the defendant had unlawfully fired its executive director due to the assumption that he could no longer perform his job because he had been diagnosed with terminal brain cancer. The former director was awarded $222,000.
- In a suit against Chuck E. Cheese on November 4, 1999, EEOC claimed that a district manager fired a custodian with a developmental disability because the company did not employ "those type of people" (*EEOC v. CEC Entertainment, Inc. a/b/a Chuck E. Cheese's* 1999, 6). A jury awarded the custodian back pay, $70,000 in compensatory damages for emotional distress, and $13 million in punitive damages (the punitive damages award was reduced on March 14, 2000, to $230,000 because of the statutory cap on damages). The judge also ordered the company to give the custodian his job back.
- In *EEOC v. Chomerics, Inc., et al.,* (August 25, 1998) the commission claimed that a chemical worker's coworkers and supervisor harassed and mocked him because of his disability (cerebral palsy). The company agreed to provide the worker with $98,000 in back pay and compensatory damages.
- In the EEOC's case involving Wal-Mart Stores, a jury found the store's hiring official had illegally asked a job applicant about his disability (amputated arm) in a job interview and then refused to hire him. On October 10, 1997, the applicant was awarded $7,500 in compensatory damages and $150,000 in punitive damages.

The Justice Department cites a decade of numerous accomplishments in enforcing ADA that include victories for people seeking access to services, facilities, jobs, and economic opportunity. Towns in North Dakota, Wisconsin, Montana, Ohio, and other locations agreed to improve and expand access to public buildings and services for people with disabilities. Courts in Utah and Washington, D.C., were ordered to improve access for the deaf and blind. The Houston, Texas, and Oakland, California, police departments agreed to take the necessary steps to ensure that people who are deaf or hard of hearing can communicate effectively with police officers. Through cases involving an injured Denver police officer, a dyslexic New York plumber, and disabled police and fire officers in Illinois, the Department of Justice enforced the employment provisions of ADA. The department worked with professional licensing and college testing services to ensure that they provided the necessary materials and devices so that deaf students and other students with disabilities could be prepared for and take the major professional and precollege exams.

Misgivings and Controversy

Despite these measures of progress, the ADA has not been without controversy, beginning with how the act defines disability, a definition that is open to a certain degree of interpretation. The ADA defines a disability as having a "physical or mental impairment that substantially limits one or more of the major life activities of the individual, having a record of such impairment (cancer, for instance), or being regarded as having such an impairment" (for instance, a disfigurement that does not actual limit major life activities but may be viewed by others as doing so). In addition, the ADA requires that "reasonable accommodation" be made in the workplace for qualified individuals with disabilities. Reasonable accommodation is considered any modification or adjustment to a job or the work environment that will enable a qualified applicant or employee with a disability to participate in the application process or to perform essential job functions. It can include providing special equipment or making a workplace more accessible. It can also mean allowing an employee to work at home or on a nontraditional schedule. Under the act, employers are not required to provide accommodations that impose an "undue hardship" ("action requiring significant difficulty or expense") on their business operations, nor are they required to hire people who are not qualified candidates simply because they have a disability. However, this provision has not been enough to allay the fears of many employers.

With the passage of the ADA, many employers feared that they would be forced to make costly accommodations for people with disabilities, hire people with disabilities who were not qualified for the job, or be sued by disgruntled workers claiming discrimination under the ADA. Many employers have overcome their fear of hiring people with disabilities, have made reasonable accommodations, and have not found the requirements of ADA to be unduly burdensome. Others have resisted making the accommodations and changes necessary for an accessible workplace. In 1995, the National Council on Disability, in its report "The Americans with Disabilities Act: Ensuring Equal Access to the American Dream," celebrated the success of ADA but cautioned that "what is needed to improve upon the implementation of the Americans with Disabilities Act is greater public awareness, further education and clarification regarding the provisions of the law, and the appropriate resources to both encourage voluntary compliance and to ensure effective enforcement" (National Council on Disability 2001, 24).

Despite the claims of the EEOC and Department of Justice, a report in the May–June 2000 issue of the American Bar Association's *Mental and Physical Disability Law Reporter* is less encouraging for advocates for the disabled. The article concluded that employers prevail more than 95 percent of the time in ADA suits and in 85 percent of the administrative complaints handled by the EEOC. In addition, a 1999 Supreme Court decision narrowed the definition of disability to exclude certain people from protection under ADA. In considering the cases *Sutton v. United Airlines, Inc.*, *Murphy v. United Parcel Service*, and *Albertsons, Inc. v. Kirkingburg*, the Supreme Court held that a person is not "disabled," and therefore not protected from discrimination under the Americans with Disabilities Act, if medication or other corrective devices diminish his or her impairment (taking medication for depression, for instance, or wearing corrective lenses).

In February 2001, the Court dealt what could be another blow to ADA protections when it ruled in favor of states' rights by deciding in the *Garrett v. Alabama* case that state employees cannot sue for money damages under ADA when they are discriminated against on the basis of disability. The decision narrows the law as written by Congress by excluding state governments as parties that can be sued for financial damages under ADA. However, state employees can still sue state governments for "injunctive relief" that requires states to take actions such as building wheelchair ramps or reinstating fired employees. In the wake of these rulings by the U.S. Supreme Court, California passed a law that restores the scope and purview of ADA within its borders, and other states may follow.

It is likely that ADA will be litigated further in the courts, as advocates for the disabled, state governments, courts, and employers continue to struggle to define the reach, scope, and regulatory requirements of the act. It is clear that the Americans with Disabilities Act was a critical step in the fight to provide unfettered access to the workplace for people with disabilities, but barriers to participation remain.

Herbert A. Schaffner and K. A. Dixon

See also Disability and Work

References and further reading

McNeil, John M. 2000. "Employment, Earnings, and Disability." Paper presented at the Seventy-fifth Annual Conference of the Western Economic Association International, Vancouver, British Columbia, June 29–July 3.

U.S. Bureau of the Census. 1997. *Disabilities Affect One-Fifth of All Americans.* Washington, DC: U.S. Department of Commerce, Economics and Statistics Administration.

U.S. Department of Justice. 2000. *Enforcing the ADA: Looking Back on a Decade of Progress.* Washington, DC: GPO, July.

U.S. Equal Employment Opportunity Commission. 2000. *Highlights of EEOC Enforcement of the Americans with Disabilities Act.* Washington, DC: GPO, , March.

Schaffner, Herbert A, and Van Horn, Carl E. 2003. *A Nation at Work: The Heldrich Guide to the American Workforce.* New Brunswick, NJ: Rutgers University Press.

The Workforce Investment Act: A Primer for People with Disabilities. New Brunswick, NJ: Heldrich Center for Workforce Development, Rutgers University.

Apprenticeship

An apprenticeship is an opportunity to learn a trade while being employed in it for an agreed-upon period of time, often at lower wages than average for the trade. Apprenticeship was the primary way to learn a trade in colonial America, but today formal schooling is required. A rough estimate of the current number of registered apprentices in the U.S. is

400,000. The dramatic fall in the number of apprenticeships since 1700 stems from automation and mass production brought on by the Industrial Revolution, as well as the rise of public schooling available for adolescents. Although the number of traditional apprenticeships that combine classroom training with on-the-job training is relatively small today, there is an increasing trend in secondary education to promote academic achievement by using work-based learning experiences.

Apprenticeships date as far back as ancient Egypt. Apprenticeships in the United States date back to the country's colonial period. Apprentices would enter a trade, such as metalworking, carpentry, shoemaking, printing, or tailoring, around the beginning of adolescence. Masters agreed to train apprentices; in return, apprentices sacrificed part of their wages and worked for room and board over a period of five to seven years. Eventually, after fulfilling their agreements, apprentices became journeymen, or qualified tradesmen, and began to save enough capital to set up a shop of their own and thus become masters of their trade. One of the best-known apprentices from colonial America was Benjamin Franklin. He established a network of printers, journeymen, and apprentices from New England to Antigua and arranged for them to serve as local postmasters. Historians conjecture that Franklin made many of his printers local postmasters to facilitate the dissemination of newspapers and political ideas. He would provide them with the capital to set up shops and received one-third of their profits for the length of their contract.

There were disadvantages to being an apprentice in colonial times. They included poor working conditions, such as long hours, abusive masters, and lengthy contracts, sometimes seven years long, which caused some apprentices to continue working for their masters long after they had mastered the trade. These hardships, combined with the availability of land on the western frontier during the eighteenth and nineteenth centuries, produced a significant number of runaway apprentices.

By the late nineteenth century, the number of apprenticeships in the United States had dramatically declined. As industrialization took hold in the late 1880s, the nature of work changed in ways that strained traditional apprenticeship arrangements. Mechanization and automation resulted in job tasks that were more specific, minimizing the need to master a trade. The large-scale commercialization of commodities eliminated the need for custom work by skilled artisans. The steam printing press displaced journeymen and apprentices trained to operate the handpress. In the plumbing trade, mass production of pipe fixtures and couplings reduced the need for traditional skills to craft pipes. In essence, small-scale craftwork was replaced by mass production and the assembly line.

Some historians also attribute the decline in apprenticeship to the absence of a guild system. Without such a system, it was difficult to blacklist apprentices who had run away to other regions of the country. The guild system is strong in Europe, which may in part explain the higher incidence of apprentices in modern-day Germany and England.

The decline in apprenticeship coincided with a rise in manual training and vocational schooling. In 1876, the Philadelphia Centennial Exposition featured an exhibit of manual training exercises coupled with classroom training from a Russian technical school. The exhibit showcased a series of graded exercises in a workshoplike environment and was soon imported by some postsecondary education institutions as a school-based alternative to apprenticeship-style learning. Manual education was not without controversy, however. Critics of manual education, such as W. E. B. Du Bois, saw manual education as a way of limiting the options available to African Americans.

Although manual education carried with it a connotation of moral reform, vocational education was associated more with skills for the workplace and their economic benefit. The rise in vocational schooling in the United States coincided with the passage of the first federal vocational act, the Smith-Hughes Act (1917). It provided federal funding to assist states in creating vocational education schools. The demand for public vocational education came from both citizens and businesses. Citizens wanted a form of "social education" that served both to mainstream the urban masses and to teach immigrant children English. Social reformers concerned with alleviating pauperism and juvenile crime looked to the school as a means of providing education for youth who otherwise would wander the streets. Parents wanted to ease access to education to increase economic opportunities for their children. Business owners wanted greater numbers of Americans to receive general training before they became workers and hoped to minimize union control of the supply of labor via apprenticeships. Consequently, the unions resisted the movement away from apprenticeships toward public schools. Eventually, the American Federation of Labor agreed that vocational education was acceptable under certain conditions: that labor had a voice in shaping how vocational education systems were built, that government should keep the system public instead of private, and that the system avoided specialization of work roles in the wider economy. Some early schools in Philadelphia and New York did involve direct employer involvement, but eventually local schools were operated by local governments, and the number of apprenticeships faded. Apprenticeships did persist in the construction trades, where work was seasonal and firms remained relatively small.

Though nationally apprenticeship was on the decline in the early 1900s, Wisconsin passed legislation in 1911 to register its apprenticeships. The federal Fitzgerald Act (the National Apprenticeship Act) of 1937 was based on the Wisconsin law. The Fitzgerald Act authorized the U.S. Department of Labor to establish standards that protect the welfare of apprentices and to bring together employers and unions to form apprenticeship programs.

Since the Fitzgerald Act, apprenticeships have been concentrated in the construction industry. As of August 2001, the occupation with the most apprenticeships is electrician, followed by carpenter and pipe fitter. In 2000, there were estimated to be 440,000 registered apprentices in the United States. Registered apprenticeships are negotiated in union collective-bargaining agreements around the country. Apprenticeships range from one to six years and typically involve 2,000 hours of supervised on-the-job training and a minimum of 144 hours per year of related instruction. The instruction may be in the form of classroom training, correspondence courses, or a self-study course approved by the sponsor/employer.

Apprenticeships are more common in Europe than they are in the United States. The apprenticeship tradition is particularly strong in Germany, where in the 1990s approximately 60 percent of adults had participated in an apprenticeship program during their youth. Upon completing secondary school, most German students enter an apprenticeship program, which lasts about three years. A weekly program typically involves two days of classroom training at a state school and three days of training at a private firm. The apprenticeship programs are offered in areas ranging from banking to crafts and are designed and administered by firms, unions, and the state. The content of apprenticeship programs, the structure of the classroom curriculum, and the nature of the certification exams all require consensus among trade unions, employer associations, and the Federal Institute for Vocational Training. The apprenticeship system in Germany is supported by historical traditions, the involvement of firms through national and state employer associations, the presence of union input, and the government through its support of vocational schools and laws. Apprenticeship systems also exist in Sweden and Britain.

Most apprenticeships in the United States take place in the construction industry, with electrician the most frequent occupation, followed by carpentry. (Corel Corporation)

In the United States, education has historically been viewed as the great equalizer, and thus there is resistance to the idea of overtly tracking adolescents into a trade. In addition, the traditional form of modern apprenticeships (on-the-job training coupled with classroom learning) has been less common than in Europe for many years. Consequently, youth job training is not a systemic part of the nation's schools but rather is handled by periodic federal legislation that provides funding for youth training programs and vocational education. School and government organizations offer numerous youth programs aimed at the school-to-work transition that model themselves after traditional apprenticeships by training youth for the workforce. During the 1960s, the federal Economic Opportunities Act (1964) created employment and training programs for hard-to-employ youth (Jobs Corps), and the Manpower Development and Training Act (1962) provided funding for union apprenticeships. The Job Training Partnership Act (1982) included funds earmarked for training out-of-school youth in basic education, occupational training, and on-the-job training.

To cope with the high dropout rate in urban areas in the 1960s, high schools that integrated academic and vocational curricula were established. A 2000 report by the U.S. Department of Education estimates that there are 1,500 "career academies" across the nation, typically established by local school districts, focusing on a range of careers from business, health, and finance to communication and video technology. Work-based learning opportunities are not offered consistently across schools, though some academies have a well-defined workplace learning component.

The School to Work Opportunities Act (1994) provided money for local school districts to better connect schools and work by emphasizing both academic achievement and work-based learning. Recognizing the concerns over programs that promote tracking, the language of the act emphasized the intent to serve all students. Across the nation, funds from the act created opportunities for students to be exposed to an array of career options through field trips to workplaces and job-shadowing opportunities. In some localities, funds were also used to support youth apprenticeships.

The most recent effort to wed classroom training and on-the-job training for youth was the Carl Perkins Vocational and Technical Education Act (1998), up for re-authorization in 2003, which provides federal funding for secondary and postsecondary vocational education programs. Title II of the act provides money specifically for Tech Prep, a program that prepares high school students for careers in a practical art or trade. Students spend their last two years of high school and two years at a community college involved in a curriculum that leads to a certificate in a career field. The legislation specifically stipulates that two years of community college can be replaced by an apprenticeship. This option is not used widely, though some localities have a well-defined apprenticeship option.

It is likely that the number of youth training programs that offer apprenticeship-style training opportunities will continue to vary across localities, with some areas having many youth training programs and others having far fewer. The variation stems from the tradition of locally controlled schools in the United States. Those localities with well-defined vocational education systems will likely have more systemic on-the-job training opportunities for youth.

Leela Hebbar

See also Building Trades Unions; Education Reform and the Workforce; Job Corps; Job Skills; Lifelong Learning; On-the-Job Training

References and further reading

Clark, Charles S. 1992. "Youth Apprenticeships." *The CQ Researcher* 2, no. 39: 905–928.

Dawson, Andrew. 1993. "The Workshop and the Classroom: Philadelphia Engineering, the Decline of Apprenticeship, and the Rise of Industrial Training, 1878–1900." *History of Education Quarterly* 39, no. 2: 143–160.

Frasca, Ralph. 1990. "From Apprentice to Journeyman to Partner: Benjamin Franklin's Workers and the Growth of the Early American Printing Trade." *Pennsylvania Magazine of History and Biography* 114, no. 2: 229–248.

Hamilton, Stephen F. 1990. *Apprenticeship for Adulthood.* New York: Free Press.

Harhoff, Dietmar, and Thomas J. Kane. 1997. "Is the German Apprenticeship System a Panacea for the U.S. Labor Market?" *Journal of Population Economics* 10: 171–196.

Hughes, Katherine L., Thomas R. Bailey, and Melinda J. Mechur. 2001. *School-to-Work: Making a Difference in Education.* New York: Institute on Education and the Economy, Columbia University.

Jacoby, Dan. 1996 "Plumbing the Origins of American Vocationalism." *Labor History* 37, no. 2: 235–272.

Kemple, James J., Susan M. Poglinco, and Jason C. Snipes. 1999. *Career Academies: Building Career Awareness and Work-Based Learning Activities through Employer Partnerships.* New York: Manpower Demonstration Research Corporation.

Kemple, James J., and JoAnn Leah Rock. 1996. *Career Academies: Early Implementation Lessons from a 10-*

Site Evaluation. New York: Manpower Demonstration Research Corporation.

Kilebard, Herbert M. 1999. *Schooled to Work: Vocationalism and the American Curriculum, 1876–1946.* New York: Teachers College Press.

Rorabaugh, W. J. 1986. *The Craft Apprentice: From Franklin to the Machine Age in America.* New York: Oxford University Press.

Silverberg, Marsha K., and Alan M. Hershey. 1995. *The Emergence of Tech-Prep at the State and Local Levels.* New Jersey: Mathematica Policy Research.

Stern, David, Marilyn Raby, and Charles Dayton. 1992. *Career Academies.* San Francisco: Jossey-Bass.

U.S. Bureau of Apprenticeship and Training. 2000. *The National Apprenticeship System Programs and Apprentices, Fiscal Year 2000.* Washington, DC: GPO.

Arbitration

Arbitration is a voluntary process for resolving disputes between employers and employees and their unions by an independent third party. There are three kinds of arbitration: (1) rights or grievance arbitration, in which the parties have a labor agreement and the arbitrator is asked to resolve a dispute that arises under that agreement; (2) interest arbitration, in which parties cannot agree on the terms of a labor agreement and ask the arbitrator, in effect, to establish the terms of the agreement; (3) employment arbitration, in which an employer either has a unilateral policy providing for arbitration of disputes with individual employees or a contract with individual employees providing for arbitration of disputes. There is no union involvement in employment arbitration.

Arbitration as it is practiced today is often said to have begun following a strike in the anthracite coalfields in 1902. President Theodore Roosevelt appointed a commission to investigate the cause of the strike. The commission produced a detailed study and established an Anthracite Board of Conciliation. This board was empowered to interpret the commissioner's award. If the board could not resolve a dispute submitted to it, then the dispute was submitted to arbitration. During World War I, the federal government created the National War Labor Board, composed of members of management, labor, and the public. It had only limited success in resolving labor disputes. Before 1935, arbitration was not widely used as a means of resolving labor disputes in the United States.

After the enactment of the National Labor Relations Act in 1935, unions began organizing many of the basic industries, such as auto manufacturing, steel, mining, and the electrical industries. Multistep grievance procedures in which arbitration was the final step became the norm in these industries. In 1942 President Franklin D. Roosevelt created the War Labor Board, whose purpose was to resolve labor disputes in any industry that might affect the war effort. The board required companies and unions to establish grievance procedures, including arbitration. Following World War II, the use of arbitration became commonplace in the basic industries.

Section 301 of the Taft-Hartley Act of 1947 authorized federal courts to enforce collective bargaining agreements. In *Textile Workers Union v. Lincoln Mills* (1957), the U.S. Supreme Court held that an agreement to arbitrate labor disputes was enforceable. Any remaining judicial hostility toward the arbitration of labor disputes was removed with the Steelworkers Trilogy, three cases in 1960 in which the U.S. Supreme Court laid down rules that had the effect of making arbitration a fully recognized and preferred method for resolving labor disputes.

Following World War II, most of the companies in the basic industries had contracts with unions representing the employees. These contracts generally contained provisions for a grievance procedure, with arbitration as the final step for resolving disputes arising in the workplace. The typical contract between a company and a union provides that all disputes arising under the contract will be submitted to arbitration. A partial list of disputes that have been submitted to grievance arbitration includes discharge and discipline, work assignments, work rules, overtime work, job classifications and rates of pay, job evaluation, hours of work, holiday pay, vacation and leave issues, fringe benefits, and management rights. For example, nearly all labor contracts contain a provision stating that the employer may discharge an employee only for just or proper cause. If a company discharges an employee and the union believes the discharge is improper, it can file a grievance. Practically speaking, the grievance and arbitration process generally includes any dispute arising in the workplace, except those specifically excluded.

Arbitration offers several advantages to employers, unions, and employees over other forms of dispute resolution. It is less expensive than litigation, and the parties can resolve disputes much more quickly in arbitration than in litigation. Arbitration's economic benefit to the employer is that it provides a mechanism for resolving disputes that might otherwise lead to strikes, slowdowns, or widespread morale problems in the workforce. For example, suppose a company and a union had a contract with a seniority clause that stipulated that in the event of a layoff, the employees would be laid off in reverse order of seniority (the newest employees would be laid off first). Suppose further that the company needed to lay off ten employees out of a workforce of 500. If a dispute arose as to which ten employees should be laid off, it could result in a strike or picketing if there was not an acceptable and expeditious way of resolving it. Arbitration's economic benefit to the union and the employees is, again, its lesser expense. For example, if an employer discharges an employee, a dispute over the propriety of the discharge can be determined in arbitration at far less cost than in a court of law. Few employees who are discharged for infractions such as absenteeism, insubordination, falsification of production records, and a host of other offenses for which employees are routinely discharged can afford to litigate the merits of their discharge in a court of law.

The typical labor contract for a union employee contains a two- or three-step grievance procedure. The first step generally directs the immediate foreman and the shop steward to seek a resolution of the dispute. The second step is often a meeting between the company's personnel manager and a business agent for the union. If the parties are unable to resolve the dispute at this level, it is submitted to an arbitrator for a final and binding decision. The arbitrator may be named in the parties' labor contract or may be selected from a list of arbitrators furnished by an appointing agency, such as the American Arbitration Association or the Federal Mediation and Conciliation Service.

Hearings before arbitrators are similar to state and federal administrative hearings. They are informal. The hearing generally opens with an attempt to agree on the question to be decided by the arbitrator. If the parties cannot agree on the precise wording of the question to be decided (that is, "Was the employee discharged for just cause, and if not, what is the appropriate remedy?"), the arbitrator will frame the issue. This process is followed by the opening statements of the representatives of the parties. Then the parties provide their proof, which usually consists of the introduction of relevant documents and oral testimony. Finally, closing statements are made, and posthearing briefs are submitted. After the case is closed, the arbitrator writes a decision and transmits it to the parties.

The fundamental responsibility of an arbitrator in a dispute that involves only the interpretation and application of a labor contract is to apply the terms of the contract to the facts presented by the parties. Although it is said that an arbitrator is not supposed to dispense his or her personal brand of industrial justice, there are many widely accepted doctrines that apply to the arbitrator's decision-making process. Where the contract is clear and unambiguous, the arbitrator must apply the words as written to the facts. If a contract is ambiguous, an arbitrator can apply the past practice of the parties or resort to their negotiating history as an aid in resolving the dispute. Prior grievance settlements in analogous situations may furnish guidance to an arbitrator. Arbitrators also rely on the decisions of other arbitrators, even though these decisions do not create binding precedent. The Bureau of National Affairs (BNA) and Commerce Clearing House (CCH) publish arbitration awards.

Many public employers at the federal, state, and local levels also have contracts with unions representing their employees. At the federal level, many workers in the Postal Service and the Department of the Treasury are represented by unions. At the state and local levels, a wide variety of employees are represented by unions, including police officers, fire fighters, sanitation workers, and schoolteachers. Most contracts between public employees and unions contain a provision for the arbitration of employee grievances. The procedures for resolving grievances in public sector labor contracts are similar to the procedures used in the private sector. Depending on the employer, there may be restrictions on the arbitrator's authority. For example, an arbitrator hearing a dispute under a public sector labor agreement cannot generally require a public employer to expend unappropriated funds to comply with a decision.

Interest arbitration is used more frequently in the public sector than in the private sector, and is often seen as an alternative to a strike. The federal government and many states have statutes prohibiting public employees from striking, and several federal and state statutes that provide for interest arbitration. When the public employer and the union representing a group of employees are unable to agree on the terms of a labor contract, the public employee collective bargaining statute may provide for an arbitrator or panel of arbitrators to establish those terms. Such disputes frequently cover the entire range of subjects usually contained in labor agreements, such as wages, holidays, vacation, sick leave, or health insurance. When the parties reach an impasse on such issues, they select an arbitrator or a panel, and a hearing is held. For example, if wages were in dispute, the government entity can present its evidence to the arbitrator as to the rate of pay it thinks is appropriate. The union presents its evidence to the arbitrator as to what it believes should be the proper rate of pay. The arbitrator or panel then determines the rate of pay for the upcoming labor contract. The arbitrator's decision thus becomes the labor agreement.

Edwin R. Render

See also Collective Bargaining; Workers' Compensation

References and further reading

Coleman, Charles J., and Theodora Haynes. 1994. *Labor and Employment Arbitration: An Annotated Bibliography.* Ithaca, NY: Cornell University, ILR Press.

Elkouri, Frank, and Edna Asper Elkouri, eds. 1997. *How Arbitration Works.* Coedited by Marlin M. Volz and Edward P. Goggin. Washington, DC: BNA Books.

National Academy of Arbitrators. *Proceedings.* Vols. 1–53. Washington, DC: Bureau of National Affairs.

Schoonhoven, Ray, Jr., ed. 1999. *Fairweather's Practice and Procedure in Labor Arbitration.* Washington, DC: BNA Books.

Asian Americans and Work

The United States has long prided itself on being, to use John F. Kennedy's words, "a nation of immigrants." And yet the history of Asian Americans and work in the United States is one of struggle. As a broad and varied group, Asian Americans have had a long history of persevering and overcoming work discrimination, anti-Asian legislation, anti-immigrant policy, exploitation, and abuse. Although many Asian Americans have been successful in their struggles, many others continue to suffer because of racism and discrimination in the United States today.

Like all categories of race, that of "Asian Americans" is artificial and misleading, in that the term encompasses a range of different nationalities, races, and thus experiences. In general, however, as the United States was settled and developed, Asian immigrants came from impoverished regions of the world as low-wage workers. Their labor was crucial to the establishment and development of the nation, but most often they were denied fair treatment and the full right of citizenship accorded to many other laboring immigrant groups.

Chinese American Workers

In the 1830s Chinese sailors and peddlers worked in New York, on sugar plantations in Hawaii, and in mining and forestry industries in the Pacific Northwest. It was not until the mid-1800s that the Chinese came to the United States in large numbers to perform menial, although dangerous and difficult work. The first large-scale wave of immigrant Chinese came to California with the hopes of cashing in on the gold rush of 1848 and to escape the economic hardships they were experiencing in China. Others went to work on the Hawaiian sugar cane plantations. In 1865, about 9,000 to 12,000 were hired as laborers on the transcontinental railroad (Asian-Nation 2002). Although Chinese men were recruited to build U.S. infrastructure and agriculture, they were often prohibited from bringing women members of their family with them to the United States. When they did immigrate, women supported men in their work but were most often not paid themselves and not counted as workers.

Despite the significant contributions early Chinese male and female workers made to the U.S. economy, they were discriminated against in many ways. In California they were subjected to a foreign miner tax, and during the building of the transcontinental railroad, they were only paid 60 percent of what other immigrant workers were earning (Asian-Nation 2002). Once the gold rush began to fade and railroad construction started winding down, the Chinese were targeted as a threat to the U.S. economy, and a widespread anti-Chinese movement began, accompanied by riots, lynching, and murders. Anti–Asian immigrant sentiments culminated in the Chinese Exclusion Act of 1882, which barred Chinese immigration and prevented both immigrant and U.S.-born Chinese from becoming U.S. citizens.

The next significant exclusionary legislation was the Act to Prohibit the Coming of Chinese Persons into the United States of May 1892. Referred to as the Geary Act, this legislation required Chinese to reg-

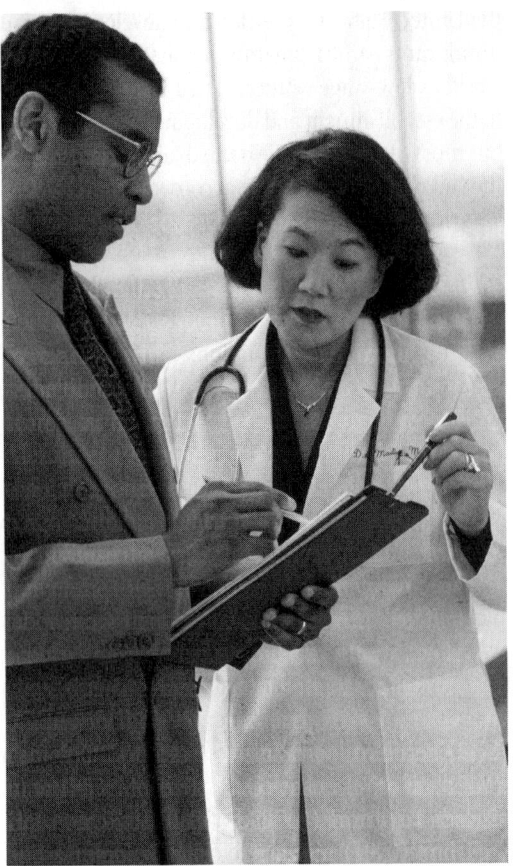

Asian Americans have had a long history of persevering and overcoming work discrimination, anti-Asian legislation, anti-immigrant policies, exploitation, and abuse. Although many Asian Americans have been successful in their struggles, many others continue to suffer because of racism and discrimination in the United States today. (Jon Feingersh/Corbis)

ister and secure a certificate as proof of their right to be in the United States. Imprisonment or deportation were the penalties for those who failed to have the required papers or witnesses. These acts were not repealed until 1943, when Franklin D. Roosevelt signed the Act to Repeal the Chinese Exclusion Acts, to Establish Quotas, and for Other Purposes and, crucially, when President Kennedy signed the Immigration Act of October 1965.

The Chinese reacted to discrimination by forming their own businesses and working in jobs that were not perceived as threats to white workers. Most Chinese on the East Cost worked in the service sector; on the West Coast, they were employed in mills, agriculture, and the fishing and forestry industries. Because few Chinese women were allowed into the United States in the early years, Chinese men also turned to what would be considered women's work and took jobs as domestics, in laundries, and in the food industries.

During the 1930s and 1940s, the Chinese again were recruited to work in large numbers, this time in the war industries. The need for workers in manufacturing, coupled with more permissive immigration laws, broke barriers for employment opportunities for Chinese men and women. Those who immigrated to the United States following World War II under the McCarran-Walter Act of 1952 were often well-educated, English-speaking professionals who had held jobs as government officials, scientists, and engineers. In 1949, 5,000 highly educated Chinese were granted refugee status in the United States after China established a Communist government (Asian-Nation 2001). These immigrants, unlike those of a century earlier, made lateral moves in employment upon their arrival into the United States, and a few took positions far below their ability. Also, following two Immigration Acts (1956 and 1965), the first establishing immigration quotas based on nationality and the second rescinding those strict quotas, the majority of Chinese immigrants who came to the United States were relatives of Chinese American citizens. These new immigrants "revitalized Chinatown" by taking jobs as tailors, salespeople, restaurant servers, and clerical workers.

Although Chinese Americans did not take part in officially recognized unions until the mid-1930s, they did organize themselves into family associations to protect themselves from discrimination in the workplace and community. The earliest organized labor group of Chinese workers formed during the mid-1800s, when they organized a strike against the Union Pacific Railroad, although the work stoppage only brought more problems for the laborers, who soon went back to work. More organized and successful labor movements came about during the mid-1900s and were spearheaded by Chinese women, whose labor guilds within the garment industry doubled their wages and offered job protection. During the Depression, Chinese women organized their own chapter of National Dollar Stores and successfully negotiated for better wages and working conditions. This group later became affiliated with the International Ladies Garment Workers Union. Chinese workers also organized the

Mutual Aid Association in the canneries of Alaska in the 1930s, and in 1995 within the Union of Needle Trades, Industrial, and Textile Employees (UNITE!), an amalgam of the Amalgamated Clothing and Textile Workers Union (ACTWU) and the International Ladies Garment Workers Union (ILGWU). More recently, Asian Americans have organized themselves into professional groups such as the National Association of Asian American Professionals and the Asian Pacific American Women Leadership Institute.

Japanese American Workers

Japanese immigrants began coming to the United States in large numbers after Chinese immigration ended in 1882. Most came as a result of the industrialization taking place in Japan, which caused many agricultural workers to lose their land. The majority of those immigrants went to Hawaii to work on the plantations; others immigrated to California as railroad workers and miners. Like the Chinese before them, many Japanese turned to agriculture, the fishing canneries, and domestic work, although a large number of women came to the United States as "picture brides." In 1907, the "Gentlemen's Agreement" between the United States and Japan barred unskilled Japanese men from entry, although it did allow for the entry of wives of Japanese men already working in the United States.

In 1893, Japanese workers formed their first trade union: the Japanese Shoemakers League. Japanese immigration to Hawaii ended under the Irwin Convention, and contracted labor practices ceased with passage of the Organic Act. As a result, many Japanese plantation workers relocated to the mainland. In 1915, the Japanese formed the Central Japanese Association of Southern California and the first Japanese chamber of commerce. Four years later, Japanese workers created the Federation of Japanese Labor in Hawaii and successfully went on strike. In 1922, a court found in *Takao Ozawa v. United States* that Japanese workers were not eligible for naturalized citizenship and, further, that any female citizen who married an "alien" would lose her own right to citizenship.

By the 1930s and 1940s, Japanese immigrants had begun to purchase large tracts of land for farming and to establish small businesses that they lost at the beginning of World War II, when Japanese and Japanese Americans were herded into detention centers because they were seen as a threat to U.S. security. Although legal measures were taken after the war to reclaim their losses, less than 10 percent was actually ever recovered (Amott and Matthaei 1996, 230). In 1952, the McCarran-Walter Act lifted a ban on Japanese immigration but restricted immigration to 100 individuals per country per year; as a result, relatively few Japanese came to the United States. Those who did immigrate dispersed both geographically and professionally. Although the Japanese continued to face discrimination, they moved quickly into the U.S. middle class.

Filipino American Workers

As early as the 1600s, Filipinos reached North America on Manila galleons, and in 1750 a group of Filipino sailors settled and began working in Louisiana. At the beginning of the twentieth century, most Filipinos were recruited to work on Hawaiian sugar and pineapple plantations, in Alaskan fisheries, and in the forest industry in the Northwest. After World War II, many of those immigrants moved throughout the mainland and began working in the same low-paying jobs in which other Asians were employed—as domestics, in agriculture, and as small business owners.

Filipinos have also remained committed to union ideals and organization. In 1911, Pablo Manlapit formed the Filipino Higher Wages Association in Hawaii; four years later, it went on strike for eight months. In 1934, the Tydings-McDuffie Act spelled out procedures for eventual Philippine independence and reduced Filipino immigration to the United States to fifty persons a year. Shortly afterward, Filipino workers created their own Filipino Labor Union in California, and after World War II, the American Federation of Labor and Congress of Industrial Organizations (AFL-CIO) created the Filipino Agricultural Worker's Organizing committee, which later merged with the Chicano Farm Workers Association to form the United Farm Workers Organizing Committee. Filipino men have been particularly visible within this union, taking on not just labor problems but social issues as well by establishing their own legal department, day care center, and medical clinics.

After the 1965 Immigration Act eliminated racial quotas, Filipinos became the second-largest Asian American population, and the number of professional Filipino workers living and working in the United States increased. Although about three-fifths of Filipino immigrants came to work in clerical, manufacturing, and service industries, the other two-fifths (40 percent) came to the United States as trained scientists, engineers, and medical professionals (Amott and Matthaei 1996, 244). Since the late 1960s, Filipinos have enjoyed relatively high earnings and employment rates.

Indian American and Korean American Workers

Large populations of workers from India, Southeast Asia, and Korea immigrated to the United States in the early 1900s. The first group of Korean workers arrived in Hawaii in 1903 to work in the sugar fields, but just a few years later their immigration was legally restricted. Those Koreans already in the United States formed the Mutual Assistance Society in 1905, and in 1909 they created the Korean Nationalist Association. New Korean immigrants didn't come to the United States en masse again until after immigration legislation in 1965; at that time they immigrated as professionals, service industry workers, and small business owners.

Indians from Southeast Asia settled primarily on the West Coast at the turn of the century. In the early 1900s, Asian Indians were denied entry into Canada under the pretext that they hadn't come "by continuous journey" from India (there were no direct shipping routes between Indian and Canadian ports). In 1917 the United States followed suit in defining a "banned zone," primarily India, from which no immigrants could hail. In the 1923 *United States v. Bhagat Singh* an appeals court determined that Asian Indians were not eligible for U.S. naturalization. Like Koreans, large numbers of Indians were not able to move to the United States until the passage of the 1965 Immigration Act. This legislation allowed Indians to immigrate, mainly to the East Coast. Today the largest concentration of Indians can be found in New York City, with 53 percent of the population living in Queens, New York (Khandelwal 2001, 3).

Many Indian immigrants have high educational and income levels, with a significant number coming from professional fields, particularly medicine and engineering. However, from the late 1970s onward, a significant part of the population worked in the service industry, running and often owning small businesses such as newsstands, retail shops, restaurants, and gas stations.

Since the latter part of the twentieth century, most Asian immigrants and Asian Americans have been called the "model minority" because of their perceived economic success and upward mobility. Today, Asian Americans have a high level of educational attainment and high median earnings, but that is not true of all Asian American workers. Many new immigrants from Cambodia, Laos, and Vietnam work at the very low end of the labor market. In 1975, more than 130,000 refugees entered the United States from these countries (Amott and Matthaei 1996, 248). In 1978 a new mass exodus of Vietnamese "boat people" arrived, and after the Vietnam War ended, thousands of Hmong immigrated to the United States. In 1990 the overall poverty rate for Asian Americans was 14 percent, but 42 percent of Cambodians and 62 percent of the Hmong people from Cambodia lived below the poverty line (Amott and Matthaei 1996, 250). Additionally, overrepresentation of Asian Americans in self-employment suggests that they still face discrimination and that racism prevents them from entering into and achieving success in certain careers and professions.

Vivyan C. Adair and Sharon Gormley

See also Affirmative Action; Green Cards; Immigrants and Work; United Farm Workers; Wage Gap; Women and Work; Working Class

References and further reading

Amott, Teresa, and Julie Matthaei. 1996. *Race, Gender, and Work: A Multi-cultural Economic History of Women in the United States.* Rev. ed. Boston, MA: South End Press.

Asian-Nation. 2002. "The First Asian Americans." *Asian-Nation: The Landscape of Asian America.* http://www.asian-nation.org/history.html (cited December).

Khandelwal, Madhulika. 2001. "Indian Immigrants in New York City." *New York Times,* September 25, B16.

U.S. Census Bureau. 2000. "Annual Demographic Survey." *Current Population Series.* Washington, DC: U.S. Census Bureau.

Automotive Industry

The most dynamic sector of the U.S. economy in the twentieth century, the automotive industry barely existed in 1900, when only 8,000 motor vehicles were registered in the United States. With more efficient production techniques, innovative marketing measures, and the introduction of auto sales on credit, however, the industry expanded in almost continuous fashion. Indeed, by the late 1990s, the automotive industry added $100 billion in gross domestic product to the U.S. economy. The automotive industry also fostered a rising standard of living for its workers by paying wages that ranked at the top of the industrial sector, beginning with Henry Ford's announcement of a Five Dollar Day in 1914. The industry's almost complete unionization by 1941, however, was even more crucial in establishing the auto worker's reputation as the elite of industrial workers. In addition to its economic and technological accomplishments, the industry transformed U.S. social and cultural life. With almost 208 million motor vehicles registered in the United States in 1997, the country ranked as one of the most automobile-dependent nations on earth, with almost 458 cars per 1,000 persons (U.S. Census Bureau 2000).

Among the numerous inventors who pioneered the use of the gasoline internal combustion engine to power a motor vehicle, Germans Gottleib Daimler and Carl Benz conducted successful trial runs in 1885 and 1886; by 1891, Benz offered the first automobiles for sale in Europe. Two years later, the Duryea brothers, Charles and Frank, made the first automobile run in the United States in Springfield, Massachusetts. In 1895 the first automobile race took place on U.S. soil, the first of many such events that generated huge public interest in the new "horseless carriage." Building on this interest as well as their reputation as automotive pioneers, the Duryeas offered the first car for sale to the American public in February 1897. They were joined by over thirty manufacturers selling over 2,500 cars just two years later.

As in Europe, the first models offered for sale to the American public were luxury automobiles, but as early as 1901, Ransom E. Olds offered the first car aimed at the lower-priced market. The car, which sold for $650, became immortalized in the popular song "In My Merry Oldsmobile" and proved that the market for automobiles extended far beyond the wealthier classes. In 1903 Henry Ford established the Ford Motor Company after two previous failures in the business; this time, Ford focused on the lower-priced market with the 1907 Model N. The following year, his company introduced the Model T, a car that revolutionized the automotive industry. Not only did Ford refine the efficiency of the assembly line process used in making automobiles, but also he used the cost savings to cut the price of the Model T in succeeding years. As he expanded the market for his product by reducing its price, Ford also used his productivity gains to increase his workers' wages. With the Five Dollar Day, announced in January 1914, Ford helped to create a mass consumer base among a broad segment of working-class Americans. By the 1920s, about 47 percent of Ford workers owned their own cars, a figure that dwarfed the figures for industrial workers elsewhere; in Chicago, a mere 3 percent of unskilled workers were auto owners, and in San Francisco, just above one-quarter of all workers owned their own cars (Cohen 1990).

Although motor vehicle registrations jumped from 8,000 in 1900 to 469,000 in 1910, the early years of the industry were filled with business failures. Unlike the success stories of Olds and Ford, over 300 of the more than 500 automobile manufacturers established between 1900 and 1908 went out of business. Although demand for the new product far exceeded the supply of automobiles, fledgling manufacturers often suffered from undercapitalization and unreasonable demands by their investors, many of whom viewed the industry as a speculative venture. Although Olds increased his production from 425 vehicles in 1901 to 4,000 in 1903—and Ford jumped from 658 cars in 1903–1904 to 8,243 in 1907–1908—most other manufacturers were either unable or unwilling to abandon the craftsmanship of traditional carriage making in favor of more efficient assembly line production (Lacey 1986). With the immediate success of Ford's Model T in 1908 and the beginning of production at his Highland Park plant the following year, it was clear that the automotive industry's trends toward mass production and mass consumption were in place. It was equally obvious, as the massive operation at Highland Park symbolized, that the automotive industry was no longer open to a few inventors-turned-prospective manufacturers.

In addition to the massive capitalization requirements, the tendency toward oligopoly in the auto industry was fostered by the thirty-two-member cartel formed to enforce the Selden patent in the early 1900s. Although the patent covering a general outline of a gas-powered vehicle was essentially unenforceable—as a court finally ruled in 1911—several automakers had banded together as the

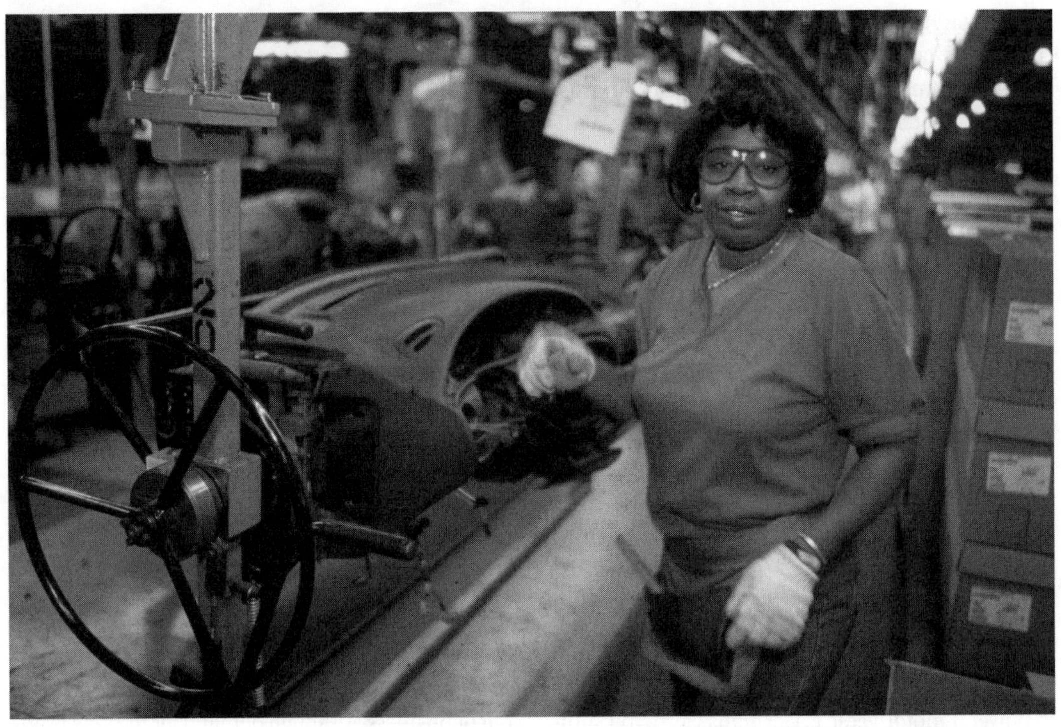

A factory worker assembles Taurus and Sable cars at the Ford assembly plant in Illinois. (Sandy Felsenthal/Corbis)

Association of Licensed Automobile Manufacturers in fear of being put out of business by its holder, George Selden. Although William C. Durant of General Motors (GM) was an avid supporter of the Selden cartel, Henry Ford was not. Despite the threats to his business, Ford fought the patent in court and eventually won, but not before many other smaller auto companies were closed, merged, or bought out.

Although Ford and his Model T quickly became household words around the world, it was another company, GM, that took the lead in mass marketing its product. Organized in 1908 by Durant as a holding company for several independent auto brands, GM attempted to offer a comprehensive lineup of cars across market segments, from the low-priced Chevrolet to the luxury Cadillac. With the creation of the General Motors Acceptance Corporation in 1919, GM also pioneered the offer of installment buying to auto buyers, a program that helped the company surpass Ford, who refused to sell on credit, after 1930; indeed, by 1921 about half of all cars sold in the United States were on the installment plan, giving Ford a serious handicap in the marketplace (Flink 1975).

Together with the Chrysler Corporation, Ford and GM eventually comprised the Big Three automakers. Although other, smaller makers continued to operate until the 1970s, the Big Three dominated the industry from the 1930s onward. In 1936 GM held 43 percent of the domestic market; Chrysler had a 25 percent share; and Ford held on to 22 percent of the market. The independent automakers—under brand names such as Hudson, Packard, Studebaker, and Willys—sold about one-tenth of all cars purchased that year (Lacey 1986).

The decade of the Great Depression was a tumultuous one for the auto industry; in addition to weathering the economic downturn—GM's stock, for example, plunged from $91 a share in 1929 to $13 per share in 1933—it also faced tremendous internal pressures from its workforce. In the wake of New Deal measures such as the National Recovery Act of June 1933 and the National Labor Relations Act (Wagner Act) of 1935, many workers were convinced that forming their own unions to engage in collective bargaining with the automakers was the best strategy for gaining job security, higher wages, and improved working conditions. The response from the Big Three was discouraging; although they felt compelled to recognize workers' unions by the federal government, their initial strategy was to form employee relations programs (ERPs) for their workers. Essentially run as company unions, the ERPs failed to stem the demands for independent labor unions in the auto industry. After a series of dramatic strikes that witnessed workers sitting down in GM plants across the Midwest in the winter of 1936–1937, the nation's largest automaker became the first to recognize the United Auto Workers (UAW) union as the collective bargaining agent of its workforce. Among the Big Three, the Ford Motor Company was the last holdout. With lucrative government contracts in the offing in the days before U.S. entry into World War II, Ford finally recognized the UAW in June 1941.

In exchange for a no-strike pledge during the war, the UAW substantially completed the unionization of the auto industry by the end of World War II. The postwar era in the auto industry focused, then, not on the issue of collective bargaining but rather on just how far the process would go. Although the UAW attempted to introduce managerial decisions into collective bargaining throughout the 1940s, the 1950 agreement with General Motors, publicized as the Treaty of Detroit, essentially drew the lines of collective bargaining for the next generation. In exchange for improved wages and benefits—including cost-of-living adjustments, pensions, and health care provisions—automakers retained all managerial prerogatives, including production and investment decisions. The arrangement allowed automakers to enjoy a measure of stability in their workforce, while autoworkers expanded their wage and benefits packages in succeeding years. Supplemental unemployment benefits were added to collective bargaining agreements in 1955, and early retirement provisions came into effect in 1964.

The U.S. automotive industry shared in the almost uninterrupted economic growth of the postwar era through the energy price hikes of 1973 and 1974. Indeed, the 1950s and 1960s are often invoked as the industry's "golden age." Faced with little foreign competition, a ready consumer market, and a stable labor force, automakers concentrated more on annual style updates on larger, more profitable models instead of technological innovation or the introduction of smaller, more efficient cars. Although some consumers turned away from the Big Three's products—which pundits likened to "the dinosaur in the driveway"—foreign automakers held just 5 percent of the U.S. market in 1963. By 1971, however, their share had increased to 16 percent, an ominous trend once gasoline prices skyrocketed after the Organization of Petroleum Exporting Countries (OPEC) imposed oil embargoes in the mid-1970s. Although many of the imported autos were luxury cars such as the Mercedes-Benz, increasingly they comprised fuel-efficient Japanese models from Honda and Toyota.

Scrambling to recapture their market share throughout the 1970s, U.S. automakers also responded with a series of cost-cutting measures that undermined their relationship with their workforce. In addition to speeding up production lines in older factories, automakers attempted to replace workers with robotic machines in their newer plants. The Big Three also relocated many of their parts and assembly plants in nonunionized, lower-wage locations outside the United States. Although GM had operated factories outside the United States since the 1920s to serve various domestic markets, it now made autos for the U.S. market in its international plants. By 1980, GM operated twenty-three plants outside the United States, a trend followed by the other members of the Big Three. Although some consumers responded with a "Buy American" campaign in the 1980s, the trend toward foreign assembly and components production continued unabated.

In contrast, foreign automakers such as Honda, Mercedes-Benz, Subaru-Isuzu, and Toyota invested billions of dollars to build assembly plants in the United States in the 1980s and 1990s, beginning with Honda's operation of a plant in Marysville, Ohio, in November 1982. Rejecting attempts by the UAW to unionize their workforces, the so-called transplant producers instead focused on quality circles and other employee involvement programs to boost production and morale in their plants. As of 1998, more than 990,000 full-time workers were employed in the automobile manufacturing sector; those in the Big Three largely remained unionized, whereas only those in joint-manufacturing operations among the transplant companies were unionized (U.S. Census 1999).

The 1990s were generally favorable to the auto industry, which remained a major contributor to the U.S. economy, with over $105 billion added to the gross domestic product in 1998 alone. Ford and Chrysler seemed to adapt to the demands of lean manufacturing to remain competitive and offered numerous successful smaller models, but GM was often criticized for organizational disarray and lackluster product development. In 1991 and 1992, the company was reckoned to have lost $15 billion in North America alone. Even its attempts to diversify its core businesses by purchasing Hughes Aircraft and Electronic Data Systems kicked off a storm of controversy and criticism. Like their transplant counterparts, however, U.S. automakers (still known as the Big Three, even after Chrysler's purchase by DaimlerBenz in 1997) have continued to emphasize the principles of total quality management to achieve impressive results since the 1980s.

Timothy G. Borden

See also American Federation of Labor and Congress of Industrial Organizations; Capitalism; Collective Bargaining; Defense Industry; Deming, W. Edwards; Ford, Henry; General Motors; Industrial Revolution and Assembly Line Work; Manufacturing Jobs; Maquiladora Zone; National Labor Relations Act; North American Free Trade Agreement; Productivity; Quality Circles; Reuther, Walter; Strikes; United Auto Workers Union

References and further reading

Chandler, Jr., Alfred D. 1990. *Scale and Scope: The Dynamics of Industrial Capitalism.* Cambridge: Harvard University Press.

Cohen, Lizabeth. 1990. *Making a New Deal: Industrial Workers in Chicago, 1919–1939.* New York: Cambridge University Press.

Critchlow, Donald T. 1996. *Studebaker: The Life and Death of an American Corporation.* Bloomington: Indiana University Press.

Flink, James. 1975. *The Car Culture.* Cambridge, MA: MIT Press.

Freeland, Robert. 2000. *The Struggle for Control of the Modern Corporation: Organizational Change at General Motors, 1924–1970.* New York: Cambridge University Press.

Graham, Laurie. 1995. *On the Line at Subaru-Isuzu: The Japanese Model and the American Worker.* Ithaca, NY: Cornell University Press.

Green, William C., and Ernest J. Yanarella, eds. 1996. *North American Auto Unions in Crisis: Lean Production as Contested Terrain.* Albany: State University of New York Press.

Hamper, Ben. 1991. *Rivethead: Tales from the Assembly Line.* New York: Warner Books.

Ingrassia, Paul, and Joseph B. White. 1994. *Comeback: The Fall and Rise of the American Automobile Industry.* New York: Simon and Schuster.

Keller, Maryann. 1989. *Rude Awakening: The Rise, Fall, and Struggle for Recovery of General Motors.* New York: William Morrow.

Lacey, Robert. 1986. *Ford: The Man and the Machine.* New York: Ballantine.

Lichtenstein, Nelson. 1995. *The Most Dangerous Man in America: Walter Reuther and the Fate of American Labor.* New York: Basic Books.

Madsen, Axel. 1999. *The Deal Maker: How William C. Durant Made General Motors.* New York: John Wiley and Sons.

Maynard, Micheline. 1995. *Collision Course: Inside the Battle for General Motors.* New York: Birch Lane Press.

Milkman, Ruth. 1997. *Farewell to the Factory: Auto Workers in the Late Twentieth Century.* Berkeley: University of California Press.

Nelson, Daniel. 1995. *Farm and Factory: Workers in the Midwest, 1880–1990.* Bloomington: Indiana University Press.

Rubenstein, Paul A., and Thomas A. Kolchan. 2001. *Learning from Saturn: Possibilities for Corporate Governance and Employee Relations.* Ithaca, NY: Cornell University Press.

Sherman, Joe. 1994. *In the Rings of Saturn.* New York: Oxford University Press.

U.S. Census Bureau. 1999. "Statistical Abstract of the United States, 1999." http://www.census.gov/prod/99pubs/99statab/sec31.pdf (cited January 7, 2001).

———. 2000. "Statistical Abstract of the United States, 2000." http://www.census.gov/prod/2001pubs/statab/sec26.pdf (cited January 7, 2001).

Walton, Mary. 1997. *Car: A Drama of the American Workplace.* New York: W. W. Norton.

Zieger, Robert. 1995. *The CIO, 1935–1955.* Chapel Hill: University of North Carolina Press.

B

Baldrige Awards

Baldrige Awards give national recognition to premier U.S. organizations exemplifying sustained performance excellence and quality. Established in 1987 under Public Law 100-107 and more formally called the Malcolm Baldrige National Quality Award, this prestigious prize is presented by the president of the United States through the program administered by the National Institute of Standards and Technology (NIST) of the Department of Commerce. The awards are named in honor of Malcolm Baldrige, who served as secretary of commerce from 1981 to 1987 and was committed to quality management as a means of ensuring long-term national prosperity, especially in more competitive and demanding world markets.

The categories for the awards originally focused on the manufacturing, service, and small business sectors. In 1998, educational and health care organizations became eligible for the annual awards as well. Up to three awards can be made in each category annually, but not all categories are necessarily used each year. The seven performance criteria upon which the awards are based include leadership, strategic planning, customer and market focus, information and analysis, human resources, process management, and organizational results.

Organizations that apply for the Baldrige Awards undergo a rigorous review, beginning with an initial eligibility certification. Applicants then submit a written organizational overview and self-study that take into account the specified award criteria for performance excellence. To avoid conflicts of interest in the assignment of reviewers to applications, candidates for the award must provide the names of their key competitors, customers or users, and suppliers. Applications for the Baldrige Awards are rated on a point value system, and a team of some six specialists gives extensive feedback, citing organizational strengths and recommending opportunities for improvement. Trained experts, who volunteer to provide feedback, conduct site visits, and even follow-up interviews for finalists, devote some 300 to 1,000 or more hours to application reviews. Award recipients are required to share nonproprietary information about their successful practices at the annual Quest for Excellence Conference and at regional conferences. This sharing encourages communication and facilitates the forging of partnerships within the business, education, and health sectors.

The Baldrige Awards program involves the combined efforts of the public and private sectors. The government commits some $5 million annually to operation of the program, but private entities, organizations, and industry have borne most of the start-up costs. The independent Foundation for the Malcolm Baldrige National Quality Award raises funds and manages an endowment for the program. Award applicants pay all required fees associated with review of their applications. More than 300 experts from all sectors volunteer annually to give presentations on the Baldrige Award, share their expertise, and critique applications.

The NIST and the media have touted the highly favorable return on investment of award-winning companies comprising the fictitious "Baldrige Index" stock fund. This was compared to a similar investment made in the Standard and Poor 500 Index, showing a return on investment at a ratio of 5-to-1. A recent longitudinal economic study by Zbigniew Przasnyski and Lawrence Tai (2002) tempers these impressive claims, however, by factoring in market and industrial considerations.

A sampling of the organizations that have received the Baldrige Awards since 1988 include Westinghouse Electric–Nuclear Fuel Division, Xerox–Business Products and Systems, Cadillac Motor Car Division, American Telephone and Telegraph (AT&T), Armstrong World Industries Building Products Operation, 3M Dental Products Division, Boeing Airlift and Tanker Programs, Merrill Lynch Credit Corporation, IBM–Rochester, and Ritz-Carlton Hotels. The 2002 winners of the Baldrige Awards were Motorola–Commercial, Government, and Industrial Solutions; Branch-Smith Printing Division; and SSM Health Care.

Less than 5 percent of all organizations applying for Baldrige Awards, since its inception in 1987, have successfully achieved this recognition. A number of organizations have even applied several times before winning. The real value of the Baldrige Award lies less in the recognition and esteem that it confers than in the applicant's active participation in the required self-evaluation and assessment process. Additionally, the constructive feedback given by experienced evaluators has a transforming effect on organizations that focus on improving their performance management and internal review systems. The success of the awards program has inspired the creation of numerous state and local quality award programs based on modified Baldrige criteria. Some sixty separate quality awards have also been established internationally. Japan's Deming Prize is a close equivalent to the Baldrige Award.

Janet Butler Munch

See also High-Performance Workforce; Quality Circles; Total Quality Management

References and further reading

Brown, Mark Graham. 1998. *Baldrige Award Winning Quality: How to Interpret the Baldrige Criteria for Performance Excellence.* White Plains, NY: Quality Resources.

Hutton, David W. 2000. *From Baldrige to the Bottom Line: A Road Map for Organizational Change and Improvement.* Milwaukee, ASQ Quality Press.

Kosko, Jan. 2000. "'Baldrige Index' Outperforms S & P 500 Almost 5 to 1." *Grand Rapids Business Journal* 18, no. 11 (March 13).

Powell, Anna S. 1997. "The Benefits of Baldrige," Pp. 7–9 in *The Total Quality Journey: A Conference Report.* Edited by Jean-Marie Martino. Report Number 1181-97-CH. New York: Conference Board.

Przasnyski, Zbigniew H., and Lawrence S. Tai. 2002. "Stock Performance of Malcolm Baldrige National Quality Award Winning Companies." *Total Quality Management* 13, no. 4 (July): 475–488.

Black Lung Disease

Black lung disease, or pneumoconiosis, is caused by continued exposure to large amounts of coal dust. The dust causes the lungs to harden, thus impairing breathing. Despite technological advancements designed to decrease the amount of dust produced by mining activities, black lung continues to affect coal miners, both active and retired. Early stages of the disease often cause no discernable symptoms. However, later stages of the disease can cause shortness of breath, coughing, pain during breathing, permanent disability, and death.

The first diagnosed case of black lung occurred in Scotland in 1831. By the 1880s, many miners knew that long exposure to coal dust could produce respiratory problems and eventually disable miners. By the first decade of the twentieth century, however, medical science could not adequately define the disease, let alone address solutions to the problem. The medical profession initially refused to accept the existence of an occupational lung disease among coal miners. According to accepted medical beliefs of the time, the only medical hazard facing miners was silica dust. Some doctors even argued that coal dust protected miners from tuberculosis.

Coal companies also downplayed black lung disease during the early 1900s. Company doctors began calling the disorder "miners' asthma," a condition that came to be expected from coal mining. Because it was undesirable for the company to grant medical attention to occupational dangers, companies ignored black lung and refused to allow miners to seek medical care for the disease. Coal companies largely refused to take measures to prevent black lung disease. Companies saw decreasing the amount of coal dust as an extra expenditure and did not invest either time or money into the effort to reduce dust levels in the mines.

After the increase in mine mechanization during the 1930s, coal dust grew to levels never seen before. As a result, black lung disease increased among miners. The United Mine Workers of America (UMWA) increased its memberships during the 1930s, but the union initially did not aid the miners in their fight for greater safety regulations, including decreasing dust levels in the mines. Then in 1950, the UMWA formed the Welfare and Retirement Fund, which strove to provide medical care and pensions for miners and their families, as well as to study occupational diseases. The fund worked to gain acceptance for the existence of black lung among the medical profession. However, UMWA president John L. Lewis did not regard the problem of black lung disease as a high priority, which hindered the efforts of the fund in promoting the recognition and prevention of the disease.

During the 1960s, the political landscape changed as collective protest against hardship became the norm. The new political reality greatly aided the black lung movement, as the political climate in the coalfields changed from resignation to one of discontent. As miners who had supported the union during the massive strikes during and after World War II came to retirement age, they realized that the UMWA leadership had not adequately represented the rank and file of the union.

The event that sparked the black lung movement more than any other factor was the 1968 explosion at Consolidation Coal Company's No. 9 mine in Farmington, West Virginia, in which seventy-eight miners died. During the UMWA convention of 1968, miners placed numerous resolutions dealing with black lung before the convention, none of which resulted in union support for dust suppression in the workplace. As a result of this lack of action by the UMWA, a group of miners in Raleigh County, West Virginia, formed the Black Lung Association (BLA). The BLA worked to bring national attention to the occupational hazards of coal mining. Although the effort faced tremendous opposition from the UMWA, the industry, and the medical profession, the BLA succeeded in getting the Coal Mine Health and Safety Act of 1969 passed, which brought national attention to the health problems of miners.

The act, however, was ineffective because it called for the diagnosis of the disease by physicians, who required scientific proof, and for workplace changes by operators to suppress coal dust, who opposed doing so for economic reasons. Although the new laws allowed benefits for miners suffering from black lung, miners had to struggle to receive any benefits. The primary tool for diagnosing black lung is the chest X-ray, and because not all miners showed significant levels of coal dust in their lungs, the government denied them compensation. Many miners felt that the Social Security Administration discriminated against them because the government did not give miners a fair chance to file for claims. These problems led to a new grassroots campaign to make the system fairer.

The 1972 amendments changed the 1969 law to prohibit the use of X-rays as the sole basis for denying a claim, among other additions. Congress passed a law that allowed for retroactive payments for claims filed before 1973, and for claims after 1973, the Department of Labor would administer them under more stringent regulations. The result was that the Department of Labor also denied benefits to miners at a very high rate (Smith 1987, 182–183). Miners tried again to mobilize for better benefits for black lung sufferers. They fought for automatic entitlement, in which miners with a certain amount of experience would get compensation. The Senate failed to act, and the black lung movement came to an end in the coalfields by 1977. Today, the debate surrounding black lung continues, but reform continues to be defeated. It is very difficult to get compensation for black lung; more than 90 percent of the claims are denied (Smith 1987, 218).

Mark Myers

See also Federal Mine Safety and Health Act; United Mine Workers of America

References and further reading

Attfield, Michael, and Robert M. Castellan. 1992. "Epidemiological Data on U.S. Coal Miners' Pneumoconiosis, 1960 to 1988." *American Journal of Public Health* 82: 964–970.

Attfield, Michael, and Noah S. Seixas. 1995. "Prevalence of Pneumoconiosis and Its Relationship to Dust Exposure in a Cohort of U.S. Bituminous Coal Miners and Ex-Miners." *American Journal of Industrial Medicine* 27: 137–151.

Brophy, John. 1964. *A Miner's Life*. Madison: University of Wisconsin Press.

Derickson, Alan. 1998. *Black Lung: Anatomy of a Public Health Disaster*. Ithaca, NY: Cornell University Press.

Dix, Keith. 1988. *What's a Coal Miner to Do? The Mechanization of Coal Mining*. Pittsburgh: University of Pittsburgh Press.

Morgan, W. K. C., et al. 1973. "The Prevalence of Coal Workers' Pneumoconiosis in U.S. Coal Miners." *Archives of Environmental Health* 27: 221–226.

Smith, Barbara Ellen. 1987. *Digging Our Own Graves: Coal Miners and the Struggle over Black Lung Disease.* Philadelphia: Temple University Press.

Blue Collar

The term *blue collar* denotes both a statistical or demographic category and a cultural experience. In the first sense, blue collar refers to a type of work or occupation. In the second sense, blue collar refers to a way of life comprising values, styles, rituals, and symbols. The two senses are, of course, related. The distinction is important, however, because it alerts us to the ways in which the meanings of work and class are never static but are instead shaped and reshaped over time.

In the early 1900s, professional and clerical workers wore white, detachable collars. The white collar thus signaled indoor, "brain" work that was clean; the spotless white collar boasted of a worker's difference from those who performed "dirty" outdoor or manual work. Collar color thus also implied certain status and power relations. As the U.S. novelist Upton Sinclair sardonically noted in his 1919 novel, *Brass Check:* "It is a fact with which every union workingman is familiar, that his most bitter despisers are the petty underlings of the business world, the poor office-clerks. who because they are allowed to wear a white collar . . . regard themselves as members of the capitalist class." (p. 114). At the time, most blue-collar men and women didn't wear collars of any color and were more often described as working-class or even proletarian. *American Speech,* a magazine devoted to tracking changes in American English, records the first popular use of *blue collar* in 1950, but blue collar in the demographic sense actually began to emerge in academic sociology a bit earlier, sometime around the mid-1940s. This usage achieved widespread, official authority over the next couple of decades. Today, for instance, the U.S. Department of Labor's Bureau of Labor Statistics divides occupations into three categories: white-collar, blue-collar, and service. Blue-collar occupations include auto mechanics, locksmiths, lathe operators, bakers, truck drivers, and garbage collectors. Blue-collar work is not defined by income; as the Bureau of Labor Statistics notes, some highly skilled blue-collar workers—like elevator repairers and master plumbers—can make more money than many professional workers (U.S. Department of Labor 2001).

As opposed to white-collar work, which generally requires educational credentials and involves the mental manipulation of symbols, words, and ideas, blue-collar work is usually defined by two major criteria: the work is largely manual, involving or supervising physical labor; and occupational skills are acquired on the job, through formal and informal apprenticeships or through vocational training. As the distinction between education and training implies, the main opposition that divides white-collar from blue-collar work centers on the opposition between mind and body or eye and hand. This point is important to note because, as we shall see later, many of the cultural values attributed to the term *blue collar* build on this fundamental distinction.

Not even statistical or demographic categories, like those used by the Bureau of Labor Statistics, are free from ambiguity, however. The basis for distinguishing between blue-collar and service occupations is, for instance, somewhat blurred. Many service occupations like firefighter, janitor, and waitress involve manual labor. Likewise, secretaries and clerks, usually included in the professional sector, rarely need higher educational credentials to perform their work. These ambiguities can be explained in several ways. Unlike pipefitters or machine operators, service workers don't produce things. And unlike carpenters and roofers, lower-level professional workers work inside and use a different, less bulky set of muscles.

Currently, blue-collar work is undergoing two major shifts. First, the core blue-collar occupations are shrinking. As the pace of technological change quickens and as companies shift their production overseas, manufacturing jobs are disappearing. Over the thirty years between 1950 and 1980, for instance, manufacturing's share of employment decreased by 11 percent and is expected to continue to decline into the near future (Kutscher 1993). Second, blue-collar workers are more likely over the next decade to be nonwhite. Because of demographic trends, minority groups will increase their workforce participation at rates faster than white Americans. By 2010, for instance, while the number of non-Hispanic white workers will decline by 4 percent, the number of Hispanic workers will increase by 3 percent (Fullerton and Toossi 2001).

A broader view of the demographics of blue-collar work would probably employ a more salient set of criteria. As opposed to salaried work, blue-collar work is paid by the hour. Even in unionized workplaces, blue-collar work is more unstable than white-collar work; in a downturn, factory workers get pink slips before managers and executives. And, finally and most importantly, blue-collar workers, whether they build skyscrapers or enter data, exercise less control over their conditions of work and enjoy less autonomy. In other words, blue-collar work is fundamentally defined by a deficit of power. One's progress up the social and occupational ladder can be measured by how much power and control one exercises over one's work and over those further down the ladder. This approach to the demographics of blue-collar work would lead to a more political definition of occupation and work, one that moves closer to an older distinction between social classes. Indeed, it is important to consider the ways in which the use of *blue collar* is a more or less implicit way to avoid using the broader, more historically and politically loaded term *working class.*

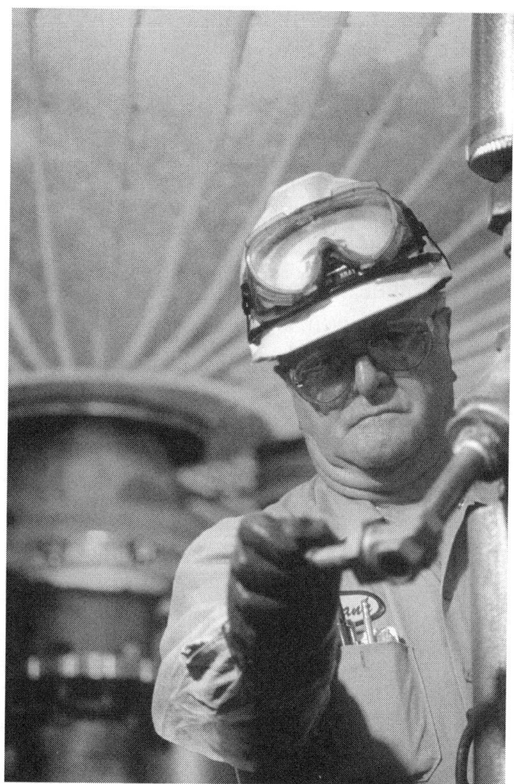

Blue-collar work is usually defined by two major criteria: the work is largely manual, involving or supervising physical labor; and occupational skills are acquired on the job, through formal and informal apprenticeships or through vocational training. (Chris Jones/Corbis)

The cultural meanings of *blue collar* are intertwined with its demographic definitions. Take, for instance, one of the most popular blue-collar workers in recent popular culture: Archie Bunker, the star of the 1970s hit sitcom *All in the Family.* Although we never see Archie at work, we know he's a blue-collar worker through a complex set of cultural cues. Archie is a burly, abrasive man who tends to dress in drab, nondescript clothes. Lacking education, Archie views the world through prejudice, stereotype, and simplified beliefs. He is racist and sexist. He is vociferous in his opinions, especially when they involve his authority at home or in the neighborhood. His loud voice flavored with an urban accent, Archie verbally bullies others less with eloquence than with taunts and gestures. Archie's home is blandly furnished, almost defiantly old-fashioned. His wife, Edith, is equally dowdy, and marriage for Archie and Edith is less about emotional fulfillment than about a battle of wills.

Archie Bunker is a caricature, but like most popular caricatures Archie's outrageous character only exaggerates prevalent cultural myths and stereotypes. His genealogy would include a whole line of popular culture "blue-collar workers," from Jackie Gleason in *The Honeymooners* through *All in the Family* and other popular 1970s sitcoms like *Sanford and Son, Good Times,* and *Chico and the Man,* up to more contemporary television shows like *Roseanne, The King of Queens,* and *Grounded for Life.* Blue-collar characters in these and other shows are comic figures because they dwell within the life of the body. Physically, these characters are depicted in terms of excess; they tend to be big, overweight, or otherwise marked as physically overpowering. They are driven by instinct, not reason. Their desires are immediate and overwhelming rather than deferred and manageable. They think in literal, borrowed terms, rather than exercising critical judgment. Like their ideas, their sense of the way the world should work is essentially conservative, looking backward to tradition and defending the way things are against change.

Ironically, however, the very childlike traits of the comic blue-collar worker can become the basis for more laudatory images of the blue-collar worker as a noble savage, guided by simple and honest beliefs and holding close to important values. This more noble version of the blue-collar worker can be found throughout the culture: in popular music, fiction, television, and in movies like *The Deer Hunter* (1978), *Wall Street* (1987), and the more recent *Good Will Hunting* (1997). Here, the physical labor that defines blue-collar work becomes a touchstone for other values like authenticity, sincerity, moral strength, community, and qualities defined in opposition to an elitist, status-driven, and uncaring social world. Reversing the "Archie Bunker" figure, this strain of blue-collar images presents, for example, the defense of tradition and old-fashioned ways as a battle against disruptive, corrosive change. Education, social mobility, and affluence threaten the more honest values to be found in tightly knit working-class communities, extended family, neighborhood, and gritty but somehow more real blue-collar experience. In this sense, *blue collar* tends to get detached from specific class meanings and instead becomes a brand of populism, expressing the virtues of the little guy, the forgotten person, and the salt of the earth.

These competing cultural images of the blue-collar worker are more often than not generated by middle-class writers, intellectuals, filmmakers, artists, and politicians. Within American popular culture, it is thus very difficult—with a few exceptions (like Paul Schrader's 1978 movie *Blue Collar* or the 1999 film *Bringing out the Dead*)—to avoid stereotypical images of blue-collar workers and work. As Barbara Ehrenreich argues in her book, *Fear of Falling* (1989), most images of blue-collar workers tell us more about the fears and desires of the middle class than about the realities of blue-collar life. Blue-collar stereotypes typically help to obscure real changes affecting working-class people; these same stereotypes also typically operate as whetstones to sharpen other symbolic identities, especially those related to nation, class, and gender.

Larry Hanley

See also Industrial Revolution and Assembly Line Work; Manufacturing Jobs; Pink Collar; Rust Belt; Working Class

References and further reading

"Blue Collar." 1960. *American Speech* 35, no. 4: 284.

Ehrenreich, Barbara. 1989. *Fear of Falling: The Inner Life of the Middle Class.* New York: Harper.

Fullerton, Howard, and Mitra Toossi. 2001. "Labor Force Projections to 2010: Steady Growth and Changing Composition." *Monthly Labor Review* (November): 21–38.

Halle, David. 1987. *America's Working Man: Work, Home, and Politics among Blue-Collar Property Owners.* Chicago: University of Chicago Press.

"The Hard Hat Riots: An Online History Project." http://chnm.gmu.edu/hardhats/homepage.html (cited March 4, 2003).

Kutscher, Ronald E. 1993. "Historical Trends, 1950–92, and Current Uncertainties." *Monthly Labor Review* (November): 3–10.

Seguin, Robert. 2001. *Around Quitting Time: Work and Middle-Class Fantasy in American Fiction.* Raleigh-Durham, NC: Duke University Press.

Shostak, Arthur. 1969. *Blue Collar Life.* New York: Random House.

Terkel, Studs. 1974. *Working.* New York: Random House.

U.S. Department of Labor, Bureau of Labor Statistics. 2001. "National Compensation Survey: Occupational Wages in the United States, 2000." Washington, DC: Government Printing Office. September.

Bonuses

Bonuses are awards granted to employees above and beyond their normal pay. The use of a bonus is one instance of the general category of pay for performance compensation systems. Other examples of pay for performance include profit sharing, gain sharing, and employee stock ownership plans. The logic of all of these pay for performance systems is the same. If employees are specifically rewarded for performing activities beneficial to the company, they will perform more of those activities.

The value of bonuses varies widely from a few dollars up to many thousands and even hundreds of thousands of dollars in some industries, such as investment banking. Bonuses come in various forms and can be categorized according to the type of award granted, the criteria for granting the award, and the award calculation method.

Cash is the most frequently used form of bonus, but many firms also provide noncash rewards to their employees. These noncash rewards are sometimes similar to cash, such as company stock or gift certificates, but some firms reward employees with travel or high-end merchandise. Another common form of bonus payment is in the form of company stock or stock options. Stock options have traditionally been reserved for more senior employees in a firm, yet recently, many firms are extending stock options to lower levels of the firm.

The criteria for granting the award differs between firms but often within firms as well, across functional groups (sales, manufacturing), or across geographically disperse groups (domestic versus international). This intrafirm variance often exists so that different groups within a firm can tailor the incentive plan to the tasks and culture of the group.

Some firms or work groups award bonuses for merit, such as for meeting a sales quota or production target. Others will provide service-based bonuses, such as a Christmas bonus that is given to all employees, or bonuses based on tenure with the firm. For merit-based bonuses, an additional distinction is the performance criteria on which the bonus is awarded. Bonuses are awarded either because of relative performance (for example, the top 10 percent of performers in a given job get rewarded) or because of absolute performance (for example, all employees in a given job reach a predetermined level of performance).

The method used to calculate the value of the bonus also varies. In many cases, there is a fixed bonus given for the achievement of the relevant goal. Awards can also be based on some percentage of the actual performance. For example, a salesperson might receive tiered bonuses based on the amount by which he or she exceeds a quota.

Bonuses are used across a wide variety of positions in a firm. Though most people think of a bonus as associated with the sales function or senior executives, firms use bonuses in many other functions and across many levels of the organization. Variable pay (bonuses, etc.) made up 10 percent of salaried exempt employees' pay in 1999; for hourly workers; that figure was 5 percent (Sunderland 1999).

The use of pay for performance systems is also on the rise. In a 2002 survey by Hewitt and Associates, spending on pay for performance as a percentage of payroll has risen from 4 percent in 1991 to over 10 percent in 2002. In addition, the percentage of firms using variable pay for performance has risen from less than 60 percent to more than 80 percent in the same time period (Hewitt and Associates 2002)

Scott A. Jeffrey

See also Compensation; Employee Stock Ownership; Profit Sharing; Stock Options

References and further reading

American Compensation Association. http://www.worldatwork.org (cited June 24, 2003).

Blinder, Alan, ed. 1990. "Paying for Performance: A Look at the Evidence." New York: Brookings Institution.

Hewitt and Associates. 2002. "U.S. Salaries Projected to Increase Slightly in 2003, While Companies Rely on Performance Pay as Key Compensation Vehicle, According to Hewitt." Press release, September 3.

Incentive Federation. "State of the Industry Report." http://www.incentivecentral.org/html/incentivemerch-study.asp.

Incentive Magazine. http://www.incentivemag.com.

Sunderland, Jennifer E. 1999. "Compensation Budget Information." *Workforce,* December 1.http://www.workforce.com.

Building Trades Unions

Since the nineteenth century, workers in the building trades—employment in jobs required for the construction of residential, corporate, and public buildings and infrastructure—have occupied a crucial niche in the U.S. economy. Building trades unions stabilized the building industry and provided training, a flexible labor pool, and uniform wage, benefit, and jobsite standards. They also wielded substantial lobbying and economic power in state and federal governments. The insular culture of the construction business and the clout of the unions and industry in various circles fostered insider practices that resisted social change and in some cases led to corruption and discrimination.

Economists, policymakers, financial analysts, corporate leaders, and many Americans closely watch the construction industry and the work it generates in the building trades. Among the reasons are the connection of the industry to the business cycle, its ability to create well-paying jobs and careers, its potential to provide training and skills to relatively uneducated and unprepared workers, and the visibility of construction projects in U.S. society.

Construction accounts for about 10 percent of business establishments in the United States and just under 5 percent of nonfarm U.S. employment; labor economists project that the industry will create over 825,000 new jobs by the year 2010 (U.S. Bureau of Labor Statistics 2002). In 2002, 6.3 million people worked in the U.S. construction industry (U.S. Bureau of Labor Statistics 2002), about 60 percent of whom were tradesmen and tradeswomen.

The building industry is exceptionally sensitive to the business cycle, expanding quickly as business growth requires new construction and modification and stopping in its tracks when business inventories stop moving. In a world of high-speed networks, cubicles, and multinational bureaucracies, the organization, distribution, and control of work in

Construction accounts for about 10 percent of business establishments in the United States and just under 5 percent of nonfarm U.S. employment. (Tom Wagner/Corbis SABA)

the building industry still follows a crafts model. In crafts production, workers have much greater control of the production process and the autonomy to resist the leverage and wishes of their employers. As Herbert Appelbaum noted, "The most striking thing about a sizeable building under construction is the myriad specialty trades working with hand tools to execute specialty hand-tool procedures based on the individual worker's knowledge and experience" (Appelbaum 1999). The main trades or crafts in the building industry include electricians, carpenters, operating engineers, plumbers and pipefitters, roofers, ironworkers, sheet metal workers, painters and paperhangers, concrete workers, and teamsters (drivers). Laborers are less skilled but essential to site construction. Pay is commensurate with skill and, to some extent, risk. Although many of these crafts have become more specialized in an economy that demands rapid turnaround, they comprise a fundamentally different work organization than manufacturing or services.

Each craft union has substantial control over who is hired for particular jobs and negotiates the rules by which work in that craft is performed. Observers identify unique attributes of the culture of building trades work that include relative autonomy and self-reliance on the work site, high pay and benefits, the importance of apprenticeship, blurred lines between supervising and supervised workers, interdependence and mutual respect among groups of variously skilled workers, insular vernacular and social codes, and a high level of job satisfaction.

The History and Dominance of the Unions

The construction industry, with its boom-and-bust cycles of business activity, is well-suited to organization by unions, which regulate labor supply and provide a negotiating partner for construction contractors. This interdependence tends to lead to long-term relationships among contractors, builders, and local union officials, who create informal structures and agreements for staffing projects.

As noted by Marc Silver in *Under Construction* (1986), the union is the principal agency for establishing wage and working conditions standards in its geographic and occupational jurisdictions. It also aids workers in handling conflicts with employers relating to the conditions and guidelines of the trade agreement covering particular job situations. Finally, the union serves as the hiring and placement agency for its members. Skilled trades workers typically have more clout in the hiring hall and on the job site, and therefore so do their union representatives. Since the late nineteenth century, union leaders formed citywide building trades councils whose signal purpose was to advocate for unionized labor and work sites.

The International Building Trades Department of the American Federation of Labor and Congress of Industrial Organizations (AFL-CIO) sets broad policies in legislative and regulatory matters and provides services and guidance to local and regional unions across the country. Until the two labor organizations merged in 1955, most construction unions were affliated with AFL. The national office develops alliances and relationships with various national and local unions and their leaders, and as with any organization, these internal political tensions and realities bear upon policy, financial, and personnel decisions.

Workers in the building and manual trades can point to one of the nation's longest traditions of union representation. Councils and leagues representing workers in major crafts were in existence shortly after the Civil War and were among the most influential unions in the founding of the American Federation of Labor (AFL) in 1886 and in pushing for the closed shop site, where only union workers may be hired. The unions formed their first national body, the National Building Trades Council, in 1897, seeking new unity and a national front against more aggressive employer efforts to stop the closed-shop movement. Interunion disagreements over jurisdiction (how unions would divide up the recruitment of new members with various skill and work areas) frayed the council, and by 1907 the council proposed to other unions that a new Department of Building Trades be formed that would allow local building trades unions to charter their own state bodies.

Unions of craft workers developed in part out of a sense that skilled, independent, and small-shop workers needed to protect their viability during the rise of an urbanized, industrial economy in the mid– to late nineteenth century. Many unions sought wholesale reforms in American life to ensure that workers' status would be protected during a time of unprecedented economic upheaval and even attempted to form a national labor political party. Eventually, some joined the Knights of Labor, a reform-minded national union that aimed to use its political power to elect supportive legislators.

Unlike in Europe, however, unionism in the United States turned away from a national political role in which unions would become the bedrock of a reform party, at least until John Lewis formed the Congress of Industrial Organizations (CIO) in the 1930s. The building trades unions would become identified with the AFL's more conservative approach that would focus for the next fifty years almost exclusively on bread-and-butter economic issues such as wages, benefits, and favorable standing in the courts, leaving aside broad social reform issues. The AFL leadership wanted a good life for its workers, as well as respectability and legitimacy among policy- and lawmakers in Congress, the White House, and the courts. That legitimacy was enhanced during World War I, when union leaders worked closely with the federal government to meet industrial targets and avoid labor and jurisdictional disputes through a War Conference Board, headed by future Supreme Court justice Felix Frankfurter.

As the United States entered a period of postwar growth fueled by highly speculative financial markets and a new wave of wealth, antiunion laws passed Congress and state legislative bodies. The construction industry declined during the late 1920s, and investors poured funds into an overspeculated stock market that crashed in 1929. Combined with already high unemployment, a disastrous tariff war, severe drought, and other concerns, the stock market crash triggered the Great Depression and extremely high unemployment for building trades and other workers across the country.

The enactment of the Davis-Bacon Act in 1931 guaranteed that the prevailing local wage was paid on all federally supported construction projects. The act was a major victory for the AFL's Building Trades Department and unions, would substantially increase the earnings of union trades workers for decades to follow, and help stabilize the industry. Franklin D. Roosevelt's (FDR's) "New Deal" programs created jobs and established an activist federal model for responding to unemployment in a declining economy. In 1935, Congress passed and FDR signed the National Labor Relations Act (Wagner Act), which made collective bargaining a right under the law.

Joseph McInerney served as president of the AFL

Building Trades Department from 1937 until his death in 1939 and was succeeded by John Coyne, who implemented a successful system for resolving jurisdictional battles and led the department during World War II. The building trades joined with all of organized labor in agreeing to no-strike pledges during the war. In addition, craft labor unions signed wage stabilization and adjustment agreements that called for wage rates to remain frozen in place for one-year increments, subject to annual renewal, and President Coyne served on the U.S. War Adjustment Board.

In an antiunion backlash after the war (as business interests lobbied to reshape U.S. policy in the postwar domestic policy vacuum), the U.S. Congress overrode President Harry Truman's signature to pass into law the Taft-Hartley Act in 1947, which restricted union activities, allowed states to pass "right-to-work" laws, and spelled out "unfair labor practices" that were prohibited by the law. Despite this antilabor mood, the baby boom and yearning for a "return to normalcy" spurred a tremendous postwar construction boom. In 1962 alone, Congress passed and President John F. Kennedy signed a series of far-reaching public laws, including the Public Works Acceleration Program, the Rivers and Harbors Projects Program, a housing program for the elderly, and the Federal Highway Act.

The building trades were instrumental in the passage of the Occupational Safety and Health Act during the 1970s, which produced substantial decreases in work-related injuries and deaths on union construction sites. Unions also founded the National Coordinating Committee on Multiemployer Plans to represent the interests of workers, employers, and beneficiaries in the difficult and byzantine challenges of managing multiemployer pension and benefit plans. From the 1970s until the present day, the national building trades unions successfully defended the Davis-Bacon Act and other legal protections against aggressive lobbying efforts to weaken wage and working standards. Robert Georgine succeeded Frank Bonadio as president of the International Building Trades Department in 1974 and has served through the present.

The economic downturn in the mid-1970s hit construction particularly hard and brought double-digit unemployment throughout the trades. These conditions began a cycle of union concessions on wages and work rules. High unemployment, combined with aggressive antiunion campaigns and the rise of double-breasted firms owning union and nonunion operations, allowed nonunion operators to gain a substantial advantage for years.

Postwar Controversy, Criticism, and Struggle

Through the late 1960s, work in the construction trades became enshrined as a path to middle-class stability. At the same time, however, Americans were experiencing the leading edges of two sweeping social and political upheavals—the civil rights movement and the Vietnam War. For the building trades labor unions, the changes unleashed by these events would trigger decades of pressure, criticism, failure, anger, and reform within their leadership and rank and file.

These events would force the construction industry and its leading unions to face a history of practices that excluded minorities and women from trades and allowed and encouraged corruption in a variety of union locals and councils, most observers agree. At the same time, contractors and large corporations would drive to break the union trades' hold over the recruitment, training, placement, and, to a large extent, supervision of organized labor.

In pulling apart the threads of reputation and reality that comprise the racially exclusive employment practices within the building trades unions and the construction industry as a whole, one needs to understand the unique nature of the construction industry, as well as immigration patterns and cultural and ethnic beliefs and practices. The "fairness" of the labor market—the supply and demand of workers in the open economy—to workers of different races and backgrounds was greatly affected by the cycles of immigration that flooded the United States during the nineteenth and early twentieth centuries.

Early immigrants from the British isles and Germany filled many of the craft and artisan jobs in the eighteenth and early nineteenth centuries, and as these organizations formalized into unions, these workers and their descendants acted to protect what they had, restricting new entrants and passing skills and opportunities down through generations.

As industrialism took hold before the Civil War, U.S. employers began recruiting immigrant workers to expand their pool of low-cost labor, and organized labor began to actively oppose what it saw as unrestricted immigration providing contract labor for industrialists. But as new workers from Ireland, Italy, Eastern Europe, and Greece found footholds in particular industries, such as textiles, they began forming their own unions to establish their rights and protect their own jobs and work standards. The AFL and building trades resisted open immigration and continued to lobby Congress for checks on immigration.

For these immigrant groups and communities, securing jobs and positions of power in organized labor was integral to the advancement and assimilation of their own community. If incoming immigrants posed a threat, so too did freed slaves and members of other minority groups. The ethnic immigration from Europe pushed the sons of the skilled black workers who had built many of the nation's cities and buildings into a lower tier of poorly paid, poorly skilled labor. Many unions created "auxiliary" or affiliate locals for lower-ranked black workers.

By the early 1920s, Congress passed new laws capping European immigration and completely barring Asian immigration. With immigration drastically reduced, U.S. workers of various ethnic groups consolidated their holds on certain industries and unions and continued to discriminate against Jews, blacks, and other people of color. Among building trades unions, many families passed down connections, training, and access to jobs, and their families and communities formed strong social ties to the industry. These strong social ties and networks became guarantors of opportunity for some—the exclusive nature of craft union employment became an "understood" right for white Irish, Italian, and other workers—but would serve as barriers to minorities and women as those Americans sought broader opportunity.

These developments harshly limited economic opportunities for blacks and minorities. The figures are stunning: in 1870, 31.7 percent of all black males in Cleveland had been employed in the skilled trades. By 1910, this figure had dropped to 11 percent (Kusmer 1976, 20, 74). Until the 1960s, building trades' unions in New York were virtually impenetrable to blacks. Each carpenters' union had its quota of two blacks who were allowed to do finish work. Plumbers Local 2 had three black members who were rarely allowed to work with other journeymen. Sheet Metal Local 28 had no black workers, ever.

The Civil Rights Act of 1964 brought a new level of legal, social, and media scrutiny to the employment policies and hiring, apprenticeship, and recruiting practices of organized labor. A series of legislative changes, federal orders, and judicial consent decrees sought to break down union resistance to hiring minority workers. The unions fiercely resisted change. They responded to lawsuits with proposals for union-controlled hometown plans based on new outreach activities, hiring goals for minorities, and hiring hall reforms. The Philadelphia Plan of 1969, the Chicago Plan of 1970, and the New York Plan of 1970 all fell substantially short of their hiring and apprenticeship goals and were resisted and circumvented in countless ways by union leaders.

The exclusive nature of construction employment came under intense scrutiny during the last three decades of the twentieth century, but the vast majority of construction unions remain dominated by whites, and black and minority workers remain concentrated in unskilled laborers' jobs, among carpenters, and in the trowel trades. The history of affirmative action policies in construction bears witness to the unions' ability to control those policies to serve their own ends (Appelbaum 1999; Waldinger 1996).

As construction workers and their union leaders confronted these many social changes, by the late 1980s and through the 1990s, lawmakers, public interest groups, prosecutors, and union reformists also focused attention on union corruption in the building trades. It had been investigated during cycles of public attention throughout the twentieth century, and there had even been crackdowns by organized labor itself, such as its removal of the International Brotherhood of Teamsters from the AFL-CIO in 1958.

By the 1980s, the topic was again the subject of wide concern. A series of federal and state investigations conducted by the Federal Bureau of Investigation (FBI), the New York Organized Crime Strike Force, and other investigative bodies found the existence of widespread illegal activity, particularly in the New York City construction industry and unions. A 1988 report by the strike force described thirty-one separate court cases initiated since 1980 that involved criminal charges and convictions in the New York metropolitan area. It was not until the 1990s that national union leaders and allied reformers working with federal officials and judges decisively cleaned up many of the worst unions and engineered the appointment of new, reform-minded union officers.

Casey Ichniowski and Anne Preston published a fascinating 1989 analysis in Cornell University's *Industrial and Labor Relations Review* that described the key economic and structural factors that facilitate corruption among industry groups, employers, and unions, including barriers to the formation of efficient markets *and* efficient firms. Production requires the coordination of numerous independently operating factors resistant to executive oversight, and the industry requires expensive, highly specialized equipment and tools that tend to limit competition (compare the competition in software development, for example, in which many experts can share the same resources for relatively low costs, with that in the manufacturing of earth-moving machines, cranes, and trucks). The industry's cyclical nature and hiring patterns tended to disadvantage larger firms, which cannot use their size and deep pockets to field a large and efficient labor force, since different crafts are needed for only one phase of a project. In addition, specific minor barriers, such as acquiring permits, can block the progress of an entire project.

The combination of these many factors created opportunities for individuals and groups that create (legal or illegal) monopolies, which are able to control and rationalize many inefficiencies. Organized crime exploited its ability to control needed labor resources at all phases of construction. Corruption can take the form of bribes, property destruction, or illegal bidding and purchasing procedures.

However, it also became apparent that the preservation of the power and perquisites of union office by individual leaders who were vulnerable to corruption charges also played a very significant role. Despite analyses by many observers that cleaning up the construction industry and unions in New York and elsewhere would be extremely difficult, by the mid- to late 1990s, the most notorious unions were undergoing reform and change, and many of the long-standing complaints about union corruption had been addressed. Turning over union stewardship to younger, proven leaders, working with various federal and judicial overseers on a joint agenda for reform, organizing new members, and focusing on cost-effective management led to genuine change that met strict monitoring standards.

One powerful example is the cleanup of the World Trade Center disaster site, where terrorists destroyed the skyscrapers on September 11, 2001. Unions and contractors worked together in an historic demonstration of dedication and efficiency to complete the cleanup and recovery under budget and ahead of schedule. As noted in a *New York Times* article by Steven Greenhouse and Charlie LeDuff:

> Now, a little more than four months into the job, those heading the cleanup and those removing the rubble at ground zero are trumpeting nothing short of a construction miracle, and with it, no small victory over cynicism about what labor can get done in New York. The cleanup, it turns out, will take no more than nine months and cost no more than $750 million.
>
> Even though it is the largest, most emotional excavation job in American history—the crews continue to sift each bucket of debris for human remains—everybody involved, including city officials, construction executives, union leaders and workers, say they are amazed at how smoothly and efficiently the job has gone.
>
> "You mention the words 'organized labor,' and they're always followed by the words 'organized crime,'" said Bob Gray of the International Union of Operating Engineers, who is in charge of all the cranes, backhoes and grapplers at the site. "This has been a good moment for us. We've shown the world what we can do."

Herbert A. Schaffner

See also American Federation of Labor and Congress of Industrial Organizations; Collective Bargaining; Davis-Bacon Act; Ironworkers; Teamsters; Workday

References and further reading

Allen, Steven G. 1986. "Union Work Rules and Efficiency in the Building Trades." *Journal of Labor Economics,* no. 2: 212–226.

———. 1988. "Declining Unionization in Construction: The Facts and the Reasons." *Industrial and Labor Relations Review* (April): 343–359.

American Federation of Labor and Congress of Industrial Organizations. 1983. *The Builders: The Seventy-five Year History of the Building and Construction Trades Department.* Washington, DC: AFL-CIO.

Appelbaum, Herbert. 1999. *Construction Workers, USA.* Westport: Greenwood Press.

Ballum, Deborah. 1994. Review of *Labor Visions and State Power: The Origins of Business Unionism in the United States* by Victoria Hattam. *American Business Law Journal* (May 1).

Bureau of Labor Statistics. 2002. "BLS 2000–2010 Employment Projections."

http://www.bls.gov/news.release/ecopro.nr0.htm (cited May 6, 2002).

Grabelsky, Jeffrey. 1995. "Lighting the Spark: COMET Program Mobilizes the Ranks for Construction Organizing." *Labor Studies Journal* (Summer): 4–22.

Greenhouse, Steve, and Charlie LeDuff. 2002. "Far from Business as Usual: A Quick Job at Ground Zero." *New York Times*, January 21.

Ichniowski, Casey, and Anne Preston. 1989. "The Persistence of Organized Crime in New York City Construction: An Economic Perspective." *Industrial and Labor Relations Review* (July): 549–565.

Kusmer, Kenneth. 1976. *A Ghetto Takes Shape: Black Cleveland.* Urbana: University of Illinois Press.

Northrup, Herbert. 1993. "'Salting the Contractors' Labor Force: Construction Unions Organizing with NLRB Assistance." *Journal of Labor Research* 14 (Fall): 469–493.

Riemer, Jeffrey. 1979. *Hard Hats: The Work World of Construction Workers.* Beverly Hills, CA: Sage Publications.

Sexton, Jean. 1989. "Controlling Corruption in the Construction Industry: The Quebec Approach." *Industrial and Labor Relations Review* (July): 524–535.

Silver, Marc. 1986. *Under Construction.* Albany: State University of New York Press.

Waldinger, Roger. 1996. *Still the Promised City?: African-Americans and New Immigrants in Postindustrial New York.* Cambridge, MA: Harvard University Press.

Zweig, Michael. 2000. *The Working Class Majority.* Ithaca: ILR/Cornell University Press.

Bureau of Labor Statistics

The Bureau of Labor Statistics is the main agency of the U.S. government for the collection, analysis, and dissemination of statistical data about labor economics. It was established in 1884 by the U.S. Congress and merged in 1913 with the newly created Department of Labor, which is today its parent organization. From its inception, the bureau collected information about the earnings and working conditions of Americans; it even mediated industrial strikes and handled workers' compensation in its earliest years.

During World War I, a cost-of-living measure was needed to adjust wages in shipyards. That led to the bureau's creation of the Consumer Price Index (CPI), a benchmark indicator monitoring monthly changes in prices paid by urban consumers for a representative basket of goods and services, including taxes and imports. This index is used in the adjustment of wages, Social Security and pension payments, and federal expenditures and grants to states and local areas. So important is the CPI that a change of as little as 1 percent would have the effect of triggering billions of dollars in federal payments.

Other key bureau indicators include: the Producer Price Index (PPI), formerly the Wholesale Price Index, which measures the average price changes paid by businesses for domestic goods and services; the Employment Cost Index (ECI), an indicator of total compensation costs, including nonwage or fringe benefit costs; and the Import Price Index (MPI) and Export Price Index (XPI), which track changes in the price of nonmilitary goods and services that are traded between the United States and the world. In addition, the bureau monitors the civilian labor force. Through a monthly survey of 60,000 households, the bureau tracks those sixteen years of age and older who are unemployed and actively seeking employment. These data form the basis for generating the unemployment rate, an important tool in assessing the health of the economy. Data from the bureau's basic indicators are incorporated in the *Handbook of Labor Statistics.* Another popular and widely used bureau source is the *Occupational Outlook Handbook,* which provides information on career and working conditions in a range of fields. Among the surveys conducted by the bureau are the Consumer Expenditure Survey, the National Compensation Survey, and the newer Job Openings and Labor Turnover Survey. Statistical sources include *Labor Force Statistics; Current Employment Statistics; Safety and Health Statistics;* and *Foreign Labor Statistics.*

The bureau has a worldwide reputation for reliability and statistical accuracy because of the scrupulous attention it pays to data-gathering methods. It demonstrates a bedrock commitment to the confidentiality of its respondents and the reporting of findings in aggregate. The purposes of bureau studies are clearly delineated so that users can understand the scope, strengths, and limitations of statistical reports and analyses. Standing research advisory councils for business and labor regularly give input on bureau studies, especially in relation to the needs of its members. They also facilitate the voluntary reporting of data from firms and individuals. The bureau's regional information offices encourage interaction with geographic locales for specialized studies and data input and provide training and technical assistance as needed. An increasing number of states and municipalities today have agreements to share their data with the bureau; and numerous federal departments and agencies cooperate as well. International participants also cooperate with the bureau's data collection efforts and rely on its expertise.

The Bureau of Labor Statistics uses the latest technology and has made its most requested publication series and detailed statistical studies, especially on employment, productivity, price indexes, and compensation, easily available through its Website (www.bls.gov). Users can read, download, and reformat timely bureau reports into customized tables for use. The U.S. Congress and numerous federal, state, and municipal government departments and agencies rely on the bureau's studies as a basis for economic decisions; and the average American directly feels the effects of these decisions in the adjusted value of the purchasing dollar, changes in the cost of living, and statuary actions affecting benefits.

Janet Butler Munch

See also Secretary of Labor, U.S.

References and further reading

BLS Handbook of Methods. April, 1997. Bulletin 2490. Washington, DC: U.S. Department of Labor, Bureau of Labor Statistics.

Claque, Ewan. 1968. *The Bureau of Labor Statistics.* New York: Praeger.

Goldberg, Joseph P., and William T. Moye. 1985. *The First One Hundred Years of the Bureau of Labor Statistics.* Bulletin 2235. Washington, DC: Bureau of Labor Statistics.

Norwood, Janet L. 1985. "One Hundred Years of the Bureau of Labor Statistics." *Monthly Labor Review* 108, 7 (July): 3–6.

Norwood, Janet L., and John F. Early. 1984. "A Century of Methodological Progress at the U.S. Bureau of Labor Statistics." *Journal of the American Statistical Association* 79, no. 388 (December): 748–761.

Business Roundtable

The Business Roundtable, an association of chief executive officers of leading corporations, is committed to promoting public policies consistent with corporate interests, including maintaining vigorous economic growth with low inflation, easing trade barriers, encouraging technological development, and, most controversially, limiting the power of trade unions.

The roundtable was the outgrowth of employers' concerns in the construction trades in the late 1960s about high wages, labor scarcity, the threat of inflation, and the idustry's decreased competitiveness in the world marketplace. Employers placed most of the blame on the growing power of the construction trades unions. In 1972 three public policy–focused organizations, the March Group, the Labor Law Study Committee, and most important, the Construction Users Anti-Inflation Roundtable, merged to form the Business Roundtable. Roger Blough, chief executive of U.S. Steel, was the driving force behind the merger.

From its inception, the association worked closely with the Nixon administration, which shared many of its concerns about the growing demands of organized labor and the impact of high wages on mounting inflation. The roundtable's relationship with the Nixon administration proved particularly helpful in dissuading the government from launching an antitrust investigation into the roundtable's activities, a very real early fear of many members.

Among the issues on the roundtable's agenda in the 1970s was the repeal of the Davis-Bacon Act (the 1931 legislation mandating that workers on public projects be paid at prevailing rates) and reform of the 1935 National Labor Relations Act (Wagner Act) to strengthen antistrike provisions. The roundtable also aided members in devising legal contrivances to allow for "double breasting," a formerly illegal arrangement in which a firm establishes a parallel nonunion operation to avoid paying workers union wages and benefits.

The roundtable also sponsored an aggressive public relations initiative to spread its message. In 1974, it purchased space in *Reader's Digest* for a monthly article (jointly written by the magazine's staff), taking up such issues as labor "terrorism" and impediments to greater productivity. Through its publicity campaign, the association managed quite successfully to link the growing threat of inflation to the supposedly unreasonable wage demands of unions, thus helping to turn the tide of public opinion against labor. The early activities of the roundtable are widely credited with contributing to the growing weakness of construction trades unions and organized labor in general during the 1970s and 1980s. Since its heyday in the 1960s, union density in the construction trades, for instance, has fallen off by 50 percent.

Business Roundtable activities are coordinated largely by the association's chairperson, in conjunction with a planning committee. A policy committee, including all roundtable chief executive officers (CEOs), also contributes. Policy research is largely performed through task forces, which take up a wide variety of industry concerns. In the early 2000s, the pressing issue of health insurance, in particular the demands of escalating costs, has occupied the association. Members meet every year in Washington, D.C., for the roundtable's annual conference. Membership dues based on company sales and stock values support the roundtable, which as the new millennium began represented corporations with a combined workforce of 12 million and $3.5 trillion in revenues.

Edmund Wehrle

See also Building Trades Unions; Davis-Bacon Act; Strikes

References and further reading

Business Roundtable. 1974. *Coming to Grips with Some Major Problems in the Construction Industry: A Business Roundtable Report.* New York: Business Roundtable.

Linder, Mark. 1999. *Wars of Attrition: Vietnam, the Business Roundtable, and the Decline of Construction Unions.* Iowa City: Fanpihua Press.

Business Schools

The first college institution to offer preparation for business was the University of London in 1827, much to the objections of Oxford and Cambridge Universities. According to the upper and middle classes of England at the time, instruction in business should be provided to the lower-class workers only. The classical curriculum should not have been tampered with or watered down with such crass, pedestrian pursuits.

In the United States, however, William Penn and Benjamin Franklin, among others, enthusiastically supported the inclusion of "useful" subjects in the college curriculum. Although the academic and utilitarian philosophies conflicted on the western side of the Atlantic too, the schism was not as great. The first business "college" (a misnomer, because it did not offer a truly college-level education) in the United States was founded by James Gordon Bennett in1824. Bennett's school did not succeed for long, however. It took Franklin, working at the same time, to establish one with any longevity.

It was not the university, however, that first accepted the concept of education for business. The first real growth was that of private business school chains, notably the fifty established by H. B. and J. C. Bryant and H. D. Stratton in 1853. But it was not until 1881, with the establishment of the Wharton School, that education for business was finally recognized as being somewhat legitimate at the undergraduate level.

The advent of the typewriter, the adding machine, the dictation machine, and the precursor to the computer, all in the late nineteenth century, fostered a different strain of business education—in the high school. To prepare a citizenry to use these new tools, typing and an introduction to business became common fare in the schools during the first half of the twentieth century. From World War I to World War II, the business education curriculum thrived in high schools.

It was not until the 1950s that schools of business established a broad foundation at the college and university levels. A clear impetus was the returning GI, who comprised a totally new college-going population. With a need to prepare for entry into their first civilian careers and a desire to make up for "lost" time, returning soldiers' demands on the curriculum to provide a pragmatic, business-oriented education were great. These fundamental changes in the curriculum have remained in place until the present.

A vast majority of two- and four-year colleges in the United States currently offer a curriculum in business (unless they are specialized institutions), fueled by the sustained demand to prepare for direct entry into the workplace. As noted below, more and more students are electing a business major each year at the undergraduate or graduate level. In fact, at the graduate level, only education degrees are more numerous than master of business administration (M.B.A.) degrees.

Since 1950, more than 1 million persons have earned the M.B.A. designation from more than 750 graduate schools. In 1970, 21,000 M.B.A. degrees were granted; by 2000, that number had increased to over 100,000 per year. About 225,000 students are currently enrolled in M.B.A. programs around the country. Two-thirds are men; one-third are women. Two-thirds are pursuing their degrees on a part-time basis (Miller 2001, lv). Overall, 19 percent of all those employed in business/management have a bachelor's degree or above in business (http://www.census.gov).

The origin of the M.B.A. is unique. Still pulled by the weight of the liberal arts curriculum, few (at least at the elite undergraduate schools) wanted to replace the liberal arts B.A. with an undergraduate degree in business. The solution was proposed by William Jewett Tucker at Dartmouth University : the three-two program. After completing three years of study in a liberal arts discipline, the student entered a two-year business program. Upon completion of the full five years, the candidate would be awarded both a bachelor's and a master's degree. With a gift from Edward Tuck (a benefactor of what would become the Amos Tuck School at Dartmouth) in 1900, the program awarded the master of commercial science (M.C.S.) degree to eight students in 1902. This full-time, two-year graduate degree served as the model for all master's programs in business well into the 1970s. Indeed, it is still the model at first-tier institutions.

However, many institutions seized on the demand for graduate-level instruction by offering students the option of studying part-time or on an accelerated basis. To increase the attractiveness of their programs to potential students, some institutions adopted a shortened degree of slightly more than thirty semester hours rather than the standard sixty-semester-hour format. In addition, "executive" M.B.A. programs proliferated. Designed to meet the demands of the upper-level executive who could not enroll full-time, concentrated weekend sessions and intensive two-week summer terms became the pedagogical models on which delivery of instruction in nontraditional timeframes was based.

The years since the 1970s have witnessed two other trends worthy of note. Although degrees are still offered in subjects such as accounting, marketing, and finance, there have been new offerings in entrepreneurship, global business, and e-commerce. At the same time, there has been more direct involvement of corporations on campus. Many have established endowed chairs, supported named departments and research centers, and served as employers of newly minted M.B.A.s. In an exhaustive listing of M.B.A. specializations, *BusinessWeek* has identified six major areas: accounting, advertising, economics, finance, marketing, and statistics. Further combinations yield a total of sixty-six specializations. From that initial cohort of eight degrees in 1902, the growth in number of business degrees awarded each successive year and the development of new curricular offerings to meet the demands of U.S. employers seem likely to continue without abating.

Salaries for newly minted M.B.A.s can vary widely. According to a recent survey conducted by *BusinessWeek,* the salaries for graduates from the top thirty institutions range from a mean $71,873 for graduates of Notre Dame to $95,012 for Harvard University graduates. Of course, these starting salaries decrease substantially for the majority of alumni of "third-tier" universities, where the range is typically from the high $30,000 to the mid-$40,000. In addition, there are clear regional differences nationally, with alumni of the more well-established institutions in the Northeast commanding higher starting salaries than those from newer, less established institutions elsewhere in the country.

The Popularity of Business Schools

The explosive gains in enrollment in business schools during the 1980s and 1990s were fueled by a national psyche that embraced a new materialism and an economy that offered new business frontiers and new opportunities for the creation of wealth. Those forces remained powerful until the collapse of the dot-com bubble and the revelation of major ethical and legal issues in the conduct of business among some of the largest U.S. corporations. There have been signs of a growing rejection of careers in business among new college graduates and displaced dot-commers. Many are choosing teaching or other service professions as career options. It is too early, however, to say whether this disillusionment with the business environment will be sustained.

Ron Schenk

See also Careers; E-learning; Job Market; Occupations; Professionals

References and further reading

Brantley, Clarice, and Bobbye J. Davis, eds. 1997. *The Changing Dimensions of Business Education.* Reston, VA: National Business Education Association.

BusinessWeek. 2002. *MBA Rankings and Profiles.* http://bwnt.businessweek.com/faqsnfigs (cited December 21, 2002).

Daniel, Carter A. 1998. *MBA: The First Century.* Lewisburg, PA: Bucknell University Press.

Miller, Eugene. 2001. *Guide to Graduate Business Schools.* 12th ed. Hauppauge, NY: Barron's.

U.S. Census Bureau. 1993. "Highest Degree and Field of Degree, by Sex, Race, Hispanic Origin, and Age for Persons With Post-Secondary Degrees: Spring 1993." Table 3. http://www.census.gov/population/socdemo/education/p70-51/table03.txt.

BusinessWeek

BusinessWeek is arguably the most powerful business magazine in the world, with a weekly global readership, as distinguished from circulation, estimated to be more than 5 million people. Its strength is underscored by its ability to consistently place itself among the world's top ten revenue-grossing magazines.

The flagship publication of McGraw-Hill, *BusinessWeek* has benefited from the growing importance and popularity of business journalism that began in the mid-1990s. Issues such as finance, stock performance, the role of technology, globalization, the rise of the Internet, and most recently, the conduct of corporate officers have all become mainstream news during this time. This interest has helped *BusinessWeek* secure wider readership and influence.

BusinessWeek fostered its new prominence by playing to its traditional strengths and placing new emphasis on emerging coverage areas, such as technology, the Internet, and e-commerce. In the late 1990s, *BusinessWeek* also began focusing more clearly on workforce issues, in both its print and online versions to leverage the increased interest in these topics. Much of this coverage appears under its "Careers" section, which deals with employment trends, salary issues, work life stories, and career strategies. The magazine has tapped into this coverage from two different directions. It has positioned itself to provide career information to individuals (usually white-collar workers) looking to enhance their own employment situations. *BusinessWeek* has also intensified its coverage of management issues relating to the workforce, including stories touching on increasing productivity, retaining employees, and aligning corporate cultures to business objectives.

The magazine's growth in the 1990s and early 2000s allowed it to invest in solidifying its position by creating a substantial editorial team that includes 200 journalists working in 11 U.S. news bureaus and 12 international offices. Its strength and reach has made it a must-read for most, if not all, executives. "Even when I don't read the magazine, or I don't have time to get through the issue, I look at the table of contents," Nokia chief executive officer and chairman Jorma Ollilia once explained in *AdAge*. "You're putting the week behind and the week ahead in context for me—and telling me what I should know." (Kaplan 2000).

BusinessWeek has used its increased prominence to expand its brand image and revenue streams through the creation of several related products: BusinessWeek online; a syndicated personal financial program, BusinessWeek TV; and BusinessWeek Events, which sponsors a series of issue-oriented global forums for senior executives.

Although prominent, the magazine has substantial competition from both *Forbes* and *Fortune*. Yet its position as a weekly magazine, in contrast to the biweekly publishing schedule of its competitors, gives *BusinessWeek* a unique advantage. Its frequency allows it to concentrate more effectively on reporting and analyzing the impact of breaking news on business and the economy.

For all its gains, *BusinessWeek*, along with its competitors, suffered when the economy began to deteriorate in the early 2000s. Although the publishing industry as a whole witnessed unprecedented layoffs and closures, magazines such as *BusinessWeek* that relied on business and technology advertising were particularly hard-hit, forcing many of them to retrench, cutting back or holding off on expansion plans and overall coverage. Coverage of workforce and career issues, however, expanded, reflecting the downturn's impact on the labor market.

John Salak

See also *Fortune*; Wall Street; *Wall Street Journal*

References and further reading

Carr, David. 2002. "Publishers Trying to Salvage Troubled Magazines." *New York Times*, September 24.

Fine, Jon. 2002. "Business Magazines Mired in Bad Business." AdAage.com. http://www.adage.com (cited June 3, 2003).

Kaplan, David. 2000. "High Tech Blueprint Sends *BusinessWeek* Soaring." AdAge.com. http://www.adage.com/news.cms?newsId=31837 (cited June 3, 2003).

C

Capitalism

Capitalism is a term used to describe economies in which capital and all other factors of production are privately held and disposed of as their owners wish. The ideal capitalist society rewards risk taking by allowing owners to accumulate more capital. The production of goods thereby leveraged creates wealth for society at large. Government places as few limits on the market as possible, and inefficient uses of capital are killed off through competition. Bonds between individuals are of the contractual type, rather than that of master and servant, as in feudal societies. In reality, there is no society anywhere that can be described as pure capitalist per laissez-faire (French for "leave alone to do") ideology, which argues for little government intervention in the economy beyond enforcing contracts. Every government places some restrictions on the movement of capital. All modern economies employ a mix of capitalist and socialist ideas. In recent years, the United States, like much of the world, has become more capitalist.

The underlying basis for capitalism is that markets will allocate resources in the most efficient manner possible if they are left alone to do so, bidding up the price of products in demand and funding their producers' search for labor and raw materials. As such, its proponents believe that capitalism as such is the "natural" state of economic affairs. It can therefore be difficult to attribute its creation to any individual or group. However, it can be said that the first documentation of capitalism as a concept, as well as the moral argument in favor of it, came with the publication of Adam Smith's *Inquiry into the Nature and Causes of the Wealth of Nations*, published in 1776. The prevalent economic theories of the time made up what was called "mercantilism," which was predicated on the use of tariffs to prevent money (usually gold) from leaving the mother country. It was carefully bound up in the empire building of the eighteenth century, and Smith's England was perhaps its leading proponent. Trade both within and without the British Empire was carefully regulated such that finished products were produced only in England and that non-English wares were taxed to be prohibitively expensive. Smith argued that the restrictions placed on the flow of capital were bad for all parties involved. If production and consumption were allowed to allocate themselves, not only would goods become cheaper, but the added efficiency would allow the economy to generate more wealth for all parties. The system was called the "free market," because it ideally would be free of government interference. The bonds between England and the colonies would become stronger because they would be based not on force but on mutual benefit. By the same token, every nation would enjoy the unrestricted flow of products of all kinds. Smith called the self-regulating mechanism the "invisible hand" because the many participants of free markets obeyed rules without knowing what they were.

The year *Wealth of Nations* was published was also the year of the American Revolution. Once the United States had dissolved the bands that held it to Britain, it found itself a nation designed to provide goods to an empire that was no longer interested in buying them. England had taken the first step on the road to the Industrial Revolution, and the new nation had no native manufacturing capable of creating the finished products of quality or quantity that England was able to turn out. Neither did it possess the capital that England, with its many banks and colonial empire, was able to raise to support new businesses. Within a few years after the U.S. Constitution was ratified, many within the Washington administration began to debate creating a national bank to issue currency. Thomas Jefferson saw the virtue of the nation in the countryside, on small family farms. Alexander Hamilton, however, believed that only by creating a strong centralized financial system would the nation be able to grow and thrive. Hamilton won the debate. The Bank of the United States was founded in 1791 in New York City. The New York Stock Exchange was founded a year later.

Both Britain and the United States saw tremendous economic growth through the first half of the nineteenth century, as did parts of continental Europe that had begun the industrialization process. Many rules on trade were liberalized, allowing for a free flow of goods between and within nations. The mercantile economy was dead. However, not all the results of capitalism were good. To continue to produce goods, capitalism requires a steady input of labor. One of the most effective means of reducing costs is to minimize labor costs. In some places, such as the industrial cities of the northeastern United States and in England, it was done by hiring poor people and immigrants, by preventing free association of labor (unionizing), and by making agreements among factory owners to keep wages low. In the agrarian South of the United States, the means was slavery. The period from the early 1840s until the late 1880s was one of great challenges to capitalism. The year 1848 in particular saw the specter of socialist revolution rise in Europe. In the United States, cheap land to the west kept the worst abuses muted for some time—the poor always had someplace else to go. However, the great abuse that was slavery was destroyed in the Civil War, after which greater investment in the South did little to stem the flow of capital northward.

One particular innovation of capitalism was that of the corporation. Wholly owned companies have upper limits on their size because of the limitations on capital that one person can attract. The corporation allowed for the leverage of "minority ownership," whereby shares of the company could be sold to the public at large. These sales allowed for tremendous influxes of capital. The growth in factories and especially in railroads was much driven by incorporation. Corporations would eventually surpass national boundaries and become multinational—indeed, in 1974, fifty-one of the 100-largest economic units in the world were corporations; the other forty-nine were countries (Trachtenberg 1982, 5). Even in the mid–nineteenth century, though, the corporation began to loom large in U.S. and European business. The sort of money it could command made it a natural target for those who feared that big business would trample the individual.

In fact, the growth of corporations in the nineteenth century led to the threat of monopoly power, the most obvious flaw in classical economics. For capitalism to function, it requires competition. But companies like Andrew Carnegie's U.S. Steel and John D. Rockefeller's Standard Oil were threatening to squelch all competitors. At the same time, greater efforts at unionization among labor and growing membership in socialist and Communist parties made many fear that capitalism was coming undone. To combat these threats, many nations, including the United States, began to regulate industry in general and corporations in particular. Perhaps most famous were Theodore Roosevelt's "trust-busting" efforts, which, although exaggerated in their accomplishments, did succeed in chastening big business.

As the twentieth century began, new innovations, such as the assembly line for Model T's implemented by Henry Ford in 1913, made mass production—and mass consumption—possible for the first time. New technology created new companies that hired more workers, drawing both agricultural families and immigrants to the industrial cities of the North. Companies like Ford Motor Company began to pay their workers enough to buy their products, guaranteeing a market and ensuring continued expansion. As the corporations and industry in general grew ever larger, regulation increased as well, limiting child labor, the length of the work week, and dangers in the workplace. Labor unions also began to implement collective bargaining agreements, whereby the threat of strikes forced industry to agree to higher wages and even guaranteed employment under certain circumstances. There was much debate in economic circles about whether unionization was legitimate under capitalism. Efforts at branding organizers as Communist, though, for the most part died a quiet death by 1950. Today most union laborers in the United States consider themselves middle class.

By 1914, many onlookers believed that free trade had united the world in peace, but that was proven wrong when World War I began in August. Nations that had been trading partners with one another exploded into hostility. When the smoke cleared, Europe's economic supremacy had come to an end, and the first Communist state had come into being after Russia's October Revolution. The United States, in order to help the war effort, had instituted its first income tax. Capitalism in the United States thrived throughout the 1920s, but in 1929 the stock market crashed and the world was plunged into the Great Depression. To combat the threat of socialism spreading across the globe, capitalism incorporated elements of state control. This process is sometimes referred to as the "Keynesian revolution," for Alfred Keynes, the English economist who first advocated it, or as "demand-side economics" because the government seeks to stimulate demand by increasing the money supply and providing jobs. In the United States, President Franklin D. Roosevelt's New Deal carried out Keynesian policies by borrowing money and creating public works agencies such as the Tennessee Valley Authority. When World War II began, government investment and regulation increased to levels even greater than at the height of the Depression.

After the war, the U.S. government continued to influence the economy both domestically and overseas. In the United States, the Truman and Eisenhower administrations promoted the move toward suburbanization and middle-class life through the GI bill and the Federal Housing Authority, which promoted education and home ownership. In Europe and elsewhere, loans and grants such as the Marshall Plan, as well as military presence of the United States, helped prevent the westward spread of communism. The U.S. corporation reached new heights in the 1950s, becoming truly multinational, diversifying, and developing the promotion-oriented company culture for which William H. Whyte coined the term "organization man" (Whyte 1956, 1).

In the 1960s, continued U.S. success led to the increasing desire to expand capitalism's bounty to the less fortunate. Lyndon Johnson's Great Society program greatly expanded the size of the welfare state while simultaneously confronting communism in Vietnam. The cost of government and the taxation of U.S. citizens became larger issues. Then, in the 1970s, U.S. capitalism seemed suddenly to struggle. Industries such as automaking and steel, which had been dominated by U.S. companies, began to see serious competition from overseas. For example, in 1970 domestic brands accounted for 85 percent of all auto sales in the United States. By 1980, that percentage had fallen to 73 percent (http://www.senate.state.mi.us). The internationalization of capitalism also meant that companies began to relocate jobs to other nations where labor was less expensive. Oil crises further threatened the U.S. economy in particular and global capitalism in general.

Toward the end of the 1970s, new theories of capitalism began to emerge. Associated with conservative economists such as F. A. Hayek and Milton Freedman, they argued (much as Adam Smith had) that capitalism was the natural state of humankind and that without government interference, it would regulate itself in the most efficient manner possible. The arguments took on a new moral component, however, with proponents arguing that state control was harmful, inequity was impossible to avoid and even good, and only the unhindered pursuit of wealth would ever provide a decent living standard to the world. Ronald Reagan in the United States and Margaret Thatcher in the United Kingdom embraced this new anti-Keynesian economics, sometimes called "supply-side economics" because it intends to address economic concerns by providing means to employers and producers in the form of tax cuts and reduced regulation. The world economy recovered in the 1980s, and when communism collapsed between 1989 and 1991, capitalism was redeemed in the eyes of many.

In the first years of the twenty-first century, capitalism has expanded. The free movement of capital has led to results both good and bad in the United States and throughout the world. As industrialization led to the decline of the small farmer as a

Trading floor of the New York Stock Exchange (Gail Mooney/Corbis)

demographic in the United States, so has the growth in globalization led to the decline of manufacturing. Even for products that are expensive to move, such as steel, it has become cheaper for companies to produce overseas and ship to the United States. In a sense, Adam Smith predicted this development more than 200 years ago, when he proposed a natural "division of labor" between nations. However, since the tendency has been to move low-paying, high-risk jobs to poorer regions of the world, this division is not entirely equitable. Further, accumulation of capital allows for individuals, companies, and nations to invest in new technologies and innovations. The newer, higher-paying, and safer jobs in computer science, aerospace, and engineering have developed almost exclusively in those countries where advanced capitalism already exists. This trend leads to substantial benefits for these nations, but less-industrialized nations tend to miss out. This combination of factors has led to charges of exploitation by antiglobalists as well as considerable dissatisfaction by native employees, who have found themselves without an industry.

In the United States and much of the most economically developed countries of the world, capitalism has created an environment of service jobs. Most employment in the United States falls into the service sector. Indeed, the Bureau of Labor Statistics (BLS) expects that the U.S. economy as a whole will create 22 million jobs by 2010; 20.2 million of these will be service positions (http://www.bls.gov). Further, the decline of union manufacturing jobs has led to a sharp division in the economy between high-paying positions that require education and social capital, such as bankers, lawyers, and managers, and low-paying positions that require little training and often offer few benefits or advancement possibilities, such as food service, retail sales, and groundskeeping. Those with education and the capital to take risks are likely to succeed in the new environment of global capitalism. Those without these advantages have few opportunities. This, too, has become a criticism of capitalism. Capital tends to accumulate where it already exists, thus depriving many of capitalism's benefits.

Although capitalism has emerged as triumphant over socialism, its flaws have led many to investigate the possibility of a "third way." In a sense, this alternative is simply an extension of the social democracies that have existed since World War II. However, in an era in which capital is globalized, the old ways of working within national boundaries have come under scrutiny. Many in the antiglobalism movement cross borders to protest. Those who advocate for a third way often do so with an eye to influencing multinational regulatory bodies to match the multinational corporations that are now economically larger than many countries. It is their hope to harness the dynamism of capitalism to a more equitable social hierarchy in which every nation can benefit from new advances in technology and no region is leveraged into exclusively performing dangerous and low-paying work. This goal becomes more important as capitalism spreads. Nations that are still Communist in name such as China and Cuba, as well as Third World countries, continue to embrace free markets in the hopes of providing for their citizens. Trade continues toward globalization, but many still hope to find a path that addresses both economic and social issues. Capitalism's great promise is that it rewards risk taking. In the twenty-first century, its critics hope not to destroy it but to extend that promise beyond those who have already benefited.

Joshua Moses

See also Democratic Socialism; Globalization and Workers; Industrial Revolution and Assembly Line Work; Socialism

References and further reading

Bureau of Labor Statistics. 2002. "Occupational Outlook Handbook." http://www.bls.gov (cited November 14).

Fainstein, Susan, and Scott Campbell, eds. 2000. *Readings in Urban Theory.* Malden, MA: Blackwell Publishers.

Freeman, Michael. 1991. *Atlas of the World Economy.* New York: Simon and Schuster.

Galbraith, John Kenneth. 1987. *Economics in Perspective.* Boston: Houghton Mifflin.

Harvey, David. 2001. *Spaces of Capital: Towards a Critical Geography.* New York: Routledge.

Hayek, F. A. 1988. *The Fatal Conceit: The Errors of Socialism.* Chicago: University of Chicago Press.

Hobsbawm, Eric. 1994. *The Age of Extremes: A History of the World, 1914–1991.* New York: Vintage Books.

———. 1999/1968. *Industry and Empire: The Birth of the Industrial Revolution.* 3rd ed. London: Penguin.

Giddens, Anthony. 1998. *The Third Way: The Renewal of Social Democracy.* Malden, MA: Blackwell Publishers.

Keynes, John Maynard. 1973. *Selected Writings of John Maynard Keynes.* Edited by Donald Moggridge. London: Macmillan.

Langford, Paul. 1989. *A Polite and Commercial People: England, 1727–1783.* New York: Oxford University Press.

Michigan State Senate. 2002. "Motor Vehicles." http://www.senate.state.mi.us (cited November 7).

Smith, Adam. 1986. *The Essential Adam Smith.* Edited by Robert L. Heilbroner. New York: W. W. Norton.

Trachtenberg, Alan. 1982. *The Incorporation of America: Culture and Society in the Gilded Age.* New York: Hill and Wang.

Whyte, William. 1956. *The Organization Man.* New York: Doubleday.

Careers

Careers are broadly defined as the evolving sequence of work-related experiences over the span of a person's lifetime (Arthur, Hall, and Lawrence 1989). This broad definition contrasts with the frequent popular use of the term *careers,* in which careers are typically thought of as involving neatly ordered patterns of jobs with consistent upward mobility, implying that engineers, programmers, and managers have careers but temporary employees, fast food workers, and janitors do not. The broad definition of careers, however, applies to the work histories of *all* workers, showing how work histories reflect employment stability and instability, skills and experience gained or made irrelevant, relationships nurtured or lost, and risks or opportunities encountered. In essence, therefore, "careers," in contrast to "jobs," "work," or "employment," involves this time dimension. Careers are thus highly complex and are shaped by both firms and individuals, activities in both work and non-work-related environments, and social relationships in both work and community contexts.

Prior to the mid-1970s, careers could be thought of as simply jobs because for much of the twentieth century, many workers could expect to have lifetime jobs working for large employers in stable mass-production industries (Hall 1982). Since the 1970s, however, rapid changes in technology, corporate structure, and economic activity have resulted in greater instability in work patterns. Few workers now can expect long-term stable employment with a single employer, and most workers instead hold many different jobs with a range of different employers over their lifetime. As a result, long-term work patterns have become more complex, with new career patterns that may be more or less beneficial to workers, their families, the economy, and society at large.

Careers are the product of both established

structures and institutions on the one hand and the choices and characteristics of individual actors on the other. The influence of both of these factors has shifted over time. In the past, stable organizations—particularly large bureaucracies and corporations—helped to create predictable "organizational careers," which emerged through orderly employment arrangements, including clearly defined job tasks, well-developed internal labor markets, and regular increases in compensation based on experience and seniority (Hall 1976; Osterman 1984; Whyte 1956). Career success in this context depended largely on gaining access to both blue-collar and white-collar jobs in this protected, primary labor market. Changing organizational structures, however, have resulted in the growth of outsourcing, the creation of complex networked production systems, and rapidly shifting economic conditions. These changes have increased the complexity and unpredictability of career opportunities and have resulted in a significant mismatch between this shifting organizational context and older labor market institutions (including employment policy, the labor relations system, and legal protections). Career opportunities have thus become more unequal, and the long-term vulnerability for many workers has increased. For organizations, the solution to these problems lies in creating new labor market institutions that can buffer workers from vulnerability, increase the portability of compensation and skills certification systems, and build more cross-firm career "staircases." To do so, organizations will need to develop multiemployer training and placement institutions that can recognize worker's experience and skills across multiple organizational contexts (Herzenberg, Alic, and Wial 1998; Osterman et al. 2001).

Individual characteristics also affect career outcomes. Attitudes, education and experience levels, demographic characteristics, and social relations are critical in shaping individual work paths over a lifetime. Historically, educational levels and demographic characteristics (for example, race, gender) have been the primary factors shaping individuals' access to entry-level jobs and thus largely determining career trajectories (Becker 1964; Mincer and Polacheck 1974). Individual psychological preferences also play an important role, as workers try through various means, including vocational counseling, psychological testing, and career advising, to find the right type of job for their personality and interests (Schein 1978). More recently, as work contexts have shifted more rapidly over time, lifelong learning opportunities and work experience seem to play a more important role than simply formal education and credentials. Furthermore, social networks have also become increasingly important in building skills and increasing workers' ability to learn in the long term, in helping workers to cope with layoffs and job loss, and in effectively dealing with a range of other issues that shape long-term employment outcomes (Wial 1991, Lave and Wenger 1991, Hull 1997, Wenger 1998). These social networks are built in both work- and non-work-related settings, leading to an increased importance of home life to work success as well (Carnoy 2000). To improve career outcomes, individuals must gain access to lifelong learning (both formal education and informal learning) and make efforts to expand their social networks.

Clearly, careers are shaped by both organizational and individual factors. Even within clearly delineated, stable organizational contexts, there is significant scope for individual career experiences, and individual career decisions also influence the creation and maintenance of formal organizations and institutions. This relationship between employers and employees, in both the formal and informal sense, is thus shifting significantly over time, with contradictory implications for career paths (Rousseau 1995). In the complex and volatile contemporary economic context, employers are expecting higher levels of engagement and commitment from their employees yet also reducing their implicit commitments to long-term employment. Workers are beginning to learn how to demand commitments on the part of their employers to promote their long-term "employability," such as expanded opportunities for training and the creation of multifirm institutions, while also facing the increased insecurity and uncertainty of contemporary career opportunities. The clearest trend in this rapidly shifting environment is that careers themselves have become more diverse and complex.

Chris Benner

See also Job Security; Labor Market; Lifelong Learning

References and further reading

Arthur, Michael, Douglas Hall, and Barbara Lawrence, eds. 1989. *The Handbook of Career Theory.* Cambridge: Cambridge University Press.

Becker, Gary. 1964. *Human Capital: A Theoretical and Empirical Analysis with Special Reference to Education.*

Chicago: University of Chicago Press.
Carnoy, Martin. 2000. *Sustaining the New Economy: Work, Family, and Community in the Information Age.* Cambridge: Harvard University Press.
Hall, D. T. 1976. *Careers in Organizations.* Santa Monica, CA: Goodyear.
Hall, Robert. 1982. "The Importance of Lifetime Jobs in the U.S. Economy." *American Economic Review* 72, 4: 716–724.
Herzenberg, Stephen, John Alic, and Howard Wial. 1998. *New Rules for a New Economy: Employment and Opportunity in Postindustrial America.* Ithaca: ILR Press.
Hull, Glynda A. 1997. *Changing Work, Changing Workers: Critical Perspectives on Language, Literacy, and Skills.* Albany: State University of New York Press.
Lave, Jean, and Etienne Wenger. 1991. *Situated Learning: Legitimate Peripheral Participation.* Cambridge: Cambridge University Press.
Mincer, Jacob, and Soloman Polacheck. 1974. "Family Investments in Human Capital: The Earnings of Women." *Journal of Political Economy,* March–April.
Osterman, Paul. 1984. *Internal Labor Markets.* Cambridge: MIT Press.
Osterman, Paul, Thomas A. Kochan, Richard M. Locke, and Michael J. Piore. 2001. *Working in America: A Blueprint for the New Labor Market.* Cambridge: MIT Press.
Rousseau, Denise. 1995. *Psychological Contracts in Organizations: Understanding Written and Unwritten Agreements.* Thousand Oaks, CA: Sage Publications.
Schein, Edgar. 1978. *Career Dynamics: Matching Individual and Organizational Needs.* Reading, MA: Addison Wesley.
Wenger, Etienne. 1998. *Communities of Practice: Learning, Meaning, and Identity.* Cambridge: Cambridge University Press.
Whyte, W. H. 1956. *The Organization Man.* New York: Simon and Schuster.
Wial, Howard. 1991. "Getting a Good Job—Mobility in a Segmented Labor Market." *Industrial Relations* 30, 3: 396–416.

Child Care

Child care refers to the care and supervision of children, usually outside the home, by someone other than a primary family member. With nearly three-quarters of women with minor children in the labor force, child care has become a subject of public concern and a key public policy issue over the past decade. Families in the United States have become more dependent on nonparental care and have made the quality, cost, and availability of such care a topic of public discourse. Child care policy was enacted on the national level in 1996 when the Personal Responsibility and Work Opportunity Reconciliation Act gave states the flexibility to design child care systems for current and former welfare recipients and other low-income families in their states.

The number of women with small children in the labor force increased drastically during the last decade of the twentieth century. Between 1990 and 2000, the percentage of women with children under age three participating in the labor force increased from 53.6 to 61 percent. During this period, the rate for women with children under age eighteen increased from 66.7 to 72.9 percent (U.S. Department of Labor 2001). Approximately 44 million children under age seventeen have both parents or their only parent in the workforce. According to the National Conference of State Legislatures, approximately 13 million children in the United States are in out-of-home child care programs (Groginsky, Robinson, and Smith 1999).

The affordability of child care has become an issue of national concern. Child care expenses can consume a large portion of a working family's income. The 1997 National Survey of American Families showed that 48 percent of working families with children under age thirteen had child care expenses. The average expense for child care was $286 per month and represented an average of 9 percent of family earnings. However, costs are greater for those with small children, and the average percentage of earnings spent on child care is greater for single-parent and low-income families. Single-parent families that paid for care spent an average of 16 percent of their family earnings, whereas two-parent families paid an average of 7 percent of their earnings. Child care expenses represent a greater hardship for poor families. For those who paid for child care, the average cost was 16 percent of earnings for low-income families versus only 6 percent for higher-earning families, and 27 percent of low-earning families spend more than 20 percent of their earnings on child care (Giannarelli and Barsimantov 2000).

Public resources for child care funding, especially for working families have historically been quite limited, although the U.S. government expanded resources for child care in the early 2000s. Child care policy has historically been tied to programs for poor families. The primary source of funding for subsidized child care is the Child Care and Devel-

According to the National Conference of State Legislatures, approximately 13 million children in the United States are in child care programs. (Vince Streano/Corbis)

opment Fund, which was created by the 1996 welfare reform law. At present, it serves only 10 to 15 percent of children who are eligible because of limited federal funds (U.S. Department of Health and Human Services 2000).

Child care has its roots in the nineteenth century, when day nurseries were created for poor mothers who were forced to work to support their families. They became more controversial in the early twentieth century, when prevailing public thought stressed the dangers of women working outside the home. This belief influenced the first federal welfare policy, Aid to Dependent Children (ADC), which was passed with the Social Security Act of 1935. ADC was established as part of President Franklin Roosevelt's New Deal to assist widowed and abandoned mothers and their children, who had little or no other means of support unless the sole parent worked. The funding allowed women to stay at home to raise their children, reflecting the cultural mores of the time.

When the Depression hit in the 1930s, many women were forced to enter the labor force to support their families. In response to public pressure, the federal government funded public nurseries across the nation. Called "emergency nursery schools," these establishments stressed the educational benefits of the experience for children. During World War II, the federal government passed the Lanham Act to fund day care centers, but the funding was not distributed systematically or equally around the nation, reflecting a lack of real cohesive policy in the area of child care. This funding was withdrawn after the war ended.

Income tax deductions for the costs of child care were first permitted in 1954, illustrating a shift in social and cultural attitudes about working women. The poverty programs of the 1960s and 1970s also provided minimal child care funding, which was targeted at the poor who entered the labor force. The 1980s saw a severe reduction in funding under the Reagan administration, but the demand for child care grew nonetheless, as more and more women entered the labor force. The private child care industry boomed, and the costs of child care skyrocketed with this increased demand.

Funding for child care was restored by the Clinton administration in the 1990s but was mainly tied to programs aimed at the poor. The welfare reform act, the Personal Responsibility and Work Opportunity Reconciliation Act of 1996 (PRWORA), requires that welfare recipients move into work within twenty-four months of first receiving assistance. Furthermore, the act imposes a five-year lifetime limit on eligibility for assistance. To deal with the millions of women who would be entering the labor force as a result of the new policy, the act established the Child Care and Development Fund (CCDF). States have been given the flexibility and the responsibility to develop child care systems to help recipients move into work and to provide services to former recipients and poor families to prevent them from going on welfare. States may use CCDF funds to aid families with incomes up to 85 percent of the state median income. In recent years, states have been allowed to use unspent funds from the welfare benefits program established under PRWORA, Temporary Assistance to Needy Families (TANF), for expanding child care services in their states. In 1999, CCDC federal and state spending was \$4.8 billion, and the total TANF spending on child care was \$2.7 billion (U.S. House Education and the Workforce Committee 2002).

Child care has been a major issue in the reauthorization of PRWORA. Child care advocates have argued for increasing the amount of funds that can be spent on child care, whereas opponents have argued that the current law provides enough flexibility for states to use funds for child care if necessary. The reauthorization of the welfare law in 2002–2003 has heated this debate by imposing stricter work requirements and longer work weeks on welfare recipients.

Denise A. Pierson-Balik

See also Family and Medical Leave Act; Mommy Track; Women and Work

References and further reading

Child Care Action Campaign. 2001. "Key Facts on Child Care and Early Education." http://www.childcareaction.org (cited October 29, 2001).

Giannarelli, Linda, and James Barsimontov. 2000. "Child Care Expenses of America's Families." Occasional Paper 40, *Assessing the New Federalism Series.* Washington, DC: Urban Institute.

Groginsky, Scott, Susan Robinson, and Shelley Smith. 1999. "Making Child Care Better: State Initiatives." National Conference of State Legislatures. http://www.ncsl.org/programs/cyf/mccexec.htm (cited October 29, 2001).

Michel, Sonya. 1999. *Children's Interests/Mother's Rights: The Shaping of America's Child Care Policy.* New Haven, CT: Yale University Press.

Rose, Elizabeth. 1999. *A Mother's Job: The History of Day Care, 1890–1960.* New York: Oxford University Press.

U.S. Department of Health and Human Services. 2000. "New Statistics Show Only Small Percentage of Eligible Families Receive Child Care Help." http://www.hhs.gov/news/press/2000press/20001206.html (cited May 7, 2003).

U.S. Department of Labor, Women's Bureau. 2001. "Work-Related Childcare Statistics." http://www.dol.gov (cited July).

U. S. House Education and the Workforce Committee. 2002. Testimony of Douglas J. Besharov before the Subcommittee on Education and the Workforce on the *Assessing the Child Care and Development Block Grant,* 107th Cong., 2d. sess., February 27.

Child Labor

Child labor has been part of American society since long before the American Revolution. For much of the early history of the United States, child labor was usually, though not always, an outgrowth of family life. Children's work was considered a good thing because it contributed to the family economy, prevented idleness and mischief (following on the Puritan heritage), and taught children trades and useful occupational skills.

This public view has radically changed over the past hundred years, as experts and eventually the broad general public identified devastating developmental and health consequences from excessive work. Child labor remains an ongoing problem that affects not only the world of work but also reflects how American society values work, the family, and childhood. Today, organizations and governments share a common vision of eliminating abusive child labor worldwide, or where child labor is woven into the fabric of community and agricultural life, ensuring fair pay and labor standards.

Beyond the Puritan ethic, there are many reasons why child labor maintained such staying power for much of American history. In addition to simply hiring children because they could pay them less and because they were more tractable (and exploitable) than adults, some employers genuinely believed that they were doing a good thing by keeping children occupied at useful tasks. Parents frequently favored their children working, whether from family tradition or because their income was genuinely needed.

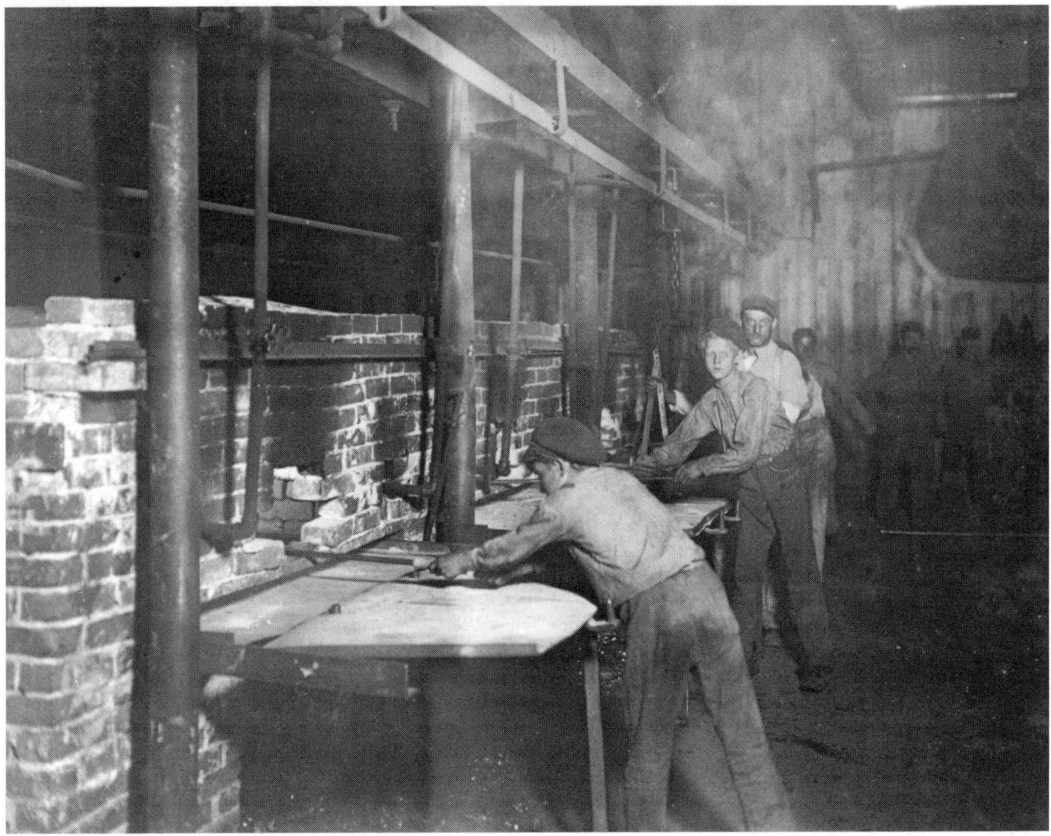

During the nineteenth century most child laborers were from the poorer classes of society. As the century wore on, many came from immigrant groups in which children working to support their families was the tradition. (Library of Congress)

The latter was especially true for families headed by widowed or deserted mothers. Finally, children themselves chose work for a number of reasons, among them the desire to help and to meet parental expectations. And at a time when the value of a sustained education to future success was less clear than in the present time, many children believed that work was more valuable than school.

For these and other reasons, the eradication of child labor has been an uphill battle throughout American history. Because most child laborers were from the poorer classes of society and, as the nineteenth century wore on, increasingly from immigrant groups in which children working to support their families was the tradition, a blame-the-victim mentality often impeded efforts at amelioration. Also, taking on the increasingly powerful industries that profited from child labor could be politically risky, especially during the Gilded Age, when capitalism grew unrestrained. Finally, in the American South, where child labor was especially rampant, issues of sectionalism and states' rights often stymied efforts to even regulate child labor.

Even during the early part of American history, the Puritan ethic emphasizing the value of work conflicted with the Puritan ethic valuing literacy, particularly the ability to read the Bible. As a result, the value of education became the first challenge to the unquestioned acceptability of child labor, and the first law legislating a minimum amount of education for working children was passed in Massachusetts in 1813. During the early nineteenth century, several states in New England and the mid-Atlantic region passed laws prohibiting child labor in factories, mines, and mills and requiring a minimal amount of education for children who worked. However, legislated minimum work ages were often as low as twelve or thirteen; inspection and enforcement were spotty; and in contrast to the North, southern states permitted work by children as young as six. As immigration increased, so did poverty, and the idea that working children could or should support their parents increasingly flew in the face of the reality of adult men losing employment (and hence genuine breadwinning ability) to children who could be paid much less, causing increased family poverty and depriving children of schooling.

"By the end of the nineteenth century, with the growth in industrialization and the increasing incidence of children performing repetitive, menial tasks that impaired their health and opportunities for education, these arguments became increasingly difficult to sustain" (Breitzer, in press). As the Gilded Age gave way to the Progressive era at the end of the nineteenth century, increased concern for child welfare in general paved the way for organized efforts to regulate child labor. Yet even as the idea of child labor regulation became increasingly accepted, laws were enforced with difficulty during the early twentieth century.

One notable nineteenth-century effort by organized labor on behalf of child workers was the creation of a union composed solely of child workers. The purpose of the Newsboys and Bootblacks' Protective Union, chartered by the Cleveland AFL, was to ensure fair pay and to reduce the number of hours worked by children and to "educate the members in the principles of trade unionism so when they develop into manhood they will at all times struggle for the product of their labor" (AFL-CIO 1902). As legislation increasingly restricted and in many cases banned child labor during the twentieth century, the unionization of child workers became a moot issue. But at the close of the twentieth century, unions were again speaking out against child labor—in Third World nations where many manufacturers have moved operations. The current activism is based on humanitarian grounds as well as concern that child labor abroad will drive down adult wages in the United States.

Most of the activism to regulate or eradicate child labor, however, was conducted by progressive activists allied with but outside of the labor movement. With increased middle-class concern for the importance of education and play to childhood and the corresponding recognition that child labor was detrimental to both, as well as to children's health, this period also sometimes became known as the "child-saving" era. Edgar Gardner Murphy, an Episcopalian minister, founded the National Child Labor Committee (NCLC) in the South in 1904. The purpose of the NCLC was first to document child labor and eventually to advocate national legislation to control it, and it focused much of its efforts on especially egregious examples, such as the illegal use of 10,000 child miners in Pennsylvania.Opposition from business leaders and southerners complicated the NCLC's task. In fact, conditions in the South contributed to the NCLC's decision to pursue federal legislation as the best solution to the child labor problem. The Keating-Owen Bill, the first successful piece of national child labor legislation passed Congress, after much effort, in 1916, but was struck down by the Supreme Court in 1918. The following year, a second national child labor law was passed, but was also struck down by the Supreme Court, in 1922. A Child Labor Amendment to the Constitution, first submitted to the states in 1924, failed to achieve ratification as late as 1950. Even so, the efforts of the NCLC were far from fruitless, and between the 1920s and 1930s, even before the New Deal, census reports showed child labor to be in decline.

Finally, in 1938, the Fair Labor Standards Act successfully established a minimum age of sixteen for nonagricultural employment, except in occupations deemed hazardous by the secretary of labor, which had a minimum age for employment of eighteen. The act exempted children employed by their parents, except in manufacturing, mining, and hazardous occupations. There were notably more lenient standards for agricultural work, allowing a minimum age of sixteen for employment during school hours, fourteen outside school hours, twelve to thirteen with parental consent, and below twelve on family farms. In 1948, an amendment to the Fair Labor Standards Act prohibited farm work during school hours while school was in session.

After World War II, child labor nearly disappeared, both in law and in fact, from the American scene. Increasing prosperity, subsequent legislation, and compulsory schooling led to the conclusion, first stated in 1950, that child labor had become "insignificant." In law and practice, the minimum age to obtain a work permit is fourteen, with a few exceptions, such as acting, modeling, and paper delivery. Federal law prohibits work by children under sixteen from 7:00 A.M. to 7:00 P.M.

and limits work during the school year to three hours per day (eighteen hours per week). When school is not in session, teenagers sixteen to eighteen may work until 9:00 P.M. and up to forty hours a week.

Although child labor has been largely eliminated, there still remain problem areas, especially in agriculture among migrant workers. It was not until 1974 that the Fair Labor Standards Act was amended to regulate child labor in agriculture, specifically prohibiting work by children under twelve and requiring parental permission for children aged twelve to thirteen. Even then, these restrictions applied only to children working on farms that were subject to minimum-wage regulations. And even then, enforcement of state and federal laws regarding child agricultural labor has remained an uphill battle, especially where migrant children were concerned. Surveys conducted by the American Friends Service Committee in the 1970s revealed high percentages of migrant children, ranging from 75 percent in Oregon to 99 percent in Washington state, working during the harvest seasons and exposed to such hazards as high temperatures and pesticides in the process. Child agricultural workers were also likely to suffer from lack of education because school attendance was not enforced in the areas where they worked. In general, the child labor problem in agriculture has been regarded as part of the larger problem of lesser labor protections for agricultural workers of all ages. For example, as of 1989, the National Labor Relations Act (Wagner Act), established in 1935, still did not grant agricultural workers the right to organize, and more progressive state laws, such as the California Labor Relations Act, have been poorly enforced. In the 1990s child labor reemerged as a public issue. Sweatshops returned to U.S. cities and city dwellers began to notice again.

Child labor has persisted as a controversial issue in recent years, with the International Labor Organization (ILO), a specialized agency of the United Nations, estimating that 211 million children between the ages of 5 and 14 were at work in economic activity worldwide in 2000 (ILO 2002). Nearly all of these children live within one of the world's developing economies, and more than half are involved in work classified as either "hazardous" or among one of the "worst forms" of child labor (ILO 2002).

It is these forms of labor—which include slavery, debt bondage, sexual exploitation, and drug trafficking, in addition to the traditional Western images of dangerous sweatshops—that continue to attract the most significant international attention. Under the system of debt bondage, for example, children have their labor rented out as a method of high-interest loan repayment, including cases in which failure to do so would mean death for the debtor. The elimination of child labor abuses such as these remains a priority of international human rights organizations such as the ILO, which has a current campaign underway to ratify worldwide an immediate ban on the worst forms.

Research has revealed that hazardous work conditions are characterized by poor or missing safety equipment, that children are often exposed to dangerous levels of toxic chemicals, and that many child laborers forgo their schooling in favor of working full time. The long-term impacts on children may be significant, with associations uncovered between child labor and reduced levels of height and weight. Stunted growth in girls has been shown to have a negative impact on the probability of giving birth to healthy children (ILO 2002).

Increased visibility of the problem is considered only the first step by advocates, however. Campaigns to combat child labor abuses generally recognize the need to solve the problems creating the demand for the labor in the first place. Indeed, many of the most flagrant abusers of child labor operate in countries where the practices in question are nominally illegal. For example, in India, estimated to house between 30 and 40 percent of the worldwide child labor population, children under the age of fourteen are prohibited from working in most industries, yet monitoring is so poor that these laws are rarely enforced (ILO 2002).

Viewing child labor through an exclusively Western framework can be problematic, however. For example, mandatory school ages differ throughout the world, and many families in developing countries realize higher standards of living when their children are permitted to work. Governments often employ children to work in fields such as agriculture, as well. As a result, some corporate-led efforts at reform have centered not on banning child labor completely, but on establishing living wage standards for adults (reducing the pressure on children to work) and on creating schooling options compatible with work needs.

In Western societies, more attention is being paid to the dangers of work for teenagers in fast-paced, highly complex societies. A 1986 study by Ellen Greenberger linked teen work to greater teen alcohol use. The study also concluded that more than twenty hours of work per week could be harmful to teenagers because it competed with schoolwork (Greenberger 1986). Teenagers are vulnerable to the dangers of retail and delivery work in fast food restaurants, convenience stores, and the like, where their inexperience makes them prey for criminals and subject to hazards in handling heavy equipment or driving. Beyond these problems, the often-cited "career-building role of teen work may be overestimated" ("Child Labor," *DAH*, Breitzer 2003) unless the work is part of a career internship or vocational education.

Susan Roth Breitzer

See also Agricultural Work; American Federation of Labor and Congress of Industrial Organizations; Capitalism; Earnings and Education; Education Reform and the Workforce; Fair Labor Standards Act; New Deal; Prostitution (Sex Work); Summer Jobs

References and further reading

AFL-CIO. 1902. "Constitution and By-Laws of the Newsboys' and Bootblacks' Protective Union, No. 8607, A. F. of L, Cleveland Ohio." Cleveland: Charles Lezius.

American Youth Work Center. 1990. *Working America's Children to Death.* Washington, DC: American Youth Work Center, National Consumer's League.

Greenberger, Ellen. 1996. *When Teenagers Work: The Psychological and Social Costs of Adolescent Employment.* New York: Basic Books.

Hawamdeh, H., and N. Spencer. 2003. "The Effects of Work on the Growth of Jordanian Boys." *Childcare, Health, and Development* 29(3): 167–172.

Hobbs, Sandy, Jim McKechnie, and Michael Lavalette. 1999. *Child Labor: A World History Companion.* Santa Barbara, CA: ABC-CLIO.

ILO. 2002. "Every Child Counts: New Global Estimates on Child Labor. Geneva: International Labour Office. http://www.ilo.org/public/english/standards/ipec/simpoc/others/globalest.pdf (cited July 30, 2003).

International Program on the Elimination of Child Labor homepage http://www.ilo.org/public/english/standards/ipec/index.htm (cited July 29, 2003).

Matthews, Rahel, Chen Reis, and Vincent Lacopino. 2003. "Child Labor." *Journal of Ambulatory Care Management* 26(2): 180–181.

Mendelevich, Elias, ed. 1979. *Children at Work.* Geneva: International Labour Office.

Miller, Sarah Rose. 2003. "Child Labor: The Real Solution." *Humanist* 63(4): 29–31.

Nardinelli, Clark. 1990. *Child Labor and the Industrial Revolution.* Bloomington: Indiana University Press.

Roth Breitzer, Susan. 2002. "Child Labor." In *Dictionary of American History.* 3rd ed. Edited by Stanley I. Kutler. New York: Charles Scribner's Sons.

———. Forthcoming. "Child Labor." In *Encyclopedia of American Labor History.* Edited by James P. Hanlan and Robert Weir. Westport, CT: Greenwood Press.

Trattner, Walter I. 1970. *Crusade for the Children: A History of the National Child Labor Committee and Child Labor Reform in America.* Chicago: Quadrangle Books, 1970.

U.S. Department of Labor. 1985. *Child Labor Requirements in Nonagricultural Occupations under the Fair Labor Standards Act,* revised. Washington, DC: U.S. Department of Labor.

U.S. House Committee on Government Operations, Employment and Housing Subcommittee. 1990. *Hearings before the Employment and Housing Subcommittee of the Committee on Government Operations,* 101st Cong., 2nd sess., March 16, June 8. Washington, DC: GPO.

U.S. Senate Committee on Appropriations, Subcommittee on Department of Labor, Health and Human Services, Education and Related Agencies. 2001. *Employment Needs of Amish Youth: Hearing Before a Subcommittee of the Committee on Appropriations,* 107th Cong., 1st sess., Special Hearing, May 3. Washington, DC: GPO.

White, Heather. 2000. "Disturbing Trends in Global Production." *USA Today Magazine* 128(2660): 26–28.

Wood, Stephen B. 1968. *Constitutional Politics in the Progressive Era: Child Labor and the Law.* Chicago: University of Chicago Press.

Civil Service

The concept of a merit system originated with the inception of the federal government in the United States in 1783; however, not until the 1883 Pendleton Civil Service Act, which created the first federal regulatory commission, were any definitive measures enacted to ensure reform for federal officeholders. Oddly enough, the act was a direct result of the assassination of President James Garfield, who had been murdered by an immigrant angry about being unable to get a government job. Initially a reaction against the abuses of the patronage system of government, in which close friends of the president or cabinet members were given jobs within the federal government, civil service reform has become a battleground of conflicting interests. Higher-level civil service positions are still a result of patronage, but acts such as the 1978 Civil Service Reform Act (CSRA) have attempted to curtail such activity. The 1883 Pendleton Act protected only 10 percent of federal positions through the merit system, forcing the merit system to continue to compete with the patronage system.

Despite efforts by each president since Garfield to diminish the patronage appointments and strengthen merit-based appointments, the increasing number of political appointees and policies such as merit pay or performance appraisal (which some people who are outside of the civil service job market consider as policies from the past) continue to alienate the concept of public service from the very members of the public it is designed to assist. In their book, *The Higher Civil Service in the United States: Quest for Reform,* William Boyer and Mark Huddleston argue that "the highly politicized U.S. system of higher administration has not worked. It has failed presidents. And more important, it has failed the American people" (Boyer and Huddleston 1995, 4). Both Huddleston and Boyer contend that Americans tend to distrust civil service because of a strong trend in the United States against elitism and distrust of a strong federal government. Despite these tendencies, the CSRA has made an attempt to create a "higher" civil service system, by establishing the Senior Executive Service (SES), although senior executives are still viewed as "necessary evils."

The underlying problem in any civil service reform effort is the strained relationship between democracy and public service. In *Democracy and the Public Service,* Frederick Mosher noted that "the accretion of specialization and of technological and social complexity seems to be an irreversible trend, one that leads to increasing dependence upon the protected, appointive public service, thrice removed from direct democracy" (Mosher 1968, 5). Therefore, during the last two decades of the twentieth century, the federal government has enacted various efforts to downsize the federal workforce and move federal government jobs into the private sector, resulting in millions of jobs being contracted out to nonprofit and private contractors and grantees. This process has essentially created a new public service workforce, one in which public servants change jobs and sectors frequently, depending on the nature of their position. Gone is the notion of job security; the challenge of a job seems to be more important. The federal government has acquired a reputation for slowness in hiring, of being extremely permissive in making promotions, and of being deficient in managing the huge workforce of private contractors. The "new public service" has become more diverse, however; in 1980, the average federal service employee was male, with relatively little experience in government; today, the average employee is female, with experience in the nonprofit sector. Recent college graduates have proven to be more eager to take jobs in the nonprofit and civil service sectors, with 25 percent of the graduates of the class of 1993 taking a postgraduate nonprofit or civil service sector job, compared to only about 10 percent of the class of 1973.

Those who condemn the public service, either in its original form or the "new" public service, contend that the federal government is in the midst of a fiscal crisis, one that has been "beset by downsizing" beginning with the military base closings after the end of the Cold War (Light 2000, 20). The increasing age of the baby boomer generation and the decline in interest in public service positions has generated calls for the development of a civil service plan that would benefit the twenty-first century.

Jennifer Harrison

See also White Collar

References and further reading

Boyer, William, and Mark Huddleston. 1995. *The Higher Civil Service in the United States: Quest for Reform.* Pittsburgh: University of Pittsburgh Press.

Ingraham, Patricia. 1995. *The Foundation of Merit: Public Service in American Democracy.* Baltimore: Johns Hopkins University Press.

Light, Paul C. 2000. "The Empty Government Talent Pool." *Brookings Review* 18, no. 1 (Winter): 20–22.

Mosher, Frederick. 1968. *Democracy and the Public Service.* New York: Oxford University Press.

Sherwood, Frank. 1996. "An Academician's Response: The Thinking, Learning Bureaucracy." *Public Administration Review* 56 (March–April): 154–157.

Civilian Conservation Corps

Founded during the Great Depression to address issues of unemployment and land conservation, the Civilian Conservation Corps (CCC) went from a controversial idea to one of the most popular programs of the New Deal. It illustrated both the problems and promises of government-sponsored work programs. Nonetheless, it was valuable for its tangible accomplishments and for the hope it provided for thousands of unemployed young men during the Great Depression.

As an environmental conservation program, the Civilian Conservation Corps had its origins in both Progressive thinker William James's "A Moral Equivalent for War," in which in 1912 he had called for a corps of "soil soldiers," and in President Franklin Delano Roosevelt's long-standing interest in conservation. The primary impetus for its founding, however, was the acute awareness of the rising problem of lack of employment or prospects for American young adults during the Great Depression. The development of the CCC neatly partnered this concern with the increased recognition of the need for conservation of U.S. natural resources, whose truly finite nature was only beginning to be seriously recognized. This recognition was accentuated by the droughts of that period, which turned areas of the Midwest into what is known as the Dust Bowl.

As a result, the Civilian Conservation Corps was founded on April 5, 1933, to provide relief for the unemployed and create public jobs that would not compete with private employment but would address the nation's needs. The CCC projects ranged from the familiar (reforestation, erosion control, and trail building) to more specialized (fighting forest fires, floods, and even insect infestation). The CCC was managed by the Department of War, which ran it along quasi-military lines, and the Departments of Agriculture and Interior devised projects. Participation in the CCC was at least initially limited to single men between the ages of eighteen and twenty-three for a period of six months, and enrollees were paid $30 a month, of which they were required to send $25 home to their families. This pay was supplemented with food, lodging in work camps, and work uniforms.

Despite initial public misgivings, especially on the part of organized labor, which opposed the low pay scale, the militarized nature of the CCC, and the possible effect of both on labor standards, it soon became the most popular and highly regarded program of the New Deal. Its surge in popularity led to its expansion, both in terms of the age range and by allowing repeat enrollment. The program diversified to include World War I veterans, African Americans, and Native Americans, although the latter groups were segregated. Women were conspicuously excluded from the CCC on the basis of the belief that women were unsuited to the type of outdoor work that was the core of the CCC program. Despite Eleanor Roosevelt's effort to promote what was laughed off as "she, she, she" camps, several work camps for women were established from which 8,500 women benefited, as opposed to the 3 million men who eventually passed through the CCC camps (Cook 1992, 88–90). Additionally, the National Youth Administration, created in response to this criticism in 1935, created a broader-based program of work and educational opportunities for both young men and young women.

Civilian Conservation Corps workers clearing the land for soil conservation, ca. 1934 (U.S. National Archives)

Exclusion and segregation were not the only criticisms of the CCC, both during its existence and in historical writing. Although the replacement of the originally proposed $1 per day wage with $30 per month allayed fear on the part of organized labor and others about setting new, low standards for wages, the military sponsorship of the program continued to draw criticism. In particular, the CCC was likened to the youth land service corps that were already a widely promoted program in Nazi Germany and Fascist Italy, a comparison the Roosevelt administration hotly opposed. Finally, there were concerns, especially early in the program, that the excessive enthusiasm for the healthy effects of work and outdoor life did not adequately recognize or address the orientation needs of young men who had never been away from their families for lengthy periods and were unaccustomed to living and functioning in a military camp setting. In fact, desertion was a significant problem, especially as job prospects improved and the possibility of military draft increased as World War II approached.

Despite these criticisms, however, the CCC quickly came to be regarded as one of the most, if not the most, worthwhile of the New Deal work relief programs. Its best-known accomplishments have remained the physical ones—reforestation and the creation of bridges, trails, reservoirs, and occasional mountain lodges, a few of which still operate as resorts today. Its services fighting fires, floods, and insect infestations were every bit as valuable both as physical efforts at conservation and as a demonstration of the effectiveness of the conservation movement in action. Yet its less tangible benefits—to the 3 million young men and 8,500 young women who benefited from the program during its existence—cannot be underestimated.

The young men who participated in the CCC had reached adulthood in an era when their prospects for employment were severely limited, so the CCC provided them not only with work and support for their families but with the improved prospects of future employment that successful completion of the program provided. Additionally, the CCC provided not only work experience but also education, ranging from vocational to college-level, and additionally taught many enrollees to read and write. Finally, as its founders had hoped, the CCC gave its participants hope, and most left better prepared to contribute to American society than when they enrolled. The CCC, despite hopes to make the program permanent, in the end became nothing more than a temporary relief agency, albeit a much more popular and less controversial one than many of the "alphabet soup" agencies. The vast economic improvement that came with arrival of World War II made jobs much more widely available, drastically reducing the need for the program, which was quietly terminated in 1942.

Susan Roth Breitzer

See also Great Depression; New Deal; Roosevelt, Eleanor; Roosevelt, Franklin Delano; Works Progress Administration

References and further reading

Cook, Blanche Wiesen. 1992. *Eleanor Roosevelt:* Vol. 2, *1933–1938.* New York: Viking.

Galo, George. 1979. *The 191st, The Civilian Conservation Corps: April 1939–April 1940.* Rutland, VT: Prime Offset Printing.

Harper, Charles Price. 1939. *The Administration of the Civilian Conservation Corps.* Clarksburg, WV: Clarksburg Publishing.

Lacy, Leslie Alexander. 1976. *The Soil Soldiers: The Civilian Conservation Corps in the Great Depression.* Radnor, PA: Chilton Book Company.

Merrill, Perry H. 1981. *Roosevelt's Forest Army: A History of the Civilian Conservation Corps, 1933–1942.* Montpelier, VT: Perry H. Merrill.

Salmond, John A. 1967. *The Civilian Conservation Corps: A New Deal Case Study.* Durham, NC: Duke University Press.

Symon, Charles A. 1983. *We Can Do It! A History of the Civilian Conservation Corps in Michigan—1933–1942.* Escanaba, MI: Richards Printing.

Collective Bargaining

Collective bargaining is a process for determining terms and conditions of employment that involves negotiations between an employer and representatives of the employees, usually a labor union. Collective bargaining can transform the employment relationship from an at-will relationship, in which workers can be fired or quit at any time for any reason, to a bilateral relationship in which workers have a voice and representation. In the latter, changes in conditions must be negotiated, valid reasons are required for discipline and discharge, and grievances are resolved in a fair manner. As such, the term *collective bargaining* is often used in the much broader sense of labor relations and captures not only the process of collective negotiations but also union organizing, labor law, dispute resolution, and contract administration.

The term *collective bargaining* is attributed to Beatrice Potter Webb in her 1891 book, *The Co-operative Movement in Great Britain;* that date coincides with the period of the development of collective bargaining. The early craft unions in the American Federation of Labor (AFL), representing various skilled occupations, were fierce proponents of collective bargaining in the early twentieth century and advocated collective bargaining by strong trade unions, instead of government regulation or corporate welfare, as the means for improving living standards and working conditions. Companies, however, usually preferred to be free of the constraints of collective bargaining, and it was not until the National Labor Relations Act (NLRA, or Wagner Act) was enacted in 1935 that collective bargaining was protected and institutionalized on a broad scale in the United States. In fact, under the NLRA, it is the policy of the United States to encourage "the practice and procedure of collective bargaining"(NLRA, section 1).

Underlying the passage of the NLRA, and the explicit support for collective bargaining, is the belief that companies are able to exploit workers through low wages, long hours, dangerous conditions, and discriminatory and capricious treatment, because of an inequality of bargaining power between corporations and individual workers. If workers can organize into unions, just as investors organize into larger corporate identities, and bargain collectively, bargaining power can be equalized and more equitable living standards and employment conditions can result.

This school of thought stands in sharp contrast to classical and neoclassical economics schools of thought in which markets are believed to operate efficiently. If markets do not have imperfections, government regulation and collective bargaining distort their operation and are bad for economic welfare. In this view, unions are monopolies in the labor market, and collective bargaining, backed by the threat of a strike, is a tool for union members to get wages in excess of what they could earn in the marketplace. How one evaluates collective bargaining is dependent on one's beliefs regarding the operations of free markets and the extent of the inequality of bargaining power between labor and management.

Collective bargaining has been embraced by modern democracies as one of the preferred methods for combating the inherent dangers of letting workers' lives be dictated by the vagaries of unregulated economic markets and managerial whim. The U.S. political system incorporates a system of checks and balances at the political level because of the belief that, as Lord Acton said in 1887, "power tends to corrupt and absolute power corrupts absolutely." The U.S. political system is also based on the right of citizens to have a voice in political decisions that affect their lives. Collective bargaining is an important vehicle for bringing these same ideals to the workplace—and is recognized internationally as a fundamental human right.

The central tenet of collective bargaining is that the unilateralism of management authority is replaced by a process of bilateral negotiations. When employees are represented by a union, employers do not get to dictate terms and conditions of employment. This does not mean that employees can dictate their terms and conditions of employment, but with collective bargaining the workers have a voice when employment outcomes are being determined.

In the United States, the process of collective bargaining in the private sector is regulated by the NLRA. It specifies that when a majority of a group of workers, or a "bargaining unit," indicate that they want a union to represent them, the employer and union must bargain "in good faith with respect to wages, hours, and other terms and conditions of employment" (NLRA, section [8d]). In other words, labor and management must negotiate to try to reach agreement on wages, fringe benefits, and other terms of employment for all members of the bargaining unit.

Wages and other terms and conditions of employment are mandatory bargaining items, and it is illegal for either labor or management to refuse to negotiate these subjects. The National Labor Relations Board (NLRB), created by the NLRA in 1935, is responsible for deciding whether a specific issue is a mandatory item or not, and negotiators can refer to many NLRB legal decisions for guidance. Mandatory items include many issues related to wages (overtime premiums, shift differentials, and call-in pay), benefits (health and retirement benefits), administrative policies (layoff procedures), and many other issues (subcontracting, in-plant food service, production standards, and rental of company housing, to name just a few). Issues that are not "wages, hours, and other terms and conditions of employment," such as benefits for retirees or internal union policies, are permissive, or voluntary, bargaining items. The parties can bargain over these subjects if they choose, but it is not illegal to refuse. The third and final category of bargaining subjects involves illegal items: issues that would violate a law, such as an antidiscrimination statute.

Although U.S. employers must bargain in good faith over mandatory bargaining items when their employees are represented by a union, the law does not require that an agreement be reached. As long as the parties have tried to reach agreement, their legal obligation has been fulfilled. If no agreement is reached under these circumstances, the employer is then allowed to change the terms and conditions of employment (to what was offered during negotiations but was rejected by the union), and employees can go on strike.

The negotiation process has traditionally been adversarial. Labor and management are viewed to have an inherent conflict of interest because improved wages, benefits, and working conditions reduce profits. The rise in international competition since the 1980s, however, has placed great strain on

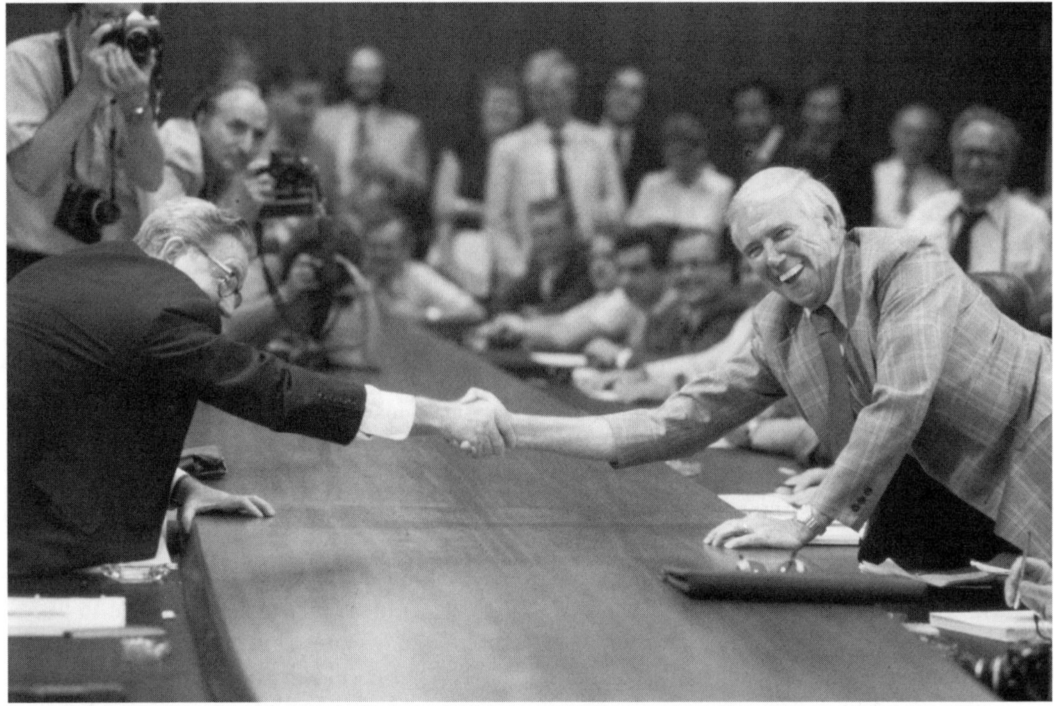

United Auto Workers union president Douglas Fraser (right) and General Motors vice president George B. Morris (left) shake hands as they begin contract negotiations, 1977. (Bettmann/Corbis)

these adversarial relationships, and many negotiators have experimented with more problem-solving, or win-win, approaches to negotiations.

Collective bargaining by government workers is controlled by the Civil Service Reform Act (CSRA) of 1978 for federal employees and by individual state laws for state and municipal employees. A number of states do not have any laws granting collective bargaining rights to public sector workers, so public sector employees in these states do not need to recognize unions or bargain with them; other states have laws similar to the NLRA. In many public sector jurisdictions, strikes are illegal, and bargaining disputes are instead submitted to arbitration, mediation, fact finding, or some combination of the three. Collective bargaining in the railroad and airline industries is controlled by the Railway Labor Act. The NLRA and these other laws govern not only bargaining, but also the union organizing process.

Collective bargaining in the United States usually results in legally binding collective bargaining agreements, or union contracts, which include wage and benefit provisions, work rules, seniority rights, transfer and layoff procedures, and other provisions dealing with employment issues important to labor and management. Nearly every U.S. union contract contains a grievance procedure in which the parties agree to resolve disputes over the application and interpretation of the contract through an orderly process that fulfills conventional standards of justice and due process. The final step of the grievance procedure is often binding arbitration. U.S. union contracts also place significant limits on the at-will relationship by specifying that management can only discipline and discharge employees for just cause, that is, for valid reasons related to job performance supported by objective evidence.

U.S. collective bargaining varies from industry to industry. Overall, 14.9 percent of U.S. workers were covered by collective bargaining agreements in 2000, though only 9.8 percent of private sector workers are covered, compared to 42 percent of government workers (U.S. Department of Labor 2001). U.S. union density (the fraction of the workforce in unions or covered by contracts) has been falling since the 1950s, though there is not agreement on the cause of this trend. Some observers cite decreased demand for unions, either because of increased government regulation or more effective corporate human resource management policies, whereas others point to increased efforts by companies to weaken and break unions, aided by weaknesses in U.S. labor law.

There are thousands of collective bargaining agreements in the United States, ranging from those that cover just a handful of employees to some that cover thousands. The American Federation of Television and Radio Artists (AFTRA) and Screen Actors Guild (SAG) contracts, the United Auto Workers' (UAW) contract with Ford, the Teamsters' contract with United Parcel Service (UPS), and the National Association of Letter Carriers' contract with the U.S. Postal Service each cover more than 100,000 workers. In the postwar period, these contracts evolved into complex, lengthy documents with numerous, very detailed provisions. More recently, corporations are trying to achieve greater levels of flexibility in the deployment of employees by trying to move away from such detailed contract language.

Research has established that U.S. workers covered by collective bargaining agreements earn approximately 15 percent higher wages than similar nonunion workers and that unionized employees are significantly more likely to receive fringe benefits. The decline in U.S. union density is also believed by many to be partly responsible for the observed increase in income inequality since the 1980s. The presence of a labor union is also associated with lower firm profits, but there is still debate over whether unionized workers are more or less productive than comparable nonunion workers and whether unions drive firms out of business.

The process and outcomes of collective bargaining can be very different across countries. In the United States and Canada, bargaining is characterized as relatively decentralized because negotiations typically cover only a single work site or company. In Western Europe, bargaining is often more centralized, with negotiations covering an entire industry. In the United States, the resulting union contract is a legally enforceable document, but that is not true in many other countries. U.S. contracts also contain many subjects, such as fringe benefit provisions or layoff procedures, that may be specified by law in other countries. U.S. contracts are often written in very detailed and precise terms, whereas agreements in other countries may simply specify acceptable minimum standards.

These differences underscore the flexibility of collective bargaining. Laws, culture, traditions, history, personalities, and the economic environment can all influence how collective bargaining is actually conducted in any given negotiation. In strong economic times, the parties can negotiate wage increases; in weak economic times, they can negotiate concessions. Many U.S. public sector unions engage in collective bargaining without the right to strike. Unions representing U.S. federal workers cannot negotiate pay levels and instead focus on policies and procedures. In an increasingly global economy, some unions are working toward transnational collective bargaining between multinational corporations and unions from more than one country. Collective bargaining allows labor and management to tailor agreements to their circumstances.

Collective bargaining can also provide industrial democracy: workers can have a voice in the workplace as terms and conditions are being negotiated and administered. Thus, collective bargaining is the cornerstone of U.S. policy to protect workers from abusive treatment and provide them a voice in the workplace. On an international level, collective bargaining is accepted as a key feature of a democratic society and as a fundamental human right. The right of collective bargaining is one of the four fundamental principles of work identified by the International Labour Organization. Article 23 of the United Nations Universal Declaration of Human Rights states: "Everyone has the right to form and to join trade unions for the protection of his interests." The primary vehicle for this protection is collective bargaining.

John W. Budd

See also Arbitration; National Labor Relations Act; Professional Air Traffic Controllers Organization Strike; Solidarity; Strikes; Working Class

References and further reading

Bluestone, Barry, and Irving Bluestone. 1992. *Negotiating the Future: A Labor Perspective on American Business.* New York: Basic Books.

Fossum, John A. 2001. *Labor Relations: Development, Structure, Process.* Boston: McGraw-Hill/Irwin.

Freeman, Richard B., and James L. Medoff. 1984. *What Do Unions Do?* New York: Basic Books.

Freeman, Richard B., and Joel Rogers. 1999. *What Workers Want.* Ithaca, NY: ILR Press.

Green, James R. 1998. *The World of the Worker: Labor in Twentieth-Century America.* Urbana: University of Illinois Press.

Gross, James. A. 1999. "A Human Rights Perspective on U.S. Labor Relations Law: A Violation of the Freedom of Association." *Employee Rights and Employment Policy Journal* 3, no. 1: 65–103.

Hoerr, John. 1997. *We Can't Eat Prestige: The Women Who Organized Harvard.* Philadelphia: Temple University Press.

Katz, Harry C., and Owen Darbishire. 2000. *Converging Divergences: Worldwide Changes in Employment Systems.* Ithaca, NY: ILR Press.

Kochan, Thomas A., Harry C. Katz, and Robert B. McKersie. 1986. *The Transformation of American Industrial Relations.* New York: Basic Books.

Turner, Lowell. 1991. *Democracy at Work: Changing World Markets and the Future of Labor Unions.* Ithaca, NY: Cornell University Press.

U.S. Department of Labor. 2001. *Employment and Earnings.* Washington, DC: U.S. Department of Labor, January.

Witney, Fred, and Benjamin J. Taylor. 1995. *Labor Relations Law.* Englewood Cliffs, NJ: Prentice-Hall.

Communications Workers of America

Communications Workers of America (CWA), founded in 1947, is the largest communications and media union in the United States, and its members are among the nation's most highly skilled union members. Affiliates of the CWA include the American Federation of Labor and Congress of Industrial Organizations (AFL-CIO), Canadian Labour Congress, and Union Network International. The union represents more than 740,000 communications and media workers across the United States, Puerto Rico, and Canada and has set up more than 2,000 collective bargaining agreements, which cover a wide range of employee interests such as wages and benefits, working conditions, job security, availability of training and education, and child and family care. Members work in a variety of occupational fields, including telecommunications, broadcasting, cable TV, journalism, publishing, electronics and general manufacturing, airline customer service, government, health care, and education. Some primary employers include American Telephone and Telegraph (AT&T), General Telephone and Electronics Corporation (GTE), Lucent Technologies, General Electric, National Broadcasting Company (NBC), American Broadcasting Companies (ABC), the *New York Times,* the State of New Jersey, the University of California, and U.S. Airways. CWA, headquartered in Washington, D.C., maintains fifty field offices and 1,200 local unions (Communications Workers of America 2002).

The CWA triangle represents the union's three primary functions, which must work in tandem to achieve union goals. At the base of the triangle is "representation." The other sides of the triangle are "organizing" and "community and political action." Joseph Beirne, the first president of the CWA, referred to this triangle as the "triple threat" (Communications Workers of America 2002) that yields unions their bargaining power. Leadership has changed little over the life of the CWA. Beirne held his title for twenty-seven years before being succeeded by Glenn Watts in 1974. President Watts retired eleven years later in 1985 and was succeeded by Morton Bahr, the union's current president.

Although officially established in 1947, CWA's roots reach back further. The International Brotherhood of Electrical Workers (IBEW), founded in 1891, was the first notable influence in the unionization of telephone workers. IBEW orchestrated frequent strikes by craftspeople and telephone operators across the United States. Although these strikes rarely resulted in employee gains, they did increase employer opposition to autonomous union activity and led to the creation of company-sponsored (and monitored) unions.

With concerns for the continued security and stability of telephone operations during World War I, the U.S. government took temporary control of the telephone industry and proceeded to freeze wages and deny unions recognition. On April 15, 1919, 9,000 New England operators walked out, discontinuing telephone service in the area for five days. Strikers won wage increases. More importantly, strikers won the right for unions to bargain with companies (Schacht 1985, 8–11).

Between 1920 and 1935, companies attempted to limit the growth of independent unions by initiating their own company-sponsored unions for their employees. These organizations provided a sounding board for employees to voice their complaints but no means with which to demand solutions. In 1935, the U.S. Congress passed the National Labor Relations Act (Wagner Act), which banned company unions and subsequently led to the rise of autonomous unions.

In 1939, twenty-seven unions representing 92,130 members established the National Federation of Telephone Workers (NFTW) (Schacht 1985, 58). Falling wages during World War II caused growing anxiety among telephone workers and the

NFTW. In November 1944, a strike in Dayton, Ohio, sparked a flurry of sympathy strikes in cities such as Detroit, Washington, D.C., and most other cities in Ohio. An estimated 10,000 strikers participated (Schacht 1985, 138). The Dayton strike yielded national attention to the union interests of telephone workers. In 1947, a strike led to the collapse of the NFTW. During this strike, AT&T offered wage increases to certain individual unions within the NFTW, contingent upon each union accepting independently of the NFTW. AT&T's tactic successfully divided the federation, yet it left room for the establishment of its successor in the same year—the more centralized CWA. Having learned from NFTW's downfall, the CWA rests on the notion that the best response to a centralized corporation is a centralized union.

One of the CWA's largest victories came in 1971, when 400,000 of its members walked out on the Bell system. The CWA secured an immediate 12.8 percent wage hike, future pay increases, gains in fringe benefits, and a cost-of-living adjustment (COLA) clause (Brooks 1977, 232). However, from its inception, the CWA's primary goal—the ability to participate in unified national bargaining—remained elusive. Bell insisted that the CWA conduct labor negotiations individually with its twenty-one operating companies, thus severely undercutting the union's ability to streamline its resources in the interests of all its members. Finally, on January 16, 1974, Bell agreed to sit down for negotiations at one national bargaining table (Brooks 1977, 231).

In 1984, the court-ordered breakup of communications giant AT&T threatened CWA membership levels. The fragmentation of AT&T and the introduction of new competitors into the market meant the CWA needed to adapt its negotiation strategies to a larger and more diverse set of employers to retain old members and attract new ones. In addition, CWA members now belonged to competing companies, creating internal conflict within the union.

One of the CWA's greatest setbacks was its loss in the 1988 U.S. Supreme Court case, *CWA v. Beck*. Beck, an employee of a company whose members were represented by the CWA, was not himself a CWA member. However, the 1935 National Labor Relations Act (NLRA, or Wagner Act) permits unions representing the employees of a particular company to take dues from both members and nonmembers. Beck charged that his dues were not being used to represent employees but rather to support political candidacies. In this landmark labor decision, the U.S. Supreme Court ruled that the NLRA does not extend a union's right to collect dues for funding of activities that go beyond the scope of representation and traditional union activities.

Over time, technological advances have threatened the power of the CWA. Its bargaining power is impaired by the development of automated systems that continue to run smoothly, whether a company's staff is on strike or not. Many suggest that the future of the CWA rests, in part, on its ability to make inroads into representing the workforces of the newest technology fields. These employees can provide high-skill services that are coveted by their employers and will provide a valuable bargaining chip in future CWA negotiations.

Sarah B. Gyarfas

See also American Federation of Labor and Congress of Industrial Organizations; American Telephone and Telegraph; Collective Bargaining; Strikes

References and further reading

Beirne, Joseph A. 1962. *New Horizons for American Labor.* Washington, DC: Public Affairs Press.

Brooks, Thomas R. 1977. *Communications Workers of America: The Story of a Union.* New York: Mason Charter.

Communications Workers of America. 2002. http://www.cwa-union.org (cited June 25).

Lopez, Julie Amparano. 1989. "Phone Automation Saps Clout of Strike." *Wall Street Journal,* August 10, B4.

Schacht, John N. 1985. *The Making of Telephone Unionism, 1920–1947.* New Brunswick, NJ: Rutgers University Press.

Weil, David. 1994. *Turning the Tide: Strategic Planning for Labor Unions.* New York: Macmillan.

Communism in the U.S. Trade Union Movement

The U.S. Communist Party (CP) played a significant role in the U.S. trade union movement from its formation in 1919 through the expulsion of the eleven CP-led unions from the Congress of Industrial Organizations (CIO) in 1949–1950. During the 1920s, the CP attempted to build left-wing opposition movements within the American Federation of Labor (AFL) craft unions. In 1929, the party's strategy shifted to organizing an industrial union federation independent of the AFL. Returning to the mainstream U.S. trade union movement in 1935,

Radical journalist John Reed organized and led the Communist Labor Party in 1919 and edited its journal The Voice of Labor. *(Library of Congress)*

the party became active in organizing the industrial unions of the CIO. Throughout World War II and in the immediate postwar period, the CP continued to either lead or exert a significant influence in many CIO unions. Political and foreign policy differences with the non-CP-led unions resulted in the expulsion of the CP-led unions from the CIO in 1949–1950.

Inspired and guided by the Russian model of revolution and initially proclaiming that capitalism was in a state of collapse, two communist parties in the United States were established in September 1919 as a left-wing split from the Socialist Party of America (SP). The first organization formed, the Communist Party, was composed mostly of foreign-born members, largely of Slavic origin. Within days, the Communist Labor Party appeared, with the vast majority of members being of native-born origin, led by the radical journalist John Reed. In May 1921, the Communist International (Comintern) ordered the two parties to merge, which led to the creation of the Communist Party of America. It renamed itself the Communist Party USA in 1929.

The first CP instrument for working within the trade union movement became the Trade Union Educational League (TUEL), founded by left-wing trade union leader William Z. Foster in 1920. When the party recruited Foster, the TUEL became the CP's labor arm in 1921. Concentrating on "boring [the AFL] from within" and building left-wing opposition movements within the existing AFL craft unions, the TUEL advocated amalgamating the craft unions into larger industrial unions and establishing a labor party. Initially, the TUEL's strongest base was in Chicago, where the organization controlled 20 percent of the seats on the AFL's Chicago Federation of Labor (CFL) (Levenstein 1981, 8). However, political blunders within the Farmer-Labor Party led to the CP's loss of power in the CFL by late 1923.

In 1926, the TUEL came close to wielding real power in the United Mine Workers of America (UMWA) when it became active in the "Save the Union" campaign, supporting John Brophy in an attempt to oust President John L. Lewis. However, after red-baiting Brophy, Lewis won easily and purged the union of TUEL activists. The CP's strongest base of support was in the New York City needle trades, where the party took control of three major International Ladies Garment Workers Union locals in 1924 and gained control of the New York Joint Board in 1926. This left-wing leadership called a strike of 40,000 cloakmakers (Cochran 1977, 40) on July 1, 1926, that was eventually defeated, leading to the party's dramatic loss of power within the union.

In February 1928, Solomon Lozovsky, head of the Communist Trade Union International (the Profintern), attacked TUEL policy and ordered the CP to organize new trade unions in a number of industries. In 1929, the TUEL transformed itself into the Trade Union Unity League (TUUL), a full-fledged dual union movement. Unlike TUEL, the TUUL program was based on the principles of class struggle as represented by the slogan "class against class." At the time of the TUUL's formation, there were approximately 9,300 members in the party (Ottanelli 1991, 15), mostly immigrants, with 80 percent of the membership being workers (Klehr 1984, 5). These workers were not concentrated in the basic industries, such as steel, mining, and chemicals: 25 percent of CP members were employed in either the building trades or needle trades, and 46 percent of party members belonged to trade unions (Klehr 1984, 5).

Prior to its formation in September 1929, the TUUL had created three new unions in industries where AFL unions existed—the National Miners

Union (NMU), the National Textile Workers Union (NTWU), and the Needle Trades Workers Industrial Union (NTWIU). Although the TUUL had more than a dozen unions affiliated to it by 1934 (Johanningsmeier 2001, 159), the NTWIU, initially composed predominantly of Jewish workers, was one of the few TUUL unions that became entrenched in the factories.

The TUUL program did not differ from the CP's program. Both organizations had adopted the major principles of "third-period communism." According to Comintern theory, the first period of communism took place from 1918 to 1923 and was a period of revolution. The second period, from 1924 to 1928, was a stage of relative stabilization of capitalism. During the third period (1929 to 1933), capitalism was in an imminent state of collapse, and therefore it was necessary to organize for the coming socialist revolution. The consequences of this analysis were that all left-wing and trade union opponents were categorized as "social fascists," including the SP and the AFL. And although the TUUL's goal in the trade union movement was to build united fronts with progressive rank-and-file members from below, the TUUL was generally unsuccessful because it attempted to organize industries that had few CP or TUUL members.

Of the 35 million workers in the U.S. labor force by 1931, 3.5 million were AFL members, although only 15,000 were in the TUUL unions (Klehr 1984, 43). Many CP members did not even join the TUUL unions. For example, in Detroit, only 15 percent of party members were TUUL members (Klehr 1984, 41). By 1932, for all intents and purposes, the TUUL was moribund, although it enjoyed an upsurge in the latter half of 1933 because of the National Industrial Recovery Act, which pushed its membership to well over 100,000 (Ottanelli, 1991, 50).

Scholars provide four major reasons for the TUUL's failure. First, because an avowed CP member led every TUUL union, these unions possessed a strongly Communist face, and few independent unionists would become involved with the organization. Second, the internal life of the TUUL unions replicated the CP's internal life. Third, the TUUL was further discredited for its revolutionary posturing. Labor issues often took second place to revolutionizing the workers. Finally, the TUUL's strategy and tactics contributed to its defeat. In most cases, spontaneous strikes occurred among workers, and the TUUL tried to rush in and lead the strikes. By the time the TUUL became involved, the strike had usually been settled in a way that did not benefit workers. After a string of such defeats, workers stayed away from the TUUL.

Debate ensued over the future of these dual unions at the preparatory meetings in Moscow for the Seventh Comintern Congress in the summer of 1934. With the abandonment of "third-period communism" and the adoption of the "popular front," a strategy designed to preserve and extend basic democratic rights within the world's industrial democracies, a recommendation was made that the TUUL revolutionary unions join the AFL, which led to the abolition of the TUUL in mid-March 1935. In some cases, the TUUL unions entered the AFL as a unit, but in others, union members were required to join individually.

Even before the TUUL's dissolution, the CP had been making inroads in the AFL unions. In 1934, a confidential CP memo claimed that Communists controlled 135 AFL locals with 50,000 members, two central labor councils, and several districts and had organized opposition groups in 500 locals (Klehr 1984, 225). At the November 1935 AFL convention, a debate occurred over the question of organizing workers industrially, as opposed to on a strictly craft basis. Eight AFL unions walked out and formed the Committee for Industrial Organizations (CIO), later to be renamed the Congress of Industrial Organizations (CIO) in 1938. At this time, the CP initially favored having the CIO unions work within the AFL to stimulate the organization of industrial workers into the craft union federation. In 1938, when the CIO began to charter unions, CP-dominated unions such as the Fur Workers, the International Longshoremen and Warehousemen's Union (ILWU), and the Transport Workers Union left the AFL for good.

John Lewis, the UMWA president and head of the CIO, invited the Communists into the CIO to help with organizing industrial workers. Lewis felt confident that he could use the CP to achieve his own purposes and that he could eliminate them from the CIO when he so desired. For example, 60 of the 200 full-time organizers on the Steel Workers Organizing Committee (SWOC) payroll were Communists (Levenstein 1981, 50).

However, the Communists' greatest help to the CIO occurred in the United Auto Workers (UAW) six-week, sit-down strike in Flint, Michigan, held from December 28, 1936, to February 11, 1937. Because the local union was infiltrated with company spies, 60 to 100 Flint CP members helped to organize the strike. The party formed the backbone of the Flint strike leadership, and all seven members of the strike committee were CP members (Klehr 1984, 232–233). In addition, a number of individual CP members played key roles in this strike, including Wyndham Mortimer and Bob Travis, who directed the strike; Bud Simons, who was the strike committee chairman; and Henry Kraus, who served as editor of *The Flint Auto Worker.*

Through the CP's contribution of organizers and leadership to other CIO unions, the party's influence continued to grow. In 1937, CP-influenced unions had 650,000 members, unions in which the CP had some presence had 600,000 members, and non-CP unions had 2 million members. Most of the unions dominated by the CP were small, except the United Electrical Workers Union (UE), which, by 1937, had 137,000 members (Klehr 1984, 233). By 1938, 40 percent of the CIO unions were either led by party members and their close allies or significantly influenced by them (Klehr 1984, 238). At this time, out of 75,000 CP members, 27,000 were members of trade unions (Klehr 1984, 240). According to 1939 figures, the strongest industrial concentrations of party members in CIO unions were in the SWOC, the UMWA, the UAW, the United Office and Professional Workers, and the Mine, Mill and Smelter Workers.

By the late 1930s, the CP had established considerable influence in the U.S. trade union movement because the party functioned as the most determined and farseeing exponent of industrial unionism. The CP attracted a host of workers on precisely that basis, becoming the nucleus around which the most fervent New Deal and trade union elements could coalesce. In addition, in 1938 and after, trade unionists viewed the party as a major force for democracy and trade unionism within the U.S. labor movement.

As the nation moved toward participation in World War II, the CP retained its leading role within a number of CIO unions. From the signing of the nonaggression pact between Joseph Stalin and Adolf Hitler in August 1939 until Germany's invasion of the Soviet Union on June 22, 1941, the CP condemned the war as an imperialist conflict and promoted the use of industrial militancy within the CIO unions as a tactic to keep the United States out of the war. However, after Germany's invasion, the CP-led unions did an about-face and called for the United States to provide aid to the Soviet Union. With the nation entering the war after the Japanese bombing of Pearl Harbor on December 7, 1941, the party became a strong supporter of the "no-strike pledge" adopted by almost all U.S. trade unions for the war's duration. In addition, the CP zealously advocated the use of piecework, a policy that the party had adamantly opposed in the past, to increase worker productivity in the wartime industries.

Throughout World War II, the CP-led unions worked on forging alliances with progressive CIO officials to help expand Communist leadership in a number of unions. At the war's conclusion, however, problems began to arise within the CIO. Certain provisions of the 1947 Taft-Hartley Act, such as the required signing of non-Communist affidavits by union officials, were designed to remove Communists from union leadership positions. Furthermore, political differences emerged within the CIO between the CP-led and the non-Communist-led unions, specifically over the CP-led unions' opposition to the implementation of the Marshall Plan and their support of Henry Wallace, the Progressive Party presidential candidate, during the 1948 elections.

The onset of the Cold War, the rise of "red" hysteria in the United States, and the splitting of Europe by the "Iron Curtain" put the CP in a defensive position. The attacks on the party intensified during the 1949 Smith Act trials, when ten of the eleven CP national board members were convicted of teaching and advocating the violent overthrow of the U.S. government. The outcome of these trials can be viewed as the beginning of McCarthyism, which led to a full frontal assault on the CP throughout most of the 1950s.

These increasing attacks on the party, combined with its support for Wallace and its opposition to the Marshall Plan, led to an irreparable rift in the CIO that culminated in the expulsion from the federation of the eleven CP-led unions in 1949–1950. Because these unions had actively organized African American workers and had fought for women workers' rights, their elimination from the CIO resulted in the loss of a powerful voice for these two groups of workers. At the beginning of the expulsions in 1949, the CP controlled about 20 percent of the CIO membership, or 1 million members, with the UE having 500,000 members (Guerin 1979, 169). Although the UE, albeit in a weakened state, and the ILWU were able to survive as independent unions and the CIO unions raided other expelled unions during the next few years, many of the remaining unions merged into non-Communist unions as a defensive strategy. By the time of the AFL-CIO merger in 1955, the CP's influence in the U.S. trade union movement as a whole had largely come to an end.

Victor G. Devinatz

See also Democratic Socialism; Lewis, John L.; Socialism; United Auto Workers

References and further reading

Cochran, Bert. 1977. *Labor and Communism: The Conflict That Shaped American Unions.* Princeton, NJ: Princeton University Press.

Draper, Theodore. 1960. *American Communism and Soviet Russia: The Formative Period.* New York: Viking.

Foner, Philip S. 1991. *History of the Labor Movement in the United States.* Vol. 9, *The TUEL to the End of the Gompers Era.* New York: International Publishers.

———. 1994. *History of the Labor Movement in the United States.* Vol. 10, *The TUEL, 1925–1929.* New York: International Publishers.

Guerin, Daniel. 1979. *100 Years of Labor in the USA.* London: Ink Links.

Johanningsmeier, Edward P. 2001. "The Trade Union Unity League: American Communists and the Transition to Industrial Unionism, 1928–1934." *Labor History* 42: 159–177.

Klehr, Harvey. 1984. *The Heyday of American Communism: The Depression Decade.* New York: Basic Books.

Levenstein, Harvey A. 1981. *Communism, Anticommunism, and the CIO.* Westport, CT: Greenwood Press.

Ottanelli, Fraser M. 1991. *The Communist Party of the United States: From the Depression to World War II.* New Brunswick, NJ: Rutgers University Press.

Rosswurm, Steve, ed. 1992. *The CIO's Left-Led Unions.* New Brunswick, NJ: Rutgers University Press.

Comparable Worth

Comparable worth is the concept that men and women in different jobs should be paid similarly if their jobs require equal skill, effort, and responsibility. Sex-based wage discrimination was prohibited by Congress in the Equal Pay Act of 1963 and Title VII of the Civil Rights Act of 1964. However, proponents of the comparable worth theory argue that these two laws and their application in Supreme Court cases have only been effective for men and women in similar job classifications. They argue further that jobs do not have to be equal but only of "comparable value" to the employer; thus the positions can be in totally different categories.

Women have historically been paid less than men. Today, women earn approximately 73 percent of what men earn. The gender wage gap had remained relatively constant through the 1960s and 1970s, with women earning approximately 60 percent of what men earned on average. The gap began to close slightly in the 1980s, and women's earnings reached 71.6 percent of male average annual earnings in 1990. Since that time, the ratio of women's to men's earning has moved up and down slightly (Institute for Women's Policy Research 2001).

Before the 1960s, it was very common for employers to pay women less than men, even if they were doing exactly the same work. This common practice was often justified by the idea that men needed to earn more because they had to support their families, but women did not. Women were working for what was often called "pin" money, or extra money in addition to their husband's income that supported her and her family. This issue was first addressed by Congress with the passage of the Equal Pay Act of 1963, which requires equal pay for equal or "substantially equal" work performed by men and women. In addition, Title VII of the Civil Rights Act of 1964 prohibits wage discrimination on the basis of race, color, sex, religion, or national origin.

Many states followed by enacting their own equal pay laws, and today women and men doing the same work usually receive the same rate of pay. However, the passage of these two laws did not alleviate the gender wage gap and only highlighted a much deeper cause of the disparity between the wages of men and women. The gender wage gap does not result only from men and women in the same occupations being paid differently but also comes from the gender-based segregation of the labor force. Women and men have traditionally been employed in different occupations and in different sectors of the labor market. Women are still overrepresented in a small number of jobs, such as clerical positions, service work, nursing, and teaching. Such jobs have historically been undervalued and underpaid. Proponents of comparable worth argue that these jobs continue to be underpaid today largely because they are still dominated by women and people of color. Thus, the Equal Pay Act, which is based upon the notion of equal pay for equal work, will not resolve the gender wage gap.

Numerous comparable worth cases have been brought before the Supreme Court, but the standard of the Equal Pay Act—equal pay for equal work—has limited its effectiveness for promoting comparable worth in most cases. In 1981, in *County of Washington v. Gunther,* the Supreme Court decided that Title VII of the Civil Rights Act is broader than the Equal Pay Act and prohibits wage discrimination even when the jobs are not identical. The Court said that women do not have to meet the equal work standard of the Equal Pay Act but have only to prove intentional discrimination. Unfortunately, this ruling was not a clear endorsement of comparable worth theory, and in fact, the majority decision claimed that the ruling had no relation to comparable worth theory.

Since *Gunther,* the courts still have not fully endorsed or rejected comparable worth theory. However, there has been legislative action at the state and federal level. Since the 1980s, states have made adjustments in their payrolls to correct for sex and race discrimination, legislation has been introduced in over twenty-five legislatures, and several states have comparable worth statutes in place. At the federal level, the Fair Pay Act was introduced by Democrats in the U.S. House of Representatives in 2001. It would extend the Equal Pay Act's protections to workers in equivalent jobs with similar skills and responsibilities, even if the jobs were not identical. In addition, the Paycheck Fairness Act was introduced by Democrats in the U.S. Senate and in the U.S. House in 2001. It would amend both the Equal Pay and Civil Rights Acts to offer better remedies for cases in which the standard of equal pay for equal work is violated.

Denise Pierson-Balik

See also Homework; Housework; Pay Equity

References and further reading

American Federation of Labor and Congress of Industrial Organizations. "The Case for Equal Pay." n.d. http://www.aflcio.org/women/equalpay.htm (cited November 2002).

England, Paula. 1992. *Comparable Worth: Theories and Evidence.* New York: Aldine de Gruyter.

The Equal Pay Act. 1963. *U.S. Code.* Vol. 29, sec. 206(d).

Institute for Women's Policy Research. 2001. "The Gender Wage Ratio: Women's and Men's Earnings." http://www.iwpr.org (cited November 2002).

National Committee on Pay Equity. http://www.feminist.com/fairpay.

Paul, Ellen Frankel. 1989. *Equity and Gender: The Comparable Worth Debate.* New Brunswick, NJ: Transaction Publishers.

Sorensen, Elaine Joy. 1994. *Comparable Worth: Is It a Worthy Policy?* Princeton, NJ: Princeton University Press.

Willborn, Steven L. 1986. *A Comparable Worth Primer.* Lexington, MA: Lexington Books.

Compensation

An individual's earnings from work have a strong connection to personal opportunity in the United States, which provides relatively weak government support for family needs such as housing, child care, health care, and education. In many industrialized democracies around the world, federal programs for basic services (such as national health care in Britain or paid leave for new parents in France) are provided to a much wider spectrum of citizens, thereby placing less emphasis on earned income as the sole determinant of status and material well-being. In the United States, historical and economic forces embedded in race, class, gender, and educational differences affect an individual's earnings. These trends were at work during the economic boom of the 1990s. Lower-income Americans, women, and African American and Hispanic American workers—groups who have historically received less compensation than others—saw general gains in earnings, but divisions remain. Through the 1990s and into the twenty-first century, senior executives at many corporations received multimillion-dollar compensation packages that were hundreds of times higher than those paid to the rest of the workforce. Employers drastically reduced health care coverage for low- and moderate-income workers during the 1980s and 1990s, which additionally contributed to slow or negative compensation growth in this period. The 1990s also manifested historic, nationwide declines in personal savings rates and company-sponsored pension benefits, further reducing the value of earned income and increasing the likelihood that Americans would work longer hours, juggle work and family, and receive less sleep—all widely documented trends in the workforce.

Income Trends

Although Americans of all income levels worked longer hours in the 1990s than they did decades ago, wealthier Americans were seeing far greater increases in wages and income than citizens further down the income ladder. The most accurate and comprehensive income data published show dramatic increases in the gaps between rich, poor, and middle-income Americans through the 1980s and 1990s. According to a 2001 Congressional Budget Office (CBO) study and a related paper by the Center on Budget and Policy Priorities (Shapiro, Greenstein, and Primus 2001), the average after-tax income of the poorest fifth of U.S. households did not grow at all between 1979 and 1997. During this period, however, average after-tax income soared by 157 percent for the richest 1 percent of U.S. households. The gap between the rich and poor and the rich and the middle class was wider in 1997 than at any other time since 1979.

Although the money gap between classes widened throughout the 1990s, the strong job growth of this period did produce gains for many U.S. households. Black household income reached an all-time high in 1997 and remained there in 1998, according to census data. In 1999, Hispanic white households recorded their highest median incomes since 1972. Because of the economic surge of the late 1990s, income gaps among minority and white households, skilled and unskilled workers, and men and women workers, were slightly moderated. During 2000 and 2001, the U.S. economy began to slow down, a decline that was accelerated by the effects of the 2001 terror attacks (U.S. Census Bureau 2000, 2001).

In 1999, non-Hispanic white households had a median household income of $44,366, compared to $30,735 for Hispanic households, $27,910 for black households, and $51,205 for Asian/Pacific Islander households. In 1986, the median income of white households was 59 percent higher than that of black households and 44 percent higher than that of Hispanic households. In 1999, Asian households had a 15 percent higher household income than non-Hispanic white households, an advantage that has held since 1988, when the U.S. Census Bureau began collecting Asian/Pacific Islander data (U.S. Census Bureau 2000, 2001).

Men historically earn more than women, a trend that persists. Although men's median income grew to $25,212 in 1997, women's median income was $13,703. When examined by *earnings* only, which excludes asset accumulation through investments, real estate, and other income where men enjoy historical advantages, full-time working women have closed the gap to seventy-four cents on the dollar in 1997 from fifty-eight cents on the dollar in 1967 (U.S. Census Bureau 1998, 81–88).

Women's roles as parents also dramatically affect their ability to receive fair and adequate compensation in the U.S. economy. When one compares the earnings of all male and female workers, both full-time *and* part-time (which includes many women in parenting and caregiving roles), the average earnings of female workers amount to only 59 percent of men's earnings (Crittenden 2001). In addition, the pay gap between women who are mothers and those who are not is growing dramatically. Studies by economists such as Jane Waldfogel of Columbia University show that during the late 1970s, the difference between men's and women's pay was about the same for all women. But by 1991, Waldfogel found, thirty-year-old American women without children were making 90 percent of men's wages, whereas comparable women with children were making only 70 percent (Crittenden 2001).

Positive trends can be found in the success of younger professional women aged twenty-five to thirty-five in white-collar occupations, who are earning the same as men in many fields, regardless of parental status or hours worked (Employment Policy Foundation 2001). Soaring participation by women in fields that include veterinarians, public administrators, math and science teachers, industrial engineers, dentists, members of the clergy, and physicians' assistants are closing pay disparities. However, gender pay gaps in these fields persist for women over the age of thirty-five, in large part because many of them leave full-time or fast track careers to raise their families.

More than any other factor, however, personal income is determined by one's education and skill attainment (see Figures 3 and 4). The information economy and globalization of production have eliminated millions of low-skilled manufacturing jobs in the U.S. and replaced them with technology-driven jobs requiring higher levels of skills. As seen in Census Bureau figures, the median income of men who have a high school degree was about three-quarters of that of men who have a bachelor's degree or higher in 1963 ($28,914 versus $38,496); that gap widened to about one-half in 1997 ($25,453 versus $47,126). Looked at another way, the economic premium for achieving a bachelor's degree grew 22 percent since 1963, while men's incomes have actually *declined* in all other educational groups (U.S. Census Bureau 1998, 83–86).

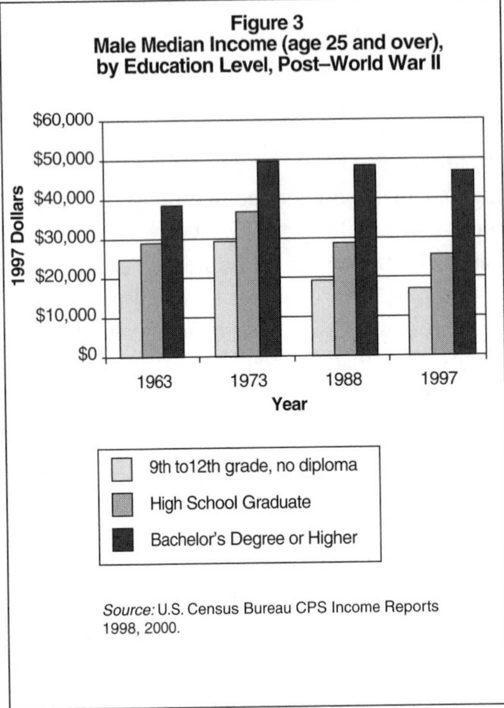

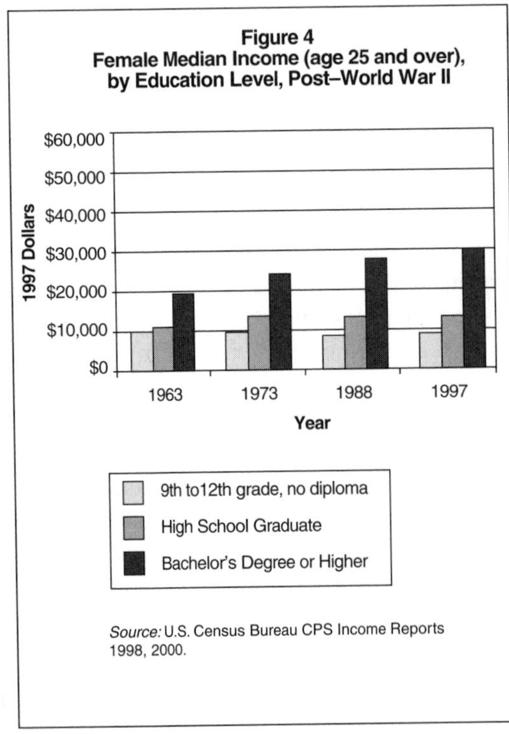

Family incomes for married couples with two earners grew since the early 1980s, as wives entered the labor force. The surge of women into the labor market reflected not only changing social mores in the United States but raw economic necessity. Until the recession of the early 1980s, the income gap between workers (particularly men) with a high school education only and those with college degrees was actually closing. Then the blue-collar recession of the early 1980s decimated the manufacturing and industrial centers of the northeastern United States. Between 1979 and 1984, about 5 percent of the U.S. labor force was displaced from their jobs, and 70 percent of these workers did not find new jobs within two years or were reemployed at lower wages (Levy 1998).

During the early 1990s, however, the country experienced a recession that affected many white-collar workers as well. Corporate mergers and downsizing, the savings and loan crisis, and federal budget cuts all combined to eliminate millions of jobs. Outplacement firm Challenger, Gray, and Christmas tabulated layoff announcements by major corporations growing from 111,285 in 1989 to 555,292 in 1991 (Levy 2001). Many of these workers eventually found new jobs in technology and service firms. Nevertheless, the U.S. job market had become less secure, heralding a new era of anxiety for all workers that fundamentally altered workers' leverage in seeking higher compensation, allowing employers to restrain salary increases with the implicit threat of downsizing (Levy 2001).

Benefit Trends and Costs

Health care and pension benefits are essential parts of the compensation packages of working Americans. From the 1950s to the early 1980s, more and more employers added health care and pension benefits for their employees. But in the last two decades of the twentieth century, this trend reversed. Increasing health care costs, growing international competition, and changes in the U.S. political and corporate environment have led employers to dramatically reduce employer-provided health care insurance and pension security.

Between 1989 and 1997, the percentage of full-time workers with medical benefits fell from 92 percent to 76 percent. The percentage of employees participating in "defined benefit" plans that guarantee a retirement benefit declined from 59 percent in

1991 to 50 in 1997 (U.S. Department of Labor, Bureau of Labor Statistics 1998). By the year 2000, 44 million Americans were uninsured, about 17 percent of the nonelderly population (Kaiser Commission on the Uninsured 2000).

The uninsured are largely low-income workers and their families. Nearly one-third of workers earning under $20,000 a year are uninsured, compared to only 5 percent of workers earning more than $50,000 a year (Kaiser Commission on the Uninsured 2000). The vast majority of workers who are uninsured (70 percent) are not offered these benefits by their employers.

Consumer Spending and Saving

Incomes rose only slightly for middle- and low-income Americans during the 1990s, but many extended their purchasing power by saving less and borrowing more. Personal savings rates (savings as a percentage of personal income) plunged from 9 percent in 1982 to 2.1 percent in 1997 and *to just 0.5 percent* in 1998, according to data from the Bureau of Economic Analysis at the Commerce Department. Consumer credit grew at a rate of 9.5 percent in 2000, exceeding 10 percent in the first quarter of 2001, as compared to 7.9 percent in 1996 (U.S. Federal Reserve Board 2001).

The long-term decline of personal savings in the United States has implications for the economic security of U.S. households. Most U.S. families have inadequate savings to see them through financial emergencies, much less help prepare them for a long-term, secure retirement. Analysis by the economist Edward Wolff of New York University and the Century Foundation shows that families with median or lower earnings, on average, have financial reserves sufficient to cover little more than one month's worth of expenses. Savings and capital gains are faraway hopes for many Americans, many of whom do not have pension assets at all. The Century Foundation analysis found that 43.5 percent of U.S. workers do not have access to an employer-sponsored pension plan, and nearly 80 percent of small business employees have no pension coverage whatsoever (Wolff 2000).

Executive Compensation, Stock Options, and Alternate Forms of Compensation

The average chief executive officers (CEO) of major corporations received a compensation package totaling $20 million in the year 2000 (Leonhardt et al. 2001), nearly 50 percent more in stock options and 22 percent more in salary and bonuses than they had averaged the year before. During this same year, the typical white-collar and blue-collar worker received raises that averaged about 3.5 percent. The average CEO made about 42 times the average blue-collar worker's pay in 1980, 85 times in 1990, and a staggering 531 times as much in 2000. Not surprisingly, these gaps contribute to poor employee morale, lost productivity, and increased turnover (AFL-CIO 2001).

The exponential growth in executive pay drew enormous criticism for economic hypocrisy because CEOs have reaped huge gains while laying off massive numbers and reducing pay for many more. Although CEO pay had been growing at an astonishing pace since the 1980s, the 1990s boom spurred a financial arms race among boards of directors that many believe fundamentally altered the compensation landscape of U.S. firms. Dangling massive compensation packages, including stock options and other perquisites, tech companies lured talent from existing employers, and firms of every nature brought out the "golden handcuffs" to secure executive talent.

During the 1990s, "short-on-cash" technology companies lured and retained talent with stock options that for a few years at least often performed well in the stock market, creating thousands of paper millionaires. CEOs and top executives were raking in options, while companies were also increasing cash and bonuses. Although options proved effective in recruiting top executives to new, riskier startups, they did not engender loyalty if the initial public offering did not perform as expected. As options became less lucrative, executives and recruiters sought to include more cash, incentive plans, restrictive stock, and other pay in their overall package.

Bonuses became popular in the 1990s for luring younger, entry-level workers as well. Louis Uchitelle of the *New York Times* wrote that signing bonuses were proliferating and reaching well beyond upper-level managers and skilled technicians (Uchitelle 1998). The booming job market of the late 1990s fueled increases in entry-level salaries for college graduates by as much as 10 percent per year in 2000 and 2001, compared with 2 and 3 percent increases in the early 1990s, according to the National Association of Colleges and Universities.

The compensation craze for young technology professionals and executives cooled down in 2000 and 2001. Many lucrative job offers made in 2000 were rescinded the next year. The repossession of luxury cars soared. Applications to law and business schools rose as college graduates returned to the traditional stepping-stones to career success. It should be further noted that the war for talent in the late 1990s occurred in small but influential high-growth sectors of the economy, where companies were chasing a small pool of highly educated workers. Only rarely does a high school graduate enjoy this kind of attention from an employer, and the same is true of many college graduates who do not graduate from Ivy League and elite institutions.

Herbert A. Schaffner and Carl E. Van Horn

See also Comparable Worth; Earnings and Education; Equal Pay Act; Living Wage; Minimum Wage; Pay Equity; Prevailing Wage Laws; Wage Gap; Wage Tax

References and further reading

AFL-CIO (American Federation of Labor and Congress of Industrial Organizations). 2001. http://www.aflcio.org/corporateamerica/paywatch/index.cfm (sited July 1, 2003).

Congressional Budget Office. 2001. *Historical Effective Tax Rates, 1979–1997.* Washington, DC: Congressional Budget Office.

Crittenden, Ann. 2001. *The Price of Motherhood.* New York: Henry Holt.

Employment Policy Foundation. 2001. "Women Breaking through Male-Dominated Fields." Press Release. Washington, DC: Employment Policy Foundation.

Kaiser Commission on the Uninsured. 2000. *Uninsured in America.* Washington, DC/Menlo Park, CA: Kaiser Family Foundation.

Leonhardt, David. 2001. "For the Boss, Happy Days Are Still Here: Executive Pay, a Special Report." *New York Times,* April 1, sec. 3, p. 1, late edition.

Levy, Frank. 1998. *The New Dollars and Dreams: American Incomes and Economic Change.* New York: Russell Sage Foundation.

Shapiro Isaac, Robert Greenstein, and Wendell Primus. 2001. *Pathbreaking CBO Study Shows Dramatic Increases in Income Disparities in 1980s and 1990s.* Washington, DC: Center on Budget and Policy Priorities.

Uchitelle, Louis. 1998. "Signing Bonus Now a Fixture Farther Down the Job Ladder." *New York Times.* June 10, sec. A, p. 1.

U.S. Bureau of Economic Analysis. 2000, 2001. *Personal Savings Rates.* Washington, DC: U.S. Department of Commerce.

U.S. Census Bureau. 2000, 2001. Historical Income Tables: Households.http://www.census.gov/hhes/income/histinc/inchhdet.html (cited July 1, 2003).

U.S. Department of Labor, Bureau of Labor Statistics. 1998. *Employee Benefit Survey.* Washington, DC: U.S. Department of Labor.

U.S. Federal Reserve Board. 2001. *Consumer Credit Report.* June, July, and August Reports. Washington, DC: U.S. Federal Reserve Board.

Wolff, Edward. 2000. *A Plan for Increasing Personal Savings.* Idea Brief No. 3. New York: Century Foundation.

Comprehensive Employment and Training Act (CETA) (1973)

In December 1973, in a time of high unemployment and after considerable negotiation with the Nixon administration, Congress enacted the Comprehensive Employment and Training Act (CETA). This legislation consolidated a variety of federal job programs that had been created during the 1960s. Community action programs such as job training, the Job Corps, and the Neighborhood Youth Corps were brought together with programs from the 1962 Manpower Development and Training Act and the Job Opportunities in the Business Sector program. Designed to move program control away from the federal government, CETA designated states and local communities as "prime sponsors" of program activities. Funds flowed to the states in block grants, and local administrative units were given considerable decision-making power over the types of training provided, the groups of individuals served, and the institutions offering training and other services.

The CETA program used two basic strategies for increasing employment of low-wage individuals: (1) Title I classroom and on-the-job training and education to provide workers with additional skills to enable them to compete in the labor market, and (2) Title II public service employment (PSE) to offer subsidized jobs to help increase worker skills while providing useful work. Three remaining titles in the legislation authorized several targeted programs for groups such as youth and migrant workers, continued the 1960s Job Corps program for youth, and created the National Commission for Manpower Policy.

Initially, CETA emphasized training activities. In fiscal year (FY) 1974, funds appropriated for Title I training activities totaled over $1 billion, compared to only $620 million for public service programs. The first CETA programs consisted of locally operated classroom and on-the-job training programs. However, just a year after passage of the original legislation, the high national unemployment rate stimulated enactment of the Emergency Jobs and Unemployment Assistance Act of 1974, which established an additional PSE program as Title VI of CETA.

Because the unemployment rate had by then topped 8 percent and the employment requirements of this new title were less restrictive than those of the original Title II, local prime sponsors quickly received enough federal funds to subsidize hiring tens of thousands of new PSE workers. John Donahue (1989) noted that by May 1975, cities and counties had hired approximately 300,000 workers with federal funds (Donahue 1989). Many had marketable skills and higher educational levels than the disadvantaged individuals for whom CETA was originally designed. These hiring practices led to the "fiscal substitution" criticism long associated with CETA—the notion that federal funds were used to subsidize the employment of individuals who would have been hired as regular employees by local governments. Nancy Rose (2001) pointed out, however, that as the recession of the mid-1970s took hold and states began to implement tax limitation initiatives, many government services might not have been provided without employees paid through CETA.

Over its nine-year life, CETA was amended several times. Although its training efforts remained relatively constant, they were ultimately dwarfed by the allocation of increasingly larger amounts of expansion funds for public service employment. At the close of the Ford administration in 1976, the Emergency Jobs Programs Extension Act responded in some measure to the substitution criticism by tightening the eligibility requirements for PSE positions. The next year, in keeping with the interests of the new Carter administration, the Youth Employment and Demonstration Projects Act (YEDPA) created three special youth training and work experience programs. Also in 1977, a Skills Training Improvement Program (STIP) was added to Title III of CETA to serve dislocated workers, and the Help through Industry Retraining and Employment (HIRE) program was added to train veterans. Passage of a supplemental appropriations bill facilitated rapid local expansion of public employment programs. A federal goal was set for creation of 725,000 PSE jobs by spring 1978.

By the time CETA came up for legislative reauthorization in 1978, the growth of PSE had generated much criticism. National employment levels had improved, yet the program was still supporting more than 200,000 public service jobs. Paul Bullock noted that the inconsistencies contained in the original CETA legislation were compounded by subsequent amendments. Congress grappled with several concerns during the reauthorization process: (1) the legislation and subsequent amendments targeted the structurally unemployed, but broad eligibility criteria allowed prime sponsors to select a wide variety of enrollees; (2) guidelines promoted "creaming" (enrollment of higher-skilled unemployed individuals); (3) CETA was designed to allow for local discretion in enrollment and services, but over time, Congress mandated services to more and more categorical groups (for example, veterans, youth, the handicapped); and (4) there was no required connection between the training and PSE components of CETA, and no funds were provided to train public service employees (Bullock 1981, 56–60).

The drafting of and debate over the 1978 CETA reauthorization legislation took several months. The compromise reauthorization bill that finally was enacted in October 1978 did not please CETA critics, nor did it clear away the legislative inconsistencies. On the one hand, an effort was made to respond to continuing concerns about creaming. PSE job tenure and salaries were limited, and the program was specifically targeted to the unemployed, underemployed, and economically disadvantaged. Eligibility for this program required unemployment of at least fifteen weeks and low family income or receipt of Aid to Families with Dependent Children (AFDC) or Supplemental Security Income (SSI).

On the other hand, Congress used Title III to add even more federal programs for special groups—this time including displaced homemakers, single parents, and those without educational credentials. Title IV extended youth programs and required creation of a youth council to advise prime sponsors. Most upsetting to PSE opponents was Title VI reauthorization of the PSE program and the addition, in Title VII, of an entirely new Private Sector Initiative Program (PSIP). The latter was designed to increase the involvement of the private sector in CETA programs and required prime sponsors to establish business-dominated private industry councils

(PICs) to oversee development, implementation, and evaluation of prime sponsor CETA programs. Finally, a new Title VIII offered conservation work experience for youth through the Young Adult Conservation Corps (YACC).

Passage of CETA in 1973 and consolidation of employment and training programs brought important changes to the employment and training field. Not only was planning and program implementation responsibility shifted from the federal level to local authorities and prime sponsors, but community-based organizations also played an increasingly important role as CETA evolved. Bullock (1981) noted that by 1981—one year prior to the termination of the CETA program—cuts in CETA appropriations and the changes included in the reauthorization legislation had resulted in significant growth in the number of PSE staff employed by community organizations. The enactment in 1978 of the new Title VII, mandating private sector involvement in CETA, represented an especially important change. The formation of PICs and orientation of businesspeople to the world of government employment and training programming took time but established the groundwork for business to play a larger role in workforce development.

The 1973 consolidation of employment and training programs under CETA brought expansion of program evaluation initiatives. Beginning in 1975, a random sample of CETA participants was tracked through the Continuous Longitudinal Manpower Survey (CLMS) and was matched with a control group of sorts from the Current Population Survey conducted by the U.S. Bureau of the Census. Throughout CETA's life, the differences in findings among evaluation studies using program statistics and economic data were considerable, especially in critical areas such as degree of fiscal substitution and economic impact of public service job creation. Bullock (1981) attributed these differences to variables such as the periods covered by studies, the number and status of prime sponsors involved, variation in assumptions, and changes in legislative requirements over time.

In his 1995 review of evaluation studies of employment and training programs, W. Norton Grubb (1995) noted that the general conclusion from the CLMS tracking studies was that women benefited the most from CETA participation, with $500 to $1,000 in increased earnings per year. Some studies actually found that the impact of the program on men was statistically insignificant and that for youth, the effects were zero or negative. Other study findings suggested that both classroom and on-the-job training had a greater impact than work experience and public service employment. Grubb noted that the various evaluations studies were "most remarkable for the range of findings" (Grubb 1995, 18).

The Brookings Institution introduced the use of field studies, conducted for the National Commission for Employment Policy in July and December 1977 with a sample of thirty-one prime CETA sponsors (Bullock 1981). The study was critical of the training component of CETA, noting that prime sponsors gave little attention to participant training needs and tended to provide mostly on-the-job training (National Commission for Employment Policy 1979). Burt Barnow's 1986 review of a number of evaluation studies in the *Journal of Human Resources* concluded that on-the-job training appeared to carry more impact than classroom training.

During the 1970s, the Committee on Evaluation of Employment and Training Programs of the National Research Council (NRC) conducted a series of studies of twenty-eight prime sponsors throughout the country, using census data, field documents and interviews, and official reports from the Department of Labor. Early studies confirmed the view of many CETA critics that only a small number of participants in the public service employment program were economically or socially disadvantaged (for example, members of families receiving welfare benefits or individuals faced with employment barriers such as low education levels or language skills) (Mirengoff et al. 1980a, 101). Evidence was also found to support claims that local governments were engaging in the practice of "substitution"—using federal funds to pay for employees who were usually supported by state and local money. During the period between June 1974 and December 1976, substitution averaged 35 percent (Mirengoff et al. 1980a, 39).

In 1979, soon after implementation of the CETA amendments began, the NRC evaluation committee undertook a new study of twenty-eight areas across the country. This study found that more economically disadvantaged individuals—women and minorities—were being hired into public service jobs. However, the committee also found that welfare recipients were underrepresented in the service population and that wage restrictions had brought average public service program wages down because prime sponsors were forced to drop higher skilled positions (Mirengoff et al. 1980b, 45–102).

The FY 1981 federal budget severely cut CETA funding, and by the spring of 1981, the new Reagan administration had already made clear that it would not support reauthorization of CETA the next year. Ironically, because such a variety of elements had been packed into CETA over the years, many were actually included in its successor legislation, the 1982 Job Training Partnership Act. Although public service employment was eliminated, local service delivery areas were preserved, as were a number of youth programs, training for disadvantaged individuals, and the involvement of the business sector in local employment and training operations.

In the years since CETA was in force, the view of the program has moderated with hindsight, and some agreement has emerged that there were a number of positive program effects. Once the CETA eligibility requirements were tightened, the program improved the skills and job prospects of lower-income participants—particularly women. An important CETA lesson, which was incorporated into future programs, was that lower-income participants needed individualized training plans and support services to succeed in employment. Although there was serious criticism of the practice of fiscal substitution, in a climate of recession and state and local tax limitations, CETA enabled towns and cities to maintain public services that might otherwise have been eliminated. Finally, Nancy Rose observed, "CETA workers developed community recreation and arts programs, set up screening clinics in hospitals, and weatherized low-income homes. They worked in law enforcement agencies, day care and senior centers, battered women's shelters, and even in some activist organizations" (Rose 2001, 4). Today's human service landscape remains populated with individuals and organizations that got their start in the days of CETA.

Natalie Ammarell

See also Job Corps; Job Training Partnership Act; Welfare to Work; Workforce Investment Act

References and further reading

Barnow, Burt S. 1986. "The Impact of CETA Programs on Earnings: A Review of the Literature." *Journal of Human Resources* 22 (February): 157–193.

———. 1999. "Job Creation for Low-Wage Workers: An Assessment of Public Service Jobs, Tax Credits, and Empowerment Zones." http://aspe.os.dhhs.gov/hsp/lwlm99/barnow.htm (cited May 15, 2003).

Baumer, Donald C., and Carl E. Van Horn. 1985. *The Politics of Unemployment.* Washington, DC: Congressional Quarterly Press.

Bullock, Paul. 1981. *CETA at the Crossroads: Employment Policy and Politics.* Los Angeles: Institute of Industrial Relations, University of California.

Congressional Budget Office and National Commission for Employment Policy. 1982. *CETA Training Programs: Do They Work for Adults?* Washington, DC: National Commission for Employment Policy.

Donahue, John D. 1989. *Shortchanging the Workforce.* Washington, DC. Economic Policy Institute.

Franklin, Grace A., and Randall B. Ripley. 1984. *CETA: Politics and Policy, 1973–1982.* Knoxville: University of Tennessee Press.

Grubb, W. Norton. 1995. *Evaluating Job Training Programs in the United States: Evidence and Explanations.* Berkeley: University of California.

Mirengoff, William, Lester Rindler, Harry Greenspan, and Scott Seabloom. 1980a. *CETA: Assessment of Public Service Employment Programs.* Washington, DC: National Academy of Sciences.

Mirengoff, William, Lester Rindler, Harry Greenspan, Scott Seabloom, and Losi Black. 1980b. *The New CETA: Effect on Public Service Employment Programs—Final Report.* Washington, DC: National Academy of Sciences.

National Commission for Employment Policy. 1979. *Monitoring the Public Service Employment Program: The Second Round.* Special Report no. 32. Washington, DC: National Commission for Employment Policy.

Rose, Nancy. 2001. "Workfare vs. Fair Work: Public Job Creation." http://www.njfac.org/us16.htm (cited January).

Computers at Work

Computers, the Internet, and other forms of information technology have changed the way Americans work. The growth of a "digital economy" has affected labor supply and demand and revolutionized methods of communication, learning, and working. It could also alter the way American society addresses such social problems as unemployment and illiteracy. Although the introduction of computers at work is widely viewed as having increased productivity and worker flexibility, it has also created new stresses and strains for workers who are now connected to their offices—through their computers—365 days a year.

Progress through technology is an enduring feature of the economic history of the United States.

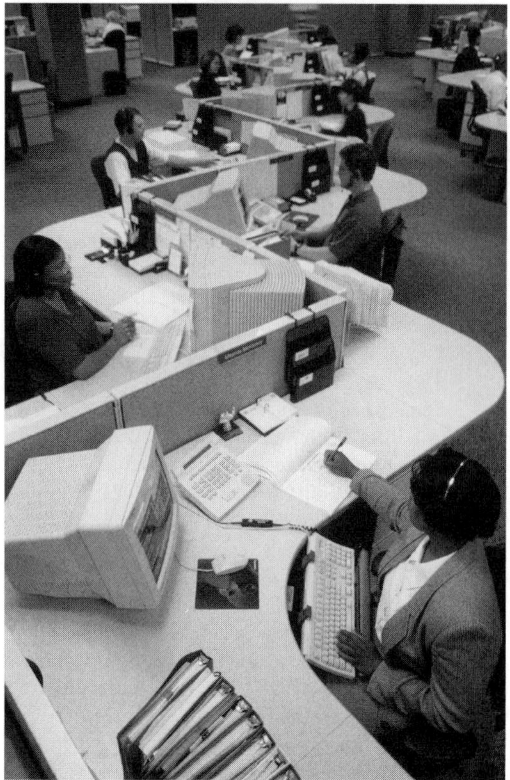

Although the introduction of computers at work is widely viewed as having increased productivity and worker flexibility, it has also created new stresses and strains for workers who are now connected to their offices—through their computers—365 days a year. (Charles Gupton/Corbis)

The transcontinental railroad, the telephone, the automobile, electricity, airplanes, and then jet travel transformed the United States economically and socially. And yet, no new technology has affected the nation so rapidly and or spread so swiftly as personal computers (PCs) and the Internet did during the last decade of the twentieth century. High-tech jobs grew explosively, and information technology was infused into nearly every other job. The information technology sector (computing and communications) accounts for more than 8 percent of the national economy and 15 percent of the rise in gross national product (U.S. Department of Commerce 1998). Today, there are more than 100 million adults using the Internet (Strategis Group 1999), and the computer and data processing industry is the fastest-growing industry in the United States (Fullerton, 1999). New services and new ways of working and communicating brought about profound changes in the workforce and in the workplace.

The U.S. economy is in the midst of an information technology revolution. Consider, for example, the findings of Work Trends surveys of U.S. workers, conducted in the late 1990s by the John J. Heldrich Center for Workforce Development at Rutgers University and its partner, the Center for Survey Research and Analysis at the University of Connecticut (Van Horn and Dautrich 2000):

1. The typical U.S. worker uses computers every day to perform his or her job.
2. U.S. workers enthusiastically support the information technology revolution.
3. U.S. workers believe that e-learning—courses taken over the Internet—will help them obtain the skills demanded by their jobs.
4. U.S. workers want to use their home computers and Internet connections to work from home—telecommute—for at least part of the workweek.
5. U.S. workers expect government and employers to help spread the benefits of information technology and require young people to get computer skills to succeed in the workplace.

In the early 1980s, personal computers were as rare as a solar eclipse. A few refrigerator-sized contraptions started cropping up in offices in the early 1980s. Just fifteen years later, personal computers were so widespread in the workplace that they changed the daily habits of millions of workers and presented new challenges for workers and their bosses (Conference Board 1998).

Today, computer use is as common for U.S. workers as the water cooler and the photocopy machine. Teenage fast food workers and pharmaceutical industry chemists depend on computers to accomplish their tasks. Nearly seven in ten workers use computers every day; eight of every ten workers use a computer at least once a month (Van Horn and Dautrich 2000). Desktop computers help workers prepare documents, send e-mails, and browse the Internet. It delivers news and information, helps people shop, and manage their finances.

Table 1
The Digital Ladder, Classifying Workers by Computer Use

Digital Ladder Classification	*Characteristics Used to Classify Workers*	*Percentage of Workers*
Exiles	Have not used a computer in the last month	19
9–5 Users	Have used a computer in the last month No home access to a computer	17
Browsers	Have used a computer in the last month Home access to a computer Have not necessarily used a computer every day Have used a computer for some but not all applications, such as e-mail, the Internet, word processing, and getting news/information	22
Power Users	Have used a computer in the last month Home access to a computer Have used a computer every day Have used a computer for some of the following applications: e-mail, the Internet, word processing, and getting news/information Do not bank and shop online	25
Technophiles	Have used a computer in the last month Home access to a computer Have used a computer every day Have used computer for all of the following applications: e-mail, the Internet, word processing, and getting news/information Do bank and shop on-line	16

Low Use/Access -- High Use/Access

Exiles *9–5 Users* *Browsers* *Power Users* *Technophiles*

Source: C. E. Van Horn and K. Dautrich. 2000. "Nothing but Net: American Workers and the Information Economy. Work Trends V Survey." John J. Heldrich Center for Workforce Development, Rutgers University, New Brunswick, NJ.

The typical worker in the United States spends about three hours every day in front of a computer screen; nearly three out of four workers use computers at least one hour a day. Half the workday is spent on personal computers for one in three U.S. workers. Computer use is very intense for those with access to a computer *and* the Internet; they spend even more time on the PC, with one in five spending half the workday on the Internet alone (Van Horn and Dautrich 2000).

Work-based computers are used for work, rather than to shop, play games, or send e-mails to relatives and friends, according to most U.S. workers. At work, employees read and send e-mails, prepare documents, and search the Internet. In fact, the e-mail is already the most popular application of information technology and the primary means of communication for more than one in four U.S. workers. Although the typical e-mail user sends or receives nine e-mails per day, the heavy e-mail communicator receives or sends more than thirty per day (Van Horn and Dautrich 2000).

The Digital Divide

As we drill a little deeper into the computer/Internet phenomenon, we discover that access and use vary greatly among U.S. workers. In fact, there is a so-called digital divide between workers and families who have access to computers and those who do not (U.S. Department of Commerce 2000; Information Technology Association of America 2000). Carl Van Horn and Kenneth Dautrich (2000) further classify workers into five categories based on their access to and use of computers and the Internet: exiles, 9–5 users, browsers, power users, and technophiles (see Table 1).

Individuals up and down the digital ladder have different demographic profiles. Power users and technophiles are younger; have more formal education and higher incomes; work for larger companies; and hold jobs in professional, managerial, or technical occupations. Technophiles are more likely to work in professional (39 percent), technical (17 percent), or managerial occupations (17 percent). Exiles are more likely to work in service (29 percent) or manufacturing (8 percent) occupations. There is a strong correlation between technology use, education level, and income. Power users and technophiles have higher incomes and education levels than browsers, 9–5 users, or exiles. Exiles and 9–5 users are much more likely to be black than technophiles, power users, and browsers. Many technophiles, and power users spend more than half their workdays using a computer. In contrast, 71 percent of browsers and 65 percent of 9–5 users do not even have access to the Internet at work.

Educational attainment provides another insight into the concentration of computer and Internet use. The higher the education level, the more likely a worker is to use the computer during the workday. Sharp increases in computer use occur for workers who have more than a high school education. Only 40 percent of workers with less than a high school education and less than half (49 percent) of high school graduates use a computer at work. In contrast, seven in ten workers with at least some college education use a computer during their workday, and nine in ten college graduates use a computer for at least a portion of the workday.

Information Technology and the Economy

The widespread introduction of computers and the Internet occurred during a period of sustained economic growth and prosperity in the mid- to late 1990s. Alan Greenspan, chairman of the Federal Reserve Bank, and other leading economists argued that the productivity gains from information technology were largely responsible for unprecedented economic growth in the United States at the time (U.S. House Education and the Workforce Committee 2000). U.S. workers echoed those sentiments at the time of the survey, expressing confidence and optimism about the new economy and the high-technology workplace.

By almost any measure, U.S. workers have embraced the Internet age. Nearly nine in ten workers do not believe that new technologies caused job reductions at their own workplace in the past year. Similarly, nine in ten are convinced that technology will not push them out of their job in the near future—within the next three years (Van Horn and Dautrich 2000). Far from fearing the dark side of technology, a majority of U.S. workers (58 percent) say computers changed their lives for the better. As expected, technophiles and power users are most enthusiastic about computers and the Internet, with overwhelming percentages touting their benefits. Only digital exiles say these new technologies have not improved their life circumstances and worry that the new technologies will threaten their job security.

Most lower-income Americans (those earning less than $40,000) and many African American workers have not reaped substantial benefits from computers and the Internet. They are much more likely than others to dwell at the bottom of the digital ladder. Yet respondents from these groups of Americans are more positive about technology's role in economic prosperity than higher-income and white workers. This optimism, which may seem misplaced to some, reflects an important fact of life: economic opportunity and personal success are closely tied to one's ability to use computers and the Internet at work. The lack of optimism among higher-income workers may reflect the integration of technology in their careers, which has led them to discount its importance. Workers who do not use those skills and tools might place a higher value on them. The lack of optimism among higher-income workers may also reflect strain they feel in managing the omnipresence of technology in their work and family lives.

Computer Know-how

For years, television and movies portrayed highly skilled computer users in an unflattering light. Most common was the computer "geek" (poorly dressed, long-haired, and bearded), who masterminded World War III or some other calamity from a computer terminal. For decades, gun-wielding good guys like James Bond spoiled these diabolical computer plots. Nowadays, however, the hero is as computer-savvy as the evildoers. Without computer skills, one can't even be an action hero anymore!

Another favorite stereotype was the bumbling fool who is "terminally challenged" by computer hardware and software. These folks couldn't even program the family videocassette recorder (VCR), let alone boot up and use Microsoft's office suite. Typically, these technophobes were proud of their condition and belittled people who chained themselves to a PC. In the early years of the twenty-first century, this stereotype is going the way of the rotary telephone, vanishing because it is no longer believable.

In reality, the United States is a digital nation, with millions of Americans smoothly handling day-to-day chores on their terminals (Carol and Sergeant 1999). U.S. workers believe they have the right stuff when it comes to computers: more than three-fourths say they have the necessary computer skills to perform their current job. Technophiles, power users, and browsers, who make up nearly two-thirds of the workforce, are very confident they can make the computers and the Internet work for them. Even one of every four computer exiles, who don't regularly use computers, think they know how to work effectively with computers (Van Horn and Dautrich 2000).

Computer and Internet tools were nearly as common as the telephone for people entering the workforce in the 1990s (Carol and Sergeant 1999). In classrooms, libraries, and homes, the personal computer played a starring role in their formative experiences. Younger workers are much more likely to be comfortable with computer basics. More than 80 percent of eighteen- to twenty-nine-year-old workers believe they are well prepared for the computer age, whereas only 70 percent of workers aged fifty to sixty-four share that belief (Van Horn and Dautrich 2000).

Computers parachuted into the lives of more mature workers in the midst of their adult careers. Often, their children nagged them into getting an Internet connection at home. Nearly everyone who started working before 1985 had no experience with personal computers in high school or college and was forced to adapt to a digital world. Nearly everyone who started working before 1993 had little or no experience with the Internet before it exploded on to the scene. Most workers learned to use a computer through informal means, with five in ten teaching themselves or learning from family or friends. Only one in four acquired their computer skills the old-fashioned way—in a classroom or through training at work. People with more formal education also have more confidence: 90 percent of college graduates are sure their computer skills are adequate for their current jobs; but only 58 percent of high school graduates believe the same (U.S. Department of Commerce 2000; and Van Horn and Dautrich 2000).

Overall, the first part of the PC/Internet age largely favored employers' interests—driving down costs, moving information more rapidly, and extending the reach of companies to every corner of the nation and the world. Three emerging applications may turn the tables, bringing significant benefits to U.S. workers. Two of these Internet-driven strategies—telecommuting and distance learning, or e-learning, are popular with U.S. workers but much less so with employers. The other—Internet-based recruiting and hiring—is a favorite of U.S. companies but thus far is viewed skeptically by most U.S. workers. It is too early to tell how these new applications will evolve (American Society for Training and Development 2001; Brown 2000; and Van Horn and Storen 2000).

The prevalence of computer use among U.S. workers has created a heightened awareness about the potential of information technology to solve problems in their workplace and work lives. The modern workplace creates new demands and challenges, and U.S. workers are turning to information technology to improve their skills and get more control over their economic destiny. Information technology has the potential to offer much needed solutions at work in this new economy. As the United States strives to remain competitive in the global economy, upgrade the skills of its workforce, help workers balance work and family, fight poverty, and provide a meaningful education for our children, its workers suggest that we embrace the technology in our midst and use it to its full potential. Continued economic expansion for the country and individual prosperity depend on workers' ability to effectively use computers, the Internet, and other technology applications.

Carl E. Van Horn

See also The Dot-com Revolution; E-Learning; Ergonomics; Telework/Telecommuting

References and further reading

American Society for Training and Development. 2001. "A Vision of E-Learning for American's Workforce—Report of the Commission on Technology and Adult Learning." Washington, DC: National Governors Association.

Brown, Justine. 2000. "Digital Education." *Government Technology: Solutions for State and Local Government in the Information Age:* 28–34.
Carol, A., and J. Sergeant. 1999. *The Digital Work Force: Building Infotech Skills at the Speed of Innovation.* Washington, DC: U.S. Department of Commerce, Office of Technology Policy.
Conference Board. 1998. *Technology's Effect on Work-Life Balance, Work-Family Roundtable* 8, no. 2.
Fullerton, H. 1999. "Labor Force Projections to 2008." *Monthly Labor Review* 122, no 11 (November): 19–34.
Information Technology Association of America. 2000. *Task Force Report: Building the Twenty-first Century Information Technology Workplace—Underrepresented Groups in the Information Technology Workforce.* Arlington, VA. Information Technology Association of America.
Strategis Group. 1999. "Internet Use Trends: Mid-Year 1999." Washington, DC: Strategis Group, October.
U.S. Department of Commerce. 1998. *The Emerging Digital Economy.* Washington, DC: U.S. Department of Commerce, April.
———. 2000. *Falling through the Net: Toward Digital Inclusion.* Washington, DC October.
U.S. House Education and the Workforce Committee. 2000. Testimony of Alan Greenspan before the Subcommittee on Education and the Workforce on *The Economic and National Importance of Improved Math-Science Education, H.R. 4272,* 107th Cong. 1st sess., September 21.
Van Horn, C. E., and Kenneth Dautrich. 2000. "Nothing but Net: American Workers and the Information Economy." Work Trends V survey. John J. Heldrich Center for Workforce Development, Rutgers University, New Brunswick, NJ.
Van Horn, C. E., and D. Storen. 2000. *Telework: The New Workplace of the Twenty-first Century.* Washington, DC: U.S. Department of Labor.

Consultants and Contract Workers

Consultants and contract workers are typically engaged in specific work assignments on a hourly or project basis. Contract workers can be from all strata of the workforce, from the most sophisticated and technologically savvy to day laborers. Consultants, however, are used because of their demonstrated expertise in a particular functional area of a business concern. They are retained to solve a problem, analyze a situation, or make recommendations for change to management. As a group, they are included among those contingent workers who have conditional or transitory employment arrangements.

This new class of worker began to burgeon in the mid- to late 1960s and has continued vigorously through the present. The largest single employer in the United States today is Manpower, Inc., the supplier of temporary labor to not only manufacturing but also to the service, technology, and professional sectors. Temporary staffing companies have evolved over time to be highly focused on the classification of workers they offer. Some specialize in placing accountants, nurses, substitute teachers, computer programmers and operators, and even medical doctors and psychologists—virtually any specialty of worker in the marketplace.

There are many reasons for a business to use contract or independent workers. In general, such arrangements allow much greater flexibility in the deployment of staff and a potential reduction in the costs of benefits and direct labor. Seasonality or the business cycle itself can make it a highly attractive option for a company. No long-term employment commitments are implied. Major corporations also find it economically attractive to "outsource" whole functions, such as human resources and various staff support services, that are peripheral to the company's core operations.

Similarly, such arrangements can be very attractive to the contract worker, who has the opportunity to move in and out of the mainstream of traditional employment, can more easily find employment during periods of job dislocation, or can explore new career fields. There are downsides, however. For contract workers, control is exerted over them by two employers—the providing company, which pays their wages and benefits, and the utilizing company. In addition, such workers typically do not have the opportunity to develop a long-term career path or avail themselves of employer-sponsored education and training. Table 1 provides information on the size of the contract workforce relative to all those employed and presents their average weekly earnings. The differences in average weekly earnings can be imputed to the skill sets the contract worker brings to the employer.

Given the steep growth in service industries during the last three or four decades of the twentieth century, it is not surprising that a full 50 percent of all contingent workers are in the service sector (Jacobs 2001, 144). Almost 40 percent of all workers included in the Jacobs data actually *prefer* their status as nontraditional workers (Jacobs 2001, 145).

All of these notions seem quite modern. Surprisingly, many of these concepts were developed

Table 2
Breakdown of Workers by Classification, Including Average Weekly Earnings

Classification	*Number**	*Average Weekly Earnings*
Traditional employment	119.02	$540
Workers provided by contract firms	0.77	$756
Workers provided by temporary agencies	1.19	$342
On-call workers	2.03	$472
Independent contractors	8.25	$640

*millions

Source: Eva E. Jacobs, ed. 2001. *Handbook of U.S. Labor Statistics*. Lanham, MD: Bernan Press, 143, 149.

by Thomas Jefferson and are contained in his papers willed to his grandson in 1826. In 1852, the Pinkerton company provided security guards for the railroads to help prevent robberies and to recover stolen property. Hoover Dam was built between 1931 and 1935 by 5,000 workers leased from a consortium of six labor-contracting firms. The Bureau of Reclamation, the designer of the dam, supervised the work with 150 inspectors, the only government employees on the project. It was not until the 1950s, however, that large companies like Olsten, Kelly, and Manpower were founded to meet industry's growing need for contract labor.

Consultants, however, are also contract workers who provide high-level assistance or guidance to others, almost always for a negotiated, predetermined fee. Consultants are not employees of the contracting organization. They work individually or as teams that are part of a larger consulting practice, depending on the scope of the assignment. The consultant's main role is to identify, diagnose, and bring about the resolution of business issues. As such, consultants do not typically guarantee the outcome of their work. Rather, they offer their best recommendations for potential success based on their skilled analysis of the client's situation.

Consulting can be very lucrative for the individual and is often the career path chosen by workers with new M.B.A.'s, particularly from top-tier institutions. After serving on a long-term consulting assignment with a client, many are later tapped to be key executives within the client's own company.

Historically, the Industrial Revolution and mass production set the stage for the ascendancy of the consulting profession as we have come to know it. The earliest consulting *firm* was probably Foster Higgins, founded in 1845; followed by Arthur D. Little in 1886; Booz, Allen, and Hamilton in 1914; and McKinsey and Company in 1926.

Although early consulting projects focused on manufacturing processes and the organization of workers to do work, consulting engagements have expanded to encompass almost any part of a business enterprise—sales and marketing, finance, research and development, human resources, innovation, globalization, quality control, distribution, communications, information technology, and product development, among many others. Clearly, wherever there is the opportunity or need for improvement or positive organizational change, there is a consulting opportunity.

The latter part of the twentieth century saw a bundling of financial accounting services with consulting services. However, in the environment following the revelations of financial mismanagement at Enron and other companies, more and more accounting firms are casting off their consulting entities for fear of accusations of conflict of interest. At the same time, too, there was a tremendous growth in e-business consulting and incubation services. The growth of these particular services has dwindled for the time being with the bursting of the dot-com bubble. However, the shrinking economy has encouraged companies to use consulting, in particular for manufacturing processes and quality management, global marketing, and information technology.

On balance, the industry continues to thrive,

ebbing and flowing with the state of the economy and emergent technologies. As long as there is an emphasis on value-added service and intellectual property, consulting as a profession will remain attractive.

Ron Schenk

See also Contingent and Temporary Workers; Part-Time Work

References and further reading

Barker, Kathleen, and Kathleen Christenson, eds. 1998. *Contingent Work: American Employment Relations in Transition.* Ithaca, NY: Cornell University Press.

Biswas, Sugata, and Daryl Twitchell. 2002. *Management Consulting.* 2nd ed. New York: John Wiley and Sons.

Jacobs, Eva E., ed. 2001. *Handbook of U.S. Labor Statistics.* Lanham, MD: Bernan Press.

Lewis, William, and Nancy H. Molloy. 1991. *How to Choose and Use Temporary Services.* New York: American Management Association.

Lozano, Beverly. 1989. *The Invisible Workforce.* New York: Free Press.

Morse, Dean. 1969. *The Peripheral Worker.* New York: Columbia University Press.

National Association of Temporary Services. 1994. *Profile of the Temporary Workforce.* Alexandria, VA: National Association of Temporary Services.

Willey, T. Joe. 1988. *The Business of Employee Leasing.* San Bernardino, CA: Aegis Group.

Contingent and Temporary Workers

Contingent and temporary workers are people with insecure or transient jobs who do not have an expectation of long-term employment. The term, however, lacks a clear definition and has been used to describe a wide variety of work arrangements, including part-time work, temporary agency employment, employee leasing, self-employment, contracting out, employment in the business services sector, and home-based work. Since the 1980s, the number of people in contingent employment appears to have increased significantly, though assessments of the scale and implications of this increase have varied, depending on the specific definition used. This increase is the result of a variety of factors, including greater volatility and unpredictability in competitive conditions in the economy and associated changes in corporate structure and human resource practices. The increase in contingent employment is thus often seen as reflective of broader changes in employment arrangements that are affecting regular, full-time workers as well. Though some workers in contingent employment have prospered, the majority of contingent workers have lower wages and poorer working conditions than similar workers in more stable, long-term employment situations. Thus, improving working conditions for contingent workers has become an important arena for innovative policy and organizing initiatives, which also provides important insights into policies that may be valuable for improving working conditions for the rest of the workforce as well.

Though the temporary help industry has existed in the United States since at least the 1930s, the term *contingent work* only first began to be widely used in the mid-1980s. Initially, it simply described a management technique of employing workers only when there was an immediate and direct demand for their services (Freedman 1985). The term, however, soon became widespread in the business and popular press. *Time* magazine, for example, ran a provocative cover story in 1993 titled "The Temping of America" (Morrow 1993), and a year later a *Fortune* cover story declared "The End of the Job" (Bridges 1994). When American Telephone and Telegraph (AT&T) vice president for human resources James Meadows declared in 1996 that "we have to promote the concept of the whole workforce being contingent [that is, on short-term contract, no promises of long-term employment] though most of our contingent workers are inside our walls" (quoted in Andrews 1996), he was describing a fundamental sea change in U.S. employment relationships that has created a widespread sense of insecurity within the entire workforce.

A more careful examination of the contingent and temporary workforce, however, reflects a more modest but still significant restructuring of employment relations that occurred in the 1980s and 1990s. Estimates of the size of the contingent workforce are at best approximations, since government statistics on contingent work are limited, there is no commonly accepted definition, and there are multiple types of employment relations that can be characterized as contingent. The easiest measure is simply to include only people employed in the personnel supply services industry, popularly known as the temporary help industry. Between 1982 and 2000, employment in this industry grew from 400,000 people to 3.5 million, rising from less than 0.5 percent to 2.7 percent of total employment. The majority of temporary help workers are in highly tenuous employment situations and are frequently the first to be laid off during economic downturns. This was clearly evident in the economic downturn of 2001. From December 2000 to December 2001, a total of 1.4 million jobs were lost in the U.S. economy as a whole, more than half of which were in the temporary help industry.

A somewhat broader approach, which includes other workers in addition to temporary workers as part of the contingent workforce, has been developed by the U.S. Bureau of Labor Statistics (BLS). In 1989 the BLS developed a conceptual definition of contingent work to include workers, regardless of their particular employment relationship, whose current job was clearly structured to be of limited duration. In other words, contingent workers are those workers who do not expect their job to last beyond a specified period or who otherwise report that their jobs are temporary. This approach distinguishes contingent employment from "alternative work arrangements," which is defined as including independent contractors, on-call workers, temporary help agency workers, and contract company workers. A worker may be in both contingent and alternative work arrangements, but that is not automatically the case, since many independent contractors have readily available work, even though it may vary from project to project. Since 1995, the BLS has developed a regular survey to try to measure the contingent workforce, using three slightly different definitions. Using the broadest definition and according to the latest estimate in February 2001, 5.4 million workers (roughly 4 percent of total employment) were in contingent employment, and a total of 12.5 million workers (approximately 9.4 percent of total employment) were in alternative work arrangements (U.S. Bureau of Labor Statistics 2001). According to these statistics, the percentage of total employment accounted for by contingent employment in 2001 was actually down from a peak of 4.7 percent in 1995, but the percentage of people in alternative work arrangements had remained roughly the same.

Other estimates of the contingent workforce have taken a broader viewpoint, trying to capture all workers who face insecure employment. One approach is to include all people who are part-time, temporary, self-employed, or subcontracted employees. One estimate from the late 1980s, for example, found that between 25 and 30 percent of the U.S. workforce were in contingent employment relationships, that the contingent workforce was growing from 50 to 100 percent faster than employment in the economy as a whole, and that between one-third and one-half of all new jobs created in the 1980s were for contingent workers (Belous 1989). This definition, however, includes many workers, such as some independent contractors and professionally self-employed people, who may have plentiful work but are just not in regular employment. As a result, it is probably more accurate to classify all these types of employment as "nonstandard" work, rather than contingent (Carre et al. 2000). Nonetheless, in recent years even workers in "standard," full-time, regular jobs have confronted higher levels of insecurity, as changing management practices have made workers at all levels more vulnerable to layoffs in the face of changing markets and competitive conditions (Abraham 1990; Cappelli et al. 1997). In this context, the standard employment contract, which used to guarantee a certain level of stability and predictability for large sectors of the workforce, can be understood as becoming increasingly contingent as well (Arthur and Rousseau 1996).

Regardless of how the contingent workforce is defined, the decline in employment stability creates significant hardships for many workers. Though again the details differ, depending on the specific definition of contingent employment used, overall contingent and temporary workers have significantly lower wages and poorer working conditions than workers in more stable employment. Using the BLS definition, for instance, median weekly income for contingent workers was $285 in 1995, compared to $416 for noncontingent workers. Similarly, one-fifth of contingent workers had employer-provided health care coverage, compared to nearly two-thirds of noncontingent workers (Hipple and Stewart 1996). Using the broader definition of nonstandard employment and comparing contingent workers to workers with similar personal characteristics in regular full-time jobs, contingent workers faced an hourly wage penalty ranging from 27 percent for part-time workers to 15 percent for temporary workers to 1 percent for independent contractors (Hudson 1999).

The reasons for the increase in contingent employment are diverse, complex, and still not fully understood. One explanation that is broadly understood is that, aside from some portion of independent contractors and the self-employed, the growth in contingent employment, and particularly the growth in temporary employment, is primarily being driven by employers, rather than by the preferences of workers (Golden and Appelbaum 1992). Clearly, one of the reasons employers have increased their use of contingent workers is the growing unpredictability and volatility of the economy. In the face of intense global competition and rapid innovation, many companies have shrunk the size of their core workforces, using various forms of temporary, contracted, and subcontracted workers to increase their ability to respond to uncertain market conditions and to take advantage of rapidly changing niche markets (Harrison 1994). Beyond the imperatives of intense competition, employers have also discovered that subjecting their employees more directly to market pressures can be an effective way of increasing workers' productivity (Cappelli 1999). In essence, rather than buffering workers from market fluctuations, companies are increasingly passing on the risks of doing business directly to significant portions of their workforce. Finally, there is also significant evidence showing that employers are increasingly using contingent employment as a way of reducing wages, not simply for the contingent workforce but for their regular permanent workforce as well (Houseman, Kalleberg, and Erickcek 2001).

If the only impact of the increase in contingent employment was an increase both in labor flexibility and in the productivity of firms and their employees, there would be little cause for concern. The low wages of contingent workers, however, along with the contribution they make to the deterioration in wages and working conditions for many regular workers as well, raise strong concerns and highlight the need for intervention. Unfortunately, the fact that all contingent employees are outside the standard employment relationship means that traditional means of assisting workers are largely ineffective for contingent workers. Their temporary and tenuous ties to employers or workplaces means that contingent workers are poorly protected by current labor legislation; often have difficulty qualifying for unemployment insurance, pension plans, and employer-provided health plans; and have difficulty gaining representation in traditional union structures. Thus, a variety of creative and innovative policy initiatives and organizing efforts have been developed to try to improve the wages and working conditions for contingent employees.

One of the most prominent areas of policy concern for contingent workers is in the arena of labor legislation. Current labor legislation is broadly based on an assumption of long-term, stable, clear ties between workers and employers, which makes contingent workers highly vulnerable. There is clearly a need, for example, to expand joint employer responsibility in cases in which temporary workers are hired through agencies to work at a third-party work site. Other reforms have been proposed to facilitate representation for contingent employees including allowing minority representation, thus enabling contingent employees to request representation even if the majority of workers at the work site do not request it; repealing prohibitions against prehire agreements, recognitional picketing, and secondary boycotts, thus facilitating nonworkplace organizing; and expanding the definition of "employee" under the 1935 National Labor Relations Act (Wagner Act) to include self-employed workers and independent contractors (duRivage, Carre, and Tilly 1998; Friedman 1994). Other policies have been proposed to expand occupational rather than workplace-based associations and to develop intermediaries that can help workers build cross-firm rather than internal career ladders (Benner 2002; Parker and Rogers 2001).

In addition, contingent workers have come together with labor and community organizers in a whole series of innovative organizing efforts. These strategies build solidarity outside the workplace among a group of workers with similarly unstable employment circumstances, typically by helping to facilitate job transitions, to improve earnings levels and stability, and to enhance access both to protection under labor and social regulations and to representation. Examples range from groups of information technology contractors in Seattle to membership associations of temporary workers in places as far apart as Silicon Valley and northern New Jersey to associations of day laborers and immigrant workers in major metropolitan areas throughout the country (Carre et al. 2000). These various local initiatives have come together in a national coalition, the North American Alliance for Fair Employment, in an effort to increase their impact on improving conditions for contingent workers. The ideas generated through this network, though focused on contingent and temporary workers, also have significant relevance for noncontingent workers facing heightened levels of insecurity and vulnerability.

Chris Benner

See also Consultants and Contract Workers; Downsizing; Employment at Will; Job Security; Manpower, Inc.; Part-Time Work; Self-Employment

References and further reading

Abraham, Katherine. 1990. "Restructuring the Employment Relationship: The Growth of Market-Mediated Work Arrangements." In *New Developments in the Labor Market: Towards a New Institutional Paradigm.* Edited by Katherine Abraham and Robert McKersie. Cambridge: MIT Press.

Andrews, Edmund. 1996. "Don't Go Away Mad, Just Go Away: Can AT&T Be the Nice Guy As It Cuts 40,000 Jobs?" *The New York Times.* February 13, D1.

Arthur, Michael, and Denise Rousseau, eds. 1996. *The Boundaryless Career: A New Employment Principle for a New Organizational Era.* Oxford: Oxford University Press.

Belous, Richard S. 1989. *The Contingent Economy : The Growth of the Temporary, Part-time, and Subcontracted Workforce.* Washington, DC: National Planning Association.

Benner, Chris. 2002. *Work in the New Economy: Flexible Labor Markets in Silicon Valley.* Oxford: Blackwell Press.

Bridges, William. 1994. "The End of the Job." *Fortune.* September 19.

Cappelli, Peter. 1999. *The New Deal at Work: Managing the Market-Driven Workforce.* Boston: Harvard Business School Press.

Cappelli, Peter, Laurie Bassi, Harry Katz, David Knoke, Paul Osterman, and Michael Useem. 1997. *Change at work.* New York: Oxford University Press.

Carre, Francoise, Marianne Ferber, Lonnie Golden, and Stephen Herzenberg. 2000. *Nonstandard Work: The Nature and Challenges of Changing Employment Arrangements.* Madison, WI: Industrial Relations Research Association.

duRivage, Virginia, Francoise Carre, and Chris Tilly. 1998. "Making Labor Law Work for Part-Time and Contingent Workers." In *Contingent Work: American Employment Relations in Transition.* Edited by Kathleen Barker and Kathleen Christensen. Ithaca, NY: ILR Press.

Fair Jobs. 2003. http://www.fairjobs.org.

Freedman, Audrey. 1985. *The New Look in Wage Policy and Employee Relations.* Conference Board Report no. 865. New York: Conference Board.

Friedman, Sheldon, ed. 1994. *Restoring the Promise of American Labor Law.* Ithaca, NY: ILR Press.

Golden, Lonnie, and Eileen Appelbaum. 1992. "What Is Driving the Boom in Temporary Employment?" *American Journal of Economics and Sociology* 51: 473–492.

Hipple, Steven, and Jay Stewart. 1996. "Earnings and Benefits of Contingent and Non-contingent Workers." *Monthly Labor Review* 118, no. 10: 22–30.

Houseman, Susan, Arne Kalleberg, and George Erickcek. 2001. *The Role of Temporary Help Employment in Tight Labor Markets.* Upjohn Institute Staff Working Paper No. 01-73. Kalamazoo, MI: W. E. Upjohn Institute for Employment Research.

Hudson, Ken. 1999. *No Shortage of "Nonstandard" Jobs.* Briefing Paper. Washington, DC: Economic Policy Institute.

Morrow, Lance. 1993. "The Temping of America." *Time Magazine.* March 29, 40–41.

Parker, Eric, and Joel Rogers. 2001. "Building the High Road in Metro Areas: Sectoral Training and Employment Projects." In *Rekindling the Movement: Labor's Quest for Relevance in the 21st Century.* Edited by Lowell Turner, Harry Katz, and Richard Hurd. Ithaca, NY: ILR Press.

U.S. Bureau of Labor Statistics. 2001. http://www.bls.gov/news.release/conemp.nr0htm (cited May 23, 2003).

Core Competencies

Simply put, the term *core competency* refers to what a company does best. It is a skill or skill set around which a company organizes itself in order to provide greater benefits for its customers. These skills are considered core competencies if they encompass and promote the central aims and expertise of a company's employees, suppliers, and, to a certain extent, its customers. Companies that effectively develop and identify core competencies are able to distinguish themselves from their competitors and gain a significant competitive advantage.

The most intriguing aspect of core competencies is that a company may be better off having fewer of them. Businesses usually have between five and fifteen core competencies, according to Gary Hamel and C. K. Prahalad in their 1994 book, *Competing for the Future.* They add that companies that truly dominate an industry generally concentrate on only a few competencies so as not to dilute their advantage. Regardless, core competencies can touch on many areas, such as marketing, production, finance, and customer service. What matters most is that a company takes advantage of its fundamental strengths. This approach is not new; it began to surface toward the end of the eighteenth century, as production, distribution, marketing, and customer service processes became more intricate and specialized. As the twentieth century dawned, many companies purposely gravitated toward developing and concentrating on core competencies. As M. S. S. Varadan explained in *Identifying and Developing Core Competencies,* the most successful efforts involved aligning workforce processes to support core aims and, to a lesser degree, securing employee buy-in through effective internal communications.

The Orvis Company's customer service approach is a prime example of a company leveraging its core competencies. Many, if not most, companies have placed increased emphasis on customer service in recent years. These efforts rely on more responsive and customized interaction with customers to explain services, address problems, build customer loyalty, and cross-market additional products and have often yielded stronger customer ties, new revenues, and an improved company image. Yet no matter how successful, they can't be considered a core competency if customer service is not a fundamental platform of a company's approach to business.

In the case of Orvis, customer service is a core competency, taking the form of online and telephone service that offers high-quality responsiveness and an almost unrelenting obsession with addressing customer product concerns. The effort is core because it is central to the company's image and its business model, which aims at developing long-standing relationships with its customers to drive sales of its expanding product line that ranges from fly-fishing and hunting gear to clothing lines and home decorations.

Almost a century earlier, one of the great business success stories in the United States was built on the ability of a fledgling company to create and leverage its own core competency. The Ford Motor Company accomplished this by developing an assembly line production process that spit out affordable cars geared for mass market consumption. Ford was by no means the first carmaker—or even a real automotive pioneer. Hundreds of carmakers were already building up-market automobiles when Henry Ford started his first car company in 1899. Ford's ultimate success was his production process that allowed him to cost effectively expand output of the Model T from its then record-breaking 10,660 units in 1908 to 54,000 cars by 1911. The jump in output came as the price of the car fell from \$950 to the even more affordable \$360. The price reduction was central to Ford's business philosophy, as Robert Shook wrote in *Turn Around* (1990, 26): "The Model T was the car he had always dreamed of building. It was uncomplicated, durable, affordable. It was a car a farmer could afford."

Leveraging core competencies was the foundation of another U.S. success story that occurred during the technology explosion of the late 1980s. In this case, Microsoft committed itself to product definition and evolution as a core competency aimed at moving software and product into the mass market. Microsoft isn't necessarily unique in these efforts. But its product development process is a core competency because it is better than that of most of its competitors: "Microsoft's approach to defining products and development processes is not particularly new," Michael Cusumano and Richard Selby explained in *Microsoft Secrets* (1995). Yet they note that Microsoft has been "extremely effective in creating a strategy for product and process definition that supports its creative strategy" (1995, 187–188).

Microsoft's approach calls for developing products for the mass market that effectively set industry technical standards, which in turn helps Microsoft maintain market share. The software maker further leverages this core competency by developing products that have relatively short development times and life cycles.

John Salak

See also High-Performance Workforce; Productivity; Total Quality Management

References and further reading

Cusumano, Michael A., and Richard W. Selby. 1995. *Microsoft Secrets.* New York: Simon and Schuster.

Hamel, Gary, and C. K. Prahalad. 1994. *Competing for the Future.* Boston: Harvard Business School Press.

Nohria, Nitan. 1998. *The Portable MBA.* New York: John Wiley and Sons.

Shook, Robert L. 1990. *Turn Around: The New Ford Motor Company.* New York: Prentice Hall.

Varadan, M. S. S. 1997. "Identifying and Developing Core Competencies." *The Hindu,* August 6.

Corporate Consolidation and Reengineering

The trends of mergers and acquisitions, consolidation, and restructuring have been a dominant theme on the corporate scene for more than two decades. Companies undertaking these activities do so to enhance profits, innovation, and competitiveness. From the employees' point of view, the net result of this trend so far has been job reduction and, far too often, alienation, outsourcing, and failure to achieve the initiative's original goals. This tension has brought employers in the United States to a crossroads, where they must learn to plan and implement strategically in a way that transcends these negatives in favor of growth and development.

There can be no doubt that the end of the twentieth century brought significant changes in the landscape of work and the workforce, including the combined effects of globalization, the increasing influence of the financial markets, and the pervasive deployment of technological innovation. The decline in certain types of jobs and the concomitant increases in productivity are easily documented. However, it is important to examine the history and some of the underlying causes of corporate restructuring and consolidation and to evaluate the effects of these trends on the experience and direction of the labor force.

Often the criteria that make restructuring successful from a business standpoint are the same factors that spell success for the firm's workforce. Just as often, mergers or consolidations have been planned with consideration for financial goals but without equal consideration for employees' needs and contributions. This is a dangerous course in an era in which reliance on the caliber of a firm's talent is ascendant. Though reengineering and consolidation efforts usually begin with lofty goals, their outcomes depend on the caliber of planning and, in particular, the attention given to execution and the nature of the work and the workforce.

Many factors have contributed to the pervasive consolidation and restructuring of U.S. firms. In the mid-1980s, many observers believed that the U.S. economy had run out of steam. Technological dominance had been lost in several manufacturing sectors, including automobiles and consumer electronics. The annual rate of increase for labor productivity, which was 2.7 percent annually in the two decades after World War II, had slipped to 1.4 percent in the 1980s. Although the U.S. standard of living was still the highest among the seven largest market economies, it had grown only one-quarter as fast as the others since 1972.

These facts led to a perception of mounting crisis and budget tightening. Japan and Germany were believed to be overtaking the United States economically, which seemed to have lost its competitive edge. Yet, as the new century began, the picture looked very different, with the United States approaching its former level of economic dominance. This phenomenon may be cyclical, or there may be fundamental changes coming about in the way U.S. businesses operate and the way the U.S. economy is structured.

There is a great deal of hope that the emerging sectors of the economy will serve as an engine for jobs, growth, and productivity. Although there were no notable productivity growth differences between the United States and Europe in the first half of the 1990s, after 1995, a noticeable change in the rate of decline in the cost of computing power enhanced U.S. productivity. Information technology was not the only source of the new productivity. Globalization, deregulation, and competition also prompted business process improvements. The *Economic Report of the President* argued that information technology, business practices, and economic policies reinforced each other (*House Miscellaneous Document no. 107-2).*

These trends are primarily responsible for the restructuring that has had such a dramatic impact in terms of job loss and the creation of winners and losers in specific industries and geographical regions. It is clear that much of the consolidation is driven solely by financial market circumstances. The key question for the future of jobs and the vitality of the economy is whether the increases we see in rates of productivity are merely cyclical (and thus likely to be reversed) or structural (and thus being capable of being sustained over long periods). The arguments over consolidation will be largely determined by the answer to that question. The financial community argued that the short term costs of loss of jobs would be offset, indeed necessitated, by increases in efficiency and productivity.

The White House Council of Economic Advisers argued that the 2.6 percent rate of growth in productivity in the second half of the 1990s was not merely cyclical and that the improvement in the ways in which capital and labor were used throughout the economy was important to the increase. The economic slowdown that began in 2000 demonstrated that the business cycle will still act as a brake on this level of growth, as will global events such as the war on terrorism.

The true vulnerability may not lie in the macroenvironment of growth and productivity but more in issues of distribution and income inequality. It is evident that the general reduction in demand for lower-skilled workers, more than declines in areas like manufacturing, has depressed wages and exacerbated structural unemployment. This is not only a question of justice but also one of whether inequality may lead to political reactions that could curb the productivity of the economy and slow the high rates of economic growth that are the foundation of a successful economy and society.

The evidence continues to suggest that worker displacement is largely the result of technology rather than import competition. Technology is not only displacing workers, it is causing workers to accept lower-paying jobs in some fields. On average, real wages are falling. There are still significant layoffs of middle managers in jobs that contribute questionable value once layers of management are reduced, and these jobs will not be replaced. Technology is also reducing jobs more rapidly in some industries than others, for example, manufacturing and utilities.

Clearly, many people admire the success of the U.S. economy, but not all extol it as a model. Government plays a lighter role in the U.S. economy, spending one-third of gross domestic product (GDP), whereas such spending in Europe is nearer one-half. Competitive market forces are stronger in the United States, but social safety nets are weaker. Unions are weaker and labor markets less regulated. Cultural attitudes, bankruptcy laws, and financial structures more strongly favor entrepreneurship. Whether it be the U.S. venture capital community of financial intermediaries that promotes leveraged buyouts or mergers and acquisitions, the environment in the United States encourages consolidation to a greater extent than elsewhere.

It is the resolution between the forces of consolidation and innovation that will determine success. The global economy simultaneously encourages and forces companies to move their activities to the lowest-cost locations. Since there are often untenable costs associated with moving, it usually pays companies to attempt to force down costs in their current locations to derive the corresponding benefits. Firms that merge often restructure with the intent of halving or eliminating previous operations, especially if they do not have a direct connection to revenue production. Simultaneously, new technologies are allowing firms to work with a very different structure of employment. The compression of layers of management and the need for many fewer workers in a centralized (corporate headquarters) location have been the driving forces in the consolidation produced by financial markets and underlying market conditions.

The same forces that were shaping the mergers and acquisitions boom and industry consolidation around the world were also forcing a revolution inside companies. Departments have been realigned, and many functions have been outsourced altogether in areas previously thought to be untouchable or "strategic." Since the 1980s and earlier in some industries, companies have been responding to competitive threats and the need to beat rivals to new opportunities and shrinking margin dollars (the money a company can make from the sale of products or services after covering the costs of production and overhead, including salaries and benefits). Internally, that translates to streamlining operations, eliminating layers of management, retraining employees, and integrating data systems. Senior teams have redefined their planning processes, performance management systems, and incentive plans. These trends have rippled through U.S. industry, usually affecting large companies disproportionately, and the effects are still occurring. Consolidation, reengineering, and downsizing have barely abated.

The early results showed gains in productivity and a net loss of jobs, even among knowledge workers. Reengineering is a variation on workplace restructuring in which the goal is to improve productivity by taking advantage of new technologies, redesigned processes, and reduced layers of management with correspondingly swifter decision making. The concept was initially popularized by Michael Hammer and James Champy in their 1993 book, *Reengineering the Corporation*. The best examples of successful reengineering delivered 30–40 percent productivity improvements in the targeted areas. Among consulting firms and academics, the concept soon had many proponents because it seemed to promise a silver lining to firms in dire need of cost trimming and better technology deployment.

Unfortunately, the concept required extensive planning and buy-in by management, including a willingness to change on the part of employees entrenched in their processes and often fearful of losing their jobs. It also required sufficient background knowledge and expertise to integrate previously disparate processes while providing sustainable customer and bottom-line benefits. The path of least resistance was simply to automate existing, often flawed or isolated processes, resulting in few or short-term benefits. Typically, cost savings were sought by changes in business operations such as information technology (IT), administration, and back office services (such as the department that processes transactions for a business' customers and creates records for these transactions). In the manufacturing arena, companies were more likely to favor more specialized quality control and quality improvement programs.

The net result has been that industries have returned to downsizing their functions and their employees. Just as firms can sometimes acquire assets or merge to obtain classes of employees, firms can integrate or hire outsourcers to eliminate categories of employees. The jobs in those categories are typically never replaced, but often the gains in productivity or customer satisfaction that should result when work is restructured are missing. New fads have appeared on the consulting scene, but some of the original cost, quality, and information technology breakthroughs portended by reengineering have been lost in the rush to make earnings goals or realize larger-scale gains from megamergers.

There is seemingly no shortcut for the strategic alignment of goals and values or for creation of an environment that encourages learning and risk taking as well as solid execution and metrics (the means of setting goals and measuring business results). Those companies or their divisions adhering to these concepts are finding ways to remain competitive. They have turned the corner toward job creation and incorporated new work into their positive culture. For them, reengineering and quality principles are a way of life. The focus is on the customer, not short-term earnings. The other way is a death spiral of rework, low morale, and increasing layoffs, ultimately resulting in buyout or bankruptcy.

Whether the weaknesses of or the opportunities presented by market-driven consolidation and restructuring will predominate cannot be known for years to come. One clear benefit is that many companies have emerged from the bureaucratic and inflexible environment of the past. But the superficial technique of paring people and functions in the name of innovation must be curbed. It seems that transition and consolidation are becoming a constant in the U.S. business environment. The key is to know what constitutes effective work restructuring and to support new ways of working with appropriate planning strategies, tools, and metrics.

Paget Berger

See also Downsizing; Job Security; Layoffs; Postindustrial Workforce; Silicon Valley

References and further reading

Champy, James. 1995. *Reengineering Management: The Mandate for New Leadership.* New York: HarperBusiness.

DiMaggio, Paul, ed. 2001. *The Twenty-First-Century Firm.* Princeton, NJ: Princeton University Press.

Hamel, Gary. 2000. *Leading the Revolution.* Cambridge, MA: Harvard Business School Press.

Hammer, Michael, and James Champy. 1993. *Reengineering the Corporation: A Manifesto for Business Revolution.* New York: HarperCollins.

Johansen, Robert, and Rob Swigert. 1994. *Upsizing the Individual in the Downsized Organization.* Reading, MA: Addison-Wesley.

House Miscellaneous Document no. 107-2. 107th Cong., 1st sess. *Economic Report of the President.* Washington, DC: Government Printing Office.

Rifkin, Jeremy. 1995. *The End of Work.* New York: G. P. Putnam's Sons.

Council of Economic Advisers

The Council of Economic Advisers (CEA) provides economic analysis and advice to the president. Primary functions of the CEA, established by the Full Employment Act of 1946, are "to maintain employment, production, and purchasing power" (cited in White House 2002).

In earlier U.S. presidential administrations, economic advice to the presidents often came largely from bankers and businesspeople, not economists. Economists were first used in the Wilson and Hoover administrations, but it was not until Franklin Delano Roosevelt's administration that great numbers of economists moved into federal employment, largely to design and staff the numerous New Deal agencies. Under the Truman administration, Leon Keyserling wrote the Full Employment Act, which was later renamed the Employment Act of 1946. This legislation commanded the government to take a proactive role in assuring maximum employment. The Council of Economic Advisers was created to work toward that goal (Sobel and Katz 1988, ix–x). The creation of the CEA is also significant because it represents one of the few aca-

George W. Bush meets with economic advisers in the Oval Office of the White House, 2001. From the right, Vice President Chief of Staff Lewis Libby, National Economic Council Director Lawrence Lindsey, and Chairman of the Council of Economic Advisers Glenn Hubbard. (Reuters NewMedia Inc./Corbis)

demic disciplines to hold such a strong presence in the executive branch of U.S. government.

The impetus for the Council of Economic Advisers grew out of the Great Depression and World War II. The experience of the Great Depression seemed to demonstrate the hazards of a laissez-faire stance toward the economy, as the United States suffered deeply from crisis levels of unemployment and a shattered business sector. Soon after, World War II seemed to demonstrate how economic recovery could be fostered by government expenditure. The dominance of Keynesian economics resulted in the CEA's creation, marking a new acceptance and expectation of government engagement in stabilization of the economy.

The Council of Economic Advisers is composed of three members who are appointed by the president and approved by the Senate. Under the Employment Act of 1946, each member held equal power in the council. However, Reorganization Plan No. 9 of 1953 altered the power structure of the council, which is now led by a designated chairperson. The chair is primarily responsible for reporting to the president as well as for administrative duties such as staff selection. The duties of the CEA include forecasting economic trends, providing the president with an economic analysis of issues, and preparing an annual economic report to the president, which is then transmitted to Congress (Porter 1983, 405). The CEA operates out of the White House complex, which allows close proximity to the president.

In addition to the three-member council, the CEA staff includes about twenty senior and junior economists, although the council has experienced minor fluctuations in size over time. Turnover is high in the Council of Economic Advisers, with most members staying around two years, because many of them are university professors who have taken leave from their positions to serve. Generally, the members of the council provide nonpartisan, objective analysis and recommendations to the president. This politically neutral tradition is evident in an election year when a change in administration party occurs. At these times, CEA staff members who have been chosen under the former party's administration are expected to remain with the council through the academic year, which overlaps for a number of months with the new presidential administration (White House 2002).

The influence of the Council of Economic Advisers has varied over time. Generally, CEA influence is dependent upon the degree to which each individual president relies upon CEA analysis and advice and the capacity of council members to work within a political environment. Although the CEA's potential for influence is great, the president is under no obligation to adhere to its recommendations.

Some suggest that the CEA reached its peak in the early 1960s under Chairman Walter Heller. At that time, the CEA initiated research that ultimately resulted in the formulation of Okun's law. Okun's law, named after CEA staff member and later chairman Arthur Okun, stated that every 1 percent decrease in unemployment is associated with a 3 percent increase in the gross national product. To test this conclusion espousing the benefits of a stimulatory fiscal policy, a large tax cut was made in 1964, signaling the potential influence of the CEA. Also during Heller's control, the CEA began attendance at periodic meetings of the newly created "troika," which included key members of the CEA as well as the Bureau of the Budget (now renamed the Office of Management and Budget), and the Department of the Treasury (Bernstein 2001, 131–137). Together, the troika is able to present powerful economic arguments to the president.

Although the Council of Economic Advisers originally placed its primary emphasis on securing maximum employment, more recent CEAs (roughly since the Nixon administration) have tended to focus on controlling inflation. In recent years, the role of the CEA has altered, and it now spends the majority of its time assessing microeconomic, rather than macroeconomic, issues for the president (Delong 1996, 49).

Sarah B. Gyarfas

See also Bureau of Labor Statistics; Federal Reserve Board; Full Employment Act

References and further reading

Bernstein, Michael A. 2001. *A Perilous Progress: Economists and Public Purpose in Twentieth Century America.* Princeton, NJ: Princeton University Press.

DeLong, J. Bradford. 1996. "Keynesianism, Pennsylvania Avenue Style: Some Economic Consequences of the Employment Act of 1946." *Journal of Economic Perspectives* 10, no. 3 (Summer): 41–53.

Hargrove, Erwin C., and Samuel A. Morley, eds. 1984. *The President and the Council of Economic Advisers.* Boulder, CO: Westview Press.

McNees, Stephen K. 1995. "An Assessment of the 'Official' Economic Forecasts." *New England Economic Review.* (July–August): 13–23.

Norton, Hugh S. 1977. *The Employment Act and the Council of Economic Advisers, 1946–1976.* Columbia: University of South Carolina Press.

Porter, Roger B. 1983. "Economic Advice to the President: From Eisenhower to Reagan." *Political Science Quarterly* 98, no. 3 (Fall): 403–426.

Sobel, Robert, and Bernard S. Katz. 1988. *Biographical Directory of the Council of Economic Advisers.* New York: Greenwood Press.

Weidenbaum, Murray. 1996. "The Employment Act of 1946: Still Working after Fifty Years." *USA Today Magazine* 125, no. 2618 (November): 68–69.

White House. 2002. *About the Council of Economic Advisers.* http://www.whitehouse.gov/cea/about.html (cited July 8, 2003).

Cowboys

The work experiences of the North American cowboy melded European, African, and Native American traditions. Cattle ranching originated in New Spain (an area encompassing present-day Mexico and the southwestern United States, including Texas) and then spread north and east. Between 1850 and 1900, the twin processes of urbanization and industrialization transformed the cowboy from a guardian to a herder. In the twentieth century, novels, movies, and television made the American cowboy into an icon of popular culture.

The American cowboy had far-reaching roots in North America and across the ocean. In 1521, Gregario de Villalobos introduced the first cows to North America. He brought cattle and other livestock to the site of Tampico, Mexico. From there, Spanish cattle herds spread from central Mexico to the rest of North America. With the proliferation of cattle in New Spain, Spanish land and cattle owners needed to protect their herds from rustlers. They hired or forced American Indians and African slaves to tend cattle. In the British colonies, colonists took cattle to Virginia and South Carolina to provide for subsistence. Cattle quickly multiplied in the South, and livestock owners found a potential market in

A wild horse roundup, ca. 1923 (Library of Congress)

the sugar plantations of the West Indies. South Carolina slaveholders sent their slaves to guard cattle on the South Carolina frontier. Slaves worked without the direct supervision of their masters, applying the knowledge they accumulated while living in pastoral societies in West Africa.

In the 1860s, the cattle industry expanded to feed urban populations and spawned the most famous aspect of a cowboy's work life: the "long drive." From 1865 to 1879, cowboys drove cattle from Texas to Kansas, where ranchers shipped the herd to the burgeoning cities in the North and Midwest. The crew consisted of a point rider, swingmen, flankmen, and the drag, simultaneously establishing the workplace hierarchy. The trail drive also included a cook and a horse wrangler. The cowboys' monthly earnings ranged from $25 to $40 on the drives. The crew was a diverse workforce, including Mexican, black freedmen, and Native Americans, in addition to white hands. It is estimated that 35,000 young men drove and trailed cattle during the heyday of the cattle drive.

By the late nineteenth century, ranch life dictated the pace of cowboy work after railroad expansion, environmental change, and economic depressions curtailed the drives. By the mid-1880s, approximately 7.5 million head of cattle grazed on ranches on the Great Plains. The cowboy followed a seasonal work cycle on ranches. In the winter, ranchers laid off cowboys, and permanent workers rode the line and repaired fences and corrals. The roundup consumed the cowboy's time and energies in the spring. Ranchers used their permanent workforce and hired temporary hands to gather, sort, and mark the cattle. In the summer, cowboys tended to the hay harvest and other duties. The fall roundup concluded the yearly events before the uncertainty and monotony of winter.

In the twentieth century, dime novels, B-movie Westerns, and prime-time television mythologized the nineteenth-century cowboy. Perhaps the most important novel was *The Virginian* by Owen Wister. Although the purveyors of popular culture romanticized the cowboy, ranchers and their workers faced a hostile world in the twentieth century. Business concentration, mechanization, and stricter environmental laws undermined the position of small ranchers and cowboys. The modern version of the cowboy is the feedlot cowboy, who tends the steers in the large feedlots before they are slaughtered. Most cowboys are poorly paid. Despite their disappearance, there remain three different cowboy cultures in North America. The vaquero is a derivative of the Spanish cattle industry in the American Southwest; the cowboy traces its origins to southern Texas and spread to the Great Plains; and the buckaroo is located in the Great Basin and Pacific Northwest. Each culture boasts different tack, clothing, and attachment to their horses. For instance, the vaquero and buckaroo use the cattle industry to train their horses, whereas cowboys view horses as a tool to work with cattle. Still, the North American cowboy faces an uncertain future in the twenty-first century.

William J. Bauer Jr.

References and further reading

Clayton, Lawrence, Jim Hoy, and Jerald Underwood. 2001. *Vaqueros, Cowboys, and Buckaroos.* Austin: University of Texas Press.

Dary, David. 1981. *Cowboy Culture.* New York: Alfred A. Knopf.

Slatta, Richard. 1990. *Cowboys of the Americas.* Norman: University of Oklahoma Press.

D

Davis-Bacon Act (1931)

The Davis-Bacon Act requires that on construction projects substantially funded by the federal government, "the minimum wages to be paid various classes of laborers and mechanics . . . shall be based upon the wages that will be determined by the Secretary of Labor to be prevailing for the corresponding classes of laborers and mechanics employed on projects of a character similar to the contract work in the city, town, village, or other civil subdivision of the State in which the work is to be performed" (U.S. Department of Labor 2002).

Since its 1931 adoption, the reach of Davis-Bacon's "prevailing wage" has expanded considerably. The federal law was amended in 1964 to include fringe benefits, and many federal programs offering grants to states and municipalities for projects like public housing and school and road construction have incorporated Davis-Bacon's prevailing wage requirements. Moreover, many states have adopted "little Davis-Bacon" acts of their own that perform a similar function for state-funded construction by requiring contractors to pay the locally prevailing wage on these projects as well.

Background and History

A government, especially a democratic one, is no conventional economic actor. Unlike a private firm, it has an obligation to the public welfare and must respond to voters as well as market signals. This requirement has led many to argue that public agencies should not try to mimic market conditions but instead should adopt model labor relations practices and demand them of public contractors as well.

In 1931, with the construction sector ailing during the Great Depression, Pennsylvania senator James Davis and New York representative Robert L. Bacon sponsored a prevailing wage law for federal construction contracts. Proponents pointed to itinerant contractors—often from the South—who relied on low labor costs to win federal construction work in other regions, wreaking havoc on local labor markets in the process. In essence, legislative supporters argued, federal dollars should not be used to further reduce local construction wages. President Herbert Hoover agreed and signed the Davis-Bacon Act into law.

The Davis-Bacon Act has become a target for conservative economists and policymakers. Their criticisms have achieved some political resonance, and some states have repealed their "little Davis-Bacon" acts. However, the federal Davis-Bacon Act remains intact and is the subject of heated debate.

Controversies

The determination of the "prevailing wage" has attracted considerable critical attention. The Davis-Bacon Act delegated this difficult responsibility to the U.S. Department of Labor (DOL), which executes this duty by conducting periodic wage surveys for each geographic area, work classification, and type of construction work. If at least 50 percent of the workers in a given classification are paid the same wage, that rate is defined as "prevailing." If not, the average wage is established as the prevailing wage.

Davis-Bacon opponents assert that the first part of this definition favors organized labor. After all, a free market will seldom generate the same wage rate for so many workers; it can only be the product of a collective bargaining agreement. A more objective definition of the "prevailing wage," they say, would be the average rate in *every* market, union or nonunion—or better yet, the wage determined by market equilibrium in the absence of Davis-Bacon altogether (Schooner 1985; Thieblot 1986). Davis-Bacon's defenders respond that a wage established by collective bargaining covering 50 percent or more of a given market better deserves the name "prevailing wage" than does an average rate actually received by few workers!

In a broader sense, Davis-Bacon opponents argue that the government should seek construction services as a private firm does—at the lowest possible cost. It is unfair, they contend, to make taxpayers shoulder the burden of government policies establishing model labor relations practices. These writers argue that prevailing wages increase the costs of public construction significantly, perhaps by as much as 20 percent (Gould and Bittlingmayer 1980, 51).

It might seem obvious that a law requiring above-market rates for construction labor would raise the cost of construction projects, but numerous studies have challenged the extent of such a differential. North Carolina State University economist Steven Allen, reviewing early research, found that Davis-Bacon critics failed to account sufficiently for either factor substitution, in which employers invest in more equipment to minimize the use of expensive labor, or for the superior quality of labor employed on Davis-Bacon projects. Simply put, when the law requires higher, union wage rates, contractors do not continue business as before. Instead, they hire a smaller number of more highly skilled workers to operate more expensive and technologically advanced equipment. Such choices tend to mitigate any increase in total construction costs (Allen 1983).

The high hourly costs associated with skilled union construction labor are integral to preserving the sector's high productivity. High wages encourage workers to make careers in their craft despite seasonal and cyclical downturns. Apprenticeship programs, although expensive, ensure a continuing investment in worker training.

The repeal of "little Davis-Bacon" acts in select states has made possible empirical studies comparing construction costs under prevailing wage polices and in their absence. One such recent study found no statistically significant difference between the cost per square foot of public school construction under "little Davis-Bacon" regulations and without them (Phillips 2001). How can this be? Perhaps part of the answer can be found in the public bidding process itself. Private sector construction users are at liberty to decline a suspiciously cheap proposal and choose a contractor whose skilled workforce, quality materials, and sound business practices ultimately make his or her work a better value. But public sector agents are often obliged by law to accept the lowest bid without taking these factors into account. Davis-Bacon wage rates may erase the competitive advantage of those marginal "lowball" contractors who depend on poorly trained workers and cheap materials to place a low bid—but whose errors, cost overruns, and poor construction mean a greater expense in the long run.

Clayton Sinyai

See also Building Trades Unions; Collective Bargaining; Prevailing Wage Laws

References and further reading

Allen, Steven G. 1983. "Much Ado about Davis-Bacon: A Critical Review and New Evidence." *Journal of Law and Economics* 26: 707–736.

Finkel, Gerald. 1997. *The Economics of the Construction Industry.* Armonk, NY: M. E. Sharpe.

Gould, John P., and George Bittlingmayer. 1980. *The Economics of the Davis-Bacon Act: An Analysis of Prevailing-Wage Laws.* Washington, DC: American Enterprise Institute.

Katz, Lawrence F., and Daniel P. Kessler. 2001. "Prevailing Wage Laws and Construction Labor Markets." *Industrial and Labor Relations Review* 54: 255–274.

Phillips, Peter. 2001. "A Comparison of Public School Construction Costs in Three Midwestern States That Have Changed Their Prevailing Wage Laws in the 1990s." Salt Lake City: University of Utah.

Phillips, Peter, Garth Magnum, Norm Waitzman, and Anne Yeagle. 1995. "Losing Ground: Lessons from the Repeal of Nine 'Little Davis-Bacon' Acts." Salt Lake City: University of Utah Economics Department.

Schooner, Steven L. 1985. "The Davis-Bacon Act: Controversial Implementation of the Fifty Percent Rule." *Employee Relations Law Journal* 10: 702–716.

Thieblot, Armand J., Jr. 1986. *Prevailing Wage Legislation: The Davis-Bacon Act, State "Little Davis-Bacon" Acts, the Walsh-Healy Act, and the Service Contract Act.* Philadelphia: University of Pennsylvania.

U.S. Department of Labor. "The Davis Bacon and Related Acts Home Page." http://www.dol.gov/esa/programs/dbra/index.htm (cited June 30, 2003).

Day Laborers

Day laborers are workers who are hired on a per-day basis to perform unskilled or manual labor. They earn low wages near, and often below, the minimum wage rate and are generally paid in cash at the end of the workday. Day laborers are very attractive workers in such industries as construction, landscaping, roofing, warehousing, and assembly facilities because they can be hired for as little as a few hours for less cost than traditional temporary workers or full-time employees. Day laborers are recruited or dispatched from day labor agencies or street corners, from regulated and unregulated facilities. The majority of day laborers are minority or immigrant men, most have low-levels of education, and many have limited English skills. Increasingly, this workforce is comprised of undocumented immigrants and/or homeless men. Because of their social and economic invisibility in the U.S. labor market, few safety oversights are provided for these workers, even though day laborers regularly perform highly dangerous tasks.

Since the 1980s, there has been an increasing reliance upon contingent labor in the U.S. workforce because contingent or temporary labor provides employers the greatest flexibility to increase and decrease the workforce very quickly at very little expense (Reynolds, Masters, and Moser 1991, 154–155). A subset of contingent labor is day labor, often considered the lowest work category because of its very contingent basis, low wages, and the physical dangers associated with manual labor. Day laborers are hired on a per-day basis as work is available. Day labor hiring sites serve as "markets" where day laborers congregate and employers come to find workers to meet that day's work/productivity demands. There are typically three types of hiring sites for day laborers.

1. Connected sites are associated with specific industries or for workers in fields including construction, moving, and painting. Some sites are related to major retailers such as Home Depot, U-Haul, and Standard Brands paints (Valenzuela 2001, 342).
2. Unconnected sites offer no ties to an industry but provide a gathering spot where employers can locate day laborers.
3. Regulated sites usually screen workers, match workers' skills to job needs, or limit the number of site participants. Many regulated sites provide workers with access to basic equipment and tools, as well as ensuring some job safety oversight. These sites include day labor agencies, civic agencies, and retailers.

The most casual day labor hiring occurs on street corners. Day labor is used by all types of employers, from the small contractor using one worker to national firms and municipalities that need larger numbers of workers but do not want to commit to the expense of full-time employment. It is difficult to determine the number of day laborers because employers do not document the hours worked by or the wages paid to day laborers.

Day laborers generally arrive at the hiring site between 4 and 6 A.M. but may not be dispatched for several hours, if at all. The day laborer's workday does not include transit time to the work site (from the hiring site) or time being processed at the work site (up to two hours), thus reducing the actual number of hours worked and at times the rate of pay (Theodore 2000, 12). The day labor rate is negotiable, usually near the minimum wage, and workers are paid on a daily basis for work performed, in cash. This under-the-table exchange means that employers provide no benefits or job security and file no reports for state or federal taxes, Social Security, or workers' compensation insurance. Estimated annual compensation for day laborers ranges between $6,000 and $9,000 (Theodore 2000, 6), well below poverty levels. Low annual compensation rates reflect work hours reduced by transportation and other on-site processes and the seasonal nature of day labor occupations such as construction and gardening. Work-related injuries also account for lost work time. The work done by day laborers does not differ in substance from that performed by regular employees; Nikolas Theodore's study indicates that over 77 percent of day laborers worked along-

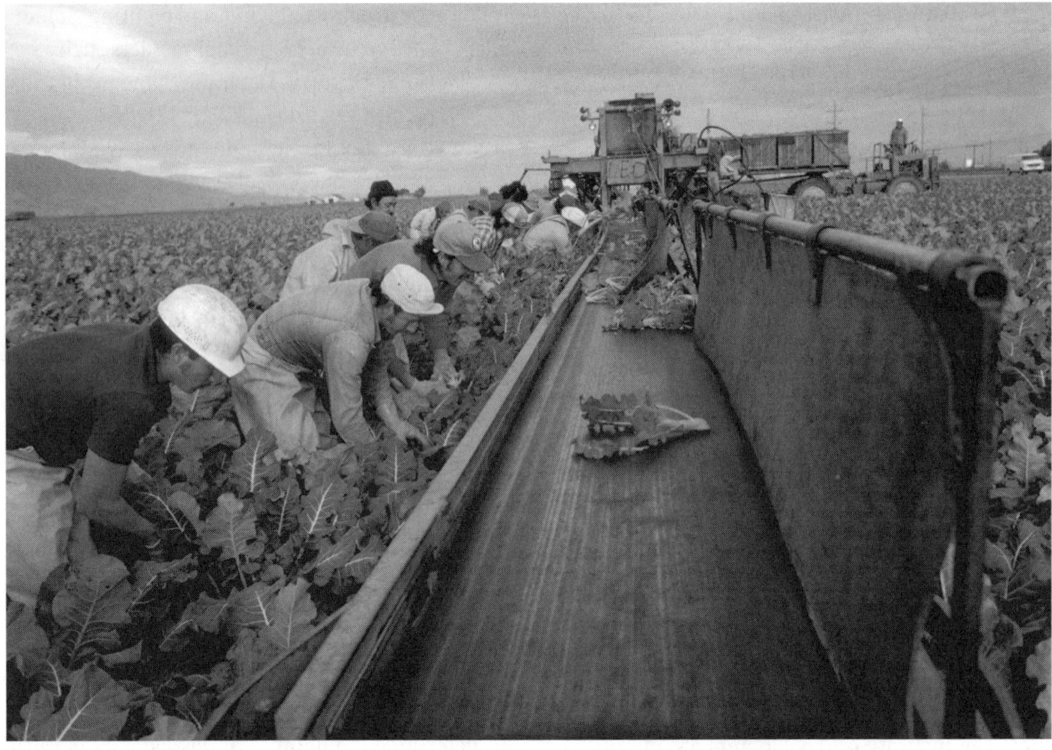

Day laborers pick broccoli in Salinas, California. Day laborers earn low wages near, and often below, minimum wage and are generally paid in cash at the end of the workday. (Morton Beebe/Corbis)

side full-time regular employees at job sites (Theodore 2000, 10).

Day laborers are more at risk for on-the-job injuries than traditional labor pools because of "inadequate training and experience, substandard safety equipment, and economic pressures that limit their capacity to avoid hazardous workplaces" (Walter et al. 2002, 224). According to Theodore, 42 percent of day laborers were worried about their safety on the job, but few voiced these concerns for fear of being fired (Theodore 2000, 16). In addition to hazardous conditions, some employers abuse day laborers by withholding wages, charging "incidental" work fees, or failing to provide any safety equipment, but their marginal existence in U.S. society provides day laborers with little recourse (Higuera 2002, D1; McNamara 2001).

Day laborers resist seeking relief from employer abuses because many are undocumented immigrants afraid of deportation, lack English proficiency, or are unaware of laws and regulations designed to protect them. In southern California Latino immigrants comprise 98 percent of the day labor work force; in the Midwest, African Americans dominate the day labor pool (Valenzuela 2001, 345; Theodore 2000, 21). Many day laborers are homeless men trying to find entry into the permanent labor market, and day labor provides the means of survival until more secure work is obtained (Theodore 2000, 18). Skilled and English-speaking workers find work more regularly. Evidence suggests that during economic recessions, minorities and immigrants are the first to become unemployed and the last to be hired, even in the day labor market (Kong 2002).

Community support of day laborers varies considerably. Some communities offer municipally sponsored day labor hiring sites and worker advocates (Valenzuela 342), whereas other communities regard day laborers as public nuisances and seek ways to outlaw areas where workers congregate to obtain jobs. In Biloxi, Mississippi, for example, a proposed ordinance likens day laborers to prostitutes and day labor hiring sites to escort services because the high number of homeless and immigrant men are viewed as public nuisances

(Wilemon 2001, A2). Therefore, Biloxi and other cities, including Kansas City and Houston, are trying to relocate day labor hiring sites to remote locales and regulate how many men a site can serve (Horsley 2002, C2).

Yet as businesses cut the regular jobs to reduce costs, more employers rely on day laborers to meet production fluctuations. Day labor, as a result, has become a major niche industry supporting national and regional day labor agencies. As day labor becomes more visible, the abuses endured by the day laborers come under increasing public scrutiny. Recent laws have been passed to address employer abuses, such as limiting the transportation fees, the job registration fees, and the check-cashing fees charged to workers (Higuera 2002, D1; McNamara 2001). Day laborers, along with advocacy groups for immigrants and the homeless, formed the National Day Labor Organizing Network to address these workplace concerns and demand reforms to "provide the basic cornerstones of a just work environment": fair wages and safe working conditions (National Employment Law Project, 2002).

Sandra L. Dahlberg

See also African American Women and Work; African Americans and Work; Contingent and Temporary Workers; Earnings and Education; Employment at Will; Green Cards; Immigrants and Work; Minimum Wage; Undocumented Workers; Work and Hispanic Americans; Workplace Safety

References and further reading

Higuera, Jonathan J. 2002. "Labor Firm Sued over Fees for Pay in Cash." *Arizona Daily Star,* July 16, D1.

Horsley, Lynn. 2002. "Panel Hears Divided Testimony about Day-Labor Businesses." *Kansas City Star,* October 16, C2.

Kong, Deborah. 2002. "Recession Toughest for Minorities." Associated Press Online, January 9. http://web.lexis-nexis.com/universe/document?_m=d591aabc73108c5b4e386(cited November 5).

McNamara, Eileen. 2001. "A High Price for Work." *Boston Globe,* September 9. http://search.epnet.com/direct.asp?an=2w61536671380&db=nfh(cited November 5).

National Employment Law Project. 2002. Press release. http://www.nelp.org/pr092602.pdf (cited September 26).

Reynolds, Lloyd G., Stanley H. Masters, and Colletta H. Moser. 1991. *Labor Economics and Labor Relations.* 10th ed. Englewood Cliffs, NJ: Prentice Hall.

Theodore, Nikolas. 2000. *A Fair Day's Pay? Homeless Day Laborers in Chicago.* Chicago: Report prepared for the Chicago Coalition for the Homeless, Chicago Interfaith Committee on Worker Issues, and Chicago Jobs with Justice.

Valenzuela, Abel, Jr. 2001. "Day Laborers as Entrepreneurs?" *Journal of Ethnic and Migration Studies* 27, no. 2: 335–352.

Walter, Nicholas, Phillippe Bourgois, H. Margarita Loinaz, and Dean Schillinger. 2002. "Social Context of Work Injury among Undocumented Day Laborers in San Francisco." *Journal of General Internal Medicine* 17, no. 3: 221–229.

Wilemon, Tom. 2001. "Sex Shops, Cabarets Targeted." *Sun Herald,* October 8, A2.

Defense Industry

Over the course of the twentieth century, paralleling the growth of the country at large, the U.S. defense industry has grown to be an ever greater part of the U.S. economy. For U.S. workers, the jobs and opportunities offered by the growing defense sector have proved a decidedly awkward blessing. Defense spending tends to be cyclical, growing with international threats and contracting during times of stability. During wartime, the demands of rapid mobilization have brought dramatic changes to the workforce—for the first time introducing women and minorities in large numbers to industrial work. Demobilization, however, often results in severe dislocation for workers. Thus instability characterizes the defense industry, even in peacetime. Likewise, critics complain that having the welfare of a large segment of the workforce tied to the defense industries encourages a needlessly hawkish, expansionistic foreign policy. Even President Dwight D. Eisenhower warned of a dangerously expanding "military-industrial complex." Meanwhile, over the course of the twentieth century, labor leaders have striven, with some limited success, to address the unstable aspects of the military-industrial complex for workers. For workers and the nation as a whole, however, the defense industry remains a source of anxiety, concern—and jobs.

Although defense industries existed from the creation of the United States, the roots of the modern defense sector can be found in early-twentieth-century Progressive efforts to reorganize and rationalize the rapidly growing economy. During World War I, "Progressivism went to war," as numerous historians have suggested. The demands of mobilization, in particular dispatching some 2 million U.S. troops to France, severely tested the U.S. economic and political apparatus. Eventually, some $33 billion was pumped into the economy. Although the federal government directly operated some defense industries, including the Emergency Fleet Corporation, private industry met most of the mobilization demand. So staggering was the buildup that virtually all industries, whether coal, steel, railroads, or other, were considered part of the defense sector. The War Industries Board, a central government agency that was subordinate to the War Labor Board, directed mobilization on a voluntary basis. To stabilize industrial relations, workers in defense industries pledged not to strike in return for new state-mandated protections, including the right to bargain collectively as well as standardized wages and hours.

During the war, women and minorities entered industrial work for the first time on a large scale, filling the void left by the millions of men at war. Nearly 500,000 African Americans left agricultural work in the South and flocked to rapidly growing northern cities. They joined hundreds of thousands of women breaking away from traditional conceptions of a "separate sphere" and taking very untraditional industrial jobs.

The sudden end of the war on November 11, 1918, brought an equally abrupt halt to the expansion of the defense sector. Demobilization meant that thousands lost their jobs. Wartime economic controls were also lifted, which led many employers to revert immediately to prewar wages, hours, and other arrangements. In response, angry strikes broke out across the country in 1919, especially in the steel industry, where employers attempted to reimpose seven-day workweeks and twelve-hour days. Race riots also broke out, brought on by the large number of blacks moving north to work in the defense industry.

The tumult and confusion caused by World War I led to a sharp reaction against the defense industries in the 1920s and 1930s. In 1935, Senator Gerald P. Nye of North Dakota held hearings assailing the practices of munitions manufacturers such as Du Pont, whose desires for profit Nye blamed for the U.S. intervention in 1917. Although dubious, the attack on big business resonated with Americans suffering the ravages of the Great Depression. Polls showed that the "merchants-of-death" scenario had wide credibility. During the interwar years, defense spending dropped off sharply. Even as circumstances in Europe grew tense, many Americans, taking an isolationist stance, desperately sought to avoid any military buildup. Despite the potential of good jobs offered by mobilization, in the 1930s, many U.S. workers viewed prosperity as not worth the risk of war.

It was only after President Franklin D. Roosevelt's reelection in 1940 that military mobilization began in earnest. In March 1941, the president dealt the isolationists a sharp setback when he pushed Lend-Lease legislation through Congress. The Lend-Lease Act allowed the president to "sell, transfer title to, exchange, lease, lend or otherwise dispose of" military supplies to any nation. The economic benefits of mobilization became almost immediately evident. Unemployment, which still stood at Depression levels in 1939, dropped sharply; labor scarcity quickly replaced labor surplus. Defense spending ended the Great Depression, and defense industries again became a leading component of the U.S. economy.

Even before the United States officially entered the conflagration, the defense industries became the venue for advances on the civil rights front. In 1941, African American labor leader A. Philip Randolph threatened a massive march on Washington, D.C., to challenge racial discrimination in defense industries hiring. Wishing to avoid a showdown, President Roosevelt banned the discrimination and created the Fair Employment Practices Committee to oversee his decree.

With the full-scale entry of the United States into World War II in December 1941, the federal government geared up, as it had during the previous war, to direct mobilization. Under government guidance, peacetime industries such as auto manufacturing shifted dramatically to wartime manufacturing. Although the federal government hoped to centralize all defense industry–related decisions under a central office, the military frequently negotiated directly with large corporations. Critics complained sharply that government practices favored large monopoly-sector industries over small competitive industries. Labor leaders argued that corporate profits far outpaced the more meager gains of workers (held to 15 percent increases). Shortages of materials, including aluminum, steel, and copper, further hampered the war effort. Nor were labor disputes absent. In 1941, before Pearl Harbor, workers at California's Long Aircraft manufacturing plant went on strike. Even after U.S. entry into the war, United Mine Workers of America president John L.

Lewis launched a strike in 1942 that earned him and his union the enmity of federal officials, the public, and other labor leaders.

Despite tensions and frequent acrimony, World War II mobilization can be counted a success. U.S. defense industries and their employees met—and often surpassed—the needs of the military and greatly exceeded the output of the Axis powers. Defense industrialists such as shipbuilder Henry Kaiser emerged as popular heroes. Again, defense mobilization brought dramatic social changes. As during World War I, women filled in for men in industrial jobs—again undermining traditional conceptions of women's roles. Record numbers of African Americans and Hispanics also worked in defense-related jobs. And again, with the coming of peace, many of these new workers left their jobs, sometimes by personal choice and sometimes not. Still, defense industries offered a venue for social advances—if only a temporary one.

After World War II, however, there was to be only a brief respite from defense mobilization. Growing tensions with the Soviet Union led to the beginning of the Cold War, which most historians see as commencing in 1947. President Harry S. Truman introduced the largest peacetime budget in U.S. history in 1948, $39 billion, with $18 billion earmarked for defense. In 1950, the National Security Council's policy planning staff drew up a proposal, NSC-68, calling for even further defense spending increases. An unprecedented peacetime military buildup had begun. Federal dollars poured into the defense sector, especially enriching larger firms. Generous contracts in particular went to the so-called "big three": Lockheed Martin, Boeing, and Raytheon. Cost-plus contracts, guaranteeing firms a profit, added to the allure of the defense sector. The Cold War military buildup clearly brought prosperity to many workers. Between 1950 and 1957, defense-related employment grew by 185 percent (a gain of over 1 million jobs). Critics complained, however, that most defense workers tended to be high-skilled white males. Contracts disproportionately went to the Southwest and Southeast, areas where organized labor tended to be weaker. Long-serving southern members of Congress proved particularly adept at procuring contracts for their districts. The rapid expansion and growing influence of the defense industry even led President Dwight Eisenhower to warn in his farewell address in 1961 of "unwarranted influence, whether sought or unsought, by the military-industrial complex."

Nevertheless, trade unions generally supported the Cold War and pushed for increased defense spending that offered jobs for their membership. With opportunities for other social spending increasingly unrealistic, organized labor essentially embraced military Keynesianism. In some cases, organized labor attempted to harness defense spending to serve social needs. During the Korean War (1950–1953), for instance, labor officials working on mobilization advisory committees drafted and helped implement Defense Manpower Policy 4, mandating that defense contracts be directed to firms in labor surplus areas. Enforcement of the provision was spotty, but it remained officially on the books into the 1960s.

Organized labor also remained concerned about the cyclical nature of defense spending. In the early 1960s, Secretary of Defense Robert S. McNamara consolidated the far-reaching procurement offices of the military into one body: the Defense Supply Agency (DSA) within the Defense Department. The guiding principle of the new DSA was keeping inventories low, "buying only what we need," and "buying it at the lowest price possible" (Neiburg 1966, 343). In the face of diminishing returns, American Federation of Labor and Congress of Industrial Organizations (AFL-CIO) economist Nathaniel Goldfinger recommended in 1964 that U.S. workers accept the decline of the defense sector and press instead for "public works, education, urban renewal, and welfare services" (Goldfinger 1964).

The advent of the Vietnam War, however, brought a new round of defense spending. Again, defense industries thrived, although the provisions implemented by McNamara did limit some profits. Fueled by tax cuts, increased domestic spending, and the war in Southeast Asia, the economy expanded rapidly. Between 1965 and 1968, over 2 million defense jobs were added to the economy. Unemployment dropped to beneath 3 percent, the full-employment level. But no sooner did the economy appear stronger than ever than a retraction began. Again the defense sector played a central role. When the Americans began to deescalate in Vietnam after 1968, the military placed fewer contracts. Defense-related employment fell from 7.8 million workers in the peak year of 1968 to 6.1 million in 1971—most of the losses coming in the private sector.

Workers test electronic military defense equipment as it passes by them on an assembly line. (H. David Seawell/Corbis)

With workers concerned about their jobs, the issue of military spending quickly moved into the political arena. In 1972 Democratic presidential candidate George McGovern promised massive cuts in defense spending—$10 billion over four years in a total federal budget of about $200 billion. AFL-CIO President George Meany, a hawk on Vietnam and concerned about the threatened cuts, privately advised President Richard Nixon that on defense, although "some people are talking about it in terms of jobs . . . our people know jobs are involved—you don't have to tell them" (Nixon 1972). Nixon took Meany's advice about the delicacy of the issue, but he did order the Defense Department to prepare a general report on the relationship between military spending and economic prosperity. The resulting study, *The Economics of Defense,* predicted difficult times for workers should McGovern get his defense cuts.

Despite Nixon's overwhelming reelection, the military emerged from the Vietnam debacle with its reputation severely damaged. Liberal Democrats, in particular, pressed successfully for cuts in defense spending, contributing to growing unemployment. President Jimmy Carter, taking office in 1977, initially did try to limit defense spending, but worsening relations with the Soviet Union forced him to call for increases.

In 1981, Ronald Reagan assumed the presidency, determined to restore U.S. military power. Between 1980 and 1985, defense-sector employment rose by 22 percent. For many workers, the increase in defense-related manufacturing jobs cushioned the impact of the general decline of U.S. industry. Indeed, defense industries accounted for a total of roughly 9 percent of all manufacturing jobs by 1985—up from 5 percent in 1977. As usual, the primary beneficiaries of increased defense spending tended to be white, skilled workers. Although organized labor vigorously opposed Reagan's antilabor policies, the AFL-CIO, at least, supported the defense buildup, offering only halfhearted reservations about its allocation and the impact on world events.

As had been the case throughout the Cold War era, certain geographic regions and their industries were the primary beneficiaries of defense spending. For instance, the largest single employer in Tacoma, Washington, is the Department of Defense, followed closely by Boeing Aircraft. Elsewhere on the West Coast, the Los Angeles and San Diego areas long have been hubs of defense-related industries. On the East Coast, millions of defense jobs have brought prosperity to Long Island. Elsewhere around the country, other smaller pockets also came to rely heavily on military contracts. The New London/Groton area of Connecticut enjoyed vigorous population and economic growth as a result of the presence of Electric Boat Corporation, builders of nuclear submarines for the U.S. Navy.

With the fall of the Berlin Wall in 1989, military spending began a decade-long contraction. From 1987 to 1995, active-duty military personnel were cut by 655,000. Defense spending fell from $421 billion in 1985 to $278 billion in 1998, and defense industries suffered accordingly. In 1987, some 3.6 million Americans worked in defense-related industries; by the end of the century the number hovered closer to 2 million. More than 100,000 defense-related jobs were lost alone on Long Island during the 1990s. The problem of the displaced defense worker became a major concern to government officials, who shifted money from the Department of Defense to the Department of Labor to finance retraining programs. As government contracts dried up, some firms, such as in the aerospace industry, attempted to shift to nondefense markets.

The horrific events of September 11, 2001, however, painfully returned the issue of national defense to the consciousness of Americans. A Gallup poll taken in July 2001 showed only 3 percent of Americans listing defense as the country's most pressing problem—on September 22, 80 percent named defense as a top priority. Even as the economy slipped into recession, new funding became available for the "war on terror." Very quickly, it became apparent that this new type of warfare would require a new type of mobilization. Observers spoke of "asymmetrical warfare" against a "shadow enemy." Although an unprecedented secrecy surrounds procurement decisions—in some cases, contractors have been warned against discussing plans—smaller firms specializing in high-tech information-gathering and weaponry and thus requiring highly skilled workers are expected to play a central role. Yet larger firms will also make contributions. Boeing, for instance, is developing more accurate guidance systems and unmanned aircraft capabilities.

In the aftermath of September 11, even the definition of defense has undergone transformation. Concern now focuses on "homeland defense," including initiatives such as equipping post offices to deliver mail safely and research into bioterrorism. As the economy increasingly goes high-tech, so will U.S. defense industries, requiring more specialized, skilled workers. With the war on terrorism, the influence and expansion of defense industries seems sure to continue—as will its ambiguous legacy for the U.S. workforce.

Edmund Wehrle

See also Military Jobs and Careers; Wartime and Work

References and further reading

Barnet, Richard. 1969. *The Economy of Death.* Atheneum: New York.

Goldfinger, Nate. 1964. Memoranda 14, July. Box 13/41, Department of Legislation, AFL-CIO, George Meany Memorial Archives, Silver Spring, MD.

Hogan, Michael. 1989. *Cross of Iron.* New York: Cambridge University Press.

Hooks, Gregory. 1991. *Forging the Military-Industrial Complex.* Urbana: University of Illinois Press.

Kaplan, Fred. 1983. *The Wizards of Armageddon.* New York: First Touchstone.

Kennedy, Paul. 1987. *The Rise and Fall of Great Powers.* New York: Vintage.

Lens, Sidney. 1970. *The Military-Industrial Complex.* New York: Pilgrim Press.

Melman, Seymour. 1970. *The Permanent War Economy.* New York: Simon and Schuster.

Nieburg, Harold. 1966. *In the Name of Science.* New York: Quadrangle.

Nixon, Richard. 1972. John Ehrlichman to Richard Nixon, August 25. Box 18, President's Office files, President's Handwriting, Nixon Archives, National Archives, College Park, MD.

Defined Benefit/Defined Contribution Plans

Financial planning for life after work is often described as a three-legged stool composed of Social Security, private savings, and pension funds and payments derived from employment. Employer-based retirement plans are classified into two main categories—defined benefit and defined contribution plans. In defined benefit plans, the employer agrees to provide the employee with a specific compensation amount upon retirement based on a predetermined formula; therefore, the final compensation amount is fixed. In defined contribution plans, the employer makes contributions to an account established for each participating employee. The final retirement payment reflects the total employer contributions, any employee contributions, and investment gains or losses; therefore, each payment to the plan is fixed.

U.S. employers are not required by law to offer retirement plans, but they remain common in the U.S. workplace. These plans are considered part of the overall compensation package provided to employees and are used by employers to attract and retain talented workers so that the company will remain competitive. In addition, employers have incentives to offer retirement plans because of their respective favorable tax consequences. Early in the first decade of the twenty-first century, approximately 68 million U.S. citizens per year were covered by about 700,000 private pension plans (U.S. Department of Labor 2001).

In defined benefit plans, participants collect a previously determined compensation amount from their employer after retirement. The amount paid may be based on the employee's length of service at the company, salary while working, or other factors determined by the employer. Employers risk investment return in this case since they must pay the specified amount, regardless of unexpected slowdowns in the market. Participants also face a different kind of risk in a defined benefit plan—inflation risk. Even if inflation escalates, the participant will be paid the same predetermined compensation amount throughout his or her retirement. With high inflation rates, participants find that the purchasing power of their retirement pay is minimized over time. This fact is especially unsettling for early retirees, who are paid the same benefit amount for many consecutive years. Defined benefit plans are more commonly found in goods-producing industries such as mining and manufacturing and are typically used in collective bargaining agreements with union contracts.

Defined contribution plans are retirement plans in which the amount ultimately paid at retirement is not predetermined. Instead, employers make a fixed contribution to the plan over the span of the employee's service with the company. Therefore, the pension funds available to the participant at retirement depend upon two factors: the amount contributed and the rate of return on the investments over time. Participants face the risk of receiving a lower than expected compensation amount if the investment returns on plan contributions are poor. In no case is an employer responsible for supplementing benefits. Many defined contribution plans also allow or require employees, as well as their employer, to make contributions to an account. Defined contribution plans include tax-deferred plans such as 401(k) and 403(b) plans, money purchase plans, stock plans (including employee stock ownership plans, or ESOPs), and deferred profit sharing plans. Traditionally, defined contribution plans are more common in service industries.

The first pension plan in the United States was established in 1759 to benefit widows and children of Presbyterian ministers. The first corporate plan was adopted more than a century later by the American Express Company. During the next century, approximately 400 plans were established, primarily in the railroad, banking, and public utility industries. However, the most significant growth in pension plans occurred during World War II, when the U.S. labor market had far more job openings than workers to fill them. Employers used pension plans as a creative incentive to attract and retain workers during wartime wage freeze rules.

In 1974 the Employee Retirement Income Security Act (ERISA) was passed to protect employee pension rights after a lengthy study of the private pension system. Today, ERISA strictly regulates the plans employers choose to offer their employees but does not mandate implementation of any specific programs. ERISA is written to prevent unfair denial or revocation of pension rights by setting minimum standards; to provide workers with protection if their pension plans cannot pay the employee's entitled benefits; and to require full disclosure of pension rights, including how and when benefits are collected, how pension funds are invested, and how benefits are accumulated. ERISA and a series of other federal provisions also limit the amount of employee and employer contributions that may be made to a plan and the maximum benefit allowed under a defined benefit plan. In 2001, the overall limit on annual compensation that can be considered for calculating benefit and contribution figures was $150,000. Since the passage of ERISA, the number of private retirement plans has more than doubled. This increase is greatly attributed to the surge in the number of participants in defined contribution plans, namely 401(k) plans, as the number of defined benefit plans has declined.

The popular 401(k) plan, named for the number of the Internal Revenue Service (IRS) regulation providing its tax-deferred status, is a defined contribution, controlled investment plan in which employees contribute a certain amount of their pretax earnings to an account that bears interest until they reach retirement age. The employees choose how their contributions are invested from a selection of funds, and often their employer matches their contributions to some extent. The popularity of 401(k) plans since the 1980s can be attributed to a number of factors. Employees no longer remain at one company for their entire career because of a more competitive job market, higher percentages of layoffs, and corporate downsizing. When each period of employment is terminated, the corresponding pension plans dependent upon long-term employment are terminated as well. In addition, survey data from the Employee Benefits Research Institute show that workers choose to invest in 401(k) plans because they are concerned about the financial stability of Social Security trust funds in the first half of the twenty-first century. At the end of 2000, there were an estimated 42,000,000 workers enrolled in 401(k) plans, holding $1.8 trillion in assets (Employment Benefits Research Institute 2001).

Elayne M. Marinos

See also Employment Retirement Income Security Act; Job Benefits; Pensions; Retirement

References and further reading

American Savings Education Council. 2001. http://www.asec.org (cited August 12).

Employee Benefit Research Institute. "401(k) Asset Allocation, Account Balances, and Loan Activity in 2000." http://www.ebri.org (cited December 2).

Gregory, Robert J. 1999. *Your Workplace Rights and How to Make the Most of Them.* New York: Amacom, American Management Association Publications.

Matthews, Joseph L., with Dorothy Matthews Berman. 1999. *Social Security, Medicare and Pensions.* 7th ed. Berkeley: Nolo.com.

Miller, Alan J. 1995. *Standard & Poor's 401(k) Planning Guide: Every Employee's Guide to Making 401(k) Decisions.* New York: McGraw-Hill.

Pension and Welfare Benefits Administration. 2001. http://dol.gov/dol/pwba (cited August 12).

Schaffner, Herbert A., and Carl E. Van Horn. 2002. *A Nation at Work: The Heldrich Guide to the American Workforce.* New Brunswick, NJ: Rutgers University Press.

U.S. Department of Labor. 1997. *Report on the American Workforce.* Washington, DC: U.S. Department of Labor.

———. 2001. U.S. Department of Labor: Employee Benefits Security Administration. http://www.dol.gov/ebsa(August 12).

Van Horn, Carl E. 1996. *No One Left Behind.* New York: Twentieth Century Fund Press.

Working Today. 2001. http://www.workingtoday.org (cited August 12).

Deming, W. Edwards (1900–1993)

William Edwards Deming, a statistician and management consultant, helped Japanese businesses learn to compete on the basis of quality in the aftermath of World War II and later sparked the quality movement in U.S. business in the 1980s. Deming grew up in rural Wyoming in modest circumstances that may have contributed to his lifelong "abhorrence of waste" (Gabor 1990, 40). After receiving a master's degree in mathematics and physics at the University of Colorado in 1924, Deming went to Yale University to pursue a doctorate in mathematical physics. He was drawn to the growing field of statistics in the belief that statistical analysis could provide government and industry leaders with information that would help them to improve their operations. After completing his education in 1928, Deming worked as a statistician for the U.S. government in the Department of Agriculture and the Census Bureau (Wren and Greenwood 1998, 205–207). In the late 1940s, he was invited to work in Japan and found an enthusiastic audience for his ideas among Japanese engineers looking to rebuild their economy. It was not until the 1980s, when many companies in the United States were struggling to compete with Japan, that U.S. business leaders discovered Deming's ideas. By this time, Deming had developed a comprehensive philosophy of management characterized by an emphasis on the benefits of pursuing quality and on the importance of building continual improvement into the operating system of any organization.

Early in his career, Deming refined the use of statistical process control (SPC), the use of sampling and statistical analysis to monitor the quality of a production process. Deming first encountered elements of SPC while working at Western Electric in the summers of 1925 and 1926. There he met Walter Shewhart, a physicist and statistician experimenting with the use of statistics to improve quality control in industry. Shewhart used statistical analysis to determine the normal, or acceptable, rate of variation in the quality of industrial production. Employees could then use statistical sampling to ensure that the production system always operated within this acceptable range (Wren and Greenwood

1998, 206). Deming built on Shewhart's approach, making a distinction between "special" and "common" causes of variation. Special causes, such as a malfunctioning machine or an erratic operator, could be addressed and eliminated immediately. Common causes, however, were built into the system and could only be addressed through study and systemic improvements (Beckford 1998, 66). Later in his career, Deming asserted that "common causes" accounted for 94 percent of all variations in the quality of production and that quality initiatives should therefore focus on improving systems (Beckford 1998, 73).

In 1947 Deming was invited to assist the U.S. occupation authorities in Japan as they prepared to conduct a census of Japan. While in Japan, Deming accepted an invitation from the Union of Japanese Scientists and Engineers to lecture on statistical quality control (Wren and Greenwood 1998, 208). Deming's time in Japan marked a turning point in his career, when he made the transition from statistician to management consultant. His message about the benefits of pursuing quality appealed to Japanese business leaders looking for a means to compete with the United States and Europe. Deming also offered Japanese managers ideas on how to use statistical analysis not simply to measure errors but also to improve production processes. At the same time, he began to learn from Japanese companies that were successfully using statistical analysis to improve quality. To honor his contributions to the development of Japanese industry, in 1951 Japan established the Deming Prize to recognize business achievement in attaining quality (Petersen 1999, 476; Beckford 1998, 66–67).

In the early 1980s, growing competition from Japan and Europe and a recession at home prompted calls for reforms in U.S. business. In this context, Deming's 1982 book, *Out of the Crisis,* found a receptive audience. The book opened with a call for the "transformation of the American style of management" (Deming 1982, ix). He emphasized the dangers of a short-term focus on quarterly profits and called on managers to adopt long-range planning procedures, to focus on satisfying customers rather than shareholders, and to abandon performance evaluations that rewarded workers for short-term improvements (Gabor 1990, 7–10). At the heart of Deming's philosophy was his passionate belief in the possibility of continual improvement at all levels of any organization (Gabor 1990, 8–9). To simplify the path to continual improvement, Deming coined the acronym PDCA, which stood for plan it; do it; check on results, and act on the new information (Wren and Greenwood 1998, 212).

Deming also hoped to transform the experience of workers in U.S. companies. In *Out of the Crisis,* he tells the story of a plant superintendent who blamed poor quality on the workers in his plant. Deming performed a statistical analysis of this plant and found that the level of mistakes from day to day was quite predictable. This meant, he explained, that there was a stable system for producing a particular percentage of defective items. The problem lay with the system and not with the individual workers (Deming 1982, 6–7). For this reason, Deming called on U.S. companies to "eliminate slogans, exhortations, and targets for the work force asking for zero defects and new levels of productivity" (65). In place of regular employee evaluations, Deming called for more teamwork, better leadership, ongoing education and training of employees, and an end to the climate of fear that he believed characterized many U.S. companies (86).

Deming's ideas about quality influenced business practices in the United States, but often in a piecemeal fashion at odds with Deming's comprehensive vision for corporate change. In the 1980s, Deming consulted with major U.S. companies, including Ford, Xerox, and General Motors, and was credited with helping such companies refocus attention on quality and on process improvements. During the same period, Deming was linked to the rise of total quality management (TQM), a theory of management emphasizing the use of statistics to monitor and improve quality. In fact, Deming was highly critical of TQM, considering it to be a superficial version of his own theory (Petersen 1999, 484). Other elements of Deming's philosophy, such as his call for the elimination of individual performance evaluations, contradicted strongly held managerial beliefs about the importance of performance feedback and the value of management by objectives (Wren and Greenwood 1998, 211). Deming's call for a long-term orientation also appears to have had limited impact on corporate practices in the 1980s and 1990s, decades characterized by the growing power of shareholders who pushed for short-term profits, by a growth in leveraged buyouts, and by an increase in mobility among top managers (Gabor 1990, 281–282).

Julie Kimmel

See also Baldrige Awards; Drucker, Peter, F.; Quality Circles; Total Quality Management

References and further reading

Beckford, John. 1998. *Quality: A Critical Introduction.* New York: Routledge.

Deming, W. Edwards. 1982. *Out of the Crisis.* Cambridge: MIT Press.

———. 1993. *The New Economics for Industry, Government, Education.* Cambridge: MIT Press.

Gabor, Andrea. 1990. *The Man Who Discovered Quality: How W. Edward Deming Brought the Quality Revolution to America—the Stories of Ford, Xerox, and GM.* New York: Random House.

Petersen, Peter B. 1999. "Total Quality Management and the Deming Approach to Quality Management." *Journal of Management History* 5, 8: 468–488.

Wren, Daniel A., and Ronald G. Greenwood. 1998. *Management Innovators: The People and Ideas That Have Shaped Modern Business.* New York: Oxford University Press.

Democratic Socialism

Democratic socialism is a nonrevolutionary, nonviolent branch of socialism that emphasizes democratic decision making, both in politics and in the running of economic entities. Unlike revolutionary socialists, democratic socialists believe that change in society will result from reform of the government and increased awareness of social issues, not through violence or revolution. Democratic socialists do not want the dissolution of the government but a stronger, better one, whose strength comes from social reforms, justice, and pressure from the people. They alone determine their own freedoms and how intrusive government should or should not be. Democratic socialists favor government programs that provide all citizens with their basic needs: food, shelter, education, clothing, health, and transportation.

Democratic socialism combines collective and private ownership of the means of production, democratic management, governmental distribution of essential goods and services, and free elections. Ideally, it is a society characterized by equality, liberty, solidarity, and participation, in which people work together to meet the needs of the whole community, not to make profits for a few. Community supersedes individualism. Production is based on social usefulness rather than profitability. People are paid according to the work done and cooperate instead of competing. Moreover, democratic socialism sees the state as the major instrument of reform. To achieve the greater goal of economic equality, democratic socialists believe that the "commanding heights" of the economy (production, distribution, and financing functions) should be owned and managed by the state.

Closely linked with this idea is the concept of state planning of the economy so as to make sure that country resources are used to produce what is most needed and to facilitate full employment. In addition, great emphasis is put on a collection of policies to provide for the most basic needs of the population (safe and reasonable working conditions, minimum income, universal basic education, decent housing, and health care services, etc.), which are generally considered to be characteristic features of the "welfare state." The democratic socialist movement has also been noted for its international outlook and the idea that the poor of the world should become united in their own interest. Moreover, democratic socialists have always favored peace and opposed war as a means of settling differences between nations and groups. Instead, they prefer to settle disagreements through constituted courts. Democratic socialists have flourished where democratic institutions are functioning well and where they have had a real opportunity to achieve their program.

The idea of state intervention in society to ensure greater economic equality has a long history, going back at least to Plato's *Republic.* The modern doctrine and practice of socialism has as its aims economic, political, and social justice for all people. The possibility of achieving these aims was first envisioned in the last quarter of the eighteenth century, a time of extraordinary social and political upheaval. Historically, socialism grew out of the French Revolution (1787–1799) and its intellectual ferment and demand for equal rights, absolute democracy, and the redistribution of property. Although modern socialism has its roots in France, it was in Germany that this theory of society and history was developed and shaped, by Karl Marx (1818–1883), with the assistance of Friedrich Engels (1820–1895).

In the last quarter of the nineteenth century, socialist parties were formed in the more powerful industrial countries (Germany, 1864; France 1880;

Eugene Victor Debs, ca. 1912. Debs organized the Social Democratic Party in 1897. (Library of Congress)

Great Britain, 1884; Italy, 1892; Russia, 1901) and in a multitude of smaller countries, mainly in Europe (Denmark, 1879; Spain, 1879; Belgium, 1885; the Netherlands, 1894) and Australasia (Australia, 1893; New Zealand, 1910), and soon they began to win mass support from the working classes. By 1914, there was a socialist party in just about every country in the world that had had some experience of the Industrial Revolution.

However, another socialist party was founded in 1877 in the United States, despite significant hostility toward the notion of collective state action to achieve greater economic equality. The U.S. Socialist Labor Party drew much of its support from workers who had migrated from the industrial cities of Europe and had its roots in the U.S. circles of Communist International (Comintern) and the Workingmen's Party of America. The Social Democratic Party, however, was largely composed of U.S.-born workers. It was organized in 1897 by the veterans of the Pullman strike of the American Railway Union, led by Eugene Victor Debs. Debs's party and the "Kangaroo" wing of the older Socialist Labor Party merged in 1906.

By the 1880s, under the rule of Daniel De Leon, the Socialist Labor Party had become increasingly intolerant of internal dissent and had suffered several splits. From the beginning, the Socialist Labor Party was the universal organization for radicals in the United States. Its membership included Marxists of various kinds, Christian socialists, Zionist and anti-Zionist Jewish socialists, foreign-language-speaking sections, and many others. On the divisive issue of reform versus revolution, the Socialist Labor Party from the start adopted a compromise formula, producing platforms calling for revolutionary change but also making demands of a reformist nature. An everlastingly unresolved issue was whether revolutionary change could come about without violence. There were always pacifists and revolutionaries in the party as well as those opposed to both those views. The Socialist Labor Party historically stressed cooperatives as much as labor unions and included the concepts of revolution by education and of building a new society within the shell of the old.

The Socialist Labor Party aimed to become a major party. In the years prior to World War I it elected two members of Congress, more than seventy mayors, and innumerable state legislators and city councilors. Its membership topped 100,000, and its presidential candidate, Eugene Debs, received close to 1 million votes in 1912 and again in 1920. But as with any ideologically mixed organization, it was drowned in internal disputes. An early disagreement occurred over the Industrial Workers of the World (IWW), which Debs and De Leon had helped create as a competitor to the American Federation of Labor (AFL). Some socialists supported the IWW, but others considered "dual unionism" to be fatal to the solidarity of the labor movement and supported the socialist faction in the AFL led by Max Hayes.

The Democratic Socialists of America (DSA) is the largest socialist organization in the United States, though it is not a political party. DSA was founded in 1983 with the purpose of bringing together U.S. supporters of left opinion. DSA's political strategy has fluctuated from electoral politics within the Democratic left (the liberal-left wing of the Democratic Party) to working with independents and the New Party, a progressive political organization, when there is no Democratic Party candidate worthy of support. The immediate goal of socialists, they argue, should be to work in a coalition with the liberal-left groups connected to the

Democratic Party, namely civil rights, environmental, and labor groups. DSA members provide the necessary base for meeting immediate goals like raising the minimum wage, making health insurance universal, guaranteeing reproductive rights, and protecting the environment. In addition, members support the idea of the democratic public controlling the dominant industries of the economy but do not support the idea of state ownership of every human enterprise.

DSA members also believe that the United States' vast wealth of must be distributed more equitably. They feel that the tax burden in the United States unfairly favors the rich, while the middle classes struggle to meet Uncle Sam's demands. Democratic socialists assume that a return to the moderately progressive tax levels before 1981 would restore close to $100 billion a year in tax revenues, yielding revenue that could be put toward restoring many of the social programs that have recently been slashed. Furthermore, increased spending on education and infrastructure, as practices in Japan and Germany have proven, can give the economy a much-needed boost.

In addition, DSA members believe that to achieve a more just society, many parts of the government and economy must become more democratic so that ordinary Americans can participate in the decisions that affect their lives. For example, during the 1930s, when existing government and regulatory structures were failing, the U.S. government increased its regulation of and intervention into the economic system, thus temporarily abandoning the capitalism system and turning toward socialism to find the answer. A complex set of economic, political, and social factors led up to the New Deal. With the economy at an all-time low, people wanted change; Franklin D. Roosevelt's legislative program represented a new role for government in capitalism in the United States. Roosevelt first used the term *new deal* when he accepted the Democratic presidential nomination in 1932. His New Deal programs aimed at relief, recovery, and reform.

Roosevelt's program was designed to assist industry, labor, and the unemployed by setting standards for prices, wages, and hours. It also guaranteed labor's right to organize unions and to bargain collectively for benefits for workers. The Roosevelt administration introduced into the United States the idea of a "welfare state," which would design safety net programs to ensure a minimal standard of living for the unemployed and working class.

In addition to supporting some version of a welfare state, the Democratic Socialists of America share a vision of a humane international social order based on equitable distribution of resources, meaningful work, gender and racial equality, a healthy environment, sustainable growth, and nonoppressive relationships. Democratic socialism also means cultural democracy. The different cultures within each society must have the same rights as every other group in that society, as well as equal access to their national and global cultural heritage. Therefore, a long-term objective of the DSA is to establish a world of "cooperative commonwealths"—a world in which nations cooperate with each other for the common good.

Although it is a capitalist nation, the United States has nevertheless adopted wide-ranging social programs. Overall, democratic socialists have implemented a variety of social programs, including improvement of parklands, unemployment compensation, Social Security, more equitable taxation, public radio and television, public libraries, and improved educational opportunities.

Recently, the collapse of Eastern European and Soviet Communist states has led socialists throughout the world to discard many of their doctrines regarding centralized planning and nationalization of enterprises. The socialist movement around the world seems to have lost much of its spirit, which brought so much success in the first part of the twentieth century. That can be attributed to the coming of new generations of leaders who have not experienced the passion of the early struggles. In addition, the advanced economies of the world appear to be gradually moving into the postindustrial age, in which the working classes, supposedly the main supporters and beneficiaries of socialist programs, are shrinking in number and are certainly no longer a majority in any of the leading industrial countries. Another factor is that with the creation of a welfare state in most industrial countries, much of the basic program of democratic socialism has been achieved already. Moreover, market economies consistently raise the standard of living and prosperity for the workers, thus lessening their desire to undermine their governments.

The main issue in recent years has been how to manage such systems efficiently—particularly in view of the rising costs caused by the aging of the population, which alters the balance between those who pay for the system and those who benefit from it. Democratic Socialists of America has undoubtedly made a contribution in the past to a more equitable and just society, and the question now is whether it still has a major role to play or will be replaced by movements more adapted to problems of the present and future.

Raissa Muhutdinova-Foroughi

See also Capitalism; Communism in the U.S. Trade Union Movement; Industrial Workers of the World; New Deal; Socialism

References and further reading

Giddens, Anthony. 1998. *The Third Way: The Renewal of Social Democracy.* Cambridge: Polity Press.

Greene, Nathanael, ed. 1971. *European Socialism since World War I.* Chicago: Quadrangle Books.

Howell, David. 1976. *British Social Democracy.* New York: St. Martin's Press.

Huddleston, John. 1989. *The Search for a Just Society.* Oxford: George Ronald Publishing.

Hunt, Nancy. 1970. *German Social Democracy, 1918–1933.* Chicago: Quadrangle Paperbacks.

Korpi, Walter. 1978. *The Working Class in Welfare Capitalism.* London: Routledge and Kegan Paul.

Le Bon, Gustave . 1899/2002. *The Psychology of Socialism.* New York: Macmillan.

Milner, Henry. 1989. *Sweden: Social Democracy in Practice.* Oxford: Oxford University Press.

Panitch, Leo. 1976. *Social Democracy and Industrial Militancy: The Labor Party, the Trade Unions, and Incomes Policy, 1945–1974.* Cambridge: Cambridge University Press.

Dilbert

The cartoon strip "Dilbert" first appeared in 1989. Set in a nameless company whose business is unspecified, it recounts the misadventures of an intelligent but geeky engineer as he deals with dimwitted bosses, troll-like accountants, surly secretaries, and occasionally headless coworkers from his cubicle in the U.S. workplace. The cast of characters includes Dilbert, the Massachusetts Institute of Technology–educated electrical engineer whose necktie curls upward; Dogbert, Dilbert's cynical talking pet and confidante; Dilbert's pointy-haired boss (also nameless but referred to by Dilbert aficionados as PHB) who cannot operate his own computer and has never met a management fad he didn't like; Dilbert's hapless colleagues Wally, Alice, and Asok the intern; and Catbert, the evil director of human resources, who revels in passing down bizarre edicts intended to make his coworkers miserable. For millions of readers, Dilbert is a workplace Everyman whose comments on the vagaries of management, the eccentricities of coworkers, and the callousness of profit-driven corporations reflect life on the job for workers in today's high-tech economy. Drawing on his seventeen years of experience working in a cubicle and that of countless workers who send him accounts of their own workplace situations, creator Scott Adams has tapped into the psyche of the U.S. worker like few other cartoonists: "No matter how absurd I try to make the comic strip, I can't stay ahead of what people are experiencing in their own workplace" (Adams 1986, 1).

Dilbert now appears in more than 2,000 papers in 61 countries, and on the web at http://www.dilbert.com.

K. A. Dixon

See also Amazon.com; Computers at Work; Postindustrial Workforce; Work in Literature; Yuppie

References and further reading

Adams, Scott. 1996. *The Dilbert Principle.* New York: HarperBusiness.

———. 2000. *Dilbert: Random Acts of Management.* New York: Andrews McNeel.

———. 2001. *Excuse Me While I Wag.* New York: Andrews McNeel.

———. 2001. *When Did Ignorance Become a Point of View?* New York: Andrews McNeel.

Disability and Work

Entry into the workplace is a right of passage for almost all Americans, a natural progression from school to work. For many, however, the transition is not so smooth. Many individuals who want to earn a living are, because of physical or mental disabilities, denied full access to the workplace.

According to the U.S. Census Bureau and the American Association of Disabled Persons, there are approximately 50 million Americans—or 20 percent of the total population—with a disability. Almost 20 million people have a severe disability, and almost 30 million Americans with disabilities are between the ages of fifteen and sixty-four. The majority of people with disabilities represent an untapped pool of potential labor for the many employers who experience staffing problems in times of a tight labor market or otherwise have difficulty finding qualified workers. However, in the past, people with disabilities were routinely excluded from the workplace. Discrimination and discomfort on the part of employers with hiring people who have a disability, combined with a lack of physical access to the workplace, prevented many otherwise qualified workers from engaging in meaningful work. In addition, federal laws regarding Social Security income and Medicare prevented many people with disabilities from entering the workplace for fear of losing their health benefits. Lack of transportation, lack of experience, and insufficient access to employment services further exacerbated the problem. Today, despite an increased awareness among employers and laws to encourage access, people with disabilities still experience higher levels of unemployment than people without disabilities.

Census Bureau data indicate that the majority (80 percent) of working-age Americans are in the labor force, and more than three-fourths are working full-time. In stark contrast, less than one-third of people with disabilities are in the labor force, and less than one-fourth of them are working full-time. At the same time, many polls show that the majority of people with disabilities who are not working would work if they could gain access to the workplace. In 2000, people with disabilities faced an unemployment rate of 9.5 percent, compared with a rate of 4.2 percent for those without a disability. According to the U.S. Department of Labor (DOL), people with disabilities are more likely to live below the poverty line than those who do not have a disability, reflecting their lower work participation. In 1995, 30 percent of working-age people with disabilities had incomes below the poverty line, three times higher than people without disabilities. In addition, people with disabilities that do work earn less than their nondisabled peers, are more likely to have jobs that pay below minimum wage, and lack opportunities for training and advancement. People with disabilities who want to work often face significant barriers to entering the workforce, even during a tight labor market. In an economy that increasingly requires technical skills and lifelong learning, many people with disabilities are entering the workforce at a disadvantage.

Since the 1960s, a number of regulations have been implemented to prevent discrimination and make the workplace and public facilities accessible to people with disabilities. One of the first was the Rehabilitation Act of 1973, which was an early attempt by Congress to enforce nondiscrimination of people with disabilities in the federal workplace. The most significant parts of the act include Section 501, which requires nondiscrimination and affirmative action in federal employment; Section 502, which requires accessibility in federal buildings; Section 503, which requires affirmative action in employment by federal contractors; and Section 504, which requires affirmative action of recipients of federal funds, including state agencies, housing authorities, educational institutions, private entities, and charitable organizations. The Rehabilitation Act contributed significantly to making the public sector more accessible to people with disabilities.

State and federal disability laws have made the workplace, the private sector, and the public sector more accessible to people with disabilities; however, people with disabilities still must contend with discrimination and fear in the workplace. (Tom and Dee Ann McCarthy/Corbis)

Perhaps the most significant law for people with disabilities in the workplace is the Americans with Disabilities Act (ADA) of 1990. The goal of the act is to make the workplace, transportation, telecommunications, and the public arena fully accessible to people with disabilities and to ensure that workers with disabilities have the same job and career opportunities as workers without disabilities. The ADA prohibits discrimination against individuals with physical and mental disabilities in employment, housing, education, and access to public services. The employment provisions of the law prohibit discrimination in hiring or firing people with disabilities who are qualified for a job, inquiring about a disability, limiting advancement opportunities or job classifications, using tests that tend to screen out people with disabilities, or denying opportunities to anyone in a relationship with a person with disabilities. Both the Equal Employment Opportunity Commission (EEOC) and the Department of Justice are responsible for enforcement of the ADA. Private employers of fifteen people or more, federal, state, and local governments, employment agencies, and labor unions are covered under the ADA.

Despite its laudable goal, the ADA has not been without controversy, beginning with how the act defines disability, a definition that is open to a certain degree of interpretation. The ADA defines a disability as a "physical or mental impairment that substantially limits one or more of the major life activities of the individual, a record of such impairment" (cancer, for instance), or "being regarded as having such an impairment" (for instance, a disfigurement that does not actually limit major life activities but may be viewed by others as doing so). In addition, the ADA requires that "reasonable accommodation" be made in the workplace for qualified individuals with disabilities. Reasonable accommodation is considered to be any modification or adjustment to a job or the work environment that will enable a qualified applicant or employee with a disability to participate in the application process or to perform essential job functions. It can include providing special equipment or making a workplace more accessible. It can also mean allowing an employee to work at home or on a nontraditional schedule. Under the act, employers are not required to provide accommodations that impose an "undue hardship" ("action requiring significant difficulty or expense") on their business operations, nor are they required to hire people who are not qualified candidates, simply because they have a disability. However, this provision has not been enough to allay the fears of many employers.

With the passage of the ADA, many employers feared that they would be forced to make costly accommodations for people with disabilities, hire people with disabilities who are not qualified for the job, or be sued by disgruntled workers claiming discrimination under the ADA. Few of these fears have been actualized. Many employers have overcome their fear of hiring people with disabilities, have made reasonable accommodations, and have not found the requirements of ADA to be unduly burdensome. At the same time, some employers have resisted making the accommodations and changes necessary for an accessible workplace. In 1995, the National Council on Disability, in its report "The Americans with Disabilities Act: Ensuring Equal Access to the American Dream," celebrated the success of ADA but cautioned that "what is needed to improve upon the implementation of the Americans with Disabilities Act is greater public awareness, further education and clarification regarding the provisions of the law, and the appropriate resources to both encourage voluntary compliance and to ensure effective enforcement" (National Council on Disability 2001, 24).

From 1993 to 1999, the U.S. Department of Justice resolved nearly 130,000 ADA charges. Conversely, according to a report in the May–June 2000 issue of the American Bar Association's *Mental and Physical Disability Law Reporter,* employers prevail more than 95 percent of the time in ADA suits and in 85 percent of the administrative complaints handled by the EEOC. In addition, a 1999 Supreme Court decision narrowed the definition of disability to exclude certain people from protection under ADA. In considering the cases *Sutton v. United Airlines, Inc., Murphy v. United Parcel Service,* and *Albertsons, Inc. v. Kirkingburg,* the Supreme Court held that a person is not "disabled," and therefore not protected from discrimination under the Americans with Disabilities Act, if medication or other corrective devices diminish his or her impairment (taking medication for depression, for instance, or wearing corrective lenses).

It is likely that ADA will continue to be litigated in the courts, as employers continue to come to terms with the regulatory requirements of the act. It is clear that the Americans with Disabilities Act was a critical step in the fight to provide unfettered access to the workplace for people with disabilities but that barriers to participation remain.

A more recent addition to disabilities law is the

Workforce Investment Act (WIA) of 1998, which regulates the federal system of job training and employment services. The overall purpose of WIA is to consolidate and improve employment, training, literacy, and vocational rehabilitation programs. Title I of WIA is enacted to meet the needs of both individual job seekers and employers by providing job seekers with access to employment and training opportunities and linking employers to a pool of qualified applicants. The main feature of Title I is the creation of "one-stop" employment centers where job seekers can access a broad range of employment-related and training services in a single central location. Designated agencies that have traditionally provided services to different groups (welfare recipients, youth, people with disabilities, displaced homemakers) are required to integrate access to their services through the one-stop career centers. Partners in the one-stop system include state vocational rehabilitation and employment service agencies.

The Workforce Investment Act (and, previously, the Job Training Partnership Act) contain nondiscrimination and equal opportunity provisions that "[prohibit] WIA Title I financially assisted grant applicants and recipients, as defined in Section 37.4, from discriminating on the basis of race, color, religion, sex, national origin, age, disability, or political affiliation or belief." It also mandates compliance with other equal opportunity and nondiscrimination regulations, including the ADA. States are required to ensure access to WIA programs and information for all participants, including people with disabilities. In conjunction with ADA, states must ensure that all one-stop facilities are physically accessible to all participants. States, in response, have adopted a number of approaches to ensure accessibility and equal opportunity for all one-stop users and most have developed a system to resolve complaints brought under ADA.

For many people with disabilities, it is not a question of finding and keeping a good job. It is a question of finding and keeping a good job and having adequate health care coverage. Many people with disabilities who want to work fear the loss of their health care coverage, should working make them ineligible for benefits such as Medicare and Medicaid. Many people with disabilities cannot obtain private health care and cannot afford to pay their medical expenses, even if they work. Not working, or working very little, is frequently in their best interests if it means holding onto their health care. In this situation, many people who want and can work choose to remain unemployed.

To remedy this situation, the federal government in 1999 passed the Ticket to Work and Work Incentives Improvement Act (TWWIA). The purposes of the act are to provide individuals with disabilities with (1) health care and employment preparation and placement services to reduce their dependency on cash benefits; (2) Medicaid coverage (through incentives to states to allow them to purchase it) needed to maintain employment; (3) the option of maintaining Medicare coverage while working; and (4) return to work tickets allowing them access to services needed to obtain and retain employment and reduce dependence on cash benefits. Under TWWIA, people with disabilities will not have to unfairly choose between a meaningful career and essential health care but can maintain their benefits and supports while working.

Other federal laws relating to hiring workers with disabilities include: the Vietnam Era Veterans Readjustment Act of 1974, which protects certain disabled veterans from being discriminated against because of a disability incurred or aggravated in the line of duty; the Architectural Barriers Act of 1968, which requires federally owned, leased, or funded buildings and facilities to be accessible to people with disabilities; the Tax Reform Act of 1976 of the Internal Revenue Code, which provides an incentive to employers for making facilities accessible to people with disabilities; the Hearing Aid Compatibility Act of 1988, which requires all telephones manufactured or imported into the United States to be compatible with hearing aids; and the Telecommunications Accessibility Enhancement Act of 1988, which requires the federal government to operate a dual party relay system for calls to, from, and within the federal government, enabling deaf employees to easily access federal government offices in their jobs. In addition, most states have statutes that make it illegal to discriminate against people with disabilities or others based on race, religion, sex, age, or other minority status.

Together, the body of state and federal disability law has made the workplace, the private sector, and the public sector more accessible to people with disabilities. However, people with disabilities still must contend with discrimination and fear in the workplace. The continued underemployment of people with disabilities means that more work remains to be done if disabled Americans are to share fully in the work and career opportunities available to Americans without disabilities. Laws such as ADA and TWWIA are necessary steps in the battle for equal rights for disabled workers, but it may be that only a tight labor market will do what regulations cannot: force employers to create disability-friendly workplaces and seek out workers with disabilities.

K. A. Dixon

See also Equal Employment Opportunity Commission; Family and Medical Leave Act; Health Insurance; Job Training Partnership Act; Medicaid; Social Security Act; Wage Gap; Workforce Investment Act

References and further reading

American Bar Association. 2001. "The American Bar Association's *Mental and Physical Disability Law Reporter,* May–June 2000." http://www.abanet.org/media/jun00/abatitle1–2.html (cited November 28).

Blanck, Peter David, and David L. Braddock. 1998. *The Americans with Disabilities Act and the Emerging Workforce: Employment of People with Mental Retardation.* Washington, DC: American Association of Mental Retardation.

Francis, Leslie Pickering, and Anita Silvers, eds. 2000. *Americans with Disabilities.* New York: Routledge.

Harris Interactive. 2001. "The Harris Poll #59, October 7, 2000. Conflicting Trends in Employment of People with Disabilities 1986–2000." http://www.harrisinteractive.com/harris_poll/index.asp?PID=121 (cited December 2).

John J. Heldrich Center for Workforce Development. 2001. "The Workforce Investment Act of 1998: A Primer for People with Disabilities." http://www.heldrich.rutgers.edu (cited November 28).

Longmore, Paul K., and Lauri Umansky, eds. 2001. *The New Disability History: American Perspectives (History of Disability).* New York: New York University Press.

Mayerson, Arlene B. 1994. *Americans with Disabilities Act Annotated: Legislative History, Regulations and Commentary.* Deerfield, IL: Clark Boardman Callaghan.

National Council on Disability. 2001. "The Americans with Disabilities Act: Ensuring Equal Access to the American Dream." http://www.ncd.gov/ (cited November 28).

Tysse, John G., ed. 1991. *The Legislative History of the Americans with Disabilities Act.* New York: L. R. P. Publications.

U.S. Census Bureau. 2001. "Disability Statistics." http://www.census.gov/hhes/www/disability.html (cited December 2).

U.S. Department of Labor. 2001. "Office of Disability Employment Policy Publications." http://www.dol.gov/odep/media/reports/main.htm (cited November 28).

Domestic Partner Benefits

Domestic partner benefits are fringe benefits provided by employers to the partners or unmarried spouses of employees, including lesbian and gay employees. The benefits may also be referred to as "spousal equivalent benefits." Possible benefits include health insurance, life insurance, disability insurance, pensions, profit sharing, family and bereavement leave, tuition reimbursement, credit union membership, and travel or relocation expenses. Employers that offer fringe benefits most often extend them to their employees' married spouses and legal dependents, but extending them to domestic partners remains a relatively new concept that is beginning to spread. Domestic partnership does not refer only to same-sex partners; unmarried heterosexual couples are also referred to as domestic partners.

In 1983, *The Village Voice,* a New York City weekly newspaper, became the first employer to offer domestic partner benefits. By 1990, less than two dozen employers provided domestic partner benefits. In 1992, Lotus Development Corporation, a computer company, became the first publicly traded company to offer domestic partner benefits to same-sex partners of its employees. Employers are increasingly recognizing domestic partners, and in 1997 an estimated 13 percent of employers offered some form of domestic partner benefits (KPMG Peat Marwick 1997). Today more than 2,500 employers, including private corporations, universities or colleges, and governments, now provide domestic partners with benefits (Human Rights Campaign 2001).

Although there are federal laws protecting employees from discrimination based on race, gender, age, disability, religion, and marital status, there are no federal laws that provide protections for employees based on sexual orientation. Individual employers, however, have the ability to prohibit sexuality discrimination by implementing nondiscrimination policies that include sexual orientation. Many employers already have polices protecting employees from racial and gender discrimination, and a few are beginning to add protections for lesbian, bisexual, and gay employees. Adopting nondiscrimination policies for gay and lesbian employees most often precedes the adoption of domestic partner benefits because it demonstrates an employer's recognition of equality for lesbian and gay employees in the workplace.

Employees are often the ones actively involved in working to achieve domestic partner benefits in their workplaces. In doing so, they try to convince employers that by not providing domestic partner benefits, they are not paying their employees equally. Benefits often comprise nearly 40 percent of employees' overall compensation. Individual employees who are married with children benefit the most from their benefits package because not only are they receiving the benefits, but their spouse and children are as well. For lesbian and gay employees, the option to marry is not available because legally binding same-sex marriages have not received political support. If domestic partner benefits are not available in a given workplace, then all the gay and lesbian employees who have same-sex partners find only themselves eligible for benefits. Unmarried heterosexual employees who have partners also find that only the employee can receive benefits. Of course, heterosexual couples do have the option to legally marry, whereas same-sex couples do not. The issue of whether to provide domestic partner benefits to both same-sex and unmarried heterosexual couples remains controversial, and many employers prefer to provide them only to same-sex domestic partners. The argument is sometimes made that heterosexual employees in particular may use the domestic partnership provisions fraudulently because they can get married.

Many employers that have not adopted domestic partner benefits argue that providing domestic partner benefits to their employees would greatly increase their benefit costs. These employers believe that an overwhelming number of employees will misuse the benefits, which has led many employers who offer domestic partner benefits to devise eligibility requirements. These requirements often involve the length of time the couple has been living together, along with other forms of proof. In a study of employers offering domestic partner benefits, less than 1 percent of each company's employees applied for the benefits (National Gay and Lesbian Journalist Association 1997). Among employers offering domestic partnership health care benefits, 85 percent reported that they have not experienced an increase in their health care costs (Society for Human Resource Management 1997).

When an employer adopts domestic partnership benefit programs (especially when they are available to both same-sex and heterosexual domestic partners), they are acknowledging that the family is changing. The number of people who are married has been decreasing. More heterosexual individuals choose to form partnerships outside marriage. Same-sex partner households are also on the rise. The Census of 2000 found that there were more than 600,000 same-sex partners sharing a home and creating a family (U.S. Census Bureau 2000).

Monica Bielski

See also Gays at Work; Job Benefits

References and further reading

Anderson, Robert M. 1997. "Domestic Partner Benefits: A Primer for Gay and Lesbian Activists." Pp. 249–260 in *Homo Economics: Capitalism, Community, and Lesbian and Gay Life.* Edited by Amy Gluckman and Betsy Reed. New York: Routledge Press.

Holcomb, Desma. 1997. "Domestic Partner Health Benefits: The Corporate Model vs. the Union Model." Pp. 103–120 in *Laboring for Rights: Unions and Sexual Diversity across Nations.* Edited by Gerald Hunt. Philadelphia: Temple University Press.

Human Rights Campaign. 2001. "Human Rights Campaign Survey." Washington, DC: Human Rights Campaign.

KPMG Peat Marwick. 1997. "Health Benefits Survey." New York: KPMG Peat Marwick.

National Gay and Lesbian Journalist Association. 1997. "Annual Survey." Washington, DC:National Gay and Lesbian Journalist Association.

Society for Human Resource Management. 1997. "Domestic Partner Benefits Mini-Survey." Alexandria, VA: Society for Human Resource Management.

U.S. Census Bureau. 2000. "Same-Sex Couples Sharing a Household." Washington, DC: U.S. Department of Commerce.

Weston, Kath. 1991. *The Families We Choose: Lesbians, Gays, Kinship.* New York: Columbia University Press.

Dos Passos, John (1896–1970)

John Dos Passos was an American poet, essayist, artist, playwright, and biographer, though he is best known for his work as a documentary-style novelist of the 1920s and 1930s. Writing in the social realist style, much of Dos Passos's modernist works examine the changing American society of the early twentieth century, as it becomes captivated by materialistic desires. Much of his work also presents a cynical view of the labor movement, which is characterized as deeply corrupt and in opposition to the interests of the worker.

John Dos Passos was born on January 14, 1896, in Chicago. His childhood was spent in numerous homes across Europe and the United States. As a

American poet, essayist, artist, playwright, and biographer John Dos Passos. Much of Dos Passos's work presented a cynical view of the labor movement. (Library of Congress)

youth, Dos Passos attended various private and boarding schools, both in England and in the United States. In 1912, Dos Passos began his studies at Harvard College.

After his graduation from Harvard, Dos Passos traveled to Europe and in 1917 enlisted as an ambulance driver for France during World War I. His experiences there influenced his bitter critique of the war in his first two novels, *One Man's Initiation* (1917) and *Three Soldiers* (1921). Dos Passos was among the postwar "lost generation" of writers. In 1925, he achieved critical success with his next novel, *Manhattan Transfer* (1925).

Dos Passos's work received acclaim for its social realism, that is, its inclusion of social and political themes. The literary techniques that he used to create such genuine novels were considered groundbreaking. Much of his work wove the fictional tales of his characters among "newsreel" sections, which drew upon pieces of contemporary news stories, popular songs, advertisements, and speeches. Dos Passos also incorporated small biographies of the lives of deceased Americans into his fictional narratives. For example, his novel *The Big Money* provides biographies of (among others) industrialist Henry Ford and the father of industrial engineering, Frederick W. Taylor, to capture the prosperity of the 1920s in which the novel is set (Nanney 1998, 191–193). His most famous work, the trilogy *U.S.A.*, included *The 42nd Parallel* (1930), *1919* (1932), and *The Big Money* (1936). This trilogy examines the lives of his fictional characters amid the grasping forces of a materialist and industrial society. In these works, unions are generally characterized unfavorably as corrupt and racketeering organizations.

Dos Passos underwent a deep transformation in ideology after publishing *U.S.A.*, moving from the political left to the political right. His later fictions were not received with the same acclaim that was garnered by his novels of the 1920s and 1930s, perhaps because of the changed political ideology represented in his work but more likely because of the change in his writing style, which did not use the more innovative literary techniques that he had developed in earlier works. His work in journalism, particularly his coverage of the Spanish Civil War and World War II, was among his more positively received writings after *U.S.A.* His late 1940s contributions to *Life* magazine clarified Dos Passos's cynicism about massive industrial societies and his belief that such societies posed a grave threat to individual liberties. In the novel *Midcentury* (1961), Dos Passos returned to his more acclaimed writing style in a scathing critique of the labor movement, towering business influences, and a consumerist society (Nanney 1998, 201–234). In this well-received work, Dos Passos characterized unions as oppressive, corrupt, and an impediment to the worker's individual freedom. Though John Dos Passos would never return to the level of his earlier successes, he continued to write until his death on September 28, 1970, in Baltimore, Maryland.

Sarah B. Gyarfas

See also Work in Film; Work in Literature

References and further reading

Dos Passos, John. 1961. *Midcentury.* Boston: Houghton, Mifflin.

———. 1996. *U.S.A.* New York: Library of America.

Maine, Barry, ed. 1988. *Dos Passos: The Critical Heritage.* London: Routledge.

Nanney, Lisa. 1998. *John Dos Passos.* New York: Twayne Publishers.
Rosen, Robert C. 1981. *John Dos Passos: Politics and the Writer.* Lincoln: University of Nebraska Press.

The Dot-com Revolution

The dot-com revolution refers to the period spanning the late 1990s through the spring of 2000, when Wall Street, corporate America, the general public, and the media caught a wave of euphoria generated by the Internet and the use of high technology for business purposes. Numerous factors all came together to create an "Internet bubble" of market speculation and frenzied investment, primarily small investors who could use Web-based trading sites to buy and sell stocks easily.

The ensuing stock market boom revolutionized the way businesses operated by providing the capital to invest in new technology. Perhaps more importantly, the dot-com revolution fundamentally changed the way people communicated through Internet-based technologies, such as e-mail, message boards, chat rooms, and others. Thus, despite the failure of most dot-com companies, the transformation continues through the use of technology and the Internet for business purposes.

In its broadest sense, the dot-com revolution served as a massive growth engine for the U.S. economy. For the first time in recent memory, the power and mystique of small, entrepreneurial companies dwarfed that of established corporations. Given the public's willingness to invest in Internet-based startups, their valuations soared.

Finally given the chance at riches gained from stock options and participation in initial public offerings (IPOs), workers flocked to dot-coms, despite the risk involved. Added to the possibility for quick riches, the quirky, decentralized culture of dot-com companies drew Generation X workers in droves. The media added fuel to the mass exodus from the Fortune 500 by regaling readers with stories of office foosball tournaments and game rooms, company-sponsored espresso machines, and a constant state of "business casual" clothing. Dot-com entrepreneurs were also able to promote work as a way of achieving a more spiritual or fulfilling state, which appealed to the sullen masses of workers awash in endless rows of drab, gray cubicles in the nation's large companies. Startups were seen as anti-authoritarian and laid-back, mirroring the lifestyle exuded in northern California since the 1960s.

The dawn of the dot-com revolution is most often linked to the premiere of the first graphics-based Web browser in early 1993, developed by Marc Andreessen, a young computer science student at the University of Illinois, and a team of researchers at the school. The Mosaic browser enabled people to surf the Net more easily and removed much of the "computer geek" mentality associated with the medium, which had ironically been created by the federal government in the late 1960s as an alternative means of communication in case of a catastrophic event. Andreessen's innovation married images, graphics, and text on the Internet and vastly improved its popularity. Soon, people began creating personal homepages, and businesses began using the Net to advertise their products and companies.

After Mosaic was released, Internet traffic increased 341,631 percent (Kaplan 1999). In 1994, Andreessen joined with computer industry veteran Jim Clark to form Netscape, one of the Web's pioneering companies. That same year, *Time* ran its first cover story on the Internet. By early 1995, a *Business Week* survey estimated that 27,000 Websites existed, with the number doubling every two months.

In early August 1995, Netscape went public, and Clark's shares were worth $565 million, making him one of the wealthiest men in the United States and coining the phrase "Internet millionaire." By the end of the year, the company's stock reached $170 a share, making it worth nearly $6.5 billion. Netscape's IPO success turned the Internet into the new Wild West, a place where fantastic wealth could be created—a capitalist nirvana on the western edge of the country, just as it had experienced during the gold rush days in the mid-1800s.

Although Netscape helped make the Internet user-friendly, the company most associated with the dot-com revolution is Amazon.com, an online bookseller and consumer goods store based in Seattle. Founded by Jeff Bezos, a former investment banker, Amazon was the first to use the ".com" suffix. Bezos's "get big fast" attitude with little care about profitability embodied the get rich fast mentality of the Internet. The main tenet of the Amazon way was to forget profits; in fact, Bezos spent more than $100 million a year to build the Amazon brand name.

Bezos became the most celebrated "new economy" cheerleader, particularly after being deemed

Time's "Person of the Year," the fourth-youngest individual ever named to the list. His story was considered the quintessential e-commerce fairytale. Amazon's lasting significance may be as a cultural force. By getting on the Web early, Amazon enabled millions of people to get comfortable with the Internet as a purchasing tool.

Based on Amazon's early success, others founded companies to capitalize on the phenomenal growth rate of the World Wide Web. College-aged entrepreneurs were some of the earliest innovators. For example, Stanford students David Filo and Jerry Yang decided that the Web required a directory to organize the plethora of new sites. In response, they founded Yahoo!, the first major portal, which attracted millions of visitors. Another young computer enthusiast, Pierre Omidyar, believed that a Web-based community could use the Net as a giant flea market. He founded eBay so that people could buy and sell collectibles and other goods. EBay is one of the few dot-com companies to become profitable and has since become the crown jewel of the Internet.

Dot-com mania reached a peak in the late 1990s, when venture capitalists started funding dot-coms based on their ability to take the company public, thus cashing in on the IPO shares. Seemingly ludicrous businesses started getting millions of dollars in seed money from a variety of investors, despite having little more than a bright idea to recommend them. The list of now defunct dot-coms reads like a comedy sketch, ranging from fashion site Boo.com, which "burned" through its $135 million investment before declaring bankruptcy, to online toy retailer eToys, online newspaper LocalBusiness.com, and the self-descriptive FurnitureAndBedding.com. Online grocer Webvan may be the biggest failure in Internet history, running through an estimated $1 billion before shutting down.

Soon, large companies started to get in on the rush. Corporations such as America Online, Cisco Systems, Sun Microsystems, and Oracle began publicizing their Net wares and purchasing startups that could add innovative technology to their portfolios. Microsoft, which had been slow to grasp the importance of the Web, debuted Internet Explorer, MSN Websites, and an online service. Fortune 500 corporations also rushed to implement e-commerce capabilities, put up Websites, and searched for methods to sell their products and services online.

The dot-com revolution coincided with and was stimulated by the year 2000 (Y2K) problem that gripped businesses worldwide. The necessity of purchasing and updating computer systems hinged on the belief that computers would not function properly when the New Year changed from 1999 to 2000. Although the switch did not cause global panic, greatly increased expenditures on corporate information technology systems added to the rationale for Internet spending.

The hysteria surrounding the Net, the get big fast mentality, and the quick grab for IPO money preordained that the bubble would burst. On paper, there was little sense in upstarts like Amazon, Yahoo, and eBay having market capitalization exceeding traditional stalwarts that had long lives on the Fortune 500. People (in many cases, really smart people) actually began to think that building a brand name or creating a flashy Website actually meant more than basic business fundamentals. Rather than adapting technology to enhance business, companies were using technology to create IPO opportunities.

The companies that flamed out at the tail end of the new economy bubble were like kindling for the recession wildfire that gripped the United States at the dawn of the new century. Over the course of one month (March 10, 2000, to April 6, 2000), the Nasdaq stock market lost $1 trillion in value. The tsunami destroyed the dreams of many dot-coms in its wake and startled tech investors back to reality. For employees at startups, from the chief executive officer (CEO) on down, stock options ended up "under water," worthless scraps of paper that would never regain their luster.

In retrospect, people should have seen the downfall coming sooner. Flying in the face of multiple warning signs, too many people still sought a shot at Web wealth and glory, unable to pass on the gamble, despite the long odds. Even after Nasdaq crashed in spring 2000, investors rushed in to buy shares of depressed stocks, many of which would rebound slightly before falling for good. The media (fueled by business cable stations like CNBC, which turned Internet CEOs into celebrities, and the plump ad-soaked tech magazines) made folk heroes out of people like Amazon.com's Bezos and Yahoo's Yang. So many Internet legends were tales of rags-to-riches glory or college students coming up with an idea in their dorm room that by focusing on them, the media made it seem easy.

All of a sudden, seemingly intelligent people (doctors, lawyers, and professors) started writing dot-com business plans in their spare time, figuring that they might be able to strike it rich by riding the venture capital wave out of Silicon Valley and into the IPO spotlight. For those who wanted to make money with less elbow grease, countless "angel" investment firms were set up to get people with money into the tech game. With enough cash, anyone could become a venture capitalist in the late 1990s, even if that person had never set foot inside a high tech startup and didn't know the first thing about building a thriving business.

By the end of 2001, thousands of dot-com companies went bankrupt, and tens of thousands of employees lost their jobs. The massive failure of the new economy and the subsequent trickle of new investments in technology companies, combined with corporate governance scandals and the September 11, 2001, terrorist attacks, sparked a recession that plagued businesses in the early years of the twentieth century. High-tech centers, such as Silicon Valley, San Francisco, Austin, Texas, Washington, D.C., and New York City, have been especially hard hit by the failure of the dot-com revolution.

Despite the meltdown, the high-tech revolution continues, though on a much more modest scale, as traditional businesses use e-commerce and the Internet to meld online and physical storefronts. Companies are using Web-based services and technologies to become more efficient and profitable. It is nearly impossible to find an industry that has not been improved through Internet-based technology, whether it is in education and nonprofits or financial services and manufacturing.

The dot-com revolution ended in early 2000, but innovation continues to propel companies into novel areas that mix business and the Internet. Figures released by the United Nations reveal that there are 655 million registered Internet users worldwide in 2002 and that global e-commerce will top $2.3 billion, doubling the figure from the previous year.

Bob Batchelor

See also Amazon.com; E-commerce; Greenspan, Alan; Layoffs; Postindustrial Workforce; Silicon Valley; Stock Options

References and further reading

Cassidy, John. 2002. *Dot.con: The Greatest Story Ever Sold.* New York: HarperCollins.

Dearlove, Des, and Stephen Coomber. 2001. *Architects of the Business Revolution.* Milford, CT: Capstone.

Kantor, Rosabeth Moss. 2001. *Evolve! Succeeding in the Digital Culture of Tomorrow.* Boston: Harvard Business School Press.

Kaplan, David A. 1999. *The Silicon Boys and Their Valley of Dreams.* New York: Perennial.

Lewis, Michael. 1999. *The New New Thing: A Silicon Valley Story.* New York: Norton.

Perkins, Anthony B., and Michael C. Perkins. 1999. *The Internet Bubble: Inside the Overvalued World of High-Tech Stocks—and What You Need to Know to Avoid the Coming Shakeout.* New York: HarperBusiness.

Public Broadcasting System. 2003. "Life on the Internet." http://www.pbs.org/internet/timeline/timeline-txt.html (cited July 1, 2003).

Spector, Robert. 2000. *Amazon.com: Get Big Fast.* New York: John Wiley.

Tapscott, Don. 1996. *The Digital Economy: Promise and Peril in the Age of Networked Intelligence.* New York: McGraw-Hill.

Downsizing

Downsizing is a relatively new term that emerged in popular vocabulary following the corporate restructuring of the 1980s. The term is commonly used to describe any layoffs or job losses. However, not all layoffs amount to downsizing. Downsizing refers to permanent reductions in an organization's workforce designed to improve efficiency. It does not apply to layoffs that are carried out in response to a weak economy or a decline in business (Wald 1999; Cappelli 2000).

Although temporary layoffs typically come in response to downturns in the economy, downsizing occurs even when the economy is expanding. The American Management Association, which conducts annual surveys on job creation and elimination in large companies, has found that companies continued to eliminate jobs at a steady rate following the recession of 1990–1991. In fact, nearly half of all firms surveyed were cutting jobs from 1998 to 2000—at the height of the late 1990s boom (American Management Association 2000).

Just as downsizing can occur at any time, so it can affect nearly anyone. Blue-collar, production workers have traditionally borne the brunt of permanent layoffs in the manufacturing sector. During the 1980s and especially the early 1990s, downsizing affected a broad range of industries, from manufacturing to services. It also spread to a wide range of occupations, including managers and other white-collar workers (Cappelli 2000).

The phenomenon of downsizing is closely linked to the waves of corporate restructuring that began in the 1980s. Rising competition, new technologies, more demanding shareholders, and other trends in the marketplace forced companies to become more competitive (Cappelli et al. 1997). In response to these pressures, firms have taken steps to restructure operations and cut costs.

The formula for restructuring tends to be the same. Companies break existing divisions into business units that focus more closely on products, services, and customers. They hand more responsibility, as well as accountability, to units far down in the organization. They reengineer business processes by modifying, outsourcing, or eliminating jobs and entire functions. And they reduce layers of middle managers and staff at corporate headquarters (Cappelli et al. 1997). Restructuring is frequently, though not necessarily, accompanied by permanent job losses.

Companies have pursued three types of strategies when downsizing. The first strategy is reducing the number of employees or the "head count" as quickly as possible to achieve short-run financial goals. Common methods include early retirements, buyouts, attrition, and, of course, immediate layoffs. The second strategy takes more time to implement and focuses on eliminating jobs and units rather than specified numbers of workers. Companies accomplish this goal by merging or eliminating functions and units. The third strategy requires systematic change, which involves long-term adjustments in the mission, culture, and processes of the organization. This approach results in an ongoing drive to simplify and improve every business function (Cappelli et al. 1997).

However implemented, downsizing imposes costs on employees. The impact on workers who are laid off is clear. Research shows that many displaced workers with years of tenure experience large and enduring earnings losses (Jacobson, LaLonde, and Sullivan 1993). They also face difficult transitions to new jobs and new careers. Workers who stay with the organization following the downsizing also face painful adjustments. These so-called survivors tend to experience heightened insecurity, increased stress, and new work demands, all of which depress morale (Cappelli et al. 1997).

The impact of downsizing on firms is more difficult to determine. Research suggests that permanent reductions in the workforce can diminish the quality of services and bottom-line financial performance (Cappelli et al. 1997). However, other studies find that downsizing as part of long-term restructuring can improve performance in some establishments. A recent study strongly suggests that the effects on organizational performance are mixed. Companies experience declining sales per employee, an outcome that hurts performance. At the same time, companies benefit from reduced labor costs as a result of job cuts (Cappelli 2000). Although evidence on its effectiveness is contradictory, downsizing is likely to remain a business practice and part of the U.S. work experience for some time.

Neil Ridley

See also Corporate Consolidation and Reengineering; Manufacturing Jobs; Postindustrial Workforce; Recession

References and further reading

American Management Association. 2000. *AMA Survey of Staffing and Structure.* New York: AMA.

Cappelli, Peter. 2000. "Examining the Incidence of Downsizing and Its Effect on Establishment Performance." Cambridge, MA: National Bureau of Economic Research.

Cappelli, Peter, Laurie Bassi, Harry C. Katz, David Knoke, Paul Osterman, and Michael Useem. 1997. *Change at Work.* New York: Oxford University Press.

Committee for Economic Development. 1996. American Workers and Economic Change. Washington, DC: Committee for Economic Development.

Congressional Research Service. 2001. *Corporate Downsizing and Other Layoffs.* Washington, DC: MII Publications.

Jacobson, Louis, Robert LaLonde, and Daniel Sullivan. 1993. *The Costs of Worker Dislocation.* Kalamazoo, MI: W. E. Upjohn Institute for Employment Research.

Wald, Michael. 1999. "Government Downsizing." *Monthly Labor Review* 122, no. 6. Washington, DC: Department of Labor, June.

Drucker, Peter F. (1909–)

Peter F. Drucker is one of the top twentieth-century intellectuals who have made significant contributions to the theory and strategy of work effectiveness and work management. For more than half a century, Drucker has served as an intellectual guide to senior business leaders all over the world. For his outstanding contributions, he has often been called the grandfather of modern management.

Drucker was born in Vienna in 1909 and was educated there and in England. Later he came to the

United States and built a distinguished career as a professor of economics and statistics first, then of history and philosophy, and finally of management and social sciences. Although he received his Ph.D. in public and international law, he is well-known for his independent analysis of politics, economics, business, and society. He has written extensively on these topics and has published more than thirty books and many articles.

How work should be organized and managed to produce results has been Drucker's major interest. His most significant contributions in this area fall in four related areas: (1) business strategy, (2) manufacturing strategy, (3) managing for economic performance, and (4) managing in turbulent times.

Business Strategy

Business in the United States experienced serious turbulence in the 1970s and 1980s. Mergers, acquisitions, and downsizing became key strategies for survival. Executives adopted other approaches as well to enhance the bottom line. Drucker stepped forward to observe that although in most cases the right things were being done, they were *not* producing the desired results. Drucker proposed a solution that he called "theory of the business." He argued that failures were happening because the basic assumptions that drove the behavior of the organizations during their period of success were no longer appropriate, because there were significant changes in the business environment and market demands. The theory of the business that Drucker proposed called on leaders to systematically and periodically check their assumptions about the environment, mission, and core competencies of the business. This periodic reevaluation would help a business to change its product and service offerings to meet the current needs of its customers. For example, IBM's decision to play a leadership role in the personal computer (PC) market is an excellent example of the company's response to a shift in the computer business environment.

Manufacturing Strategy

From the days of the Industrial Revolution, the factory has been a center of economic activity and employment. Therefore, the success of the factories has always had an important impact on the success of the economy. In the 1980s, however, technological change and intense competitive pressure caused many manufacturing companies to falter in productivity. Several concepts of manufacturing principles and processes, such as statistical quality control (SQC) or systems design, were proposed, but no coherent strategy had emerged to guide the thinking of the engineers. Drucker provided a cogent analysis of the key processes being followed by different organizations and suggested a synergistic process in an article on the theory of manufacturing. He recommended that management of people and business economics should be integrated into the total manufacturing process to lower cost and enhance quality. Traditionally, they have existed as separate disciplines, receiving varying degrees of importance, depending on the leaders.

Managing for Economic Performance

Throughout his career, whether teaching, writing, or consulting, Peter Drucker has always reminded his students or clients that economic performance (that is, producing results) is the specific function and the fundamental responsibility of a business. Doing so requires a disciplined approach, and Drucker's *Managing for Results* (1964) is the first book to describe a straightforward approach for achieving results. He recommends a simple three-step process to manage for economic performance: (1) understanding business realities, (2) identifying and focusing on opportunities, and (3) engaging in purposeful performance. According to Drucker, there is only one resource that makes a business distinct or provides a niche in the marketplace—knowledge. Other resources, such as money or physical assets, cannot differentiate a business. Therefore, success in business depends on the ability of the business to use knowledge in a creative way to provide value to the customer. Today, almost forty years after Drucker wrote his book, knowledge management has become an important topic of the executive parlor.

Exploiting outside opportunities is key to business success. Yet, much too often, Drucker observed, managers allocate critical resources to solve only internal problems. Such management practices can only lead to poor results. Maximization of opportunities is key to entrepreneurial success. Focusing on the outside—the market and the customer—is a fundamental requirement of good leadership. And leadership, in Drucker's view, is what differentiates one business from the other.

Managing for results requires that managers know how to allocate resources and reduce cost effectively. According to Drucker, 90 percent of resources are frequently allocated to activities that produce only 10 percent of the results, so a great deal of resource allocation simply leads to waste. Furthermore, executives often work on solving or handling problems of the past, when their precious time is needed to prepare the organization to meet the challenges of the future. A process needs to be in place that will engage leaders in continuous reappraisal and redirection as new environmental trends appear on the horizon.

Business earns money by selling a product to a customer, so deciding on what product to sell is a critical decision. But Drucker places equal importance on two other areas—the market and the distributive channel. These two are outside the business and therefore cannot be modified by the business; therefore managers and workers must acquire a thorough knowledge of the market and the distributive channels, although they are outside the day-to-day reality of the organization. Managers must keep in mind that the distributive channel is also a customer of the business. In essence, the Drucker model says that there must always be a good fit between the product on the one hand and the market and the distributive channel on the other. A poor fit will always result in poor economic performance.

Managing in Turbulent Times

The first two decades following World War II saw unprecedented economic growth in the United States and other nations in Western Europe. Multinational corporations dominated business during this period, with a strategy based primarily on financial control. The business environment was fairly stable. The future was planned more or less as a continuation of the past.

Economic and world events brought sudden changes in the mid-1970s. Inflation, productivity challenges, technology shifts, and global competition all hit the business world at about the same time and made the classical planning methods suddenly obsolete. Peter Drucker's 1980 book, *Managing in Turbulent Times,* was perfectly timed to serve as a guide to executives managing complex businesses.

Maintaining productivity is a fundamental requirement of managers in times of chaotic changes, and it has to be done for four key resources—capital, crucial physical assets, time, and knowledge. Successful companies, such as General Electric and Siemens, have beaten their competition by significantly increasing the productivity of capital, Drucker has noted.

Strategic assignment of critical resources is another effective way of managing in turbulent times. Managers need to be smart about choosing areas of potential results and allocating resources accordingly. In chaotic times, there is a natural tendency to use resources to solve current problems, but the top priority should be the areas of potential opportunities. Drucker's maxim in situations like this has been "Feed the opportunities; starve the problems."

Drucker was also influential in convincing managers to avoid working on issues that had been important in the past but not expected to be profitable in the future. An exit strategy needed to be carefully developed so that resources would be allocated to areas with the highest probability of future success for the business. A critical activity that contributed to GE's success during the Jack Welch period of the early 1990s was called the "work out" program. This activity was designed to eliminate work that no longer met the strategic needs of the corporation. Drucker recommended this approach almost a decade earlier, as he had done in so many cases in the past. Stimulating innovation while managing change is a critical managerial competence needed in turbulent times.

Perhaps the most challenging task for managers is to respond effectively to what Drucker referred to as "unique events" that are unanticipated and therefore cannot be planned for ahead of time. The situation becomes more complex when one has to function in a global business environment. Doing so requires leaders to have a good understanding of the shifts in politics, customer expectations, employee values, population structure and dynamics, currency values, economic trends, technology, and other critical factors. Managers must be prepared to lead in this environment of multidimensional changes and prepare their organizations to function effectively while overseeing a transformation of their organizational culture.

Drucker's Impact on Business and Economic Trends

Drucker was the most prolific writer on business during the last half of the twentieth century. His thinking and teaching significantly influenced business and economic outcomes during this period. Perhaps his most influential contribution is the vision of a knowledge society comprised of knowledge business and knowledge workers. Drucker produced this vision almost thirty years before the knowledge society and the knowledge economy became a reality in the 1990s. The knowledge economy also produced, as Drucker had predicted, a new breed of capitalists, the knowledge workers themselves, because they now own the means of production.

Two other important trends followed the creation of the knowledge economy. Knowledge workers need formal and advanced schooling, and therefore the educational strategy needed to build a stronger link between the world of learning and the world of work. Drucker also predicted that the knowledge economy would be global and borderless and that instead of workers migrating to other countries to find work, now work would migrate to other countries where knowledge workers are available. Globalization of knowledge work has indeed become a reality in the twenty-first century. China, India, and several countries of Europe are now attracting Fortune 500 companies to perform their computer work as well as some research and development activities, with a lower price and a high standard of quality.

Tapas K. Sen

See also Core Competencies; Deming, W. Edwards; High-Performance Workforce; Taylor, Frederick Winslow

References and further reading

Drucker, Peter F. 1964. *Managing for Results.* New York: Harper and Row.

———. 1980. *Managing in Turbulent Times.* Harper and Row.

———. 1981. *Toward the Next Economics and Other Essays.* New York: Harper and Row.

———. 1990. "The Emerging Theory of Manufacturing." *Harvard Business Review* 68, no. 3.

———. 1994. "The Theory of the Business." *Harvard Business Review* 72, no. 5.

Kripalani, Manjeet. 2002. "Calling Bangalore." *Business Week,* November 11.

Drug Testing and Substance Abuse in the Workplace

Alcohol has been part of working life in America since colonial times, when rum was doled out as part of workers' wages. In the last quarter of the twentieth century, drugs joined alcohol as disruptive forces on the job, increasing safety problems and contributing to lost productivity and increased absenteeism. Drugs entered the workplace with less obvious encouragement since they were generally illegal. The generation of the 1960s brought marijuana to work, and as other drugs like cocaine, PCP (phencyclidine), methamphetamine, heroin, and the like swept various communities, it was inevitable that they found their way into the workplace. The annual costs of alcohol abuse alone are estimated at $148 billion, almost double the amount spent for purchasing alcohol (U.S. Department of Health and Human Services 2000, 364–371). Employers responded to these costs with drug and alcohol testing many consider invasions of privacy, but Congress has mandated such testing in the transportation industry. Considered a disease by the medical community, drug and alcohol addiction has been the springboard for a growing treatment industry and for a variety of self-help and support group options, of which Alcoholics Anonymous (AA) is the most well known.

Substance-abusing employees are late to work and absent more often than other employees, make more mistakes and have more accidents, produce less, use more sick leave and file more workers' compensation claims, cause increased medical premiums for their employers, and often endanger themselves and their coworkers. Numerous employers find that an employee assistance program (EAP) more than pays for itself. When an employer offers treatment options rather than simply discharging an employee with a drug and/or alcohol problem, the risks and costs to the employer are reduced, and valuable employees are retained (Bureau of National Affairs 1986). Some companies report a 60–85 percent decrease in absenteeism among abusing employees when treatment is offered, along with a 45–75 percent decrease in workplace accidents (Inaba and Cohen 1993, 219–220).

Certain occupations have long been associated with drinking on the job. Drinking was not only accepted but deemed part of the costs of a job. Providing alcohol to workers building the first stone government building in Albany, New York, in 1656 ran almost 6 percent of the total building costs. Drinking bonded workers together in olden days, and in modern times military personnel, journalists, automobile assembly-line workers and building tradespeople retain a reputation for mixing alcohol and work. Professional and managerial employees are often expected to drink at the business lunch (Sonnenstuhl 1996, 3–6). Contrary to popular stereotypes, most abusers and addicts are not living in the streets but are functional members of society, as long as their need for drugs or alcohol is being filled. For many, filling that need involves not only the illegal activity of buying drugs but often criminal activity to raise the money for ever-increasing drug costs.

There is continuing debate about legalizing drugs, partly because alcohol and nicotine are legal, with Prohibition, that experiment in banning alcohol by constitutional amendment (1919–1933), cited as proof of the failure of proscription. Although Prohibition brought about a rise in organized crime as a source of illegal liquor for those who wanted it, it is also true that cirrhosis of the liver declined by almost two-thirds as one of the leading causes of death, domestic abuse went down, and there were fewer automobile accidents (Inaba and Cohen 1993, 145–146). Legalizing drugs would, in the opinion of proponents, allow regulation and remove the criminal aspect with its related violence. Critics of legalization ask if such problematic drugs like crack cocaine and PCP would be included on the legalization list and if the experience with legalized alcohol and nicotine does not suggest that legalization makes use and abuse more attractive? The alcohol industry spends over $1 billion a year on advertising; in a survey of fifth- and sixth-grade children, 59 percent could correctly identify a brand of beer from an edited commercial (U.S. Department of Health and Human Services 2000, 412–423).

In response to growing problems at work, Congress adopted the Drug-Free Workplace Act in 1988, mandating employers to ensure that their workplaces were drug-free. Many employers began testing for drug and alcohol use; court cases and workplace arbitrations have laid out three general areas where testing is legally appropriate: job applicants can be tested if the applicant has been offered the job and if all applicants are treated similarly; testing is allowed in the event of an accident; and testing is allowed in the event of impaired job performance observed by management. Random testing, except as mandated by legislation, is generally viewed as an invasion of privacy by the courts, except where there are critical safety or national security issues. Random testing has been allowed for employees with national security clearances, police and prison officers, and employees at chemical weapons and nuclear power plants (Repa 2000, 18–20 [chapter 6]).

In 1994 Congress adopted drug and alcohol random testing requirements for safety-sensitive employees in the transportation industry. Employees who test "dirty" are evaluated and, if appropriate, offered treatment. If there is no indication of a substance abuse addiction, they may simply be terminated for using prohibited substances. Early concerns about the reliability of tests have faded as newer technology reduces the margin for error.

Treatment for alcohol or drug addiction varies. Expensive hospital-based programs have often been found to be less effective than social-model programs that incorporate the twelve steps developed by AA and applied to many other addictions. Social-model programs are less costly than hospital-based treatment programs and are thus favored by insurers. They often use recovering addicts/alcoholics on their staff.

Some courts, citing AA's reliance on a "higher power," have ruled that the AA fellowship is religious in nature. AA has also been criticized for its requirement of total abstinence from alcohol (and Narcotics Anonymous's requirement of total abstinence from drugs); other programs attempt to turn alcoholics into moderate drinkers.

Albert Vetere Lannon

See also Outplacement; Stress and Violence in the Workplace

References and further reading

Alcoholics Anonymous. 2001. *Alcoholics Anonymous: The Story of How Many Thousands of Men and Women Have Recovered from Alcoholism.* 4th ed. New York: Alcoholics Anonymous World Services.

Bureau of National Affairs Staff. 1986. *Alcohol and Drugs in the Workplace: Costs, Controls, and Controversies.* Washington, DC: Bureau of National Affairs.

Elkhouri, Frank, and Edna Elkhouri. 1993. *Resolving Drug Issues.* Washington, DC: Bureau of National Affairs.

Inaba, Darryl S., and William E. Cohen. 1993. *Uppers, Downers, All Arounders: Physical and Mental Effects of Psychoactive Drugs.* 2nd ed. Ashland, OR: CNS Productions.

Repa, Barbara Kate. 2000. *Your Rights in the Workplace.* 5th ed. Berkeley: Nolo Press.

Sonnenstuhl, William J. 1996. *Working Sober: The Transformation of an Occupational Drinking Culture.* Ithaca, NY: ILR Press.

U.S. Department of Health and Human Services. 2000. *Tenth Special Report to the U. S. Congress on Alcohol and Health.* Washington, DC: U.S. Department of Health and Human Services, Public Health Service, National Institutes of Health, National Institute on Alcohol Abuse and Alcoholism.

Dunlop Commission

This influential national commission was formed in 1993 by the labor and commerce secretaries of the United States to address the need for modern, new approaches to labor relations and policy in the United States. Chaired by respected former labor commissioner and Harvard University faculty dean John Dunlop, the commission published a final report in 1995 that addressed the importance of a strong workforce for the United States' economic future and issued ten major recommendations. They included enhancing workplace productivity through cooperation between bosses and workers, reducing unneeded conflict and delay in negotiations between labor and management, and helping to ensure that workplace problems are resolved directly by the parties themselves, if at all possible, rather than the courts or government. Although the report went too far for some in management and not far enough for many in organized labor, it focused policy and public debate on improving equity and productivity in the workplace. The report earned long-standing influence among many officials, managers, union leaders, employers, and experts in the labor management and labor policy fields.

The report made a number of noteworthy recommendations, as judged by their influence over time. The commission supported changing the 1935 National Labor Relations Act (Wagner Act) to encourage greater labor-management cooperation and employee participation in decisions and called for greater employee participation in key workplace topics regulated by public law, such as workplace health and safety. The Dunlop Commission also encouraged unions and professional associations to expand and diversify the services and benefits provided to workers, the approach used in the early twenty-first century by a number of professional and trade unions.

In the area of worker representation and collective bargaining—the process by which unions and professional associations negotiate work standards, pay, and benefits for their members—the report stated its concern about a number of trends. Many new collective bargaining agreements were enacted in a highly adversarial environment, too many workers were discharged or discriminated against for exercising their rights to organize, as many as one-third of workplaces voted to be represented by a union but did not obtain a collective bargaining agreement, and nationally, far more workers would like to belong to a union than were ever offered the chance to join one. The commission recommended a series of steps to address this erosion of worker rights, including increased penalties for violations of law, reductions in delays in the collective bargaining process, stronger protections against employee discharge, and a strong federal presence in the mediation and arbitration of the first union contract in a workplace. Under the Clinton administration, the National Labor Relations Board made progress in shortening the time period from a "yes" vote for a union to the actual contract. The commission also recommended expanded use of mediation, arbitration, and other dispute resolution tools to resolve workplace disputes and widen participation in key employer-worker concerns.

The Occupational Safety and Health Administration (OSHA) and other major regulatory bodies were encouraged to develop guidelines that included greater employee participation. The commission also recommended that more study and investigation take place regarding the growth of part-time and contingent work, among workers who wish to work full-time and enjoy health benefits.

Herbert A. Schaffner

See also Arbitration; Collective Bargaining; Democratic Socialism; Employee Stock Ownership; Fair Labor Standards Act; Job Benefits; Labor Force; Pensions; Workplace Safety

References and further reading

Kochan, Thomas. 1995. "Using the Dunlop Report to Full Advantage: A Strategy for Achieving Mutual Gains." MIT Working Paper No. 95-003WP.

U.S. Department of Commerce and U.S. Department of Labor. 1995. *Final Report, Dunlop Commission on the Future of Worker-Management Relations.* Washington, DC: U.S. Department of Commerce and U.S. Department of Labor. (Cathwerwood Libarary Electronic Archive, Cornell School of Industrial and Labor Relations, www.ilr.cornell.edu/library/e_archive).

E

Earned Income Tax Credit

The federal earned income tax credit (EITC) program was developed and established by the U.S. government in 1975 to help low-income families cope with high Social Security and Medicare payroll taxes and decrease poverty. It has enjoyed high marks for effectiveness and enjoys bipartisan political support at the national and state levels. The EITC is often referred to as the "making work pay" policy because it is grounded in the theory that every family that has an adult working full-time deserves to live above the poverty line. Nearly 20 million families and individuals filing federal income tax returns—roughly one tax return in six—claim the federal EITC. Congress and the White House have expanded the income and family criteria three different times since 1975 (in 1986, 1990, and 1993) to allow more working Americans to participate, including those without children. Since 1997, fifteen states have joined the federal government in providing incentives to work by allowing poor families to be eligible for a state EITC in addition to their federal tax credits.

The EITC is refundable at the federal level and in most states. Based on income from employment and family size, a family is eligible for a particular amount of money in credit. If the family's credit amount exceeds their tax liability, the family would receive a refund in the form of a check. Unlike other benefits, the EITC allows families' credit eligibility to increase as income increases, until they reach a specified maximum credit benefit. Once a family's income increases enough to afford them their maximum benefit level, the value of their credit decreases. The family is still eligible for some credit, however, until its earnings reach a particular amount. For example, a family of two or more children in 1999 would have received forty cents per dollar earned until their income reaches $9,540, at which time the family will be eligible for $3,816 in credit. As the income of that family continues to increase, the credit decreases until the family's income is $30,580 at which time the credit is entirely phased out (Center on Budget and Policy Priorities 1999).

Even with minimum wage increases, the regressive nature of most state taxes is enough to push working families into poverty. Although the federal EITC provides help in defraying the cost of federal income taxes, low-income people still pay a disproportionate amount of their income in state and local income taxes. As a response to this problem, fifteen states have supplemented the federal EITC with their own state EITCs: Colorado, the District of Columbia, Illinois, Iowa, Kansas, Maine, Maryland, Massachusetts, Minnesota, New Jersey, New York, Oregon, Rhode Island, Vermont, and Wisconsin. The state EITC can be either refundable or nonrefundable. Nonrefundable EITCs offset a family's tax liability until it reaches zero. If a family's credit exceeds its tax liability, that amount is forfeited, whereas with refundable credits, a family would receive that money in the form of an actual check.

A significant body of research has been conducted on the EITC, largely confirming its economic and social benefits. A 1998 study by Northwestern University economists Bruce Meyer and Dan Rosenbaum found that a large share of the increase in employment of single mothers since the mid-1980s can be attributed to expansions of the EITC. According to their study, *Welfare, the Earned Income Tax Credit, and the Labor Supply of Single Mothers* (1998), expanding the EITC accounted for more than half of the increase in single mothers who went to work between 1984 and 1996, a larger effect than all other factors combined.

A series of reports by a leading poverty think tank show that the EITC is one of the federal government's most effective programs for fighting poverty (Porter, Primus, Rawlings, and Rosenbaum 1998). Because the EITC is targeted to working families with low incomes and because its largest benefits go to working families below the poverty line, it is more likely to lift families out of poverty than programs that provide their largest benefits to families with little or no earnings. Data from the Census Bureau show that in 1998, the EITC lifted more than 4.8 million people in low-income working families above the poverty line. Of this number, more than half—2.6 million—were children. The EITC lifts more children out of poverty than all other means-tested benefit programs (including food stamps and housing subsidies) combined.

During the mid-1990s, some members of Congress and outside organizations publicized concerns about the relatively high rates of error and fraud (20.7 percent) in tax returns requesting the EITC. The Internal Revenue Service (IRS) investigated the rates of error and fraud and found that although a small percentage of returns were prepared fraudulently by individuals seeking to earn a credit who did not qualify, the vast majority of incorrect returns were filled out in error caused by taxpayer mistakes and misunderstandings in filling out the form. Federal laws passed in 1997 contained a series of measures designed to reduce error and fraud that observers to date regard as successful in reducing the error rates.

Herbert A. Schaffner

See also Minimum Wage; Wage Gap; Wage Tax

References and further reading

Greenstein, Robert, and Isaac Shapiro. 1998. *New Research Findings on the Effects of the Earned Income Tax Credit.* Washington, DC: Center on Budget and Policy Priorities.

Johnson, Nicholas. 1999. *A Missouri Earned Income Tax Credit Would Build on the Strengths of the Federal Credit.* Washington, DC: Center on Budget and Policy Priorities.

Meyer, Bruce D., and Dan Rosenbaum. 1998. *Welfare, the Earned Income Tax Credit, and the Labor Supply of Single Mothers.* Evanston, IL Northwestern University.

Mishel, Lawrence, Jared Bernstein, and John Schmitt. 1999. *The State of Working America: 1998–1999.* Ithaca, NY: ILR Press.

Porter, Kathryn, Wendell Primus, Lynette Rawlings, and Esther Rosenbaum. 1998. *Strengths of the Safety Net: How the EITC, Social Security, and Other Government Programs Affect Poverty.* Washington, DC: Center on Budget and Policy Priorities.

Schaffner, Herbert A., and Carl E., Van Horn. 2002. *A Nation at Work: The Heldrich Guide to the American Workforce.* New Brunswick, NJ: Rutgers University Press.

Earnings and Education

An individual's earnings tend to rise with the amount and quality of his or her education. Consequently, education is a highly prized commodity. It is important to the individual worker, who must view his or her decisions regarding how much education to pursue as a fundamental indicator of future earnings. Similarly, education is highly valued by employers, who interpret the educational level of their workforce as an indicator of company productivity and, by extension, profit. The positive relationship between education and earnings offers strong support to arguments for increasing not only the quantity of schooling but also its quality. Finally, education is of tremendous importance to the overall society, for it serves as an investment toward the achievement of enhanced global competitiveness and a higher standard of living.

The wide distribution of earnings in the labor market is explained, in part, by variations in individuals' levels of education. In 1997, the average hourly wage of Americans with less than a high school degree was just $8.23. That is just over one-third of the average hourly wage of Americans with an advanced (graduate) degree, who earn an average of $24.09 an hour. Americans with a high school degree average an hourly wage of $11.03, those with some college receive $12.44, and those with a college degree earn $18.41 an hour (Mishel, Bernstein, and Schmitt 1999, 156).

The positive relationship between earnings and

education has received substantial research attention—most notably from such economists as Gary Becker. He explained this correlation between education and earnings within a simple investment framework in his classic text, *Human Capital.* In this work, Becker compared the immediate costs of further education with future gains. With greater quantities of education, an individual's skills are enhanced and so too is his or her productivity. This greater productivity is reflected in higher earnings, and thus the costs associated with obtaining an education are recovered.

Americans with a high school degree earn an average hourly wage of $11.03, while those with some college receive $12.44, and those with a college degree earn $18.41 an hour. (Paul Barton/Corbis)

One application of Becker's theory of human capital lies in the example of the decision-making process of an individual considering whether to pursue a college education. In this analysis, the primary direct costs of education are the costs of tuition and books, and the primary indirect costs are forgone earnings during the period as a student. If these total costs are less than the expected gains in lifetime earnings from holding a bachelor's degree (in today's dollars), then one would expect the individual to pursue further education. Certainly, other factors, such as values, family expectations, and mental ability, influence an individual's consumption decisions for education. For example, an individual's desire to pursue more education is expected to lessen as he or she reaches higher levels of education because at some point, an individual's productivity gains from education will be limited by his or her inherent intellectual ability.

Jacob Mincer, another pioneer in the development of human capital theory, identified three advantages associated with higher education—higher wages, greater employment stability, and greater potential for pay raises. A more highly educated individual will capture a higher wage, thus making his or her exit from employment more costly. Consequently, more highly educated workers are associated with both more hours on the job and less chance of turnover, making them an attractive candidate to receive job training. Job training, in turn, enhances skills, which increase productivity—further enhancing the return on the initial educational investment.

The *quality* of education is an important determinant on future earnings, more so than the *quantity* of education one receives. A 1998 study by David Card and Alan Krueger found that decreases in the pupil-teacher ratio, an indicator of school quality, are associated with increases in the returns on education (Card and Krueger 1992). Indeed, concerns over poor quality of schooling, particularly in the nation's poorer school districts, have led to grassroots movements across the states for a more equitable financing of public education.

In addition to quantity and quality, the type of education undertaken must also be considered when assessing gains on earnings. For example, returns on education are particularly profitable for students in relatively lucrative fields such as computer science and engineering. Data from the U.S. Department of Education reveal that students in these fields receive a starting salary that exceeds the median starting salary of all college graduates by 35.8 percent (U.S. Department of Education, National Center for Education Statistics 1998).

Human capital theory has a number of implications. First, given this positive correlation between education and earning, a decrease in the cost of education leads to an increased consumption of education. One study has found that an increase in the cost of college by $1,000 leads to a decrease in enrollment by 16 percent (McPherson and Schapiro 1991). Governments, seeking to enhance the quality and productivity of their workforces, have long recognized this simple supply-and-demand effect. Consequently, public policy has been crafted to achieve the desirable effects produced by increased consumption of education—for example, the provision of grants and low-interest student loans. This connection also suggests that the most frequent recipients of high earnings are those who can afford the initial educational investments. The cost of education is greater for those who do not have the funds on hand but instead must seek loans. Thus poorer individuals, who must pay the basic costs of education plus the interest to finance it, pay more for education than wealthier individuals, who avoid the interest cost. Given their comparatively lower costs for education, the wealthiest individuals tend to consume greater quantities of education, further reinforcing the existing income distribution.

Second, applications of the human capital theory are evident in the concentrated consumption of education among the young. Individuals are more likely to consume education in their youth because they will then have a longer period in the workforce during which to make a return on their investment. If an eighteen year old and a sixty-five year old each begin college, the eighteen year old will have a longer career over which to recover the costs of education and, most likely, turn a profit.

Third, given that the return on education is enhanced by the length of time in the workforce, those individuals who expect to have greater continuity in the labor force can expect the greatest return on their education investment. Women's traditional role as caretaker causes great disruption in their labor force participation. Consequently, women tend to have fewer years in the workforce over which to recapture the costs of their educational investment, and thus their return on education can be expected to be less than that of men. U.S. women in their thirties spend more than three times as much time out of the labor force than men in their thirties (Kaufman and Hotchkiss 2000, 380).

Discrimination plays an important role in individuals' investment decisions. If they believe they will be subjected to future discrimination in the labor market, they will likely perceive their return on any educational investment to be lower than that of an unaffected individual. Such diminished future benefits of education may diminish an individual's willingness to pursue further education.

Another explanation for the positive relationship between education and earnings rests on the application of education as a proxy for productivity. Within the screening framework, an individual's productivity is difficult to quantify, and so employers must look instead to educational attainment as an indicator of such desirable worker qualities as intelligence, commitment, and communication. Some research has indicated that although earnings grow with each additional year of schooling, this trend jumps most dramatically for certain important years, such as the completion of year twelve and sixteen, which generally indicate the receipt of high school and college credentials respectively. This finding suggests that gains on earnings can be explained jointly by the human capital theory and the screening method. One study hypothesized that if the theory of human capital were accurate, then two sets of recent college graduates, both majoring in economics but one seeking employment in a related field and another seeking employment in an unrelated field, would earn different starting salaries (Miller and Volker 1984). However, both groups earned similar salaries, suggesting that it was not the specific skills learned in college that determined their earnings but rather their completion of the program that signaled other desirable qualities (most likely, the ability to be trained) to the employers.

Indeed, a 1995 survey conducted by the Bureau of Labor Statistics indicated that employees with higher levels of education were more likely to be the beneficiaries of employer-provided training than lesser-educated employees, thus further concentrating the impact of an individual's earlier education decisions on his or her earnings. The study reported that over a six-month period, employees with a high school diploma or less received 10.9 hours of formal training from their employers. Not surprisingly, employees with a bachelor's degree or more received 16.1 hours of formal training (or 48 percent more than the lower educated group) over the same period (Frazis et al. 1998).

The impact of education on earnings, or the education-earnings premium, has increased in recent decades. One study found that each additional year of schooling yielded an increase in wages of 6.2 percent in 1979, but the same education investment increased earnings in 1993 by nearly 10 percent (Ashenfelter and Rouse 1999). Certainly, Americans in different educational groups have experienced vastly different changes in their real wages between 1979 and 1997. Those with less than a high school degree have seen their real wages decline by 26.2 percent between 1979 and 1997, whereas those with an advanced degree have enjoyed real wage gains of 12.4 percent over the same period. Americans with a high school degree or some college (but no degree) have also experienced declines in their real wages in this period, by 11.7 percent and 8.6 percent, respectively. The only other group to gain in real wages over this period has been Americans with college degrees, gaining 5.6 percent.

The heightened wage vulnerability of the lower-educated groups in the United States has been influenced by a number of factors. First, the advancement of technology in virtually all sectors has increased the need for educated workers, thus driving up the wages of that group and leaving the less educated behind. Second, the sectoral restructuring of the U.S. economy has shifted the lower-educated groups away from high-paying manufacturing jobs and into lower-paying service industry positions. Third, the trend of deunionization in recent decades has hit the lower-educated groups most severely. A falling minimum wage and an increase in import competition has also threatened this group's wages since the 1970s (Mishel, Bernstein, and Schmitt 1999).

The education-earnings relationship is an important foundation of many key social and economic policies in the United States. The government's investments in the education of its workforce (or future workforce) are evident in major investments in public schooling, state universities, community colleges, and the provision of federal student aid, to name a few. The government's deep investment in education speaks, in part, to its recognition of the positive relationship between education and earnings. If education at the individual level increases one person's earnings, then education at the societal level raises a nation's global competitiveness and the standard of living for its citizens.

Sarah B. Gyarfas

See also Education Reform and the Workforce

References and further reading

Ashenfelter, Orley, and Cecilia Rouse. 1999. "Schooling, Intelligence, and Income in America: Cracks in the Bell Curve." New York: National Bureau of Economic Research, Working Paper 6902.

Becker, Gary S. 1975. *Human Capital.* 2nd ed. New York: National Bureau of Economic Research.

Card, David, and Alan Krueger. 1992. "Does School Quality Matter? Returns to Education and the Characteristics of Public Schools in the U.S." *Journal of Political Economy* 100, no.1 (February): 1–40.

Frazis, Harley, Maury Gittleman, Michael Horrigan, and Mary Joyce. 1998. "Results from the 1995 Survey of Employer-Provided Training." *Monthly Labor Review* 12, no. 6 (June): 3–17.

Kaufman, Bruce E., and Julie L. Hotchckiss. 2000. "Education, Training, and Earnings Differentials: The Theory of Human Capital." Pp. 337–406 in *The Economics of Labor Markets.* 5th ed. Fort Worth, TX: The Dryden Press.

Kosters, Marvin H, ed. 1991. *Workers and their Wages: Changing Patterns in the United States.* Washington, DC: AEI Press.

McPherson, Michael S., and Morton Owen Schapiro. 1991. "Does Student Aid Affect College Enrollment? New Evidence on a Persistent Controversy." *American Economic Review* 81, no. 1 (March): 309–318.

Miller, Paul W., and Paul A. Volker. 1984. "The Screening Hypothesis: An Application of the Wiles Test." *Economic Inquiry* 22, no. 1 (January): 121–127.

Mincer, Jacob. 1974. *Schooling, Experience, and Earnings.* New York: National Bureau of Economic Research.

Mishel, Lawrence, Jared Bernstein, and John Schmitt. 1999. *The State of Working America: 1998–1999.* Ithaca, NY: ILR Press.

Thurow, Lester. 1975. *Generating Inequality.* New York: Basic Books.

U.S. Congress. 2000. "Investment in Education: Private and Public Returns." Joint Economic Committee Study. Washington, DC: U.S. Congress:

U.S. Department of Education, National Center for Education Statistics. 1998. *Condition of Education 1998.* NCES 98–013. Washington, DC: U.S. Department of Education.

E-commerce

Electronic commerce, or "e-commerce," is a term broadly used to describe transactions conducted over the Internet, whether completed by individuals, organizations, or companies. E-commerce is usually used to refer to individual purchases made via the World Wide Web, though it is also applicable for business-to-business applications, such as selling inventory online or general procurement activities.

Before e-commerce could become a phenomenon, the general public first had to become acquainted and comfortable with the Internet. Marc Andreessen and a team of computer scientists at the University of Illinois cleared the first hurdle to mass acceptance in 1993, when they introduced the Mosaic browser. Mosaic married graphics and images to the predominantly text-based World Wide

Web and made usage more easy through point-and-click access.

Based on the tremendous success of Mosaic, Internet users multiplied geometrically. The Web grew so quickly that the potential for commercializing it became a reality. Countless entrepreneurs founded Internet-based startup companies, funded by Silicon Valley venture capitalists. The feeding frenzy for startups reached a peak after several early innovators filed initial public offerings (IPO) and turned their founders into paper millionaires. Corporations also jumped into the mix, funding startups on their own and acquiring technology firms that would expand their capabilities. Internal corporate information technology departments gained power within businesses, and investments in this area skyrocketed.

The company that embodied both the Internet stock market bubble and the promise of the dot-com revolution was Amazon.com. Founded by Jeff Bezos, a former investment banker, the Seattle-based company sold books online and then expanded into other consumer goods, including music, movies, clothing, and much more. Initially, Bezos thought that selling books via the Web would exploit the power of the Internet, since the company would not have to stock inventory.

Bezos adopted a "get big fast" mentality, which emphasized building Amazon's brand name, despite the negative effect it had on earnings. Bezos saw the battle as one of market share, not profitability, and other Web entrepreneurs and investors followed suit. Soon, nearly every industry had Internet-based startups fighting with traditional competitors, and any corporation on the Fortune 500 was suddenly deemed stodgy if it didn't have a viable Web component.

For online businesses, the Internet held several built-in advantages, including a global audience, greater product selection, and focused marketing that could be quickly tailored to individual shoppers. As consumers became more Web-savvy, e-commerce grew rapidly, doubling every year throughout the late 1990s. In 1998, online retailers sold $7.2 billion in merchandise, up 50 percent over the previous year. Amazon alone topped $1 billion in 1998, spurred by a strong holiday shopping season. America Online also generated $1.2 billion in the holiday season. These figures scared traditional retailers into pushing their own online capabilities. The thought was that if a company did not find a way to sell goods and services online, it would be destined for history's dustbin.

Corporations also rushed to establish e-commerce sites in the late 1990s. Business-to-business (B2B) e-commerce, or electronic transactions between companies, was hyped as the future of corporate America. Long the U.S. business bellwether, General Electric (GE) soon grasped the significance of the Internet, despite some early resistance. GE chief executive officer Jack Welch caught e-commerce fever with a vengeance. In early 1999, he demanded the company become an e-business and directed the company's top 500 executives to execute that goal within several months. Adopting the famed GE competitiveness, the plan was dubbed "destroy yourbusiness.com." When he charted out GE's advantages over dot-coms, Welch realized that the company wouldn't have to increase advertising or build warehouses, and GE's Six Sigma quality assurance program already put it ahead of the curve. GE would use its size to its advantage.

Welch understood that large corporations did not want upstart dot-coms getting between themselves and their customers, especially when big companies could build or implement technology on their own. For example, GE Aircraft Engines built a procurement Website by hiring a cadre of 125 programmers, knowing full well that it already had a slew of paying customers. As a result, by December 1999 all 500 of GE Aircraft Engine's suppliers replaced their traditional delivery scheduling and billing with online systems through sites GE programmers built for them.

GE's Global eXchange Services (GXS) assembled online exchanges and auctions. Welch fueled the growth of GXS by investing several hundred million dollars in the unit, which provides software, infrastructure systems, and consulting services to companies that want to build online exchanges. In short order, GXS became the largest B2B community in the world, gaining 100,000 trading partners, including 17,000 suppliers, and handling 1 billion transactions and accounts for $1 trillion in goods and services a year.

By applying technology to its own internal operations, GE realized $150 million of benefits in 2000. GE also took significant steps to sell online, and the revenues easily placed it as one of the top e-commerce companies in the world—if not the top. The company sold $7 billion online in 2000.

In 2000, U.S. Census Bureau analysts showed that B2B e-commerce accounted for 94 percent of all e-commerce transactions. The manufacturing arena alone reported $777 billion in e-commerce shipments for the year. E-commerce is an attractive method for selling goods and services for companies of all sizes because it reduces the overhead costs associated with conducting business transactions. Sending an order online over the Internet is cheaper, faster, and more convenient than completing the same deal via the mail or phone. Even security issues, which initially made companies hesitant to send sensitive data over the Internet, have been greatly alleviated. As a matter of fact, resolving security issues has become an important online business sector.

The economic recession gripping the United States in the early years of the twenty-first century slowed e-commerce, despite its geometric growth in the late 1990s. Some estimates show online retail sales falling for the first time in the third quarter of 2002, basically keeping in line with the sluggish state of the world economy. Online sales for the quarter reached $17 billion, down from $20 billion in each of the first two in 2002. E-commerce stalwarts Amazon and eBay continued to post impressive gains, however. Amazon's quarterly sales reached $851 million, up 33 percent over the same period in 2001, and eBay revenues hit $3.77 billion, jumping 60 percent.

Interestingly, in its quarterly report on e-commerce trends, the U.S. Commerce Department reported that third-quarter 2002 online sales increased 7.8 percent from the previous quarter to $11.06 billion. The government survey concluded that the figure constituted a 34.3 percent increase from the third quarter of 2001, the largest e-commerce year-to-year gain since the first three months of 2001, when sales rose 42 percent.

These kinds of contrasting statistics reveal the inconsistencies inherent in trying to calculate e-commerce revenues. The definition of what constitutes e-commerce is broad, which hinders entirely accurate statistics about its overall impact on the national and global economies. Different analysts use varying methods for calculating total sales, but they estimate that online sales accounted for approximately $50 billion to $60 billion in revenue in 2001. Experts expect the figure for 2002 to top $72 billion, a 41 percent increase from the previous year. E-commerce leaders anticipate that sales will continue to expand through 2007, but at a more measured pace than in the early years of the new century.

For e-commerce to grow faster, companies will have to gain market share in industries where no strong foothold has yet been established, such as new automobile sales. For example, most vehicle buyers still want to visit a dealership to complete the transaction. These kinds of changes, however, will only occur as the buying public becomes more confident in big-ticket purchasing via the Web. Also, since the dot-com meltdown eliminated hundreds of online retailers and other technology companies, heightened consumer suspicion will have to be overcome as well.

Traditional sales dwarf those made online, which account for only 1 to 1.5 percent of total retail sales, but the Internet's percentage of overall retail sales in the United States is increasing. Online retail sales growth rate also outstrips the percentage offline. Companies like Bed Bath and Beyond and Lowe's are melding their online and traditional sales efforts to post significant gains on the Web.

Some of the most successful e-commerce organizations are catalog retailers. With existing warehouses, logistics operations, and call-center locations, catalog companies have the built-in infrastructure that enables them to thrive online. The strongest retail e-commerce markets at the turn of the twenty-first century are book sales, music and video sales, travel, and event tickets.

The Internet is a technological marvel, but as the Web was commercialized, the hype overtook reality. Too many people began viewing the Internet as a way to quick riches, and e-commerce was at the heart of the effort. Rather than use the Web as an additional tool for selling goods and services, startups believed that they were "revolutionizing" business.

Backed by venture capitalists and a general public willing to buy tech stocks, e-commerce companies soon realized that a sustainable business required much more than a jazzy Web site. When the Internet bubble burst, many of these companies were exposed as little more than empty shells. It is little wonder that some of the best examples of how e-commerce has transformed business are from large corporations like GE, Hilton Hotels, and Home Depot. Using size to their advantage, these companies employed e-commerce to squeeze costs out of their infrastructures and make their organizations more efficient.

In the future, e-commerce will remain a vital part of the economy as technological innovations push into new areas. Wireless communications over the Web, nanotechnology, and online gaming are some examples of industries that will necessitate an e-commerce infrastructure. Both new startups and established companies are looking at these opportunities, along with a host of others, to generate new e-commerce business.

Bob Batchelor

See also Dot-com Revolution; Greenspan, Alan; Layoffs; Postindustrial Workforce; Silicon Valley; Stock Options

References and further reading

Cassidy, John. 2002. *Dot.con: The Greatest Story Ever Sold.* New York: HarperCollins.

Dearlove, Des, and Stephen Coomber. 2001. *Architects of the Business Revolution.* Milford, CT: Capstone.

Kantor, Rosabeth Moss. 2001. *Evolve! Succeeding in the Digital Culture of Tomorrow.* Boston: Harvard Business School Press.

Kaplan, David A. 1999. *The Silicon Boys and Their Valley of Dreams.* New York: Perennial.

Lewis, Michael. 1999. *The New New Thing: A Silicon Valley Story.* New York: W. W. Norton.

Perkins, Anthony B., and Michael C. Perkins. 1999. *The Internet Bubble: Inside the Overvalued World of High-Tech Stocks—and What You Need to Know to Avoid the Coming Shakeout.* New York: HarperBusiness.

Spector, Robert. 2000. *Amazon.com: Get Big Fast.* New York: John Wiley.

Tapscott, Don. 1996. *The Digital Economy: Promise and Peril in the Age of Networked Intelligence.* New York: McGraw-Hill.

Education Reform and the Workforce

Throughout history, American children have received preparation for the workforce from public schooling. Initially, the U.S. educational system schooled only the elite, leaving children from the poorer classes to look to apprenticeships for their career education. As labor force training became more respected and as business and growing technology began to demand a more highly skilled workforce, apprenticeships gave way to vocational education. This form of schooling, often separate from traditional academic education, served to connect students with the needs of the labor market and train them specifically for entry into careers of their choice. Vocational education has developed over time into a highly funded and regulated means of training future workers. Increasing collaboration among business leaders and training providers has established an expanding system of vocational education in the United States. Recent legislation has both expanded and amended career education in the United States while also changing the way the educational system and workforce interact.

Education and the Workforce in Early America

In American colonial times, education was common only in the elite classes of society. Education was not free or accessible for all persons, and therefore, only a small percentage of Americans had any sort of formal schooling. At that time, education did not respond to the specific needs of the workforce but rather served as a means for enlightening the elite classes of society (Bolino 1973, 21). Instead, it was apprenticeships that provided the practical education that prepared some students for the workforce.

Apprenticeships

Initially, apprenticeship programs were completely separate from formal schooling. An institution distinct from servitude, apprenticeships allowed employers to train workers in exchange for their labor. These apprenticeships provided a particularly advantageous opportunity for children from poor families, since the programs consisted of both training in a particular skill and basic educational skills such as reading and writing. Until the Industrial Revolution, apprenticeships remained the sole source of employee education in the United States. For many disadvantaged children, apprenticeships became the only chance to improve their position in society (Gordon 1999, 4).

The early 1800s brought the Industrial Revolution to the United States, and with it an increasing demand for workers skilled in operating machines. Fewer skilled tradespeople were required in the workforce as society increasingly demanded manufactured goods. Free public education was introduced at this time as well, thus causing the number of apprenticeships to decline. For the majority of children, public education replaced apprenticeships as the major source of education in the United States. In addition, the introduction of machine-based work allowed many workers to learn their trade on the job. Apprenticeships were no longer relied upon to train the nation's workforce (Gordon

1999, 6). As manufacturing jobs increased in number, the need for education in manual labor emerged in the U.S. educational system in order to continue to align education with the needs of the nation's workforce.

Manual Training Education

When businesspeople from Massachusetts visited the 1851 World's Fair in London, they observed the ways in which other countries used the arts and sciences to improve industrial techniques. Inspired by these new advances, U.S. businesspeople began to demand the instruction of technical drawing in public schools, thus sparking a movement toward manual training in U.S. public schools and opening new debate for practical education in the United States (Bolino 1973, 28–29).

Agricultural growth also increased the need for a skilled workforce, thus prompting the proposal of the Morrill Act of 1862 by Senator Justin Morrill (R-VT). It was the first legislation to support vocational and practical education in the United States. The bill set aside 300,000 acres of land per senator and representative for each state. These lands were then sold and profits from the sales used to establish and sustain colleges of agriculture and mechanical arts in each state. These colleges educated agricultural technicians, farmers, and homemakers in the technological advances that would ensure success in the workforce (Gordon 1999, 36–37, 46).

In 1868, the Worcester Polytechnic Institute in Worcester, Massachusetts, became the first school to incorporate the manual labor school movement into its curriculum. The school required all students to perform manual labor in exchange for their education and tuition costs. A combination of theory and practical experience left students immediately prepared to enter the workforce upon completion of their studies (Gordon 1999, 10). Similarly, the Massachusetts Institute of Technology (MIT) incorporated manual instructive techniques into its curriculum in 1877 and observed great success among its students. Graduates no longer needed to complete apprenticeships to supplement their theory-based studies (Gordon 1999, 10–11).

The Debate over Practical Education

Although many viewed the movement toward manual and practical education as a great success, its presence in the U.S. educational system sparked intense debate over the role of education within society. Some argued that the purpose of education was to promote and protect democratic values while also educating young persons in order to preserve American culture.

This school of thought rejected the idea of using education to prepare a stronger workforce, arguing that skills or career-based education would diminish the stature of society (Bolino 1973, 27).

Those advocating for manual training in public schools stressed the development of strong skills that resulted from manual education, pointing out that these skills related to the teachings of the natural sciences. However, their opponents argued that these skills were vocational in nature and thus appropriately taught only through apprenticeships. At the very least, this school of thought maintained, separate schools were necessary for teaching such manual skills (Gordon 1999, 11).

As a result of this debate, early manual training programs were often regarded as separate from the realm of regular academia. Although many public schools did incorporate manual arts into their school programs, manual training was seen as vocational in nature and thus different from academic learning (Bolino 1973, 31; Gordon 1999, 11). At this time, several manual arts–based academies were also created. For example, the Baltimore Manual Training High School was established in 1884 and provided both manual and academic training for its students (Gordon 1999, 11).

Although manual training programs grew in number throughout the country, attacks continued against the usefulness and quality of manual arts curricula. National Education Association president and later U.S. commissioner of education William E. Harris spoke out against the way in which manual arts were taught. Harris argued that current curricula lacked the teaching of intelligence. Men, he charged, needed instruction not just in how to work machines but also in how machines themselves work. He believed that intellectual instruction should take precedence over manual training and that men deserved training in both kinds of education (Bolino 1973, 31–32). In addition to Harris's assertions, others claimed that manual training, although it could be valuable, was not taught properly. Outdated machines were often used to teach students, teachers lacked appropriate knowledge of new advances in technology, and students were not provided proper instruction in their future occupational options (Bolino 1973, 32).

Douglas Commission

In the early 1900s, the Massachusetts legislature established the nine-member Douglas Commission to study the state of manual and vocational training. The commission determined, in accordance with previous criticisms, that the majority of manual training schools were outdated in both their teachings and equipment. Although the commission's report determined that, overall, these training schools provided beneficial opportunities to educate students from poorer classes, even easing social conditions, the fact remained that outdated programs were graduating students ill-prepared to enter the workforce (Bolino 1973, 35).

Wide distribution of the Douglas Commission's report sparked enough discussion that industrial education became the biggest education issue in 1908 (Bolino 1973, 37). Eventually, manual and vocational programs fell out of favor. Students were sent to trade schools when they did not keep up with regular academic classes, thus making trade schools a haven for poor and slow students. Soon these programs were widely seen as undemocratic, since, it seemed, students were not provided with an equal opportunity to learn scholarship (Bolino 1973, 27–28). Eventually, vocational programs became primarily academic programs with a minimal amount of training included (Bolino 1973, 38).

U.S. Businesspeople and Vocational Education

The elimination of actual training in trade schools sparked more debate from U.S. businesspeople as to the need for vocational education in the United States. Business leaders, through the American Manufacturers' Association and the National Association of Manufacturers, contended that a strong vocational education system was vital to the success of U.S. business throughout the world. U.S. businesses, they argued, could not compete with other nations unless a highly skilled workforce emerged (Bolino 1973, 35). The public education system in the United States was filling the needs of the higher-level scientific demands of the workforce but ignoring the need to train skilled workers for shops and factories (Bolino 1973, 27).

Economists and business leaders pointed out that the simultaneous growth of U.S. industry and the decline in apprenticeships made this occupational education an absolute necessity for the success of U.S. industries. Similarly, U.S. labor leaders made the case that, in a democracy, public schools should prepare all kinds of students for all kinds of employment. They claimed that it went against democratic ideals to provide training in college programs while leaving non-college-bound students with few options for the future (Bolino 1973, 38).

Although some dissenters brought up the fact that U.S. industry had grown successfully without including career education in school curriculums, business leaders quickly rebutted their arguments. They pointed out that until that time, skilled immigrants and apprenticeships supplied the workforce for the growing industry. However, since apprenticeships were dying out and skilled immigrants were becoming fewer in number, the nation's businesses needed a new means of supplying educated, skilled workers (Bolino 1973, 34). Economists and businesspeople encouraged the use of public schools to fill this need in the U.S. workforce. Eventually, their arguments won favor in Congress, starting what would be a long line of workforce and education-based legislation.

U.S. Labor Unions and Vocational Education

The historical relationship between labor unions and career education has varied as circumstances surrounding educational and labor issues changed over time. In the late 1930s and early 1940s, trade schools were generally supported by labor unions, which saw training classes as a means for producing acutely skilled workers for the future labor market. During this time, some vocational schools were established to train students to participate in the war effort. Labor unions generally supported the aim of these classes, even though they were separate from the public school system, because they did not train enough workers to flood the market yet provided well-trained future union recruits (Katznelson and Weir 1985, 172).

These independent schools and classes enjoyed far greater support than did the vocational education classes provided in public schools. Labor unionists were left out of the curriculum-building process for many in-school programs and thus regarded them with great skepticism (Katznelson and Weir 1985, 173–174). The formalization of industrial arts classes, moving them more toward the realm of vocational education, was received poorly by many union members. However, in general, the labor union's support or lack of support for vocational education programs varied from city to city depending upon the way the programs were run. The more an occupational education program was enmeshed with the public school program, the less support it got from the labor union. Programs that associated loosely with the public school curriculum, thus allowing more labor union influence over the vocational program, fared better in gaining the support of unions (Katznelson and Weir 1985, 150–151).

Legislation and Major Reports

The 1917 Smith-Hughes Act

In 1917, Congress answered the pleas of U.S. businesspeople and passed the first law to provide funding specifically for career education programs. The 1917 Smith-Hughes Act (or Vocational Education Act of 1917) was created to train non-college-bound students for entry into the workforce (Bolino 1973, 39; Gordon 1999, 67–68, 195). Proposed by Senator Hoke Smith (D-GA) and Representative Dudley M. Hughes (D-GA), the Smith-Hughes Act advocated for the separation of vocational education from the traditional academic curricula in place in most schools (Gordon 1999, 67). The act mandated that in order to get federal funds for vocational education programs, states were required to establish a board of education for vocational programs. Many states created this board of education in addition to and separate from existing state boards of education, thus making an immediate distinction between the business of academic schooling and vocational education (Gordon 1999, 67).

Once the board of education was established, the state was entitled to the $7.2 million annual grant that the act provided for home economics, trade and industrial, and agricultural education (Gordon 1999, 67). Finally, the Smith-Hughes Act established a Federal Board for Vocational Education, consisting of the secretaries of commerce, agriculture, and labor, the commissioner of education, and three appointed citizens. The Smith-Hughes Act remained a grant in perpetuity until its repeal in 1997 (Gordon 1999, 68).

The onset of World War I brought new challenges to the U.S. educational system. The Federal Board for Vocational Education played a significant role in the preparation of troops for war. War classes were needed to train individuals for battle, and the Federal Board for Vocational Education was called upon to oversee this endeavor. New advances in war technology required a highly skilled group of mechanics, technicians, and supervisors. Vocational education, as established by the Smith-Hughes Act, played a significant role in the preparation of these soldiers (Gordon 1999, 49).

The Walter F. George Acts

The success of the Smith-Hughes Act inspired a set of workforce-centered education laws from Georgia senator Walter F. George. Senator George argued that few high school students went on to college, thus making career-based education necessary for the employability of non-college-bound youth (Gordon 1999, 68). After the passage of the Smith-Hughes Act, Senator George sponsored every piece of vocational education legislation proposed throughout the remainder of his term in office. During the Coolidge administration, George cosponsored the George-Reed Act of 1929 with Representative Daniel A. Reed of New York. This legislation provided a national annual increase of $1 million for three years to develop vocational programs in home economics and agriculture (Gordon 1999, 68).

Senator George cosponsored two pieces of legislation during Franklin Delano Roosevelt's administration. The George-Ellzey Act of 1934 was cosponsored by Representative Lawrence F. Ellzey of Mississippi. Renewing and expanding upon the previous George-Reed Act, this legislation provided for an annual increase of $3 million for three years for education in agriculture, home economics, trade, and industrial education (Gordon 1999, 68). George then cosponsored the George-Dean Act of 1936 with Representative Braswell Dean of Georgia. This act authorized $14 million for the expansion of vocational and career education programs. Included in this legislation were programs in marketing occupations and teacher education (Gordon 1999, 68).

Senator George then cosponsored one piece of legislation during the Truman administration. The George-Barden Act of 1946 was cosponsored by Representative Graham A. Barden of North Carolina. This legislation amended the George-Dean Act, calling for the expansion of career education programs to serve the needs of the growing population of World War II veterans in the United States (Gordon 1999, 68).

The National Defense Act of 1958

The late 1950s brought a new issue to bear upon U.S. education. Although international competition had influenced schooling in the past, a new kind of competition marked a time when the education of U.S. students and the resulting success of U.S. workers was linked with the defense of the nation. In 1957, the Soviet Union successfully launched Sputnik I into outer space. This created a rush to reform U.S. education, particularly in the sciences, to ensure that the United States would catch up to and eventually surpass Soviet accomplishments (Gordon 1999, 68–70).

The National Defense Act of 1958 stressed improvements in math, foreign languages, science, and technical competencies (Gordon 1999, 70). Improvement required more intense instruction in these subjects so that students would be better prepared for careers in scientific and technical professions. These reforms were aimed not just at youth but also at adults and older workers (Gordon 1999, 68). Finally, the National Defense Act called for better guidance counseling, improved testing methods, increased funds for higher education, and more effective use of mass media for educational purposes (Gordon 1999, 70).

The Vocational Education Act of 1963

Also known as the Perkins-Morse Bill, the Vocational Education Act of 1963 was unprecedented in terms of U.S. vocational education. The legislation mandated that all persons, regardless of background or financial situation, should have access to high quality vocational training. In this capacity, the act expanded upon existing programs while also establishing a program of part-time employment for students who needed assistance to fund their schooling. Specific funds were also set aside to aid persons from disadvantaged backgrounds who might otherwise be kept from completing vocational education programs (Gordon 1999, 71). Funds from the Vocational Education Act were distributed to states based on the number and type of persons in each state enrolled in vocational education programs. Thus, for the first time, vocational education was planned around the needs of individuals instead of around the needs of the nation's workforce (Gordon 1999, 71).

The Vocational Education Amendments of 1968

A revision of the Vocational Education Act of 1963, the Vocational Education Amendments served to replace all previous vocational education legislation except the Smith-Hughes Act. The Smith-Hughes Act was retained in an effort to honor the nation's first legislation on vocational education (Gordon 1999, 72). The 1968 amendments expanded the way vocational education was defined in the United States, making it more similar to general education programs. In addition, the act introduced vocational education programs into postsecondary schools and furthered the goal of the Vocational Education Act of 1963 to ensure access to vocational programs to students of all ages and backgrounds (Gordon 1999, 72).

The Comprehensive Employment and Training Act of 1973

The Comprehensive Employment and Training Act of 1973 (CETA) replaced the Manpower Development and Training Act of 1962, which granted funds for the training of employees alienated by technological changes in the workforce (Gordon 1999, 70–72). One of the main provisions of CETA served to transfer authority from the federal government to the state and local levels. Those governments were given more power to determine the use of funds and the development of programs for their areas (Gordon 1999, 74). Although CETA did not make changes to traditional U.S. schooling as such, it affected the education of U.S. workers by providing funding for on the job training, classroom training, and employment counseling (Gordon 1999, 74).

The Vocational Education Amendments of 1976

The Vocational Education Amendments of 1976 addressed several issues related to satisfying the needs of all types of workers. The act mandated that states implement a better system of planning their career education programs to attract a more diverse set of outside agencies willing to assist in educating students, which would ensure a wider set of options for students enrolled in vocational education programs. Also, the act stipulated that actions must be taken to alleviate sex discrimination and stereotyping within vocational education programs. The Vocational Education Amendments of 1976 then increased and lengthened the funding established through the 1963 and 1968 vocational education legislation (Gordon 1999, 74).

The Job Training Partnership Act of 1982

The Job Training Partnership Act (JTPA) replaced the Comprehensive Employment Training Act, which expired in 1982. The act served to create programs that would aid youth and unskilled adults in entering the workforce. In addition, the JTPA provided training for individuals having trouble securing gainful employment as a result of their economic situation (Gordon 1999, 76).

The JTPA afforded state governments and private industries a larger role in the development of training programs while also giving them a larger responsibility for the quality of these programs (Gordon 1999, 76). It required a strong relationship between vocational education and job training programs. Overall, the JTPA expanded the role of career education in job training programs and encouraged states to explore a stronger link between private businesses and job training programs. These improved and expanded programs were then offered to more disadvantaged individuals in need of job training or retraining (Gordon 1999, 76–77).

A Nation at Risk: The Imperative for Education Reform

During the Reagan administration, Secretary of Education Terrell H. Bell commissioned a report from the National Commission on Excellence in Education on the condition of education in the United States. The resulting report, *A Nation at Risk: The Imperative for Education Reform,* brought education reform to the forefront of the nation's attention (Bell 1986, 3–4). The report described failing schools, poor test scores, and probably most notably, the fact that children in the United States were not able to compete with students from other countries, who were educated more efficiently in the areas of math and science (Levy 1996, 127).

Prior to the release of *A Nation at Risk,* the Reagan administration had planned to dissolve the Department of Education (DOE). Reagan and other conservatives considered the DOE far too cumbersome and argued that it took too much decision-making power away from states and localities (Congressional Quarterly 1981, 21). However, the resurgence of interest in education policy created by the release of *A Nation at Risk* spurred several new policies aimed at improving the global competitiveness of U.S. students. As a result, education policies during the remainder of the Reagan years focused primarily on the improvement of students' skills and competencies in mathematics and sciences and on adult education (Thomas 1983; Ronald Reagan 1984).

The Carl D. Perkins Vocational Education Act of 1984

The Carl D. Perkins Vocational Education Act of 1984 amended the Vocational Education Act of 1963 and replaced the Vocational Education Act Amendments of 1968 and 1976. There were two main goals of the 1984 legislation, named for Representative Carl D. Perkins of Kentucky, who was a strong supporter of vocational education during his tenure in office (Gordon 1999, 67): it was designed to enhance the skills of labor force participants and to ensure that adults could have equal access to vocational education programs (Gordon 1999, 77). This bill shifted the aim of vocational education legislation from establishing vocational education programs to improving and expanding programs to serve different types of populations not previously considered (Gordon 1999, 77).

The Forgotten Half

The Forgotten Half: Pathways to Success for America's Youth and Young Families, released by the William T. Grant Foundation in 1988, was a two-year study of sixteen to twenty-four year olds in the United States. Non-college-bound youth, the report claimed, were forgotten in the sense that they had one of the highest unemployment rates of any section of the population. Of workers aged twenty to twenty-four in 1988, 6.8 percent of whites, 11 percent of Hispanics, and 20.3 percent of blacks were unemployed, and the real income of these workers was on a ten-year decline (William T. Grant 1988, 2). According to *The Forgotten Half,* employment statistics skewed the view of unemployment and ignored many of the endogenous factors that caused such high unemployment for this age group (William T. Grant 1988, 1–2).

In addition, *The Forgotten Half* argued that as the world changed, the U.S. educational system had failed to change along with it, graduating students who were ill equipped to enter the ranks of the changing workforce. Young families were left to survive on dead-end, low-paying jobs that held them at or below the poverty level (William T. Grant 1988, 3). This inequity, the report argued, was a result of the amount of attention focused on college-bound students over non-college-bound students. According to *The Forgotten Half,* the U.S. educational system became so preoccupied with preparing students who choose to attend colleges that it failed to provide direction for those who did not. These students then graduated unprepared to enter the workforce and unable to participate in society in a productive manner (William T. Grant 1988, 3).

The Forgotten Half made four proposals that invoked a new perspective on the education of non-college-bound students. First, the commission sought a stronger relationship between the youth and adults of the country. More support was advocated for single-parent families to ease the burden of raising children. Businesses and educational institutions were asked to work toward a more flexible system that would serve the needs of these families and encourage strong youth-parent relationships (William T. Grant 1988, 5–6).

Second, the commission suggested more community-based leadership opportunities for young community members. Young people were recommended for involvement in the implementation and development of programs serving their needs and the needs of others. The idea behind this suggestion was to involve youth in their communities so that they would in turn care more about their communities later in life (William T. Grant 1988, 6–8).

The commission's third recommendation was an appeal to state and national government leaders to find a place for these issues on state and national legislative agendas. A number of existing and successful community-based programs served as examples of successful new practices, and the improvement of skills and employment opportunities for area youth provided evidence that these recommendations would work. The call to legislators asked them to encourage businesses and employers to take an interest in educating and training employees and future employees (William T. Grant 1988, 9).

Finally, the commission proposed the Fair Chance: Youth Opportunities Demonstration Act, a piece of legislation that established a national demonstration program to expand admission to training and education programs for postsecondary students. The program would be administered by the state and would provide counseling, academic support, and financial aid (William T. Grant 1988, 10). This piece of legislation would encourage and expand the opportunities for all students for training both during and after high school, providing youth with the accredited skills needed to obtain gainful and steady employment in the workforce.

The National Education Goals

In the fall of 1989, President George Bush met with the National Governors' Association to discuss education policy and to raise awareness of the need for education reform (Greene 2000; Levy 1996, 128). No formal policies resulted from the conference, but President Bush and the nation's governors emerged calling for a system of national standards in the United States (Levy 1996, 128). The six national education goals that emerged from the summit mandated excellence in all U.S. schools. In theory, graduating students needed better preparation for entry into higher education or the workforce.

The Choice: High Skills or Low Wages

The Commission on the Skills of the American Workforce presented the *America's Choice* report in June 1990. According to the report, the working poor were getting larger in number, and productivity was growing more slowly as the nation approached the final decade of the twentieth century. Income levels for the lowest 70 percent of salary earners had steadily decreased since the late 1970s; only income levels for the top 30 percent of salary earners had steadily increased. To combat these problems, the commission recommended a more employment-ready system of education. This new system would mandate an educational standard of excellence that all students should meet by age sixteen (Commission on the Skills of the American Workforce 1990). Successful students would then receive a certificate indicating proficiency in a number of different subject areas and training programs, thus proving to employers that they were hiring a more highly skilled worker. The aim was to give non-college-bound students a direction about which they could feel proud, similar to the technical programs for youth that already existed in Europe (Foster 1990, 8).

A team of twenty-three executives, along with the U.S. Department of Labor, came together to produce *America's Choice* and spent eight months researching the training techniques of different industries in countries around the world. A comparison of these programs and those in the United States showed that in the United States, "the lack of any clear, direct connection between education and employment opportunities for most young people is one of the most devastating aspects of the existing system" (Foster 1990, 8). Similar to the findings in *The Forgotten Half,* the commission found that youth were entering the workforce lacking both the necessary skills to gain long-term employment and the skills to keep the United States competitive in the global economy. *America's Choice* also made a plea for action, in the form of financial incentives for companies to retrain their workers for high-productivity work (Foster 1990, 8).

The Carl D. Perkins Vocational and Applied Technology Education Act of 1990

The Carl D. Perkins Vocational and Applied Technology Education Act of 1990 (familiarly called Perkins II) amended the Carl D. Perkins Vocational Education Act of 1984 and brought new prominence to the need for a highly skilled workforce in a world growing more technologically advanced (Gordon 1999, 79). Perkins II emphasized a three-tiered approach to establishing a more prepared workforce. The first tier dealt with the incorporation of vocational education into academic education. Perkins II intended to better integrate these two traditionally separate forms of schooling (Gordon 1999, 79). The second tier mandated more efficient communication among different types of training programs, and similarly, the third tier mandated more efficient linkages between educational programs and the needs of the workforce. This law deviated from past legislation that perpetuated the separation of vocational programs from traditional academic curricula (Gordon 1999, 79).

The Secretary's Commission on Achieving Necessary Skills (SCANS)

The Secretary's Commission on Achieving Necessary Skills (SCANS) released its initial report, *What Work Requires of Schools,* in June 1991. In this report, the commission determined the skills necessary for students to become successful employees while also outlining the teaching methods that educators might use to ensure that students achieve these skills. The report determined what kinds of employees businesses need in order to become high-performance workplaces and then made recommendations as to how schools can help students to obtain those skills. The objective of the report was to encourage high-paying jobs for highly skilled workers in a highly productive workplace (SCANS 1991).

The report also emphasizes the interpersonal skills that employees must have to be successful employees and encourages the development of these skills within the realm of public education. The main point of the report was to emphasize a three-part academic foundation necessary for the success of all students and future employees, as well as the five most important workplace competencies that SCANS determined are necessary for employees in a highly productive workforce (SCANS 1991). Teachers and organizations helping to develop stronger curriculums for schools now often use the foundation recommended by the SCANS report as a reference for change. Subsequent SCANS reports built upon the initial report and continue to encourage the teaching of skills that will help to develop a successful U.S. workforce.

The School-to-Work Opportunities Act of 1994

The School-to-Work Opportunities Act of 1994 (STWOA) revised the national framework for vocational education. Under the act, states received seed money for the formation of programs that assisted youth in acquiring vocational skills for gainful employment. Individual states applied for federal grant money to start each program, indicating how they would finance the program after federal grant funding discontinued. States and communities then formulated and implemented school-to-work systems in their areas (U.S. Senate 1993). Proponents of the act expected states to establish links between secondary and postsecondary education, in the process giving students the chance to engage in a "career major" in an occupational field of their choice (Fuhrman 1994, 85). The intention of this legislation was to provide non-college-bound students with a more secure direction, allowing them to gain high-paying, long-term employment.

The details of how to implement the initiative were left up to individual states, and consequently school-to-work (STW) programs looked different in each state. The act provided funds for state STW projects and articulated three broad-based activities that states should pursue: work-based learning, school-based learning, and connecting activities (Erlichson and Van Horn 1999, 1). Thus, an unusual opportunity was left for states to set their own STW goals and the means by which they wanted to achieve those goals. However, this discretion served as an impediment for implementation in many states that found themselves stuck in battles over local and state control over education reforms.

The National Skills Standards Act of 1994

The National Skills Standards Act of 1994 established the National Skills Standards Board to encourage the development of a national voluntary system of standards and assessments for skill attainment. The aim of the legislation was that this new system of standards and assessments would help to enhance the skill level of the nation's workforce. The board would also serve as a liaison among prospective employees, training providers, and prospective employers. Thus, the board would ensure that training providers were kept aware of the changing needs of current employers, and current employers would be made aware of the highly skilled workers emerging from training programs. The board would also call upon employers to accept a role in the development of training programs and to provide employees with portable credentials and skills that would enhance their job security. Finally, the National Skills Standards Board would assist in the overall enhancement of the national workforce by overseeing successful transitions from school to the workplace and secondary and postsecondary vocational and technical education (U.S. Department of Education 2002).

Goals 2000: Educate America Act

The Goals 2000: Educate America Act was proposed by the Clinton administration in 1994. The most notable section of Goals 2000 put forth a set of national education goals that required a system of standards and assessments for schools throughout the nation. Student achievement, school readiness, adult literacy, math and science, teacher education and professional development, and parental participation were just some of the categories defined in the legislation as marked for improvement. Other sections of the bill called for the funding of programs to aid parents and states in achieving systemic reform in their local schools (Thomas 1994). This legislation sparked widespread debate over the use of standards and assessments in the U.S. educational system. Although perhaps not directly related to workforce preparation, these new education goals served to promote more efficiently educated students for entry into the labor market and the world of global competition.

The Carl D. Perkins Vocational and Technical Education Act of 1998

The Carl D. Perkins Vocational and Technical Education Act of 1998 (familiarly known as Perkins III) amended and extended Perkins II. The act further promoted the training of students in ways that would ensure their preparedness for work. Perkins III recognized the reforms taking place in U.S. schools and encouraged the realignment of vocational and technical education programs with the changing nature of academic programs. Along with provisions stipulated in the Workforce Investment Act of 1998, Perkins III was involved with workforce training programs within state "one-stop" centers for education and workforce development (U.S. Department of Education 2002).

Perkins III lifted several previous restrictions, granting more flexibility to states, postsecondary institutions, and school districts. This flexibility was allowed so that training providers would be able to design better programs that were more specific to the needs of their local populations. Perkins III also called for greater accountability from training programs and providers. Annual reports were required to encourage continual improvements from training programs. Finally, Perkins III sponsored the continued use of work-based learning programs and encouraged stronger linkages among businesses, training providers, and labor organizations so that students could benefit from the collaborative programs they developed (Department of Education 2002).

The Workforce Investment Act of 1998

Title I of the Workforce Investment Act of 1998 (WIA) established the development of one-stop centers for employment services to provide a central location where clients could access multiple resources that aid in the attainment of gainful employment. Information resources, education, and training services were provided at one-stop centers for individuals who wish to advance in or pursue longtime careers (McNeil

1999, 1). Under the WIA and Perkins III, training programs can provide services in these comprehensive one-stop centers. Training providers covered under both Perkins III and WIA are required to provide certain core services at local one-stop centers in place of or in addition to the programs offered at their regular place of training (McNeil 1999, 3, 8). However, grantees of WIA and Perkins III have several options for using their funds, including, but not limited to, professional development programs, curricula development, and programs geared toward underserved populations (McNeil 1999, 4). Finally, programs funded through WIA and Perkins III are required to provide certain performance data to ensure quality and continued improvement within the training programs (McNeil 1999, 5).

Karin A. Garver

See also Comprehensive Employment and Training Act; Earnings and Education; E-learning; Job Training Partnership Act; Lifelong Learning; Workforce Investment Act

References and further reading

Bell, Terrell H. 1986. "Education Policy: An Inside View of the Reagan Administration." *Education Digest* 52 (November): 2–6.

Bolino, August C. 1973. *Career Education: Contributions to Economic Growth.* New York: Praeger.

Commission on the Skills of the American Workforce. 1990. *America's Choice: High Skills or Low Wages!* Rochester, NY: National Center on Education and the Economy.

Congressional Quarterly. 1981. "Reagan: Actor to President." In *President Reagan.* Edited by Nancy Lammers. Washington, DC: Congressional Quarterly.

Erlichson, Bari Anhalt, and Carl E. Van Horn. 1999. "School to Work Governance: A National Review." *The National School-to-Work Learning and Information Center.* Philadelphia, PA: Consortium for Policy Research in Education.

Foster, Catherine. 1990. "Modernizing the Work Force." *Christian Science Monitor,* June 19, 8.

Fuhrman, Susan H. 1994. "Clinton's Education Policy and Intergovernmental Relations in the 1990s." *Publius: The Journal of Federalism.* 24: 83–97.

Gordon, Howard R. D. 1999. *The History and Growth of Vocational Education in America.* Boston: Allyn and Bacon.

Greene, John Robert. 2000. *The Presidency of George Bush.* Lawrence, KS: University Press of Kansas.

Katznelson, Ira, and Margaret Weir. 1985. *Schooling for All: Class, Race, and the Decline of the Democratic Ideal.* New York: Basic Books.

Levy, Peter B. 1996. *Encyclopedia of the Reagan-Bush Years.* Westport, CT: Greenwood Press.

McNeil, Patricia W. 1999. *Program Memorandum: Responsibilities and Opportunities Created by Title I of the Workforce Investment Act of 1998.* Washington, DC: United States Department of Education. http://www.ed.gov (cited August 18, 2002).

Ronald Reagan Presidential Library. 1984. "Statement on Signing the Education Amendments of 1984." http://www.reagan.utexas.edu (cited April 3, 2001).

SCANS (Secretary's Commission on Achieving Necessary Skills). 1991. *What Work Requires of Schools: A SCANS Report for America 2000.* Washington, DC: U.S. Department of Labor.

Thomas: Legislative Information on the Internet. 1983. "H.R. 1310—Public Law: 98–377." http://thomas.loc.gov (cited April 11, 2001).

Thomas: Legislative Information on the Internet. 1994. "H.R. 1804: Goals 2000: Educate America Act." http://thomas.loc.gov (cited March 1, 2001).

U.S. Department of Education. 2002a. *Carl D. Perkins Vocational and Technical Education Act of 1998 (Public Law 105–332) Summary.* http://www.ed.gov/offices/OVAE/CTE (cited August 18, 2002).

———. 2002b. *National Skills Standards Act of 1994.* http://www.ed.gov/legislation/GOALS2000/TheAct/sec502.html (cited June 22, 2002).

U.S. Senate. 1993. *School-to-Work Opportunities Act of 1993 Report.* 103rd Cong., 1st sess.

William T. Grant Foundation Commission on Work, Family, and Citizenship. 1988. *The Forgotten Half: Pathways to Success for America's Youth and Young Families.* Washington, DC.: William T. Grant Foundation.

Elder Care

Elder care is the care of older adults as they face disability and health issues brought on by aging. It is provided in institutional or community settings or in the home. The provision of elder care will be affected by several trends over the next fifty years. The number of older Americans is increasing as the baby boom generation ages. Two of the major government programs funding elder care, Social Security and Medicare, are facing possible insolvency, partially because the number of working adults in the labor force who pay for these programs cannot keep up with the increasing number of retirees. Costs for health care, which are intimately related to the costs of elder care, continue to rise. Corporations, although responding to the needs of workers who are caring for an elderly relative, are cutting back in their contributions to health insurance for both pensioners and current employees. There is a shortage of elder care workers, including nurses, home health aides, and nursing assistants. Increasing their numbers may require improving salaries and benefits to attract workers, which in turn will further increase elder care costs. Providing and funding elder care will be a major concern for workers, employers, and the government as the effect of these trends is felt across the country.

Historically, families cared for older relatives. Elder care evolved as people lived longer and families moved apart. The first old-age homes were established in the late nineteenth century, as well as some retirement communities (Brown 2002). Many elderly without families lived in poorhouses. The rise of private, for-profit nursing homes is often linked to the Social Security Act of 1935, which limited the flow of social security dollars to public institutions. Elderly living on their own became more prevalent as a result of the income available through the Social Security program. Home health care and visiting nurse associations, which were set up in the late nineteenth century, grew as the elderly lived longer on their own. The Older Americans Act of 1965 established federal money for community-based elder care. Medicare and Medicaid were also established in 1965, bringing the federal government solidly into the role of financing health care for the elderly.

Elder care in the United States currently consists of a combination of institutional and community-based services. Nursing homes provide short-term and long-term care for those who have intensive needs and can do little for themselves. Assisted living facilities and continuing care retirement communities provide a range of services at various levels of intensity, offering older adults the opportunity to maintain an independent life but the safety of having more intensive medical care available. Frail elderly are also cared for in their own homes by relatives, visiting nurses, and other home health care workers. Some 85 percent of frail elderly are cared for by their friends or family (Seki 2001, 91). The number of adult day care facilities is growing across the nation, and these programs offer more intensive services for the frail elderly on a daily basis, providing respite for caregivers or caring for an elder while a caregiver is at work. Other community services include nutrition programs like Meals on Wheels, which delivers food to older adults in their homes, and senior centers, which provide social and nutritional opportunities for older adults who can travel to the centers.

Many who work in the field of elder care advocate a continuum of care, providing the appropriate level of services to meet changing levels of health and independence as older adults age. This continuum would include affordable housing options that allow people to age in place and possibly receive services in their homes. It is generally predicted that elder care services are underprovided in the United States, particularly in relation to the aging of the population over the next half century.

Elder care can be expensive to provide, particularly in terms of long-term care for the frail elderly. There is debate over whether community-based programs will allow financial savings by helping older adults remain independent and in their own homes for as long as possible. Federal and state governments currently provide funding for both community-based care and institutional care, but levels of funding are extremely varied. Medicaid and Medicare, both public health insurance programs that support health care–focused elder care services, are beginning to look at ways to fund community-based services, but in general most of the funding for elder care from these two sources goes to acute or long-term care. Some, like the National Council on Aging, argue that funding patterns create a preference for institutionalized care, which may not be cost-effective or preferred by older adults (National Council on Aging 2001). Medicare will only pay for home health care if it is ordered by a medical doctor and provided by a skilled nurse or physical or occupational therapist. Thus Medicare only usually supports home health care after an older person suffers a major health problem, and its funding for home health care is generally short-term and for only a few hours a week.

The Older Americans Act (OAA), which became law in 1965, governs the federal provision of elder care services and does support some community-based care. OAA created the Administration on Aging (AOA), housed in the federal Department of Health and Human Services. The AOA supports community programs that allow older adults to avoid institutionalization and remain in their homes. Funding distributed by AOA provides for services such as transportation, nutrition, senior centers, disease prevention, case management, and in-home services for the frail. The OAA's reauthorization in 2000 focused on the needs of low-income and minority elderly. New in the 2000 reauthorization was a caregiver support program to provide counseling, information, and respite care for those tending a relative. Appropriations under the OAA totaled $1.1 billion in 2001 (Consolidated Appropriations Act 2001).

Although it does not directly support elder care services, Social Security is another way that the government participates in the care of the older population. Workers pay into this system and after a certain age can begin to receive monetary payments, the amount of which is determined by income level. Many older Americans are heavily dependent on Social Security to survive, with 63 percent of those over sixty-five years of age depending on Social Security for 50 percent or more of their income (Seki 2001, 91). Social Security faces possible bankruptcy in 2040 because fewer numbers of younger workers will be paying into the system and large numbers of older Americans will be dependent on the system.

The government also provides health insurance for adults over sixty-five through the Medicare program. All adults who paid Medicare taxes while working, or whose spouse did so, are automatically enrolled in Medicare Part A when they turn sixty-five. Medicare Part A covers hospital stays and other intensive health needs. Adults over sixty-five also have the option of purchasing Medicare Part B, which provides insurance coverage for outpatient health care. Neither Medicare Part A nor Medicare Part B provides for long-term care, though Medicare Part A may pay for a short-term stay in a nursing facility if a patient requires skilled nursing or rehabilitation services (Kaplan 2001, 66). Older adults can also buy Medigap coverage to help with needs, such as prescription drugs, that Medicare does not cover. Some rely on either Medigap coverage or an employer-sponsored health plan to which they continue to subscribe to provide additional benefits, but many struggle to pay for medications.

As with Social Security, the future of Medicare is in jeopardy because of the decreasing ratio of working-age Americans to retirees. According to the National Bipartisan Commission on the Future of Medicare, the Medicare trust fund, which finances most Medicare expenditures, will disappear by 2008. Without that funding, costs to Medicare beneficiaries will rise. The portion of elder care that Medicare currently supports will have to be provided by another source, and whether most retired older adults can afford to support their own health care needs is a serious question.

Older Americans who qualify based on their income are also eligible for Medicaid, the government health insurance program for the poor, which does cover long-term care. Over three-quarters of Medicaid spending on the elderly goes to long-term care (Liska 1997, 2). Older adults who enter long-term care facilities often spend all assets and then depend on Medicaid. Researchers have found that 67 percent of those in nursing homes spend all assets within a year of entering and that Medicaid pays for 38 percent of all nursing home care in the United States (Seki 2001, 91).

As the population in the United States becomes older, the demand for elder care will increase. The baby boom generation is aging, and the labor force will be smaller in comparison to the number of older retired adults. In the year 2000, there were 35 million people aged sixty-five and over, but the Census Bureau projects that by 2016, 47 million Americans will be sixty-five and over (Federal Interagency Forum on Aging-Related Statistics 2000). By 2050 almost 82 million Americans will be over age 65 (Federal Interagency Forum on Aging-Related Statistics 2000). The population over eighty-five is the fastest growing segment of the older population as life spans increase (Federal Interagency Forum on Aging-Related Statistics 2000).

The older population will also become more ethnically diverse over this period, with the percentage of whites among those over sixty-five expected to drop from 84 percent to 64 percent between 2000 and 2050. The Hispanic elderly are the fastest-growing older population, growing from 2 million in 2000 to over 13 million by 2050. Women are expected to continue outnumbering men among older adults, especially among those over eighty-five. By 2050, women will comprise 61 percent of the over-eighty-five population (Federal Interagency Forum on Aging-Related Statistics 2000). Responses to elder care needs will have to take these demographic realities into account.

Other demographic trends also shape elder care. Like child care, elder care responsibilities once fell largely to women. Traditional methods of elder care are no longer available following the mass entrance of women into the labor force during the last half of the twentieth century. Two-income families must look to other ways to care for their elders or juggle elder care while working, causing concern for employers whose workers may be facing difficult elder care problems that affect productivity.

The government and corporations are both beginning to create programs and services that assist workers caring for frail relatives. The Family and Medical Leave Act of 1993 allows employees to take up to twelve weeks per year of leave, with job protection, to deal with a family or medical situation. Such leave can be taken in larger units or for as little as a few hours. This law can help employees cope with elder care issues. Companies are also helping employees handle the care of an elderly relative through such means as seminars, newsletters, handbooks, referral services, and personnel policies that allow for flexible schedules and time off (Scharlach, Lowe, and Schneider 1991, 61–85).

As increasing numbers of people live longer, the need for expensive long-term care will increase. The rise of chronic diseases, such as Alzheimer's, also contributes to the increased demand for and cost of long-term care. Long-term care insurance is one option to help older adults and their families cover high costs. It is beginning to gain more attention but continues to be fairly expensive and includes many limitations because the ultimate cost of the care is substantial. Some people see continuing care communities as a type of long-term care insurance, and insurance companies have actually partnered with continuing care communities to provide coverage for people who move into the community when they are independent and relatively healthy, for any future long-term needs they may have (Sherwood et al., 7).

The increasing demand for elder care means a greater need for workers who will provide such care. Some researchers have gone so far as to call the need for long-term care workers a crisis (Stone and Weiner 2001). The Bureau of Labor Statistics predicts that home health work will be a high-growth occupation, growing by 21 to 35 percent between 2000 and 2010 (Bureau of Labor Statistics 2003). With the sharp increase in population over sixty-five during the next half-century, this demand will only rise. The majority of such jobs are for paraprofessional workers, including home health workers and nursing assistants, are not well respected, pay poorly, and have extremely high turnover. Many do not provide benefits, including any career development opportunities that may help workers remain in the field. Under many government workforce development programs, training for such positions may in fact be ignored because starting salaries are below requirements for the programs (Stone and Weiner 2001). The nation also faces a critical shortage of registered nurses, and hospitals have begun extensive recruiting campaigns to attract nurses (Janofsy 2002). This workforce shortage, combined with the considerable concerns about the funding of long-term care and the solvency of Medicare and Social Security, means that elder care will rise to the forefront of public policy agendas and necessitate a response both from the government and from employers because of the impact of these pressures on the entire workforce.

Ariana Funaro

See also American Association of Retired Persons; Family and Medical Leave Act; Health Insurance; Medicaid; Older Workers; Social Security Act

References and further reading

Angel, Ronald J., and Jacqueline L. 1997. *Who Will Care for Us? Aging and Long-Term Care in Multicultural America.* New York: New York University Press.

Brown, Karen Stevenson. 2002. "A History of Long Term Care." http://www.elderweb.com/history (cited October 6).

Bureau of Labor Statistics. 2003. *Occupational Outlook Handbook.* Washington, DC: Bureau of Labor Statistics. http://www.bls.gov/oco/home.htm (cited July 2, 2003).

Federal Interagency Forum on Aging-Related Statistics. 2002. *Older Americans 2000: Key Indicators of Well-Being.* http://www.agingstats.gov/chartbook2000 (cited June 3).

Janofsy, Michael. 2002. "Shortage of Nurses Spurs Bidding War in Recruiting Industry. *New York Times,* May 28.

Kaplan, Richard L. 2001. "Financing Long-Term Care in the United States: Who Should Pay for Mom and Dad?" Pp. 65–82 in *Aging: Caring for our Elders.* Edited by David N. Weisstub, David C. Thomasma, Serge Gauthier, and George F. Tomossy. Dordrecht: Kluwer Academic Publishers.

Liska, David. 1997. *Medicaid: Ten Basic Questions Answered.* http://www.urban.org/news/factsheets/medicaidFS.pdf (cited June 24, 2002).

National Bipartisan Commission on the Future of Medicare. 1999. *The Facts about Medicare.* http://medicare.commission.gov/medicare/factpage4.html (cited June 3, 2002).

National Council on Aging. 2001. *2001 National Council on Aging Public Policy Agenda.* Washington, DC: National Council on Aging. http://www.ncoa.org.

Public Law 106–554, Consolidated Appropriations Act 2001. 2002. http://thomas.loc.gov/cgi-bin/query/z?c106:H.R.4577.ENR (cited June 24).

Scharlach, Andrew E., Beverly F. Lowe, and Edward L. Schneider. 1991. *Elder Care and the Work Force: Blueprint for Action.* Lexington, MA: Lexington Books.

Seki, Fusako. 2001. "The Role of Government and the Family in Taking Care of the Frail Elderly: A Comparison of the United States and Japan." Pp. 83–105 in *Aging: Caring for our Elders.* Edited by David N. Weisstub, David C. Thomasma, Serge Gauthier, and George F. Tomossy. Dordrecht: Kluwer Academic Publishers.

Sherwood, Sylvia, Hirsch S. Ruchlin, Clarence C. Sherwood, and Shirley A. Morris. 1997. *Continuing Care Retirement Communities.* Baltimore, MD: Johns Hopkins University Press.

Stone, Robyn I., with Joshua M. Wiener. 2001. *Who Will Care for Us? Addressing the Long-Term Care Workforce Crisis.* Washington, DC: Urban Institute and American Association of Homes and Services for the Aging.

U.S. Census Bureau. 2001. *The 65 Years and Over Population: 2000: Census 2000 Brief.* Washington, DC: U.S. Department of Commerce.

E-learning

Recent technological advances have resulted in a learning revolution that revolves around the concept of e-learning, defined by the Commission on Technology and Adult Learning as "instructional content or learning experiences delivered or enabled by electronic technology" (Pantazis 2001). E-learning appears in various forms, including online learning, computer-based training, information and learning technology, and virtual learning. This new type of learning, used by both corporations and academia, has raised numerous questions about its validity; although the key to a quality education may once have been hands-on exercises and face-to-face feedback in the physical classroom, the opportunity to learn online and receive feedback by both asynchronous (interaction between learner and instructor via communication such as e-mail) and synchronous communication (interaction between learner and instructor in "real time" or live chat sessions) is a new avenue for exploration. The "just-in-time" nature of e-learning, as well as the changing nature and needs of twenty-first-century learners, has revolutionized the concept of both learning and instruction.

E-learning is in its infancy in the twenty-first century. The terms *e-learning* or *online learning* have become catchwords to refer to courses that cover marketability in the corporate world, for example, or courses in fields such as history or business for those individuals interested in beginning or completing a degree program.

The self-directed nature of e-learning has encouraged individuals to learn at their own pace and to choose courses that interest them. Leslie Darling, chief learning officer at Element K, an online learning portal, contends that e-learning "forces participants into a needs analysis role; they're expected to bring something back, so they try to be more efficient with their time" (Salopek 2002, 73). Ideally, the combination of work and e-learning in the workforce challenges individuals to accomplish more in both the work environment and in the classroom. E-learning, however, involves the creation of high expectations; the instructor needs to set boundaries on the first day of the class and maintain control of the classroom. The focus in the corporate e-learning environment is on the specific nature of an individual's job, which, in turn, facilitates the transfer of what had been learned online into the workplace.

E-learning has resulted in a revolution in methodology; the question of how information and communications technology can be used to enhance and strengthen human interaction is at the forefront of the e-learning field. Although formal learning has always been associated with time and location, e-learning can occur at the discretion of both instructor and student. Simon Mauger of the National Institute of Adult Continuing Education noted that e-learning "require(s) a smart environment. This involves not simply the delivery of materials online with some online support from competent online tutors. It needs a supporting cast of other staff who understand what is going on for the learner and who are themselves e-functional" (Mauger 2002, 12). For e-learning to be effective, there must be some sort of evaluation system in place, as well as training and support for both learners and instructors. The "smart" environment to which Mauger refers is one that must refer to the "outcome end" of an e-learning system, or one that is results-oriented and retention-focused.

For corporations that buy into the e-learning environment, the emergence of e-learning portals marked the beginning of an e-learning industry. The Masie Center, which evaluates new educational venues, ranks the emergence of e-learning portals as the second most important innovation in corporate America. However, as is often the problem with new innovations, corporate buyers may have

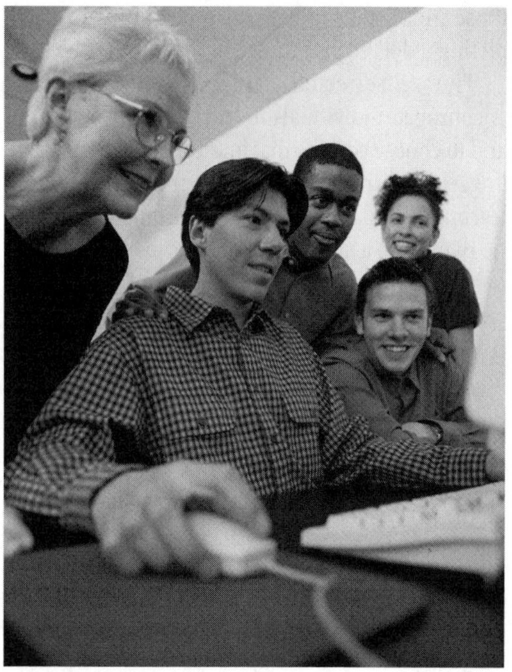

E-learning appears in various forms, including online learning, computer-based training, information and learning technology, and virtual learning. (Getty Images)

a somewhat unsophisticated interpretation of the e-learning environment, particularly of the somewhat transient nature of some e-learning portals. Various networking solutions can provide flexibility and affordability to a company since most of the services offered allow consumers to avoid disabling firewalls on their computers. E-learning portals such as Click2learn.com; Learn2.com; Knowledge Planet.com, THINQ, Headlight.com, and eMind offer a wide variety of learning opportunities. Yet one of the downfalls of e-learning portals and the e-learning environment in general is the sheer volume of available course material. Often, the information is not consistently updated, and depending on the vender, the same type of course could offer different information. Corporate spending on e-learning is expected to increase to an estimated $18 billion by 2005, more than four times the current spending. E-learning is also advantageous because corporations can cut travel budgets by not sending employees to training conferences, as in the case of International Business Machines (IBM), which saved $350 million in 2000 by not spending money on a training budget.

Not necessarily only a corporate advantage, e-learning has become a controversial part of academia. A combination of profit and not-for-profit ventures, e-learning in academia can lead to associates, bachelor's, master's, or even doctoral degrees. The University of Phoenix, the largest for-profit university in the United States, saw an increase in revenue by 76 percent for the fiscal year 2000–2001, to $181 million, with an increase in profits of 82 percent to $32 million. The U.S. Army offers degree-based courses through ArmyU, and students receive a free laptop and printer, as well as free tuition; as a result, the army expects enrollment to hit 80,000 by 2005 (Symonds 2001, 76). Approximately one-half of the nation's colleges and universities offer courses over the Internet toward a degree or at least use the Web to enhance on-campus courses. Estimates show that the numbers of students taking online courses could increase to approximately 5 million by 2006, more than double the estimated 2 million students currently involved in e-learning (Symonds 2001, 77). Nearly half the distance education population are adult learners with one or more children, and most are employed, so the ease and convenience of the online environment allows them to pursue their degrees.

Those who doubt the efficacy of online learning contend that the online environment lacks quality and cite situations in which students dropped out of online classes because of an inability to manage time well. Many colleges that offer both traditional and nontraditional venues for learning struggle with just how much time faculty should devote to e-teaching, and many schools, including Harvard University, feel that the preparation for the online environment is more hassle than it is worth. However, many schools, such as those sponsored by the test-preparation corporation Kaplan, including Kaplan College and Concord Law School, are primarily devoted to online learning, with a few students taking the traditional route. Yet accreditation is essential, and many students look for an accredited school in which to take classes. Those schools that lack both name recognition and accreditation have to work harder to attract more students. Capella University took five years to gain accreditation; Concord Law School allows its students to sit for the California Bar Exam, although the American Bar Association has yet to grant it accreditation. Online programs can also be costly; for example, Duke University's Fuqua School of Business offers the opportunity to earn a master's in business administration (M.B.A.), but for an estimated cost of $90,000 for the program, versus approximately $60,000 for the traditional residential M.B.A.

Economic considerations, particularly of the cost for the individual or the corporation, are essential. However, the economic cost advantage depends on the future of e-learning and the reliability of and variability in course offerings. As a potential tool for reducing the cost of workplace education (as in the case of IBM, mentioned earlier), e-learning has promise. With the advantage of offering all that the Internet (or intranet) can provide, e-learning offers a process of continuing improvement. Yet, there are problems with this medium and its development, primarily because of its relative state of infancy and the lack of good business practices or even industry models. Therefore, e-learning is in a constant state of reevaluation. As Elisabeth Goodridge noted, "Companies know that e-learning is no longer just about immediate cost savings but about increasing worker productivity, driving operational efficiencies, and streamlining corporate training" (Goodridge 2002, 64). The American Red Cross made a seven-year deal worth more than $10 million with Plateau Systems in April 2002, and Toyota Corporation plans on its partnership with Vuepoint Learning System saving the company $11.9 million over the average five-year spending period. In addition, General Motors also developed a partnership with Thomson Corporation to offer an M.B.A. program to its managers, which was formulated by schools such as Carnegie Mellon, Columbia University, and the London School of Economics.

Standards are essential when evaluating the efficacy of e-learning programs. Those who purchase relationships with e-learning portals expect a promising return on their initial investment, and the companies that invest in e-learning partnerships want to reuse courses from the online environment. To encourage both, the Department of Defense and the White House Office of Technology created the shareable content objective reference model (SCORM) in early 2000, in part because of the need for reusable content. Yet there are no e-learning standards; each institution or e-learning portal provides its own. However, as Kevin Oakes, the chief executive officer of Click2learn noted, "The ability to reuse content pieces will enable companies to create high-quality courses more quickly and update their curriculums more easily. With e-learning standards, buyers should eventually have the flexibility to mix course content from different publishers" (Oakes 2002, 70).

Two essential problems with e-learning have been identified, including poorly designed e-learning courses and insufficient focus. In the former, traditional courseware is often just reformatted for the online environment, without real consideration for the difficulties with integration into the online environment, thereby creating limited learning and no real hope for learning transfer. In the latter, course creators do not focus on the environment of the entire learning system to ensure a change in work performance, primarily for the better; they do not grasp that learning on its own will not guarantee a change in performance. It is the application of those skills that is most essential for e-learning to be effective. Relying on a single learning solution to create a change in performance only creates more problems.

Considering the emphasis on the outcome, the question of e-learning reliability and permanence remains. A Michigan State University study released in March 2002 demonstrated that onsite employee education programs offered better results than online education programs. Economics professors Carl Liedholm and Byron Brown discovered that students in a virtual education program fared worse on examinations than their traditional counterparts, a problem the professors traced to the inability to develop complex analytical skills. Liedholm argued, "These classes are not the huge success stories that they're touted to be"; employees are often "used to classroom experiences in high school and college, where they absorb material in a more hands-on way. That's what you're missing in an e-learning environment" ("Poor Grade for E-Learning" 2002). The study, based on thirty-seven questions related to the subject material for the classes the students were taking, did not result in a consensus that e-learning should be eradicated but that more emphasis should be placed on motivation and the use of live classroom environments. The study also found that female students performed better in the online environment than in the traditional environment; female students scored an average of 6 percentage points lower than their male counterparts in the traditional classroom ("Poor Grade for E-Learning" 2002).

The e-learning industry of the early twenty-first century has been characterized by a wide variety of course offerings, yet barriers to widespread adaptation remain. In 2000, classroom training accounted for 77 percent of corporate training, but experts predict that by 2004, traditional classroom training will occur about one-third of the time. The customer service industry has begun to rely on e-learning; since the service department is often the customer's first point of contact, corporations such as First Union have employed e-learning to strengthen their call center employees' customer service skills. In 1995, for example, customer service representatives handled fewer calls than at present and did not have to deal with numerous product lines, but once First Union consolidated its over sixty toll-free numbers into one main toll-free number, used at its five call centers, service representatives were taking calls regarding more than just checking accounts. The 6,000 call service representatives needed to be trained by a uniform method, so First Union called on the e-learning portal Cognitive Arts to organize a training program. After spending $350,000 to train the first half of its 6,000 agents for the pilot test, training time decreased by 16 percent, and the graduates were found to make 20 percent fewer errors than before.

Despite their infancy status in the early twenty-first century, e-learning programs are beginning to promote more productivity in the corporate environment. The public and private partnerships in the conduct of research on the results of e-learning will dissipate some of the barriers between public and private academic and business environments. Much of modern society is knowledge-based, and as Donnee Ramelli, president of General Motors University, noted, "the faster you can ship it around, the more value to major companies" (Goodridge 2002, 65). Current research suggests that e-learning, both in the corporate world and in academia, will continue to strengthen and gain accreditation, making it a viable resource for public and private partnerships in education and in the corporate world.

Jennifer Harrison

See also Computers at Work; On-the-Job-Training

References and further reading

Cone, John W. 2001. "The Power of E-performance." *T + D* 55, no. 8 (August): 32–41.

Goodridge, Elisabeth. 2002. "E-Learning Struggles to Make the Grade." *Information Week* 888: 64–66.

Mauger, Simon. 2002. "E-learning Is about People, Not Technology." *Adult Learning* 13, no. 7 (March): 9–12.

Oakes, Kevin. 2002. "The One Question You Should Ask Before You Purchase E-learning. Hint: Think Standards." *T + D* 56, no. 4 (April): 68–71.

Pantazis, Cynthia. 2001. "Executive Summary: A Vision of E-learning for America's Workforce." http://www.learningcircuits.com/2001/aug2001/pantazis.html (cited August 4).

"Poor Grade for E-learning." http://www.workforce.com.

Salopek, Jennifer. 2002. "E-Mentality: Is E-learning Affecting Classroom Behavior?" *T + D* 56, no. 4 (April): 73–76.

Symonds, William. 2001. "Giving It the Old Online Try." *Business Week* 3760: 76–81.

Weggen, Cornelia. "E-learning Portals: Who Needs Them?" http://www.learningcircuits.org/sep2000/weggen.html (cited August 4).

Employee Retirement Income Security Act (ERISA) (1974)

The Employee Retirement Income Security Act (ERISA), enacted in 1974 and amended a number of times since, is the primary federal law regulating employee benefit plans, which include both pension and welfare plans. Although ERISA does not require employers to establish a plan, any plans that are created must meet certain minimum standards. ERISA is divided into four sections: Title I deals primarily with the protection of employee rights; Title II amends the Internal Revenue Code to provide favorable tax treatment for contributions to qualified plans under ERISA (plans that satisfy ERISA's standards are referred to as "qualified plans"); Title III divides the enforcement of ERISA among the Department of Labor (DOL), the Internal Revenue Service (IRS), and the Pension Benefit Guarantee Corporation (PBGC); and Title IV establishes a system for plan termination insurance that provides benefits to participants in a plan that is unable to meet all its benefit obligations. ERISA is a complicated law that is extremely difficult to understand and interpret.

Employers had provided employee benefit plans for employees long before the passage of ERISA. These plans were largely unregulated for many years, however, and employees' expectations were often dashed when they did not get the benefits they expected. For example, at an assembly plant in South Bend, Indiana, in the 1960s, employees were given numerous assurances that their pension benefits were secure. Then, in 1966, the plant closed, and many employees—some of whom had spent their entire working lives at the plant—discovered that they would actually collect considerably less than they had been led to believe. In another case (*Hablas v. Armour and Co.*, 1959), an employee had worked for more than forty years for a company but lost all of his pension rights because he was fired one year before retirement, even though he was fired *for no apparent reason.* After stories such as these caught the attention of several prominent members of Congress, ERISA was introduced and championed by Senator Jacob Javits to regulate these plans.

ERISA covers virtually any employee benefit plan maintained by an employer or union. According to the act, the two types of employee benefit plans are pension plans and welfare plans. A pension plan is any program that provides employees with postretirement income; a welfare plan is a program that provides any other type of income or benefit to employees or their beneficiaries (for example, medical benefits, vacations, training, education, or unemployment income). There are more rules governing pension plans than there are for welfare plans. For pensions, ERISA rules govern reporting and disclosure, fiduciary responsibilities, civil enforcement provision, funding and participation, and vesting. Welfare plans are subject to ERISA reporting and disclosure provisions, fiduciary responsibility provisions, and civil enforcement provisions but not to ERISA participation, vesting, or funding rules.

ERISA has extensive disclosure provisions. First, it requires the person who oversees and administers the benefit plan (the plan administrator) to report certain plan information to the IRS, the DOL, and the PBGC and to cooperate with surveys made by the General Accounting Office. Perhaps more importantly, administrators must provide a great deal of information about benefit plans to all plan participants (some information must be provided automatically, and other information must be disclosed upon request). These rules are designed to ensure that anyone who participates in a benefit plan has access to all the information about the plan.

ERISA designates certain people who are involved with benefit plan administration as "fiduciaries." They are persons who have discretionary authority or control with respect to plan administration or plan assets. In other words, persons who have authority over other people's money or benefits are considered fiduciaries. Since fiduciaries have control over other people's money and benefits, they are subject to strict rules regarding what they may and may not do. First, ERISA has a detailed list of "prohibited transactions" rules. These rules make it illegal for fiduciaries to engage in certain specific behaviors (for example, to borrow money from the plan). Also, the act states that all fiduciaries are required to adhere to a general standard of care and loyalty.

The disclosure rules and fiduciary responsibilities just discussed apply to both pension and welfare plans. ERISA has even more rules governing pension plans. In the pension plan area, ERISA distinguishes between "qualified" and "nonqualified" plans. Qualified pension plans meet tax qualification requirements established by the Internal Revenue Code and offer substantial tax advantages to both employers and employees. To achieve these tax advantages, however, a pension plan must follow extremely complex rules governing issues such as the percentage of the firm's employees that must be permitted to participate in the plan, the age at which an employee must be allowed to participate in the plan, when a participant's benefits under the plan become "vested" (that is, nonforfeitable), and so on. In fact, a firm must spend a great deal of time and money to establish a qualified plan and more money to maintain that plan, since the requirements are so numerous, detailed, and complex.

There are two types of pension plans that can be qualified under ERISA: defined contribution pension plans and defined benefit pension plans. In a defined contribution pension plan, the employer makes contributions to accounts established on behalf of individual employees. The retirement benefits of each employee depend entirely on the value of that employee's account. Thus, the employee bears the investment risk, because the value of the employee's final benefit depends on the investment choices made by the employee. A defined benefit pension plan includes any other type of pension plan. Essentially, a defined benefit pension plan promises to pay a dollar amount at retirement, based upon a formula specified in the plan. In other words, when the employee retires, he or she gets a benefit based on things such as age, years in the plan, salary at the time of retirement, and so on.

Among the biggest problems facing workers before ERISA was passed was the number of people who expected to receive a pension benefit upon retirement, only to receive nothing when they did retire because there was no money left in the plan to pay the benefits to which they were entitled. ERISA attempts to protect benefits due under defined benefit plans in a number of ways. With defined contribution plans, there is always a possibility that plan participants will receive nothing upon retirement, but this outcome is of less concern under ERISA because participants have some control over what they receive. Participants' contributions to the plan are guaranteed, and if they make appropriate investment choices, they will receive benefits upon retirement. With defined benefit plans, ERISA has several mechanisms to ensure that participants receive plan benefits upon retirement. First, there are minimum funding rules that require the plan sponsor (the employer who established the plan) to contribute enough money to the plan to reduce the risk that there will not be enough money to pay the benefits that come due. In addition, the PBGC provides a type of insurance for defined benefit plans. The PBGC collects insurance premiums from employers whose plans are covered by PBGC insurance and pays out benefits to participants who would otherwise receive little or nothing in the way of promised plan benefits because the plan does not have sufficient funds to pay the required benefits.

Finally, ERISA has broad preemption provisions, which means that any benefit plan that is covered by ERISA has to satisfy ERISA's requirements only; the plan need not satisfy any state laws that would apply if ERISA were not in effect. In other words, if a plan is covered by ERISA, the sponsor of the plan may be able to avoid satisfying other laws that would apply if the plan were not covered by ERISA. Many critics of ERISA find this to be a major flaw with the statute, especially in the area of welfare plans. These critics believe that the regulations ERISA imposes on welfare plans are insufficient to protect these plans adequately. Further, there may be state laws that would better protect these plans. Because of ERISA's broad preemption provisions, however, the plans need not satisfy the state laws and can get away with satisfying ERISA's less stringent requirements.

Steven E. Abraham

See also American Association of Retired Persons; Defined Benefit/Defined Contribution Plans; Job Benefits; Older Workers; Pensions; Retirement

References and further reading

Cunningham, Joseph F. 1996. "ERISA: Some Thoughts on Unfulfilled Promises." *Arkansas Law Review* 83–101.

Department of Labor. 1978. *What You Should Know about the Pension and Welfare Law.* Washington, DC: U.S. Department of Labor.

Employee Retirement Income Security Act. 1974. *U.S. Code.* Vol. 28, sec. 1001 et seq.

Hylton, Maria O'Brien. 1998. "Recent Developments in ERISA Law." *Labor Law Journal* 49, no. 6 (June): 1065–1073.

Iezman, Stanley L. 1997. "Complying with ERISA: A Primer for Pension Plan Trustees." *Real Estate Review* 27, no. 1 (Spring): 18–25.

Jorden, James F., J. Pflepsen Waldemar Jr., and Stephen H. Goldberg. 1999. *Handbook On ERISA Litigation.* 2d ed. Aspen, CO: Aspen Law and Business.

Marty, Denis. 1993. "ERISA 'Plans': How Informal Can They Be?" *Employee Relations Law Journal* 18, no. 4: 603.

McAlpine, Patrick. 1998. "Survey: ERISA." *University of Arkansas at Little Rock Law Journal* 20 (Summer): 1089.

Rouco, Richard. 1994. "Available Remedies under ERISA Section 502 (a)." *Alabama Law Review* 45 (Winter): 631.

Sayre, David A., and Anthon A. Harris, eds. 1989. *ERISA: The Law and the Code.* Edison, NJ: Bureau of National Affairs.

Employee Stock Ownership

At the end of 2002, 24.1 million U.S. employees owned approximately $395 billion worth of stock in 11,561 companies where they were employed. There are six principal forms of employee stock ownership in the United States. Many of these forms are defined contribution retirement plans, in which employees or companies make contributions to a retirement benefit plan that invests in certain assets. Upon retirement, the employee receives the then current value of these investments. Many employers have multiple plans. The estimates that follow indicate the total employee ownership of all types in companies with a specific dominant plan.

The first type is the employee stock ownership plan (ESOP), a defined contribution retirement plan that allows an employer to concentrate virtually all the assets of this retirement plan in company stock. In 2002 6,431 corporations offered pure ESOPs to 3.4 million workers; those plans contained $58 billion of total employee-owned stock of all kinds (Blasi, Kruse, and Bernstein 2003, 249). ESOPs were created by the Employee Retirement Income Security Act of 1974 (ERISA), when Senator Russell Long (D-LA) introduced the idea of the San Francisco investment banker Louis Kelso into law. Kelso had elaborated on the theory of ESOPs in his 1958 book, *The Capitalist Manifesto,* written with philosopher Mortimer Adler.

In an ESOP, companies make contributions each year to fund stock for employees, or they borrow money to buy company stock on behalf of employees. In the first case, called a "nonleveraged ESOP," companies contribute cash or stock to an ESOP on behalf of employees. This is similar to a stock bonus plan. Company contributions allow the ESOP to slowly accumulate company stock year after year. In the second case, called a "leveraged ESOP," a company borrows funds from a lender to purchase stock for employees. In a leveraged ESOP, a large block of stock can be purchased in one single transaction. Thus, a company can use a leveraged ESOP to transition from little employee ownership to significant employee ownership in a very short time.

When a company uses a leveraged ESOP to create employee ownership, both principal and interest payments on a loan to buy company stock for employees are deductible from the company's income for tax purposes. In the 1980s, Congress provided an additional tax benefit. Owners of private companies were excluded from capital gains taxes on the sale of more than 30 percent of their firm to a broad group of employees. The combination of these incentives spawned thousands of largely employee-owned firms from 1980 to 2002. Other tax incentives followed. In general, corporations whose stock is publicly traded on the three stock markets (New York Stock Exchange, American Stock Exchange, and NASDAQ) have ESOPs holding less than 15 percent of the company's common stock, whereas corporations that are closely held tend to have larger employee ownership and represent most of the ESOPs that hold stakes in excess of 51 percent. Some of these firms are entirely employee-owned. Employees do not use their savings to buy stock in an ESOP. The ESOP benefit generally adds compensation on top of the typical compensation an employee would receive. The exceptions are the small number of cases in which unionized employees trade wage and benefit and work rule concessions for ESOP stock, as was common in the steel and airline industries in the 1980s and 1990s.

The second type of employee ownership is the KSOP, a combination of an ESOP and a 401(k) plan. In 2002, a total of 1,397 corporations employing 4.8 million workers provided KSOPs, holding $174 billion worth of employer stock (Blasi, Kruse, and Bernstein 2003, 249). A 401(k) plan is a retirement plan in which employees make pretax contributions to an individual account that are invested in stocks, bonds, and money market funds. Employers often match these contributions in company stock and also encourage employees to use their savings to purchase more company stock. When an ESOP is combined with a 401(k) plan, the employer adopts a leveraged ESOP to borrow funds to buy a large block of employer stock that is used over a number of years to match employee contributions to the 401(k) plan. Such plans are common in large publicly traded corporations. To the extent that an employee uses a KSOP to accumulate company stock solely as a result of the stock that the company provides to match the employee's retirement contributions, the KSOP provides a low-risk opportunity to invest in company stock. However, when employees also choose to invest their own individual retirement contributions in purchasing additional company stock, the KSOP can become a source of personal risk.

The third type of employee ownership is the 401(k) plan that is not combined with an ESOP. There are 2,813 corporations that have employer stock in pure 401(k) plans, covering 13.6 million workers and holding $147 billion of employer stock. As noted, a 401(k) plan is a defined contribution retirement plan in which employees make pretax contributions to an individual account that are invested in stocks, bonds, and money market funds. Employers match these contributions in company stock and also encourage employees to use their savings to purchase more company stock. A common match is for an employer to offer an employee a fifty cent company contribution for each dollar of employee contribution. Like KSOPs, 401(k) plans can also become a source of personal risk to employees.

The fourth type of employee ownership is the deferred profit-sharing trust. A total of 174 corporations provide profit-sharing plans that hold employer stock, covering 0.9 million workers and holding $12 billion worth of employer stock (Blasi, Kruse, and Bernstein 2003, 249). In a deferred profit-sharing trust, the employer agrees to share profits with employees according to a set formula, or discretion, on an annual basis. These profits are typically paid into the retirement plan that is a defined contribution plan. In some plans, these profits are partly or wholly invested in company stock. In addition, employees may make additional individual contributions that they can use to buy more company stock. Deferred profit-sharing trusts were far more common before the 1970s. In fact, many companies had made liberal profit-sharing contributions to their employees in most years that constituted a significant proportion of their annual compensation. However, after the rise of 401(k) plans, the federal government mandated certain ceilings for employer contributions to all retirement plans. Many employers determined that they could not afford to make meaningful profit-sharing contributions and also fund employer matching contributions to employee contributions to the increasingly popular 401(k) plans. As a result, many profit-sharing plans were converted to 401(k) plans, and authentic profit sharing fell into abeyance in many companies.

The fifth type of employee ownership is the employee stock purchase plan (ESPP). There are 746 corporations that have ESPPs, in which 1.4 million workers own $4 billion worth of employer stock. In an ESPP, the employer gives employees the opportunity to contribute funds from their regular paychecks to purchase company stock during certain buying periods. Typically, the stock is offered at 15 percent below the market price, and the employer absorbs brokerage costs. ESPPs are entirely based on employee savings, with the exception of the stock discount. However, some employees use ESPPs like short-term stock option plans. They accumulate payroll savings to buy stock but only purchase the stock in a buying period when they are assured of a clear profit. They also take advantage of the 15 percent discount. They sell the stock, pocket the profits, and do not hold large proportions of their portfolio in company stock on an ongoing basis.

The sixth form of employee ownership is individual market purchases. Employees can purchase stock in their companies on the open market through a broker. At present, there are no reliable estimates of the extent to which U.S. citizens own their company stock through such individual purchases that are unconnected to organized company retirement or benefit plans. However, it is widely observed that many companies have a "culture of employee ownership" that encourages such purchases.

KSOPs, 401(k) plans, profit-sharing trusts, and ESPPs became controversial in the 2000–2002 recession because some employees used their personal savings to purchase quite large personal holdings of their company stock. Whatever the motive or level of company encouragement for the practice, some employees clearly went way beyond the rules of diversified investing, maintained such holdings over a number of years, and allowed these holdings to represent a large proportion of their retirement portfolio. When the stock market crashed and some companies failed (for example, Enron, Worldcom), many employees experienced devastating losses. In addition, many employees reported that they were prevented from selling their shares in Enron's 401(k) plan as the shares' value fell, even as higher-level managers were able to bail out of their shares. After much public debate about whether the 401(k) form of employee ownership should be curtailed, the Bush administration issued new regulations in 2002 that gave employees added protections.

Another public policy issue surrounding employee stock ownership is whether stock should be purchased mainly by employees with their savings and retirement assets or whether it should be provided as a benefit on top of regular pay and benefits. Before 1929, many corporations strongly encouraged employees to use their savings to purchase company stock. Most of these holdings were wiped out by the stock market crash. In the 2000–2002 stock market correction, it is estimated that employees lost $261 billion in the value of employee ownership stock from March 2000 to August 2002, which again raised the problem of excessive risk in employee ownership. These concerns were resolved in several ways. Employees were encouraged to distinguish between forms of employee ownership not based on the use of personal savings, such as ESOPs and company stock matches in 401(k) plans, and those based exclusively on personal savings. ESOPs and company stock matches are usually offered in addition to normal pay and benefits. In the late 1980s and early 1990s, many companies in the technology industry began to offer stock options to rank-and-file employees as a way to gain the benefits of employee ownership without the excessive risk of tying up personal savings. Options allow employees the opportunity for the upside gain in the stock without the risk of losing capital if the share price goes down. During the 1990s, more and more nontech companies began to adopt this approach. As a result, a form of employee equity began to emerge at the beginning of the twenty-first century that emphasized less risky stock options and the low-risk ESOP and company stock matches. Employees and companies were encouraged to educate employees to take care that company stock bought directly with their savings represent only a modest and reasonable proportion of their overall portfolio.

There is extensive evidence that broad employee ownership can result in better corporate performance over the long term. In general, empirical research using large samples of corporations and adequate statistical controls suggests that broad-based employee ownership can result in one-time but sustainable increases in total shareholder return of 2 percentage points and productivity of 4 percentage points. Some studies suggest that returns on equity go up 14 percent, returns on assets rise by 12 percent, and profit margins go up by 11 percent (Blasi, Kruse, and Bernstein 2003, 153–184; Kruse 2002). A number of studies strongly suggest that these effects are the result of combining employee ownership with a participatory and team-oriented corporate culture.

Joseph Blasi and Douglas Kruse

See also Compensation; Defined Benefit/Defined Contribution Plans; Profit Sharing; Stock Options

References and further reading

Beyster Institute. 2002. *The Entrepreneur's Guide to Equity Compensation.* La Jolla, CA: Beyster Institute for Entrepreneurial Employee Ownership.

Blair, Margaret, Douglas Kruse, and Joseph Blasi. 2000. "Employee Ownership: An Unstable Form or a Stabilizing Force?" Pp. 241–298 in *The New Relationship: Human Capital in the American Corporation.* Edited by Margaret Blair and Thomas Kochan. Washington, DC: Brookings Institution.

Blasi, Joseph, Douglas Kruse, and Aaron Bernstein. 2003. *In the Company of Owners: the Truth about Stock Options and Why Every Employee Should Have Them.* New York: Basic Books.

Blasi, Joseph R., Douglas Kruse, James Sesil, Maya Kroumova, and Ed Carberry. 2000. *Stock Options, Corporate Performance, and Organizational Change.* Oakland, CA: National Center for Employee Ownership. (The full research report is available at www.nceo.org/library/optionreport.html)

Kelse, Louis O., and Mortimer Adler. 1958. *The Capitalist Manifesto.* New York: Random House.

Kruse, Douglas. 2002. "Research Evidence on the Prevalence and Effects of Employee Ownership." *Journal of Employee Ownership Law and Finance,* 14, no. 4: 65–98.

National Center for Employee Ownership. 2002. *Selling to an ESOP.* Oakland, CA: National Center for Employee Ownership.

National Industrial Conference Board. 1928. *Employee Stock Purchase Plans in the United States.* New York: National Industrial Conference Board.

Rosen, Corey, Katherine Klein, and Karen M. Young. 1986. *Employee Ownership in America: The Equity Solution.* Lexington, MA: D. C. Heath, Lexington Books.

Sesil, James, Maya Kroumova, Joseph Blasi, and Douglas Kruse. 2002. "Broad-based Employee Stock Options in U.S. New Economy Firms." *British Journal of Industrial Relations* 4, no. 2 (June): 273–294.

U.S. Department of Labor. 2000. Press Release: "Pilot Survey on the Incidence of Stock Options in Private Industry in 1999." Washington, DC: U.S. Department of Labor, Bureau of Labor Statistics, USDL 00-290.

Weeden, Ryan, Ed Carberry, and Scott Rodrick. 2001. *Current Practices in Stock Option Plan Design.* Oakland, CA: National Center for Employee Ownership.

Weitzman, Martin. 1986. *Share Economy: Conquering Stagflation.* Cambridge, MA: Harvard University Press.

WestwardPay.com. "Biotechnology Stock Compensation Practices." 1998. http://www.WestwardPay.com, March (cited May 20, 2003).

Employment and Training Administration (ETA)

The Employment and Training Administration (ETA) was established in February 1963 and acquired its current name in 1975. When the agency was created, John F. Kenney was president and W. Willard Wirtz was secretary of labor. Just nine months before, the Manpower Development and Training Act, the first major piece of manpower legislation since 1946, had been enacted. The Kennedy administration and members of Congress developed this legislation to address concerns about continuing unemployment and the impact of new technologies and automation on the U.S. workforce.

One of nearly twenty agencies comprising the U.S. Department of Labor (DOL), ETA was reorganized into its present structure as a requirement of the Workforce Investment Act of 1998. The national office includes four program offices focusing on adult, youth, employer/labor services, and workforce security. Each of six U.S. regions has a parallel structure. The principles guiding the work of ETA include encouraging business growth through creation of an "agile workforce," equipping individuals with career information and skills, helping the less fortunate to make sound economic decisions, administering a workforce system that partners with the education system, and combining youth training programs and education. The primary programs and activities of ETA include youth education, training, and apprenticeship programs; the Senior Community Service Employment Program (SCSEP); management of the U.S. Employment Service; responsibility for the federal side of the unemployment insurance system; management of the labor market information system; and many adult programs, including welfare-to-work, training, one-stop centers, and programs for Native Americans and migrant and seasonal farm workers.

From its inception, an important goal of ETA was to build a quality workforce capable of adapting to the changing economic and technological conditions of the times. At any given moment, how the agency seeks to achieve this goal is influenced by the particular federal legislation in force and the priorities of the presidential administration in office. For example, from 1982 through 1997, the Job Training Partnership Act (JTPA) was a central element of the legislative framework within which ETA worked. JTPA mandated a core of employment and training services to be provided for specific groups of economically disadvantaged or dislocated adult workers and youth. Although the requirements of JTPA had much to do with ETA's agenda, under the Reagan administration in the mid-1980s, the long-term competitiveness of the U.S. workforce and the dislocation of workers by technology were also key concerns that helped shape ETA's activities. Under President George H. W. Bush, the agency developed a "New Century Workplace" plan emphasizing youth apprenticeship programs; an overhaul of the Job Corps program for youth; job training for the homeless; training, job readiness, and unemployment insurance for dislocated workers; and workplace literacy programs.

Soon after President Bill Clinton took office in January 1993, amendments to JTPA took effect, and the DOL and ETA declared their intention to focus on "preparing workers to meet the demands of increasingly complex and challenging workplaces" (U.S. Department of Labor 1996, 3). An important goal was to enhance both the basic and higher-level skills of workers available to U.S. companies. ETA sought to consolidate and reform workforce education and training programs around two core concepts: school-to-work (for youth) and "one-stop" workforce development centers.

The 1998 Workforce Investment Act (WIA) required a major realignment of delivery of job training, education, and employment services so that both employers and individuals needing information or services would have a single point of contact (one-stop center) in a local neighborhood area. Individuals ("customers") were to be given more choice about the services they might use, and "individual training accounts" were to be established to pay providers for the services chosen by customers. Three separate funding streams were created for adults, dislocated workers, and youth. Certain core services (for example, job search and placement assistance, assessment of skills and needs) were to be available to *all* adults, with no eligibility restrictions. More intensive services (including the possibility of skill training) were to be provided to those who could not find a job using core services.

The WIA became fully effective in July 2000. Early implementation came in a strong economic climate at the end of the Clinton administration. The national unemployment rate in early 2000 was under 3.5 percent. ETA quickly moved to develop its strategic plan for fiscal years 1999–2004 (U.S. Department of Labor 2000), outlining agency reorganization plans and establishing goals and strategies for development of a national workforce investment system. Despite the events of September 11, 2001, and an economic downturn in 2001–2002 (the unemployment rate reached 5.4 percent in October 2001), the new administration of George W. Bush retained and continued to build on the one-stop center concept. According to the ETA 2003 Performance Plan, a key ETA focus is on "business as a principal customer of the workforce system" (U.S. Department of Labor, Employment and Training Administration 2002, 2). Agency priorities include reform of the unemployment insurance system, improving adult and dislocated worker services provided by one-stop centers, increasing the accountability of service providers, and generally tightening many aspects of the services and programs under ETA oversight.

The Workforce Investment Act will be up for congressional reauthorization at the end of the program year that begins July 2003. Although there appears to be consensus among most interested parties that the concept of one-stop centers should be retained and developed, several aspects of WIA have been criticized. For example, states and localities are finding it difficult to develop and sustain one-stop centers without funding specifically allocated for that purpose. In addition, critics note that the emphasis on job placement over training and the tiered system of access to services exclude many people from programs. There are also concerns about efforts by the Bush administration to cut funding for youth programs and to overemphasize the role of businesses in local policy development and program management.

In August 2002, President Bush signed the Trade Adjustment Assistance Reform Act of 2002 (TAA Reform Act), which extended the TAA program and repealed the North American Free Trade Agreement (NAFTA)–TAA program. This legislation targets workers affected by the movement of production to other countries or by increased imports and requires greater coordination of services between the WIA and TAA programs. It also allows employers more flexibility to determine the types of on-the-job and custom training that might be needed by workers. The Alternative TAA Program for workers fifty years and older and provision of health insurance benefits represent new features of the TAA program that will be implemented during 2003.

As ETA looks to the future, a vital theme in its plans is the maximization of use of information technology and resources to achieve both program and management goals. ETA is revamping its automated performance management systems and has developed a sophisticated website (http://www.doleta.gov) that offers a wide range of user-friendly information and resources. Here, one can access up-to-date information and news about ETA, descriptions and links to the network of one-stop centers and other workforce development partners, details about the programs and activities for which ETA carries responsibility, and many links to other organizations and information. In addition, the researcher can tap into a workforce security research database, the full text of policy and research reports from 1983 to present, workforce security research publications from 1997 to 2002, and other policy and research papers and materials.

Finally, ETA is also participating fully in the federal government's "e-government" initiative, which seeks "the transformation of public sector internal and external relationships through Internet-enabled operations, information technology, and communications that optimize government service delivery, constituent participation, and governance" (U.S. Department of Labor, Employment and Training Administration 2001, 2). The agency has created a website (http://www.egovernment.doleta.gov), where its strategies for becoming digitally based and fully Internet-accessible are outlined and a forum for discussion has been established.

Natalie Ammarell

See also Comprehensive Employment and Training Act; Job Training Partnership Act; Occupations and Occupational Trends in the United States; Trade Adjustment Assistance Program; Workforce Investment Act

References and further reading

National Coalition for the Homeless. 2002. *NCH Recommendations for the Reauthorization of the Workforce Investment Act.* http://www.nationalhomeless.org/wia/recommendations.html (cited December 30).

Occupational Information Network (O*NET). 2002. A wide variety of resources and occupational information are available at http://online.onetcenter.org (cited December 30).

U.S. Department of Labor. 1996. *Training and Employment Report of the Secretary of Labor Covering the Period July 1992–September 1993.* Reports dating back to the July 1986–September 1987 period are accessible through the Internet. The most recent reports cover the periods July 1995–September 1996 and July 1996–September 1997. http://wdr.doleta.gov/opr/FULLTEXT/default.asp?titlesort=yes (cited June 15, 2002).

U.S. Department of Labor, Employment and Training Administration. 2000. *Strategic Plan: FY 1999–2004.* Washington, DC: U.S. Department of Labor, September.

———. 2001. *An E-government Strategy for America's Workforce Network.* http://www.egovernment.doleta.gov (cited May 13, 2003).

———. 2002. *Serving American Businesses and Workers: 2003 Annual Performance Plan for the Committee on Appropriations.* http://www.doleta.gov/perform (cited February 21).

U.S. General Accounting Office. 2001. *Workforce Investment Act: Better Guidance Needed to Address Concerns Over New Requirements.* October. GAO-02-72. Available at http://www.gao.gov (cited June 15, 2002).

U.S. Office of Workforce Security. 2002. *Leading Change under the WIA One-Stop System.* Final report prepared for the U.S. Department of Labor Employment and Training Administration under contract L6826-8-00-80-30. New Brunswick, NJ: Rutgers University, John J. Heldrich Center for Workforce Development.

Employment at Will

Employment at will is the legal doctrine that wage-earning or salaried employees may be terminated for good cause, bad cause, or no cause at all. Although it lacks a statutory basis, it was codified in U.S. common law (that is, case law or the accumulated precedents of court decisions) in the late nineteenth century and reflects that era's commitment to laissez-faire economic principles. In theory, barring an express contract, employment may be ended freely at any time, by either employer or employee, without liability or injury to either. Thus, exceptions to the at-will doctrine have consisted of that minority of the U.S. workforce working under contract or collective bargaining agreements.

For decades, employers' right to terminate at-will employees on any grounds was essentially absolute. Yet, by the mid–twentieth century, influential lawyers and others were challenging the structural imbalance and potential for abuse in the at-will doctrine. These critics felt that the courts had erred in treating the employment relationship as one in which firms and employees had equal bargaining power, and they began to question both instances of what might be considered wrongful discharge and appropriate remedies by which employee interests might be protected. In this effort, much of the impetus came from the example of postwar union contracts in which "just cause" for termination, forms of progressive discipline, and grievance procedures (such as arbitration) were detailed (Getman and Pogrebin 1988, 213–215). Similarly, the more pro-labor governments of postwar Europe had enacted protections against wrongful discharge, leaving the United States alone among the industrialized nations in its laissez-faire stance (see Summers 1976). However, there was no collective voice calling for statutory protection. At-will employees were not an organized force. Employers formed a well-organized lobby against interference with management's prerogatives, and unions had a stake in arguing that employees must seek unionization to protect themselves against unjust termination. Legal specialists argued that changes to the common law doctrine must emerge from within the courts themselves (see Blades 1967).

Indeed, beginning fitfully in the 1950s, accelerating in the 1980s, and continuing into the present, employment at will has been successfully challenged in numerous court cases. Employers' right of discharge has been curtailed by three important exceptions (see Muhl 2001). The most widely adopted has been the public policy exception, which does not allow an employer to fire an employee in violation of public policy (such as terminating someone who refuses to break the law at the employer's behest). The second major exception involves an implied contract (such as an employee handbook that promises adherence to just-cause guidelines). Finally, courts in a few states have recognized a covenant of good faith and fair dealing as the basis for any employment relationship, thereby eliminating the employer's unilateral right to fire with bad or no cause.

Many employees rely for protection on state and federal statutes covering specific employment situations, such as prohibiting discrimination (as by age, sex, or race) or retaliatory discharge of whistleblowers. However, though draft law exists in the Model Employment Termination Act (requiring a showing of "good cause" for discharge), comprehensive legislation overturning the principles of the at-will doctrine has not been forthcoming. Indeed, the challenges to employment at will, though impressive, have resulted in a patchwork of legal interpretations across the states. Much remains in question, such as what may be considered "public policy." Similarly, firms have found it relatively easy to avoid providing an implied contract for jobs, simply by rewriting employee handbooks. Enforcement of statutory and judicial protections is uneven (see Hananel 2002; Henry 1989), even as conservative objections to interference with "markets" have become insistent and well articulated (see Reynolds and Reynolds 1995).

At this time, employment at will remains the doctrine affecting most U.S. employees. Most courts continue to favor employer rights under the at-will doctrine, and few employees can meet the legal tests or afford the legal battles to define their situation as protected by law. Further, those protections leave untouched broad areas of ordinary employment experience. For instance, people fired for "business necessity," even if top executives reap millions from the firm's downturn, are not protected from at-will presumptions (see Greenhouse 2002). Nor are those fired for commonplace reasons ranging from personality conflicts to technological change.

Jacquelyn H. Southern

See also Arbitration

References and further reading

Blades, Lawrence E. 1967. "Employment at Will v. Individual Freedom: On Limiting the Abusive Exercise of Employer Power." *Columbia Law Review* 67: 1404–1435.

Getman, Julius G., and Bertrand B. Pogrebin. 1988. *Labor Relations: The Basic Processes, Law, and Practice.* Westbury, NY: Foundation Press.

Greenhouse, Steven. 2002. "The Mood at Work: Anger and Anxiety." *New York Times,* October 29.

Hananel, Sam. 2002. "Whistle-Blower Report Cites Abuses." *Washington Post,* September 1.

Henry, Sandra Perry. 1989. "Can You Recognize the Wrongful Discharge?" *Labor Law Journal* 40, no. 3: 168–176.

Muhl, Charles J. 2001. "The Employment-at-Will Doctrine: Three Major Exceptions." *Monthly Labor Review* (January): 3–11.

Reynolds, Cameron D., and Morgan O. Reynolds. 1995. "State Court Restrictions on the Employment-at-Will Doctrine." *Regulation* 18, no. 1. http://www.cato.org/pubs/regulation/reg18n1e.html.

Summers, Clyde W. 1976. "Individual Protection against Unjust Dismissal: Time for a Statute." *Virginia Law Review* 62: 481–520.

Equal Employment Opportunity Commission (EEOC)

The Equal Employment Opportunity Commission (EEOC) is the primary federal administrative agency that deals with employment discrimination. The EEOC has enforcement authority over several federal discrimination laws: Title VII of the Civil Rights Act of 1964, the Age Discrimination in Employment Act (ADEA), Titles I and V of the Americans with Disabilities Act (ADA), the Equal Pay Act (EPA), and Sections 501 and 505 of the Rehabilitation Act of 1973. The commission's authority differs from statute to statute, however. In other words, the EEOC is involved with each of the laws just mentioned in slightly different ways.

The EEOC is headquartered in Washington, D.C., and has fifty offices throughout the country. It is composed of five persons who are appointed by the president with the advice and consent of the Senate. Members of the commission serve for five-year terms, and no more than three members of the commission can be from the same political party.

The EEOC was created by Title VII of the Civil Rights Act, which also gave the commission certain enforcement powers with respect to Title VII. When it was first created, the EEOC had no enforcement authority over the ADEA or the EPA, however. Enforcement powers over the EPA and the ADEA were transferred to the commission in 1978, and the ADA delegated enforcement responsibility to the EEOC when the law went into effect in 1991.

The EEOC has five primary functions: charge processing, litigation, interpretation of federal discrimination laws, adjudication of complaints by federal employees, and resolution of complaints by state governmental policymakers. Employees wishing to enforce rights created by Title VII, the ADEA, or the ADA must file a charge of discrimination with their local EEOC office (charges are not required by the EPA or Section 501 of the Rehabilitation Act). A lawsuit may not be filed unless the individual first files a charge and then lets the EEOC's administrative process run its course (this is referred to as exhausting the "administrative remedies"). Once a charge has been filed, the commission will investigate the matter.

In connection with its investigation, the EEOC has broad powers to obtain a wide variety of documents from any party to the charge. The commission will often hold an administrative hearing in an attempt to resolve the charge as well. At the conclusion of its investigation, the EEOC will reach a determination as to whether the discrimination alleged in the charge actually occurred. If it determines that the alleged discrimination did not take place, it will notify the charging party of its decision and send a "right-to-sue letter" to that person. A right-to-sue letter notifies the charging party that he or she has ninety days to file a lawsuit against the employer in federal court. In other words, even if the EEOC believes that the employer did not discriminate against the person who filed the charge, that person can file a lawsuit in court anyway.

If the EEOC determines that the discrimination complained of did occur, it will notify both parties and attempt to settle the matter. The commission meets with everyone involved and tries to help them reach an out of court settlement. The EEOC cannot force either party to settle, however. If the EEOC believes that discrimination occurred but its conciliation efforts fail, it will do one of two things. It is authorized to commence lawsuits against private (that is, nongovernmental) employers. In other words, if the commission believes that discrimination took place but the employer is unwilling to settle, the EEOC may bring a lawsuit against the employer on behalf of the complaining party. This

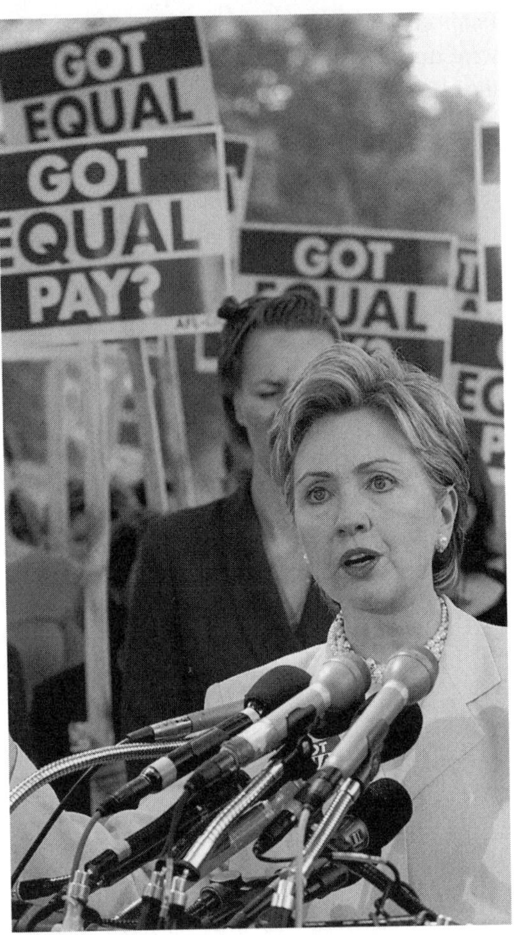

Senator Hillary Rodham Clinton (D-NY) speaks outside the U.S. Capitol, June 12, 2001. Clinton called for working women to receive equal pay and for increased penalties and enforcement of the Equal Pay Act. (AFP/Corbis)

action makes it unnecessary for the complaining party to file his or her own suit. In actuality, however, the commission files suit in only a small percentage of these cases. If the EEOC decides not to commence a lawsuit against the employer, it will send the charging party the same right-to-sue letter mentioned above. Again, the charging party then has ninety days to file a lawsuit against the employer.

When an employee of the federal government sues under Title VII, the process works slightly differently. Federal employees file their discrimination charges with their own employing agency (that is, their own employer), not the EEOC, and the employing agency investigates the matter. The person who filed the charge may request an EEOC officer to serve as a neutral fact finder, and a hearing in front of an EEOC officer may be requested. The ultimate decision about whether discrimination occurred is made by the federal agency, not the EEOC. If the individual is not satisfied with the agency's decision, however, he or she may demand a full adversarial hearing before the EEOC. If such a hearing is requested, the commission does reach a formal decision. Then, if the individual is dissatisfied with the EEOC's decision, he or she may file suit against the employing agency in federal court. The individual does not have to have a hearing in front of the EEOC, however. He or she may bypass the EEOC entirely and file suit in federal court immediately after receiving the agency's determination.

Section 321 of the 1991 Civil Rights Act provides protection against discrimination for persons chosen by an elected state or local government official to serve in what are referred to as "personal staff" positions, for appointees at the "policymaking level," and for those serving as an "immediate advisor with respect to the exercise of the constitutional or legal powers of the office" (Civil Rights Act 1991). Such employees are required to proceed with a complicated process of mediation and conciliation that does not involve the EEOC. If that process is unsuccessful, however, the complaining party is authorized to file a complaint with the EEOC. The commission will hold a hearing to determine whether a violation exists, issue a decision and order, and provide for appropriate relief if a violation is found. Although the commission's orders in these cases may be appealed to federal court, the grounds for overturning its orders are quite limited.

The EEOC has issued many interpretations of discrimination law, known as guidelines, in accordance with the formal regulatory process that must be followed whenever a federal agency issues guidelines of this type. Its guidelines are maintained in the Code of Federal Regulations, where all federal regulations are kept. Unlike guidelines issued by certain agencies (for example, the Securities and Exchange Commission), those issued by the EEOC are not legally binding. The U.S. Supreme Court has held that the commission's guidelines are entitled to "great deference," however, meaning that employers take great risk in ignoring them (*Albermarle Paper Co. v. Moody,* 1975). The commission also issues numerous less formal statements referred to as "policy statements" that deal with the law and maintains a Web page (http://www.eeoc.gov) with a great deal of advice and information about the laws it enforces.

Steven E. Abraham

See also Affirmative Action; African Americans and Work; Equal Pay Act; Glass Ceiling; Work and Hispanic Americans

References and further reading

Bales, Richard A. 1999. "Compulsory Employment Arbitration and the EEOC." *Pepperdine Law Review* 27 (December): 1–51.

Calvasina, Gerald E., Richard V. Calvasina, and Eugene J. Calvasina. 2000. "Management and the EEOC." *Business Horizons* 43, no. 4 (July): 3–8.

Casellas, Gilbert F. 1998. "The Equal Employment Opportunity Commission: Challenges for the Twenty-First Century." *The Trustees of the University of Pennsylvania Journal of Labor and Employment Law* (Spring): 1.

Civil Rights Act. 1991. Public Law 102–166. November 21, 1991, 105 Stat. 1071.

Kilberg, William J. 1997. "Whither Goest the EEOC?" *Employee Relations Law Journal* 23, no. 2 (Autumn): 1–4.

Payne, Dinah, Sandra J. Hartman, Maurice F. Villere, Beverly H. Nelson, and Gregory Baxter. 1992. "Is Big Brother Watching? Perception and Research on the Effectiveness of the EEOC." *Labor Law Journal* 43, no. 4 (April): 249–256.

Wood, B. Dan. 1990. "Does Politics Make a Difference at the EEOC?" *American Journal of Political Science* 34, no. 2 (May): 503.

Equal Pay Act (EPA) (1963)

The Equal Pay Act (EPA) was enacted as an amendment to the Fair Labor Standards Act in 1963. The act makes it unlawful for an employer to discriminate on the basis of sex in the payment of wages for jobs that require equal skill, effort, or responsibility and are performed under similar working conditions, except where the differential is justified by one of four statutory defenses. The act protects the majority of employees working in the United States.

The EPA was the culmination of years of crusading by women's groups for the goal of "equal pay for equal work." In the congressional debates leading to the passage of the act, there were detailed hearings on the specific problem of relatively depressed wages earned by women, and this testimony was supported by volumes of statistics detailing how women were paid less than men, even if they were doing the same jobs.

The EPA was not the first attempt to legislate a requirement of equal pay for equal work. In 1870, Congress enacted legislation that, among other things, adopted the principle of equal pay for equal work in the federal civil service. This principle was not generally implemented, however, until the Classification Act of 1923, when Congress established a uniform system of job grades and salaries. This early legislative response to sex-based pay discrimination was largely limited to the federal sector, however, although two states (Michigan and Montana) enacted broad equal pay laws in 1919 that applied to private employers.

The first major application of the concept of equal pay for equal work in the private sector did not occur until World War II, when the National War Labor Board approved wage increases that were designed to correct gross inequities based on sex, race, or age. Their guiding principle was this: "If it shall become necessary to employ women on work ordinarily performed by men, they must be allowed equal pay for equal work." This principle was reaffirmed by the National War Labor Board on November 24, 1942, in General Order No. 16, which stated, "Increases which equalize the wage or salary rates paid to females with the rates paid to males for comparable quality and quantity of work on the same or similar operations . . . may be made without approval of the National War Labor Board" (National War Labor Board 1943).

Based on the experience of the War Labor Boards, a comprehensive federal equal pay bill was introduced in Congress in 1945. At that time, there were six states with similar legislation, and there was substantial support from both the government and the public for a federal bill. As proposed, the 1945 bill, S. 1178, provided, "It shall be an unfair wage practice for any employer . . . to discriminate between the sexes—(a) by paying wages to any female employee at a rate less than the rate at which he pays or has paid wages to male employees for work of comparable quality and quantity." The 1945 legislative effort failed, however, and, although similar bills were introduced in every subsequent session of Congress, it was not until 1963 that an equal pay bill was finally approved.

The bill that eventually became the EPA would have prohibited sex discrimination in compensation for "work of comparable character on jobs the performance of which requires comparable skills," but the act was approved only when the sponsors of the legislation agreed to change the language in the bill from "work of comparable character on jobs the performance of which requires comparable skills" to "equal work on jobs the performance of which requires equal skills." This change greatly narrowed the types of wage discrimination that would violate the act (Equal Pay Act 1963).

To proceed successfully with an EPA claim, an employee must show that a male and a female employee who work in the same establishment are paid different wages, on the basis of sex, for equal work (although most EPA cases are brought by females, the act protects males as well). The plaintiff has the burden of showing that the work involved was equal. According to the act itself, the term *equal* means that the jobs require "equal skill, effort, and responsibility" and that they "are performed under similar working conditions." A plaintiff's burden of proof in this regard was made much less onerous by *Shultz v. Wheaton Glass Co.* (1970), which held that the word *equal* in the EPA does not require that jobs be identical but only that they be "substantially equal." Further, it is the actual content of the work that is important. The fact that two jobs have the same title does not mean that they will be found substantially equal for purposes of the act, and the fact that two jobs have different titles does not foreclose the possibility that they will be found equal under the act.

If the plaintiff succeeds in proving that he or she was paid less than a person of the opposite sex despite the fact that he or she was doing equal work, the employer will be able to avoid liability by proving that the wage differential is due to one of four statutory exceptions in the act itself: "(i) a seniority system; (ii) a merit system; (iii) a system that measures earnings by quantity or quality of production; or (iv) a differential based on any other factor other than sex" (Equal Pay Act 1963). The first three defenses are fairly straightforward, but much litigation has taken place concerning whether an employer can justify sex-based wage differentials because they are "based on any other factor other than sex." As the wording suggests, this is a catch-all exception. The words "a differential based on any other factor other than sex," could embrace an almost unlimited variety of possible factors. Among the factors employers have used to justify different wages paid to the opposite sexes are temporary assignments (that is, a higher-paid employee is temporarily assigned to a normally lower-paid job but continues to be paid at the higher rate), training programs (employees receive different pay rates while they are going through a training program), shift differentials (employees working more difficult shifts are paid more than employees working easier shifts), market forces (an employee is paid more to lure him away from another, higher-paying, job), and education or experience (employees are paid more because they have more education or experience than other employees). The list just mentioned is not exhaustive, and in fact, any of the factors just enumerated might be unsuccessful in any given case.

An employee wishing to sue for discrimination under the EPA can file his or her lawsuit in federal court. The administrative procedures required by Title VII are not applicable to the EPA. The EEOC also has the authority to file its own lawsuits under the EPA, even if no charge has been filed. If a violation of the EPA is established, the employer is required to compensate the plaintiff in several ways. First, the defendant must raise the pay rate of the lower-paid employee to that of the employee receiving the higher rate. (It is impermissible for the employer to reduce the wages of the higher-paid employee.) In addition, the defendant must pay the plaintiff the difference between what he or she earned and what the higher-paid employee earned as "back wages." Finally, the defendant must pay the plaintiff "liquidated damages" in an amount equal to the back wages mentioned in the previous sentence, unless the employer can prove that it acted in good faith and that it had reasonable grounds for believing that its actions were lawful.

Finally, it should be noted that many people contend that the Equal Pay Act is too narrow and does not do nearly enough to rectify the compensation discrimination suffered by women. One criticism of the law is that it does not cover a lawsuit based on the theory of "comparable worth." Comparable worth proponents argue that it should be illegal for employers to discriminate in compensation if two jobs are "worth" the same (that is, equal in value), even if the jobs themselves are different in content. Currently, the act does not support such a claim; the jobs themselves must be equal.

Legislation was introduced in the 1990s to amend the act and prohibit a broader class of claims. The Paycheck Fairness Act would correct weaknesses in the Equal Pay Act by amending it to prohibit employers from penalizing employees for sharing information about their salaries, to make it easier to file class action suits, and to allow compensatory and punitive damages. (Compensatory damages make the person "whole," or place that person in the position he or she would have been in without the discrimination, and cover both monetary losses and nonmonetary losses, such as pain and suffering. Punitive damages may be awarded to punish the employer and deter it from future discriminatory conduct.) The Paycheck Fairness Act would also direct the Department of Labor to develop and distribute information, such as voluntary pay guidelines for implementing pay equity.

The Fair Pay Act would amend the Equal Pay Act by requiring employers to pay equal wages to employees in equivalent jobs. The act would apply to both public and private employers. In addition, the Fair Pay Act requires employers to submit reports to the EEOC with wage information and prohibits retaliation against employees or others who discuss wages or pursue their rights under the act. The Fair Pay Act and Paycheck Fairness Act, introduced in Congress in 1999, have not passed the House or the Senate.

Steven E. Abraham

See also Comparable Worth; Equal Employment Opportunity Commission; Glass Ceiling; Pay Equity; Pink Collar; Women and Work

References and further reading

Bland, Timothy S., and Michele L. Fowler. 1999. "Anatomy of an Equal Pay Act Case." *Employee Relations Law Journal* 25, no. 3 (Winter): 17–39.

Brady, Teresa. 1998. "How Equal Is Equal Pay?" *Management Review* 87, no. 3 (March): 59–63.

Director, Jerald J. 2001. "Annotation: Construction and Application of Provisions of the Equal Pay Act of 1963 (29 USCA § 206(d)) Prohibiting Wage Discrimination on the Basis of Sex." *American Law Review.* Fed. 7: 707–749.

Equal Pay Act. 1963. *U.S. Code.* Vol. 29, sec. 206d.

Freed, Mayer G., and Daniel D. Polsby. 1984. "Comparable Worth in the Equal Pay Act." *University of Chicago Law Review* (Fall): 51.

Hamburg, Jeanne M. 1989. "Note: When Prior Pay Isn't Equal Pay: A Proposed Standard for the Identification of 'Factors Others Than Sex' under the Equal Pay Act." *Columbia Law Review* 89 (June): 1085–1103.

Narol, Mel. 1998. "A New Defense to the Old Defenses? The EEOC Equal Pay Act Guidelines." *Marquette Sports Law Journal* 9 (Fall): 175 –195.

National War Labor Board. 1943. "Chapter 24: Equal Pay for Women." Pp. 290–291 in *The Termination Report of the National War Labor Board: Industrial Disputes and Wage Stabilization in Wartime.* Vol. 1. Press Release no. B 693.

Sneirson, Amy M. 1994. "Case Comment: One of These Things Is Not Like the Other: Proving Liability under the Equal Pay Act and Title VII: *Tidwell v. Fort Howard Corp.,* 989 F.2d 406 (10th Cir. 1993)." *Washington University Law Quarterly* 72: 783–802.

Whitley, L. Tracee. 1997. "'Any Other Factor Other Than Sex': Forbidden Market Defenses and Subversion of the Equal Pay Act of 1963." *Northeastern University Forum* 2: 51–84.

Ergonomics

Ergonomics is the science of designing the work process and environment to correspond to the natural movements of the worker. It is also known as "human factors" or "biotechnology." Its goals are to improve employee efficiency, productivity, and morale; enhance the quality of work; and limit avoidable injuries, illnesses, and stress on the job that often result when workers are forced to contort themselves to meet the regimented requirements and pacing associated with standardized work processes. Ergonomics studies the relationship between work and human factors such as the musculoskeletal system, the nervous system, and variations in body weight and size; the impact of heavy work, handling loads, fatigue, stress, boredom, and improving job design to avoid monotonous, repetitious tasks; the impact of natural and electric lighting on vision; the relation of noise and vibration to stress; and the effect of environmental factors such as climate, ventilation, indoor air pollution, colors, and music on the mood and effectiveness of the worker and the work environment.

Poorly designed work processes and stations often result in work-related repetitive strain illnesses (RSIs), which are progressive illnesses affecting the muscles, nerves, tendons, ligaments, joints, cartilage, and spinal discs caused by repeated motions in awkward positions. There are more than twenty types of RSIs, including bursitis, carpal tunnel syndrome, DeQuervian's syndrome, epicondylitis, ganglions, lower back pain, synovitis, tendonitis, and tenosynovitis. RSIs are also known as "cumulative trauma disorders" and "musculoskeletal disorders." Although many repetitive motion jobs are performed by women, work stations and machinery are usually designed with men in mind. This helps to explain why women suffer a disproportionate percentage of RSIs (Kome 1998, 5; Mogensen 1996, 15).

The problem of RSIs in the workplace resulting from poorly organized work processes were recognized by the Italian physician Bernardino Ramazzini, the father of occupational medicine, in his pioneering 1700 work, *De Morbis Artificum Diatriba* (Diseases of workers). Observing the unnatural motions and postures of scribes and notaries, he wrote that "certain morbid affections gradually arise from some particular posture of the limbs or unnatural movements of the body called for while they work" (Franco 1999, 859). Cumulative trauma disorders were also observed in shoemakers, telegraphers, clerical workers, writers, seamstresses, farmers who milked cows, and others during the nineteenth century. Today, a wide range of workers suffer from RSIs, including meatpackers, poultry cutters, food processors, assembly line workers, warehouse and delivery workers who must repeatedly lift and move heavy loads, construction workers (especially jackhammer operators), clerks using price scanners, textile workers, and office workers typing on computer keyboards (Pascarelli and Quilter 1994; Mogensen 1996; Kome 1998).

The modern study of ergonomics evolved out of the effort to redress the deleterious impact of the Industrial Revolution's one-size-fits-all production techniques on workers' health. Ergonomics began to be taken seriously as an applied science during World War II, when engineers and planners realized that taking the variability of human factors, such as body type, height, and weight, into account when designing military machinery and equipment resulted in improved efficiency, operation, and morale. After the war, it became readily apparent that ergonomic principles could be applied to a wide variety of industrial work processes and environments (Dembe 1996).

Ergonomics has grown in importance as the computerization and automation of work processes have resulted in the increase of repetitive work processes and the number of work-related RSIs, which have been the fastest-growing occupational illness in the United States since the 1980s. According to the U.S. Bureau of Labor Statistics (BLS), RSIs account for approximately 60 percent of all reported occupational illnesses—up from only 18 percent in 1981 (Mogensen 1996, 14). As the RSI problem became widespread during the 1990s, the Occupational Safety and Health Administration (OSHA) declared it to be "the most important occupational safety and health problem in the United States today" (Dainoff 1992, 27).

The economic and social costs of RSIs are enormous. They are the largest single cause of workplace injury in the United States. The BLS reports that more than 1.8 million U.S. workers suffer from RSIs annually, one-third of which are serious enough to force workers to miss at least one workday. Workers who are afflicted with carpal tunnel syndrome lose an average of thirty-two workdays. Some observers maintain that these figures are low because many workers are unorganized and afraid to report injuries for fear of losing their job or because they haven't been properly educated about the causes and symptoms of RSIs. The economic cost to society of RSI-related injuries in terms of workers compensation claims, lost work time, and lost productivity is estimated to be $50 billion a year, and RSI-related costs account for one-third of all workers compensation expenditures (National Academy of Sciences 2000; National Institute for Occupational Safety and Health 1995, 7).

In the early 1980s, the enormous scope of the problem led to calls by organized labor, women's groups like 9to5, the National Association of Working Women, and local committees for safety and health such as the New York Committee for Occupational Safety and Health for a federal ergonomics regulation to limit the human damage done by RSIs. The resulting political battle with capital has lasted for twenty years and is still going strong. Throughout the 1980s, organized labor petitioned OSHA, whose mission it is to protect workers from preventable hazards on the job, to promulgate an ergonomics rule designed to prevent RSIs. The Reagan and Bush administrations, computer manufacturers, and other corporate interests that were opposed to safety and health regulation of their industries were successful in blocking labor's proposal until RSIs, especially in the meatpacking industry, reached crisis proportions and could no longer be ignored. In August 1990, OSHA issued a proposal for an ergonomics rule and embarked on the long and complicated path of rule making. OSHA's proposed ergonomics regulation would require employers to examine their workplaces for the existence of five "signal risk factors" that are commonly associated with the onset of RSIs: performance of the same motion or motion pattern for a specified period of time, use of vibrating or impact tools, use of forceful hand exertions over a set period of time, unassisted frequent or heavy lifting, and fixed or awkward postures for more than a certain number of hours.

In large part because of intense opposition on the part of corporate interests and the Republican Party, OSHA spent ten years developing the ergonomic standard. Corporate opposition was led by the National Coalition on Ergonomics, an alliance of more than 300 corporations and trade associations formed by the National Association of Manufacturers. Together with the U.S. Chamber of Commerce, the National Federation of Independent Business, the Labor Policy Association (over 225 business members), and the Small Business Survival Committee (40,000 members), they constitute a formidable lobbying alliance in Washington. Corporate-financed think tanks such as the Heritage Foundation and the Cato Institute have played important roles in defining the policy agenda along corporate lines. Eugene Scalia, a corporate lawyer and son of U.S. Supreme Court justice Antonin Scalia, illustrates the linkage between corporate interests and think tanks. He lobbied to defeat the OSHA ergonomics rule for his corporate clients, including United Parcel Service, Anheuser-Busch, and the National Coalition on Ergonomics; and he wrote position papers opposing the ergonomics standard for the Cato Institute. He is now the solicitor general in President Bush's Labor Department.

Corporate interests opposed the ergonomics regulation on three grounds. First, they claimed that the RSI crisis was essentially an employee "comfort" problem that is best dealt with by employers on a voluntary basis, not a serious public health problem that needed government regulation. Second, they claimed that it would be too expensive to implement. These arguments are rebutted by the aforementioned data that showed RSIs to be an enormous occupational health problem that is largely being borne by injured workers and their families. Finally, they claimed that ergonomics is not a science. Scalia criticized ergonomics as "junk science," writing that "OSHA wants to entrench the questionable science of ergonomics in a permanent rule" (Scalia 2000). But Scalia's claim was without merit. In their attempt to discredit and defeat OSHA's proposed ergonomic standard, congressional Republicans twice asked (in 1997 and 1998) the prestigious National Academy of Sciences (NAS) to evaluate whether or not it was based on sound science. Both times the NAS found that it rested on a solid foundation of over 2,000 soundly conducted scientific studies of workplace conditions (Mogensen 2001, 4–5).

Although corporate opponents were unable to derail the ergonomic standard on scientific grounds, they did succeed in delaying its release until the 2000 presidential election. Republicans, who controlled Congress at the time, threatened to shut down the federal government if President Bill Clinton issued the ergonomics regulation before the election. Clinton responded by issuing the ergonomics standard on November 14, 2000, after Congress recessed for the election. It took effect on January 16, 2001, just four days before George W. Bush was sworn in as president. More than 27 million workers were to be covered under the standard in approximately 6 million workplaces.

Although it was long in the planning, the ergonomics standard was short-lived. George W. Bush's first official act as president was to issue an executive order freezing all pending regulations, but since the ergonomics standard had just gone into effect, another tactic was necessary to stop it. Corporate interests urged Republican leaders to utilize the previously unused Congressional Review Act (CRA) of 1996 to repeal the ergonomics standard. The CRA gives Congress and the president the power to overturn regulations without lengthy debate, amendment, Senate filibusters, or other parliamentary delays. On March 7–8, 2001, Congress used the CRA to pass a "resolution of disapproval," and on March 20, President Bush signed it, repealing the ergonomics rule. Under the CRA's stringent provisions, OSHA is prohibited from promulgating it again without congressional approval.

However, California, North Carolina, and Washington have established their own ergonomics standards. Washington and California take an education and implementation approach, whereas North Carolina takes the enforcement and citations approach.

In the eventuality that a new ergonomics rule is promulgated, policymakers should take into account that ergonomic studies have demonstrated that giving workers more control over the work process can reduce stress and prevent injuries. For safety and health regulations to be effective, workers must be included in the design of the work process. Not only do they have firsthand experience with work problems that many managers lack, but OSHA has found that workers are more likely to follow ergonomic instructions if they are included in their preparation.

This finding also has important political implications for the health of our democracy. Citizens are forced to check many of their democratic rights at the door when they enter the workplace, but prominent political theorists such as Carole Pateman and Benjamin Barber stress that a strong, vibrant, democracy requires citizens who are empowered in the workplace as well as the civic culture. Workplace ergonomics may, therefore, be a means of promoting both safety and health and participatory democracy.

Vernon Mogensen

See also Black Lung Disease; Occupational Safety and Health Act; Stress and Violence in the Workplace; Workers' Compensation; Workplace Safety

References and further reading

American Federation of Labor and Congress of Industrial Organizations. 1997. *Stop the Pain! Repetitive Strain Injuries: An AFL-CIO Background Report.* Washington, DC: AFL-CIO.

Dainoff, Marvin J. 1992. "The Illness of the Decade." *Computerworld,* April 13, 27.

Dembe, Allard E. 1996. *Occupation and Disease: How Social Factors Affect the Conception of Work-Related Disorders.* New Haven: Yale University Press.

Franco, G. 1999. "Ramazzini and Workers' Health." *The Lancet* 354: 858–861.

Kome, Penney. 1998. *Wounded Workers: The Politics of Musculoskeletal Injuries.* Toronto, Canada: University of Toronto Press.

Mogensen, Vernon L. 1996. *Office Politics: Computers, Labor, and the Fight for Safety and Health.* New Brunswick, NJ: Rutgers University Press.

———. 2001. "Trust Us, We're Experts! RSIs Aren't Real and Other Tales of Voodoo Science." *Hazards* 75: 4–5.

National Academy of Sciences, Panel on Musculoskeletal Disorders and the Workplace, Commission on Behavioral and Social Sciences and Education. 2000. *Musculoskeletal Disorders and the Workplace: Low Back and Upper Extremities*. Washington, DC: National Academy Press.

National Institute for Occupational Safety and Health. 1995. *Cumulative Trauma Disorders in the Workplace: Bibliography.* Cincinnati: Department of Health and Human Services.

Pascarelli, Emil, and Deborah Quilter. 1994. *Repetitive Strain Injury: A Computer User's Guide.* New York: John Wiley and Sons, Inc.

Putz-Anderson, Vern, ed. 1988. *Cumulative Trauma Disorders.* Philadelphia: Taylor and Francis.

Scalia, Eugene. 2000. "OSHA's Ergonomics Litigation Record: Three Strikes and It's Out." Cato Institute. Policy Analysis No. 370, May 15.

Estate Tax

Estate taxes facilitate the transfer of wealth, and such taxes have existed in the United States for the past 200 years. Controversy regarding estate taxes has existed for nearly as long. Proponents' arguments regarding the societal fairness of wealth redistribution from the rich to those less fortunate clash sharply with opponents' dislike of taxes in general (they derisively refer to estate taxes as a "death tax") and a distrust of government intervention in the workings of capitalism.

Early in U.S. history, estate taxes were designed to raise revenue, not to redistribute wealth, and the chronology of the estate tax follows a path of enactment and repeal. One of the first estate taxes to be implemented by the nascent U.S. government was enacted in 1898 to defray the costs of the Spanish-American War. Four years later, this tax was repealed. It was not until 1916 that estate taxes became a more permanent fixture of the U.S. tax code. But since the estate tax applied only to transfers at death, many wealthy taxpayers adroitly avoided paying the tax by giving away their wealth before they died. In 1924, Congress amended the tax law (in the form of a "gift tax") to blunt this practice. The gift tax was later repealed in 1926, but, in the midst of the Great Depression, President Franklin Delano Roosevelt and Congress reenacted the gift tax in 1932.

Roosevelt was the first U.S. president who viewed the estate tax as a remedy for the unequal distribution of wealth (Bartlett 2000). President Roosevelt supported very high estate taxes (up to 70 percent) to circumvent the dangers he saw inherited wealth posing (the Founding Fathers saw a similar danger in inherited power and government). With the introduction of the concept of fairness as an argument in favor of estate taxes, battle lines were drawn between proponents and opponents that exist to this day. Traditionally, Democrats are in favor of estate taxes, but Republicans are vehemently opposed to them.

Our current system of estate and gift taxes took form in 1976, with the unification of the two systems in the Tax Reform Act of 1976. In 1976, the estate tax exemption was $120,667. Since that time, various tax reform acts have gradually raised the exemption rate, to $225,000 in 1981 (Economic Recovery Act), $600,000 in 1986 (Tax Reform Act), and $1,000,000 in 1997 (Taxpayer Relief Act). Partial marital deductions, instituted in 1948, are unlimited under the current tax code (that is, a spouse can be given unlimited wealth without incurring estate taxes. However, when that wealth is passed onto children or other beneficiaries, the whole amount over the exemption is subject to estate taxes).

The most recent tax reform gradually increases the estate tax exemption amount, from $1 million in 2002 to $3.5 million in 2009. In 2010, if current legislation remains unchanged through several congressional sessions, the estate tax will be repealed. It remains to be seen which side will win the battle of the estate tax.

K. A. Dixon

See also Federal Unemployment Tax and Insurance System; Great Depression; Wage Gap; Wage Tax

References and further reading

Bartlett, Bruce. 2002. National Center for Policy Analysis. "Estate Tax History vs. Myth." http://www.ncpa.org/oped/bartlett/jul1900.html (cited August 12).

Cataldo, Anthony J., and Arline A. Savage. 2001. *U.S. Individual Federal Income Taxation : Historical, Contemporary, and Prospective Policy Issues.* New York: Amsterdam Press.

Center on Budget and Policy Priorities. 2002. "Estate Tax Repeal: A Costly Windfall for the Wealthiest Americans." http://www.cbpp.org/5–25–00tax.htm (cited August 12).

McCaffery, Edward J. 2002. *Fair, Not Flat : How to Make The Tax System Better and Simpler.* Chicago: University of Chicago Press.

Office of Tax Policy Research. 2002. "Working Papers," http://www.otpr.org/ (cited August 12).

Planned Giving Today. 2002. "The Practical Newsletter for the Gift Planning Professional." http://www.pgtoday.com/ (cited August 12).

Slemrod, Joel B., ed. 2000. *Does Atlas Shrug? The Economic Consequences of Taxing the Rich.* New York and Cambridge, MA: Russell Sage Foundation and Harvard University Press.

Export-Processing Zones (EPZs)

Export-processing zones (EPZs) are industrial and assembly areas in lesser developed countries (LDCs), where foreign investors and employers pay low-skill, low-wage labor to assemble, process, or manufacture goods for export while enjoying tax and regulatory incentives and a favorable labor market.

EPZs soared in popularity since the 1980s (and have been used since the 1960s in Mexico) but have come under intense criticism for exploiting human labor and degrading natural resources for the benefit of low-cost western consumer goods. EPZs have been discussed interchangeably with terms such as *industrial free zones, free trade zones,* or *maquiladoras.* Although the broad concepts underlying these trade instruments are the same—primary materials are imported tax-free; goods are assembled or manufactured in labor-intensive processes and then exported for consumption in developed countries—the World Bank has strictly defined the EPZ as an industrial area, usually fenced-in, that specializes in manufacturing for export and offers free trade conditions and a liberal regulatory environment (Madani 1997). By the late 1990s, there were at least 500 EPZs worldwide by this strict definition, and more than 2,000 when including related entities such as export-processing firms and other facilities enjoying tax and export incentives. The International Labor Organization estimates EPZs and related "free trade" areas employ about 27 million people worldwide (van Heerden 2002). Nations throughout East Asia, the Indian subcontinent, Central and Latin America, and Africa have implemented EPZs. As an example, the Cavite Export-Processing Zone located near Manila, Philippines, is a 682-acre walled-in facility employing 50,000 workers at 207 factories producing goods strictly for the export market (Klein 1999).

EPZs became influential economic development tools for three leading reasons, most experts agree. Nations hoped to expand their foreign exchange earnings, create jobs, and attract new foreign direct investment that would fund technology development, policies that reflected dominant neoliberal economic development models that emphasized export-led growth. Although the willingness of western firms to seek low-cost, low-oversight facilities for manufacturing is well-documented, what benefits do EPZs bring to host countries? Zones do create nontraditional jobs, particularly for women and younger workers (World Bank 1998). Although these workers receive some job training, the vast majority of new jobs are low-skilled and low-tech. EPZs are a catalyst for host nations to build basic industrial infrastructure, such as roads and plumbing, in the immediate area of the EPZ. Typically, host countries have sought "linkages" between EPZ activity and increased growth of production and services in local economies, but most EPZs remain enclave economies with few tiebacks to the host nation's economy. And although EPZs increase foreign exchange earnings, these earnings do not always recapture physical investments and opportunity costs for the host nation.

EPZs and related free trade zones have received strong criticism. Within many EPZs, labor unions and other forms of labor organizing are banned. Most EPZs fight unionization at any cost. Advocates have accurately documented widespread poor working conditions within the zones, including mandatory overtime, lack of health care, discrimination against and harassment of pregnant workers, and lack of adequate housing and food. It should be noted that across the developing world, young women are favored for EPZ employment because they have higher turnover rates and therefore tend not to get involved with unions, they are paid less, and they are viewed by many employers as more diligent and dexterous than males. However, zone employers have been found to discriminate against pregnant women and mothers. Human Rights Watch found that women applying for jobs in Mexican maquiladoras were routinely given pregnancy tests; other studies have documented these and other abuses.

As noted in Naomi Klein's landmark book *No Logo,* a 1998 study of brand-name manufacturing in the Chinese special economic zones, found that more than ten U.S. brand-name companies were paying only a fraction of the 87 cents an hour labor experts say would be a living wage for Chinese workers. During the late 1990s and early 2000s, the National Labor Committee in Support of Worker and Human Rights and other advocacy groups publicized and sought changes in work conditions at the Bangladesh Beximco factory in the Dhaka Export-Processing Zone, among a number of EPZs. Investigators found young women sewing clothing for Wal-Mart were paid just 20 cents an hour, while their helpers were paid just 9 cents an hour. These wages were far below the regulation wage set for the Dhaka Export-Processing Zone, which itself was far below subsistence levels. In addition, investigators found that the young workers were forced to work twelve-hour shifts seven days a week, women were cheated out of maternity benefits, and worker savings were misappropriated. There were almost no health services available for workers. Wal-Mart and its contractor pay no taxes whatsoever; the low wages and rents they pay are their sole contributions to Bangladesh. Reformers called for Wal-Mart to work with the contractor at the site to improve conditions, rather than withdraw their contracts and eliminate the jobs, thereby turning the workforce back onto the street.

Most experts agree that the continuing rise of globalization increases competitive pressure for the "EPZ dollar," fueling yet another race to the bottom for developing world governments seeking western investment. This competition will tempt EPZs into further weakening of labor and regulatory standards in hopes of attracting the EPZ investment dollar.

Herbert A. Schaffner

See also Manufacturing Jobs; *Maquiladora* Zone; North American Free Trade Agreement

References and further reading

Co-op America. 2003. "Urge Wal-Mart to Support Labor Justice." http://www.sweatshops.org/action/action_wal-mart.html (cited May 15, 2003).

Klein, Naomi. 1999. *No Logo.* New York: Picador.

Madani, Dorsati. 1998. *A Review of the Role and Impact of Export Processing Zones.* Washington, DC: World Bank.

van Heerden, Auret. 2002. *What Are Export Processing Zones?* Geneva, Switzerland: International Labor Organization.

F

Fair Labor Standards Act (FLSA) (1938)

The Fair Labor Standards Act (FLSA) is the U.S. law that establishes a federal minimum wage, overtime pay requirements, and restrictions on child labor. Most employees are currently entitled to the minimum wage of $5.15 per hour (2002) and overtime pay at a rate at least one and one-half times their regular rate of pay after forty hours of work in a week. The child labor provisions place restrictions on dangerous working conditions and the numbers of hours some youths can work. The FLSA also mandates a minimum level of record keeping by employers.

The FLSA was enacted in 1938 during the troubled economic decade of the Great Depression. Many believed that corporate power created sweatshop conditions of low wages and long hours and contributed to the high unemployment levels and continued economic depression of the 1930s. The FLSA was intended to combat these conditions and create basic standards of protections for employees. Along with the 1935 National Labor Relations Act (Wagner Act), the FLSA established a new legal and philosophical framework for government regulation of employment that continued with the Civil Rights Act (1964), the Occupational Safety and Health Act (1970), the Family and Medical Leave Act (1993), and other laws.

All employees covered by the FLSA must be paid at least the mandated hourly minimum wage. If employees are not paid on an hourly basis, such as salaried workers or those paid on commission, the employee's pay divided by hours worked must equal at least the minimum wage. There are minimum wage exceptions that can apply to disabled workers, students, tipped employees, and others.

Employees who are not exempt from the FLSA are also entitled to an overtime premium of one and one-half times their regular rate of pay for hours worked in excess of forty hours in a week. A workweek is seven consecutive twenty-four-hour periods starting on any day. There are a number of regulations on determining hours of work—questions can arise, for example, pertaining to sleep time, meal periods, or travel time. The most significant issue for many employers and employees, however, is exempt status.

Professional, executive, and administrative employees are exempt from the overtime provisions of the FLSA. Some jobs may fit clearly into these categories or be clearly excluded, but for many there can be questions. A number of clarifying regulations have been issued, and in broad terms, individuals are exempt if they have the authority to hire and fire or make recommendations affecting other employees or they regularly exercise independent judgment in their work. Some salespersons and other occupations are also exempt. Exempt employees are usually salaried, but making someone a salaried employee does not by itself make him or her exempt.

The child labor provisions prohibit individuals under the age of eighteen from working in seventeen

Spindle boys working in a Georgia cotton mill, ca. 1908. The Fair Labor Standards Act set restrictions on child labor, regulating the number of hours children can work and protecting children from dangerous working conditions. (Bettmann/Corbis)

hazardous nonfarm jobs. Examples of these jobs include mining, meatpacking, roofing, demolition, excavation, and working with explosives and various forms of power-driven machinery. Youths sixteen and seventeen years old may work unlimited hours in nonhazardous jobs, but fourteen and fifteen year olds face additional restrictions. In particular, fourteen and fifteen year olds may work, outside school hours, in nonmanufacturing, nonhazardous jobs up to three hours on a school day, eighteen hours in a school week, eight hours on a nonschool day, and forty hours in a nonschool week These young workers can also work only between 7:00 A.M. and 7:00 P.M., except during the summer, when they can work until 9:00 P.M. All states also have child labor laws that in some cases may be stricter than the FLSA. For example, a number of states also restrict the hours of sixteen and seventeen year olds during the school year.

The effects of the FLSA, especially the minimum wage requirement, have been widely debated and researched. Standard economic theory implies that if employers are forced to pay higher wages, employment levels will fall. Recent research, however, does not always find strong evidence that increases in the minimum wage hurt employment. The required overtime premium is intended, among other things, to encourage work sharing, that is, to cause employers to hire new workers rather than pay overtime to existing employees. The FLSA's effectiveness in promoting work sharing, however, is questionable.

The FLSA is enforced by the Wage and Hour Division of the U.S. Department of Labor's Employment Standards Administration (http://www.dol.gov/dol/esa/public/whd_org.htm). The Department of Labor and individual employees can sue to recover unpaid minimum wage and overtime compensation. Willful or repeat violators can also be subject to fines and criminal prosecution. The FLSA covers many workplaces, but small businesses are exempted. Most states, however, have similar laws that cover workplaces not covered by the FLSA. Employers must comply with the state law if it is stricter than the FLSA.

When the FLSA was enacted in 1938, the minimum wage level was set at 25 cents per hour, and the standard workweek was set at forty-four hours. The workweek was reduced to forty hours in 1940. The minimum wage has been increased about twenty times since 1938. In the early twentieth century, some states passed minimum wage laws for women and children, but the Supreme Court ruled in 1923 that they were unconstitutional because they violated individual freedom to enter into contracts without government interference. Legal sentiments changed during the Great Depression, though not universally, and the FLSA was ruled constitutional in 1941.

In recent years, the FLSA has come under attack for being antiquated in today's economy. The regulations pertaining to exempt employees were developed long before jobs such as computer programmers emerged. Provisions pertaining to the calculation of overtime payments predate recent increases in employers' use of incentive bonuses and stock options for nonexecutive employees. Recent bills in Congress have also considered revising the FLSA to allow employees to receive time off instead of cash compensation for overtime hours and to allow employers and employees to develop more flexible work schedules (such as eighty hours over two weeks rather than forty hours per week). Although employers would be prohibited from coercing their employees from making a certain choice about their workweek or form of overtime compensation, opponents argue that abuses would still occur and that effective labor standards are still needed.

John W. Budd

See also Child Labor; Compensation; Health Insurance; Job Benefits; Minimum Wage; National Labor Relations Act; Overtime and the Workweek; Pensions

References and further reading

Card, David, and Alan B. Krueger. 1995. *Myth and Measurement: The New Economics of the Minimum Wage.* Princeton, NJ: Princeton University Press.

Hart, Vivian. 1994. *Bound by Our Constitution: Women, Workers, and the Minimum Wage.* Princeton, NJ: Princeton University Press.

Hunnicutt, Benjamin Kline. 1988. *Work without End: Abandoning Shorter Hours for the Right to Work.* Philadelphia: Temple University Press.

Kearns, Ellen C., ed. 1999. *The Fair Labor Standards Act.* Washington, DC: Bureau of National Affairs.

Levin-Waldman, Oren M. 2001. *The Case of the Minimum Wage: Competing Policy Models.* Albany: State University of New York Press.

Nordlund, Willis J. 1997. *The Quest for a Living Wage: The History of the Federal Minimum Wage Program.* Westport, CT: Greenwood Press.

Sovereign, Kenneth L. 1999. *Personnel Law.* Upper Saddle River, NJ: Prentice Hall.

Family and Medical Leave Act (FMLA) (1993)

The Family and Medical Leave Act of 1993 (FMLA) allows workers to take unpaid leave from work when they or someone in their family needs medical care. The law covers individuals who have worked for the same company for at least twelve months, have worked for at least 1,250 hours in the past year, and work for a company with at least fifty employees. The law allows employees to take unpaid leave if they are having or caring for a new baby; adopting a child or getting a foster child; are very sick or unable to work; or have a very sick parent, child, or spouse. Under FMLA, workers who meet these conditions are eligible to take a total of twelve weeks off without pay. The leave may be used all at once, intermittently, or as part of a reduced work schedule. Employees are also guaranteed the maintenance of their health coverage during the time off as well as the ability to return to their old job or a job with equal pay, status, and benefits after the leave. FMLA requires employers to keep records of leave and protects employees who request such time off. Unlike most federal laws, FMLA does not preempt state laws in this area. The act requires that the employer follow the more generous leave policy and the least burdensome procedures for obtaining leave.

Approximately two-thirds of the U.S. labor force work for employers covered by FMLA, and more than 35 million Americans benefited from taking family and medical leave between 1993 and 2000 (Cantor et al. 2001). Prior to passage of the Family and Medical Leave Act, employees had access to leave only under voluntary employer policies, those set by collective bargaining, and state laws. According to the Department of Labor, only about one-quarter to one-third of formal employer policies matched FMLA in scope.

FMLA established the bipartisan Commission on Family and Medical Leave to study the impact of the new policy on workers and employers. This commission administered surveys to workers and employers in 1995 and again in 2000. The 2000 surveys revealed that the number of individuals who took leave in the previous eighteen months for FMLA reasons had increased since 1995 to about 16.5 percent of the labor force. Of those eligible workers who claimed they needed to take leave but did not take it, the most common reason was "lack of money." Although FMLA does guarantee a worker's job position and health coverage during the time off, it does not require employers to provide pay for this period. Furthermore, although employees are not receiving a paycheck, they must still pay for their health insurance premiums during their time off. According to employee surveys, 88 percent of those who needed leave but did not take it said they would have taken leave if they had received some pay.

Knowledge of eligibility under FMLA is also a barrier to employee use of its benefits. Reports show that very few employees in covered establishments are aware of the law, although under the act, covered employers are required to notify their employees of their rights for unpaid leave.

FMLA supporters have long argued that with the increasing number of dual-earner families and working mothers, FMLA provides the opportunity for workers to care for their family medical needs without the fear of losing their job. Indeed, the benefit has been accessed widely by employees with young children. According to the Family and Medical Leave surveys, three-fourths of covered female employees with young children and almost one-half of covered male employees with young children took advantage of the benefits in the eighteen months prior to the survey.

Although government is considering expanding the law to cover employees in establishments with twenty-five or more employees, employers not currently covered under the act are increasingly offering unpaid leave as well. In addition to expanding the scope of coverage, the law has had some effect of removing the stigma of requesting family leave, even for men, who represent one out of every eight employees requesting time off to care for a new baby or adopted child (Wilcox 2000).

Denise Pierson-Balik

See also Fair Labor Standards Act; Glass Ceiling; Pay Equity; Women and Work

References and further reading

Cantor, David, Jane Waldfogel, Jeffrey Kerwin, Mareena McKinley Wright, Kerry Levin, John Rauch, Tracey Hagerty, and Martha Stapleton Kudela. 2001. *Balancing the Needs of Families and Employers: Family and Medical Leave Surveys.* Funded by U.S. Department of Labor. Rockville, MD: Westat.

Kalet, Joseph E. 1994. *FSLA and Other Wage and Hour Laws.* 3rd ed. Washington, DC: BNA Books.

U.S. Department of Labor, Commission on Leave. 1996. *A Workable Balance: Report to Congress on Family and Medical Leave Policies.* Washington, DC: U.S. Department of Labor.

U.S. Department of Labor, Women's Bureau. 2001. *Know Your Rights: Family and Medical Leave.* http://www.dol.gov/dol/wb/public/wb_pubs/fmla.htm. (cited September 17).

Wilcox, Melynda Dovel. 2000. "Have Your Job and Leave It, Too (Facts about Family Medical Leave Act)." *Kiplinger's Personal Finance Magazine* (October).

Federal Mine Safety and Health Act (1977)

The Federal Mine Safety and Health Act (Mine Act) became public law on November 9, 1977, to promote safety and health in the mining industry and prevent recurring disasters. The legislation expanded two previous acts, the Federal Metal and Nonmetallic Mine Safety Act of 1966 and the Coal Mine Health and Safety Act of 1969, to expand the rights and entitlements of miners and to amend the Coal Mine Health and Safety Act to include coal and noncoal mining. The legislation transferred the functions of the Mine Enforcement and Safety Administration (MESA) from the Department of Interior into the Department of Labor. It also established a Mine Safety and Health Administration (MSHA) in the Department of Labor. The purpose of MSHA is to enforce the rules and regulations of the Mine Act and to provide technical service to mine operators.

The first federal legislation that governed coal mines was passed in 1891. That law established minimum ventilation requirements and prohibited mine operators from employing children under twelve. By the time the 1966 act was passed, there were nearly twice as many metal and nonmetal employees working as coal miners and nearly three times as many nonmetal mines as coal mines as in the 1890s.

Although mine work has played a significant role in the development of the United States, it is considered one of the world's most dangerous occupations. Miners face numerous diseases and health hazards in the workplace. One of the primary diseases that afflicts coal miners is black lung disease, which is caused by an accumulation of coal dust particles in the lung. It can lead to disability and premature death. Mine workers also are at risk of developing silicosis, a respiratory disease, from inhaling crystalline silica dust when drilling rock. Workers who develop either of these diseases may be eligible for federal aid.

Mining disasters can occur in ore or copper mines or in rock quarries in the forms of floods, fires, explosions, or roof cave-ins. When the Mine Act was introduced in the 1970s, the chance of a mine worker getting killed on the job was much greater than that of a worker in the manufacturing industry. Mine workers in the United States have faced high health and safety risks—and numerous fatalities—since the late 1800s and the early 1900s. One of the most disastrous coal mining accidents occurred in 1907, when explosions in two mines in Monongah, Virginia, resulted in 362 deaths. Thirteen days later, 239 died in Jacobs Creek, Pennsylvania (Graebner 1976, 15). The Monongah mines were considered well-equipped and safe; the company controlling the mines had a reputation for safety. The *United Mine Workers Journal* challenged that belief, however, stating faulty mine inspection was responsible for the accident and that the mines were operated without two openings. This disaster spurred scientific research on coal-mining safety, and it also led to public awareness and the passage of the Organic Act of 1910, which established the U.S. Bureau of Mines (USBM).

In 1942, there were 71,035 accidents, of which 1,471 were fatal (U.S. House 1947, 5). By 1945, the coal industry was experiencing declining fatality rates. Regulation and mechanization brought about a significant drop in death rates. In the Rocky Mountain states, 157 miners died in major disasters from 1934 through 1945 and 183 in all explosions (Whiteside 1990, 173). In 1946, the Bureau of Mines found more than 90,000 safety code violations among twenty-seven government-operated mines. Two of the twenty-seven mines were found to have complied with the Federal Mines Safety Code (U.S. House 1947, 13).

Numerous deaths among coal miners led to passage of the bill that governs mine workers today. In 1972, the Sunshine silver mine fire killed several workers in Kellogg, Idaho. This tragedy led the Department of the Interior to spot weaknesses in safety programs for metal and nonmetal mine workers. The U.S. Bureau of Mines identified nine major factors that led to the deaths.

The 1977 Mine Act was established to direct the secretary of health, education, and welfare and the secretary of labor to develop mandatory health and safety standards for all mines. Each U.S. mine must have an approved worker-training program in health and safety issues. Each program must include at least forty hours of basic safety training for new miners in surface mines. The training provides instruction about respiratory devices, escape routes, ventilation, and first aid and promotes awareness of various hazards. Each miner also must receive at least eight hours of refresher safety training every year. MSHA conducts classes on health, safety, and mining methods. Mining machinery manufacturers also offer courses in machine operation and maintenance.

Although mine work has played a significant role in the development of the United States, it is considered one of the world's most dangerous occupations. Miners face numerous diseases and health hazards in the workplace. (Library of Congress)

The Mine Act also required that each mine operator and each miner comply with health and safety standards and that every state develop and enforce health and safety programs. The law also was established to improve and expand research and development and training programs aimed at preventing accidents and occupational diseases.

Besides MESA and MSHA, other agencies investigate occupational hazards. The 1970 Occupational Safety and Health Act created the National Institute for Occupational Safety and Health (NIOSH) and the Occupational Safety and Health Administration (OSHA). NIOSH investigates hazardous work conditions, and OSHA sets safety regulations. USBM investigates hazards and promotes accident prevention and mine rescue. These agencies have mandated physical changes in the workplace such as improved ventilation and dust suppression in mines, safer equipment, safer work practices, and improved training of health and safety professionals.

Cynthia E. Thomas

See also Black Lung Disease; United Mine Workers of America

References and further reading

Adams, Adele L. 2001. "What's Happening at MSHA?" *Professional Safety* 46, no. 9: 66–70.

Graebner, William. 1976. *Coal-Mining Safety in the Progressive Period: The Political Economy of Reform.* Lexington: University Press of Kentucky.

Greer, M. E. 2001. "90 Years of Progress in Safety." *Professional Safety* 46, no. 10: 20–24.

"Improvements in Workplace Safety—United States, 1900–1999." *Journal of the American Medical Association* 282, no. 4: 319–321.

Mine Safety and Health Administration. 2002. http://www.msha.gov (cited November 19).

U.S. Department of the Interior. 1977. "After Years of Effort, Accident Rates Are Still Unacceptably High in Mines Covered by the Federal Metal and Nonmetallic Mine Safety Act." GAO Report B-166582. Washington, DC: U.S. Department of the Interior, July 26.

U.S. House, Committee on Education and Labor. 1947. "Testimony of John L. Lewis before the House of Representatives Subcommittee on Miners' Welfare of the Committee on Education and Labor, April 3, 1947 and Subcommittee of the Senate Committee on Public Lands to Investigate the Centralia Mine Explosion, April 17, 1947." Washington, DC: Labor's Non-Partisan League.

———. 1969. *Benefits to Employees in the Mining Industry: Hearings on H.R. 111476.* 91st Cong., 1st sess.

———. 1972. *Federal Metal and Nonmetallic Mine Safety Act (Oversight): Hearings on Federal Metal and Nonmetallic Mine Safety Act (Public Law 89–577), and the Sunshine Silver Mine Disaster in Kellogg, Idaho.* 92nd Cong., 2nd sess.

———. 1976. *The Federal Metal and Nonmetallic Mine Safety Act: Hearing before the Subcommittee on Manpower, Compensation and Health and Safety. 94th Cong., 2nd sess.*, May 5.

———. 1979. *The Federal Mine Safety and Health Act of 1977: Hearings on H.R. 4287.* 95th Cong., 1st sess.

U.S. Senate, Committee on Human Resources, Subcommittee on Labor. 1978. *Legislative History of the Federal Mine Safety and Health Act of 1977.* 95th Cong., 2nd sess., July.

Whiteside, James. 1990. *Regulating Danger: The Struggle for Mine Safety in the Rocky Mountain Coal Industry.* Lincoln: University of Nebraska Press.

Federal Reserve Board

The Federal Reserve (often called the Fed) is a federal banking system established by the U.S. government in 1913 to regulate the money supply of the nation and to place some control on banking activities. The Federal Reserve provides the nation with a more stable and secure financial and monetary system. In fact, the Federal Reserve is the central bank of the United States, which establishes banking policies, interest rates, and the availability of credit. It also acts as the government's fiscal agent by regulating the supply of currency.

The main supervisor, regulator, and administrator of the Federal Reserve is the Board of Governors, which has a staff of about 1,700 people located in Washington, D.C. The seven members of the board are appointed by the president of the United States and confirmed by the Senate. From the members of the board, the president appoints a chairperson and a vice chairman, which the Senate then approves. Both the chair and the vice chair serve four-year terms; other board members serve fourteen-year terms, which expire on January 31 every even-numbered year. They are long enough to prevent day-to-day political pressures from influencing the formulation of monetary policy and the supervision of the operations of the regional reserve banks. The board is audited annually by a major public accounting firm and is also subject to audit by the General Accounting Office (GAO), an arm of Congress. Monetary policy, which is exempt from audit by the GAO, is monitored directly by Congress through written reports prepared by the board.

The Board of Governors is responsible for conducting the nation's monetary policy by influencing the money and credit conditions in the economy. It supervises and regulates banking institutions to ensure the safety and soundness of the nation's banking and financial system. In addition, it provides certain financial services to financial institutions, the public, and foreign official companies. The overall duties of the Board of Governors include keeping the wheels of business rolling with currency, coin, and payments services, such as electronic funds transfer and check clearing. It also administers banking- and finance-related consumer protection laws.

All these activities the Federal Reserve Board of Governors executes through the central bank and twelve Federal Reserve districts, or regions, throughout the United States. Regional headquarters are located in Boston, New York, Philadelphia, Cleveland, Richmond, Atlanta, Chicago, St. Louis, Minneapolis, Kansas City, Dallas, and San Francisco. Additionally, there are branches of reserve banks in twenty-five other cities. Each of the twelve reserve banks has a board of nine directors. The president of each bank is appointed by its board of directors and approved by the Board of Governors in Washington, D.C. Reserve bank directors oversee the operations of their bank and are subject to the overall supervision of the Board of Governors. The nine directors of each reserve bank are evenly divided into three classes, designated A, B, and C. Class A directors represent commercial banks that are members of the Federal Reserve system. Class B and C directors represent the public interest and cannot be officers, directors, or employees of any bank. They encompass the broad economic interests of the Federal Reserve district, including industry, agriculture, services, labor, consumers, and the nonprofit sector. Class A and B directors are elected by member commercial banks in the district. The Board of Governors appoints class C directors.

Each of the twenty-five Federal Reserve branches has its own board of directors of five or seven members, depending upon the size of the branch. A majority of the branch directors are appointed by the district reserve bank of the branch. The Board of Governors appoints the remainder.

National banks chartered by the federal government are, by law, members of the Federal Reserve system. State-chartered banks may choose to become members of the Federal Reserve system if they meet the standards set by the Board of Governors. Each member bank is required to subscribe to stock in its regional Federal Reserve bank, but holding Federal Reserve stock is not like holding publicly traded stock. Reserve bank stock cannot be sold, traded, or pledged as collateral for loans. As specified by law, member banks receive a 6 percent annual dividend on their Federal Reserve bank stock; member banks also vote for Class A and B directors of the reserve bank.

The Federal Reserve Board of Governors also has responsibilities for writing rules and enforcing a number of major laws that offer consumers protection in their financial dealings. Federal Reserve regulations govern such areas as truth in lending, equal credit opportunity, home mortgage disclosure, community reinvestment, and electronic fund transfer. Truth in lending regulations ensure that accurate information about the cost of credit is available to consumers. Equal credit opportunity prohibits discrimination in lending. Home mortgage disclosure requires depository institutions to disclose the geographic distribution of their mortgage and home improvement loans. Community reinvestment encourages depository institutions to help meet the credit needs of their communities, including low- and moderate-income neighborhoods. Electronic fund transfer identifies the rights, liabilities, and responsibilities of consumers and financial institutions for electronic transfer services, such as automated teller machines (ATMs).

The most crucial role of the board is to keep the economy healthy through the proper application of monetary policy. The objective of monetary policy is to influence the country's economic performance to promote stable prices, maximize sustainable employment, and balance economic growth. Thus, the Federal Reserve's monetary policy actions affect prices, employment, and economic growth by influencing the availability and cost of money and credit in the economy, which in turn influences consumers' and businesses' willingness to spend money on goods and services.

To influence the availability and cost of money and credit, the Federal Reserve Board of Governors uses three monetary policy tools: open market operations, the discount rate, and reserve requirements.

Open market operations are a tool of monetary policy for buying or selling government securities. The Federal Open Market Committee (FOMC) sets the Federal Reserve's monetary policy, which is carried out through the trading desk of the Federal Reserve Bank of New York. If the FOMC decides that more money and credit should be available, it directs the trading desk in New York to buy securities from the open market.

The discount rate is the interest rate a reserve bank charges eligible financial institutions to borrow funds on a short-term basis. Unlike open market operations, which interact with financial market forces to influence short-term interest rates, the discount rate is set by the boards of directors of the Federal Reserve banks, and it is subject to approval by the Board of Governors. Under some circumstances, changes in the discount rate can affect other open market interest rates in the economy. Changes in the discount rate also can have an announcement effect, causing financial markets to respond to a potential change in the direction of monetary policy. A higher discount rate can indicate a more restrictive policy, whereas a lower rate may be used to signal a more expansive policy.

Reserve requirements are the requirements that are imposed on financial institutions by the Federal Reserve Board of Governors. Reserve requirements compel the financial institutions to set aside a percentage of their deposits as reserves to be held either as cash on hand or as reserve account balances at a reserve bank. Such financial institutions comprise commercial banks, savings banks, savings and loans, credit unions, and U.S. branches and agencies of foreign banks. Altering reserve requirements is rarely used as a monetary policy tool. However, reserve requirements support the implementation of monetary policy by providing a more predictable demand for bank reserves, which increases the Federal Reserve's influence over short-term interest rate changes when implementing open market operations.

Until the twentieth century, the United States was without a central bank, although there were two attempts to establish one in the early 1800s. A poorly regulated banking system and the lack of a flexible money supply caused bank failures, business bankruptcies, and economic downturns. Lacking a money manager, the nation's financial system was like the nation itself—diverse and subject to uneven growth. Consequently, there were frequent economic depressions and financial panics. The Bank Panic of 1907 finally convinced the public that a central bank was necessary to balance the financial needs of the country. Reform was difficult. Business leaders in the more established eastern cities wanted to create a national financial system, but small businesses and farmers in the West and South feared that idea. They worried that it would not provide enough easy credit to support their developing economies. However, on December 23, 1913, after considerable debate, President Woodrow Wilson signed the Federal Reserve Act, and Congress passed it. Since then, Congress has set forth the Employment Act of 1946, and the Full Employment and Balanced Growth (Humphrey-Hawkins) Act of 1978. Over the years, deficiencies in the original act have been addressed in further legislation. The Humphrey-Hawkins Act included an update of the objectives of the Federal Reserve. The update was designed to achieve economic growth in line with the economy's potential to expand, a high level of employment, stable prices (meaning stability in the purchasing power of the dollar), and moderate long-term interest rates.

Since its founding, the Federal Reserve has expanded in size and function. It continues to affect the economic and financial decisions of virtually everyone—from a family buying a house to a business increasing its operations or to a consumer choosing a sound financial institution. However, the monetary policy cannot target specific industries or regions within the country but affects the overall level of prices, economic growth, and employment as a whole. Stable prices help create jobs and raise incomes, whereas fluctuating prices distort consumer and investment decisions, thereby adversely affecting employment and growth in the economy. Therefore, the Federal Reserve influences short-term interest rates in the economy to achieve its goals of stable prices, maximized sustainable employment, and steady economic growth. Besides, global interdependence, fostered through international trade, investments, and exchange rate fluctuations, compels the Board of Governors to consider economic conditions in other countries in its monetary policy. In the global economy, the actions of the Federal Reserve have significant economic and financial effects not only inside the country but also around the world.

Raissa G-Muhutdinova

See also Bureau of Labor Statistics; Council of Economic Advisers; Greenspan, Alan

References and further reading

Anderson, Clay J. 1965. *A Half Century of Federal Reserve Policymaking, 1914–1964.* Philadelphia: Federal Reserve Bank of Philadelphia.

Bach, George Leland. 1950. *Federal Reserve Policy-Making: A Study in Government Economic Policy Formation.* New York: Carnegie Institute of Technology, Alfred A. Knopf.

Beckhart, Benjamin Haggott. 1972. *Federal Reserve System.* New York: American Institute of Banking. Distributed by Columbia University Press.

Federal Reserve Board. 2002. http://www.federalreserve.gov (cited September 24).

Federal Unemployment Tax and Insurance System

The Federal Unemployment Tax Act (FUTA) imposed an excise tax upon employers that is used to fund the federal unemployment program. The tax is calculated as a percentage of wages the employer has paid to the employee. Unlike Federal Insurance Contributions Act (FICA) taxes, the federal unemployment tax is charged only to the employer and not to the workers themselves. This program confers monetary benefits to workers during temporary periods of unemployment. Benefits ordinarily consist of twenty-six weeks of partial wage replacement for workers, with extensions of the benefit period under certain select circumstances. Although the amount a worker previously earned plays a role in determining the amount of benefits paid out under the system, financial need is essentially irrelevant under the unemployment insurance system. The triggering event is involuntary job loss, which happens to workers at all income levels and with varying amounts of savings. The purpose behind the program and thus the tax is to provide a safety net for those who find themselves unemployed through no fault of their own (workers fired for cause do not receive compensation).

There was interest in a federal unemployment compensation program early in the twentieth century and especially during the depression of 1914–1915, but a strong momentum did not build behind unemployment insurance legislation until the beginning of the Great Depression. Franklin D. Roosevelt's pledged, as part of his presidential platform, a thorough study of unemployment insurance. During the early 1930s, unemployment insurance legislation was introduced in as many as twenty-five states and the District of Columbia. No legislation was passed, presumably because state legislatures feared the comparative disadvantage such legislation would impose upon their economies. If one state led the way in establishing an unemployment compensation fund, with an accompanying tax on employers, that state assuredly faced some degree of alienation of business interests and employers' flight to other states with no unemployment tax obligations. Those in favor of unemployment insurance recognized the paralyzing effect that interstate competition would have on the establishment of state-based unemployment insurance programs. Thus, they took their plight to Congress, seeking a federal unemployment insurance program. In response, Congress passed Title III of the Social Security Act of 1935, which included FUTA.

Congress was unwilling to establish a national unemployment insurance program, preferring that the states themselves institute and manage such programs. To force states to do just that, FUTA established an unemployment compensation system that is jointly administered by both the federal government and state governments. Under FUTA, states are "permitted" to create their own unemployment legislation. All states have done so, in no small part because states failing to establish systems in conformance with the mandates of the FUTA risk losing federal administrative funds and paying higher payroll taxes for state businesses. The U.S. Supreme Court upheld the constitutionality of the federal unemployment insurance tax scheme in 1937, explaining that without federal imposition of such requirements, individual states were highly unlikely to establish such programs on their own because of the comparative disadvantages inherent in doing so.

The federal government funds the unemployment insurance program by imposing an excise tax on all employers based on the wages they pay to their employees. An "employer" is defined as any person who paid wages of $1,500 or more or who employed at least one individual for twenty weeks during the relevant calendar year. By statutory definition, "wages" under the federal unemployment tax refers to only the first $7,000 paid to an employee. For wages paid in the calendar years 1988 through 2007, the rate of the federal unemployment tax is 6.2 percent. The tax rate drops to 6.0 percent for wages paid in and after the year 2008. Thus, for each employee that earned over $7,000 per year from 1998 through 2007, the employer must pay $434 in federal unemployment taxes.

Under this federal-state unemployment insurance system, employers are required to pay taxes to both the federal government and the state government. State tax rates vary from state to state. If the state's unemployment system conforms to the requirements set forth in FUTA and related regulations, the state's unemployment compensation program will be certified by the Department of Labor, a determination made annually by the secretary of labor. The employer receives a credit on his or her federal unemployment tax liability for certain contributions made to certified state unemployment compensation funds. Additionally, the employer may enjoy lower tax liability depending upon his or her "experience rating." The experience rating is a measure of the degree to which the employer maintains a stable work force or, conversely, the extent to which the unemployment compensation system has faced claims from an employer's former employees. The maximum credit permitted to each employer is 90 percent of the federal tax. For the years between 1998 and 2007, that means the employer could pay as little as $43.40 per employee per year in federal unemployment tax.

Although the federal government imposes the federal unemployment tax, it does not directly handle unemployment claims. States administer unemployment insurance programs under a variety of different departmental designations, and the federal government allocates the funds collected under FUTA to the states. The federal legislation allows each state a wide measure of discretion in how to administer unemployment insurance programs, including how to define and decide whether claimants are eligible for compensation, whether they are disqualified from receiving benefits, the amount of benefits to award, and the number of weeks to award benefits. Typically, state programs provide for a maximum of twenty-six weeks of benefits. Though a claimant may in fact need benefits beyond that period, eligibility for unemployment benefits is determined without reference to financial need.

In 2002, Congress enacted the Temporary Extended Unemployment Compensation Act as part of the Job Creation and Worker Assistance Act. This temporary legislation provided up to thirteen weeks of federally funded unemployment insurance benefits to workers in all states who had exhausted their state unemployment compensation benefits. In addition, the legislation provides for thirteen more weeks of federally funded benefits to workers in states with especially high unemployment rates.

Debra L. Casey

See also Job Security; Layoffs; Unemployment Rate

References and further reading

Becker, Joseph M. 1980. *Unemployment Benefits: Should There Be a Compulsory Federal Standard?* Washington, DC: American Enterprise Institute.

Chiu, W. Henry, and Edi Karni. 1998. "Endogenous Adverse Selection and Unemployment Insurance." *Journal of Political Economy* 106: 806–827.

Corson, Walter. 1982. *The Federal Supplemental Benefits Program: An Appraisal of Emergency Extended Unemployment Insurance Benefits.* Kalamazoo, MI: W. E. Upjohn Institute for Employment Research.

Federal Unemployment Tax Act, 26 U.S.C. 3301–3320 (2001).

Harrington, Kirsten. 1993. "Employment Taxes: What Can the Small Businessman Do?" *Akron Tax Journal* 10: 61–87.

Lester, Richard A. 1960. "Financing of Unemployment Compensation." *Industrial and Labor Relations Review* 14: 52–67.

Rubin, Murray. 1983. *Federal-State Relations in Unemployment Insurance: A Balance of Power.* Kalamazoo, MI: W. E. Upjohn Institute for Employment Research.

U.S. Department of Labor, Employment and Training Administration. 2002. "About Unemployment Insurance." http://workforcesecurity.doleta.gov/unemploy/aboutui.asp (cited December 18).

Flood, Curt (1938–1997)

This 1960s-era star outfielder for the St. Louis Cardinals baseball club changed the course of labor and race relations in major league sports by mounting a legal challenge to the control over labor relations given to baseball team owners by the "reserve clause" of player-team agreements. Flood's crusade came at great personal cost and set a precedent for economic change that required courage many compare to that of Jackie Robinson.

Curt Flood played in an era that may be difficult for many younger people to understand. Owners ruled their organizations with near-dictatorial powers; every major league baseball player was "owned" by his team, who could trade, waive, pay, or not pay the athlete entirely as management saw fit. Only the most celebrated stars enjoyed any leverage in negotiating a contract. Discrimination against black and Latino players was often accepted and in the open, with de facto limits for the numbers of minority players on major league rosters.

Flood was a special player, a three-time All-Star and seven-time winner of the Golden Glove for his defensive excellence in center field. He hit more than .300 six times during a fifteen-year major league career, largely spent with the St. Louis Cardinals. He also was a painter, writer, and entrepreneur. Despite Flood's central role in helping the Cardinals win three pennants and two World Series in five years, the Cardinals traded Flood to the Philadelphia Phillies after the 1969 season, a decision Flood heard about from a newspaper reporter first. Infuriated by the decision and motivated by a strong intellect, sensitivity to the struggle for civil rights, and opposition to the war in Vietnam, Flood believed he had the right to exercise some control over his career. To win some self-determination and dignity, Flood took on 100 years of precedent in labor-management relations in professional sports. He would initiate a court challenge to baseball's infamous "reserve clause," arguing that the stricture violated the federal antitrust laws written to limit monopoly power. The reserve clause bound the player, one year at a time, in perpetuity to the club owning his contract. As Flood wrote in his extraordinary autobiography, *The Way It Is:*

> Required to negotiate his contract in individual, eye-to-eye discussion with the general manager, without the helpful presence of a lawyer or a talent representative, the ordinary player is outgunned. His inexperience as a bargainer is only one of his disadvantages. The know-how of the general manager is another. But the fundamental handicap is baseball's reserve system, the iron provisions of which make individual negotiation a mockery. The player who refuses to sign on the employer's terms remains bound to the club. He can be forced to work at reduced wages without signing, unless he chooses to abandon his career altogether. No other team can hire him until his official owner clears the way by selling or trading his contract, which then becomes the exclusive property of the new owner.

With the backing of the nascent Baseball Players Association and Arthur Goldberg, a former U.S. Supreme Court justice, Flood took his lawsuit against the reserve clause the entire way to the Supreme Court, which ultimately ruled against him. Flood's first letter to Baseball Commissioner Bowie Kuhn stated the heart of his case: "After 12 years in the major leagues, I do not feel that I am a piece of property to be bought and sold irrespective of my wishes. I believe that any system that produces that result violates my basic rights as a citizen and is inconsistent with the laws of the United States and several states." Flood's crusade helped to change public opinion and open the way for the emergence of free agent rulings and activism of the Baseball Players Association in the 1970s.

Flood's courage inspired many of his fellow players, but he paid enormous financial and emotional costs for his crusade. The stress and exhaustion of the legal fight crippled his ability to play the major league game, leading to his retirement shortly after his return to baseball. He left baseball to travel to Europe, where he spent much of his time painting and writing. He died in 1997 of throat cancer, at the age of fifty-nine. Advocates, economists, observers, and journalists have praised his courage for confronting baseball's owners over fundamental inequities in labor-management relations.

Herbert A. Schaffner

See also Arbitration; Collective Bargaining

References and further reading

Flood, Curt. 1972. *The Way It Is.* New York: Pocket Books, Simon and Schuster.

Miller, Marvin. 1991. *A Whole Different Ball Game.* Secaucus, NJ: Birch Lane Press.

Staudohar, Paul. 2000. *Diamond Mines.* Syracuse, NY: Syracuse University Press.

Food Stamp Program

Without the federal food stamp program, millions of children, elderly, and poor Americans would likely go to bed hungry—many in households where an adult works. Administered by the U.S. Department of Agriculture (USDA) in partnership with state and local governments, the food stamp program reaches low-income Americans regardless of age, family status, or health, although changes in the 1996 welfare law made many legal immigrants ineligible for food stamps. Historically, a large number of working poor Americans have relied upon food stamp assistance to provide an adequate diet for their families. Researchers and analysts in the nonprofit, academic, and government sectors have published numerous detailed studies showing the effectiveness of the food stamp program in helping low-wage working families meet their needs in a cost-effective manner. For decades, substantial bipartisan support and the advocacy of skilled experts and public interest groups led the way to the expansion of food stamps into a sophisticated, well-run government benefit program. However, the congressional drive to reduce and reform welfare and other safety net programs during the 1990s generated substantial controversy over the funding, administration, and work requirements of the food stamp program.

How the Food Stamp Program Works

In an average month during fiscal year 2000, the food stamp program provided benefits to more than 17 million people living in 7.3 million households across the United States, according to USDA figures (U.S. Department of Agriculture 2001). The total cost of the program over fiscal year (FY) 2000 was $17.1 billion, $15.0 billion of which went for food stamp benefits. Food stamp benefits are funded by the U.S. government, and administrative costs are shared by federal, state, and local levels of government.

The average monthly food stamp allotment provided in FY 2000 was $158 per household. Stamp benefits are provided in books or as cash value through electronic benefit transfer cards. In FY 2000, slightly over half of all food stamp participants were children, 39 percent were nonelderly adults, and 10 percent were elderly. About 68 percent of the children in food stamp households were school age, and 70 percent of adult participants were women.

In 2000, nearly 90 percent of food stamp households lived in poverty, and about one-third of food stamp recipients lived in the poorest U.S. households (U.S. Department of Agriculture 2000a). Historically, federal studies have shown that for single-parent families earning the minimum wage for example, food stamps can provide from 25 to 40 percent of that family's total purchasing power (U. S. Department of Agriculture 2000b).

Food stamp participation fell dramatically during the 1990s, however, not only as a result of a growing economy. The USDA has shown that participation in the program declined from more than 27 million recipients per month in 1994 to 18 million per month in 1998 and 17 million in 2000; only part of this decline is attributed to economic conditions (U.S. Department of Agriculture 2001). As the economy slowed in 2001 and 2002, however, food stamp participation increased moderately.

Households needing food assistance either seek it or are directed by case workers to local food stamp offices, where detailed applications for benefits are reviewed and certified. As of 2001, families generally had to have gross incomes before deductions of no more than 130 percent of the federal poverty line ($1,848 per month for a family of four). Their net incomes could be no more than 100 percent of the poverty line ($1,421 per month for a family of four) to receive stamps.

Evolution of the Food Stamp Program

The federal government first provided food stamps to low-income individuals during the 1930s, when it issued orange stamps that individuals purchased dollar-for-dollar to buy retail food items; with those stamps, people also received free blue stamps that could be used to purchase surplus food commodities. By 1942, the two-stamp program was available in about half the counties in the United States. As noted by James Ohls and Harold Beebout in *The Food Stamp Program* (1993), the initiative had drawbacks: "Requiring households to purchase a substantial proportion of food stamps with their own money placed heavy emphasis on encouraging food consumption, but it also significantly reduced access to the program, particularly among very poor households."

The food stamp pilot program was phased out as the Eisenhower administration placed a new emphasis on distributing free commodities, to help low-income Americans, to be sure, but also to reduce growing stockpiles of unsold agricultural goods. The commodities program would continue for decades. Food stamps were reintroduced by the Kennedy and Johnson administrations in a new initiative that went nationwide in 1964. With the passage of the Food Stamp Act, families paid a fraction of the base value of the stamps, through a formula based on income. Food stamps were made available as an alternative to commodities distribution nationwide, but counties were not required to offer either program. The food stamp program expanded dramatically during the 1960s, as more and more localities dropped direct commodities distribution in favor of food stamps.

By the late 1960s, the influence of civil rights activism and related social consciousness, disquiet over the war in Vietnam, and greater social mobility combined to spark a national outcry over hunger and poverty in the United States. New cadres of committed public interest activists such as Ralph Nader had become more influential in Washington, D.C., and within the national media, leading to the formation of a loose antipoverty lobby in Washington. The Nixon administration felt the public pressure and worked with factions in Congress, agriculture, and public interest groups to expand benefits and access to food assistance. Although the food stamp issue was swept up in acrimonious battles over federal welfare policy, eventually a new food stamp law was passed in 1971 that substantially expanded the program and incorporated elements of the program still in force today: uniform income and asset eligibility standards, a federal obligation to pay 50 percent of the program's administrative cost, indexing of benefits, and standard maximum benefits (Ohls and Beebout 1993, 15). The program grew rapidly, with more than 16 million Americans receiving benefits by 1975.

By the late 1970s, Congress required all states to serve all eligible people who applied for food stamps—making the program essentially an entitlement. The Food Stamp Act of 1977 eliminated the food stamp purchase requirement. Instead of paying cash for a portion of the value of the food stamps received, households would receive fewer food stamps for the full value of their subsidy, without any cash changing hands. The dollar value of the subsidy remained the same, but households no longer had to pay anything out of their own pocket to obtain stamps.

The food stamp program expanded dramatically between the early 1970s and mid-1990s, serving 28 million people in 1994. This low-income nutrition safety net generally received stronger political support than other entitlement programs such as welfare, for a number of reasons. Providing "in kind" food assistance to hungry people has wider public support than cash assistance. In addition, because food support ultimately sells more agricultural commodities and produce, the food stamp program found political leverage among rural southern and midwestern members of Congress and senators, who often allied with urban politicians to forge coalitions on agricultural policy and food stamps. Finally, food assistance policy was shaped and influenced by an extremely effective network of public interest and advocacy groups, as well as cadres of government experts, resulting in highly sophisticated, detailed regulations and administrative procedures. Food stamps are widely regarded as an efficiently run government program.

The Politics of Food Assistance during the Reagan, Bush, and Clinton Administrations

The presidency of Ronald Reagan brought profound changes in the political and media climate surrounding federal spending and policy. Elected by a landslide in difficult economic times, President Reagan's stated goal to "get government off the backs of the American people" included treating low-income "welfare" assistance programs as fair game for budget reductions. Although ultimately Reagan allowed federal deficits to increase over the long-term rather than forgo new tax cuts or confront Congress over deeper spending reductions, he undoubtedly enjoyed a gust of political momentum and public support for cutting social programs. During the 1980–1982 budget cycles, the Reagan administration cut food stamp benefits somewhat, delayed inflation adjustments, reduced deductions for earned income (which allowed households that were working but still poor to discount some of what they made in qualifying for food stamps), and reduced first-month benefits. Other rule and administrative changes also were enacted to reduce costs and benefits.

The consequences of these decisions had a discernible impact on the well-being of low-income families and served to galvanize the loose confederation of public interest and advocacy lobbyists, experts, and groups to protect the program. Jeffrey Berry noted in his 1984 analysis of food stamp politics and advocacy, *Feeding Hungry People:*

> The second reason for the growing hunger problem is the reduction of funding levels for the government nutrition programs. These reductions . . . restricted eligibility and reduced benefits. The Reagan Administration's rhetoric aside, the savings have not been accomplished largely through administrative belt tightening or by eliminating fraud and waste. In fiscal year 1982, over $3 billion was cut from government nutrition programs. As noted earlier, the food stamp program alone has lost approximately $11 billion for fiscal years 1982–1985 from the cuts made (earlier). (Berry 1984, 132)

The deep 1980s recession brought a public opinion backlash against cutting benefits for poor families. Combined with effective lobbying and renewed congressional interest in food assistance, the public mood helped swing the legislative pendulum back by the mid-1980s to increases in benefits and access to food stamps. Congress restored cuts in maximum benefit levels and passed a comprehensive food stamp employment and training program that required and supported training and job search activities for able-bodied food stamp recipients. During the administration of George H. W. Bush, a major bipartisan effort to increase food stamps benefits in 1990 eventually fell apart in the face of mounting budget deficits.

When Republicans gained control of Congress in 1994, led by House Speaker Newt Gingrich, the ground was set for another major confrontation over "reform" and reduction of social and entitlement programs targeted at low-income people. The new law that would replace Aid to Families with Dependent Children (AFDC)—the system commonly known as "welfare"—was titled the Personal Responsibility and Work Opportunity Reconciliation Act of 1996 (PRWORA). This new sweeping national welfare law was also intended and did indeed affect federal nutrition programs in several ways. The Food Stamp Program was substantially scaled back through adjustments in the Thrifty Food Plan, a low-cost food budget used to calculate food stamp awards; elimination of benefits to most legal immigrants; creation of time limits for benefits to able-bodied adults without dependents; and changes in eligibility and income criteria for families. The new law also mandated that all states convert benefit awards from paper coupons to electronic benefits transfer (EBT) systems by 2002. In subsequent legislation, Congress restored some benefits to selected populations and gave states options to restore benefits and provide work and training opportunities to able-bodied adults without dependents and other populations excluded from the federal program.

Participation in the food stamp program declined until 2001, when rolls began to increase with the slowdown of the economy. In an USDA report published in 2001, *The Decline in Food Stamp Program Participation in the 1990s,* the authors noted a number of factors contributing to declines in food stamp enrollment. States were given wider mandates to set their own rules. They included reducing food stamp benefits as a "sanction" for households failing to comply with public assistance rules, setting requirements for job search activities before permitting applications for welfare benefits, and offering applicants lump-sum "diversionary" payments to forestall applying for benefits for some time period. In three states, the USDA identified specific practices intended to deter potential food stamp recipients from signing up for the program. In New York City, low-income applicants were forbidden from applying for food stamps during their first visit to a social agency. However, the 1996 law and its aftermath did shift the terms of legislative debate to making "work first" a cornerstone of social policy, and many advocates and experts noted that food stamps provide essential in-kind income for working poor families. In looking toward the next decade, virtually all policy analysts and officials concur that the food stamp program will continue to receive wide political support and play a role in reducing hunger in the United States, which remains widespread among tens of millions of adults and children across the land.

Herbert A. Schaffner

See also Earned Income Tax Credit; Living Wage; Welfare to Work

References and further reading

Berry, Jeffrey M. 1984. *Feeding Hungry People: Rulemaking in the Food Stamp Program.* New Brunswick, NJ: Rutgers University Press.

Center on Budget and Policy Priorities. 2001. *The Food Stamp Program Can Be Improved for Working Families.* www.cbpp.org.

Gundersen, Craig., Michael LeBlanc, and Betsy Kuhn. 1999. *The Changing Food Assistance Landscape: The Food Stamp Program in a Post-Welfare Environment.* Washington, DC: Food and Rural Economics Division, Economic Research Service, U.S. Department of Agriculture.

Ohls, James, and Harold Beebout. 1993. *The Food Stamp Program: Design Tradeoffs, Policy, and Impacts.* Washington, DC: Mathematica/Urban Institute Press.

Super, David. 2001. *Background on the Food Stamp Program.* Washington, DC: Center on Budget and Policy Priorities.

U.S. Department of Agriculture. 2000a. *Trends in Food Stamp Participation: 1994–1999.* www.fns.usda.gov/oane/menu/Published/fsp/FILES/Participation/Trends94–99.htm.

———. 2000b. *The National Nutrition Safety Net.* Washington, DC: USDA Food and Nutrition Service.

———. 2001. *The Decline in Food Stamp Participation: A Report to Congress.* http://www.fns.usda.gov/oane/menu/Published/fsp/FILES/Participation/PartDecline.htm (cited July 14, 2002).

Food-service Industry

Since the first tavern was built, Americans have enjoyed eating out. A 2002 exhibit at the New York Public Library entitled "New York Eats Out" traces the history of dining in that city, from the opening of Delmonico's, the first real restaurant in the United States, in 1827, to the rise of popular dining following Prohibition. Although "high-style" restaurants such as Delmonico's served a wealthy clientele, ordinary people flocked to a varied assortment of eating houses, including oyster cellars, cafeterias, street carts (serving such interesting items as coconut milk and roasted sweet potatoes), and the earliest Chinese and other ethnic restaurants. Prohibition, the Depression, and the war eras eclipsed both popular and fine dining, but Americans enthusiastically returned to both in the following years. Today, with almost 850,000 eating and drinking establishments in the United States to choose from (up from 491,000 in 1972), Americans are eating out more than ever.

More than 11 million people are employed by the food-service industry (National Restaurant Association 2001). At the same time, nearly everyone has eaten in a restaurant, cafeteria, school lunchroom, or snack bar, and millions of Americans do so on a daily or weekly basis. According to the 2001 National Restaurant Association's (NRA) "Restaurant Industry Operations Report," based on an analysis of the Bureau of Labor Statistics's Consumer Expenditure Survey, the amount consumers are spending on food away from home is increasing. In 1998, the average American household spent $2,030, or $812 per person, on food away from home. In 1999, that figure rose to $2,116, or $846 per person. The restaurant industry's share of today's food dollar is 46 percent, compared to only 25 percent in 1955. That number is expected to rise to more than half by 2010, when the NRA predicts consumers will spend 53 percent of every food dollar on food eaten away the home. As a result, the food-service industry has grown into a billion-dollar industry that generates millions of dollars a day in restaurant sales and sales in related businesses such as agriculture, transportation, wholesale trade, and food production. It also employs millions of people. To satisfy the nation's growing demand for "away from home" food service, the labor market in the food-service industry has grown dramatically in recent years.

Millions of Americans have been on the service end of the food-service industry. For many, work at a restaurant, snack bar, or fast food joint was their first job. According to the National Restaurant Association, one-third of all adults in the United States have worked in the restaurant industry at some time during their lives. The combined workforce in the nation's quick-service (fast food) restaurants, full-service restaurants, caterers, snack bars, commercial cafeterias, bars, and taverns makes the food-service industry one of the nation's largest private sector employers, generating sales equal to 4 percent of the U.S. gross domestic product. Food service involves millions of workers, even more consumers, and a dizzying array of products and venues.

The "typical" employee in a food-service occupation, according to the National Restaurant Association, is a young woman (58 percent) under the age of thirty (59 percent), who is single (71 percent) and is living in a household with two or more wage earners (80 percent) while working part-time, averaging 25.5 hours a week. This typical worker has a range of options when considering a job in the food-service industry.

The food-service industry is very labor-intensive, with sales per full-time-equivalent employee at $44,656 in 1999, notably lower than other industries (National Restaurant Association 2001). Workers in the food-service industry fill a wide variety of positions, including restaurant managers, chefs and kitchen staff, snack bar attendants, caterers, bartenders, and wait staff. Food-service occupations have education and training requirements that range from entry-level (busboys, waitresses) to high-skilled (executive chefs). For some positions, such as restaurant managers and operators, a college or business degree is required or preferred. Chefs require specialized culinary training. Food preparation staff, waitresses, and busboys require little or no specialized training, although prior experience is often necessary or preferred. Some high-end establishments offer wait staff special training in areas such as wine service.

As a rule, pay is relatively low throughout all sectors of the food-service industry for both salaried and nonsalaried workers, except at the very top of the career ladder (that is, executive chefs, restaurant owners) or in high-priced, high-status restaurants, where full-time wait staff can make more than $60,000 a year. Many establishments, particularly those in tourist areas or associated with season-dependent activities (such as summer resorts or ski areas), provide employees with seasonal job opportunities that may create hardship in the off-season. Tips make up the majority of some food-service employees' wages. Benefits for entry-level workers are rare.

Labor shortages are a constant challenge for all sectors of the food-service industry. Turnover is substantial in a field where job-hopping is common among all occupation levels, as wait staff, bartenders, managers, and food preparers jockey for position among the top-paying posts at the most lucrative establishments. In addition, for many workers, the food-service industry is not a full-time, permanent career. High school students looking for summer jobs, college students looking for part-time work, and people needing a temporary source of income regularly move in and out of the food-service job market.

More than 11 million people are employed in the food-service industry nationwide. (Jeff Zaruba/Corbis)

Work conditions in the food-service industry are such that many workers soon look for other employment. The flexible hours offered in many food-service venues benefit students, homemakers, part-time workers, and others who cannot or prefer not to work a traditional 9-to-5 schedule. However, this benefit is offset by the late night, weekend, and holiday work that food service demands. Hours can also be unpredictable, depending on the season, the type of establishment, and the state of the economy. In addition, the work in the food-service industry is often physically demanding. Chefs, cooks, and kitchen staff work in kitchens that, with multiple, industrial-size ovens, can reach 115 degrees in the heat of the summer. Wait, bar, and bus staff spend the majority of a shift on their feet, often lifting heavy trays of food or dishes. Finally, the work itself can be onerous. Food-service employees must interact daily with a public that can be demanding and often irate. Bars and restaurants with smoking sections are often smoke-filled. The pace of many food-service jobs is brisk, even breakneck, particularly during certain rush hour times. Food preparation and cleanup is often unpleasant. The uniforms are almost always polyester-based and unattractive. However, despite these drawbacks, the food industry employs millions of people in a wide range of jobs.

At the top of the food-service industry hierarchy are the managers. According to the U.S. Department of Labor's (DOL) Occupational Outlook Handbook (2000–2001), restaurant and food-service managers held about 518,000 jobs in 1998. Most managers are salaried, but about one in six are self-employed. Most work in restaurants or private food-service companies, and educational institutions, hospitals, and nursing and personal care facilities employ a smaller number.

Managers perform a wide range of duties ranging from menu planning to bookkeeping. Good communication, customer service, and organizational skills are important, as well as a knowledge of food preparation and service. To attain these skills, many colleges offer degrees in restaurant, hotel, and food-service management. According to the DOL, the median earnings of food-service managers were $26,700 in 1998, with the lowest-paid 10 percent earning $14,430 and the highest-paid 10 percent earning over $45,520. In addition, managers, as salaried staff, typically receive health benefits.

Food-preparation positions range from executive chefs in the nation's most expensive and highly regarded restaurants to fry cooks in the local fast food franchise. According to the DOL, more than 20 percent of food-preparation employees are between sixteen and nineteen years old, and about 35 percent work part-time. Almost one-third (33 percent) of chefs/cooks and 40 percent of kitchen and food preparation workers work part-time, compared to 16 percent of other workers. More than 3.3 million food preparation and kitchen workers are employed by the food-service industry, with 60 percent working in restaurants, 20 percent in institutions, and 20 percent in the remainder of food-service establishments. Food preparation employees vary by establishment and skill attainment and include institution chefs and cooks who work in places such as businesses, hospitals, and schools; restaurant chefs and cooks; short-order cooks in diners and coffee shops; and fast food cooks. Culinary school or other advanced training (including apprenticeships) is required for most chefs, but short-order cooks may have little or no experience before being hired. Not surprisingly, the career ladder for highly trained chefs is the most developed in the industry, with many chefs advancing to high-level jobs that pay up to six-figure salaries. However, the median hourly earnings in 1998 of restaurant cooks were $7.81 and $6.12 for short-order and fast food cooks, respectively.

On the front line of the food-service industry are the food and beverage service workers, the waitresses, waiters, bartenders, and busboys who wait on tables and work behind counters, take orders, and serve the food and drinks. Restaurants, coffee shops, bars, and other retail eating and drinking places employ the overwhelming majority of food and beverage service workers. Others work in hotels and motels, country clubs, schools, and other institutions.

Food and beverage service workers derive their earnings from a combination of hourly wages and customer tips. Earnings vary greatly, depending on the type of job and establishment. For example, fast food workers and hosts and hostesses usually do not receive tips, so their wage rates may be higher than those of waiters and waitresses and bartenders, who may earn more from tips than from wages. Hourly wages may also vary according to shift, with those working less lucrative shifts earning a higher hourly wage. In many restaurants, tip earners share a portion of their earnings with those staff, such as busboys, who do not earn tips but are people the wait staff need to do their job.

According to the DOL, food- and beverage-service workers held over 5.4 million jobs in 1998. Waiters and waitresses held about 2,019,000 of these jobs; counter attendants and fast food workers, 2,025,000; dining room and cafeteria attendants and bartender helpers, 405,000; bartenders, 404,000; hosts and hostesses, 297,000; and all other food preparation and service workers, 280,000.

In 1998, median hourly earnings (not including tips) of full-time waiters and waitresses were $5.85. The middle 50 percent earned between $5.58 and $6.32; the top 10 percent earned at least $7.83. For most waiters and waitresses, the bulk of their earnings are their tips (usually between 10 percent and 20 percent of the customer's check). As such, competition to work in busy and/or expensive restaurants can be fierce (some people argue that service should be built into the check and wait staff should be paid appropriate salaries, a common practice in European countries). Full-time bartenders had median hourly earnings (not including tips) of $6.25 in 1998. The middle 50 percent earned from $5.72 and $7.71; the top 10 percent earned at least $9.19 an hour. Like waiters and waitresses, bartenders employed in public bars may receive more than half of their earnings as tips. According to the DOL, median weekly hourly earnings (not including tips) of full-time dining room attendants and bartender helpers were $6.03 in 1998. The middle 50 percent earned between $5.67 and $7.11; the top 10 percent earned over $8.49 an hour. Again, tips make up a significant portion of wages.

Full-time counter attendants and fast food workers, except cooks, had median hourly earnings (not including tips) of $6.06 in 1998. The middle 50 percent earned between $5.67 and $7.14, and the highest 10 percent earned more than $8.45 an hour. Counter attendants at snack bars sometimes earn extra wages in the form of tips, but fast food workers, as a rule, do not.

In establishments covered by federal law, most workers beginning at the minimum wage earned $5.15 an hour in 1998. However, the law provides employers with a variety of ways to circumvent the minimum wage, such as including tips as part of the employee's wages. Employers have the option of deducting the cost of meals and uniforms from an employee's paycheck, but many food-service establishments do provide each shift with a free meal, and some cover the cost of the uniform. Some workers in the food-service industry receive benefits, particularly full-time staff and workers in institutions such as hospitals, schools, and corporate establishments. However, the majority of part-time employees do not, and even many full-time wait and service staff are not offered benefits. In some large restaurants and hotels, food and beverage service workers are unionized and are members of either the Hotel Employees and Restaurant Employees International Union or the Service Employees International Union. However, union membership among food-service workers is not the norm.

For many, work in the food-service industry is temporary. High school students working a summer job, college students working their way through school, graduates (and actors) waiting for a "real" job to come along know that this job is a transition to a career in their chosen field. For 11 million others, serving or preparing food is their career. As Americans eat out in ever-increasing numbers, the food-service industry will continue to be an important part of the nation's economy and a significant portion of the labor force.

K. A. Dixon

See also Blue Collar; Contingent and Temporary Workers; Job Benefits; Minimum Wage; Part-time Work; Summer Jobs; Women and Work

References and further reading

Axler, Bruce H., and Carol Litrides. 1990. *Food and Beverage Service.* New York: John Wiley and Sons.

Culinary Institute of America. 2001. *Remarkable Service: A Guide to Winning and Keeping Customers for Servers, Managers, and Restaurant Owners.* New York: John Wiley and Sons.

Ehrenreich, Barbara. 2001. *Nickel and Dimed: On (Not) Getting by in America.* New York: Henry Holt.

Hayes, David K., Jack D. Ninemeier, and Stephen C. Barth. 2001. *Restaurant Law Basics: Wiley Restaurant Basics Series.* New York: John Wiley and Sons.

National Restaurant Association. 2001a. "Restaurant Industry Operations Report 2001." http://www.restaurant.org/research (cited December 11).

———. 2001b. "2002 Restaurant Industry Forecast." http://www.restaurant.org/research (cited December 11).

New York Public Library. 2002. "New York Eats Out," on view from November 8, 2002, through March 1, 2003, at the New York Public Library's Humanities and Social Sciences Library, Edna Barnes Salomon Room. Information accessed at http://www.nypl.org/press/ (cited December 16).

Spang, Rebecca L. 2000. *The Invention of the Restaurant: Paris and Modern Gastronomic Culture.* Cambridge: Harvard University Press.

U.S. Department of Labor, Bureau of Labor Statistics. 2002–2003. *Occupational Outlook Handbook.* http://www.bls.gov/oco/home.htm (cited December 11, 2001).

Ford, Henry (1863–1947)

From how Americans work and socialize to where they live, few have changed the American landscape as much as Henry Ford. Although he did not invent the automobile or originate assembly line manufacturing, his innovations in manufacturing and marketing made the automobile into a true mass consumer item and the assembly line into the hallmark of mass production. Ford was also hailed as a visionary for his announcement in 1914 of the Five Dollar Day—in reality, a base wage with incentives added on for qualifying employees—at the Ford Motor Company. Although his stance against U.S. entry into World War I, the obvious anti-Semitism of the Ford-owned *Dearborn Independent,* and the company's violent opposition to labor unions eventually dimmed Henry Ford's reputation in his later years, he remained a hero to many Americans for the sheer magnitude of his accomplishments. Generations after his death, the company that Ford established remains one of the largest corporations on earth.

Although Ford later liked to emphasize his humble origins as a Michigan farm boy, he was born into the relatively prosperous family of William and Mary (Litigot) Ford in the then village of Dearborn on July 30, 1863. After immigrating from Ireland in the 1840s, William Ford had worked as a railroad carpenter before establishing considerable land holdings in Dearborn, where other members of his family had already settled. Ford passed along his mechanical aptitude to his first surviving son, Henry, who made extra money as a child by repairing neighbors' watches. Although he later considered opening up a watch-making business, Ford's encounter as a youngster with a steam-driven engine used for threshing and sawing proved pivotal in his aspirations. With his mechanical aptitude already obvious, Ford left home in 1879 to work in the Flower and Brothers Machine Shop in nearby Detroit. After a few months as an apprentice, Ford then worked at the Detroit Dry Dock Company's engine works until 1882, when he returned to his family's Dearborn farm.

Between 1882 and 1891, Ford derived much of his income as a mechanic and operator of a portable steam engine for farmers around Dearborn. After marrying Clara Bryant on April 11, 1888, the couple built their own home on an 80-acre site in Dearborn. The Fords welcomed their only child, son Edsel, in 1893. By that time the family had relocated back to Detroit, where Henry Ford obtained a position with the Detroit Illuminating Company. Eventually, Ford rose to the position of chief engineer with the power company while teaching mechanical courses at Detroit's Young Men's Christian Association (YMCA). All this time—inspired by the self-propelled vehicle he had witnessed years earlier and his own experience as a farm mechanic—Ford experimented with gasoline-powered internal combustion engines. By June 1896, Ford was ready to test out his first automobile. Christened the Quadricyle—its structure resembled two bicycles harnessed together with an engine—the machine was too large to be brought out the door of Ford's tool shed where he had constructed it with the help of some colleagues. Knocking out the door and a portion of the wall, Ford and his friends took the Quadricyle for its first successful run in the early morning of June 4, 1896.

Although Ford was not the first person to make a successful automobile run in Detroit, his connections to the business establishment of the city paved the way for the establishment of the Detroit Automobile Company in August 1899. With Ford serving as mechanical superintendent, the company was the first automobile company to be established in Detroit. Like numerous other early auto companies, however, the Detroit Automobile Company closed just a year after it had set up shop. Undaunted by the failure, Ford regained his reputation in an auto race held at Grosse Pointe, Michigan, on October 10, 1901. Although he was not favored to win—and in fact trailed in the early stages of the race—the mechanical soundness of Ford's car proved to be decisive. After winning the race, Ford once again had ready access to capitalize another car company. The Henry Ford Motor Company was duly established on November 30, 1901, although Ford's tenure there was brief. After a series of disagreements with the company's investors, Ford left the company in March 1902. Renamed the Cadillac Motor Company, the company that Ford had once led later became part of the rival General Motors Corporation (GM).

Henry Ford, leaving the White House after calling on President Calvin Coolidge, 1927. (Library of Congress)

Ford's third try at entering the automobile business was far more enduring than his previous attempts. Established on June 16, 1903, in Detroit, the Ford Motor Company produced moderate-priced automobiles at the rate of twenty-five cars per day. Using carriage bodies made by the Dodge Brothers and other parts from its suppliers for the final product, the first Ford factory on Mack Avenue was more of an assembly plant than a manufacturing operation. Under Ford's guidance, however, the company's debuting Model A offered a number of innovative mechanical features, including engine cylinders that operated vertically—and with more power and less friction—instead of horizontally. With 658 Model A cars sold in the 1903–1904 season, the Ford Motor Company was profitable from its very first year. In 1905 Ford also established a separate Ford Manufacturing Company to produce engines, gears, and other components; not only would the division ensure timely delivery of quality parts, but it would also increase Ford's share of the company, a cause for concern on the part of his fellow investors. In 1919 Ford ended years of bickering among his partners by buying out the other shareholders.

The Ford Motor Company added other automobiles to its lineup in its early years, although it remained focused on the midpriced market. Against the conventional wisdom of the day—which predicted that a move into the luxury car market would be more profitable—Ford decided around 1906 that the future of the automobile industry lay in the lower-priced automobile market. Refining the company's Model N with the use of lighter and stronger vanadium steel and a powerful four-cylinder engine, the company offered the car for the price of $600 in 1907. Following Ford's new approach, sales topped $4.7 million on 8,243 Model N automobiles that sales season, and the Ford Motor Company cleared more than $1 million dollars in profit. The following year, the Model T—even lighter, stronger, and more innovative than the Model N—passed the 10,000 sales mark at a price of $825.

With more orders than could possibly be filled for the Model T after its introduction, Ford opened a new factory in Highland Park, Michigan, in December 1909. The factory utilized every aspect of Ford's decade of experience in the automobile business as well as his knack for simplifying the mechanical aspects of automobile production. Although the assembly line production of the Highland Park plant was not the first time such a setup had been used, Ford's routinization of each step in the process and use of machinery instead of skilled, hand labor as much as possible throughout the factory set a new standard for industrial mass production.

Ford's simplification of the assembly process and use of machines deskilled much of the labor needed in the Highland Park plant, but the rapid speed of the assembly line and routine nature of much of the work meant that the new factory was plagued by a high turnover rate among workers. By 1913, after the Highland Park operations had been further mechanized and routinized, daily absenteeism reached 10 percent of the work force, and the yearly turnover rate approached 380 percent. Although unskilled workers performing assembly line work did not require much training, replacing them on such a scale nevertheless represented a significant cost to Ford's production.

To stabilize his work force, Ford came up with an incentive pay plan that carried his name around the world as a visionary of labor relations: the Five Dollar Day. Although the new wage scheme kept the basic daily wage rate at $2.34, profit-sharing incentives allowed Ford workers to earn far more than the typical unskilled industrial worker for an eight-hour day. The fact that the bonus would be paid only to workers with six months of service and after investigations of workers' home lives and moral conduct by the Ford Sociological Department did not stop thousands of prospective workers from streaming to the Highland Park plant immediately after the announcement of the Five Dollar Day. Although his contemporaries predicted economic disaster for the Ford Motor Company, the move proved decisive in setting a pattern for the automotive industry. Although job security and workplace safety remained elusive for most workers in the era before labor unions, the high wages alone were enough to keep many on the assembly line in spite of its frenzied pace. Seeing the measure of stability achieved by the Five Dollar Day, other industrial manufacturers eventually caught up with Ford's wage. The era of mass consumerism had begun.

Between 1908 and 1927, the Ford Motor Company sold over 15 million Model T automobiles. Although it faced competition in its low-priced market segment from the Chevrolet division of GM, it still held 57 percent of the U.S. car market as late at 1923. The introduction of the Model A in 1927 revitalized the company for a brief period, but after 1930 Ford ceded its dominance to GM. GM surpassed Ford not only because of its annual style changes and innovative marketing tactics but also for its willingness to allow purchasers to buy its cars on credit. Further, Henry Ford's attentions were increasingly divided as his company reached maturity. Although he expanded the Ford Motor Company's vertical integration of automobile manufacturing—buying up iron ore supplies and building blast furnaces at the company's giant River Rouge complex in the 1920s, for example—Ford's public role took him far afield from automaking. Arguing against U.S. entry into World War I, Ford participated as a delegate on a so-called Peace Ship that traveled to Oslo to foster negotiations to end the war. The trip was a failure, and Ford soon took on lucrative war contracts that aided the United States after it entered the war in 1917.

Far more controversial was Ford's ownership of the *Dearborn Independent,* a newspaper he bought in November 1918. Soon after the purchase, the paper began running a series of articles alleging an international conspiracy for control of U.S. business, political, and cultural arenas on the part of the Jews. From 1920 through 1927, the *Dearborn Independent* ran numerous such articles, until a lawsuit for libel—and possibly, Ford's own plans to run for national political office—brought the open anti-Semitism of the paper to an end. Ford issued an apology and considered the matter finished, but it came back to haunt him later, when the Nazi Party championed the automaker's former views to legitimize its own anti-Semitic program in Germany.

A staunch individualist, Ford's opposition to labor unions also tarnished his reputation in the

1930s. The violent tactics of the company's Service Department under Ford lieutenant Harry Bennett against the nascent United Auto Workers (UAW) at the Battle of the Overpass at the Rouge Plant on May 26, 1937—in addition to its routine brutalization of workers suspected of supporting the union—caused a public uproar at a time when the other major auto manufacturers had already signed agreements with the union. Ford resisted unionization until June 1941, when the company suddenly reversed its course and entered into collective bargaining with the UAW.

Although Edsel Ford had gradually assumed managerial control of the Ford Motor Company in the 1930s, his untimely death in 1943 brought Henry Ford back as the leader of the company he founded. In declining health himself after a stroke in 1938, Ford's stewardship of the company lasted until his grandson, Henry Ford II, took over as president in 1945. Henry Ford died on April 7, 1947, at his Fair Lane estate in Dearborn, its grounds adjacent to the Greenfield Village historical site and museum that he had established in 1928.

Timothy G. Borden

See also American Federation of Labor and Congress of Industrial Organizations; Automotive Industry; Collective Bargaining; General Motors; Industrial Revolution and Assembly Line Work; Manufacturing Jobs; Productivity; Strikes; Taylor, Frederick Winslow; United Auto Workers Union

References and further reading

Alvarado, Rudolph, and Sonya Alvarado. 2001. *Drawing Conclusions on Henry Ford.* Ann Arbor: University of Michigan Press.

Baldwin, Neil. 2001. *Henry Ford and the Jews: The Mass Production of Hate.* New York: Public Affairs.

Batchelor, Ray. 1995. *Henry Ford, Mass Production, Modernism, and Design.* Manchester: University of Manchester Press.

Hooker, Clarence. 1997. *Life in the Shadows of the Crystal Palace, 1910–1927.* Bowling Green, OH: Bowling Green State University Popular Press.

Ingrassia, Paul, and Joseph B. White. 1994. *Comeback: The Fall and Rise of the American Automobile Industry.* New York: Simon and Schuster.

Lacey, Robert. 1986. *Ford: The Men and the Machine.* New York: Ballantine Books.

Lichtenstein, Nelson. 1995. *The Most Dangerous Man in America: Walter Reuther and the Fate of American Labor.* New York: Basic Books.

Norwood, Stephen. 1996. "Ford's Brass Knuckles: Harry Bennett, the Cult of Muscularity, and the Anti-Labor Terror—1920–1945." *Labor History* 37, no. 3: 365–391.

Fortune

Fortune has been at the forefront of the business press for almost seventy-five years. It is recognized as one of the most powerful magazines in the United States, in part because its standing in the publishing world grew rapidly during the 1990s, in the face of a booming national economy and an insatiable demand for information on business issues and the people that shape them.

The magazine's strength and influence is built on several factors. It benefits from the marketing and financial resources that come with being a part of the largest magazine holding group in the world, AOL Time Warner. The group's holdings include *People* and *Time.* Yet *Fortune*'s editorial strength comes from other factors as well. Its editorial product is sophisticated and well produced, effectively targeting upper management with a mix of compelling yet informative articles. The per capita wealth of its readership, in fact, allows *Fortune* to secure disproportionately high advertising revenues compared to its circulation. The magazine consistently places in the top ten of all publications in terms of revenue, but it doesn't rank among even the top 100 magazines in terms of circulation.

The magazine's strength also stems from its impressive pedigree. It is the brainchild of publishing magnate Henry Luce, who is largely responsible for creating the Time, Inc., empire and using its publications to advance his own largely conservative political and social beliefs. *Fortune* claims its own place in Luce's advance. It was created at the outset of the Great Depression in an effort to lionize "America's new royalty—businessmen and industrialists—and the engine of power that they commanded," William A. Swanberg wrote in *Luce* (1972, 75). Little wonder that the magazine's first suggested name was *Power.*

Fortune immediately began to assert its influence with a landmark series in 1932 on the Soviet Union, which although acknowledging the nation's achievements under communism, left little doubt of Luce's lowly opinion of Russia, the Russian people, and totalitarianism. Yet Swanberg is quick to point out that although *Fortune* hailed the achievement of capitalism and business leaders, it provided a wider range of opinions than its more conservative counterpart *Time.* During the 1930s—a period of enormous economic and political upheaval—*Fortune* at times would run articles critical of conservatives like Herbert Hoover and complimentary of liberals such as Franklin D. Roosevelt.

The magazine's contemporary focus is less opinionated and runs the gamut of business issues. One of its greatest coups came more than a decade ago, when it was at the forefront of breaking information regarding insider trading scandals in the mid-1980s. Despite this, unlike many of its competitors, *Fortune*'s trademark is its "terrifically memorable features" rather than its breaking news stories, as one former managing editor noted.

In line with its evolution, the magazine's editorial effort has increasingly been directed toward workplace issues. The magazine has leveraged its strength in publishing top-grade business features to constantly explore a range of workforce subjects, such as the impact of stress, technology, and employee education and input on the workplace. This coverage has also touched on employment trends and emerging workplace motivational tactics. Admittedly, these subjects are usually presented from a management perspective. However, *Fortune* supports its efforts with substantial data to drive home its points.

For all its editorial strength and financial muscle, the magazine's greatest fame comes not from the words written on its pages but rather from the rankings of companies and individuals it produces. The business world completely understands the significance of being identified as a Fortune 500 company or, better yet, a Fortune 50 enterprise. The magazine's rankings also cover where international firms stand with the "Global 500" ranking, as well as listings for "America's Most Admired" and "Washington's Power 25." The listings also designate the "100 Best Companies to Work For" and the "50 Best for Minorities," which identify companies that not only compensate employees well but create working environments that promote worker morale.

Fortune has repeatedly been named among the country's best magazines by *AdWeek* and *AdAge*. Consequently, it is considered to be one of the most influential business magazines in the country. "Perhaps the most influential magazine journalism is being produced by business magazines such as *BusinessWeek, Fortune,* and *Forbes,* which cover financial news authoritatively and aggressively," Leonard Downie Jr. and Robert Kaiser wrote in *The News about the News* (Downie and Kaiser 2002, 24).

Like its main rivals, *BusinessWeek* and *Forbes, Fortune*'s growth mirrors the general rise in the U.S. economy during the 1990s. Its revenues soared during this time. Unfortunately, the downturn in the economy undercut a large portion of these gains. In fact, all business and technology magazines suffered severe decreases in revenues in the early 2000s, well outstripping the setbacks seen in other sectors of the magazine publishing industry. But *Fortune* held up better than *BusinessWeek* and *Forbes* because its coverage and advertising base were less tied to companies involved in the dot-com boom and bust. *Fortune,* however, faced other challenges in the early 2000s. Most specifically, it had to deal with management changes and the uncertain impact of the AOL Time Warner merger. The combination of these information-centric groups forced all the properties involved to come to grips with how various media—print and Internet—can be used to market, distribute, and drive revenue streams for all AOL Time Warner products. The resolution of this issue is especially critical to mainstream magazines, such as *Fortune,* which may no longer be able to count on traditional revenue streams such as print advertising and subscriptions.

John Salak

See also *BusinessWeek; Wall Street Journal*

References and further reading

Carr, David. 2002a. "Is the Slumber Over?" *New York Times,* July 08.

———. 2002b. "Inheriting the Burden of Success at Time Inc." *New York Times,* July 22.

Deutschman, Alan. 1993. *Fortune Cookies.* New York: Vintage Books.

Downie Jr., Leonard, and Robert G. Kaiser. 2002. *The News about the News.* New York: Alfred A. Knopf.

Fine, Jon. 2002. "Business Magazines Mired in Bad Business." *AdAge.com* (cited July 01).

First Day Staff. 2000. "Time Warner, AOL Merger Gives Few Magazine Clues." *Folio,* January 12.

Swanberg, W. A. 1972. *Luce and His Empire.* New York: Charles Scribner's Sons.

Full Employment Act (1946)

The Full Employment Act of 1946 was established during the organized labor movement as a result of the high rate of unemployment in the United States in the 1930s. President Harry S. Truman signed the act into law February 20, 1946, after approval by an overwhelming majority of both parties in Congress. The act was created to direct lawmakers to pursue policies to reduce joblessness, to create and maintain full employment (zero unemployment), and to reduce inflation or to keep price levels stable. It was originally introduced as the Full Employment Bill of 1945, after President Franklin D. Roosevelt outlined an economic bill of rights in his State of the Union address. The 1945 bill called for the federal government to even out the business cycle by doing the following: (1) establish the principle of the right to work and the government's obligation to ensure full employment, (2) place responsibility on the president for seeing that the economy be analyzed from time to time, (3) commit the federal government to enact safety measures when faced with economic challenges, and (4) commit Congress to enact full employment (or zero unemployment) policies.

Before the bill was introduced, economist John Maynard Keynes had already theorized about employment in his 1936 work, *The General Theory of Employment, Interest, and Money.* Keynes attempted to explain why economies became depressed. His ideas gained influence among policymakers who had tried to increase employment opportunities by stimulating business. Keynes believed that government had to intervene when individuals and businesses could not. Economists and policymakers believed Keynes's theory was a guarantee to sustain economic growth as well as full employment.

The employment act promoted close cooperation between the federal government and industry, agriculture, labor, and state and local governments in pursuing its objectives. In addition to committing the government to keep the U.S. economy on the path of economic growth, the Full Employment Act of 1946 instructed the federal government to intervene and use resources to ensure economic stability. The passing of the 1946 act also meant that a means existed to determine the level of unemployment and employment. The law would require information on the number of jobs needed to accommodate those unemployed and attempt to find a remedy to the nation's unemployment status.

As head of the executive branch, the president is responsible for fulfilling the objectives of the Employment Act. It commits the federal government to create and maintain conditions for individuals to seek useful employment opportunities, including self-employment. The bill is known to have provided ten presidents with a charter for economic policy (Weidenbaum 1996, 880). During the first few years of the law's existence, certain policies contributed to the adoption of anti-inflationary measures, as well as to measures aiding in recovering from a recession.

Government work programs were created during the 1930s to create jobs for the unemployed. Some of those initial programs included the Federal Emergency Relief Administration (FERA), founded in 1933; the Civil Works Administration (CWA), founded in 1933; and the Works Progress Administration (WPA), founded in 1935. Later, other work programs aided the unemployed. They included the Public Employment Program (PEP) and Public Service Employment (PSE), which were begun in the New Deal era and reintroduced by President Nixon through the Emergency Employment Act of 1971; the Comprehensive Employment and Training Act (CETA, 1973); and the Job Training Partnership Act (JTPA, 1982). PSE was incorporated as a title of CETA as a key element of the program and eventually eliminated through the formation of JTPA after a firestorm of political criticism.

The Full Employment Act of 1946 also established two institutions—the Joint Economic Committee (JEC) and the Council of Economic Advisers (CEA)—to monitor the overall performance of the U.S. economy. The CEA tends to be the more visible and influential body. It informs the president, Congress, and the public on economic problems and policies; gives the president the economic advice needed to anticipate and avoid future recessions; and aids him or her in writing the annual economic report, which includes analyses of economic issues and the latest data on production, prices, purchasing power, money, credit, and monetary policy. It also is used by members of Congress, economists, and businesspersons to promote economic understanding and stability. The JEC holds hearings on the president's economic report and issues findings. Some of the hearings and committee reports have been influential in generating public and congressional support for reforms in monetary and fiscal policy, international economics, defense procurement, taxation, and budget matters.

Today, economists and theorists continue to debate to what extent the federal government should continue to emphasize full employment at the expense of economic growth and efficiency.

Cynthia E. Thomas

See also Comprehensive Employment and Training Act; Humphrey-Hawkins Act; Job Training Partnership; New Deal; Workforce Investment Act

References and further reading

Bailey, Stephen Kemp. 1950. *Congress Makes a Law: The Story behind the Employment Act of 1946.* New York: Columbia University Press.

Bancroft, Gertrude. 1958. *The American Labor Force: Its Growth and Changing Composition.* New York: John Wiley and Sons.

Baumer, Donald C., and Carl E. Van Horn. 1985. *The Politics of Unemployment.* Washington, DC: Congressional Quarterly.

Colm, Gerhard, ed. 1956. *The Employment Act Past and Future: A Tenth Anniversary Symposium.* Washington, DC: National Planning Association.

Garraty, John A. 1978. *Unemployment in History: Economic Thought and Public Policy.* New York: Harper and Row.

Keynes, John Maynard. 1936. *The General Theory of Employment, Interest, and Money.* London: Macmillan and Company.

Neufeld, Charles M. 1983. *A Short History of the Unemployment Rate: Its Uses and Misuses.* Charleston, SC: The Citadel.

Prywes, Ruth W. 2000. *The United States Labor Force: A Descriptive Analysis.* Westport, CT: Quorum Books.

Rose, Nancy E. 1999. "Jobs for Whom? Employment Policy in the United States and Western Europe." *Journal of Economic Issues* 33, no. 2: 453–460.

Thorbecke, Willem. 2002. "A Dual Mandate for the Federal Reserve: The Pursuit of Price Stability and Full Employment." *Eastern Economic Journal* 28, no. 2: 255–268.

Weidenbaum, Murray L. 1996. "The Employment Act of 1946: A Half Century of Presidential Policymaking." *Presidential Studies Quarterly* 26: 880–886.

G

Garment/Textile Industries

The garment and textile industries have been among the most important industries in the United States throughout much of its history. Yet at the same time, these industries have been the most difficult for those who work in them. As the garment and textile industries have developed throughout U.S. history, they have become the industries in which it is easiest to drive down wages and to export jobs overseas, owing largely to the continuous subdivision and deskilling of what had begun as skilled crafts, especially garment trades. The textile industry is fairly broadly drawn and may be defined to include the garment industry, which is primarily concerned with the manufacture of clothing, sometimes including hats, furs, and leather goods. Beyond clothing, however, textiles include a wide range of products, ranging from cloth itself to linens, furniture upholstery, and rugs. The textile industry has also historically been subdivided into different stages of production, such as spinning, weaving, and dyeing, although these components have become increasingly integrated. Although synthetic textiles have gained importance in the second half of the twentieth century, the largest and most important branch of the nongarment textile industry has always been cotton cloth manufacturing.

Throughout much of U.S. history, the garment trades have been primarily located in major cities on the Eastern Seaboard and in the Midwest. The primary center of the garment trades has been New York City, but other centers of note include Chicago, Baltimore, Philadelphia, and St. Louis. Textile manufacturing, by contrast, has been identified with small towns and regions rather than cities. For most of the nineteenth century, the majority of textile manufacturing was located in New England and only from the early twentieth century onward made a broad regional shift to the South. The South has subsequently remained the primary locus of the U.S. textile industry, until recent decades when garment and textile manufacturing, along with other U.S. manufacturing industries, has increasingly moved overseas.

The development of the garment and textile industries in the United States go back nearly to the founding of the American nation. Even after the success of the American Revolution, Britain sought to dominate the new nation economically, especially through its domination of the U.S. textile market. Textiles were initially homemade, but home manufacturing was largely displaced by the early nineteenth century. Although the first cotton cloth factory appeared in Beverly, Massachusetts, as early as 1787, it was in 1790 that Samuel Slater, popularly known as "the father of American industry," engineered a new, efficient textile mill in Pawtucket, Rhode Island, that established the cotton industry. In more than one way, however, the U.S. textile industry was truly born in Lowell, Massachusetts, with the building of the first factory at Wameset Falls in 1813.

The garment and textile industries have been among the most important industries in the United States throughout much of its history, but they have become the industries in which it is easiest to drive down wages and to export jobs overseas.(Corel Corporation)

The Lowell Mills are justly famous in U.S. history, not only because they were the largest textile outfit of its time that produced the most and employed the most workers, but also for the workforce it attracted and for decades maintained. The young women who worked for the Lowell Mills generally came from rural New England and found working at the mills to be an attractive way to work for a few years and save money before marrying. The mills offered these women an opportunity to live away from their families, in the carefully supervised boardinghouses the company provided for its employees. The attractive community that the Lowell Mills provided came at the price of long hours and eventually speed-ups and pay cuts, however. As early as 1834, the women workers organized as the Factory Girls Association and by the late 1840s had allied themselves with the New England Workingmen's Association. By that time, the management began increasingly to replace "native-born" women with immigrants who worked under less pretense of benign paternalism. Other centers of the nineteenth-century New England textile industry included Lawrence and Fall River, Massachusetts.

As the textile industry grew during the nineteenth century, the garment trades emerged from the home comparatively slowly, with the work of independent tailors and dressmakers long preceding mass production, especially in the women's garment trade, which only began to emerge following the Civil War. Many of the early clothing manufacturers were German Jewish immigrants who arrived in the wake of the 1848 revolution that helped create the nation of Germany. Between the 1860s and the 1880s, the manufacturing outfits grew in scale and, paradoxically, began increasingly contracting out work from "inside shops" to small subcontractors with low overhead. During this period, the growing workforce in the garment factories changed from primarily "native-born" women and girls to men, initially Irish and German American, and then increasingly Eastern European Jewish immigrants. It was during this period that an increasing division emerged between the all-male minority of cutters (following the invention of the cloth-cutting knife) and the majority of mostly female workers, whose tasks became increasingly subdivided and deskilled.

It was from the late 1880s through the first decade of the twentieth century, the period of the greatest expansion of both the garment and the textile industries, that its workforce was subject to some of the worst abuses. Workers were required to work longer hours and to tend increased numbers of machines in what became known as the speedup-stretchout. As garment manufacturing was increasingly subdivided, pay was often on a piecework basis, with fines for mistakes and losses. During this period, workers were also charged for the cost of needles, thread, power for the sewing machines, and even for the rental of their chairs and lockers.

Urban garment employers frequently played different groups of immigrant employees against each other, encouraging ethnic divisions as a way of preventing the formation of class solidarity. Similarly, the New England textile industries increasingly exploited immigrants, predominantly from Eastern and southern Europe, and made use of language barriers and ethnic prejudices to keep workers divided. The situation of predominantly white Anglo-Saxon textile workers in the U.S. South, however, was hardly better. As the South rebuilt economically after the Civil War, it became the new center of the U.S. cotton textile industry, owing to the immediate availability of raw materials as well as of cheap labor. The Southern mill owners brought in poor white tenant farmers to work in the mills, with promises of a better life in exchange for unquestioning loyalty to the mill. The mill owners sought to maintain control over their workforce through the creation not only of company housing but also company towns, where the mill owners controlled even schools and churches. The few African Americans who were hired worked the most menial jobs and were paid the least of what were already abysmally low wages. As in the U.S. garment industry, inhumanely long hours and child labor were both rampant in the U.S. textile industry.

The earliest efforts at organizing the textile industries North and South coincided with the rise of the Knights of Labor (KOL) in the 1880s. Most of the early organizing efforts during this period were on a craft basis, with little in the way of successful mass organization until 1885. The first effort to organize textile workers on an industrial basis was the socialist-leaning National Union of Textile Workers (NUTW), founded in 1891, and affiliated with the American Federation of Labor (AFL). The AFL, however, provided little support for the strikes that took place during the early years, and by 1901, the NUTW was absorbed into the United Textile Workers (UTW), which was more tightly controlled by the AFL and its craft philosophy. During this same period, in the garment centers, Jewish, Italian, and other garment workers began fomenting strikes and other job actions that tended to die out once the immediate objective was achieved; the first sustained garment trades union was the United Garment Workers (UGW), founded by immigrant tailors in 1891 and quickly dominated by "native-born" skilled workers. By 1900, however, a broader-based garment trades union movement began to achieve sustainability with the founding of the International Ladies Garment Workers Union (ILGWU) in New York City.

The early decades of the twentieth century were a period of pitched battles and dramatic progress, especially in the garment trades. The first successes were the "Uprising of the 20,000," a fourteen-week strike conducted by predominantly female shirtwaist workers, followed by the "Great Revolt" of New York City garment workers in 1910, that resulted in the establishment of the "Protocols of Peace," the first serious effort to achieve fair labor standards in the garment industry. The following year, 1911, however, saw a fire at the Triangle Shirtwaist Factory that resulted in the death of 146 workers, mostly immigrant women. The factory had previously resisted ILGWU organizing efforts. The general outcry over the fire resulted in a movement for new protective laws and spurred further organizing. At the 1914 convention of the United Garment Workers in Nashville, Tennessee, urban immigrant workers in the men's clothing trade, having been increasingly ignored by the UGW leadership, held a breakaway convention to found what would become the Amalgamated Clothing Workers of America (ACWA). In 1919, the ACWA achieved its first successful settlement from the Chicago men's clothier, Hart, Schaffner, and Marx.

During this period, textile workers were hardly quiescent either, whether in New England or the South. The 1912 "Bread and Roses" strike in Lawrence, Massachusetts, which brought together 20,000 working men and women of several nationalities, drew national attention (Cahn 1977, 9). And even as textile mills increasingly migrated South to take advantage of the lack of unionism, workers managed to keep up a sporadic struggle that included a failed 1914 strike in Atlanta, led by the Industrial Workers of the World, and the first "legitimate" strike in Anderson, South Carolina, in 1919. Despite this activism, however, by the late 1920s, factors ranging from the red scare to the rise of corporate welfare led to the decline of union activity in both the garment and textile industries. Additionally, both the established clothing and textile unions experienced competition from rival left-led unions that further divided the ranks.

The onset of the Great Depression decimated union membership in all industries, but the arrival of the New Deal brought labor reforms that contributed to a resurgence in both organizing and activism. For example, in 1934, textile workers throughout the South staged the largest industrial strike in U.S. history. Nonetheless, as wages and conditions improved for garment workers and northern textile workers throughout the New Deal and war years and as prosperity increased after World War II, the wages of southern textile workers visibly lagged below the national average, and the labor pool decreased as textile workers, both black and white, took better jobs in other regions and industries.

Efforts to organize southern textile workers persisted, however, with the formation of the Textile Workers Organizing Committee (TWOC) by the ACWA in 1937 and then the founding of the Textile Workers Union of America (TWUA) in 1939. Although the northern textile industries declined during the postwar decades, efforts at organizing in the South remained an uphill battle, including the long-drawn-out effort to organize the J. P. Stevens textile mills, which was immortalized in the 1979 movie *Norma Rae.* In 1976, the TWUA merged with the ACWA to form the Amalgamated Clothing and Textile Workers Union (ACTWU).

By the 1970s, however, the gains of textile and garment industries were reversed, as manufacturers fighting unionization began to move overseas, a trend that has continued to the present day. By the 1990s, sweatshops were also reappearing, not only overseas, but also in New York City, now staffed by illegal immigrants. The textile industry fared somewhat better, with organizing successes at resistant companies such as J. P. Stevens and Fieldcrest Cannon. Even then, as the unions have continued to consolidate, culminating in the 1995 merger of ACTWU and the ILGWU to form the Union of Needle Trades, Industrial, and Textile Employees (UNITE!), stemming, let alone reversing losses has remained an uphill battle, causing UNITE! to "go global" in focus with efforts such as the 2001 inauguration of the Global Justice for Garment Workers Campaign.

Susan Roth Breitzer

See also American Federation of Labor and Congress of Industrial Organizations; Globalization and Workers; Homework; Immigrants and Work; Lowell Strike: Piecework; Socialism; Strikes; Sweatshops; Triangle Shirtwaist Fire

References and further reading

Brietzer, Susan Roth. 2002. "Amalgamated Clothing Workers of America." In *Dictionary of American History,* 3rd ed. Edited by Stanley Kutler. New York: Charles Scribner's Sons.

Cahn, William. 1977. *Lawrence: The Bread and Roses Strike.* Introduction by Paul Cowan. New York: Pilgrim Press.

Carpenter, Jesse T. 1972. *Competition and Collective Bargaining in the Needle Trades, 1910–1967.* Ithaca: New York State School of Labor and Industrial Relations.

Kulik, Gary, Roger Parks, and Theodore Z. Penn, eds. 1982. *The New England Mill Village, 1970–1860.* Cambridge, MA: MIT Press.

Liefermann, Henry. 1975. *Crystal Lee: A Woman of Inheritance.* New York: Macmillan.

McCreesh, Carolyn Daniel. 1985. *Women in the Campaign to Organize Garment Workers, 1880–1917.* New York: Garland Publishing.

Mitchell, George Sinclair. 1931. *Textile Unionism in the South.* Chapel Hill: University of North Carolina Press.

Page, Dorothy Myra. 1929. *Southern Cotton Mills and Labor.* Introduction by Bill Dunne. New York: Workers Library Publishers.

Stein, Leo, and Annette K. Baxter, eds. 1974. *Women of Lowell.* New York: Arno Press.

———. 1977. *Out of the Sweatshop: The Struggle for Industrial Democracy.* New York: Quadrangle/ New York Times Book Company.

Tyler, Gus. 1995. *Look for the Union Label: A History of the International Ladies' Garment Workers' Union.* Armonk, NY: M. E. Sharpe.

Union of Needle Trades, Industrial, and Textile Workers (UNITE!). 2001. "UNITE! A New Union with a Long History." http://www.uniteunion.org/research/history/unionisborn.html," (cited January 13).

Woloch, Nancy. 1984. *Women and the American Experience.* New York: Alfred A. Knopf.

Gays at Work

Historically, gay, lesbian, and bisexual workers have experienced extreme hardship because employers and coworkers discriminated freely against anyone suspected of being gay. This discrimination can be traced back to the earliest periods of U.S. employment history, when almost all gay workers were forced to keep their sexuality hidden for fear of termination and harassment. Beginning in the 1950s and 1960s, gay activists began making concerted efforts to gain civil rights. The right to be free from employment discrimination was one of their demands, and they were able to achieve some success. For example, in 1967 the American Civil Liberties Union formally opposed the federal government's ban on hiring gay employees for federal jobs, after lobbying from gay rights organizations such as the Matttachine Society. This ban was enacted in 1953 by the U.S. government because officials argued that gay people were emotionally unstable and susceptible to blackmail. After the Stonewall riots of June 1969, in which gay individuals resisted a police raid at the Stonewall bar in New York City and protested for equal treatment, gay issues became more visible. By the mid-1970s, thirty municipalities in the United States had passed nondiscrimination laws. Progress for gay and lesbian workers continued throughout the 1980s and 1990s, but the struggle for equal rights for gay workers still continues.

Today gay, lesbian, and bisexual employees are becoming increasingly more visible but still face challenges in the workplace. Studies have estimated that approximately 10 percent of the U.S. population is gay, lesbian, or bisexual. Based on this percentage, gay individuals are working in almost every workplace and contributing to the overall productivity of the labor force. Many gay individuals, however, do not feel comfortable openly expressing their sexual orientation, or "coming out," in the workplace because there is no federal legislation that protects workers from employment discrimination or harassment based on sexual orientation.

Coming out at work is often one of the most difficult challenges for gay, lesbian, and bisexual workers. Gay individuals may choose not to announce their sexual orientation at work because they fear that their employers and managers will begin discriminating against them once they know they are gay. This employment discrimination could involve denial of promotion, unequal pay, or intentional firing. Besides employment discrimination, once gay employees enter a workplace or come out at work, they often face harassment from both coworkers and managers. Verbal abuse and physical violence directed at gay employees can result, which causes gay workers to feel threatened and uncomfortable in their workplaces. Some even decide to voluntarily leave the hostile workplace. Not having the assurance that one's workplace will be safe and accepting creates yet another challenge for gay workers. Some occupations and industries have proven to be more accepting of gay workers, such as: the health care industry, college and universities, and libraries. Other occupations and industries have proven to be more hostile to gay workers, such as: manufacturing work, construction, and public school teaching. As a result, gay and lesbian workers may feel limited in where they can choose to work than do heterosexual workers, who do not have to fear workplace harassment because of their sexual orientation.

Employment discrimination and workplace harassment against gay individuals frequently goes undetected or unreported because many gay workers fear publicly addressing their sexuality and choose not file a complaint when they do face discrimination. Still, there are numerous accounts of gay employees being treated unfairly after their sexual orientation becomes known at work. The Human Rights Campaign has been collecting accounts of discrimination based on sexual orientation in U.S. workplaces. It documented 130 cases and found that discrimination against gay workers occurred in every region of the county and in a variety of jobs and occupations.

In attempts to avoid discrimination and harassment in the workplace, gay, lesbian, and bisexual workers may decide not to come out at work. Others in their workplaces then often assume that they are heterosexual. To maintain these assumptions, gay individuals often must avoid discussing their private lives with coworkers, which creates social tension for gay workers because they may feel isolated. They might also be excluded from social networks formed at work because they do not feel comfortable spending time with coworkers outside the workplace. The lack of social connection for gay employees could also leave them excluded from networks within the workplace, making them less connected to information and support, which in turn might hurt their chances for career advancement.

Unequal treatment for gay workers also exists in the distribution of workplace benefits, including health care insurance, pensions, and family leave. Because gay individuals cannot legally marry, the partners of gay and lesbian employees do not have access to benefits provided by employers. Married partners of heterosexual employees do, however, have full access to benefits. Benefits often account for 40 percent of an employee's wages, so not giving gay workers equal access to employer-provided benefits for their partners leads to unequal pay based on sexual orientation. Some employers have implemented domestic partner benefits or spousal equivalent benefits for their unmarried employees. Domestic partner benefits extend the same benefits available to married spouses of heterosexual employees to the partners of gay employees. (In some workplaces, domestic partner benefits may also be provided to the partners of unmarried heterosexual employees.) A 1997 survey found that only 13 percent of employers extend health care benefits to domestic partners, but that the number has steadily been increasing (National Gay and Lesbian Task Force 1997).

To combat employment discrimination based on sexual orientation, gay and lesbian workers have in some cases formed gay employee groups or caucuses in their workplaces. Corporations such as American Telephone and Telegraph (AT&T), Boeing, Chevron, Eastman Kodak, Hewlett-Packard, Levi Strauss, Microsoft, Motorola, Polaroid, United Airlines, Walt Disney, and Xerox all have gay and lesbian employee groups. These groups enable workers to discuss ways to promote the equal treatment of gay employees in their workplaces. Their activities may involve employees lobbying or bargaining for domestic partnership benefits. They may also pressure the employer to pass a nondiscrimination policy that prohibits discrimination against gay, lesbian, and bisexual workers. This is often the first step toward equality for gay individuals in a workplace and may lead employers to pursue more efforts to promote equality for gay employees.

A majority of the American public believes that discrimination against gay workers is wrong. Polls have found that more than 75 percent of voters in the United States oppose workplace discrimination because of one's sexual orientation, and 83 percent of Americans believe gay individuals should have equal job opportunities. Despite public opinion, employment discrimination directed at gay and lesbian individuals is not legally prohibited by federal law. Unlike other minority groups (women, racial minorities, and the disabled), there is no federal antidiscrimination law for gay, lesbian, and bisexuals, making them a particularly vulnerable group. Twelve states, the District of Columbia, and 229 cities and counties throughout the United States include sexual orientation (or a similar term) in their antidiscrimination employment legislation. (The states are California, Connecticut, Hawaii, Maryland, Massachusetts, Minnesota, Nevada, New Hampshire, New Jersey, Rhode Island, Vermont, and Wisconsin.) Most Americans (62 percent of the U.S. population) are not covered by these state or local laws, leaving them unprotected from employment discrimination based on sexual orientation. The Employment Non-discrimination Act (ENDA), a bill that would have protected gay and lesbian workers against discrimination in the workplace, failed to pass Congress in 1996. The effort to pass ENDA, however, has not ended, and gay rights and gay labor activists have placed the passage of this bill at the top of their agenda.

Even with the challenges gay employees face at work, many gay individuals do make the decision to come out at their workplaces. In recent years, the number of openly gay, lesbian, and bisexual employees has been increasing. If more gay workers continually choose to come out in their workplaces, the progression toward an end to sexual orientation–based employment discrimination may begin to accelerate. Then employers and the government might begin to recognize the true presence of gay workers in the U.S. workforce and adopt policies and laws to protect the rights of gay individuals at work.

Monica Bielski

See also Domestic Partner Benefits

References and further reading

Baker, Daniel B., Sean O'Brien Strub, and Bill Henning. 1995. *Cracking the Corporate Closet: The 200 Best (and Worst) Companies to Work For, Buy From, and Invest In If You're Gay or Lesbian—and Even If You Aren't.* New York: Harper Business.

Ellis, Alan L., and Ellen D. B. Riggle, eds. 1996. *Sexual Identity on the Job: Issues and Services.* New York: Haworth Press.

Friskopp, Annette, and Sharon Silverstein. 1995. *Straight Jobs Gay Lives: Gay and Lesbian Professionals, the Harvard Business School, and the American Workplace.* New York: Scribner Press.

McCreery, Patrick. 2001. "Beyond Gay: 'Deviant' Sex and the Politics of the ENDA Workplace." Pp. 31–51 in *Out at Work: Building a Gay-Labor Alliance.* Edited by Kitty Krupat and Patrick McCreery. Minneapolis: University of Minnesota Press.

McNaught, Brian. 1993. *Gay Issues in the Workplace.* New York: St. Martin's Press.

National Gay and Lesbian Task Force. 1997. http://www.NGLTF.org.

Pride at Work (the AFL-CIO's national constituency group for gay, lesbian, bisexual, and transgender/sexual workers). http://www.prideatwork.org.

Rasi, Richard A., and Lourdes Rodriguez-Nogues, eds. 1995. *Out in the Workplace: The Pleasures and Perils of Coming Out on the Job.* Los Angeles: Alyson Publications.

Weston, Kath, and Lisa B. Rofel. 1997. "Sexuality, Class, and Conflict in a Lesbian Workplace." Pp. 25–44 in *Homo Economics: Capitalism, Community, and Lesbian and Gay Life.* Edited by Amy Gluckman and Betsy Reed. New York: Routledge.

General Agreement on Tariffs and Trade (GATT)

An international body for regulating world trade, the General Agreement on Tariffs and Trade (GATT) was initially drawn up as a provisional trade agreement in 1947 during a session of the preparatory Committee of the United Nations Conference on Trade and Employment. Twenty-three countries participated. From its inception, the GATT's main purpose (later incorporated into the World Trade Organization, or WTO) was to promote "freer trade" as well as help construct the least restrictive and the most stable trading environment by reducing trade barriers and dismantling protectionist policies.

The GATT was intended to be a short-term, single round of negotiations to provide a forum for the first multilateral tariff-reduction negotiations in 1948 and, more importantly, to draw up a transitional set of rules during the drafting and ratification of the International Trade Organization (ITO) treaty, as Donald Beane has noted (2000). The ITO treaty, including the GATT, was drafted in the spirit of the Bretton Woods meetings, discussions, and organizations that also chartered the World Bank and the International Monetary Fund. The principles embedded in these institutions and agreements were oriented toward establishing a stable international economic order to avoid the financial chaos that preceded World War II. More specifically, ITO's purpose was to promote trade liberalization policies and reduce the impact of domestic protectionist policies. However, when the ITO treaty was not ratified by the United States, who was its biggest proponent, the ITO was effectively dead. Consequently, the mere transitional organization GATT took its place since legally it was not a treaty requiring ratification but rather an executive agreement that could be implemented without legislative support.

From 1948 to the early twenty-first century, negotiators have held eight rounds of negotiations involving growing numbers of countries (called "contracting parties"). There are presently over 100 member countries in the WTO. Most of the rounds have dealt solely with tariff reduction, with a few exceptions. The Kennedy Round (held in Geneva from 1964 to 1967) produced an agreement on antidumping and dealt with problems of developing nations. The Tokyo Round (1973–1979) was intended to extend and improve the system overall. It dealt with nontrade barriers such as subsidies and countervailing measures, technical barriers to trade, import licensing procedures, government procurement, and other nontariff areas of concern. The most recent as well as most comprehensive round of negotiations was the Uruguay Round (1986–1994). The Uruguay Round agreements expanded the GATT Agreement on Trade in Goods by adding the General Agreement on Trade in Services (GATS), the Agreement on Trade-Related Aspects of Intellectual Property (TRIPS) and three other agreements pertaining to agriculture.

Most importantly, it was during this round that the World Trade Organization was established as a legal institution to replace the provisional GATT. The creation of the WTO was prompted by the contracting parties' belief that although each of the previous "rounds" successfully further reduced trade barriers, the increasing complexity of international economy required a more formal, powerful international trade regime. Consequently, the WTO was created to be a permanent organization that would be imbued with much greater powers to settle trade disputes than its predecessor, which was not a recognized international body. Furthermore, as a body of law, the WTO encompasses the GATT 1994 agreements, as well as others. (Now that the updated version of the GATT agreement—GATT 1994—has been incorporated into the new WTO agreement, the older version is called GATT 1947.)

In addition to increasing the scope of trade covered, the WTO also differs from the GATT in two other ways that specifically reflect the desire of negotiators to enable the WTO to address a much broader agenda. The first is the elimination of a special class of membership known as de facto membership. De facto membership was only open to independent countries that were former territories of a contracting party. De facto members benefited from reduced trade barriers on their exports but did not have to pay for the operations of GATT. Under the GATT 1947, contracting parties could be selective in the GATT provisions they implemented, a practice often called "GATT a la carte," but under the newly created WTO, member countries are required to accede to all major GATT provisions. The second difference is the authority of the WTO to settle trade disputes, a power not given to the GATT.

The two basic principles that govern the GATT philosophy are most-favored-nation (MFN) status and nondiscrimination. The MFN principle states that a contracting party cannot restrict or promote imports of certain goods from country "A" if it does not do so from country "B, C, D . . . Z." In other words, all countries' imports must be treated the same way. The nondiscrimination principle says that once a good has entered the country, it must not be treated differently than a domestically produced good. The other guiding principles that drove GATT agreements were to protect tariff concessions against nontariff barriers (NTBs), to establish a code of trade conduct, to institute consultation procedures and joint action to carry out the basic purposes of the agreement, and lastly, to create a waiver exception-exemption-escape process to promote survivability and flexibility of the agreement against the stringency of the code of conduct (Beane 2000, 63). Furthermore, contracting parties are called upon to work for the steady reduction of trade barriers and the elimination of quotas; member nations agree any concession granted to any one member must be granted to all and that a tariff concession once made cannot be rescinded without an agreed-upon compensation (Beane 2000, 21). The four major provisions of GATT reflect these principles. They deal with tariff and MFN status, quantitative restrictions, trade and development, and a set of smaller provisions covering procedural matters and concealed protection.

Since GATT was intended to be only a transitional agreement, its initial structure was ad hoc and less defined than the structures of other multilateral organizations. For one, its administrative body belonged to the never-ratified ITO. Additionally, its general agreement was also contained in that nonexistent organization. Yet, despite its ad hoc nature, it has evolved beyond a loose negotiating structure into a complex trade organization.

There are a number of explanations for GATT's survivability and expansion. It is primarily argued that GATT has remained viable by adherence of the member countries to the aforementioned set of principles, as well as the system's emphasis on process over structure, policy over institution, and pragmatism over idealism (Beane 2000, 270). This adherence is crucial since the system exists only at the discretion of the member countries. In other words, there is no mechanism or enforcement capability to prevent a country from withdrawing from the system. It is assumed that a common desire for international economic stability among member countries that simultaneously allows each to pursue its own economic goals has worked to ensure some degree of adherence to the system's basic principles. GATT succeeded in retaining its members. It has also attracted new members who believe either that "freer" trade is economically optimal or simply that it is more advantageous to be part of the system than outside it. For instance, some argue that developing nations have joined GATT in the belief that it would help them gain access to the markets of larger industrialized countries, such as the United States and the European Union, as well as assist in developing their domestic markets.

The GATT's successful evolution into the world's leading trade organization may also be attributed to its pragmatic nature as embodied in its exceptions, exemptions, waivers, and the escape clause. The waivers and exceptions process allows for a series of exceptions to reciprocity (that is, MFN status) and nondiscrimination. For example, Article 21 states: "Nothing in this agreement shall be construed" to negatively affect what any nation defines as a risk to its own security. Furthermore, in Article 24, allowances are made for certain kinds of discrimination, that is, the establishment of regional trade alliances that exclude other members (for example, the European Union, Association of Southeast Asian Nations, etc.). The contracting parties all vote to decide who is granted exceptions, waivers, exemptions, and exercise of the escape clause. This procedure allows for behavior that may undermine the GATT's/WTO's other constituting principles. Since its survival is dependent on its members, the WTO accommodates such disruptive actions. Consequently, the form and structure of WTO has been built on actual practices instead of prior directives. The decisions to reduce tariffs or to allow an exception are only reached through collective negotiations. All members meet to negotiate a self-governing agreement. Also, WTO operates on a one-country, one-vote rule. Thus, each and every contracting party, regardless of its share of global trade, has one vote.

Although it is generally believed that GATT/WTO has contributed to the growth of the global economy, it has also been criticized for a number of shortcomings. The most vocal WTO critics include groups concerned with democracy and the environment, as well as labor organizations and Third World countries. Such critics argue that the neoliberal model promoted by the WTO undermines health safeguards and environmental and labor regulations while providing transnational corporations (TNCs) a cheap labor source. First, the WTO has been reproved for not dealing adequately with worker rights, which is illustrated by the absence of a provision in the agreement to protect workers' rights such as safety standards, living wages, and reasonable working hours. Furthermore, unions such as the American Federation of Labor and Congress of Industrial Organizations (AFL-CIO) have criticized the WTO for lacking effective programs to assist workers dislocated by or adversely affected by trade. However, in 1996 during the WTO's first summit, steps were taken to create standards regarding worker rights. These standards were not made binding because many developing world nations opposed standards that would reduce their wage-cost advantage in the global market.

Second, since international concern about the relationship between trade and the environment has been steadily growing, the fact that WTO also lacks a provision regarding the environment has made it a focal point in the debate over free trade and the environment. This concern is further highlighted by the fact that to date, every credible environmental and public health challenge made to WTO agreements has been found to violate the WTO agreements. Environmentally minded citizen groups and politicians also decry the fact that since trade negotiations are conducted in secrecy, business groups have far greater access to the trade negotiating table than do either environmental groups or public interest groups. They believe that without measures in international trade agreements to protect environmental standards and regulations, economic growth created will be unsustainable and impose heavy costs on an already burdened environment.

A third set of GATT/WTO detractors believe that an international agreement on trade seriously weakens the functioning of democratically elected bodies across the globe. They fear that world governments are relinquishing the power of democratically elected bodies over decisions regulating commerce and setting labor, health, and environmental standards to a secretive and unelected global organization. Last, many critics believe the WTO largely carries out the agenda of wealthy industrialized nations at the expense of developing ones. Although most developing nations are in favor of liberalizing trade policies, many are also in opposition to WTO policies that they believe discriminate against developing economies. Such countries believe that the WTO agenda reflects only the industrialized countries' desire to gain even greater access to markets in the developing world without any interest in ensuring that the most pressing concerns of these nations are addressed.

Although, historically, the United States has been one of the most enthusiastic supporters of free trade and economic liberalization, its championing of free trade has not always garnered domestic political support, as is evident in recent debates over legislation granting the president trade promotion authority (TPA) and China membership in the WTO. Proponents of the TPA legislation (formerly known as fast track authority), such as U.S. trade representative Robert Zoellick, argue that TPA is necessary to ensure that the United States will not be left out of international trade agreements and thus unable to reap the economic benefits of free trade. The bill renewing TPA was eventually passed in September 2002, despite some resistance from Democrats in both chambers of Congress, who opposed its constraint on their ability to amend trade agreements and called for provisions to ensure that other nations uphold minimum labor and environmental standards.

U.S. domestic opposition to granting China membership in the WTO has been more successful, however, than criticism of the TPA. Many economic sectors in the United States advocate China's inclusion into the WTO to gain access to an untapped market for U.S. products. Yet objections to China's inclusion by groups expressing concern over China's poor human rights and environmental record have also had sway in Congress. The debate over TPA and China's membership to the WTO demonstrate that domestic pressures, not only in the United States but across the globe, will affect the deepening and widening of free trade agreements and the future of the WTO.

Meredith Staples

See also Trade Adjustment Assistance Program; World Trade Organization

References and further reading

Basgen, Brian, and Andy Blunden. 2002. *Encyclopedia of Marxism.* Marxist Internet Archive. http://www.marxists.org/glossary.

Beane, Donald G. 2000. *The United States and GATT: A Relational Study.* New York: Pergamon, Elsevier Science.

Collins, Susan M., and Barry P. Bosworth. 1994. "GATT: Where Are the Trumpets?" *Brookings Review* (Fall).

Evans, John W. 1968. "The General Agreement on Tariffs and Trade." *International Organization* 22, no. 1: 72–98.

French, Hilary F. 1993. "Costly Tradeoffs Reconciling Trade and the Environment." *World Watch Paper* 113, March.
Hoekman, Bernard M., and Michel M. Kostecki. 1995. *The Political Economy of the World Trading System from GATT to WTO.* Oxford: Oxford University Press.
Howse, Robert. 2000. "Adjudicative Legitimacy and Treaty Interpretation in the International Trade Law: The Early Years of the WTO Jurisprudence." Pp. 35–70 in *The EU, the WTO, and the NAFTA: Towards a Law of International Trade.* Edited by J. H. H. Weiler. Oxford: Oxford University Press.
Lovell, William S. 2001. "GATT (Now the WTO)." http://www.cerebalaw.com/gatt.htm (cited December 12, 2002).
Magnusson, Paul, and Dexter Roberts. 2000. "Sleepless after Seattle: The Political Battle for Most Favored Nation Status for China." *BusinessWeek,* January 24, 122.
Moore, Patrick M. 1996. "The Decisions Bridging the GATT 1947 and the WTO Agreement." *American Journal of International Law* 90, no. 2: 317–328.
Page, Sheila. 2001. "Developing Countries in GATT/WTO Negotiations." London: Overseas Development Institute, October.
Sobel, Russell S. 1997. "The Distinction between True and Induced Free Riders: An Application to GATT De Facto Membership." *Public Finance Review* 25, 4: 366.
Trade Observatory. 2002. http://www.tradeobservatory.org/pages/home.cfm.
United Press International. 2002. "Bottom Line: A GOP Free Trade Comeback." Nov 7, 2002.
US Newswire. 2002. "DeLay Applauds House Passage of Trade Bill: Free Trade Is the Vehicle that Carries Our Democratic Principles." July 27.
Zeiler, Thomas. 1997. "GATT Fifty Years Ago: U.S. Trade Policy and Imperial Tariff Protections." *Business and Economic History* 26, no. 2 (Winter): 709–717.

General Motors

Long the largest of the Big Three U.S. automakers, General Motors (GM) ushered in the age of mass consumerism with its installment buying and credit programs for car buyers in the 1920s. Coupled with its expansive lineup of cars—from the humble Chevrolet to the mighty Cadillac—and yearly style changes, GM's approach to selling cars was adapted throughout the industry as the standard for mass marketing durable goods to the U.S. consumer. Although it posted record profits in the 1980s, GM came under criticism for its failure to adapt to changing consumer tastes and competition from foreign automakers. It remained among the largest corporations in the world but was no longer held up as the model of corporate planning and efficiency.

In an era of fierce competition among numerous small, fledgling automakers, the idea of grouping together different automobile companies had been discussed by numerous investors in the early 1900s. After William C. Durant, a major shareholder in the Buick Motor Car Company, failed to convince Henry Ford and Ransom E. Olds to join him in such an organization, Durant decided to form his own holding company, General Motors, in the fall of 1908. Within a year, GM added the Oldsmobile brand to its lineup, with the Oakland (later renamed Pontiac) and Cadillac divisions included by the following year. From the start, Durant's vision was clear: in contrast to Henry Ford's approach of developing one leading automobile, GM would offer a spectrum of cars at different price levels. Longtime GM chairman Alfred P. Sloan later described the strategy as "a car for every purse and purpose," a dictum that remained at the heart of GM's mission years later. The company also pioneered the use of credit buying for its products through its General Motors Acceptance Corporation; by facilitating consumer spending, the company not only expanded its market but benefited from the additional revenue that the interest payments brought in.

For all of Durant's vision, the rapid and sometimes chaotic growth of GM led to his ouster in 1910; he returned to the company from 1916 to 1920, but he had effectively lost control of the company to its investors, including the Du Pont family, which controlled about 30 percent of GM's stock through the 1950s. Durant's successor, Alfred P. Sloan, instituted rigorous financial and planning controls, and his rationalization of GM's operations led to a then-record corporate profit of $235 million in 1927. Although GM suffered a downturn during the Great Depression, it nevertheless enlarged its market share and after 1930 was ranked as the nation's largest carmaker, ahead of rival Ford Motor Company and the Chrysler Corporation.

After a series of sit-down strikes in its plants during the winter of 1936–1937, GM became the first automaker to enter into collective bargaining with the United Auto Workers union. In 1950, the two parties signed an agreement hailed as the Treaty of Detroit: in exchange for a five-year contract, GM granted a 20 percent wage hike and established a pension plan and partially paid health insurance plan. The contract also included a cost-of-living adjustment for workers' wages, the first such agreement in the auto industry. In an era of almost uninterrupted economic expansion, however, the guarantee of labor stability was well worth the price. GM increased its share of the domestic auto market to 60 percent, and the company was often invoked as the symbol of the modern U.S. corporation for its planning, efficiency, and profitability.

Publicity surrounding a series of hearings on the safety of GM's 1964 Corvair model, however, called into question GM's corporate decision making. After consumer advocate Ralph Nader published *Unsafe at Any Speed* in 1965, which alleged that GM knowingly put the Corvair out even after it was aware of its design defects, the company's reputation was tarnished. Even worse for the bottom line, GM's product lineup in the early 1970s increasingly veered away from consumer tastes that favored smaller and more fuel-efficient cars, often made by foreign automakers. Because compact cars offered GM less profit per sale but cost just as much to push through product development, the company continued to design and manufacture cars that fell out of step with the times. Although the company remained the largest of the Big Three automakers, it gradually lost its market share. In 1980, the company held 46 percent of the domestic market, but by 1994, the figure had slipped to 33 percent. The company also suffered from the negative publicity generated by the documentary film *Roger & Me,* made by Flint, Michigan, native Michael Moore. Taking aim at GM's decision to close its operations in Flint, Moore criticized GM's diversification strategy—including its purchase of Hughes Aircraft and Electronic Data Systems—as a shortsighted one.

Although GM remained a profitable company in the 1980s—with a record profit of $4.5 billion announced in 1988—the company remained plagued by internal conflicts among its divisions, which often acted in their own interests at the expense of GM's general economic health. Despite a reorganization attempt by chairman Roger Smith in 1984, the company continued to struggle for a long-range plan to counter increased competition by foreign automakers and more efficient manufacturing processes and better marketing strategies by its rivals in the Big Three. With the creation of a new GM division, Saturn, which started operating in 1992, GM hoped to regain both its market share and its reputation for organizational innovation. Based on a cooperative labor management style that fostered a partnership between workers and the company, Saturn generated reams of good publicity for GM after its debut. However, it was questionable whether the new emphasis on quality circles, profit sharing, and customer satisfaction had transformed GM as a whole. As the company approached its centennial, it remained under fire for its perceived lack of focus, organizational reform, and long-range planning.

Timothy G. Borden

See also American Federation of Labor and Congress of Industrial Organizations; Automotive Industry; Collective Bargaining; Industrial Revolution and Assembly Line Work; Manufacturing Jobs; Productivity; Quality Circles; Strikes; United Auto Workers

References and further reading

Chandler, Alfred D., Jr. 1990. *Scale and Scope: The Dynamics of Industrial Capitalism.* Cambridge: Harvard University Press.

Drucker, Peter. 1995. *Managing in a Time of Great Change.* New York: Truman Talley Books.

Freeland, Robert. 2000. *The Struggle for Control of the Modern Corporation: Organizational Change at General Motors, 1924–1970.* New York: Cambridge University Press.

Ingrassia, Paul, and Joseph B. White. 1994. *Comeback: The Fall and Rise of the American Automobile Industry.* New York: Simon and Schuster.

Keller, Maryann. 1989. *Rude Awakening: The Rise, Fall, and Struggle for Recovery of General Motors.* New York: William Morrow.

Lichtenstein, Nelson. 1995. *The Most Dangerous Man in America: Walter Reuther and the Fate of American Labor.* New York: Basic Books.

Madsen, Axel. 1999. *The Deal Maker: How William C. Durant Made General Motors.* New York: John Wiley and Sons.

Maynard, Micheline. 1995. *Collision Course: Inside the Battle for General Motors.* New York: Birch Lane Press.

Nader, Ralph. 1965. *Unsafe at Any Speed: The Designed-in Dangers of the American Automobile.* New York: Grossman.

Rubenstein, Paul A., and Thomas A. Kolchan. 2001. *Learning from Saturn: Possibilities for Corporate Governance and Employee Relations.* Ithaca, NY: Cornell University Press.

Sherman, Joe. 1994. *In the Rings of Saturn.* New York: Oxford University Press.

GI Bill

The Serviceman's Readjustment Act of 1944, better known as the GI Bill, provided returning U.S. veterans of World War II educational, housing, and unemployment benefits, thus helping to encourage the growth of higher education and the middle class in the postwar era. The bill, authored by the American Legion among others, supported by President Franklin D. Roosevelt, and passed by Congress with little opposition, was arguably the greatest expansion of the U.S. welfare state in the postwar era. Designed to avoid problems with readjustment and economic reconversion, as well as potential social unrest among unemployed veterans, the GI Bill enabled millions of veterans of working-class background to join the growing postwar suburban middle class.

The Serviceman's Readjustment Act, signed by President Franklin Roosevelt in June 1944, provided approximately 16 million veterans with education and training; loan guarantees for the purchase of homes, farms, and businesses; unemployment insurance; and job-finding assistance. Soldiers that had served at least 90 days and had been honorably discharged were eligible for all benefits. As early as the fall of 1943, Roosevelt had called for liberal unemployment, Social Security, and educational benefits for veterans. After a series of unsuccessful bills, the American Legion, a veterans' interest group, proposed an omnibus measure in January 1944 that later became known as the GI Bill of Rights. It sailed through the Senate unanimously in March 1944 but tripped temporarily over the issue of race in the House, where Mississippi congressman and chair of the Committee on World War Veterans Legislation John Rankin worried about the generosity of benefits to black veterans. Nonetheless, the GI Bill passed the House in June 1944, representing a tremendous victory for the American Legion, which had lobbied heavily for the law, and for a larger and better-funded Veterans Administration (VA) (Polenberg 1972, 96–97).

Higher education as well as job training was made available through the VA, which in addition to providing a monthly stipend of up to $50 a month, paid educational institutions directly for tuition. All qualified veterans received at least one year of full-time training or education, plus a period equal to their time in service (Nash 1992, 154). By the time the program ended in July 1956, the VA had spent $14.5 billion to educate and train nearly 8 million veterans. Continuing and expanding the policies of the Federal Housing Administration (FHA), created in 1934, the VA also agreed to insure mortgage loans to veterans so that they could purchase homes, businesses, and farms. Nearly 4 million veterans purchased homes under the law (Sherry 1995, 109). The bill provided veterans with $20 per month of unemployment benefits for up to fifty-two weeks and gave them job-finding assistance as well as hiring preferences.

Historians who study the GI Bill and its effects struggle to separate the reasons for its passage from its eventual impact, much of which was unanticipated. It is generally acknowledged that the law passed because of a sense of obligation to those who served, a fear of postwar depression and unrest, and the need for a well-trained and broadly educated postwar work force. The public pronouncements of political leaders tended to emphasize the bill's provisions as a reward to veterans from a grateful American public. President Roosevelt argued that the GI Bill gave "emphatic notice to the men and women in the armed forces that the American people do not intend to let them down" (Nash 1992, 154). Administration officials described the law both as a reward for deserving citizens and a means to maintain morale among the troops. Veterans who took advantage of the opportunities the law provided eventually came to see it as a kind of entitlement, as did much of the American public; indeed, the bill played a critical role in the growing perception of middle-class Americans in the postwar era that the opportunity for home ownership and higher education were rights to which all were entitled.

Although the desire to provide veterans with a just reward undoubtedly motivated many of the legislators who voted for the law, the GI Bill was also passed out of fear of those same veterans and the possible social and economic consequences of flooding the postwar labor market with 16 million untrained service people of largely working-class background. Many U.S. legislators and voters had keen memories of 4 million demobilized World War I veterans sleeping under bridges and standing on street corners during the unrest and depression of 1919, as well as of the infamous "Bonus March" of veterans to Washington in 1932. Wartime surveys indicated a deep anxiety among both citizens and soldiers about the postwar economy and a possible return to depression. The precedent of the previous war aside, the worry was not unfounded; by the end of 1947, the federal government had paid nearly $2.5 billion to unemployed veterans (May 1988, 77). A massive strike wave and housing shortage at the end of the war, as well as the rapid growth of socialist politics among veterans in Europe, provoked fear of unemployed and potentially radical soldiers in the United States. It was hoped that the educational and home loan provisions in particular would prevent both the flooding of the labor market and the growth of unrest and political radicalism (Sherry 1995, 112).

Finally, the bill was driven by the perceived need for a better-trained and educated workforce. As early as 1942, the federal government initiated plans to anticipate the problems of the postwar economy and society. The National Resources Planning Board studied manpower needs and in June 1943 recommended programs for the education and training of demobilized soldiers. This study provided a model for the American Legion, when it authored the basic framework of what would become the GI Bill the following year. In particular, it was hoped that retraining veterans in new skills like aviation and electronics would strengthen not only the economy but U.S. military might as well (Sherry 1995, 109).

Of all the provisions in the GI Bill, the education and homeownership provisions had by far the greatest impact, both in the long term and the short term. Both benefits were used by many more veterans than had been anticipated when the measure was passed. Based on surveys of servicemen, the federal government expected that 7 percent to 12 percent of veterans would take advantage of job training and college aid, with perhaps 700,000 going to college over a period of years. Indeed, given the large percentage of veterans of both working-class and immigrant background, university officials worried about the effect the law's educational provisions would have on academic standards. Stunningly, over 2.2 million veterans attended colleges and universities under the bill, with over 1 million in attendance in 1946 and 1947 alone. In 1947, veterans accounted for 49 percent of all college enrollment, helping to greatly accelerate a century-long expansion in higher education attendance generally. A 1988 congressional study later estimated that 40 percent of those who went to colleges and universities under the GI Bill would not have otherwise done so. Although most Americans associate the GI Bill with helping veterans go to college, far more veterans utilized the benefits to attain job training or to attend other kinds of educational institutions (May1988, 77). The success of the GI Bill's educational provisions led to the creation of similar measures for the veterans of the U.S. wars that followed. Although it is difficult to determine just how many who attended college under the law actually graduated—the VA didn't keep such statistics—its impact on the opportunities of veterans and their descendants is undisputed. It was indispensable to the rapid growth of the middle class in the postwar era and also played a critical role in the assimilation of immigrants and their children into the mainstream of American life (Baritz 1982, 185).

Section 505 of the GI Bill underwrote the economic risk inherent in the construction and finance of low-cost homes for veterans by insuring their mortgages. The program also allowed veterans to borrow the appraised value of a home without a down payment. A massive housing shortage after the war—Senate investigations found veterans living in garages, trailers, and barns in 1946—provided a strong incentive for veterans to make use of this benefit (Wright 1983, 242). By 1948, 1.4 million had taken out guaranteed loans to buy houses. By insuring home loans to veterans, the bill encouraged private investors to enter the housing mortgage market by reducing their financial risk. Federal tax benefits for homeowners made Section 505 especially attractive. Housing starts went from 114,000 in 1944 to nearly 1.7 million in 1950 (Jackson 1987, 231–232). Suburban real estate developers like William Levitt argued that homeownership would help to domesticate the veteran and create social and political stability. Historians have generally concurred that the rapid growth of single-family suburban homeownership in the postwar era has not only expanded the U.S. middle class but has increased the extent to which Americans identify themselves politically and culturally as middle class (Hayden 1984, 41–42). The GI Bill played a critical role in ending the postwar housing shortage and greatly accelerating the growth of suburbs in the United States, as well as the flight of the white middle-class from older northeastern and midwestern cities (Baritz 1982, 185).

Unfortunately, even though the GI Bill aided millions of U.S. veterans, it did not aid all of them. African American veterans, particularly in the South, had a difficult time claiming and making use of the law's entitlements to improve their socioeconomic condition. Importantly, Section 505 continued the practice initiated in the 1930s by the Home

Owners' Loan Corporation (HOLC) and the Federal Housing Administration of showing a strong bias for the purchase and construction of single-family homes largely in suburbs and against insuring loans in urban areas. This attitude had the unfortunate consequence of encouraging the flight of white families, jobs, and capital out of cities. It also had the unfortunate consequence of largely excluding black veterans from GI Bill mortgage benefits because black families were prevented both by law and custom from living in suburban areas throughout the country. Until 1948, for example, black veterans were legally excluded from Levittown, New York, the quintessential postwar veteran suburban development, because of the insertion of racially restrictive covenants into home property deeds. As a result, the buildup of home equity that vaulted so many white veterans and their families into the middle class did little for black veterans or for the prosperity of U.S. cities. In this sense, perhaps the greatest and most effective piece of social legislation in U.S. history had the effect of reinforcing, rather than eliminating, racial inequality.

Mark Santow

See also Earnings and Education; Education Reform and the Workforce; Federal Unemployment Tax and Insurance System; Labor Force; Labor Market; Levittown; New Deal; Roosevelt, Franklin Delano; Veterans

References and further reading

Baritz, Loren. 1982. *The Good Life: The Meaning of Success for the American Middle Class.* New York: Harper and Row.

Bennett, Michael. 1999. *When Dreams Came True: The G. I. Bill and the Making of Modern America.* New York: Brasseys.

Hayden, Dolores. 1984. *Redesigning the American Dream: Gender, Housing and Family Life.* New York: W. W. Norton.

Jackson, Kenneth. 1987. *Crabgrass Frontier: The Suburbanization of the United States.* New York: Columbia University Press.

Kelly, Barbara. 1993. *Expanding the American Dream: Building and Rebuilding Levittown.* New York: State University of New York Press.

May, Elaine Tyler. 1988. *Homeward Bound.* New York: Basic Books.

Milford, Lewis, and Richard Severo. 1990. *The Wages of War: When America's Soldiers Came Home—from Valley Forge to Vietnam.* New York: Touchstone Books.

Olson, Keith. 1974. *The G.I. Bill, the Veterans and the Colleges.* Lexington: University Press of Kentucky.

Polenberg, Richard. 1972. *War and Society: The United States, 1941–1945.* New York: Lippincott.

Ross, Davis. 1969. *Preparing for Ulysses: Politics and Veterans during World War II.* New York: Columbia University Press.

Sherry, Michael. 1995. *In the Shadow of War: the United States since the 1930s.* New Haven, CT: Yale University Press.

Wright, Gwendolyn. 1983. *Building the Dream: A Social History of Housing in America.* Cambridge: Massachusetts Institute of Technology Press.

Glass Ceiling

Glass ceiling is a phrase often used to refer to "invisible barriers" that prevent women and minorities from assuming positions at the top of corporate hierarchies in the United States. Although the term *glass ceiling* currently refers to invisible barriers that impede *any* underrepresented group from advancing, the phrase was first used in reference to women. The glass ceiling was first mentioned in an article that appeared in the *Wall Street Journal* on March 24, 1986, and subsequently has appeared in the 1991 Civil Rights Act and in a number of reports issued by different federal agencies.

On March 24, 1986, a special report appeared as a cover story in the *Wall Street Journal,* entitled "The Corporate Woman." The subtitle to the report was "The Glass Ceiling: Why Women Can't Seem to Break the Invisible Barrier That Blocks Them from the Top Jobs." The report discussed the fact that women had failed to reach top positions in most U.S. corporations, gave both statistical and anecdotal evidence of the glass ceiling phenomenon, and proffered reasons why the glass ceiling existed. The *Wall Street Journal* story received a great deal of notoriety.

In 1989, the Department of Labor (DOL) set out to investigate the glass ceiling. Nine Fortune 500 firms were selected for review, and the findings from the department's investigation were published in a report released in 1991, entitled *A Report on the Glass Ceiling Initiative.* The essential finding of the report was that there was a point beyond which minorities and women have not advanced in some companies, with minorities reaching plateaus lower than those reached by white women. The definition of glass ceiling that the Department of Labor reached was that the term encompassed artificial barriers that built upon biases and attitudes within organizations that prevent qualified individuals from advancing into management-level positions (U.S. Department of Labor 1997).

On August 11, 1992, the DOL issued a follow-up report on barriers to advancement in the workplace, entitled *Pipelines of Progress: An Update on the Glass Ceiling Initiative.* This report reviewed the past year's efforts to eliminate barriers to job advancement and identified ongoing and innovative efforts in various corporations to promote women and minorities to higher levels. The report noted that, although corporate America had become increasingly diverse, inquiries made by the DOL showed that women and minorities who had advanced to upper-level management jobs remained an exception to the rule. *Pipelines of Progress* also focused on steps companies could take to remove glass ceiling barriers.

The findings of the DOL's investigations led to the inclusion of the Glass Ceiling Act of 1991 as Title II of the 1991 Civil Rights Act. The act created a twenty-one-member commission known as the Glass Ceiling Commission "to conduct a study and prepare recommendations concerning: (1) eliminating artificial barriers to the advancement of women and minorities; and (2) increasing the opportunities and developmental experiences of women and minorities to foster advancement of women and minorities to management and decisionmaking positions in business." The act required the commission's report to be delivered to the president and the appropriate congressional committees within fifteen months.

The commission released two reports as a result of its investigations. The first, released in March 1995 and entitled *Good for Business: Making Full Use of the Nation's Human Capital,* was an "environmental scan" that presented the findings of the commission. The commission's report "confirm[ed] the enduring aptness of the 'glass ceiling metaphor'" (U.S. Department of Labor 1995). The overall conclusion was similar to those that had been reached in other glass ceiling reports: few women or minorities had reached positions in the highest levels of corporate America and, even if they had reached such positions, their compensation was lower.

The commission's second report, released in November 1995 and entitled *A Solid Investment: Making Full Use of the Nation's Human Capital,* was a "strategic plan" that presented the commission's recommendations based on its findings. Recommendations were made for businesses to dismantle barriers within corporate structures; for government to do its part to break glass ceiling barriers; and for society to enlist schools, media, community organizations, and other institutions to break the glass ceiling.

Finally, in June 1997, the Office of Federal Contract Compliance Programs (OFCCP) released a report entitled *The Glass Ceiling Initiative: Are There Cracks in the Ceiling?* This report was a further follow-up to *A Report on the Glass Ceiling Initiative* and consisted of fifty-three reviews conducted in 1993 and 1994. The first conclusion this report reached was that a glass ceiling does exist. It went on to note, however, that "there are cracks in the glass ceiling." In other words, there were increases in the proportion of both women and minorities in corporate management.

Apart from these governmental initiatives, the glass ceiling phenomenon induced discussion, commentary, and empirical research as well. In the January–February 1989 issue of *Harvard Business Review,* Felice N. Schwartz, president and founder of Catalyst, a not-for-profit group that works with corporations to foster women's careers, published an article entitled "Management Women and the New Facts of Life." Schwartz's article contained a number of provocative ideas, including the assertions that it costs companies more to employ women than men because women have greater turnover than men in similar management positions and women's careers are often interrupted—or ended—when they have children.

Schwartz's ideas were dubbed "Mommy track" because Schwartz suggested that corporations should create a two-tiered system for women employees, one for career-oriented women and one for those who divide their attentions between home and work. For the former group, Schwartz suggested that all obstacles to advancement should be cleared. For women who are both career- and family-oriented, Schwartz argued that companies must become more flexible to make the best use of these employees. They must plan for and manage maternity better, provide greater workplace and work-hour flexibility, and make high-quality day care available.

Schwartz's article generated a great deal of criticism from women's rights advocates and other feminists who believed her work would be used as ammunition by companies seeking any excuse to avoid hiring and promoting women. These critics argued that corporations would use Schwartz's article to justify all types of discrimination against women (for example, women would be paid less, given less important jobs, promoted less frequently). Schwartz countered her critics by pointing out that her goal was merely to make things easier for women by inducing corporate America to recognize and be sensitive to the many different motivations that could be important to women.

Finally, the glass ceiling idea has generated academic research as well, as researchers have sought to identify causes of the glass ceiling phenomenon. For example, in 1989, Belle Rose Ragins and Eric Sundstrom developed a model of over thirty unique factors that potentially could affect sex segregation patterns at three different levels: individual, interpersonal, and organizational. Other research looked at whether there might be biological and/or cultural differences between the genders that would help explain the glass ceiling. These studies found differences between the genders (or races, etc.) that would account for different performance on the job.

Steven E. Abraham

See also Comparable Worth; Mommy Track; Pay Equity; Pink Collar; Wage Gap; Women and Work

References and further reading

Baron, Tracy Anbinder. 1994. "Comment: Keeping Women Out of the Executive Suite: The Courts' Failure to Apply Title VII Scrutiny to Upper-level Jobs." *University of Pennsylvania Law Review,* November, 143–267.

Bridge, Diane L. 1997. "The Glass Ceiling and Sexual Stereotyping: Historical and Legal Perspectives of Women in the Workplace." *Virginia Journal of Social Policy and the Law* (Spring), 4.

Chicago Area Partnerships. 1996. "Pathways and Progress: Corporate Best Practices to Shatter the Glass Ceiling." Executive Summary.

Corsun, David L., and Wanda M. Costen. 2001. "Is the Glass Ceiling Unbreakable? Habitus, Fields, and the Stalling of Women and Minorities in Management." *Journal of Management Inquiry* 10, no. 1 (March): 16–25.

Eyring, Alison, and Bette Ann Stead. 1998. "Shattering the Glass Ceiling: Some Successful Corporate Practices." *Journal of Business Ethics* 17, no. 3 (1998): 245–251.

Kende, Mark S. 1994. "Shattering the Glass Ceiling: A Legal Theory for Attacking Discrimination against Women Partners." *Hastings Law Journal* (November): 17.

Moore, Dorothy P., and E. Holly Buttner. 1997. "Women Entrepreneurs: Moving beyond the Glass Ceiling." Thousand Oaks, CA: Sage.

Paetzold, Ramona L., and Rafael Gely. 1995. "Through the Looking Glass: Can Title VII Help Women and Minorities Shatter the Glass Ceiling?" *Houston Law Review* 31 (Spring): 1517.

Ragins, Belle Rose, and Eric Sundstrom. 1989. "Gender and Power in Organizations: A Longitudinal Perspective." *Psychological Bulletin* 105: 51–88.

Rhode, Deborah L. 1994. "Gender and Professional Roles." *63 Fordham Law Review 39.*

Schwartz, Felice N. 1989. "Management Women and the New Facts of Life." *Harvard Business Review* (January–February): 65–76.

U.S. Department of Labor. 1991. *A Report on the Glass Ceiling Initiative.* Washington, DC: U.S. Department of Labor.

———. 1992. *Pipelines of Progress: An Update on the Glass Ceiling Initiative.* Washington, DC: U.S. Department of Labor.

———. 1995. *Good for Business: Making Full Use of the Nation's Human Capital.* Washington, DC: U.S. Department of Labor.

———. 1995a. *A Solid Investment: Making Full Use of the Nation's Human Capital.* Washington, DC: U.S. Department of Labor.

———. 1997. *The Glass Ceiling Initiative: Are There Cracks in the Ceiling?* Washington, DC: U.S. Department of Labor.

Weiler, Stephan, and Alaxandra Bernasek. 2001. "Dodging the Glass Ceiling? Networks and New Wave of Women Entrepreneurs." *Social Science Journal* 38, no. 1 (January): 85–106.

Globalization and Workers

Globalization is a process of growing mutual dependence between countries that links nations together economically, socially, and politically. People interact through free trade, capital flow, migration, and exchange of information. Although globalization is not a new phenomenon, by the end of 1990, it became a hot topic of widespread debate. The dispute has divided the public into proponents of globalization and its opponents.

Most economists highlight the net benefits of free trade to national economies, such as lower prices for consumers, greater efficiency in the overall economy, and an improvement in the total welfare of citizens. Besides, they argue that globalization has brought about higher wages, better working conditions, more jobs, and access to education and technology. They cite many countries of Asia, where internal market-oriented labor policy improved job opportunities for millions of working people and left them far better off. Yet those economists also agree that trade liberalization reduced the income of some producers and workers. In other words, the distribution of the benefits from free trade—across industries, occupations, regions, and ultimately individuals—is unequal.

Even workers in the United States are concerned over the gigantic steps of globalization that in some instances leave them worse off. The highly visible nature of job loss, along with the failure of current federal adjustment programs to compensate workers for their losses, weakens popular support for the view that economic integration brings widespread global benefits. Many Americans clearly feel that U.S. workers are getting short shrift in the process of growing international trade. Opening to trade with low-wage countries encourages U.S. companies to relocate outside the United States in low-wage countries, thus taking away jobs and directly affecting U.S. workers. For instance, despite the promises of politicians and heads of industry that U.S. jobs would be safe after the North American Free Trade Agreement (NAFTA) entered into force in January 1994, far more jobs have been created in Mexico than the United States, where median wages remain stagnant for workers. On the contrary, with cheap labor abroad and NAFTA trade agreements smoothing the way, many U.S. workers have seen their jobs exported or have been forced to agree to wage and benefit reductions to save their employment. U.S. workers are forced to compete more directly with foreign workers, which has a globally equalizing effect that disadvantages the former. The actual shift of capital abroad and the use of the external option to drive hard bargains at home has weakened labor. In addition, deliberate government policies of tight money and restrictive budgets to contain inflation, which have reduced unemployment, have also weakened organized labor.

Even many of globalization's leading enthusiasts acknowledge that the outsourcing of production from the United States to facilities around the world has created downward wage pressures for U.S. workers. But the damage done by this defining feature of globalization is widely thought to be confined to the economy's low-wage, low-skill sectors. Public opinion on this issue is also divided. Some argue that skilled workers in a relatively high-skilled country like the United States would benefit from trade liberalization. Unskilled workers, however, would suffer real wage losses. The survey data reveal that skilled workers in the United States are more likely than unskilled workers to support trade liberalization because since the 1980s, the U.S. labor market has been characterized by stagnant real wages of lower-skilled workers and increased wage inequality. This division between high-skilled and low-skilled U.S. workers adds heat to the progressing debate over the benefits and costs of globalization. Workers blame the global economy for the relatively poor performance of less-skilled workers in the labor market over the last three decades of the twentieth century.

Moreover, the observed pattern of preferences toward trade policy reflects recent trends in the U.S. labor market. The view that losers from trade and globalization are economic losers is heard most often in connection with U.S. trade with low-income, Third World countries. Usually, these countries are recognized as major competitors for U.S. workers in labor-intensive industries such as apparel, textiles, toys, auto parts, and electronics assembly. Likewise, U.S. jobs have been lost in industries such as automobiles, steel, textiles, footwear, and consumer electronics, as goods produced abroad have increasingly come into competition with domestically produced items. At the same time, the growth of foreign markets through exports has benefited other industries, including aircraft, computers, entertainment, and finance.

Another issue that causes disputes is income distribution. Economists from the World Bank have noted that income inequality has risen considerably both within and between countries. The gap between the richest 20 percent and the poorest 20 percent worldwide grew from 30 to 1 in 1960 to 82 to 1 in 1995, and Third World conditions have in many respects worsened. Per capita incomes have fallen in more than seventy countries since the 1980s; some 3 billion people—half the world's population—live on less than $2 a day; and 800 million suffer from malnutrition. In the United States, despite a 35 percent increase in productivity between 1973 and 1995, the median real wage rate was lower in the latter year. Inequality rose to levels of seventy years earlier, along with underemployment, job insecurity, and benefit loss. Moreover, some Americans believe that the growth of international trade has increased the gap between rich and poor in their country and that U.S. policymakers are not adequately addressing the needs of U.S. workers. These Americans want government to help workers adapt to international trade through retraining and education.

Therefore, those who reject further globalization have gained considerable ground. Serious opposition was demonstrated during the 1999 World Trade Organization (WTO) ministerial conference in Seattle and the 2000 meetings in Washington of the World Bank and the International Monetary Fund (IMF). The protesters opposed the negative outcomes of globalization brought about by liberalization of trade, increased foreign investment, and rising immigration. The demonstrators particularly disproved of the activities of three main institutions that govern globalization, the IMF, the World Bank, and the WTO. Each of these organizations has its own mission and role to play on the international arena. The IMF, for instance, was created to facilitate the expansion and balance growth of international trade and contribute thereby to the promotion and maintenance of high levels of employment and real income. The World Bank and WTO were created to advance liberalization of the trade regime and capital markets and to promote imports and exports. The overall objective is to open the economies of the Third World (and now the transitional economies such as those of the former Soviet Union and Eastern Europe, including Bulgaria, Hungary, and Romania) and enable the corporations of the developed world to sell their goods and services in the markets of the developing countries.

Other institutions that influence the expansion of the globalization include the United Nations, the International Labour Organisation (ILO), and the World Health Organization (WHO). ILO promotes its agenda around the world under the slogan "decent work." WHO is concerned with improving health conditions in the developing world. In addition, many other institutions play a role in the international economic system. They include a number of regional banks, smaller and younger sisters to the World Bank, and a large number of UN organizations, such as the UN Development Program or the UN Conference on Trade and Development (UNCTAD). These organizations often have views that are markedly different from those of IMF and the World Bank. The ILO, for example, worries that the IMF pays too little attention to workers' rights, and the Asian Development Bank argues for "competitive pluralism." According to the views of the general American public, as well as political analysts and economic specialists, not all of these institutions have worked perfectly. The promises of more jobs, higher wages, and better opportunities were not fulfilled, at least in some parts of the world.

Numerous public opinion surveys through the late 1990s and early 2000s indicate that Americans are concerned about the impact upon jobs and incomes within the United States of continued liberalization of trade, foreign direct investment, and immigration. This view has been commonly characterized as reflecting the interests of small groups whose diverse agendas have very little connection, if any, to the economic consequences of policy liberalization. However, one recent study of U.S. public attitudes show that a broad section of U.S. workers are concerned about the trade's effects on workers, because most Americans are either working or are being supported by someone who works. At first glance it seems obvious that Americans are concerned with the effects of globalization, but that does not necessarily mean that all Americans feel personally threatened by it. Despite the voices of protest and criticism, globalization is continuing at a rapid pace.

Raissa Muhutdinova-Foroughi

See also Export Processing Zones; North American Free Trade Agreement; Trade Adjustment Assistance Program; World Trade Organization

References and further reading

Bradshaw, York W., and Michael Wallace. 1996. *Global Inequalities.* Thousand Oaks, CA: Sage.

Friedman, Thomas L. 1999. *The Lexus and the Olive Tree.* New York: Farrar, Straus, and Giroux.

International Labor Organization. "Report: Globalization." http://www.ilo.org/actrav.

Program on International Policy Attitudes. 2000. "Americans on Globalization: A Study of U.S. Public Attitudes." http://www.pipa.org/publist.html (cited March 28).

Waters, Malcolm. 1995. *Globalization.* London: Routledge.

World Bank. 2001. *World Development Report 2001.* New York: Oxford University Press.

Gold Watch

The presentation of a gold watch has become a symbolic memento of retirement from one's career. As a custom, its origins are unclear. It has been attributed to the presentation of a railroad conductor's watch to retiring railroad workers, who were among the first U.S. workers covered by any sort of pension or retirement program.

From the 1900s through the 1950s, the practice spread to other industries and companies. The watch was seen as a source of recognition for the retiring employee's long-term contributions and loyalty to his or her employer. Typically, the award was personalized with the recipient's name and corporate logo, hopefully strengthening the symbolic bond between the employer and employee.

However, the meaningfulness of the gold watch to the retiree has declined precipitously since then. Employees no longer spend their entire careers with only one or two employers, nor are their lives defined by their employment. Contemporary workers are understandably more concerned about their own economic welfare after retirement than the symbolic recognition afforded by a watch.

For some retirees, the "gold watch" presentation—or plaque or gift purchased by their coworkers—along with their 401(k)s and retirement programs, are the only symbols of the end of a workaday career. However, for some senior level executives, the recognition is considerably more expansive: use of corporate jets, lifetime income, lucrative consulting contracts, office and secretarial expense, cars and drivers, forgiveness of loans, and other lavish perks continue well into retirement.

Although clearly not the norm, these once unquestioned arrangements between the board of directors and the retiring executive have drawn much criticism, particularly from shareholders, as these arrangements have been exposed in the popular press in the wake of Enron, WorldCom, Tyco, and other corporate scandals of 2001 and after. One retired chief executive officer of a major U.S. corporation publicly renounced them (once they were made known), and others have followed suit.

Ron Schenk

See also American Association of Retired Persons; Retirement

References and further reading

Awardville. 2002. "Recognition Tips." http://www.awardville.com/symbolism.asp (cited August 10).

Great Depression

The Great Depression was a period of economic, political, and social change in the United States, initiated by the stock market crash of September 1929, reaching its peak in 1932 and 1933, and lasting until economic recovery and the nation's entry into World War II in 1941. Numerous events contributed to the "Great Crash" that was connected to and exacerbated by worldwide changes of the era. Legislative, policy, and social responses to the Great Depression reshaped the ways that Americans think about unemployment and the role of their government in enduring ways.

After the end of World War I in 1918, the United States experienced a brief postwar depression, and then the economy began to grow at an unprecedented rate. Prior to 1929, the Federal Reserve Board made credit increasingly available, created more than $500 million in new money (Kelley 1990, 595), reduced interest rates and lowered taxes, and enforced little trade or antitrust regulation. As a result, money poured into the stock market from millions of investors in the United States and Europe, creating record profits and growth. Many investors purchased stock "on the margins"—with less than 10 percent down—and by 1929 almost 2 million Americans had invested in the volatile and largely unregulated securities market (Kelley 1990, 594).

In September 1929, the Bank of England raised its rediscount rate to 6.5 percent, reducing the flow of capital to the United States and causing many U.S. and European investors to slow their U.S. purchasing, sell out, and protect themselves. Confidence in the market began to wane. Wall Street was deluged with "sell orders," and prices began to tumble. A selling panic resulted, and within a month of "Black Tuesday" (September 29, 1929), the total value of stocks listed on the New York Stock Exchange had dropped by $26 billion (with a total loss of $16 billion), or to 40 percent of their former value (DeLong 1997, 3).

Despite the shock of the economic crash of 1929, a recession had in fact already been underway. In 1928, production outpaced consumption, and many factories shut down operations and laid off workers. Some analysts have sited underconsumption as the principal cause of the Depression, positing that an increasing disparity in income prohibited working Americans from consuming the huge overproduction of the nation. Other observers argued that the wages of the period were more evenly distributed than they had been at any earlier period. Thus the potential demand for goods was still high, and the federal government could have used its existing resources to stop the downward economic spiral of the Great Depression.

An idle man dressed in a worn coat, lying on a pier in the New York City docks, c. 1935. During the Great Depression, unemployment rates increased from about 3.2 percent in 1929 to 24.9 percent in 1933. (U.S. National Archives)

Analysts also single out a failure on the part of the Federal Reserve Board as a cause of the Great Depression. Prior to the crash, the Federal Reserve Board fueled speculation by responding to demands for more funds, not by regulating but by increasing the ease with which investors could secure credit. Then, after the stock market crash, the board made borrowing money more difficult by raising the discount rate and sharply decreasing the money supply, in an attempt to curtail the amount of capital leaving the United States. Both actions proved disastrous.

In response, consumers slowed their rates of consumption from $203.6 billion annually in 1929 to $141.3 billion in 1933, and business reduced its investments from $40.4 billion annually in 1929 to $5.3 billion in 1933 (New Deal Network 2002, 1). The Dow Jones average of industrial stock prices fell from 381 to 41 between 1929 and 1932. Simultaneously, workers were laid off; unemployment rates increased from about 3.2 percent in 1929 to 24.9 percent in 1933 (Kelley 1990, 596). Six months after the crash, some 3 million Americans were unemployed, and by 1933 the number had reached almost 14 million (Kelley 1990, 590; DeLong 1997, 2).

From 1929 to 1933, thousands of banks were dissolved, approximately 110,000 businesses closed down, and aggregate corporate profit was reduced from almost $8.5 billion to $3.4 billion (Kelley 1990, 617; New Deal Network 2002, 1). Within one year, from 1929 to 1930, industrial production was reduced by 25 percent, and two years later, it had dropped by 50 percent (Kelley 1990, 618). These stark statistics scarcely convey the distress of the millions of Americans who lost their jobs, their homes, and their savings during the Depression.

President Herbert Hoover framed the events of the market crash and ensuing economic, social, and cultural instability, as a "temporary disequilibrium" about which the government could do little. Rather, he encouraged the business community to be "unselfish," asked citizens to have "faith in the system," and informed Americans that he had no intention of interfering with private enterprise.

Hoover and the Republican Congress did cut the prime interest rate (from 6 percent to 4 percent), expanded the money supply, softened antimonopoly legislation, and revised the tariff upward to further exclude foreign producers from the U.S. market. His objective was to allow government to equalize the costs of production, but the result was that the Hawley-Smoot Tariff Act of 1930 increased rates on more than 1,000 imports and decreased international trade. In 1930, under a newly Democratic congress, several legislative actions, including the passage of the Federal Employment Stabilization Act, had little impact on a depressed economy and people. Finally, in 1931, when it was clear that the Depression would not correct itself on its own, Hoover called for the establishment of a Reconstruction Finance Corporation that would attempt to save collapsing banks and industry by lending money. Met by much criticism, the measure was nevertheless passed, allocating $500 million in capital to more than 5,000 companies in 1932 (Kelley 1990, 597). Still, in 1930 the gross national product fell a record 13.4 percent, unemployment rose to 23.6 percent, banks continued to fail, capital gains investments and international trade were reduced, and industrial stocks continued to lose their value at alarming rates (New Deal Network 2002).

President Hoover became known as "heartless Hoover" and was chided for caring more about his principles of political theory than he did for the fate of his own people. In the elections of 1932, Franklin D. Roosevelt was easily elected president. Roosevelt responded to his most pressing challenge by enacting the 1933 Emergency Banking Relief Act, empowering the federal government to assess all the banks in the nation and delivering additional funds to the Federal Reserve Bank. In doing so, he put the word of the federal government behind banks in an attempt to regain public trust in the system as a whole.

Roosevelt next proposed sweeping initiatives in the spring of 1933, during which time Congress enacted reform legislation dealing with banking, the gold standard, work and relief programs, mortgages, the stock market, industry, and agriculture. Hoover's Reconstruction Finance Corporation was reshaped by President Roosevelt. In addition to lending out more than $8 billion, the corporation was also used to fund state and local relief programs, public works, homeowner loans, public housing construction, rural electrification, and even support for public schools (Leuchtenburg 1963, 18). These actions illustrated Roosevelt's commitment to using the federal government to reverse the economic depression.

In his "Second New Deal for America," in 1934, Roosevelt crafted legislation dealing with banking, social supports, and organized labor. Congress authorized the creation of the Federal Communications Commission, the National Mediation Board, and the Securities and Exchange Commission. The Securities and Exchange Act and the Trade Agreement Act were also passed. Roosevelt's Banking Act of 1935 increased the federal government's power to regulate the money supply. In 1935, he additionally supported legislation that created the Social Security Act, establishing matching federal and state old-age pension insurance; unemployment and public health insurance; and support to mothers with dependent children, the blind, and the disabled.

Finally, Roosevelt addressed the issue of labor and union protection. In the 1920s, aggressive, often violent, antiunion crusades were launched, and by the early 1930s, 36 million workers, or only one in ten Americans, belonged to a union (Bernstein 1970, 12). The 1930 Norris-LaGuardia Anti-injunction Act had allowed workers the right to organize, but these laws were seldom enforced, and violent "class warfare" had caused much antiworker sentiment. National policy changed dramatically when Roosevelt created the National Labor Relations Board and supported the 1933 National Industrial Recovery Act, which provided for collective bargaining. Moreover, the 1935 National Labor Relations Act (Wagner Act) guaranteed not just the right to organize but also the right to fair and equitable collective bargaining conditions. From 1935 through 1940, the National Labor Relations Board handled over 30,000 cases, settled 2,000 strikes, and organized and supervised 24,000 elections. As a result of this change in legislation and sentiment, labor spies and antiunion propaganda were prohibited, and peaceful picketing was protected by law, as was the establishment of closed union shops (Kelley 1990, 618).

Under the National Recovery Administration, "fair trade" codes were established regulating prices and production and creating new minimum wage and maximum working hours restrictions. Within weeks of Roosevelt's plan, some 2.5 million employers had signed codes regulating labor standards, so that 16 million workers came under the program's protection (Kelley 1990, 611). Although the codes were critiqued and ignored by many, they did establish the idea of workers' protections and reframed the public's view of vigorous federal regulation.

Roosevelt's second New Deal also included programs designed to aid tenant farmers and migrant workers. Farms had been overworked, which had caused disastrous farming conditions, exacerbated by dry land farming practices and natural disasters. In the 1930s, farm income stood at about one-third of what it had been prior to the market crash, and prices had dropped by more than 50 percent (Brownlee 1979, 118). The parity ratio (the ratio of prices received versus prices paid for manufactured farm goods) had also fallen from 89 in 1929 to 55 in 1932 (Kelley 1990, 611). In response, Roosevelt created the Agricultural Adjustment Administration, to raise farm income to 100 percent of parity by restricting production. As a result of compulsory crop controls, gross farm income rose by 50 percent in 1935 (Kelley 1990, 611). The benefits of this program were shared unequally; the poorest farmers, and especially tenant farmers, lost farms and were expelled by farm owners.

The Great Depression and ensuing New Deal also led to the creation of the Works Progress Administration (WPA), designed to employ 3.5 million people and to stimulate the economy. In 1941 the WPA spent more than $11 billion on small construction projects, building hospitals, schools, air fields, and playgrounds (Leuchtenburg 1963, 18). The programs employed writers and artists creating publications, recording history, and fostering a national working-class culture. The project also supported an ambitious Rural Electrification Project.

As a result of much of this legislation, the U.S. economy did begin to recover from the Great Depression. From 1933 to 1937, national productively soured to an astounding 12 percent a year. In 1937, real income was higher than it had been in 1929; per capita income reached the 1929 level in 1939; half of those without jobs in 1933 had work in 1937. In 1939 the country borrowed and spent about $1 billion to build up its armed forces, the gross national product rose 7.9 percent, and unemployment fell to 17.2 percent (Kelley 1990, 621).

Although successful, the New Deal did not solve all of the economic problems of the poor and minority workers. For example, the WPA did not provide assistance to the poor. In 1936, about 60 million people (close to half of the U.S. population) lived below the poverty level (Bernstein 1970, 126). Depression-era policies set the stage for further economic stratification. By 1929, the richest 1 percent of the population owned 40 percent of the nation's wealth. Despite the fact that worker productivity rose during this period, the bottom 93 percent of the working population experienced a 4 percent drop in their per capita incomes (Bernstein 1970, 202).

WPA programs also failed to address the employment needs of women and minorities. By 1932, approximately half of all African Americans were out of work, discrimination in employment and social support programs was rampant and sanctioned by law, and racial violence was common (Kelley 1990, 623).

Vivyan C. Adair

See also African American Women and Work; African Americans and Work; Federal Reserve Board; New Deal; Roosevelt, Franklin Delano; Social Security Act; Unemployment Rate; Women and Work

References and further reading

Bernstein, Irving. 1970. *The Turbulent Years: A History of the American Worker, 1933–1941.* Boston: Houghton Mifflin.

———. 1985. *A Caring Society: The New Deal, the Worker, and the Great Depression, 1933–1941.* Boston: Houghton Mifflin.

Brownlee, Elliott. 1979. *Dynamics of Ascent: A History of the American Economy.* New York: Prentice Hall Books.

DeLong, J. Bradford. 1997. "The Great Crash and the Great Slump." In *Slouching Toward Utopia? The Economic History of the Twentieth Century.* Berkeley: University of California.

Kelley, Robert. 1990. *The Shaping of the American Past.* Englewood Cliffs, NJ: Prentice Hall.

Leuchtenburg, William E. 1963. *Franklin Roosevelt and the New Deal, 1932 –1940.* New York: Harper and Row.

New Deal Network. 2002. "The New Deal and the Great Depression in the United States." http//Newdeal.feri.org (cited December 28).

Green Cards

Green card is the common name for the permanent resident card (Form I-551 or I-151), a form of identification issued by the U.S. Immigration and Naturalization Service (INS) that indicates the holder's authorization to live and work permanently in the United States. The term *green card* originated with the issuance of the green alien registration receipt card (INS Form I-151) in 1951, which bestowed similar benefits on its holder. Despite the fact that the color of the card has changed several times since this original card was issued, the term *green card* has remained the popular name for the card.

Green cards are generally available to the immediate family members of U.S. citizens, refugees and persons seeking political asylum, investors, green card lottery winners, educated professionals, and individuals with employment offers for certain positions that are in demand by U.S. employers. In addition to gaining the right to reside and work permanently in the United States, individuals who are issued green cards will eventually be able to apply for U.S. citizenship, a process referred to as "naturalization."

Precursors to the green card developed during a time when the United States was concerned with increasing the number and scope of immigration laws in general, in an attempt to better classify and track foreign visitors, immigrants, and other noncitizens within its borders. At the beginning of the twentieth century, most immigration laws were solely concerned with those defining conditions, such as physical and mental illness, that were used to deny entry to certain persons. Several laws passed in the early part of the century, such as the Naturalization Law of 1906 and the Immigration Act of 1921 (also known as the First Quota Law), however, attempted to limit immigration based on other factors and to track the number and types of immigrants seeking entry into and already living within the United States. Increasing needs to classify groups of immigrants necessitated the development of identification cards for some types of individuals, such as "border commuters," who worked in the United States or visited often but whose official residence was in Mexico or Canada.

As a result of the Alien Registration Act of 1940, the first standardized immigrant identification card, the white Form AR-3, was created. Designed as a national defense measure, the act required all aliens (non-U.S. citizens) within the United States to register with the U.S. government at post offices. After processing, a receipt card (Form AR-3) was mailed to each registrant as proof of his or her compliance with the law. The Alien Registration Act, however, did not discriminate between legal and illegal alien residents. All were registered, and all received AR-3s in return. Therefore, the AR-3 represents a precursor to the green card, insofar as it was the government's first attempt to produce a standard form of identification for immigrants. However, this card did not carry with it the same benefits or level of security normally associated with the green card.

In 1951, however, the Security Act of 1950 produced the original green card, the green alien registration receipt card (Form I-151). This card was created to provide some classes of legal immigrants the permanent right to live and work in the United States. By 1952, the Immigration and Nationality Act required that the card, now also referred to as INS Form I-551, be carried by all eligible immigrants. This card represented security to its holder and was recognized as a standard form of permanent resident status identification by government officials and employers. Therefore, the term *green card* came to refer not only the card itself but also to the official permanent resident status desired by so many individuals.

In fact, the status that the green card conferred became so desirable that the Immigration and Naturalization Service began to experience serious counterfeiting problems. To deal with this issue, between its introduction and the present, the INS issued a series of different designs for the card in various colors. The color of the form was first changed from green to another color in 1964,when the card became a pale blue. The permanent resident card, the latest version of the green card, is pink and was issued in 1997. Regardless of color or design, however, the I-151 and I-551 continue to carry the benefits associated with the term *green card.*

In 1998, the INS granted permanent resident cards to over 660,000 immigrants, a 28 percent decrease from 1996 levels and the lowest number since 1988. This decline is attributable to a sharp increase in the number of pending immigration status adjustment applications. A notable spike in the number of persons receiving green cards occurred between 1989 and 1992, when over 2.6 million former illegal aliens were granted permanent resident status under the Immigration Reform and Control Act of 1986.

Jennifer M. Cleary

See also Globalization and Workers; Immigrants and Work; Immigration Reform and Control Act

References and further reading

Corwin, Arthur F. 1978. *Immigrants and Immigrant Perspectives on Mexican Labor Migration to the U.S.* Westport, CT: Greenwood Press.

U.S. Department of Justice, Immigration and Naturalization Service. 1986. "The History of

Immigration and Nationality Legislation." Extension Training Program Lesson 1.1.
———. 1988. "A Temporary Resident's Guide to Applying for Permanent Residency." M-306, September.
———. Office of Business Relations. 1997. "Discussing Common INS Documents." Employer Information Bulletin 97-02, April.
———. 2000a. "1998 Statistical Yearbook of the Immigration and Naturalization Service." M-367, 13–15.
———. 2000b. "Systematic Alien Verification for Entitlement (SAVE) Program User Manual." M-300, September.
———. 2001. "Why Isn't the Green Card Green?" http://www.ins.usdoj.gov/graphics/aboutins/history/articles/Green.htm (cited December 7).

Greenspan, Alan (1926–)

Since his appointment as chair of the U.S. Federal Reserve Board, Alan Greenspan has elevated the position to one of unprecedented visibility. A larger-than-life figure, Greenspan is a hero to some and a scourge to others. Ronald Reagan first appointed him in 1987, in a noticeable break from his strict laissez-faire ideology. As Federal Reserve chair, Greenspan's job, strictly speaking, is to adjust short-term interest rates, the rates at which banks may loan money to each other. Yet Greenspan, perhaps more than any previous Federal Reserve chair, has created an image of the job as one of safeguarding the health of the U.S. economy in general and protecting it against inflation in particular.

Alan Greenspan, chairman of the Board of Governors of the Federal Reserve (Corbis)

Alan Greenspan was born in New York City on March 6, 1926. His early interests included music, which he studied briefly at the Juilliard School. After receiving his bachelor's and master's degrees from New York University, he enrolled in the Ph.D. program in economics at Columbia University. During his years in the program, which he eventually left without finishing, he was greatly influenced by the writings of Ayn Rand, which shaped his views on capitalism and the role of government in regulating the economy. After leaving Columbia in 1954, Greenspan began his career as a partner in a private economic consulting firm, where he remained until his appointment as Federal Reserve chair in 1987 and where he developed his impeccable reputation as an economic forecaster. Prior to his appointment as Federal Reserve chair, he had also served as the chairman of the Council of Economic Advisers in the Nixon and Ford administrations and as chair of the National Commission on Social Security Reform in the 1980s.

As Federal Reserve chair, Greenspan first received acclaim for his handling of the stock market crash of 1987. Taking over as chair in what had already become an unsound economy, he was able to minimize long-term damage by drastically lowering interest rates and creating liquidity in the financial system. Since that time, Greenspan has made a name for himself by adjusting the short-term interest rates in response to a speedup or a slowdown in the economy. Although his efforts have hardly been without controversy, he has generally been credited with the simultaneous economic expansion and curbing of inflation in the 1990s. Few would disagree that Greenspan has never wavered from his view that keeping inflation under control has been the key to maintaining the overall health of the economy.

Greenspan has tenaciously clung to this view in the face of political pressures from numerous quarters. Despite the controversy that surrounds him as a result, he has enjoyed a level of renown unparalleled by any Federal Reserve chair in history through the Federal Reserve's seemingly contradictory accomplishments of job growth and price stability under his leadership. The financial world and free market conservatives have lionized him for it. His reputation among liberal thinkers and working people, by contrast, has been notably more mixed, given the attention he gives the stock market and his concern for the effects of wage increases on inflation.

So is Allan Greenspan the friend or foe of the working man and woman in the United States? Despite his image as being solely concerned with the needs of investors, Greenspan has been keenly aware of and concerned with the effects of the changing economy on the U.S. worker.He believes, however, that the solution to worker displacement in the new economy is increased education and job training and has further argued that keeping inflation under control will ultimately improve the economic situation for *all* Americans. In reality, however, although the boom of the 1990s brought prosperity to increasing numbers of Americans, the gap between rich and poor also visibly widened and continues to do so.

In any case, Greenspan is well aware of the myth surrounding him and how it obscures the actual limits of what he—or the Federal Reserve—can do to influence the direction of the U.S. economy. He is even aware of how the effect of his public utterances can spread well beyond the Federal Reserve to influence the market, as was the case with his public warning against "irrational exuberance" and the overvaluation of stocks. This statement, which was not an official announcement but merely part of a speech at the American Enterprise Institute for Public Policy, became the stuff of public legend and was blamed for the subsequent drop in stock prices worldwide. Although incidents like these have not deterred Greenspan from publicly airing his views when he deems it necessary, in matters of policy, he remains guarded enough to resist outside pressure not to adjust rates one way or another but simply to announce that he is going to do so. This careful managing of his public statements and persona, therefore, is part of what has made Greenspan so effective in guiding the U.S. economy between the Scylla of inflation and the Charybdis of recession to what he has termed a "soft landing."

As the economic boom of the 1990s receded, he remained Federal Reserve chair into the George W. Bush administration, despite fears that his popularly perceived omnipotence could be turned against him. He still remains widely respected as an economic forecaster, known both for gathering all necessary information before making pronouncements and for his willingness to take politically risky measures, such as raising interest rates even when the danger of inflation does not appear to be imminent. Greenspan, therefore, shows remarkable staying power in U.S. finance for the foreseeable future.

Susan Roth Breitzer

See also Capitalism; Consultants and Contract Workers; Council of Economic Advisers; Federal Reserve Board; Wall Street

References and further reading

Beckner, Steven K. 1996. *Back From the Brink: The Greenspan Years.* New York: John Wiley and Sons.

Jones, David M. 1991. *The Politics of Money: The Fed under Alan Greenspan.* New York: New York Institute of Finance.

Kahaner, Larry. 2000. *The Quotations of Chairman Greenspan: Words from the Man Who Can Shake the World.* Holbrook, MA: Adams Media.

Lindsey, Lawrence B.1999. *Economic Puppetmasters: Lessons from the Halls of Power.* Washington, DC: AIE Press.

Martin, Justin. 2000. *Greenspan: The Man Behind Money.* Cambridge, MA: Perseus Press.

Sicilia, David B., and Jeffrey L. Cruikshank. 2000. *The Greenspan Effect: Words that Move the World's Markets.* New York: McGraw-Hill.

Woodward, Bob. 2000. *Maestro: Greenspan's Fed and the American Boom.* New York: Simon and Schuster.

Guilds

Guilds are a means of structuring businesses so that workers hold ownership of industries, thus abolishing the use of wages for payment (Carpenter 1922, 1–2). Proponents of guilds argue that workers should have "collective ownership" over the means they employ to do their work. Without this collective ownership, employees are cheated out of the total value of the industry in which they work. This, proponents claim, establishes an unequal distribution of profits between management and laborers (Carpenter 1922, 1; Hutchinson 1998, 134).

Guild socialists (those who advocate for a guild system) propose the decentralization of authority and power to create a more democratic structure of industry (Hutchinson and Burkitt 1997, 14). As a movement, guild socialism marks the desire to return to times of medieval "gilds," in which working conditions and pay were regulated for all workers in a given trade (Hutchinson and Burkitt 1997, 15). Guild socialists often pit themselves against capitalism, viewing it as a force that serves to enslave workers (Hutchinson and Burkitt 1997, 16).

Modern industrialization was viewed negatively by guild socialists. The mechanization of industry marginalizes the art of craftsmanship in which guild workers once took great pride. It turns attention away from the individual creativity at the core of trade occupations toward the mass production of goods. This economic shift demoted craftsmanship from an art into mere tasks that any person can perform (Hutchinson and Burkitt 1997, 15).

Main Arguments for the Guild Structure

Four main arguments were generally used by guild socialists to advocate for the establishment of a guild work structure: the moral/psychological argument, the aesthetic argument, the political argument, and the economic argument. The moral and psychological argument held that wage systems encouraged the "commodification" of employees (Carpenter 1922, 143). Guild socialists contended that wage systems served to characterize workers as objects or servants that could be bought and sold and used to achieve a particular end, rather than as humans working toward a common goal (Carpenter 1922, 143; Hutchinson 1998, 132).

The aesthetic argument forwards the notion that industrialization has led to a system in which monetary gain drives decision making in business. Guildspeople purport that quality work and pride in workmanship have declined seriously since management began to dictate to employees what and how they must create their products (Carpenter 1922, 146). Crafters are no longer able decide what to create based on their own intuition but are instead dictated to by managers who make decisions according to potential monetary gains. Thus workers are unable to take pride what they produce.

The political argument says that servitude leads to apathetic citizens. When workers cannot think for themselves in the workplace, this oppression carries over into their political behavior. Guild socialists argue that commodified workers participate less in the democratic processes to which they have access (Carpenter 1922, 146–7; Glass 1966, 18).

There are two strains to the economic argument for guild work structures. The first, known as the Marxian analysis, stresses the idea that managers make profits based on what workers produce and pay workers their wages based on what they think their labor is worth. The manager, according to Marxian principles, is afforded an enormous amount of power in that he or she determines what workers are paid based on the eventual profits he or she wishes to make (Carpenter 1922, 150; Hutchinson 1998, 132). In effect, capitalism gives managers the opportunity to pay workers less than they are worth to increase their own profits.

The second strain of the economic argument relies upon the Douglas-Orage analysis, which states that economic democracy is only possible when the majority are able to set policy priorities. A capitalist system thwarts true economic democracy because a small few hold decision-making power over the larger majority (Carpenter 1922, 151).

The Fall of Guild Socialism

The eventual fall in the popularity of guild socialism is largely attributed to impractical goals within the movement. First, the guild system required that all employers and business owners either be driven out of authority or voluntarily give up the control they held over industry for so long. Second, the guild movement required the unlikely support of white-collar workers before guilds could be instituted in place of capitalism (Glass 1966, 58). Third, after overcoming these first two obstacles, the movement would still need to convince the government that capitalism should be derailed in favor of a system ruled by worker control (Glass 1966, 58–59). The decline in the guild movement is attributed to the failure of guild socialists to accomplish these necessary goals.

Karin A. Garver

See also Democratic Socialism; Industrial Revolution and Assembly Line Work

References and further reading

Carpenter, Niles. 1922. *Guild Socialism: An Historical and Critical Analysis.* New York: D. Appleton.

Cole, G. D. H. 1980. *Guild Socialism Restated.* New Brunswick, NJ: Transaction Books.

Glass, S. T. 1966. *The Responsible Society: The Ideas of Guild Socialism.* London: Longmans, Green.

Hutchinson, Frances. 1998. *What Everybody Really Wants to Know about Money.* Oxfordshire, UK: Jon Carpenter Publishing.

Hutchinson, Frances, and Brian Burkitt. 1997. *The Political Economy of Social Credit and Guild Socialism.* New York: Routledge.

Hawthorne Plant Experiments

Conducted at Western Electric's Hawthorne Works in Cicero, Illinois, between 1924 and 1933, the Hawthorne Plant experiments changed the direction of labor-management relations as they influenced generations of management experts with their findings. In the age of assembly line production through the 1920s, scientific management had emphasized the routinization of tasks to increase efficiency. In the wake of the Hawthorne experiments, however, a more complex set of variables was viewed as equally, if not more, important in increasing worker productivity. The most important conclusion of the experiments pointed to the social interaction among workers and between workers and managers as a significant factor in affecting productivity levels. When worker satisfaction was improved through active participation in structuring the work environment, productivity levels also increased, even if work conditions were made worse. In the decades since the findings were publicized, scholars have criticized the study for its methodological flaws and the subjective interpretation of the data that researchers invoked. The study has even given rise to the term *Hawthorne effect* to denote a study that leads to increased (yet short-lived) levels of worker productivity based on employees' gratification for being chosen to participate in the project. Despite these critiques, however, the conclusions of the Hawthorne Plant experiments continue to echo through contemporary labor-management theories, including participatory decision making, quality circles, and total quality management.

First built in 1905 by American Telephone and Telegraph's (AT&T) Western Electric (WE) division, the Hawthorne Works in Cicero, just west of Chicago, Illinois, employed 12,000 workers by World War I. As the primary site of AT&T's manufacture of telephones and telephone switching equipment, the plant expanded its operations to employ over 22,000 workers in the massive factory site by 1927. Known for its welfare capitalism measures, WE instituted a number of programs in the Hawthorne Works to foster satisfaction and company loyalty among the workforce. In addition to offering medical care onsite and educational courses after working hours, WE sponsored numerous sports teams and social programs for its employees. It also instituted numerous efficiency measures in the Hawthorne Works to improve productivity. Like other manufacturers, these efforts typically focused on the scientific management of the workplace to simplify production tasks and make each worker's job more routine and easier to perform.

As part of its efforts to study how work conditions affected job performance, WE agreed to sponsor an experiment to determine the effects of lighting levels on assembly line workers' productivity. Begun in November 1924, the lighting experiments were cosponsored by the National Research Council of the National Academy of Sciences, a federal agency that undertook the project after being lobbied by several manufacturers of industrial lighting equipment, and foundations supported by the Rockefeller Family. Although the researchers hypothesized that reduced lighting would lead to similar reductions in output by workers, there proved to be no correlation between the amount of lighting on the assembly line and worker output. Even as the amount of lighting decreased to dismal levels, productivity actually continued to increase. Although the results from the first experiments were inconclusive, researchers tentatively concluded that factors other than lighting were influencing productivity.

After the National Research Council withdrew from the studies, Clair Turner and George E. Mayo joined the research team in conjunction with the Harvard Business School in April 1928. Intrigued by the outcome of the first study, the research group set up another set of thirteen experiments with a group of five women assembly line workers. Once again changing a number of variables such as lighting, rest periods, and the length of the working day and week, the researchers found no specific correlation between the variables and productivity, which increased a total of 46 percent over the five years of the subsequent studies. From these observations, the researchers concluded that factors such as increased participation by employees in managing the workplace were more important than incentive pay schemes or physical conditions in improving productivity. From this early conclusion, WE followed up the experiments by conducting over 10,300 interviews with its employees to discuss their opinions about their work environment. The experiments themselves continued until they were curtailed as an austerity measure in 1933, as the Great Depression unfolded.

The emphasis on employee participation instead of scientific management of work conditions made an immediate impact on the fields of industrial and labor relations after the researchers' studies began to appear from the late 1920s onward. Elton Mayo in particular became the leading expert on industrial human relations and psychology, although it was not long before significant critiques of his work appeared. To many scholars, it was clear that Mayo and his colleagues were far from objective in their interpretation of the data and often ignored workers' statements about their motivations and satisfaction. With an ideological bias that argued against worker self-organization and in favor of managerial prerogatives, Mayo's subjectivity also seemed to predict the conclusions he drew from the evidence. In one instance, Mayo labeled a worker he deemed troublesome as a "Bolshevik," even though there was no evidence that the woman had demonstrated any political leanings. The woman was quickly replaced as a test group member, and the experiments continued.

By suggesting that worker satisfaction—and therefore, productivity—could be improved by a more participatory management style, the Hawthorne experiments nonetheless ushered in a new age of labor-management relations for many employers. Even those who criticized the conclusions agreed that the experiments were a breakthrough in terms of treating the workplace as a complex social environment. Although the results of the Hawthorne experiments did not completely replace the scientific management school in the arena of industrial relations (which held that in-depth mathematical and motion analysis provided the key to worker productivity), they did mark an innovation in the theory and methodology of industrial management studies and their implementation. The contemporary interest in cooperative decision making through practices such as quality circles demonstrates the continuing influence of the Hawthorne experiments.

Timothy G. Borden

See also Blue Collar; Bonuses; Consultants and Contract Workers; High-Performance Workforce; Industrial Revolution and Assembly Line Work; Manufacturing Jobs; Productivity; Quality Circles; Taylor, Frederick Winslow

References and further reading

Gillespie, Richard. 1991. *Manufacturing Knowledge: A History of the Hawthorne Experiments.* Cambridge: Cambridge University Press.

Greenwood, Ronald G., Alfred A. Bolton, and Regina A. Greenwood. 1983. "Hawthorne a Half Century Later: Relay Assembly Participants Remember." *Journal of Management* 9: 217–231.

Milkman, Ruth. 1997. *Farewell to the Factory: Auto Workers in the Late Twentieth Century.* Berkeley: University of California Press.

Schatz, Ronald W. 1983. *The Electrical Workers: A History of Labor at General Electric and Westinghouse, 1923–1960.* Urbana: University of Illinois Press.

Sonnenfeld, Jeffrey A. 1985. "Shedding Light on the Hawthorne Studies." *Journal of Occupational Behaviour* 6: 111–130.

Trahair, Richard C. S. 1984. *The Humanist Temper: The Life and Work of Elton Mayo.* New Brunswick, NJ: Transaction Books.

Waring, Stephen P. 1991. *Taylorism Transformed: Scientific Management Theory since 1945.* Chapel Hill: University of North Carolina Press.

Haymarket Square Incident

The Haymarket Square Incident of 1886, traditionally known as the Haymarket Square Riot, was a local event that quickly gained national significance. Both the event itself and the trial and execution that followed had enormous impact on the history of Chicago and on U.S. labor history in general. Subsequent views of the Haymarket Square Incident have changed noticeably, both in scholarship and in popular thought. For example, the "consensus" school of historical writing regarded the event at Haymarket Square as a deviation from the social order, whereas the "conflict" school viewed it as the outcome of an unjust social hierarchy.

There is ample historical evidence to suggest that the Haymarket Square Incident was an example of both, as well as conflicting ideas about the place of work and workers in the social order. By the late 1880s, Chicago had rapidly grown from a frontier outpost to an urban industrial power and was full of the increasing social stratification that accompanied such a change. The growing socialist and anarchist movements, as well as the eight-hour day movement and the nascent labor unions, were increasingly trying to address the growing social and economic inequality, often experiencing violent repression in return. Just prior to the Haymarket Square Incident, the McCormick Harvester strike was just the latest in a series of incidents in which management responded to worker protest with police and privately hired guards.

So perhaps it was not surprising that what began on the evening of May 4, 1886, as a peaceful meeting ended in a bloody confrontation between workers and police with dead on both sides. The meeting in Haymarket Square, though poorly planned and starting late, was unusually well attended thanks to the official approval of Chicago mayor Carter H. Harrison, who also was present for much of the meeting. By 10:00 P.M., seeing that the meeting, peaceful throughout, was almost over and that people were dispersing, Harrison ordered Police Captain John Bonfield to send the police guard present at the meeting home. Instead, Bonfield, taking advantage of the progressive Harrison's absence, sent 170 police troops to the meeting, where on arrival, Captain William Ward ordered the remaining crowd to disperse "immediately and peaceably." When Samuel Fielden, one of the organizers of the meeting, countered that the meeting *was* peaceable, Ward simply repeated his order. Then, an unknown person suddenly threw a homemade bomb into the crowd, which wounded several people and killed police officer Mathias Degan when it exploded. The explosion, in turn, sent the policemen on a rampage of shooting and clubbing, during which time they managed to shoot several of their own men, as well as many in the fleeing crowd. The event left seven policemen and an unknown number of civilians dead. There were soon citywide calls for revenge against the perceived anarchist violence.

The following morning, May 5, the police arrested hundreds of people in a series of raids on meeting halls, printing offices, and even private homes. The police issued no warrants, and people were harassed and interrogated into confessing to crimes they didn't commit and to serving as states' witnesses against others. Of the eight who were finally brought to trial, anarchist leader Albert Parsons voluntarily turned himself in from the safety of Wisconsin. The ensuing trial made little pretense of fairness. To begin with, the accused, Parsons, Samuel Fielden, August Spies, Louis Lingg, Adolph Fischer, George Engel, Oscar Neebe, and Michael Schwab, were tried as a group, increasing the sensational nature of the trial and making it impossible to render fair judgment on each individual. Furthermore, the jury selection process was purposefully skewed to select jurors with admitted biases against the defendants. The chosen trial judge, Joseph E. Gary, skewed the proceedings even more by allowing the prosecution vastly greater latitude in the case than the defense, in terms of line of questioning and introduction of evidence. Finally, State Attorney Julius Grinnell went so far as to admit that the eight accused were on trial for their ideas rather than their actions, proclaiming to the jury that they had been selected by the grand jury and indicted because they were the leaders. Grinnell urged the jury to convict the men and to make examples of them. Predictably, all eight were convicted and seven sentenced to hang, with Neebe receiving fifteen years with hard labor.

Wood engraving (ca. 1886) of the Haymarket Square Incident in Chicago—a homemade bomb exploding among the police (Library of Congress)

Their sentences were not carried out without public protest. Although the hanging was delayed because of an appeal to the Illinois State Supreme Court (it was later unsuccessfully appealed to the Supreme Court), trade unions across the United States mounted protests and published petitions against the sentence. This in turn inspired protests in Europe and by many prominent Americans outside of the labor movement to speak out. The day before the execution, American Federation of Labor president Samuel Gompers personally made a final appeal to Illinois governor Richard Oglesby. Although Oglesby agreed to commute the sentences of Schwab and Fielden to life imprisonment, the others remained sentenced to hang. The morning of the hanging, November 11, 1887, Lingg killed himself with a smuggled dynamite capsule. The remaining men shouted final declarations from the gallows; concluding with Parsons's "Let the voice of the people be heard!" Two days later, a funeral parade of thousands of workers marched and bore the bodies to Waldheim Cemetery, where the executed men's defense attorney, Captain William P. Black, eulogized them as martyrs.

In the months and years following the execution, public opinion slowly shifted to recognize the unjust nature of the trial and execution. Nonetheless, when the newly elected Governor John P. Altgeld decided in 1892 to pardon Fielden, Schwab, and Neebe, the ensuing controversy cost him reelection. Although the Haymarket Square incident had an immediate dampening effect on labor and radical movements in Chicago, it failed to permanently halt the growth of organized labor. The worldwide attention the incident, trial, and execution drew furthermore spurred the growth of May Day, a workers holiday observed today mostly outside the United States.

Susan Roth Breitzer

See also Immigrants and Work; Knights of Labor; Socialism

References and further reading

Adelman, William J. 1986. *Haymarket Revisited: A Tour Guide of Labor History Sites and Ethnic Neighborhoods Connected with the Haymarket Affair.* Chicago: Illinois Labor History Society.

Avrich, Paul. 1984. *The Haymarket Tragedy.* Princeton: Princeton University Press.

David, Henry. 1958. *The History of the Haymarket Affair: A Study in the American Social-Revolutionary and Labor Movements.* New York: Russell and Russell.

Lum, Dyer D. 1969. *The Great Trial of the Chicago Anarchists.* New York: Arno Press.

Nelson, Bruce C. 1988. *Beyond the Martyrs: A Social History of Chicago's Anarchists, 1870–1900.* New Brunswick, NJ: Rutgers University Press.

Smith, Carl. 1995. *Urban Disorder and the Shape of Belief: The Great Chicago Fire, the Haymarket Bomb, and the Model Town of Pullman.* Chicago: University of Chicago Press.

Health Insurance

Health insurance enables avoidance of large unforeseen medical expenses: in exchange for an annual insurance premium from members of a group, the insurer pays all or most of any medical expenses that any of the members of this group may incur over the year. Based on reports from the National Center for Health Statistics, about 16 percent of the population under sixty-five years of age, or close to 40 million people, were uninsured during the1990s. About 70 percent of the population under sixty-five years of age had private insurance, and 90 percent of these had coverage through their workplaces. About one-fifth of those sixty-five and older were covered by private insurance in addition to Medicare. The Medicaid program, which pays for health insurance coverage for the poor, paid for close to 10 percent of the population younger than sixty-five and about 8–9 percent of the population aged sixty-five and older through the 1990s. (Note that an individual can have more than one form of coverage at any time.) In practice, those who have no insurance coverage are eligible for emergency care because emergency rooms cannot legally turn away anyone just because of inability to pay. Access to health insurance, however, usually ensures access to preventative care that might circumvent the need for some of these emergency room visits.

Employee group plans, the most common source of health insurance in the United States, are tax-sheltered employee benefits that are sponsored and maintained by an employer or a union for employees of the firm and possibly their dependents, and retirees. The federal government provides health insurance to the elderly and the disabled through the Medicare program. State governments provide health insurance to poor families through the Medicaid program and to children of families ineligible for Medicaid through the State Children's Health Insurance Program (SCHIP). Those who are not covered by any of these sources have the option of purchasing insurance privately from an insurance firm. Premiums on individually purchased insurance plans are typically more expensive than premiums under employee group plans. Some associations offer the option of purchasing individual insurance through them at discounted rates. For example, universities offer students, who are too old to be covered under their parents' medical plans, the opportunity to purchase individual insurance. Some states maintain plans for people who have a poor health history and are ineligible to purchase health insurance on the open market; the state, therefore, bears the burden of the risk.

Origins

Health insurance made its earliest appearance in the late 1800s, in the form of accident and disability insurance. However, until the early 1900s, most health insurance plans were still restricted to compensation of lost wages for illness. Modern health insurance originated with the hospital insurance plan for schoolteachers of Dallas public schools at Baylor University Hospital in 1929. In exchange for a monthly payment, the schoolteachers were guaranteed some hospitalization services if needed.

All modern health insurance plans have some combination of indemnity insurance and service benefits. Indemnity insurance reimburses plan members for some proportion of medical expenses incurred. Most physician services and out-of-hospital expenses are treated as indemnity insurance. Service benefits pay for the entire cost of a service, as is typical with hospital expenses.

During the 1930s, several hospitals began to offer insurance plans similar to the one at Baylor University Hospital, and these plans were brought together within the framework of the American Hospital Association (AHA) and eventually evolved into the Blue Cross Association, which was independent from the AHA. The Blue Shield plans were similar insurance plans that paid for physician services. The first of these plans originated in California in 1939, and over the years, the physician payment plans came together to form the National Association of Blue Shield Plans. State level legislation allowed them to act as nonprofit corporations and thereby enjoy tax-exempt status and freedom from regulations imposed on other insurance firms. In 1982, the two merged to form the Blue Cross and Blue Shield Association that exists to this day.

Employer-Provided Health Insurance

Employer-provided health insurance made its appearance during World War II. Increases in the monetary component of the wage were prohibited by a wage freeze. Therefore, employers attracted workers by offering health insurance coverage. Commercial, for-profit insurance firms were spurred on by the success of the Blue Cross and Blue Shield plans to expand their offers of health insurance. Employer contributions to health insurance were exempt from payroll tax and from personal income tax, which made them a very attractive component of compensation packages.

For a given set of benefits, the cost of insurance per covered person is lower in an employer-provided group health insurance plan than the premium on privately covered insurance. The premium is the price paid for the insurance coverage, and the rate is contracted for a specified period, for example, one year or one month. The actual premium consists of a pure premium component and a loading charge. The pure premium is the average cost per group member of all expenses paid out by the insurance firm. The administrative costs, marketing costs, and any profit margin that the insurance company takes for itself make up the loading charge. The pure premium component is calculated in one of two ways: by experience rating or community rating. Experience-rated premiums are set at the average expected medical costs of the group that is being insured, and these expected costs are based on past experience and any other observed characteristics of the population. Community-rated premiums are set at the expected average medical costs of the entire community of which the beneficiary is a part, for example, everyone in that age cohort living in the state.

The difference in premium between employee group plans and individual plans occurs for two main reasons. Health insurance, like many other nonmonetary benefits provided by the employer, is exempt from personal income tax. The second advantage is associated with the health status of the enrollee mix in employee plans. In the case of insurance plans sold to individual purchasers, the people who buy health insurance are more likely to be the ones who need it the most, in other words, those who expect to have above-average medical costs. The presence of such people in the group raises the average cost of insuring the entire group. This phenomenon is called the "adverse selection problem." If premiums are experience-rated, or based on the average costs of the insured group, the adverse selection of enrollees into the group raises premiums for the group. In contrast, employee group plans cover the entire group of employees, not just the ones with the greatest need. Therefore, the insured group does not have higher-than-average risk of medical expenses, and the employee group avoids the adverse selection problem. Since the employee group is healthy enough to work, the group probably has lower-than-average costs. As a result, the per-employee premium costs that the firm incurs are lower than the cost that an insurance firm incurs when selling insurance to an individual purchaser.

Large establishments tend to self-insure. In other words, the firm assumes the risk of unexpected medical expenses for its employees. In doing this, the firm might save on loading charges and can often avoid the legislative restrictions that are imposed on insurance firms, such as restrictions on preexisting condition exclusions. Some self-insuring firms might avail themselves of administrative services only (ASO) contracts with third parties to handle the administrative details of the plan and to manage the employer's funds and pay claims. Smaller firms do not find it convenient to self-insure because they are more vulnerable to fluctuations in costs than larger firms. They purchase insurance from insurance firms that are regulated, and the insurance firms pass on their costs to the firms purchasing insurance from them. Consider two firms A and B with the same expected probability of a catastrophic claim per employee, say 1 in 1,000. But firm A has 1,000 employees, and form B has 100 employees. Therefore, we expect firm A to have one catastrophic claim per year, and firm B to have one every ten years. However, if any one employee in firm B incurs a large medical expense in any year, the burden placed on the firm is very great. This expense might be large enough that it is impossible for firm B to afford to provide insurance to its employees in the following year. With larger firms like firm A, the occurrence of such an expense in any year is spread across a large group of plan members, and the average premium per employee does not fluctuate as much.

Managed Care

National health spending increased rapidly through the 1970s and 1980s. Rising costs, which made it increasingly difficult for many firms to offer health benefits to their employees, were partly caused by the development of new and expensive medical procedures and partly by the institutional structure of health insurance.

Most insurance plans in the 1970s and early 1980s were traditional fee-for-service plans, such as those provided by the Blue Cross and Blue Shield. Under these plans, the insurance firm paid for all but a fraction of the cost of procedures, without much restriction on the services or health care providers used. The physician and patient alone made the decisions regarding what services should be provided to the patient. The patient only bore a small fraction of the costs and therefore had no incentive to be cost-conscious. Health care providers were paid for all administered procedures. The physician was the beneficiary of any service for which the patient decided to opt and was an adviser to the patient on what procedures to undertake. With these conflicting interests, physicians had an incentive to encourage patients to go in for expensive procedures, even if they were not absolutely essential. Such an incentive system naturally led to an annual growth rate of 13.5 percent in per capita private health expenditures (Eberhardt et al. 2001).

The need for cost control led to the growth and popularity of managed care plans. Managed care coverage provides insurance with intervention in either services or providers used or both, in an attempt to contain costs. A managed care plan may be administered like a fee-for-service plan, with utilization review and prior authorization for large expenses, such as hospitalization costs. At the other end of the spectrum, the patient could be in a health maintenance organization (HMO), which requires patients to be restricted to a closed panel of physicians and to pay all or a large percentage of any expenses incurred from physicians outside the network. There is usually a primary care physician who coordinates all the care that a patient needs. Some HMOs charge a fixed capitation fee per customer for a time period for coverage and provide any service that might be required during that time period. Since that payment does not depend on the services provided, there is less of a tendency for physicians to overprescribe specialized tests that are expensive. Physician compensation packages in HMOs may be designed with incentives that encourage cost-consciousness. In addition to these, there are preferred provider organizations (PPOs) that are less restrictive than HMOs but more restrictive than traditional fee-for-service plans. PPOs allow patients to choose from a panel of providers. The insurer reviews utilization in some cases and uses financial incentives, such as lower copayments, to induce patients to use PPO providers. The insurer controls costs by negotiating lower fees with PPO providers in exchange for a guaranteed volume of patients. The growth of these plans appears to have made the provision of health insurance more affordable for employers. Participation in HMOs increased rapidly in the 1990s, from 19 percent of the population in 1989 to 28 percent in 1998 (Eberhardt et al. 2001).

Another institutional development in response was the emergence of flexible benefit, or cafeteria, plans. With an increase in the number of dual-earner families, most families had double coverage. The overlapping coverage was an unnecessary expense for most firms. Therefore, firms started offering flexible benefit plans that allowed employees to pick any combination out of an array of benefits. These plans took some time to become popular. They originally emerged in the 1970s and slowly gathered popularity through the 1980s and the 1990s.

It is important to note that although managed care providers may offer increased access to care, they have also been accused of paying little or no attention to the quality of care. Although fixed payments discourage overprescription of unnecessary treatments, they also leave little incentive for the physician to provide quality care. Under traditional fee-for-service plans, physicians competed in terms of the quality of care since insurance companies paid for all services rendered, and concerns of employers and policymakers centered on the sky-rocketing costs. In contrast, increasing complaints regarding the low quality of managed care have sparked debates regarding the necessity for consumer protection in managed care.

Legislative Protection to Beneficiaries

The Employee Retirement Income Security Act (ERISA) was enacted in 1974 to protect the interests of participants and beneficiaries in these private benefit plans. ERISA set minimum standards for these plans, ensured disclosure of plan information to the beneficiaries, and established processes for addressing grievances and appeals from beneficiaries.

The Consolidated Omnibus Benefits Reform Act (COBRA) of 1986 was an amendment to ERISA. COBRA enabled health insurance beneficiaries to keep their employment-based insurance benefits for up to eighteen months after they ceased to be eligible for them. The beneficiary had to pay for these benefits, but he or she paid the employee group rate as opposed to the individual rate. Most typically, COBRA covered employees whose employment had been terminated, but it also extended to dependents who lost their coverage because of death of a spouse or divorce.

The Health Insurance Portability and Accountability Act (HIPAA) of 1996 was another amendment to ERISA. HIPAA further facilitated continued insurance for individuals and dependents between jobs and guaranteed coverage to some small businesses and individuals. Insurers were no longer permitted to refuse issuance or renewal of coverage to an individual or a group based purely on health status. Since small firms are usually at a disadvantage in their ability to provide insurance to their employees, this was an important policy development for them. In addition to federal statutes, states passed their own mandates through the 1980s and 1990s to protect the rights of small groups. These mandates specified service obligations for insurance firms and regulated managed care networks.

Many insurance plans deny or limit coverage for medical conditions that the person had prior to purchasing the insurance coverage. These types of exclusions are called preexisting condition exclusions. Typically, such conditions are not covered for the first few months of uninterrupted coverage with the insurer, during which time the patient is liable for the entire expense associated with the preexisting condition. HIPAA restricted the duration for which a preexisting condition could be excluded from coverage to twelve months. Current legislative efforts are geared toward establishing a patient's bill of rights to determine the extent to which consumers are protected.

Public Health Insurance

After extensive debate during the 1950s and 1960s, Congress passed legislation in 1965 establishing Medicare and Medicaid programs as part of the Social Security Act to provide health care to the elderly (persons age sixty-five or older) and the poor, respectively. In 1973, Medicare extended coverage to some individuals with a disability or end-stage renal disease.

Medicare traditionally consists of two main parts: Part A, or hospital insurance (HI), which pays for hospitalization expenses, and Part B, or supplementary medical insurance (SMI), which pays for physician and other services. HI is primarily funded through a mandatory federal payroll tax. SMI is financed partly through premium payments from beneficiaries and partly through contributions from the general fund of the U.S. Treasury. Since 1998, a third part, Medicare+Choice, has been available to beneficiaries who want to expand their options for participation in private-sector health care plans.

Medicaid pays for hospitalization, physician and other medical services, and prescription drugs for the poor. The program is administered by state governments within guidelines established by federal statutes, and the federal government partially reimburses states for their costs. In 1997, the State Children's Health Insurance Program was created with federal funding to enable states to offer health insurance coverage to children from families with incomes that were too high to be eligible for Medicaid but too low to be able to afford private health insurance coverage.

The Politics of Health Care

Health care reform or, in particular, the provision of universal health insurance has been a highly visible public policy issue in the political process of the United States, particularly in most of the elections of the 1990s. For instance, Clinton successfully ran for the presidency on a universal health care platform in 1992, the failure of the same cost the Democrats control of Congress in 1994, and several segments of the debate featured in the 1996 and 2000 presidential elections as well.

In the U.S. health care system, several interest groups represent a diverse array of interests, and the current system is the outcome of a constant bargaining process among them. Employers and unions that provide health insurance to their employees and members have faced rising medical costs through most of the last decades of the twentieth century. Since employers have to offer health insurance to stay competitive in the market for workers, they lobby for policy aimed at keeping expenses down. Physicians and hospital associations favor proposals that result in increased demand for medical services, resist management of costs and patient care by nonphysicians, and oppose cutbacks in government payments for Medicare and Medicaid. (Most private payers follow Medicare guidelines in determining payments to physicians; hence, Medicare payments are an important focal point for lobbying efforts by health care providers.) Health insurance firms favor any plan that retains the system of private health insurance. Large insurers favor reforms like portability of coverage when employees switch jobs; small insurers oppose them because these reforms add to their costs. Health insurance firms favor nationally established technology assessment panels to establish the cost-effectiveness of experimental procedures and seek protection against malpractice suits in the context of patients' rights legislation. The elderly seek Medicare reform in the form of prescription drug coverage. The middle class, which is mostly covered by employer-provided insurance, seeks continuous coverage with minimal restrictions and low out-of-pocket payments but is predominantly unwilling to vote for additional taxes to pay for universal coverage. With the interaction of such a diverse array of interests, most changes in health policy tend to be slow and incremental as opposed to sweeping and large scale.

The Structure of Health Insurance

In any insurance plan, the patient is liable for a deductible and a copayment, and the insurance company pays for the rest of the expenses. The deductible is a fixed dollar amount for which the patient is liable. One could have a zero deductible plan or have a deductible only for some types of expenses, such as hospital bills. For indemnity insurance plans with a deductible, say $500, the patient pays the first $500 of expenses during the year. The insurer is liable for any expenditure in excess of the deductible. The deductible exists to ensure that insurance claims are reserved for the truly large expenses, or catastrophic claims, leaving the patient to pay for most of their smaller expenses that arise in any year. Plans with higher deductibles typically cost less than plans with no deductible. The copayment, or coinsurance, is the amount that the patient pays every time a medical service is used; the insurer pays for the rest of the bill for the service. Stop-loss is a clause in indemnity insurance that pays 100 percent of expenses, once the sum of deductible and copayment reach a prespecified maximum for the patient. The stop-loss clause protects the patient from unlimited liability.

Mythreyi Bhargavan

See also Compensation; Domestic Partner Benefits; Employee Retirement Income Security Act; Job Benefits; Medicaid; Social Security Act

References and further reading

Bureau of Labor Statistics. 1999. *Employee Benefits in Medium and Large Private Establishments: 1997.* Results of Employee Benefit Survey. Washington, DC: Bureau of Labor Statistics.

Center for Medicare and Medicaid Services. 2002. "What Is HIPAA?" http://www.hcfa.gov (cited February 1).

Cunningham, Robert III, and Robert M. Cunningham Jr. 1997. *The Blues: A History of the Blue Cross and Blue Shield System.* DeKalb: Northern Illinois University Press.

Custer, William S., and Pat Ketsche. 1999. *Health Insurance Coverage and the Uninsured, 1990–1998.* Washington, DC: Health Insurance Association of America.

Eberhardt, Mark S., et al. 2001. *Health, United States, 2001: With Urban and Rural Health Chartbook.* Hyattsville, MD: National Center for Health Statistics. (Updated tables can be found online at http://www.cdc.gov/nchs/products/pubs/pubd/hus/01hustop.htm, cited August 2002.)

Feldstein, Paul J. 1999. *Health Policy Issues: An Economic Perspective on Health Care Reform.* 2nd ed. Ann Arbor: Health Administration Press.

———. 2001. *The Politics of Health Legislation: An Economic Perspective.* 2nd ed rev. Chicago: Health Administration Press.

Hoffman, Earl D., Jr., Barbara S. Klees, and Catherine A. Curtis. 2000. "Overview of the Medicare and Medicaid Programs." *Health Care Financing Review* 22, no. 1: 175–193.

Mills, Robert J. 2001. *Health Insurance Coverage: 2000. Current Population Reports.* Washington, DC: U.S. Census Bureau.

Phelps, Charles E. 2002. *Health Economics.* 3rd ed. Boston, MA: Addison-Wesley.

U.S. Department of Labor. 2002. "Health Plans and Benefits: Employee Retirement Income Security Act—ERISA." http://www.dol.gov (cited February 1).

High-Performance Workforce

The concept of a high-performance workforce comes from research on high-performance work systems (Nadler and Tushman 1988; Nadler and Gerstein 1992). Although these production systems go by many names, such as high-commitment work systems and high-involvement work systems, they all share some common elements. Essentially, a high-performance work system is a bundle of human resource and job design practices implemented to maximize worker productivity.

This topic has received a great deal of academic and practitioner coverage since the 1970s. By some estimates, firms that engage in the activities believed to lead to high-performance workforces outperform their industry counterparts by as much as 50 percent, after controlling for all other differences between firms.

History

For the first half of the twentieth century, the dominant paradigm for human resources and job design was based on the work of Frederick Taylor. Taylor believed that there existed a "one best way" to perform every job, and if smart engineers studied those jobs, this way would be discovered. Once this way of doing things was discovered, these engineers would design narrow and specialized jobs for the employees to perform.

This method of job design had a number of implications. Jobs would be mechanized as much as possible, using tools like Henry Ford's assembly line. Also, since these "smart engineers" had already figured out the best way to do things, employees were given little, if any, discretion over how to perform their jobs. This method also led to the separation of production and quality assurance, away from the employees making the product. The unfortunate assumptions were that employees were either stupid, lazy, or both, and the natural implication was that they had to be told specifically what to do and be extensively monitored in their work (Taylor 1911).

The human relations and human resources schools laid the early foundation for high-performance work systems by challenging these basic assumptions and asserting that employees wanted to do a good job and that there were rewards for good work beyond monetary compensation (see, for example, Herzberg 1987; Herzberg, Mausner, and Snyderman 1959; McGregor 1960; Hackman and Oldham 1980). Researchers at the Tavistock Institute of Human Relations undertook the first fundamental steps in high-performance work systems. Rather than studying individual jobs, these researchers focused on the entire productive system. Sociotechnical systems theory, as it is now called, was first applied in British coal mines. Instead of the normal narrow and highly controlled jobs, these workers were placed into semiautonomous work groups, with some discretion over how they performed their jobs. In addition, these workers often interchanged their roles, what is now more formally called "job rotation." These coalminers dramatically outperformed those who worked under a more traditional organizational design.

Components

The theory of high-performance work systems is broad and open-ended, with a great deal of leeway in the design of the production system. Most scholars emphasize that the bundle of practices must be internally consistent and fit with the organization's goals (MacDuffie 1995). Although there is some disagreement over the exact composition of a high-performance work system, they generally include most of the following characteristics.

Employee Participation

This practice may be as simple as an employee suggestion box but is generally taken much farther in the design of most high-performance work systems. These participation programs have also taken on many names, such as "quality of work life," "*kaizen*," or continuous improvement programs. The basic element remains the same; the employees that will be performing the work are given a great deal of voice in how the work is designed, organized, and carried out.

Open Systems Designed with the Environment in Mind

High-performance workforces and work systems are designed to be one activity in a chain of events. A high-performance work system design is not an insular design that takes only the firm or the individual production center into account; it begins with the customer. Such systems are also designed for smooth connection to the firm's suppliers and the entire value chain. The system must be flexible enough to react to new customer needs or to new technological or logistical developments in the firm's supply chain. To better see the signs from the environment, all buffers (for example, inventory, slack time) should be removed. This goal is at the heart of the lean manufacturing movement (Womack, Jones, and Roos 1990).

Minimal Design, Developing over Time

To make effective use of employee input and meet the needs of customers, only the essential elements of a production system should be designed in advance. Sociotechnical theorists call this "minimal critical specification," and scholars of HPWS state that this essential level is all that should be specified in advance, with the rest allowed to develop over time. As the employees learn about the system, their roles, tasks, and responsibilities are further defined and codified. Minimal design at the beginning does not imply that the production system is loose or unspecified. On the contrary, the procedures of high-performance work systems are often just as tightly controlled as traditional work systems, sometimes even more so. For example, the Toyota production system was refined over many years and is now considered the most strictly controlled production line in the automobile industry (Adler 1993).

Integration of Social and Technical Systems

This principle follows directly from the work at the Tavistock Institute. People and equipment are inextricably linked in production, and thus compatibility between the machinery and the workers is emphasized. The entire facility must be designed with this principle in mind. A firm should not just experiment with small pockets of high-performance work systems; rather the entire facility must be converted, or in the case of a newly built factory, high-performance work systems must be implemented across the entire new plant.

Control of Variance at the Source

Variances are unexpected events, for example, quality problems. When they are handled close to their source, employees are able to receive key feedback about their performance, allowing them to learn better ways to perform their jobs. In addition, employees develop a heightened sense of responsibility, which often leads to a decreased need for management supervision as well as higher performance.

Autonomous Work Groups

Teams are an essential element of a high-performance workforce. The autonomy granted to these teams varies a great deal among organizations, from minimal autonomy (for example, scheduling activities and routine maintenance) to fully self-managed teams that have responsibility for hiring and termination decisions, discipline, promotion decisions, and work assignments. These teams are most often assigned a "complete" task, such as the assembly of a full subsystem, or the delivery of a complete service, such as the processing of an insurance claim.

Boundary Control

Closely related to the control of variance and the deployment of autonomous work groups is the need to define and defend clear boundaries. Empowered employees who are expected to control their own variances need to be clear on what is and is not within their sphere of control. It is important to ensure that complementary and/or interdependent tasks fall within the group's boundary. Doing so will allow the group to function effectively, with less need for outside intervention and less need to disturb other work groups.

Enriched Jobs

The theory of enriched jobs states that correct job design can increase worker motivation. J. Richard Hackman and Greg R. Oldham (1980) demonstrated that jobs high in task variety, task identity, and task significance (the importance or impact of the end product) were more motivating than more narrow jobs. Although the task significance is related to the product itself and is difficult for the firm to control, other management practices can affect task variety and task identity. By allowing employees to use and develop multiple skills, the job becomes more motivating.

Task identity is often achieved by having an employee or group of employees responsible for the whole process. Higher levels of task identity also create a learning environment in which employees feel a heightened sense of responsibility for their output, which also increases motivation. These enriched jobs lead to more committed and motivated employees, contributing to the environment of a high-performance workforce.

Associated Practices

There are some additional modifications to human resources systems that often go along with a high-performance work system. Arguably, the most important is careful employment screening. A highly empowered work environment is not for everyone; many employees do not like the added responsibility and the heavy workload that is often associated with a high-performance workforce. Careful preemployment screening will assist with successful implementation. In addition, there are often compensation changes that come along with a high-performance work system. Often, pay for performance or pay for knowledge schemes replaces traditional salary-based plans for workers. This allows a firm to ensure that the skills required for effective functioning of the work system are in place in the workforce. Finally, since a high-performance workforce is expected to continually improve the work process, many firms pursuing a high-performance workforce have adopted some form of job security provisions so that employees do not feel that they are going to design themselves out of a job by continually improving the work process.

Problems with High-Performance Work Systems

Even though they have been shown to be successful, high-performance work systems have their drawbacks. Because organizations that have implemented these types of systems generally eliminate many layers of management, traditional career paths are not available to ambitious employees who want to "advance" to management roles. If paying for skill acquisition becomes the norm, then what happens after all "skills" are learned? Management needs to be certain that there is always room for advancement. Finally, there are often boundary disputes regarding the role of the team and the role of management. As teams become more autonomous, they tend to become less tolerant of what they view as inappropriate management intervention. There may be increased resistance to any new rule that company management tries to implement. Also, as noted above, a high-performance workforce is generally a high-stress environment.

Scott A. Jeffrey

See also Automotive Industry; Baldrige Awards; Compensation; Job Skills; Lifelong Learning; Profit Sharing; Quality Circles; Taylor, Frederick Winslow; Total Quality Management

References and further reading

Adler, Paul. 1993. "Time and Motion Regained." *Harvard Business Review* 71, no. 1: 97–108.

Becker, Brian E., and Barry Gerhart. 1996. "The Impact of Human Resource Management on Organizational Performance: Progress and Prospects." *Academy of Management Journal* 39, no. 4: 779–801.

Becker, Brian E., and Mark A. Huselid. 1998. "High-Performance Work Systems and Firm Performance: A Synthesis of Research and Managerial Implications." *Human Resource Management* 16: 53–101.

Garvin, David A. 1993. "A Note on High-Commitment Work Systems." Harvard, MA: Harvard Business School Press.

Hackman, J. Richard. and Greg R. Oldham. 1980. *Work Redesign.* Reading MA: Addison-Wesley.

Herzberg, Frederick. 1987. "One More Time: How Do You Motivate Employees?" *Harvard Business Review* 65, no. 5: 109–120.

Herzberg, Frederick, Bernard Mausner, and Barbara B. Snyderman. 1959. *The Motivation to Work.* 2nd ed. New York: John Wiley and Sons.

Huselid, Mark. A. 1995. "The Impact of Human Resource Practices on Turnover, Productivity, and Corporate Financial Performance." *Academy of Management Journal* 48, no. 3: 635–672.

Kling, Jeffrey. 1995. "High Performance Work Systems and Firm Performance." *Monthly Labor Review* 118 (May): 29–36.

MacDuffie, John P. 1995. "Human Resource Bundles and Manufacturing Performance: Organizational Logic and Flexible Production Systems in the World Auto Industry." *Industrial and Labor Relations Review* 48: 197–221.

McGregor, Douglas. 1960. *The Human Side of Enterprise.* New York: McGraw-Hill.

Nadler, David A., and Marc S. Gerstein. 1992. "Designing High-Performance Work Systems: Organizing People, Work, Technology, and Information." In *Organizational Architecture: Designs for Changing Organizations.* Edited by David Nadler, Marc S. Gerstein, and Robert S. Shaw. San Francisco: Jossey-Bass, 195–208.

Nadler, David A., and Michael L. Tushman. 1997. *Competing by Design: The Power of Organizational Architecture.* New York: Oxford University Press.

Neal, J. A., and C. L. Tromley. 1995. "From Incremental Change to Retrofit: Creating High Performance Work Systems." *Academy of Management Executive* 9, no. 1: 42–54.

Taylor, Frederick. 1911. *The Principles of Scientific Management.* New York: Harper and Brothers.

Varma, Arup, Richard W. Beatty, Craig E. Schneier, and David O. Ulrich. 1999. "High Performance Work Systems: Exciting Discovery or Passing Fad?" *HR. Human Resource Planning* 22, no. 1: 26–37.

Womack, James P., Daniel P. Jones, and Daniel Roos. 1990. *The Machine That Changed the World.* New York: Rawson Associates.

Home Economics/Domestic Science

Home economics—also known as "scientific housekeeping," "sanitary cookery," and "domestic science"—is one of the most influential and far-reaching movements in women's labor history. From the mid-1800s to the present, the leaders of domestic science have sought to reshape the fundamental nature of women's unpaid work in the home—in essence, the food production, cooking, cleaning, sewing, and child rearing that have occupied women since the beginning of written history. Though home economics has had many factions and phases, its overarching theme has been to free women from "drudgery," mainly by educating them to go about their domestic labors with scientific knowledge. Once properly educated, the theorists believed, women would apply order, up-to-date technology, cleanliness, labor-saving efficiencies, and higher standards of health to their homes. In the process, they would improve themselves, their families, and the nation at large. Millions of American women have received home economics education—either formally in classrooms across the nation or informally through women's guides and magazines.

Home economics traces its roots back to "domestic economy," which became a national concern during the first decades of the new republic. Fresh from the revolution, the former colonies faced the awesome task of building a nation, and most U.S. leaders agreed that education would be essential to achieving a great citizenry. A public school system slowly emerged for boys, at first on a local basis. By the 1820s, a few schools opened for girls as well, and with them came public debate over what sort of education was appropriate and whether it made sense to provide schooling for females. Some progressive female seminaries emphasized academics, others the practical skills of housewifery. Many encouraged a combination of both. In any case, there was a growing sense in the United States that women needed to be more intelligent so that they would run better homes and raise better sons.

During this era, Americans were in love with science and its possibilities for improving the world, and women wanted to share in the trend. By the 1840s and 1850s, cookbooks and household guides were appearing with increasingly intellectual and scientific content, such as the biological functions of the body, detailed charts showing chemical analyses of food, and diagrams of mechanical systems in the family home, including stoves, furnaces, and chimneys.

Most historians consider Catharine Beecher to be the first great visionary of domestic science. In her enormously popular household guides—*Treatise on Domestic Economy* (1842) and later her 1869 book *American Woman's Home* (coauthored with her famous sister, Harriet Beecher Stowe, best-selling author of *Uncle Tom's Cabin*), Beecher derided the irrational methods of housekeeping taught by old-fashioned mothers and grandmothers. Instead, she called for the professionalization of housework, with dramatically higher standards of cleanliness, order, and beauty—all achieved by a dogged devotion to details aided by enlightenment of science. With nitty-gritty, step-by-step instructions, she outlined a job description for the middle-class housewife, one that covered such diverse topics as how to heat and ventilate a house; build an "earth closet" (a toilet); clean rooms and keep away bugs; care for the aged, infants, and children; garden; organize the laundry closet; and decorate, entertain, and cook healthful meals.

Such high levels of performance approximated those previously attainable only by the wealthy. Now, Beecher suggested that all women in the United States could achieve fine homes if they sought professional instruction in schools. And so she set about establishing several seminaries where women could learn such skills and gain social status as competent housewives and managers of their own homes.

Beecher's prescriptions (and those of other domestic writers of the era) codified housework for the masses and held wide appeal for a new generation of women seeking to leave behind traditional rural life and enter the middle class. And so, as industrialism transformed the world, domestic science transformed women's work—from that which met the biological and economic needs of a family to that which achieved social and emotional goals, such as middle-class respectability, upward social mobility, morality, personal happiness of children and husbands, and in some cases, morality, Christianity, and ideal womanhood. The mother of the Christian family, Beecher insisted, should become a "self-sacrificing laborer" in her home. A woman's "great mission is self-denial" (Beecher and Stowe 1994/1869, 18, 19).

The great popularity of domestic science cannot be separated from larger forces at work during the

A group of young girls posed in a home economics class in Washington, D.C., ca. 1899 (Library of Congress)

nineteenth and early twentieth centuries. Domestic science existed because of and contributed to the emergence of a market economy, the growth of the professional class, U.S. faith in science, the fervor of Protestant reformism, and of course the "doctrine of separate spheres," in which women replaced men as the chief authority of the home once industrialism pulled husbands to distant clerical and factory jobs. Historians such as Jeanne Boydston (1990) have noted that the rising standards of housework for women enabled men to go more willingly to paid workplaces and therefore made the rise of capitalism possible. Indeed, proper home life became a symbol of social status—achieved by unpaid and seemingly invisible female labor.

After the Civil War, domestic science gained immense national momentum. Many middle-class U.S. women now wanted a larger part of public life, and a new generation sought university degrees and careers. This transition to higher education and paid work seemed easier and more socially acceptable when women went into positions that did not veer too far from their traditional roles as helpers, healers, and feeders of the human race. U.S. women embarked on the Progressive era, their well-known period of social activism and charity.

Like teaching, nursing, and social work, domestic science offered middle-class women some of their first paid jobs helping those less fortunate. Indeed, it was a time of vast human suffering and one that called for answers. Freed slaves needed education and housing. Displaced Indians had lost their homes. Millions of foreign-born immigrants flooded U.S. cities, living impoverished lives in unsanitary tenements.

The white, Anglo-Saxon majority in the United States widely believed that these people suffered from poor diets and poor living habits because they came from uncivilized cultures and their women did not know how to run proper homes. If lower-class girls—future mothers of their races—could be taught to create order and better work habits in their own homes, so the theory went, they would uplift their families from poverty and ignorance. Domestic science teachers were particularly concerned about the inferior diets of the lower classes, whom they believed ate too much starch and not enough meat or milk.

During the 1870s, three hugely successful cooking schools opened, providing early training grounds: the New York Cooking School, the Philadelphia Cooking School, and the Boston Cooking School. The original mission of all these enterprises was to teach poor and working-class girls about proper nutrition and cleanliness and how to cook with scientific rigor. But eventually, all of them offered classes to middle-class women as well. Many housewives and young women wanted to do a better job at their daily labors and sought self-improvement. Others wanted to become teachers of the subject.

Many colleges began admitting women and established domestic science curricula. Some offered highly practical vocational classes on how to cook and preserve foods. Others took a more academic approach, requiring theoretical classes in chemistry, biology, and bacteriology. Always, the goal was to lighten the burdens of housework through efficiency, science, and the use of new kitchen gadgets, products, and tools.

As the domestic science movement continued, thousands of U.S. women were graduating each year from cooking school courses and degreed programs that qualified them to teach domestic science. And so they spread across the nation like an army.

Many were hired by the nation's growing public education system, which embraced domestic science for its girls, setting up kitchen "laboratories" in elementary and high schools from coast to coast. There were jobs to be found, also, at hundreds of settlement houses across the nation, many of which offered immigrants some form of cooking classes or domestic science. The goal was to convert newcomers to the foods and expectations of American life.

Former slaves and their children also received this training. After the Civil War, the Freedmen's Bureau (a federal agency), the American Missionary Society, and various churches set up training institutes and colleges throughout the South. Almost always, these schools included kitchen laboratories and a domestic science curriculum for girls, just as boys almost always learned agriculture. One of the most famous of these schools was the Tuskegee Institute, founded by former slave Booker T. Washington. Some critics, such as W. E. B. Du Bois, assailed Washington for teaching a vocational curriculum rather than a liberal academic education. According to Du Bois, places like Tuskegee were creating better-educated field hands and servants. Instead, he believed that blacks needed liberal academic education and should agitate for power.

Domestic science teachers also found jobs on Indian reservations as far away as Alaska. Federally funded Indian schools systematically sought to strip thousands of native children of their cultures, religions, and economies. Domestic science was a useful tool in this endeavor. Teachers scorned the hunting, gathering, and outdoor cooking labors of Indian women. They disdained traditional homes and native diets of whole grains and roots and buffalo. Domestic science classes taught young Indian girls how to set a table with European style utensils; bake yeasted bread; and cook roasts, puddings, and cakes according to middle-class protocol.

Domestic science had a phenomenal reach that went far beyond classroom education and reform efforts for the poor. In fact, its most ardent supporters were probably middle-class women who were willing to spend money on cookbooks, household guides, and new products that would save them labor. Cooking school teachers such as Juliet Corson, Maria Parloa, Mary Lincoln, and later Fanny Farmer became household names, churning out cookbooks, household guides, and magazines that sold by the millions. *The Boston Cooking-School Cook Book* by Fanny Farmer, a principal of the Boston Cooking School, would sell 4 million copies. Many of the great culinary women of the era endorsed commercial food products and appliances.

In this way, domestic science was a remarkable vehicle for transforming cooking—one of the most ancient of women's domestic labors. Across the nation, women began, most remarkably, to cook according to the exact specifications of proven formulas—that is, written recipes, rather than tradition, taste, and culture. Instead of learning housewifery from the oral traditions of mothers and grandmothers, they turned to outside authorities and experts for advice. This led them to compute calories and protein grams when planning meals, to embrace new gadgetry and appliances, to put extra efforts into making foods that looked dainty and pretty on the plate, and to buy instead of make essential ingredients. All these principles were essential in almost all domestic science curricula and have remained a guiding focus of women's work in the home to this day.

The mass appeal of domestic science became abundantly clear at the 1893 World's Fair in Chicago—one of the first great marketing events in U.S. history. Cooking lectures and demonstrations were prominent throughout the fairgrounds, as the nation's most famous cooking teachers gathered for the first time to spread their doctrine of scientific cookery. The power of this message seemed irrefutable amid the dazzling presentations of science and technology. Most marvelous of all were Thomas Alva Edison's displays, including a futuristic electrical kitchen of the future. Hundreds of thousands of women attended these exhibits, taking home pamphlets and new ideas.

These events ultimately led to the founding of the American Home Economics Association six years later at a conference in Lake Placid, New York. At this historic event, the nation's foremost nutritionists and domestic science teachers formally established a new academic discipline called "home economics" (the term *euthenics* was almost chosen). They founded a scholarly journal, *The Journal of Home Economics,* and curriculum standards for elementary, secondary, and college education. Ellen Swallow Richards was elected the first president of the association in 1908. She was distinguished as the first female graduate of the Massachusetts Institute of Technology (MIT), a champion of women in science, a pioneer in ecology, the founder of a public kitchen to help the poor, and the author of texts like *The Chemistry of Cooking and Cleaning* (1882).

If all this were not remarkable enough, by 1914, the federal government got in the domestic science business when it passed the Smith-Lever Act, which required that all the nation's "land-grant" colleges "extend" their agricultural and home economics knowledge to local communities. The U.S. Department of Agriculture's home economics department hired women to write books and pamphlets on nutrition, cleanliness, sewing, and all other aspects of efficient housework. Land-grant colleges sent economists home to rural communities as "extension agents" to teach efficient methods of cooking and housekeeping. They found an eager audience. In the early part of the twentieth century, farmers' wives still carried out immense physical labors in isolated homes—they were expected to bake bread, cook large meals, preserve garden produce, and manufacture clothing and housewares. Many were thrilled to have the opportunity to gather with friends and neighbors to learn labor-saving techniques for canning, butchering, mattress making, and home decoration to make their lives easier.

With academia, the federal government, and public school systems behind it, home economics now offered women a bona fide field of their own, one with a body of professional expertise and nationally recognized academic credentials. This prestige opened many new doors. During the twentieth century, women trained as home economists got paid jobs in universities, food businesses, publishing, and government. Through home economics, women got Ph.D.'s and developed national standards for child care. They pioneered the earliest school lunch programs and demanded pure food and a cleaner public milk supply. Home economists also developed the first vitamin-fortified cereals and, as the century moved on, encouraged the inclusion of more fruits and vegetables in the U.S. diet. Their advice was greatly needed when during two world wars and the Great Depression, food and material shortages demanded that all women in the United States economize and carry out extra labors in their homes.

But home economics claims a mixed historical legacy—one that has drawn criticism from scholars. As we have seen, the movement overtly sought to Americanize and erase the ethnic foodways of immigrants. Famous home economists promoted convenience foods and commercial products that ultimately deskilled future generations of cooks. By the middle of the twentieth century, feminists charged that home economics training in public schools was a conspiracy to limit the career options of women. In addition, food critics have blamed the field for creating a bland American diet, featuring gray sodden roasts, gelatin molds, overboiled vegetables blanketed in white sauce, and far too much trust in food factories that promised technological progress.

Certainly, the early home economists wanted to create a national palate and lighten women's burdens. These goals overlapped conveniently with the goals of companies interested in developing mass markets and selling products. As consumer goods and appliances exploded during the 1920s and then again during the 1950s, home economists acted as mediators between U.S. women and companies. On radio and television shows, in paid advertising, and in women's magazines and product brochures, home economists demystified new products and goods, teaching women how to use new inventions such as refrigerators, electric stoves, toasters, chafing dishes, Pyrex, blenders, and unusual new products like biscuit mixes, self-rising flour, gelatin, and a unique new invention known as shortening. In many ways, the original domestic scientists accomplished their goals. Homemaking required less arduous physical labor and more emotional and intellectual attention. Middle-class American homes now lay claim to some of the highest standards of cleanliness and technology known in the world.

Ironically, by the 1970s, these achievements enabled women to leave the home and abandon homemaking as a full time pursuit. Feminism and a new economy drew many mothers, wives, and daughters into new fields of paid employment. Women's domestic labor once again underwent vast readjustments, responding to and contributing to dramatic social change.

On the surface, home economics, per se, now seems less present in public education and universities and daily life than it was 100 years ago. But this may be, in fact, because the values of the movement were long ago woven into American life. Indeed, the home economics agenda is still alive and well under many names and venues—and in some ways with even larger breadth and scope.

Today dozens of universities and colleges across the nation continue to teach home economics under the old and various new monikers, such as human ecology, dietetics, health and human sciences, and family and consumer sciences. Home economists continue to work in university extension programs and in 4-H clubs, teaching baking and sewing in rural areas. All across the United States, a wide variety of human service programs teach low-income families to adopt healthy diets and manage food budgets, and all schoolchildren today still learn lessons of health and food.

Millions of middle-class U.S. women and a growing number of men expend immense amounts of labor, time, and money on cookbooks and household guides to help them achieve perfect homes. Cooking institutes have surged in popularity. Magazines and newspapers of all sorts continue to advise women on how to declutter their homes and cook meals with nutrition as the primary guide. Manufacturers promise less mess and labor with convenience products, which have been embraced by Americans. Domestic gurus such as Martha Stewart tell us how to better our families through expert housekeeping and step-by-step guides remarkably reminiscent of *The American Woman's Home* by Catharine Beecher. With expert help, women entertain and decorate in ways that bring social respectability and upward mobility.

As during the nineteenth century, a heady but small intellectual wing of the movement exists with a national agenda to advocate for higher standards in U.S. homes and educate professionals who will elevate women's traditional work. In 1994, the American Home Economics Association was renamed the American Association for Family and Consumer Sciences (AAFCS). According to the organization's Website, it helps "professionals develop, integrate and provide practical knowledge about the things of everyday life—human growth and development; personal behavior; housing and environment; food and nutrition; apparel and textiles; and resource management—that every individual needs every day to make sound decisions which contribute to a healthy, productive, and more fulfilling life" (AAFCS 2003). Among other things, the AAFCS advocates for high-quality child care for working mothers, environmental issues, pure food, the primacy of family relationships, and the application of scientific research to solve problems in daily life.

Laura Schenone

See also Housework; Mommy Track; Pink Collar; Servants and Maids; Women and Work

References and further reading

AAFCS. 2003. American Association for Family and Consumer Sciences Homepage. http://www.aafcs.org (cited August 20, 2003).

Adams, David Wallace. 1995. *Education for Extinction: American Indians and the Boarding School Experience, 1875–1928.* Lawrence: University Press of Kansas.

Beecher, Catharine Esther. 1842. *A Treatise on Domestic Economy: For the Use of Young Ladies at Home and at School.* New York: Harper and Brothers.

Beecher, Catharine Esther, and Harriet Beecher Stowe. 1994/1869. *American Woman's Home.* Hartford: Stowe-Day Foundation.

Boydston, Jeanne. 1990. *Home and Work: Housework, Wages, and the Ideology of Labor in the Early Republic.* New York: Oxford University Press.

Corson, Juliet. 1877. *Fifteen-Cent Dinners for Families of Six.* New York: the author.

Ellis, Pearl Idelia. 1929. *Americanization through Homemaking.* Los Angeles: Wetzel Publishing.

Farmer, Fannie Meritt. 1997/1896. *Boston Cooking-School Cook Book.* Reprint with a new introduction by Janice (Jan) Bluestein Longone. Mineola: Dover Publications.

Francke, Maria. 1916. *Opportunities for Women in Domestic Science.* Prepared under the direction of Susan M. Kingsbury. Philadelphia: Association of Collegiate Alumnae.

Kander, Mrs. Simon, comp. 1987. *The "Settlement" Cookbook: The Way to a Man's Heart.* Facsimile of 1903 edition. New York: Gramercy Publishing.

Levenstein, Harvey. 1988. *Revolution at the Table: The Transformation of the American Diet.* New York: Oxford University Press.

Lincoln, Mary J. 1915. *The School Kitchen Textbook: Lessons in Cooking and Domestic Science for the Use of Elementary Schools.* Boston: Little, Brown.

New England Kitchen Magazine. April 1894.

Reed, Estelle. 1901. *Course of Study for the Indian Schools of the United States, Industrial and Literary.* Washington, DC: Government Printing Office.

Schenone, Laura. 2003. *A Thousand Years over a Hot Stove: A History of American Women Told through Food, Recipes, and Remembrances.* New York: W. W. Norton.

Schwartz, Ruth Cowan. 1983. *More Work for Mother: The Ironies of Household Technology from the Open Hearth to the Microwave.* New York: Basic Books.

Shapiro, Laura. 1986. *The Perfection Salad: Women and Cooking at the Turn of the Century.* New York: Farrar, Straus and Giroux.

Weigley, Emma Seifrit. 1974. "It Might Have Been Euthenics: The Lake Placid Conferences and the Home Economics Movement." *American Quarterly* 26, no. 1 (March).

Welter, Barbara. 1966. "The Cult of True Womanhood, 1820–1860." *American Quarterly* 18 (Summer): 151–174.

The cover of Frank Leslie's Illustrated Weekly, *depicting the 1892 strike at the Homestead steel plant in Pennsylvania (Library of Congress)*

Homestead Strike

The deadly strike at the Homestead steel plant in Pennsylvania embodied the class struggle endemic to the late-nineteenth-century United States. Working-class men and women confronted perhaps America's leading industrialist on the banks of the Monongahela River. Workers used the tools at their disposal—a strike and violence—but the vast forces arrayed against them—capital and the national government—proved too much for the workers.

In 1882, Andrew Carnegie purchased the Homestead steel mill. Seven years later, the Amalgamated Association of Iron, Steel, and Tin Workers union went on strike and secured union recognition, a pay raise, and a three-year contract. Immediately after losing this labor battle, Carnegie plotted to undermine the union and made Henry Clay Frick chairman of his steel company. The two industrial leaders did not agree on ways to bring the union to heel. Carnegie favored locking out workers until they capitulated, whereas Frick preferred using force.

In 1892, the union's contract expired. The slowing of railroad construction burst the steel boom and weakened the union's position at the bargaining table. As it prepared for another strike, Carnegie left the United States for Scotland and gave Frick unilateral control over the labor situation. Frick proposed lower wages and longer hours to Amalgamated, and when the union refused and issued a strike notice, Frick closed the mill. He fortified the complex and announced that no more unions were welcome at Homestead. Two days later, workers stormed the mill and cordoned off the town to prevent strikebreakers from entering. On July 6, Frick hired a squad of Pinkerton detectives to restore order. Striking workers, their families, and sympathetic townspeople attacked the Pinkerton's boat with rifles, dynamite, and fireworks left over from the Fourth of July. In the ensuing gun battle, three Pinkertons and seven workers perished. The Pinkertons surrendered, and the workers forced them to run a gauntlet of protestors.

The workers' famous victory proved ephemeral. Days later, 8,500 members of the Pennsylvania National Guard arrived in Homestead to protect private property and preserve law and order. They occupied the town for ninety-five days. The presence of the National Guard allowed Frick to open the plant with strikebreakers. Police arrested 167 Homestead residents on charges of murder, rioting, and conspiracy for their role in the attack on the Pinkertons. Few of these men were tried, and no one was convicted for his participation. On July 23, 1892, Alexander Berkman, a Russian anarchist, shot and stabbed Frick in his office, but the redoubtable Frick survived the assassination attempt. Workers received renewed support in early fall, when prominent members of the Democratic Party campaigned in Homestead, but by election time, the strike had weakened considerably. In October, strike leaders declared the strike over. The result of the strike was a complete loss for the union and its workers. Frick slashed tonnage rates, imposed longer hours on workers, and decreased the number of breaks workers could take, and the increasing mechanization of the plant slashed jobs. Carnegie and Frick also employed a hierarchical management system, thereby curtailing workers' control over the production process.

William J. Bauer Jr.

See also American Federation of Labor and Congress of Industrial Organizations; Solidarity; Steel/U.S. Steel

References and further reading

Krause, Paul. 1992. *The Battle for Homestead, 1880–1892: Politics, Culture and Steel.* Pittsburgh: University of Pittsburgh Press.

Montgomery, David. 1987. *The Fall of the House of Labor: The Workplace, the State, and American Labor Activism, 1865–1925.* New York: Cambridge University Press.

Homework

Homework, paid labor that is performed within the employee's home, includes a wide range of occupations with a variety of working conditions. Farmers, professionals pursuing careers at home through telecommunications, and individuals performing clerical and industrial piecework in their homes are all categorized as "homeworkers" by the Department of Labor. Historically, however, homework has been an important source of income for immigrant and working-class women, who have toiled under difficult, if not illegal conditions.

Since the 1980s, growing public demand for flexible, family-friendly work schedules has led numerous businesses to promote homework as the perfect solution for working mothers. Company brochures often portray homework with pictures of compliant toddlers resting quietly beside mothers who work undisturbed, sewing window treatments, typing envelopes, or reviewing insurance claims.

The reality is far less idyllic for women and minority homeworkers, who are disproportionately employed in low-paying, low-status jobs such as clerical and industrial piecework. Industrial textile and apparel homeworkers are almost exclusively women, and growing numbers of legal and illegal immigrants perform homework for these industries. Industrial homeworkers are often paid by the piece. This system enables employers to avoid paying full-time salaries. Though employers rarely provide overtime compensation, low piece-rate wages often require homeworkers to toil long hours to make ends meet. Homeworkers hired as "independent contractors" are denied health insurance, unemployment compensation, paid vacations, and Social Security. Homework also transfers the overhead costs of machinery, electricity, floor space, heating, and air conditioning to the employee. For workers paid by the piece, these numerous expenses erode often small, undependable paychecks. Finally, most female homeworkers retain primary responsibility for child care and housework. As a result, they lengthen their workday to fulfill multiple roles.

Although sometimes described as a modern innovation, the combination of wage and domestic work within the home has long been a practice of working-class families and a strategic form of employment for manufacturers. Eighteenth-century households often depended on female family members' wages, and homework, known then as the "putting out system," was a primary form of female employment. During industrialization, homework was supported by a domestic ideology that celebrated the home as a haven of personal, nonmarket relations. Deemed "natural" caretakers, women were expected to stay home and care for their families and households. Necessity forced many working-class and immigrant women to seek paid labor, however. In a time when limited occupational opportunities existed for women outside the home, many found employment as homeworkers.

Nineteenth- and early-twentieth-century industrial homeworkers helped their families eke out a living through long hours weaving and spinning, rolling cigars, fashioning artificial flowers, sorting nuts and coffee beans, and setting teeth into carding combs. Wage-cutting and withholding and underpayment were just a few of the notorious ills endured by struggling homeworkers, whose isolation within their homes made organized redress difficult. Despite the vigorous efforts of union leaders and philanthropists anxious to rid the domestic sphere of sweatshop labor, homework remained a necessary evil for thousands of urban poor who were offered few other realistic options for family survival.

Katie Otis

See also Consultants and Contract Workers; Immigrants and Work; Piecework; Telework/Telecommuting; Women and Work

References and further reading

Boris, Eileen. 1994. *Home to Work, Motherhood, and the Politics of Industrial Homework in the United States.* New York: Cambridge University Press.

Boris, Eileen, and Cynthia R. Daniels, eds. 1990. *Homework: Historical and Contemporary Perspectives on Paid Labor at Home.* Chicago: University of Illinois Press.

Boris, Eileen, and Elisabeth Prugl. 1996. *Homeworkers in Global Perspective: Invisible No More.* New York: Routledge.

Christensen, Kathleen. 1988a. *Women and Home Based Work.* New York: Holt.

Christensen, Kathleen, ed. 1988b. *The New Era of Home-Based Work: Directions and Policies.* Boulder, CO: Westview Press.

Costello, Cynthia B. 1987. *Home-Based Employment: Implications for Working Women.* Washington, DC: Women's Research and Education Institute.

Dublin, Thomas. 1994. *Transforming Women's Work.* Ithaca, NY: Cornell University Press.

Prugl, Elisabeth. 1999. *The Global Construction of Gender: Home-Based Work in the Political Economy of the Twentieth Century.* New York: Columbia University Press.

Stansell, Christine. 1987. *City of Women.* Chicago: University of Illinois Press.

Housework

The term *housework* is generally used to signify unpaid work predominantly performed by women in and around a home. The broadest definition of housework includes many different forms of unpaid labor done to maintain a family and home—cleaning, child care, repairs, yard work, shopping, planning, cooking, serving, and sometimes subsistence farming or gardening and volunteer work. Wages for Housework, an international advocacy group, estimates the value of housework done in the United States at $1.4 trillion per year, if it were paid work (Wages for Housework 2001). In the twentieth century, in western industrialized countries like the United States, housework is generally used to denote cleaning, cooking, child care, and shopping. Whatever activities are included under housework, three things are clear: this work is by definition unpaid, it is generally held in low esteem, and it is predominantly performed by women.

Because most housework is generally maintenance work (it does not produce an original product), is unpaid, and is done within the privacy of the home, it is a type of work that is largely invisible. Housework is often viewed as a labor of love—it is not seen as work having a direct bearing on the economic systems of countries or family units. Under this view, housework is done on behalf of society, children, and families, not on behalf of capitalism or patriarchy, and women tend to do it because it is the natural or proper role of women to do the nurturing and maintenance work that families and homes require.

Yet a number of theories have emerged that attempt to make housework more visible as a form of labor, many of which are inspired by Marxist analyses of paid labor. A number of Marxist feminists (for example, Heidi I. Hartmann) have attempted to apply Marxist analyses to housework and often begin with the notion that the work that women tend to do within the home is reproduction (as opposed to production, which is done in the industrial workplace). This reproductive work includes bearing and raising children and tending to the daily bodily and emotional needs of household members that is necessary to maintain the laborers who work outside the home for wages. In this way, women serve capital just as much as men paid to labor outside the home do, just in a different way. This labor is not generally considered production in the classical Marxist sense because it does not directly produce a distinct product. Exceptions to this are gardening, if it produces food for the family, and the trend by which consumers are increasingly made to do more of the work that producers and shopkeepers used to do—self-service, self-check-out, or self-assembly. In this way, it is argued, consumers become unpaid workers for capital. But most housework processes are transformative rather than productive, turning materials (baking goods and cloth) into usable forms, or are maintenance work—cleaning, repairing, or restoring.

Reproductive work done by women does not just reproduce and maintain the labor force but also reproduces traditional (heterosexual, nuclear) family forms. Wives become necessary to do this work within the home while husbands are necessary to earn money. The necessity of reproductive work to maintain a paid labor force leads Marxist accounts to note that when an employer pays wages to one person, he or she is generally purchasing the work of another laborer, this one invisible, within the home. This system may allow employers to keep wages low, lower than if the paid employee would have to pay fair market prices for someone to cook, clean, and tend to any children.

Marxist feminist theories of housework posit that the definition of housework is to a large extent historically and geographically specific. To suggest this is to recognize the evolutionary processes in industrialized, western countries that led up to housework in the form in which we know it. Although work has always been done to maintain homes and families, householders, even those with little or no property, often had servants do it for them in the early stages of developing capitalist societies. As capitalism has advanced, historically, the material base that maintained a servant class whose services could be bought cheaply has been eroded away. Although there are still many today who either employ domestic servants or work as domestic servants, the middle and lower middle classes are no longer able to purchase these services to the same extent as was previously possible. Instead, the housewife or homemaker has emerged as a new historical phenomenon. Martha Gimenez describes the housewife as the lady of the house and the servant all rolled up into one, when previously there would have been two separate people filling these roles. Housework, now, is the set of tasks she performs without wages.

Marxist accounts of housework go far to explain a phenomenon that many other theories of labor do not take seriously, yet there are still questions that a

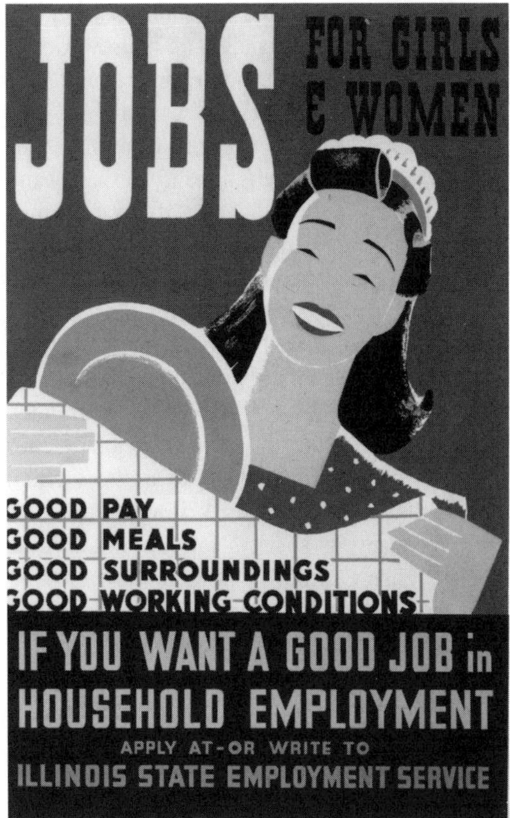

A WPA poster created for the Illinois State Employment Service promoting jobs for women and girls as domestics (Library of Congress)

Marxist analysis alone cannot answer easily. For instance, why is it specifically women who tend to do housework? Even when women hold paid jobs outside the home, if they are married or partnered to a man, on average they will still spend twice as many hours on housework as their spouse or partners (Robinson and Godbey 1999, 100). Is housework only done for capitalism, or are there other social values attached to it that Marxist-inspired analyses do not account for well? Can the "social reproduction" performed through the rearing of children really be understood through such economic analyses? What explains the roles of the church, state, and civil society in the valuation of housework and its gender specificity? Because of these questions, some feminist theorists have come to the conclusion that capitalist social relations alone cannot explain the phenomenon of gender oppression through the undervaluation of housework and the women who predominantly do it.

Even when women hold full-time jobs, they still bear the primary responsibility for housework and child care. This is the phenomenon often referred to as the "double day" or the "second shift." The feminist approach to housework recognizes this fact as a barrier to women's equality in society and posits that this sexual division of labor ensures male superiority or patriarchy in social relations. To eradicate women's inequality, feminists argue that widespread, perhaps state-funded child care services are needed, as well as generous family leave policies that would allow both women and men to hold jobs and care for family members. Within the home, feminists argue the sexual division of labor needs to change; men need to assume equal responsibility for housework if women are to achieve equality in society. Not only would these changes ensure a more equitable view of what "women's work" is, but it would also allow women to participate more fully in paid labor and achieve more economic independence.

Social scientists of all theoretical persuasions who study housework note that it seems to have a sort of elasticity about it. Marxist feminist analyses note that when paid wages decline in value, many household units compensate by intensifying work done around the house—more meals are cooked at home rather than bought at restaurants, and clothes are mended and handed down rather than replaced. Yet there is another form of elasticity about housework in that it seems to expand to fit the time available. Feminists have long noted that the advent of new, supposedly time-saving appliances eventually do little to reduce the hours spent by women on housework. Instead, the standards of cleanliness seem to rise with every new piece of technology or cleaning product available, so that women using these devices still put in just as many hours on housework as they did previously.

Concomitant with this phenomenon is the historical deskilling of the housewife. Part of her work may include time spent buying clothes, but today she is less likely to have the skills to make them herself, even though a tailor can make a living wage with this skill. The same is true for meals—more and more items in grocery stores are at least partially processed so that the person who prepares them is required to heat or cook them but may not know how to turn raw materials into finished products from beginning to end anymore, though a person who finds work as a chef can be paid for this type of knowledge. This deskilling can have serious consequences for a woman who was once a housewife but who later finds herself having to support herself and children with her own wages. Additionally, when a housewife has more skills, she is able to maintain a family if the primary wage earner becomes unemployed without having to purchase goods and services if she can perform them herself. These skills serve as a buffer for the family in the case of a loss of a job; as these skills are lost, cash is increasingly needed to purchase goods and services elsewhere.

The fact that women tend to do most of the shopping for families is often overlooked when people consider housework. Yet women are estimated to buy 80 percent of all goods and services (Greer 1999, 146). The links between "women's work" and the economy are such that women are vitally necessary as consumers. Although this important role would suggest that women should have a good deal of political leverage over producers and sellers, Germaine Greer points out that the political action most likely to be taken by a consumer is boycott. Although boycotts can be very effective if they are launched on a massive scale, they require more time and more money spent by women to accomplish their shopping for their families. Alternative products may be hard to find or more expensive. Boycotts actually require a lot of effort by a lot of people, whereas a protest drawing media attention could be more effectively staged by fewer people and last only a few hours or a day. She argues that the political tool most associated with consumers, the boycott, is comparatively the most laborious and least effective form of political action, requiring the coordinated efforts of huge groups of people. An individual consumer or a small group of consumers with a concern is unlikely to have much effect on the producers and sellers of the products they buy.

Feminist accounts of housework around the world often make links to environmental concerns. In part, this connection has to do with the waste produced in the consumption that women do on behalf of families and with the types of household chemicals they are expected to use to accomplish their housework. With new products and new technologies available, the expectation has grown that bathrooms and kitchens be surgically sterile. Yet there is concern that bleaches and detergents can have harmful effects both on the people who come directly into contact with them through daily use and on ecosystems, once these chemicals are drained out of homes. Additionally, as more and more women are expected to buy products needed for the maintenance of their families (rather than produce things on a much smaller scale for their own use) concerns with factory farming techniques and the production of goods on a mass level leave many feminists concerned with the effects of consumerism on environments around the world.

For decades, feminists around the world have been arguing that governments should include the value of unpaid housework in calculations of gross national product (GNP). They argue that including the monetary value of this unpaid work in these national statistics requires governments to recognize the contributions women make to nations. With this recognition, it is argued that women will be able to establish their entitlement to welfare benefits, higher wages, Social Security, educational opportunities, social services, child care, health care, land, and technology. The fact that much of the work that women do is unpaid allows it to be invisible. Making it visible in GNP gives women a basis on which they can make claims on their governments to further their equality. In 1985, the United Nations agreed to count women's unwaged work in GNP calculations but has yet to do so.

Jennifer Schenk

See also Blue Collar; Home Economics/Domestic Science; Homework; Pink Collar; White Collar

References and further reading

Collins, Jane L. 1990. "Unwaged Labor in Comparative Perspective: Recent Theories and Unanswered Questions." Pp. 3–24 in *Work without Wages: Domestic Labor and Self-Employment within Capitalism.* Edited by Jane L. Collins and Martha Gimenez. Albany: State University of New York Press.

Friedan, Betty. 1963. *The Feminine Mystique.* New York: Dell.

Gimenez, Martha E. 1990. "The Dialectics of Waged and Unwaged Work: Waged Work, Domestic Labor, and Household Survival in the United States." Pp. 25–45 in *Work Without Wages: Domestic Labor and Self-Employment within Capitalism.* Edited by Jane L. Collins and Martha Gimenez. Albany: State University of New York Press.

Glazer, Nona. 1990. "Servants to Capital: Unpaid Domestic Labor and Paid Work." In *Work without Wages: Domestic Labor and Self-Employment within Capitalism.* Edited by Jane L. Collins and Martha Gimenez. Albany: State University of New York Press.

Greer, Germaine. 1999. *The Whole Woman.* New York: Anchor Books.

Hartmann, Heidi I. 1981. "The Unhappy Marriage of Marxism and Feminism: Towards a More Progressive Union." Pp. 1–41 in *Women and Revolution.* Edited by Lydia Sargent. Boston: South End Press.

Landry, Bart. 2000. "Husbands and Housework: A Stalled Revolution?" In *Black Working Wives: Pioneers of the American Family Revolution.* Los Angeles: University of California Press.

Robinson, John P., and Geoffrey Godbey. 1999. *Time for Life: The Surprising Ways Americans Use Their Time.* 2nd ed. University Park: State University of Pennsylvania Press.

Shelton, Beth Anne. 2000. "Understanding the Distribution of Housework between Husbands and Wives." Pp. 343–355 in *The Ties That Bind: Perspectives on Marriage and Cohabitation.* Edited by Linda J. Waite. New York: Aldine de Gruyter.

Wages for Housework. 2001. "International Wages for Housework Campaign." http://ourworld.compuserve.com/homepages/crossroadswomenscentre/WFH.html (cited October 24).

Humphrey-Hawkins Act (1978)

Also known as the Full Employment and Balanced Growth Act of 1978, the Humphrey-Hawkins Act was envisaged by some legislators as an effort to breathe life into the essentially obsolete Employment Act of 1946. The Employment Act of 1946 committed the federal government to becoming the employer of last resort and maintaining a macroeconomic policy of full employment, economic growth, and price stability. Thirty-two years later, the Humphrey-Hawkins Act committed the federal government to shrink the unemployment rate to no more than 4 percent by 1983 and then went even further, stating that the federal government would maintain that unemployment rate thereafter and reduce the inflation rate to zero by 1988. In addition, the Humphrey-Hawkins Act required the chair of the Federal Reserve Board to testify before Congress twice a year on the state of macroeconomic matters and the Federal Reserve's policies. History has shown that the lofty goals established by the Humphrey-Hawkins Act were not realized, possibly because of the complete absence of either supports or penalties in the legislation itself to ensure achievement of its ideals.

Congress passed the Employment Act of 1946 in response to the Great Depression of the 1930s. The initial proposal, the Full Employment Bill of 1945, stirred much debate about whether the government could or should guarantee citizens the right to employment. That bill put the onus on the government to even out the business cycle through government spending if necessary, guaranteeing full employment for Americans. Business and agricultural interests defeated this more stringent version, and the Employment Act of 1946 (without the term *Full*) was passed as part of Truman's "Fair Deal." The Employment Act committed the federal government to a macroeconomic policy of fostering full employment, economic growth, and price stability. It required the president to estimate the macroeconomic future of the United States, establishing both the president's Council of Economic Advisers and the Congress's Joint Economic Committee. For about twenty years after enactment of the Employment Act, unemployment in the United States remained at generally low levels. Even today, there is much debate over the economic impact of the 1946 Employment Act.

Unemployment levels began to rise in the 1970s. The bill proposing the Fair Employment and Balanced Growth Act was formally introduced in June 1974 by Representative Augustus Hawkins (D-CA). In debates on the Act, Hawkins described its goal as "an authentic full employment policy, rejecting the narrow, statistical idea of full employment measured in terms of some tolerable level of unemployment—the percentage game—and adopting the more human and socially meaningful concept of personal rights to an opportunity for useful employment at fair rates of compensation". Senator Hubert Humphrey (D-MN), stated that the goal of the bill was to reduce unemployment to 3 percent within four years. The key provision of the bill was section 102, which amended the Employment Act to state that "the Congress declares and establishes the right of all adult Americans able, willing, and seeking work to opportunities for useful paid employment at fair rates of compensation." If passed, the federal government would have become the guarantor of employment opportunities, or the last-ditch employer.

Opponents of the bill argued that a nationwide full employment policy, or any government-sponsored reduction of unemployment to the proposed minimal levels, would necessarily result in inflation. Economic advisers to President Jimmy Carter's administration admitted there would be an inflationary impact, and Republicans projected the costs of the proposed legislation to be $30 to $60 billion annually. These objections necessitated extensive changes to the bill to ensure its enactment. The Humphrey-Hawkins Act, as modified, passed the House on March 16, 1978, and the Senate on October 13, 1978.

Congress declared the act's goal as "the fulfillment of the right to full opportunities for useful paid employment at fair rates of compensation of all individuals able, willing, and seeking to work." In addition to stating the specific target of 4 percent for the unemployment rate within five years, the Full Employment and Balanced Growth Act of 1978 stated that *full* employment and a balanced budget were sought "as soon as practicable." The act required "the President to initiate, as the President deems appropriate, with recommendations to the Congress where necessary, supplementary programs and policies to the extent that the President finds such action necessary to help achieve these goals." In striving for full employment, reduced inflation, price stability, and increased real incomes for workers, the act set a precedent for later efforts to mandate a living wage.

The Humphrey-Hawkins Act is an example of Congress's power to adopt legislation regulating the U.S. Federal Reserve Board. Because the Board does not enjoy constitutional status, Congress can mandate certain goals or policies for it. Throughout history, Congress has rarely done so. Under this act, the chair of the Federal Reserve Board must report to Congress its monetary targets for the upcoming year and reconcile those targets with the administration's economic projections for the year. Doing so exposes the Federal Reserve's actions to the public and was designed to improve coordination of monetary and fiscal policies. Monetary policies (raising or lowering interest rates to control the volume of borrowing and lending) and fiscal policies (raising or lowering taxes and/or spending) are the essential mechanisms of federal economic stabilization policies. There is some debate as to the extent of the Federal Reserve's compliance with the act's policy coordination disclosures.

There is, however, little debate that the act has not achieved its economic purposes. The statute creates no enforceable rights and almost no procedural requirements. Although the legislative history is replete with statements lauding the importance of full employment and balanced growth, experience has not borne out the aspirations of the act. The existence of unemployment insurance systems and the actions of the Federal Reserve Board indicate a national resignation, and perhaps a commitment, to inevitable unemployment levels, even among those ready, willing and able to work.

Debra L. Casey

See also Compensation; Full Employment Act; Unemployment Rate

References and further reading

American Enterprise Institute for Public Policy Research. 1976. *Reducing Unemployment: The Humphrey-Hawkins and Kemp-McClure Bills.* Washington, DC: American Enterprise Institute for Public Policy Research.

DeLong, J. Bradford. 1996. "Keynesianism, Pennsylvania Avenue Style: Some Economic Consequences of the Employment Act of 1946." *The Journal of Economic Perspectives* 10, no. 3: 41–53.

Eisner, Robert. 1998a. *Investment, National Income, and Economic Policy.* Northampton, MA: Edward Elgar.

———. 1998b. *The Keynesian Revolution, Then and Now.* Northampton, MA: Edward Elgar.

Harvey, Philip. 2000. "Combating Joblessness: An Analysis of the Principal Strategies That Have Influenced the Development of American Employment and Social Welfare Law During the Twentieth Century." *Berkeley Journal of Employment and Labor Law* 21: 677–758.

———. 2002. "Human Rights and Economic Policy Discourse: Taking Economic and Social Rights Seriously." *Columbia Human Rights Law Review* 33: 363–471.

Keyserling, Leon H. 1984. "The New Deal and Its Current Significance in National Economic and Social Policy." *Washington Law Review* 59: 795–841.

Krashevski, Richard S. 1998. "What Is So Natural about High Unemployment?" *American Economic Review* 78: 289–293.

Mucciaroni, Gary. 1990. *The Political Failure of Employment Policy, 1945–1982.* Pittsburgh: University of Pittsburgh Press.

Quigley, William P. 1998. "The Right to Work and Earn a Living Wage: A Proposed Constitutional Amendment." *New York City Law Review* 2: 139–182.

Schantz, Harvey L. and Richard H. Schmidt. 1980. "Politics and Policy: The Humphrey-Hawkins Story." Pp. 25–52 in *Employment and Labor-Relations Policy.* Edited by Charles Bulmer and John L. Carmichael, Jr. Lexington, MA: Lexington Books.

U.S. Congress, Joint Economic Committee. 1995. *The Humphrey-Hawkins Act and the Role of the Federal Reserve: Hearing before the Joint Economic Committee.* Washington, DC: U.S. GPO.

I

Immigrants and Work

Immigrants and work have always been closely tied together in U.S. labor history. The question of whether immigrants in general—and from which countries—are good or bad for the U.S. working class and working conditions has been hotly debated, with employers traditionally supporting increased immigration and labor organizations frequently favoring immigration controls. Work and immigration issues, however, have always been affected by larger political, economic, and social trends. Furthermore, the situation has never been uniform for all immigrant groups, with certain groups at different times being considered more desirable than others. Finally, as immigrant groups have assimilated into American society, they have at times contributed their voices to the debate.

Immigration has also figured prominently in the study and discussion of work in the United States because of how it has affected and complicated U.S. labor and working-class history. Most prominently, it has been blamed for the lack of a sustained, cohesive working-class movement in the United States, for there has been plenty of evidence that ethnicity has tended to trump class when it comes to how immigrant workers perceive themselves. Yet in the larger U.S. working class that includes immigrants, native-born workers, and racial minorities, ethnicity has been just one of several factors in the creation of what has become known as "American exceptionalism." Throughout history, down to the present day, both this phenomenon and the role of immigration in its creation have been subject to continuous debate.

Immigrants, therefore, have been regarded as both a problem and a solution in the U.S. workplace. Employers have long used immigrants willing to work for much less and in worse conditions than native-born workers to undercut union organizing efforts. Similarly, employers have made use of prejudice against and between certain groups to discourage workers from uniting even long enough to form a viable union, let alone a working-class movement. In slack times, immigrants have been resented either for taking jobs from U.S. workers or for becoming public charges on account of their failure to find jobs. Yet immigrants who proved their willingness to start from the bottom and to work and save have also been regarded as a boon to the U.S. economic system. And throughout U.S. history, one immigrant group after another has gone from being regarded as unorganizable to being recognized for its contributions to the U.S. labor movement.

Discrimination and Exploitation

Nonetheless, the intertwining of job competition and immigration has remained as much reality as perception throughout U.S. history. Employers, it should be added, were willing not only to exploit various immigrant groups and play one off another but to similarly divide and conquer by fostering competition between immigrants and African

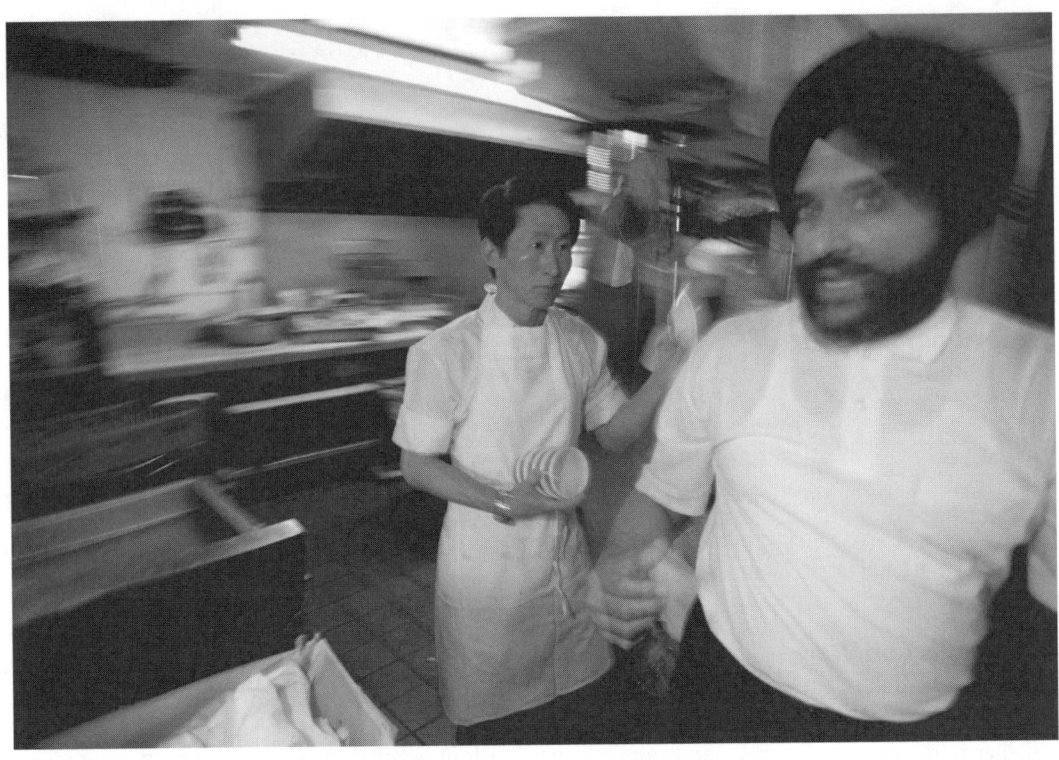

Indian and Vietnamese workers in a restaurant kitchen. Immigrant workers have been regarded as both a problem and a solution in the U.S. workplace; their willingness to work for lower wages and under worse conditions than native-born workers has undercut union organizing efforts, but they have provided a pool of labor that has been a boon to the U.S. economy. (David H. Wells/Corbis)

Americans. Another, less widely acknowledged phenomenon of immigrants was the role immigrant women played in the labor market and whether gender was a substantial factor in the exploitation of immigrant labor. In the garment trades during the early twentieth century, the willingness of immigrant men to work for less than native-born women generated conflict. Finally, although illegal immigration and its uses by employers have largely been regarded as a modern problem, historical precedents can be found in disputes over whether immigrants may be brought to the United States specifically to work (and which immigrants).

For immigrants themselves, making it in the "land of opportunity" depended not only on skill and individual initiative but on ethnic background and family tradition, as well as how these influenced the purpose of immigration. For example, Eastern European Jewish immigrants were most noted for seeking (and encouraging their children to seek) education to advance from the working to the white-collar class. In the late twentieth century, Asian immigrants have similarly promoted the virtues of education. Other immigrant groups, by contrast, have been slower to accept the idea of children straying too far from the occupational choices of their parents.

Racial discrimination against and exploitation of vulnerable immigrant groups are recurrent patterns in the history of work in the United States. Discrimination can affect all aspects of the workplace, from hiring to union representation. Historically, it has been possible for any given immigrant group to be both the oppressor and the oppressed. (At times, even those who have "made it" from a certain group have discriminated against their own, in order to protect their position and supposedly prevent prejudice.) In all its forms, prejudice can both prevent and discourage members of a group from pursuing a given occupation, yet paradoxically it can also inspire them to break barriers through individual effort or to seek redress from discrimination, as individuals or as groups.

Beyond prejudice, however, numerous factors fig-

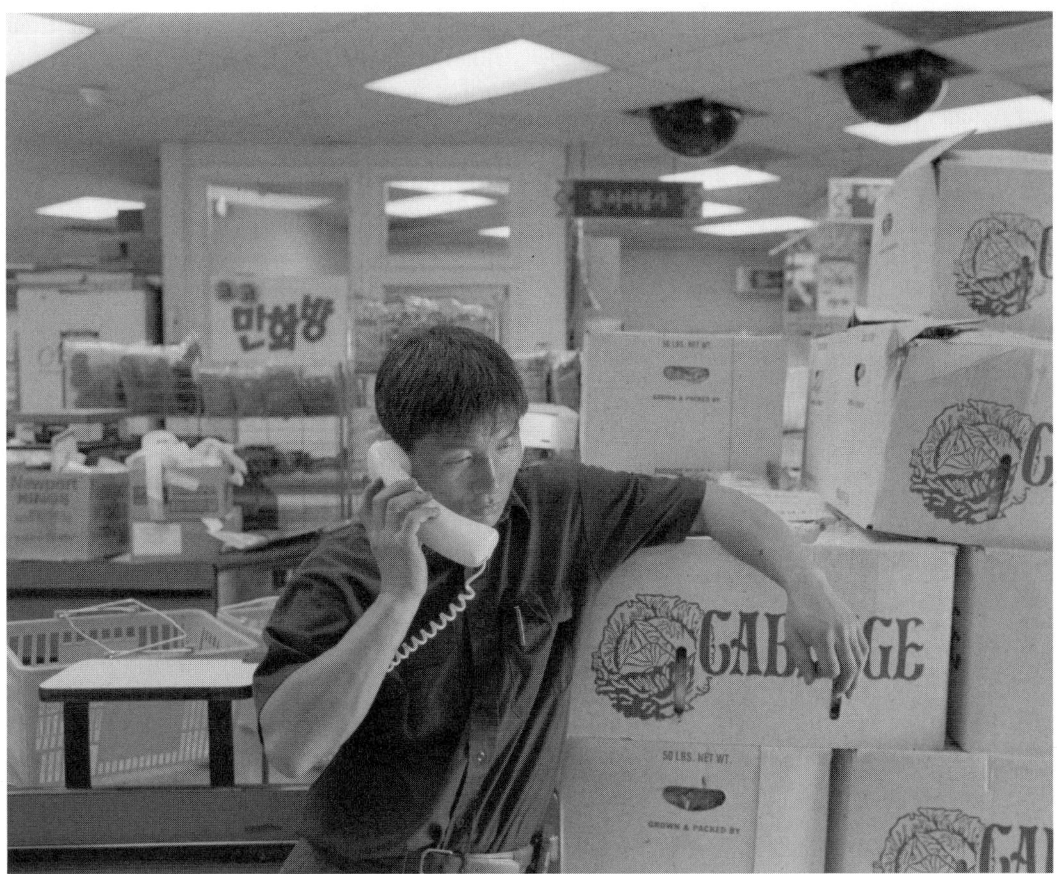

A grocer at The Korean Korner, a supermarket in Wheaton, Maryland (Paul A. Souders/Corbis)

ured into why different ethnic groups clustered into certain occupations, including preimmigration conditions, preimmigration patterns of occupation, family and cultural traditions, levels of education, purpose of immigration, time of arrival in the United States, postimmigration conditions such as language barriers, and the desirability (or undesirability) of a given line of work. For example, "old immigrant" groups from Britain and northern and Western Europe faced fewer barriers in seeking work in a new, sparsely populated nation. Many in these groups became small farmers and entrepreneurs and carried on the artisanal traditions of their families. Among "new immigrant groups," from Jews and Italians to Chinese and Japanese, for whom urban living was more likely to be a given condition, ethnic enclaves within the city could provide sources of employment and community services but limit opportunities by making it possible to avoid learning English and otherwise assimilating into American society. Chinese immigrants famously made the laundry trade their own in part because little English was required, and it provided a valuable service to the general population for what was then backbreaking work. The heavy Eastern European Jewish participation in the needle trades has been attributed to the low overhead required for these trades and to an adherence to the religious prohibition against mixtures of wool and linen: becoming tailors ensured these immigrants that the clothes they wore met religious requirements.

Gender and Immigration

Recent studies of immigration and work have highlighted the role of gender in determining occupational choices. Although gender roles limiting women's primary responsibility to home and family have been widespread, society has made room for variations in the acceptability of women going to work for pay, especially unmarried women. For most of U.S. history, the only acceptable place for married women to work (especially if they had children) was at home, to help support the family. This conditional acceptability has been further influenced by considerations of ethnicity and class. Immigrant families typically gave sons (who had the greatest future earning capacity) priority in educational opportunities, until families reached an economic and social level that made it possible for young women to choose education (or leisure) over work. Additionally, the acceptable purposes of women's work and, more concretely, how much, if any, of her earnings the working daughter was permitted to keep for herself, has varied significantly according to ethnic group and period of history. Finally, circumstances of immigration—namely whether an immigrant arrived alone or as part of a family—often influenced the occupational choices of single immigrant women far more than those of their male counterparts, regardless of marital status.

For example, Irish women frequently immigrated alone and were more likely to seek employment as domestic servants, in large part because of the pay and comparative job security (and ease of finding employment it offered). By comparison, Jewish and Italian women were much less likely to choose domestic work because they were more likely to arrive in the United States with their families. Factors that mitigated against choosing to work as domestic servants ranged from the generally degrading nature of the work to the sense of isolation necessitated by living in the place of employment. Factory work appealed to young immigrant women of many backgrounds because at the end of the day, the factory worker had comparative freedom of movement, despite the job's low pay (sometimes less than domestic work), long hours, and often terrible working conditions. Regardless of choice of work, however, if immigrant daughters lived with their families, a near-universal expectation was that they would turn over their pay envelopes to their parents without so much as opening them. In practice, however, as work increasingly became a matter of personal independence and especially as immigrant Jewish women became more Americanized, daughters became increasingly likely to keep part of their earnings, even over parental objections.

By contrast, for much of U.S. history, married women, whether immigrant or native-born, almost never worked outside the home. Working from within the home, however, gained an acceptability born as much of economic necessity as cultural tradition. For example, immigrant women who came from rural peasant backgrounds would have previously contributed to their household economies in the form of production of goods; so for them, home-based work for cash wages became an acceptable practice. Common options included doing "homework" for manufacturers, keeping boarders, and working in family-owned small businesses. These women tended to assimilate less quickly because of the lack of interaction that work outside the home provided. Even then, especially from the late nineteenth century onward, some immigrant wives had no choice but to go out to work, leaving their older children to care for younger siblings.

For men and women alike, ethnicity has affected levels and types of militancy and protest against work conditions. Gender has been significant in this area too, not the least because of gender stereotypes and expectations. Aside from the assumed greater docility of immigrant women, because women generally expected and were expected to work for only a few years at the most before marrying, they were considered more likely to endure substandard pay and working conditions, rather than fight to improve jobs in which they had no permanent investment. Union organizers, therefore, were more likely to dismiss women workers as unorganizable, and employers hired them in place of men (at lower wages) for the same reason. Although many immigrant women fulfilled these low expectations, many more went on to play important roles as labor activists, though few were permitted by the union hierarchies to assume formalized roles of leadership, except of all-women locals and actions.

For immigrant workers of both sexes, organized labor played an important but at times frustrating role in the assimilation and Americanization of their workers. Employers hired the newest, most vulnerable groups of immigrants for their tractability in the workplace and took pains to keep them this way. They appealed to immigrants' desire to fit in with American society by presenting unions as un-American and labor activism as the province of foreign agitators. They mixed ethnic groups to hinder worker solidarity. Unions did not always welcome immigrants to their ranks. This reluctance can be attributed to the simple prejudice of members or leaders, the desire to distinguish themselves as "American" by excluding foreigners, or the pragmatic effort to protect their hard-won gains by limiting the labor supply (and therefore job competition). This mix of prejudice and pragmatism was especially endemic to the first, craft-based unions.

Two labor organizations most committed to inclusive organizing, the Knights of Labor (KOL) and the Industrial Workers of the World (IWW), also proved to have the least ability to endure in the U.S. labor movement (Breitzer 2002). Yet immigrants themselves formed unions and protective associations, most notably the Jewish- and Italian-led clothing unions, which strove to be inclusive (based on class consciousness) by forming locals organized by language or ethnic group. As the decades passed, these unions then became vehicles for Americanization, offering classes, recreational activities, and other support services that helped ease the adjustment to life and work in the United States. The success in organizing immigrants turned the notion of "foreign" unionism on its head by appealing to immigrant beliefs in the promise of U.S. democracy, justice, and equality.

Immigration Trends in History

In early America, the issue of work and immigration was comparatively unproblematic, at least among white immigrants, and during this period immigration was essentially open and unrestricted. Most immigrants from the prerevolutionary period through the early republic started as farmers, craftspeople, or shopkeepers, and class distinctions at the time were still fairly fluid. Englishmen and -women who could not afford the ship's passage often came to America as indentured servants, working off the price for a few years after arrival. During this early period, Africans began arriving, far less voluntarily. Although initially it was possible for black as well as white servants to work for their freedom, by the early nineteenth century, the African immigrant experience was one of forced immigration as part of the North American slave trade.

As long as the American population remained relatively small and homogeneous and the frontier open, immigration was not regarded as a threat to American society in terms of competition for scarce employment or resources. As early as the 1850s, however, the rise of industry and the arrival of newer (and larger) groups of immigrants began to seriously alter the picture and make the question of how immigration affected work (and society as a whole, for that matter) much more pertinent. German immigrants, both Jewish and non-Jewish, became identified with peddling and small commerce across the expanding country, although it was German Jews who bore the brunt of the money-grubbing peddler stereotype. Irish immigrants filled the ranks (and fueled the stereotypes) of common laborers and housemaids. In industries such as the New England textile mills, as concern for profits increasingly displaced paternalism, the predominant composition of the workforce correspondingly changed, in this instance from Anglo-American to Irish to French Canadian, in addition to becoming increasingly diverse and less "American."

The 1870s was still an era of economic growth and an age of confidence. Full-blown xenophobia, whether on the part of labor or management, was comparatively uncommon. In fact, prior to the Civil War, U.S. business owners large and small regarded immigrants as an economic boon, and their attitude led to the passage of the Contract Labor Law of 1864, which allowed employers to pay the passage of employees they had hired from abroad. Furthermore, before the Civil War, slavery was a far more contentious issue in the labor market, overshadowing virtually all others. During the Civil War, 500,000 immigrants fought, mostly (though not entirely) on the Union side, both as part of the regular army and in separate companies (Higham 1984, 12–13). Following the Civil War, immigration and the work issues affected by it underwent further shifts. At first, the post–Civil War westward expansion made the nation even more hospitable to increasing immigration, especially in the more sparsely populated West and South. The South, struggling to rebuild its economy following the Civil War, especially sought immigrants to take the place of newly freed slave labor. Still, most immigration was concentrated mainly in the northern urban centers.

If economic and physical expansion provided a conducive environment for immigration, economic contraction, beginning with the panic of 1873 and the closing of the western frontier, proved capable of increasingly turning Americans against immigration, especially as immigration began to swell and diversify by the 1880s. It should be noted, however, that sentiment regarding immigration during this period was far from a simple matter of big business favoring it and labor opposing it. By the early 1880s, U.S.-born workers understandably viewed laborers imported to work for less as a threat to their own conditions. This fear and loathing was expressed in a number of ways, ranging from petty harassment and even violence against immigrant workers, such as that perpetrated by the Pennsylvania coal miners against Slavic and Italian immigrants brought in as strikebreakers by the mining companies, to congressional legislation restricting immigrant labor eligibility.

Some of the latter activities, such as the support of legislation prohibiting Chinese immigrants from certain occupations or the American Federation of Labor's (AFL's) general anti-Oriental tone and its support of the Chinese Exclusion Act of 1882 was motivated as much by xenophobia and even racism as much as concern over job competition (Breitzer 2002). In most cases, U.S. workers of this period, increasingly of immigrant background themselves, and U.S. labor organizations were not so much opposed to *immigration* in itself as to immigrants brought in for contract labor, whom they regarded as beholden to or even enslaved by their employers. Even Samuel Gompers, later noted for his anti-immigrant sentiment, argued that voluntary immigration was not the problem. This distinction, especially promoted by the KOL, led to a new Contract Labor Law, passed in 1885, forbidding employers to pay for the transportation of workers hired abroad.

During this period, unions also became increasingly composed of immigrants and furthermore increasingly embraced the idea of international worker solidarity. As even the supposedly docile contract labor immigrants proved their potential for militancy when pushed, the positions of labor and management regarding immigration underwent a gradual but significant shift. As the nineteenth century drew to a close and immigrants from diverse backgrounds went from the exploitable "huddled masses" to an important part of an increasingly militant labor movement, fear and loathing of foreign radicalism and the labor disruption it presumably could inspire caused many industrialists to significantly revise their views of immigrants and immigration. This fear was further stoked by incidents such as the Haymarket Square Incident in 1886, in which German-born anarchists were blamed for a bomb explosion that occurred at the conclusion of what had begun as a peaceful meeting in Chicago's Haymarket Square. Notably, exceptions to the rising anti-immigrant settlement on the part of industrialists came from the South, fitting in with the desire to build the "New South" in part by increasing the white population as well as building industry. Furthermore, during this period, anti-immigrant sentiment from whatever source (with the exception of anti-Orientalism) was about opposing immigration in general, rarely singling out particular groups.

The situation worsened by the 1890s, however, as the rapid influx of immigration (and by 1896 a corresponding decline in "old immigration" from the British Isles and northern and Western Europe) ran up against the increased hardening of class divisions in American society. The depression of 1893 darkened the American mood and fueled the need for scapegoats. Even the South by this time was shifting its singularly favorable stance on immigration. Labor and capital alike began to favor immigration restrictions, with labor no longer distinguishing between voluntary and employer-induced immigration (because employees could simply recruit workers abroad without paying for transportation) and business seeing the new hordes of immigrants less as potential employees and more as unemployed (and unemployable) potential troublemakers. In 1892, the KOL publicly supported immigration restrictions. The AFL, historically regarded as the more conservative, exclusive body, in fact held out longer, not officially endorsing immigration restriction until 1896, although many of its leaders (including Samuel Gompers) and constituent unions were speaking out in favor of it much earlier. At the same time, states, at the behest of their citizens, were increasingly passing laws prohibiting employment of all aliens in public works, whereas previously only immigrants who had not declared their intentions to become citizens were restricted. Labor also participated in promoting more specific limitations on immigrants, such as literacy tests.

The debate over immigration and its effect on work in the United States continued to wax and wane through the turn of the twentieth century and was further affected by the economic upturn after 1896, the rise of the Progressive movement, and the efforts of immigrants themselves to fight back against the discrimination of literacy tests and other restrictions. At the same time, the rate of immigration soared and stood at an annual average of

650,000 between 1907 and the onset of World War I (Higham 1984, 159). As the debate raged, immigrants increasingly filled the ranks of the U.S. industrial workforce, which became more and more open to them as increased mechanization lessened the demand for skilled labor in major U.S. industries. As new immigrants filled the ranks of unskilled labor, however, more acculturated immigrants and their children, especially Jewish and Italian immigrants faced de facto and sometimes even legal discrimination as they attempted to move into the ranks of white-collar and professional work. Furthermore, although the problems of immigration and job competition were concentrated in the northern cities, these problems were also found on the Pacific Coast between European and Asian immigrants and in the South between African Americans and the increasing number of Italian immigrants.

As the craft union constituency of the AFL became increasingly native-born, immigrant workers became a part the growing unionization efforts among unskilled workers in industries ranging from mining to textiles. Immigrants also played an important role in the rise of labor activism (and accompanying political radicalism) in the early decades of the twentieth century. The garment trades provided the most visible example of labor unrest. In New York City alone, thousands of immigrant garment workers struck in what became known as the "Great Uprising" and the following year the "Great Revolt," winning increasing union recognition in the men's and women's garment trades. But the plight of the immigrant worker in the clothing sweatshops was brought to more general public recognition by the Triangle Shirtwaist Factory fire in 1911, in which over 100 Jewish and Italian immigrant workers died, most of them young women. Beyond the garment trades, the 1912 textile workers' strike in Lawrence, Massachusetts, popularly known as the "Bread and Roses" strike, brought together 20,000 working men and women of nationalities ranging from French Canadian to Portuguese (Cahn 1977, 9).

The arrival of World War I had several important effects on work and immigration in the United States. The sheer number of immigrants dropped as a result of wartime conditions in Europe and the increased hazards of sea travel posed by newly introduced submarine warfare. An economic downturn that coincided with the war increased competition for even the lowliest jobs between immigrant and native-born workers, spurring further pushes for literacy tests and immigration restrictions. Also, well before U.S. entry into the war, a new prejudice against "hyphenated Americanism" arose and especially targeted German Americans, at the time the most numerous and generally prosperous segment of the U.S. immigrant population. Even before the October Revolution of 1917 in Russia, fear of foreign radicals stoked by the strikes and antiwar activities of the IWW had a dampening effect on labor activism, which was further held in check in key industries by war labor boards. Yet at the same time that business boomed and immigration declined, employers such as Henry Ford sought to Americanize foreign-born workers, sponsoring classes and other programs for them, which in turn was part of the growing practice of "welfare capitalism" in which employers sought to discourage unionism by cultivating worker loyalty.

Finally, proponents of restriction continued to lobby Congress against the day when war would no longer provide an automatic check on immigration. A 1917 law permitted the Department of Labor (DOL), which then contained the Bureau of Immigration, to deport aliens for radical activity, regardless of length of residence. Then the end of the war brought a new outburst of labor unrest across U.S. industry from garment trades to steel, with significant immigrant participation. The resulting red scare of 1919 brought about the Palmer Raids against subversive organizations and contributed to the decline in labor activism in favor of postwar "labor peace." At the same time, a postwar economic downturn decreased enthusiasm for Americanizing immigrants and helped provide the final push toward restriction. As early as 1918, the AFL advocated a two-year moratorium on immigration, now for nationalist as well as economic reasons. The postwar resurgence of immigration (and an increasingly literate group of immigrants) rendered literacy tests largely ineffective as a deterrent. Then in 1921, a new immigration bill, created by Senator William Dillingham of Vermont, imposed the first-ever legal limitations on European immigration (migration of labor from Canada and Latin America was unaffected, but Asian immigration was completely restricted).

The new quota law was at first enforced with difficulty and was initially contested by big business, especially as returning prosperity once again tightened the labor market. What finally led industrialists to abandon their promotion of immigration to gain cheap labor was the increased use of something even cheaper—automation. As a result, Congress was able to press ahead with the passage of the Johnson-Reed Act, which became law in 1924. This new bill limited European immigration to 2 percent of the foreign-born population counted in the 1890 census (after 1927, quotas were distributed by national origin) and completely barred Asian immigration. Shortly after the passage of the Johnson-Reed Act, Congress established the U.S. Border Patrol to deter the illegal immigration that dramatically rose in the wake of restrictions on legal immigration.

The Johnson-Reed Act achieved the desired results of severely reducing immigration from southern and Eastern Europe and reducing immigration in general, owing to the sparse immigration from the northern and Western European countries favored by the quota. The issue of work and immigration therefore subsided. First- and second-generation Americans saw fewer of their fellow compatriots and became increasingly Americanized and less differentiated in the workplace, although discrimination against certain groups, notably Jews and immigrants of color, remained. Immigration and work did not become a national issue again until the rise to power of the Nazi regime in Germany caused many Jews to attempt to seek asylum in the United States, only to be barred by the 1924 quotas (which the State Department enforced so strictly that some went unfilled). Despite efforts to lower the barriers to allow at least temporary refuge, a common argument that helped opposition to these efforts prevail was that these immigrants could take U.S. jobs (at the same time, those few who were admitted had to provide proof that they would not become public charges). Those who were admitted, furthermore, predominantly educated German Jews, were forced to seek employment well below their qualifications. Yet as immigration from Europe was restricted for this reason, the U.S. government began unofficially bringing in guest workers from Mexico to take the place of U.S. agricultural workers who had gone to war.

In the years following World War II, special bills were passed to address humanitarian postwar needs, such as the War Brides Act of 1945 and the Displaced Persons Act of 1948, and these efforts continued into the Cold War, with measures such as the Hungarian Refugee Act of 1956. General immigration policy, however, was slower to change and was merely recodified with the Immigration and Nationality Act of 1952. In 1951, however, the U.S. government made the unofficial Mexican guest worker program fully legal as the bracero program. It was not until 1965 that the national origins system was legally scrapped and replaced with a system that gave priority to both reunifying families and bringing skilled workers to the United States (in fact, scientific or cultural contribution to the United States became a new category of preference). By this time, the sources of immigration had largely shifted from Europe to Latin America and Asia.

Since the 1960s, the issues surrounding work and immigration have both dramatically changed and remained remarkably similar. Immigrants, increasingly of color, were both welcomed for their contributions to the U.S. economy during flush times and scapegoated during economic downturns. Illegal immigrants in particular were victimized by unscrupulous employers and unable to speak out for fear of deportation. However, as the 1960s progressed and the civil rights movement became a driving force in American society, the attitude of organized labor toward immigration made a slow but significant shift. One important event that changed the relationship between immigration and organized labor was the rise of the United Farm Workers (UFW) in the 1960s. Although the bracero program stipulated that no guest agricultural worker could replace a domestic worker, in practice many California growers who benefited from the bracero program did just that, to the detriment of the predominantly Latino and Filipino domestic agricultural workers. Early efforts of domestic farmworkers to organize in the 1940s and 1950s had suffered defeat through the growers' use of bracero scab labor. Then, in the 1960s, the charismatic Cesar Chavez succeeded in building the United Farmworkers Movement from the Community Service Organization (CSO), a Latino movement designed to eliminate the exploitation of migrant farmworkers (Breitzer 2002) and that helped bring about the end of the bracero program in 1964.

In the decades since the rise of the UFW, public perception of the problem of work and immigration, especially work and illegal immigration, has increasingly shifted the blame from immigrants themselves to employers, and the law has followed accordingly. For example, in 1986, the Immigration Reform and Control Act made the Immigration and Naturalization Service responsible for investigating and prosecuting employers who employed undocumented aliens. Although under the new law working illegal aliens were still routinely deported, some were permitted to obtain legal residence. Still, the use and abuse of illegal immigrants by employers continues, including the return of sweatshops. But by the end of the twentieth century, organized labor had shifted its position in regard to immigrants and immigration, with the American Federation of Labor and Congress of Industrial Organizations electing its first Latina vice president in 1994 (Breitzer 2002), and its recent stepped-up drive to organize the unorganized is increasingly conducted with the recognition and even celebration of the diversity of the U.S. workforce. Most recently, the U.S. labor movement has supported laws that would grant amnesty to undocumented workers and prohibit employers for threatening these workers with deportation when they try to organize.

Susan Roth Breitzer

See also Agricultural Work; American Federation of Labor and Congress of Industrial Organizations; Garment/Textile Industries; Green Cards; Servants and Maids; Sweatshops; Undocumented Workers; United Farm Workers; Work and Hispanic Americans

References and further reading

Barrett, James. 1982. "Americanization from the Bottom up: Immigration and the Remaking of the Working Class in the United States, 1880–1930." *Journal of American History* 79 (December): 996–1020.

Bodnar, John. 1985. *The Transplanted: A History of Immigrants in Urban America.* Bloomington: Indiana University Press.

Breitzer, Susan Roth. 2002. "Discrimination: Race." In *Dictionary of American History.* 3rd ed. Edited by Stanley L. Kutler. New York: Charles Scribner's Sons.

Cohen, Lizabeth. 1990. *Making a New Deal: Industrial Workers in Chicago, 1919–1939.* Cambridge: Cambridge University Press.

d'A. Jones, Peter, and Melvin G. Holli, eds. 1981. *Ethnic Chicago.* Grand Rapids: William B. Eerdmans.

Diner, Hasia. 1983. *Erin's Daughters in America: Irish Immigrant Women in the Nineteenth Century.* Baltimore: Johns Hopkins University Press.

Ewen, Elizabeth. 1985. *Immigrant Women in the Land of Dollars: Life and Culture on the Lower East Side, 1890–1925.* New York: Monthly Review Press.

Handlin, Oscar. 1951. *The Uprooted: The Epic Story of the Great Migrations That Made the American People.* New York: Grossett and Dunlap.

Higham, John. 1984. *Send These to Me: Immigrants in Urban America.* Rev. ed. Baltimore: Johns Hopkins University Press.

Keil, Hartmut, and John B. Jentz, eds. 1983. *German Workers in Industrial Chicago, 1850–1910.* DeKalb: Northern Illinois University Press.

Kossak, Hadassa. 1994. *Strangers in the Land: Patterns of American Nativism, 1860–1925.* New Brunswick, NJ: Rutgers University Press.

———. 2000. *Cultures of Opposition: Jewish Immigrant Workers, New York City, 1881–1905.* Albany: State University of New York Press.

McCaffrey, Lawrence J., Ellen Skerrett, Michael F. Funchion, and Charles Fanning. 1987. *The Irish in Chicago.* Urbana: University of Illinois Press.

Nelli, Humbert S. 1970. *Italians in Chicago, 1880–1930: A Study in Ethnic Mobility.* New York: Oxford University Press.

Saxton, Alexander. 1971. *The Indispensable Enemy: Labor and the Anti-Chinese Movement.* Berkeley: University of California Press.

United Farm Workers. 2002. "UFW History: The Rise of the UFW." http://www.ufw.org/ufw.htm (cited January 29, 2002).

U.S. Department of Justice, Immigration and Naturalization Service. 2002. "Overview of INS History." http://www.ins.usdoj.gov/graphics/aboutins/history/articles/OVIEW.htm (cited January 30, 2002).

Van Reenan, Antanas J. 1990. *Lithuanian Diaspora; Konigsberg to Chicago.* Lanham, MD: University Press of America.

Immigration Reform and Control Act (IRCA) (1986)

The Immigration Reform and Control Act of 1986 (IRCA) established sanctions for employers who knowingly hire undocumented workers. IRCA's purpose was to limit and control the number of illegal immigrants in the United States. The employer sanctions strove to reduce the demand for illegal immigrants among employers. To lower the number of illegal immigrants residing in the country, the law also included an amnesty program. Protections against employment discrimination that might result from employer sanctions and a temporary worker program were also included.

The passage of IRCA was a fifteen-year process, beginning with a series of hearings about illegal immigration in 1971. Political pressure for these hearings grew from concerns that undocumented migrants take jobs from U.S. citizens, drive wages down, and use social services without paying taxes, though empirical studies about these concerns varied widely in their conclusions. Others expressed worries over an "underclass" of easily exploited undocumented immigrants during this debate.

The hearings were also a response to the consequences of the Immigration Act of 1965. This law had lifted historical bans on immigration against citizens of countries in the Southern and Eastern Hemispheres. The 1965 law shifted the focus of U.S. immigration policy to family reunification, allowing larger numbers of immigrants to enter the country. Some theorists suggest that xenophobic responses to these increases in legal, non-European immigrants, particularly Asians and Latinos, were played out in the increased concerns over illegal immigration that led to IRCA (Hayes 2001).

Although there was little agreement on the number of illegal immigrants in the United States during the 1970s, the press and politicians began to insist that large numbers of undocumented immigrants were in the country. Much of the debate was fueled by Mexicans illegally crossing the southern border to work in the Southwest, Texas, and California. Illegal crossings had increased after the abolition of the bracero program in 1964, which had allowed Mexicans to legally enter the United States as temporary workers.

In 1978 the Select Commission on Immigration and Refugee Policy was created to study the effects of undocumented migration to the United States. The commission's 1981 report laid the groundwork for the final provisions of IRCA, recommending employer sanctions, a temporary worker program, and amnesty for current undocumented immigrants.

IRCA was finally passed in 1986. Under IRCA, any employer of four or more employees must certify that all new hires are legally allowed to work in the United States. This requirement led to the creation of the I-9 form that all workers must complete when starting a job. It requires a combination of identification materials to prove eligibility for employment. Forms of identification include passports, driver's licenses, Social Security cards, voter registration cards, and various Immigration and Naturalization Service (INS) documents, such as an alien registration card (better known as a green card). Employers that knowingly hire unauthorized workers are subject to civil and criminal liability, including monetary fines and possible jail time. There is no process for employers to verify the validity of identification, and employers are not liable if employees use falsified or stolen documents to attain eligibility.

In response to concerns at the time of IRCA's passage that employer sanctions would lead to discrimination against legal workers who are foreign-born or have an accent, IRCA contains provisions against discrimination. Employers cannot require any certain combination of documents or prefer certain documents for the I-9. Employers cannot require that job applicants or employees are U.S. citizens. IRCA directed the General Accounting Office (GAO) to conduct audits of discrimination related to the employer sanctions program. The law authorizes the termination of employer sanctions, should the GAO find evidence of widespread discrimination. In March 1990, the GAO found that discrimination was occurring as a result of IRCA's requirements. However, since the discrimination was not "widespread," the employer sanctions remained in effect. Recent studies continue to find evidence of discrimination based on country of origin, including significant negative earnings effects on Latino workers in the short term (Bansak and Raphael 2001).

Under IRCA's general amnesty, any undocumented immigrant who arrived in the United States prior to January 1, 1982, and could prove continuous residency for at least five years could become a legal immigrant. Those eligible could apply for legalization from May 1987 to May 1988. In 1981, the Select Commission on Immigration and Refugee Policy had recommended that any amnesty provision contain a recent arrival date, since failing to do so would mean a substantial number of recent immigrants would remain undocumented. However, political pressures led to the requirement that only those who had resided in the United States for five years were eligible. This requirement may have caused fewer immigrants to request amnesty because illegal immigrants may have had difficulty proving continuous residence. Some immigrants' families included ineligible members who arrived more recently, and those who were eligible may have been reluctant to expose them by applying for amnesty (Hayes 2001, 68). According to a 1990 analysis of IRCA, 1.7 million people were legalized through the general amnesty program, which is approximately two-thirds of those who would have been eligible, based on estimates of the undocumented immigrant population at the time (Passel and Woodrow 1990, 66).

Many employers, particularly agricultural employers, opposed passage of IRCA and its predecessor bills because they stood to lose a major labor pool. To obtain final passage of the bill, a compromise was created by then Congressman Charles Schumer (D-NY), creating a temporary worker program known as the special agricultural workers (SAW) program. Any undocumented immigrants who had worked for ninety days or more in agriculture between May 1985 and May 1986 were eligible to receive temporary residency in the United States and later become permanent resident aliens. Some 1.2 million undocumented immigrants were legalized under the SAW program, rivaling the number legalized through the general amnesty provision of IRCA (Portes and Rumbaut 1996, 279).

IRCA also included a visa lottery for 10,000 visas for countries negatively impacted by the 1965 immigration law. This lottery was later expanded in 1988 and continues to allow immigrants from underrepresented countries a possible opportunity for permanent residency.

Although researchers and policy analysts still have difficulty measuring the number of illegal immigrants currently residing in the United States, it is generally agreed that significant illegal immigration continues, despite IRCA's attempts to lessen undocumented immigration. IRCA's employer sanction provisions remain in effect, but some argue their impact is seriously weakened by the use of forged or stolen documents and enforcement difficulties.

Ariana Funaro

See also Green Cards; Immigrants and Work; Undocumented Workers

References and further reading

Bansak, Cynthia, and Steven Raphael. 2001. "Immigration Reform and the Earnings of Latino Workers: Do Employer Sanctions Cause Discrimination?" *Industrial and Labor Relations Review* 54, no. 2: 275–296.

Bean, Frank, Barry Edmonston, and Jeffrey S. Passel, eds. 1990. *Undocumented Migration to the United States: IRCA and the Experience of the 1980s.* Washington, DC: Urban Institute.

Government Accounting Office. 1990. *Immigration Reform: Employer Sanctions and the Question of Discrimination.* Washington, DC: Government Printing Office.

Hayes, Helen. 2001. *U.S. Immigration Policy and the Undocumented: Ambivalent Laws, Furtive Lives.* Westport, CT: Praeger.

Meissner, Doris M., and Demetrious G. Papdemetriou. 1986. *The Legalization of Undocumented Aliens: A Third Quarter Assessment.* Washington, DC: Carnegie Endowment for International Peace.

North, D. M., and Alejandro Portes. 1988. *Through the Maze: An Interim Report on the Alien Legalization Program.* Washington, DC: Trans Century Development Associates.

Passel, Jeffrey S., and Karen A. Woodrow. 1990. "Post-IRCA Undocumented Migration to the United States: An Assessment Based on the June 1988 CPS." Pp. 33–72 in *Undocumented Migration to the United States: IRCA and the Experience of the 1980s.* Edited by Frank Bean, Barry Edmonston, and Jeffrey S. Passel. Washington, DC: Urban Institute.

Portes, Alejandro, and Ruben G. Rumbaut. 1996. *Immigrant America: A Portrait.* Berkeley: University of California Press.

Reimers, David M. 1985, 1992. *Still the Golden Door: The Third World Comes to America.* New York: Columbia Press.

Industrial Engineering

Industrial engineering is an integrated approach to identifying the resources that will create the greatest possible outcome or product. A number of different definitions exist for industrial engineering. The following definition has been developed by the Institute of Industrial Engineers: "Industrial engineering is concerned with the design, improvement and installation of integrated systems of people, material, information, equipment and energy. It draws upon specialized knowledge and skills in the mathematical, physical, and social sciences, together with the principles and methods of engineering analysis and design to specify, predict and evaluate the results to be obtained from such systems" (Institute of Industrial Engineers 2002).

Frederick Winslow Taylor (1856–1915), known as the father of industrial engineering, fostered a movement toward the increased application of scientific methods in the production process in his work, *The Principles of Scientific Management* (1911). For example, Taylor applied stopwatch time studies on workers and advocated the use of a differential piece rate system, whereby faster workers earn greater compensation than do slower workers. Taylor was an active promoter of scientific management, but not until the onset of World War I were the principles of scientific management widely applied in the United States, as industries sought to enhance their production capacity for the war effort.

Although much of the foundation of industrial engineering is attributed to Taylor, numerous other individuals were involved in its development. For example, Frank and Lillian Gilbreth examined the human components of production and contributed greatly to motion studies—analyses undertaken to eliminate wasteful movements in the production process. Statistician Walter Shewhart introduced the control chart, which plots performance data across time. The work of another statistician, William Edwards Deming (who was a student of Shewhart), emphasized the enhancement of product quality and an understanding of production systems.

A primary goal of industrial engineering is to maximize worker productivity. Although this goal has obvious benefits that are realized through increased profits, critics argue that the methods developed through industrial engineering dehumanize labor. Industrial engineering analyses, such as wage and salary administration systems and job evaluation programs, scrutinize the behavior and abilities of workers. Again, although such assessments help identify the best utilization of resources, they may also be seen as a hostile threat to the job security and earnings potential of workers. Opponents argue that by specifying the pace and process of the worker, industrial engineering has eliminated the individualism of the worker. In addition, labor interests are fearful of industrial engineering because they suspect the discipline seeks to identify ways to substitute capital for labor, as advances in machinery and technology progress. Doing so, they claim, results in the demoralization and heightening vulnerability of the working class.

Although much of the analysis of industrial engineering on the worker centers on the negative impacts, industrial engineering is also credited with increasing worker satisfaction. For example, it was Taylor who promoted the provision of break times for workers. Although some industrial engineering approaches use techniques such as a quota system (generally viewed with dread by workers), others explicitly recommend against it. Some parts of industrial engineering stress the importance of on-the-job training and others on increasing workforce morale. Though the bottom line for industrial engineers is enhanced productivity, a wide variety of techniques exist, some of which may enhance worker satisfaction and others may not.

According to the U.S. Bureau of Labor Statistics, there were about 198,000 industrial engineers (including health and safety) in the year 2000. Although the majority of these professionals are employed in the manufacturing industry, industrial engineers may work in other areas, including engineering and management services, utilities, business services, and government agencies. The Bureau of Labor Statistics predicts that, through 2010, overall employment of industrial engineers will grow more slowly than the average for all occupations, but a strong need is expected in both the manufacturing industry and in the financial services sector. In 2000, the median earnings of industrial engineers were $58,580 (Bureau of Labor Statistics 2003, 112). The Institute of Industrial Engineers is the largest trade organization for this occupational group, representing more than 17,000 members and 150 chapters worldwide

Sarah B. Gyarfas

See also Deming, W. Edwards; Postindustrial Workforce; Taylor, Frederick Winslow; Total Quality Management

References and further reading

Bureau of Labor Statistics. 2003. *Occupational Outlook Handbook, 2002–2003.* http://www.bls.gov/oco (cited October 1, 2002).

Institute of Industrial Engineers. 2002. "About IIE." http://www.iienet.org (cited October 1, 2002).

Kanigel, Robert. 1997. *The One Best Way: Frederick Winslow Taylor and the Enigma of Efficiency.* New York: Viking.

Salvendy, Gabriel, ed. 2001. *Handbook of Industrial Engineering: Technology and Operations Management.* 3rd ed. New York: Wiley.

Shenhav, Yehouda. 1999. *Manufacturing Rationality: The Engineering Foundations of the Managerial Revolution.* New York: Oxford University Press.

Spender, J. C., and Hugo Kijne, eds. 1996. *Scientific Management: Frederick Winslow Taylor's Gift to the World?* Norwell, MA: Kluwer Academic Publishers.

Taylor, Frederick Winslow. 1911. *The Principles of Scientific Management.* New York/London: Harper and Brothers.

Industrial Psychology

Industrial psychology uses methods and concepts from psychology to study workers and their interactions with their work, work environment, and employers. The field of industrial psychology first emerged in the early twentieth century as one of many responses to the challenges of managing workers in large, hierarchical industrial organizations. The earliest advocates of industrial psychology, led by Harvard University psychologist Hugo Munsterburg (1863–1916), emphasized the importance of finding new ways to fit individuals into their proper place in the industrial hierarchy. If the "fit" between the worker and his or her job was wrong, they warned, the outcome would be inefficiency and possibly even industrial unrest. During World War I, industrial psychologists pioneered the use of job classification and job-specific skills testing to assign army recruits to units and positions in the armed forces, winning respect for the new field and greater opportunities to apply their tests in industry. Industrial psychologists also drew attention to the importance of noneconomic motives for work and, in popular as well as scholarly writing, called on employers to appeal to these motives. In the 1930s and 1940s, psychologists working with other social scientists developed human relations, a new approach to managing workers that emphasized the importance of social relationships as a factor influencing worker behavior. The rise of human relations launched a new branch of psychology, organizational psychology. Today, industrial psychology continues to be centrally concerned with the relationship between the individual and his or her job, whereas organizational psychology focuses on the social relations in the workplace.

In 1913, Hugo Munsterburg published *Psychology and Industrial Efficiency,* arguing that psychologists could help workers choose the "best possible man" for each position and elicit the "best possible work" from each employee (Munsterburg 1913, 169). He drew on ideas from the vocational guidance movement as well as scientific management. In the late nineteenth century, advocates of vocational guidance were the first to argue for the importance of using expertise to fit individuals to their jobs, an idea that would later become central to industrial psychology. These men and women believed that, in the newly industrialized world of work, it was difficult for young people to find their calling. They drew on the tenets of social Darwinism, which emphasized the significance of individual difference and the importance of fitting each individual into the right place in a social or, in this case, employment hierarchy (Jacoby 1985, 78). This idea that employment hierarchies conformed to natural hierarchies of talent found further expression in the movement for scientific management. In his classic 1911 work, *The Principles of Scientific Management,* Frederick W. Taylor argued that some men were well suited to menial tasks, but others were not. He identified the "scientific selection of the workman and then his progressive development" as the second principle of scientific management (Taylor 1911, 44–47). Munsterburg claimed that experimental psychology could develop mental tests to aid in hiring and placing workers (Hale 1980, 123). This emphasis on mental testing to determine job placement continued as a central component of industrial psychology through the 1930s.

When mapping the future of the field of industrial psychology, Munsterburg imagined that industrial psychologists would assist industry not only in choosing the best possible worker but also in eliciting the "best possible work" (Munsterburg 1913, 169). Again, Munsterburg and his followers linked industrial psychology to scientific management, a management fad in the 1910s and 1920s. Advocates of industrial psychology pointed out that Taylor's system of closely managing workers contributed to worker unrest. Taylor's system, they argued, would work only if managers paid greater attention to the "human element" and worker psychology (Noble 1977, 297). In the 1920s, for example, some industrial psychologists drew on "instinct psychology" to argue that all workers had basic emotional needs and desires and that workers were more productive when these needs and desires were satisfied (Bendix 1963, 290). Walter Dill Scott, a psychologist at Northwestern University, called on psychologists to aid employers in their efforts to motivate workers and was the first to identify "attitudes" as crucial to worker motivation (Scott 1911, 135–136).

Industrial psychology received a boost during World War I, when several psychologists were recognized for their service to the armed forces. Robert M. Yerkes, an assistant professor of psychology at Yale University, developed and administered intelligence tests to U.S. Army recruits, sparking nationwide interest in intelligence testing. At the same time, Walter Dill Scott led the Army Committee on Classification, a group that developed a system for classifying jobs according to the required skills and for surveying and testing recruits to place them into jobs. Scott's focus on job classification, job placement surveys, and job-specific testing would ultimately have a more lasting impact on the field of industrial psychology than Yerkes's work on intelligence testing (Von Mayrhauser 1989, 60–72).

In the 1930s and 1940s, industrial psychologists began experimenting with new approaches to managing the "human element" at work. Testing had not delivered industrial peace, and fitting the worker to the right job did not seem pressing for industries hiring large numbers of semiskilled workers (Baritz 1960, 67–69). Industrial psychologists were looking for other avenues for applying psychology to the workplace. Specifically, they began borrowing from sociology and anthropology to consider the importance of social interactions at work. By the 1950s, the new field of "human relations" dominated academic and business discourse on how to manage workers (Gillespie 1991, 210). The new experts in the field of human relations were more likely to invoke organizational psychology than industrial psychology, emphasizing their interest in the web of social relations in the workplace. Organizational psychologists used tools from psychology, like surveys and interviews, to gather information about employee attitudes and social aspects of the work environment. Industrial psychology did not disappear, however, and students of business and psychology today are likely to take a class in industrial/organizational psychology (I/O).

Critics and advocates of industrial psychology agree that this field contributed to important changes in the way employers and others perceived the modern workplace (Jacques 1996, 141). Critics charge that industrial psychology provided employers with a politically expedient means of dismissing workers' concerns by assuming all problems were psychological in nature and that a better adjustment between the worker and his or her work would solve the problem (Bendix 1963, 288–297; Noble 1977, 317). Even so, industrial psychologists also played an important role in highlighting the importance of noneconomic incentives for work.

Today, I/O psychologists provide research and theory that underpins the practice of personnel management, also called human resource management. I/O psychologists publish on issues including job design, job training, performance assessment, teamwork, leadership, stress management, and diversity in the workplace. Earlier generations of I/O psychologists valued stability in employment relations, focusing on techniques for boosting employee loyalty to organizations. Faced with trends like downsizing and temporary work, I/O psychologists have had to reevaluate their understanding of the ideal relationship between individuals and organizations. Some I/O psychologists have begun counseling individuals on how to manage careers that span many organizations, and others have begun to carve out a role for themselves as experts who can help organizations deal with change (Kraut and Korman 1999, 148, 275).

Julie Kimmel

See also Taylor, Frederick Winslow

References and further reading

Arnold, John, Gary L. Cooper, and Ivan T. Robertson. 1995. *Work Psychology: Understanding Human Behavior in the Workplace.* London: Pitman Publishing.

Baritz, Loren. 1960. *The Servants of Power: A History of the Use of Social Science in American Industry.* Middletown, CT: Wesleyan University Press.

Bendix, Reinhard. 1963. *Work and Authority in Industry: Ideologies of Management in the Course of Industrialization.* New York: Harper and Row.

Drucker, Peter. 1954. *The Practice of Management.* New York: Harper and Brothers.

Gillespie, Richard. 1991. *Manufacturing Knowledge: A History of the Hawthorne Experiments.* New York: Cambridge University Press.

Hale, Matthew. 1980. *Human Science and Social Order: Hugo Munsterburg and the Origins of Applied Psychology.* Philadelphia: Temple University Press.

Herriot, Peter. 2001. *The Employment Relationship: A Psychological Perspective.* East Essex, PA: Routledge.

Jacoby, Sanford. 1985. *Employing Bureaucracy: Managers, Unions, and the Transformation of Work in American Industry, 1900–1945.* New York: Columbia University Press.

Jacques, Roy. 1996. *Manufacturing the Employee: Management Knowledge from the Nineteenth to the Twenty-first Centuries.* London: Sage Publications.

Kraut, Allen, and Abraham Korman, eds. 1999. *Evolving Practices in Human Resources Management: Responses to a Changing World of Work.* San Francisco: Jossey-Bass.

Munsterburg, Hugo. 1913. *Psychology and Industrial Efficiency.* New York: Houghton Mifflin.

Noble, David F. 1977. *America by Design: Science, Technology, and the Rise of Corporate Capitalism.* New York: Oxford University Press.

Scott, Walter Dill. 1911. *Increasing Human Efficiency: A Contribution to the Psychology of Business.* New York: Macmillan.

Taylor, Frederick W. 1985/1911. *Principles of Scientific Management.* Easton, PA: Hive Publishing.

Von Mayrhauser, Richard T. 1989. "Making Intelligence Functional: Walter Dill Scott and Applied Psychological Testing in World War I." *Journal of the History of Behavioral Sciences* 25: 60–72.

Industrial Revolution and Assembly Line Work

The Industrial Revolution was the transformation of the old methods of creating consumer goods into new ways of production through introduction of new technologies and machines. In simple words, the Industrial Revolution changed the way people produced the goods for their own consumption and the consumption of other people. Before the Industrial Revolution, many families made their own furniture, clothes, and shoes. All these crafts were handmade, and because the process was slow, craftspeople produced very few items. This in turn made these items very expensive. Only people with enough money could afford to buy things they needed from craftspeople.

The situation dramatically changed when new devices and machines started to replace hand labor. With the help of new devices, craftspeople could produce more goods at a lower price. In addition, the development of bigger machines gave rise to factories. Thus from making goods by hand in small shops or homes, people moved to making them in factories and later on assembly lines. These changes made goods more affordable to a greater number of people.

With the introduction of new technologies and machines, workers became more efficient and productive, which in turn resulted in higher profits and the rise of national income per capita as well as changes in the distribution of income. It also affected the living and working conditions of the workers. Technology, organization, and manufacturing were key features of the Industrial Revolution. The Industrial Revolution grew more powerful each year as new inventions and manufacturing processes added to the efficiency of machines and increased productivity.

The Industrial Revolution first began in Great Britain during the eighteenth century and later spread across the Atlantic, reaching the United States by the nineteenth century. Although it began in England, it established what was known by the 1850s as the "American system of manufacturing." Actually, the transformation of the United States into an industrial nation took place largely after the Civil War. This rapid economic change has sometimes been called the New Industrial Revolution. It had a great impact on American society, turning the country from an agrarian to an urban and industrial society.

More importantly, the Industrial Revolution had changed the face of the United States, giving rise to urban centers. Urban growth was about as dramatic as the growth in production. It meant in turn that during the Industrial Revolution, millions of people abandoned a traditional life in the countryside and moved to cities, which created a specialized and interdependent economic life and made an urban worker more dependent on the will of the employer than the rural worker had been. Moreover, industrial cities themselves changed the landscape, with smokestacks becoming the new urban symbol, dominating the countryside. These fundamental changes took place first in agriculture and then spread to manufacturing, transportation, communication, economic policies, and the whole social structure.

The progress of the Industrial Revolution can be divided into four distinct periods. From 1730 to 1770, cotton textiles were the key industry, and all inventions made at this time were designed to increase production in cotton textiles and make the work of producing textiles faster and more efficient. John Kay constructed the flying shuttle for weaving (1733), Richard Arkwright created a water-powered spinning frame (1769), and James Hargreaves thought up the spinning jenny (1764).

All these tools revolutionized not only textile industries but also such industries as manufacturing and transportation. It was also during this time that Watt developed a steam engine that was more efficient and much safer than the engine developed by Thomas Newcomen in 1705. The application of steam to transportation, for instance, led to the development of the railroad system, vastly increasing the amount of goods that could be moved over long distances, as well as the speed and reliability of their transport.

The advancement of the cotton industry continued during the second period of the Industrial Revolution, which lasted from 1770 to 1792. During this time, the earlier mechanical tools were modernized, and new devices were introduced. A spinning mule was constructed by Samuel Crompton in 1779, and later in 1785, Edmund Cartwright came up with the power loom. The major problem that further industrialization faced at this time was the limitation on location of textiles industries. Factories had to be located by water because of the need to use water wheels to drive the machinery. That problem was solved by several innovations that were developed during the next part of the Industrial Revolution.

During the period 1792–1830, more innovations were put to use in the textile and other industries. Steam power, Eli Whitney's cotton gin, Samuel Herrick's dressing machine, and the throttle made production more efficient. In the early nineteenth century, Eli Whitney, subsidized by the U.S. government, perfected the precision measuring and machining techniques required to create weapons with interchangeable parts. In 1798, Whitney had secured a U.S. government contract (for $134,000) to produce 10,000 army muskets. Whitney refined and successfully applied the "uniformity system" of production, using interchangeable parts. However, he failed to convince army bureaucrats, who delayed implementing his ideas. He overcame these obstacles by convincingly demonstrating to President John Adams the workability of the interchangeable parts concept. He showed Adams that randomly selected parts would fit together as a whole working musket. Previously, a gunsmith had to make all the parts for each musket separately. Whitney showed how he could use the same parts to build ten different muskets. The machine-made parts always fit together perfectly, which made building muskets much faster and cheaper. Whitney then single-handedly designed and built all the machinery to produce the weapons. Soon it was used in building clocks and many other products. Whitney's idea was the origin of the phrase "the American system of manufacturing."

Other Americans, including Isaac Singer, who perfected sewing machines, Cyrus McCormick, who developed harvesters, and Henry Ford, who designed automobiles, used Whitney's concept of interchangeable parts in their own inventions and innovations. More specifically, Elias Howe built the first practical sewing machine in 1845 using Whitney's invention. Howe's machine could sew 250 stitches per minute, much faster than humans could sew. It greatly speeded up the work of sewing clothes. Now fewer people could make more clothes in the same amount of time.

Another aspect of the third period of the Industrial Revolution is that the precision of metalworking technology improved steadily, allowing for increasingly accurate stamping, forging, and machining.

During the fourth period, from 1830 to the early 1900s, steam power was further applied to modes of transportation. During the first decade of the nineteenth century, several steam carriages known as locomotives were built and were mainly used for transportation of coal and ore out of the mines. These locomotives were one of the most important elements in reducing transportation time and costs and in allowing trade to flourish on inland routes. In addition, within decades, steam-powered boats were making transatlantic crossings, providing merchants with an increased ability to exchange their goods for foreign resources. Dozens of other technical innovations brought changes in iron and steel manufacturing, bridge building, and communication.

In the 1840s, the factory system spread from the textile industry to the chemical and metallurgical industries and, by the 1860s and 1870s, to all market-oriented industries. By the end of the nineteenth century, machine processes dominated the American model of manufacturing, which included mass manufacture by power-driven machinery and the use of interchangeable parts. Machine processes dictated the nature and organization of production, although there was no uniformity in production layout or methods between different industries. For example, in the textile industry, machines almost immediately created a sequential manufacturing process that was characteristic of that industry. In iron manufacturing, however, a standard factory layout took a long time to develop, and there was little uniformity in factory organization until the end of the nineteenth century.

By the end of the nineteenth century, electricity and the internal combustion engine opened a door to a new period of automobile production. Thus, the construction of automobiles began the Post-Industrial Revolution era. By the mid-twentieth century, middle-class and working-class people owned automobiles in Europe as well as in the United States, and the motorcar began to transform social patterns. It has been said with some truth that Americans in the twentieth century carried on a love affair with their automobiles. Certainly, motorcars were marketed as status symbols. But at the same time, the growth of the automobile industry created large fields for investment, produced new types of service occupations, and revolutionized road making. These changes occurred in Western Europe as well as in the United States after World War II.

The Industrial Revolution gave rise to the idea of mass production, the process companies use to produce the same product at a very efficient and inexpensive rate. The mechanization movement had a significant impact on how people worked. In the

The technology and manufacturing processes of the Industrial Revolution made workers more efficient and productive, leading to higher profits, goods that were more affordable, and an increased standard of living. (Corbis)

years just before the emergence of the automobile, U.S. bicycle makers made quantum leaps in metal-forming skill. During the same period, engineers in other industries began to use conveyors to move raw materials around in foundries and flour mills. The next great change in the organization of work occurred as a result of the development of scientific management and the assembly line.

The concept of assembly line production is so familiar today that we sometimes overlook that, until the early twentieth century, it was relatively unknown. An assembly line is an arrangement of machines, equipment, and workers for a continuous flow of pieces in mass production operations. In an assembly line, workers attach the same parts day after day along a conveyor belt, knowing that all of the parts taken together will complete the entire product. There is a disassociation between the worker's job and the final product, since the workers no longer make the entire product. Instead, they work repeatedly on one tiny portion of the manufacturing process. An item is sent down a line, and at each point, there is someone to work on one aspect of it. One person punches a hole, and the next person puts in a screw, and so on, down the line, until the item is completed. Devices used on the assembly line include conveyor-belt systems, monorail trolleys, and various pulley arrangements.

A transfer machine, a landmark in progress toward complete automation, moves pieces from one station to another. A U.S. firm, the Waltham Watch Company, built the first known transfer machine in 1888. It fed parts to several lathes mounted on a single base. By the mid-1900s, transfer machines were widely in use within the automotive, appliance manufacturing, electrical parts production, and many other industries because they cut labor costs and ensured uniformity and precision.

Automatic controls represented an innovation when applied to the aspects of the production process. The cam, a device that automatically adjusted the position of a lever or machine element, was an important device in many early machines. During the nineteenth century, it was used to make many tools automatic, as opposed to manual. However, the cam had severe limitations in range of movement, number of changes, speed, size, and sensitivity. "True automatic control" could not be accomplished unless the machine was sensitive enough to adjust to varying conditions. Nevertheless, even those imperfect assembly lines changed the way things were made. They changed not only the price for consumers but also the working conditions for workers.

The first assembly line ideas came from nineteenth-century meatpacking industries in Cincinnati, Ohio, and Chicago. Overhead trolleys connected with chains were used to make a "disassembly line." This minimized unnecessary moving and increased productivity. After that, assembly line techniques were used elsewhere in manufacturing, including bicycles and armaments. In the 1890s, Westinghouse used an assembly line for the manufacture of railway brakes. Even before that, assembly lines were used in shoemaking. At one time, a skilled shoemaker did all the work of making a pair of shoes, one step at a time. This process changed in the 1820s, as workers were brought together in shoe factories and organized into assembly lines. On the assembly line, one worker used a machine to cut out heels. A second worker used a sole-making machine. A third made shoelaces. Other workers put the parts together to make the shoes. The assembly line allowed workers to work on lots of pairs of shoes at the same time. It also made it easier to train workers. Each worker only had to learn one task.

Indeed, two key developments led to the creation of the assembly line: standardized parts and the factory system of work. Both of these developments occurred in Europe, but they were merged with the greatest success in the United States. Today, mass production gives us everything from our clothes to our cars, making them affordable to almost everyone. The first cars were so expensive that only rich people could afford to buy them. In the early 1900s, most people still walked or rode horses. Then, in 1913, Henry Ford introduced the moving assembly line, and things changed.

Ford's objective was to create an affordable automobile, and all his experiments with the assembly line were designed to meet this objective. Ford's use of the assembly line was not necessarily innovative. Nevertheless, his goal to produce inexpensive products on a mass basis definitely was original. Once Ford proved that the assembly line could reduce production costs, his techniques were followed by other industries, and the United States experienced an explosion in the production of inexpensive consumer products. Ford wrote that the assembly line should be based on three basic principles. First, the commodity should progress through the shop in a planned, orderly, and continuous manner. Second, the work should be delivered instead of leaving it to the worker's initiative to find it. Third, the operations should be reduced to the elements of their constituent parts. Ford began experimenting with his assembly line on April 1, 1913. He had one worker assemble a new magneto using the usual method. He accomplished his task in approximately twenty minutes. This job was then split into twenty-nine individual jobs, which cut down assembly time to thirteen minutes and ten seconds. In 1914, the height of the assembly line in Ford's factory was raised 8 inches, lowering the amount of time it took to build a magneto to seven minutes. With further experimentation, the time was cut to five minutes.

These results stimulated Ford to apply the technique to chassis assembly. The fastest the pre-assembly line workers were able to produce a stationary chassis was twelve hours and twenty-eight minutes. Ford experimented with the production of a chassis by drawing one going down the line with an open windlass and a rope. Six assemblers moved along with the chassis and added parts as they went along. This experiment reduced the production time of an individual chassis to five hours and fifty-five minutes. Ford then elevated the assembly line so that it was waist-high and subdivided the work further, reducing the assembly time to one hour and thirty-three minutes. Ford was then able to lower the price of cars drastically, putting the purchase of a car within reach of a working-class person. Ford's use of the moving assembly line opened the door to mass production and automation.

The term *automation* was coined in the 1940s within the Ford Motor Company and was first applied to the automatic handling of metalworking processes. It is logically the ultimate step in the evolution of mass production processes. In its ideal form, it implies elimination of any manual labor and the introduction of automatic controls, assuring efficiency among the production of the product. Perfect automation has never really been accomplished, however. Tasks normally performed by workers operating equipment have been replaced with machines that require only maintenance personnel, engineers, and production control specialists. Automation may be described as a "revolutionary" development, but it is actually the result of mechanization, which began with the Industrial Revolution.

U.S. mathematician Norbert Wiener gave automation a broader meaning when he wrote about cybernetics, which he explained as control and communication in the animal and the machine. He predicted the application of computers to manufacturing situations and an increase in unemployment. This caused a considerable amount of alarm in the 1950s and the 1960s, when his prediction became most popular.

Automation "evolved" from three trends in technology: the development of powered machinery to perform production tasks; the introduction of powered equipment to move materials and pieces during the production process; and the perfection of control systems that were used to regulate handling, distribution, and production. The assembly line illustrates the fundamental principles of mechanization: standardization, continuity, constraint, and the reduction of work to simple labor. Taken together, these principles form the core of industrial culture in the mid-twentieth century in the United States. In addition, these fundamental principles form the basis of the "American production system," which until recently was the undisputed leader in global manufacturing.

There is no doubt that inventions and technology were the key elements of the Industrial Revolution. It changed the way things are made, it changed the prices of things, and it changed the conditions for workers. It was indeed revolutionary. The Industrial Revolution in the United States changed society profoundly. It caused a complete change in working conditions and the relationship between the working and middle classes. Unfortunately, working conditions became very harsh during the Industrial Revolution. Assembly lines led to mass production, which led to the division of labor. The division of labor was a method of working that involved doing the same task repeatedly. It was totally mindless and led the working class to feel bitter toward the middle class. Factory managers, who were members of the working class, became more concerned with profit and expenses after learning about mass production and started to cut wages to make a quick buck, which also led to bitterness on the part of the working class.

The Industrial Revolution affected not only the economy but also the whole stability of a nation. As discussed earlier, it affected not only the relationships between classes, but also the relationships between countries. The most important aspect of the Industrial Revolution is how all of these concepts are very much applicable to today's economy, which is why the Industrial Revolution was such an important period of time in the history of the world.

The Industrial Revolution has had massive effects on politics, economics, culture, and society. The emergence of the factory system, for instance, radically changed not only the organization of work but also its very meaning. Huge complexes, job specialization, massive increases in productivity, regimentation, and eventually the assembly line all revolutionized the work experience for millions of people. For many, it meant substantial improvements in family income. For many others, the factory system meant the loss of craftsmanship and the de-skilling of the workforce. The reduction of work to the simplest, repetitive motions eliminated the mastery and personal satisfaction traditionally associated with labor and often substituted unskilled for skilled workers.

The mountains of manufactured goods made available through the technological achievements of the Industrial Revolution also altered virtually everyone's lifestyle and standard of living. More goods in more varieties were available than at any other time in human history. Except for the most impoverished, nearly any ordinary person could afford to own devices, tools, and appliances available only to the wealthiest classes in earlier centuries. Rapid economic growth and spreading prosperity were among the positive effects of the Industrial Revolution.

In addition, the Industrial Revolution affected social behavior. With the development of new forms of transportation, such as railroads, steamships, automobiles, and airplanes, people became used to migration, thus altering cultural norms and values. Although in earlier times it would be unusual for an individual to travel much beyond the county or state of his or her birth, with the appearance of new forms of transportation, whole new prospects of travel, cultural exchange, and commerce appeared. Moreover, improvements in communications technologies, from the early telegraph to the telephone to radios, televisions, and computers, have greatly expanded the array of information sources accessible to ordinary people and have allowed huge improvements in the coordination of very large organizations scattered over the entire face of the globe.

Other cultural changes are more worrisome, however. Where frugality, savings, and staying out of debt were once thought to be fundamental virtues, after the Industrial Revolution, consumption became the watchword. If too few people purchased the rapidly expanding array of goods, store shelves would never be empty, factory orders would fall, and people would be laid off as factories closed. The only way to stave off economic ruin was to reeducate the population to become intensive consumers, buying many things they would never have imagined before.

To encourage such consumption, the advertising industry was created, developing sophisticated techniques for inducing new desires and needs among ordinary people. Often using manipulation, sex appeal, and other emotional inducements, advertisers have been able to get people to purchase objects and services they never felt any need of before the advertising appeared. And they could be induced to throw away still functioning items in order to buy the "latest, improved" models. Rapid improvements in transportation, warehousing, shipping, record keeping, and bookkeeping led to the creation of giant department store chains and supermarkets. And, in the later years of the twentieth century, the booming mail-order catalog market aimed at moving goods rapidly and efficiently from stores to consumers.

But along with these great leaps in technology occurred an overall reduction in the socioeconomic and cultural situation of people. The growth of cities was one of the major consequences of the Industrial Revolution. Many people were driven to the cities to look for work and ended up living in cities that could not support them. With the new industrial age, a new quantitative and materialistic view of the world took hold, which caused people to consume as much as they could. Living on small wages required small children to work in factories for long days.

The Industrial Revolution brought with it an increase in population and urbanization, as well as new social classes. The increase in population was nothing short of dramatic. In the United States, the annual increase was more than 3 percent, which might have been disastrous, had it not been for its vast amounts of land and fabulous natural resources. The general population increase was aided by a greater supply of food made available by the agricultural revolution and by the growth of medical science and public health measures, which decreased the death rate and added to the population base.

The Industrial Revolution and the factory system brought wonderful new products into U.S. homes. But they also created new problems, such as pollution and overcrowded cities. Workers, too, paid a price. Workers in factories worked long, hard hours. They had bosses instead of working for themselves. Often they fought bitterly with their companies over low pay, unsafe conditions, and other problems. In addition, work itself changed. Before the Industrial Revolution, craftspeople took great pride in their skills and in their handmade products. In factories, workers did simpler jobs, repeatedly. They were not attached to the final product and therefore were deprived from having pride for the item they produced.

Each of the three major aspects of the Industrial Revolution—the division of labor, specialization, and mechanization—helped to create modern industrial society, with its vision of mass production and the assembly line. A great deal of what it means to be modern—both good and bad—derives from the Industrial Revolution and the technologies it spawned.

Raissa Muhutdinova-Foroughi

See also American Federation of Labor and Congress of Industrial Organizations; Automotive Industry; Capitalism; Democratic Socialism; Ford, Henry; Garment/Textile Industries; Manufacturing Jobs; Railway Labor Act; Solidarity; Working Class

References and further reading

Hindle, Brooke, and Steven Lubar. 1986. *Engines of Change: The American Industrial Revolution, 1790–1860.* Washington, DC: Smithsonian Institution Press.

Hobsbawm, Eric. 1999. *Industry and Empire: The Birth of the Industrial Revolution.* Rev. ed. New York: New Press.

Hunter, Louis C. 1979–1985. *A History of Industrial Power in the United States, 1780–1930.* Charlottesville: Published for the Eleutherian Mills-Hagley Foundation by the University Press of Virginia.

White, John H., Jr. 1978. *The American Railroad Passenger Car.* Baltimore: Johns Hopkins University Press.

Woodbury, Robert S. 1972. *History of the Lathe to 1850: A Study in the Growth of a Technical Element of an Industrial Economy.* Cambridge: MIT Press.

Industrial Workers of the World (IWW)

Organized in 1905, the Industrial Workers of the World (IWW), also known as the "Wobblies," was formed in order to organize all workers, regardless of skill, race, ethnicity, or gender, into one big industrial union in opposition to the craft-oriented American Federation of Labor (AFL) unions. Promoting the practice of revolutionary syndicalism, or the use of direct action tactics on the shop floor as preparation for a worldwide general strike, the IWW successfully led a couple of major strikes in the United States. Opposition to U.S. participation in World War I and the advocacy of strikes in war-related industries resulted in the federal government's harassment of the organization during the war. By 1920, continuing government repression, for all intents and purposes, led to the IWW's downfall.

IWW was founded in Chicago on June 27, 1905. Opening the founding convention was William "Big Bill" Haywood of the Western Federation of Miners, who announced to the crowd, "Fellow Workers. This is the Continental Congress of the Working Class" (Conlin 1969, 2). From this opening speech, the IWW offered an alternative in both structure and ideology to the AFL, which dominated the U.S. trade union movement at the beginning of the twentieth century.

As opposed to the AFL's strategy of organizing only native-born, white, skilled, male workers, the IWW believed in organizing on an industrial basis (that is, skilled, semiskilled, and unskilled workers) into one big union, thus opening the door to the organization of immigrant, African American, and women workers. The IWW outlined its basic ideology in the preamble to its constitution, which proclaimed: "The working class and the employing class have nothing in common" (Werstein 1969, 15). Believing that the historical role of the working class was to abolish capitalism, the IWW advocated the use of revolutionary syndicalism in its struggle to overthrow capitalism and replace it with socialism. Doing so involved workers using direct action tactics on the shop floor (such as sit-down strikes, work slowdowns, threatened sabotage, etc.) to achieve immediate demands; these tactics also served to train workers for the organization of a worldwide general strike, culminating in the destruction of capitalism.

Although more than 900 locals of the IWW had been chartered by September 1907 (Renshaw 1999, 75), the organization experienced little success in its first two years. Membership turnover was extremely high, and the total number of members shrank to 6,000 by the fall of 1907 (Renshaw 1999, 75). In these early years, the IWW achieved some success in Goldfield, Nevada, a gold-rush town of 30,000 residents. By the end of 1907, virtually all wage workers in the town, including miners, clerks, stenographers, teamsters, dishwashers, waiters, general laborers, and even newsboys, were organized into IWW Local 77. The Wobblies achieved real gains for its members, including a minimum wage of $5.00 per day for miners and a dramatic increase in wages for railroad workers, from $1.75 for a ten-hour workday to $4.50 for an eight-hour workday (Renshaw 1999, 78). With an economic depression sweeping the nation in 1908, businesses folded, and unemployment skyrocketed, turning Goldfield into a ghost town. The economy's downturn eliminated the IWW not only in Goldfield but also in other areas throughout the United States.

The IWW roared back to life in July 1909, when a spontaneous strike among unskilled immigrants occurred at the Pressed Steel Car Company in McKees Rock, Pennsylvania, over the implementation of a pay plan based on piecework. After the AFL Machinists Union, which represented the company's skilled workers, refused to help the strikers, they appealed to the IWW, who immediately sent organizers to support the strike. Although the state police and employer-hired deputies physically attacked strike meetings and picket lines, the strikers fought back. With public sentiment on the strikers' side, Pressed Steel Car Company capitulated to the union within two months, restoring the previous payment system and resolving the strikers' immediate grievances. Achieving this major victory led to additional organizing successes and a rebirth for the organization on a national level.

The major activity that the IWW concentrated on from 1909 to 1912 was participation in "the free speech fights," in which union leaders propagandized on street corners to publicize the poor working and living conditions of migratory laborers that it sought to organize. However, the IWW led a second major strike in January 1912 to protest wage cuts in the American Woolen Company textile mills in Lawrence, Massachusetts. With 23,000 men, women, and children on strike (Dubofsky 1969, 249), this work stoppage was the first time so many immigrant, unskilled, and unorganized workers had struck any U.S. employer.

Demonstration of the Industrial Workers of the World, New York City, 1914 (George Grantham Bain Collection/Library of Congress)

Even with the presence of state militia and state police in Lawrence, the strikers stood fast throughout the winter, marching under the slogan, "We want bread and roses, too!" For economic reasons, hundreds of strikers' children were sent to New York City and Philadelphia to live with union supporters, helping to publicize the strike. With Congress investigating the strike in March, public sentiment continued to mount against the American Woolen Company. On March 12, 1912, the company gave in to all the strikers' demands.

The last major strike led by the IWW, the 1913 silk strike in Paterson, New Jersey, did not end as well as the Lawrence strike. After the implementation of a work speedup at the end of January, more than 25,000 workers went on strike within a month and idled the city's 300 silk mills (Renshaw 1999, 113). By July, the strikers were weakening and went back to work without achieving any gains.

With the U.S. entry into World War I, the IWW faced harassment by the U.S. government for its opposition to the war and its advocacy of conducting strikes in war-related industries. On September 5, 1917, Department of Justice agents raided the IWW headquarters, and on September 28, 1917, nearly 200 IWW leaders across the nation were arrested for alleged antiwar activities (Werstein 1969, 122). This federal government repression against the IWW continued after the war, with the Palmer raids, launched by Attorney General Mitchell Palmer on November 7, 1919. Federal agents raided many radical groups' headquarters and arrested individuals in numerous cities.

However, government repression was not the only reason for the IWW's downfall by 1920. Although the union led successful strikes, it was not able to consolidate strike gains because of its refusal to sign collective bargaining agreements that the organization felt would bind the workers' hands on the shop floor. Nevertheless, the IWW served as an important precursor to the Congress of Industrial Organizations, which utilized the Wobblies' syndicalist tactics in building stable and successful industrial unions during the mid- to late 1930s.

Victor G. Devinatz

See also Communism in the U.S. Trade Union Movement; Democratic Socialism; Mother Jones; Socialism

References and further reading

Cannon, James Patrick. 1967. *The I. W. W.* New York: Merit Publishers.

Conlin, Joseph Robert. 1969. *Bread And Roses Too: Studies of the Wobblies.* Westport, CT: Greenwood Publishing.

DeCaux, Len. 1978. *The Living Spirit of the Wobblies.* New York: International Publishers.

Dubofsky, Melvyn. 1969. *We Shall Be All: A History of the Industrial Workers of the World.* Chicago: Quadrangle Books.

Foner, Philip S. 1965. *A History of the Labor Movement in the United States.* Vol. 4, *The Industrial Workers of the World, 1905–1917.* New York: International Publishers.

Renshaw, Patrick. 1999. *The Wobblies: The Story of the IWW and Syndicalism in the United States.* Chicago: Ivan R. Dee.

Werstein, Irving. 1969. *Pie in the Sky: An American Struggle: The Wobblies and Their Times.* New York: Delacorte Press.

International Business Machines (IBM)

Formerly Computing-Tabulating-Recording Company (C-T-R), International Business Machines Corporation (IBM) was founded in February 1924 by Thomas J. Watson Sr. (1874–1956), a former executive with National Cash Register Company who joined C-T-R as general manager in 1914 at the age of forty. Watson redirected an organization specializing primarily in butcher scales, time clocks, and early tabulating machines to devote its corporate development to core business values oriented to customer service in the burgeoning market for data processing. An extraordinary gamble to expand the company and stockpile inventory during the Great Depression paid off, when IBM was positioned to capitalize on two historic events critical to the company's future growth and industry dominance.

The passage of the Social Security Act in 1935 required employers to establish record-keeping practices on a scale previously unimagined, and Watson's prescient commitment to parts and personnel enabled IBM to provide the equipment nationally almost immediately. Another crucial element of the company's breakaway success occurred during World War II, as government and manufacturers demanded both the technology and the service necessary to conduct the war effort. IBM emerged from the war years with a philosophy oriented to the requirements of its customers and the infrastructure to deliver the product. In the postwar economic environment, the company's phenomenal growth began to dominate domestic and international markets by adapting to evolving technology, particularly in the emerging computer industry. Establishing schools for junior executives and line managers in the early 1950s, IBM innovated management techniques involving communication, human resources, and capital assets to match a powerfully marketed reputation for commitment to product performance and customer relations. IBM also maintained employee loyalty with generous performance benefits and the promise of a job for life. Thomas J. Watson Jr. became chief executive officer in 1956, epitomizing the corporate strategy to promote from within rather than rely on employees not groomed to manage in the IBM tradition.

Critics of the highly structured IBM corporate model focused on its towering market presence, employee dress code and relocation policies, and obsessive adherence to unchanging philosophical standards, although the company insisted that refusal to compromise basic beliefs was the most important factor in its dominant stature. IBM's success, some charge, was the result of anticompetitive practices such as price discrimination, allowing the company to monopolize information-related industries. The dominance unraveled in the 1980s and early 1990s, however, as IBM committed itself to mainframe processing with a tremendous expansion of personnel and facilities, misjudging the technology shift to microprocessors. The company exacerbated customer and employee disillusionment with downsizing and decentralization, damaging its reputation for productivity and service. New management in the late 1990s recalibrated the company's product line to the rapidly evolving information technology market and reestablished its commitment to a service-oriented management philosophy. IBM entered the twenty-first century with invigorated purpose, powerful but no longer the domineering industry force of the past.

Darrell A. Hamlin

See also Computers at Work; Great Depression; Industrial Engineering; Silicon Valley; Social Security Act; Time Cards

References and further reading

Carroll, Paul. 1994. *Big Blues: The Unmaking of IBM.* New York: Crown.

DeLamarter, Richard Thomas. 1986. *Big Blue: IBM's Use and Abuse of Power.* New York: Dodd, Mead and Company.

Garr, Doug. 1999. *IBM Redux: Lou Gerstner and the Business Turnaround of the Decade.* New York: HarperBusiness.

Mills, D. Quinn. 1988. *The IBM Lesson: The Profitable Art of Full Employment.* New York: Times Books.
Rodgers, F. G. "Buck," with Robert L. Shook. 1986. *The IBM Way: Insights into the World's Most Successful Marketing Organization.* New York: Harper and Row.
Watson, Thomas J., Jr., and Peter Petre. 1990. *Father, Son and Co.: My Life at IBM and Beyond.* New York: Bantam.

International Labour Organization (ILO)

The International Labour Organization (ILO) is a specialized agency of the United Nations that promotes social justice and internationally recognized human and labor rights. The ILO is the chief international authority on labor standards and formulates international labor standards pertaining to union organizing and collective bargaining, forced labor, discrimination, and other conditions of work. The ILO also provides technical assistance in areas such as vocational training, employment policy, labor law, social security, and occupational safety and health.

The ILO was created with the League of Nations in 1919 by the Treaty of Versailles at the conclusion of World War I. It was founded on the beliefs that after making great sacrifices in World War I, the workers of the world deserved decent working conditions and that poor working conditions are a threat to political stability and therefore global peace. The ILO is the only surviving organization of the League of Nations, and at the end of World War II, it became the United Nations' first specialized agency. Most countries are now members. The overarching premise of the ILO is that "universal and lasting peace can be established only if it is based upon social justice" (International Labour Organization 1919).

To this end, a fundamental activity of the ILO is adopting conventions that specify minimum labor standards. For example, the Discrimination (Employment and Occupation) Convention (No. C111, 1958) calls for countries "to declare and pursue a national policy designed to promote, by methods appropriate to national conditions and practice, equality of opportunity and treatment in respect of employment and occupation, with a view to eliminating any discrimination in respect thereof" (International Labour Organization 1958). Member countries are obligated to submit the conventions to their national legislatures for ratification and to fulfill their provisions. As of the year 2000, the ILO has passed 183 conventions. Technical assistance to help implement these standards is also provided.

The ILO has worked with numerous countries to establish national and local policies to reduce unemployment, combat employment discrimination, improve safety standards, and eliminate child labor. For example, in recent years the ILO has helped the government of Vietnam launch a national safety week to bring awareness to worker safety; trained local officials in Indonesia to recognize child labor problems, resulting in the placement of 3,000 children into local schools; helped design and implement low-cost loan programs in France and Germany to help unemployed workers start their own businesses; created posters to promote women workers' rights in India; and worked with the government of Costa Rica to update its labor laws to protect workers' rights to unionize.

In light of the growing linkages between labor issues and globalization, the ILO adopted the Declaration on Fundamental Principles and Rights at Work in 1998. It champions the belief that all countries have an obligation to promote certain fundamental rights: freedom of association and the effective recognition of the right to collective bargaining, elimination of all forms of forced or compulsory labor, effective abolition of child labor, and elimination of discrimination in respect of employment and occupation.

The ILO comprises three main entities: the International Labour Conference, the Governing Body, and the International Labour Office. The International Labour Conference is an annual meeting to establish international labor standards and elect the Governing Body, the ILO's executive council. Each member country is represented by two government delegates, one employer delegate, and one worker delegate. The International Labour Office comprises the ILO's permanent staff. The ILO's unique tripartite structure of government, employers, and workers is apparent in all three bodies. It is headquartered in Geneva, Switzerland, and has forty field offices around the world. On its fiftieth anniversary in 1969, the ILO won the Nobel Peace Prize for its work on promoting social justice in employment—including reducing poverty and discrimination—and therefore peace, around the world.

The United States was involved in the ILO's founding, but its commitment to the ILO has been questioned. In fact, the United States withdrew from the ILO between 1977 and 1980 because of a perception that the ILO's agenda was overly politicized by Communist countries. In many areas, the United States does not have a strong record of ratifying international treaties—either because of constitutional concerns or a desire to act unilaterally—and the U.S. experience with ILO conventions is no different. The United States has only ratified a handful of ILO Conventions and has been criticized for ratifying only one of the seven core or fundamental conventions.

John W. Budd

See also American Federation of Labor and Congress of Industrial Organizations; General Agreement on Tariffs and Trade; World Trade Organization

References and further reading

Coxson, Christopher R. 1999. "The 1998 ILO Declaration on Fundamental Principles and Rights at Work: Promoting Labor Law Reforms through the ILO as an Alternative to Imposing Coercive Trade Sanctions." *Dickinson Journal of International Law* 17, no. 3: 469–504.

Galenson, Walter. 1981. *The International Labor Organization: An American View.* Madison: University of Wisconsin Press.

Ghebali, Victor-Yves, Roberto Ago, and Nicolas Valticos, eds. 1989. *The International Labour Organisation: A Case Study on the Evolution of UN Specialised Agencies.* Boston: Nijhoff.

Gross, James A. 1999. "A Human Rights Perspective on U.S. Labor Relations Law: A Violation of the Freedom of Association." *Employee Rights and Employment Policy Journal* 3, no. 1: 65–103.

International Labour Organization (ILO). 1919. "Preamble." *ILO Constitution.* Written and adopted at Peace Conference of 1919. Paris and Versailles: International Labour Organization.

———. 1958. Discrimination (Employment and Occupation) Convention, no. C111. Session 42. June 25. Geneva: International Labour Organisation.

Valticos, Nicolas, and Geraldo von Potobsky. 1995. *International Labour Law.* The Hague: Kluwer Law and Taxation Publishers.

Internships

An internship, in the strictest sense of the word, refers to the occupational experience required for certification in professional fields such as education, medicine, law, and accounting. The term is commonly applied, however, to a wide variety of educational programs that involve student employment. Related to the ancient but declining tradition of craft guilds and apprenticeship systems, internships gained popularity at the end of the nineteenth century as a way to teach students practical skills in an educational environment that dealt increasingly with abstract theory.

The internship has been considered a vital part of many professional programs since the late 1800s and early 1900s. Professional internships typically occur after the completion of academic coursework but before graduation, thereby allowing students to apply classroom learning in working world situations. The first teachers' internship, established by Brown University in 1909, offers one example. Brown's education graduates worked for a year as closely supervised, part-time salaried teachers in Providence city schools before earning positions as full-time, professional educators. Similar internships were soon established for student teachers in Cincinnati, Boston, Cleveland, Seattle, and Minneapolis. By the 1930s and 1940s, the internship had become a recognized prerequisite for beginning teachers in school systems across the country.

More recently, the term *internship* has come to describe a form of "experiential education" at the high school and college levels. Experiential education, or "learning by doing," encourages the integration of real-world experience with classroom-style instruction. Internships provide students with the opportunity to explore career options by participating in and observing work in a selected field. They may enhance classroom learning by honing students' practical knowledge, developing their interpersonal skills, and increasing their self-esteem. Student internships are available in corporate, nonprofit, and government settings. They may be part-time or full-time, paid or unpaid, and often include a formal assessment of the student-worker in the form of a recorded grade and academic credit.

Although undergraduate programs in agriculture, engineering, and other curriculum with direct connections to nonacademic careers have encouraged internships since the early twentieth century, they are a fairly new addition to most liberal arts disciplines. Internships gained popularity across college campuses during the 1970s and 1980s, when a declining economy and shrinking job market encouraged students to gain occupational experience within their field of interest before graduation. Humanities majors, worried about their employment prospects after college, hoped that an internship would help them stand out in the job market. A number of recent advice books and studies have supported such decisions. In a 1995 survey by the National Center on the Educational Quality of the Workforce, for example, employers described internships and other job experience as an important factor in the selection of entry-level personnel.

Of course, internships benefit employers as well as students. Interns provide companies with inexpensive or free labor. They often supply nonprofit organizations with program and administrative assistance that such groups otherwise might not be able to afford. Internship programs also infuse the workplace with energetic, creative new minds and provide employers with a ready source of qualified, company-trained recruits.

Katie Otis

See also Apprenticeship; Child Labor; Education Reform and the Workforce; Summer Jobs

References and further reading

Ciofalo, Andrew, ed. 1992. *Internships: Perspectives on Experiential Learning.* Malabar, FL: Krieger Publishing.

Gardner, Harrison. 1969. "Internship in Historical Perspective." *The Education Digest* vol. 34, no. 7 (March): 42–45.

Green, Marianne Ehrlich. 1997. *Internship Success: Real-World, Step-by-Step Advice on Getting the Most Out of Internships.* Lincolnwood, IL: NTC/Contemporary Publishing.

Kaston, Carren O., and James M. Heffernan. 1984. *Preparing Humanists for Work: A National Study of Undergraduate Internships in the Humanities.* Washington, DC: Washington Center.

Mason, Ralph E., and Stewart W. Husted. 1997. *Cooperative Occupational Education: Including Internships, Apprenticeships, and Tech-Prep.* Danville, IL: Interstate Publishers.

Sweitzer, Frederick H., and Mary A. King. 1999. *The Successful Internship: Transformation and Empowerment.* Pacific Grove: Brooks/Cole Publishers.

Ironworkers

Workers in U.S. iron mills experienced the most fundamental changes that accompanied industrialization and urbanization in the late nineteenth century. Before the Civil War, skilled ironworkers exercised independence in the workplace and strived to make connections with unskilled workers. Mechanization, managerial transformations, and technological innovations weakened the skilled worker's place in the production of iron and later steel, as well as the ties that bound skilled and unskilled workers. Ironworkers formed one of the largest and most powerful labor unions of the late nineteenth century, but the concerted power of industrial capitalists and the federal government brought the union to heel. Iron- and steelworkers entered the twentieth century severely weakened, working in deplorable situations, and powerless in U.S. society.

Before the Civil War, iron was made in rolling mills. The Englishman Henry Cort (1740–1800) developed the process in 1784, and a further refining process became popular in the 1830s. Iron production relied on a large pool of skilled workers, which contributed to the hierarchical labor organization in the mills. Skill divided the workplace into craftspeople and common laborers. Common workers carried materials, shoveled ores, and cleaned up the mill. Employers paid these workers by the hour or day. Craftspeople influenced the outcome of the finished product with their knowledge, skill, and expertise. Puddlers, for instance, poured off the slag and shaped the molten iron into balls, which sometimes weighed 200 pounds. The ball was flattened into the "muck bar" and then heaters, rollers, and nailers transformed the iron into the finished product. Employers paid craftspeople by the tonnage of iron produced.

Skilled ironworkers attempted to overcome workplace divisions that skill levels imposed. Craftspeople hired "helpers" (typically relatives, thus keeping the skill hereditary), taught them their craft, and decided how much each member of a crew made. Although some workers received more money than others, workers controlled the distribution of wages. Skilled ironworkers also decided about how much iron the crew produced in a day, a practice known as the "stint." They enforced the stint through peer pressure. Ironworkers derided those employees who were too eager to please the boss by calling them unkind names and questioning their masculinity. Lastly, a code of "mutualism" existed in the ironworks. Unskilled workers clung to the opportunity for upward mobility, and skilled workers did not forget their unskilled brethren when they went on strike.

The emergence of the steel industry in the late nineteenth century undermined the autonomy, skill, and influence of craftspeople. Between 1865 and 1892, iron and steel production exploded in the United States. The continental railroad system required an enormous amount of iron for tracks. Iron also provided for the growth of city transportation and the construction of skyscrapers. Beginning in the 1850s, business proponents in the

Inside an iron mill, 1865. Between 1865 and 1892, iron and steel production exploded in the United States, supplying the building of the continental railroad system and city transportation systems and skyscrapers. Mechanization in iron mills made iron production more efficient, but it eliminated many jobs. (Hulton Archives)

United States wanted to make iron production more efficient. Frederick Overman argued that the United States needed to mechanize the iron industry to generate more profits, liberate production from skilled workers, and improve managerial techniques. In 1856, Henry Bessemer introduced the process of blowing cold air onto molten pig iron, thus strengthening the metal and creating steel. Bessemer promised that the new metal-making technique would eliminate puddling from the process. Businesspeople also improved management techniques. Beginning in the Civil War, engineers took over the duty of hiring workers and instituted workplace rules, which trumped the worker's stint. Lastly, mechanization eliminated jobs in mills. The three-high rail mill, lifting tables, and hydraulic pushers made iron and steel production more efficient and required fewer skilled workers.

Mechanization, managerial innovations in the workplace, and the proliferation of steel mills exacerbated divisions in the workplace. Steel production organized labor differently than iron. In contrast to the iron mills, which had an equal number of unskilled laborers and craftspeople, steel mills relied on a large pool of common workers and a few highly specialized workers. This difference increased the divisions between skilled and unskilled workers. "New immigration" (that of northern and eastern Europeans) and the northern migration of African Americans created a dual-labor system in steel mills. Old-stock immigrants worked in the specialized crafts and obtained positions as helpers. New-stock immigrants experienced more difficulties in moving up the job ladder, tended to associate in their own communities, and attended non-Protestant churches. African Americans held the worst jobs in the factory; those closest to the furnace. They were an extremely mobile population in the mills, and job turnover was high because of the poor working conditions. In addition, the size of steel mills contributed to problems of labor organization. Steel mills were much larger than iron mills and made the process of organizing workers cumbersome. Finally, the transformation to steel affected each craft differently. Puddlers, for instance, suffered a loss of autonomy and influence in the workplace, whereas rollers earned more money under the new process.

Ironworkers did not take the assault on their livelihood lightly. They formed the Amalgamated Association of Iron, Steel, and Tin Workers, and by the 1870s, it was one of the most powerful craft unions in the nation. Nevertheless, Amalgamated's influence waned after Andrew Carnegie and Henry Clay Frick broke the union in the Homestead Strike of 1892, and steelworkers did not have an active organizing voice until the twentieth century. After the Homestead strike, steel mill owners adopted Carnegie's and Frick's relentless workplace schedule. Steel workers worked seventy-two-hour weeks and received low wages. In 1919, worker discontent exploded in a strike that encompassed much of the Midwest. This strike produced the same results as the Homestead struggle: a defeat for the workers. Steel workers did not form an active and powerful voice until the 1930s, with the formation of the Congress of Industrial Organizations.

Ironworkers entered the Gilded Age of the 1890s with autonomy in the workplace. Despite the hierarchical organization of the workplace and the influence of craftspeople, ironworkers dictated the day-to-day conditions in the workplace and linked all workers with a code of mutualism. However, the economic changes of the Gilded Age undermined their position in the workplace. The Bessemer process transformed iron and steel making and touched off nearly thirty-five years of labor strife.

William J. Bauer Jr.

See also American Federation of Labor and Congress of Industrial Organizations; Building Trades Unions; Guilds; Industrial Revolution and Assembly Line Work

References and further reading

Bennett, John. 1977. "Iron Workers in Woods End and Johnstown: The Union Era, 1865–1895." Ph.D. diss., University of Pittsburgh.

Dubofsky, Melvyn. 1996/1975. *Industrialism and the American Worker, 1865–1920.* 3rd ed. Wheeling: Harlan Davidson.

Krause, Paul. 1992. *The Battle for Homestead, 1880–1892: Politics, Culture, and Steel.* Pittsburgh: University of Pittsburgh Press.

Montgomery, David. 1987. *The Fall of the House of Labor: The Workplace, the State, and American Labor Activism, 1865–1925.* New York: Cambridge University Press.

J

Job Benefits

Job benefits are the nonmonetary components of employee compensation. They may include voluntary benefits, such as paid and unpaid leave, health care, life and disability insurance, retirement plans, supplemental pay benefits for overtime or bonuses, and intangible benefits, such as flexible workday schedules or the opportunity to telecommute. In addition, employers are legally mandated to contribute to unemployment insurance and Social Security and to purchase workers' compensation insurance. The U.S. Bureau of Labor Statistics (BLS) collects information on the provision of these benefits through the Employee Benefits Survey and the National Compensation Survey.

Voluntary Benefits

Leave

Paid leave includes days available for vacation, personal use, funerals, jury duty, military service, family obligations, and the employee's or family member's sickness. Leave has never been federally mandated in the United States, but 80 percent of all employees in 2000 had paid vacation, and 77 percent had paid holidays. On average, Americans have had about ten days of leave per year through the 1980s and 1990s. In 1993, the Congress passed the Family and Medical Leave Act, which entitles eligible employees to twelve weeks of unpaid leave in any twelve-month employment period for the purpose of caring for a newborn or newly adopted child or because of a serious health condition suffered by the employee or a family member. Although some employers may choose to provide paid leave for part or all of the twelve-week duration, the law guarantees only that workers can return from leave to their old jobs or to a similar job with the same salary and benefits.

Retirement Benefits

The original pension plans were designed for disabled veterans. The first full-fledged pension system was the Civil War pension program of 1862, which started off as a plan to provide for disabled veterans, widows, and orphans, and it was eventually extended to all disabled and old veterans. Private pension plans also began to make an appearance in the late 1800s; for example, American Express established a private pension plan in 1875.

The federal government enacted the Employee Retirement Income Security Act of 1974 (ERISA) to provide protection for individuals (employees and their dependents) in voluntarily established pension and health plans provided by employers in private industry. It entitles plan participants to plan information, responsible management of plan assets, and a grievance and appeals process.

Today, employers offer one or both of two types of employment-related retirement plans in addition to making federally mandated contributions to Social Security: defined benefit or pension plans and defined contribution or tax-deferred retirement savings plans. Traditional defined benefit plans require employers to make annual contributions to a fund and pay out retirement benefits based on each employee's compensation and years of service. Defined contribution plans permit employees to contribute pretax funds to a savings account, with taxes on those savings deferred until the time the person withdraws money from the fund on retirement. There are early withdrawal penalties for funds withdrawn before retirement age (currently at age fifty-nine and one-half). Contributions to such plans are usually made in the form of salary withdrawals, and employers may match employee contributions up to a limit.

The tax-deferred retirement savings plans (that is, the 401[k] plans for for-profit firms and 403[b] plans for nonprofit firms) allow employees to put away some portion of their pretax incomes in a portfolio of accounts. The money in these accounts and the income from them are not taxed until they are withdrawn. These plans originated in the Revenue Act of 1978, which stipulated that employees should not be taxed on the portion of compensation that was deferred in profit-sharing plans and that these contributions should be made through salary reductions. Internal Revenue Service (IRS) regulations promulgated in 1981 sanctioned the use of salary withdrawals for retirement plans. Subsequent reforms changed the maximum amounts that could be contributed, regulated transfers of funds when employees changed jobs, and regulated the administration of these plans. The Pension and Welfare Benefits Administration was established in 1986 to educate and assist participants, beneficiaries, and sponsors of pension, health, and other employee benefit plans. It administers and enforces the provisions of the ERISA.

Health Care Benefits

Health insurance enables avoidance of large unforeseen medical expenses in exchange for an annual insurance premium from members of a group; the insurer pays all or most of any medical expenses that any of the members of this group incur over the year. Employer-provided health insurance benefits emerged as a means of getting around the wage ceiling during World War II and expanded over the following decades. National health care spending increased rapidly in the 1970s and 1980s. The rising costs made it increasingly difficult for many firms to offer health benefits to their employees, which led to the emergence and propagation of managed care. The Health Maintenance Organization (HMO) Act of 1973, signed into law by President Richard Nixon, required all firms with twenty-five or more employees to offer an HMO plan.

Under ERISA, beneficiaries are entitled to health care plan information and responsible management of health care plans, just as they are for pension plans. The Consolidated Omnibus Budget Reconciliation Act of 1986 (COBRA) is an important amendment to ERISA that guarantees continuation of health insurance coverage at the rate available to the employer for some limited duration after loss of eligibility for benefits under certain situations, such as job loss or the death of the primary beneficiary. The Health Insurance Portability and Accountability Act of 1996 (HIPAA) protects those with preexisting conditions from discrimination in health coverage.

Some employers offer supplemental insurance benefits to retirees, either to cover those as yet ineligible for Medicare or to pay for services not covered by Medicare for the Medicare-eligible. Of late, the trend has been for employers to pay for less of retiree health insurance premiums since costs are rising. So although employers continue to pay current employee premiums to stay competitive, they may not always pay for those for retirees.

Flexible Spending Plans

In addition to providing health insurance coverage, some employers allow employees to put away money in pretax accounts to cover medical expenses such as copayments and services not covered by health insurance. Fewer employers offer health promotion plans to their employees, such as reimbursements for memberships to fitness clubs and paid time and reimbursement for annual medical checkups.

Overtime, Bonuses, and Profit Sharing

Compensation for overtime work is regulated by the Fair Labor Standards Act of 1938, which has been amended over time. In addition, employers offer bonuses based on performance and the opportunity to share profits and to own company stock as a means of retaining employees.

Flexible Schedules and Telecommuting

A flexible work schedule is an alternative to the traditional 9-to-5, forty-hour workweek. It allows employees to vary their arrival and/or departure times. Under some policies, employees must work a prescribed number of hours per pay period and be present during daily "core times," which might involve compressed workweeks in which employees work longer days in exchange for a day off every other week or so. Alternative work arrangements such as flexible work schedules are a matter of agreement between the employer and the employee (or the employee's representative). Because of increasing urban sprawl and growing commute times and to facilitate improved work-life balance for their employees, many employers allow their employees to "telecommute," or work from their homes.

Life and Disability Insurance

A number of employers offer life insurance plans whereby dependents and survivors of the employee get some amount of benefits if the employee dies. Similarly, disability insurance plans pay some proportion of the employee's income if disability prevents the employee from being able to work. Insurance plans for employee groups cost less per person than would a corresponding plan offered by an insurance firm on the open market, and these costs are not taxable, so it is advantageous to the employee to obtain insurance plans from work. Some employers provide employees with the option of purchasing insurance for nursing home care during old age.

Miscellaneous Benefits

Some large employers, such as the federal government and universities, offer employees the option of saving in thrift plans. In addition, employers may pay tuition or offer interest-free loans for educational expenses. Others offer subsidies to pay for child care. Some employers offer low-cost access to legal services plans.

Flexible Benefits or Cafeteria Plans

Under Section 125 of the Internal Revenue Code of 1986, employers can allow employees to choose taxable cash benefits by opting out of certain qualified nontaxable benefits offered to employees. Although employees have the option of opting into or out of certain benefits, any cash compensation they obtain in exchange for benefits they give up is not exempt from income tax.

Federally Mandated Benefits

Social Security

In 1935, the Social Security Act set up a federally mandated retirement fund that was funded through payroll taxes from employers and employees and paid out benefits out of those funds to those who were retired. Social Security benefits were subsequently extended to the disabled and then to all those over retirement age (which is currently at sixty-five and will soon be extended to sixty-seven), irrespective of retirement status. The benefits vary based on lifetime earnings and age at retirement (with reduced benefits for early retirees and additional credits for late retirees).

Medicare

Employers contribute to Medicare taxes for all their employees. These contributions entitle employees to Medicare coverage after they retire, which pays for hospital expenses and, at a small premium, physician services.

Unemployment Benefits

Union-based unemployment insurance made its appearance in 1831, but it was not until 1932 that Wisconsin became the first state to enact state-based unemployment insurance. The unemployment insurance system was established as part of the Social Security Act of 1935. In combination with the Federal Unemployment Tax Act of 1939 and subsequent state unemployment tax legislation, a partnership was established whereby taxes are collected primarily from employers and redistributed among the unemployed by individual states within guidelines established by the federal government.

Workers' Compensation

This is a federally mandated, state-regulated employment benefit, whereby employees who are made sick, injured, or killed on the job receive benefits to cover medical expenses, lost wages, vocational rehabilitation, and death benefits. These plans were established for maritime workers and others in 1927. Today employers are required to purchase workers' compensation insurance, which is a no-fault insurance system, to pay for these benefits. Requirements for the amount of insurance and employers that may be exempt are determined by legislation at the state level.

Mythreyi Bhargavan

See also Bureau of Labor Statistics; Employee Stock Ownership; Fair Labor Standards Act; Family and Medical Leave Act; Federal Unemployment Tax and Insurance System; Health Insurance; Overtime and the Workweek; Profit Sharing; Retirement; Social Security Act; Workers' Compensation

References and further reading

Bureau of Labor Statistics, U.S. Department of Labor. 2002. "National Compensation Survey." http://www.bls.gov/ncs/ebs/home.htm (cited September 12, 2002).

Chao, Elaine L. 2001. *Report on the American Workforce.* Washington, DC: U.S. Department of Labor.

Employment Benefits Research Institute. 1997. *Fundamentals of Employee Benefit Programs.* 5th ed. Washington, DC: Employment Benefits Research Institute.

U.S. Department of Labor. 2002. *Find It! By Audience—Workers.* http://www.dol.gov/dol/audience/aud-workers.htm (cited September 12, 2002).

Job Corps

Job Corps is one of the nation's largest and most intensive education and training programs for low-income youth. Launched in 1964 as part of President Lyndon B. Johnson's War on Poverty, its purpose is to help eligible youth become responsible, employable, and productive citizens. About 70,000 new students enroll in Job Corps every year.

The program targets economically disadvantaged youth between sixteen and twenty-four years of age. Nearly 80 percent of students are high school dropouts, and about 70 percent come from minority groups. About 20 percent come from families who receive public assistance. The typical Job Corps student is an eighteen-year-old high school dropout who reads at slightly above the seventh-grade level and has never held a full-time job (U.S. Department of Labor 2001).

Job Corps is widely recognized for its intensive battery of education, training, and support services. Most participants receive a variety of services, including social skills training, academic instruction, and vocational training and counseling, as well as other support services. Students spend an average of seven to eight months in the program, but the length of stay varies, depending on the pace of each student's progress. Just over 20 percent of all new participants drop out within the first sixty days for a variety of personal reasons (U.S. Department of Labor 2001).

A distinctive feature of Job Corps is its residential setting and commitment to personal development. About 80 percent of students live in dormitories at one of 118 Job Corps centers across the country (U.S. Department of Labor 2001, 2–4). All students develop social skills through a structured program that covers forty-five topics, such as responsibility to self and others, teamwork, and respect for diversity. Students also have access to a variety of activities and support services, including health care, meals, counseling, and student government. Nonresidential students have access to all the support services except dormitory living.

In addition to personal development, Job Corps emphasizes acquisition of academic and vocational skills. Upon entering the program, students, with assistance from counselors, develop an individualized plan that lays out an appropriate mix of academic and vocational training.

Vocational training prepares students for jobs in specific occupations or trades. Following an assessment, students are matched with training in a range of trades, such as health occupations, automotive maintenance, culinary arts, and construction. Vocational curricula encourage students to build specific skills or competencies that will meet the needs of employers and labor organizations in that trade. As they advance in their training, students have an opportunity to apply their newly acquired skills through unpaid positions with local employers.

Most students also receive academic instruction while they are learning a trade. The aim of academic instruction is to boost students' reading, math, computer, and Internet skills, laying a solid foundation for employment or further education. In addition, students receive training in workplace communications, such as following instructions, preparing resumes, and writing memos. Participants who lack high school diplomas are encouraged to acquire them or to enter high school equivalency classes leading to Graduate Equivalency Degree (GED) certificates.

The Job Corps administrative structure is as distinctive as its mix of services. Unlike most federal job training programs, which are administered by states and localities, Job Corps is a national program that is directly managed by the U.S. Department of Labor. Federal staff issue policy and program guidance and contract for the operation of centers. In 2000, there were 118 centers run by a combination of federal agencies and private organizations.

Federal administrators set high expectations for

performance. The program has a sophisticated performance measurement system that tracks the results of center operators, training providers, and other contractors. Contracts are awarded based on success in achieving outcomes for students and meeting quality and compliance standards for center operations.

Recent evaluations demonstrate that the program is indeed achieving results. The National Job Corps Study, released in 2001, found that the program has many positive impacts on participants' lives, including increased education and training equivalent to about one year of school, higher earnings following program participation, reduced receipt of public assistance, and reduced arrest and conviction rates. However, Job Corps has little effect on the chances that participants will attend or complete postsecondary education. Most of the measured gains go to students who stay in the program long enough to complete vocational training or obtain a GED.

The study also found that Job Corps generates a strong return on the public investment. The program is expensive, costing the federal government about $16,500 per participant. Still, the benefits of the program, such as increased productivity of the participants and reduced use of public programs, exceed program costs by nearly $17,000 per participant. As a result, the program generates about two dollars in benefits to society for every dollar spent on services (Mathematica Policy Research 2001). The positive impacts on participants, combined with the high return on investment, make Job Corps one of the most effective job training programs for disadvantaged youth ever designed.

Neil Ridley

See also Comprehensive Employment and Training Act; Employment and Training Administration; Workforce Investment Act

References and further reading

James, Donna Walker, ed. 1997. *Some Things Do Make a Difference for Youth: A Compendium of Evaluations of Youth Programs and Practices.* Washington, DC: American Youth Policy Forum.

Lerman, Robert I. 2000. "Employment and Training Programs for Out-of-School Youth." In *Improving the Odds: Increasing the Effectiveness of Publicly Funded Training.* Edited by Burt S. Barnow and Christopher T. King. Washington, DC: Urban Institute Press.

Mangum, Garth, Stephen Mangum, and Andrew Sum. 1998. *A Fourth Chance for Second Chance Programs.* Baltimore, MD: Johns Hopkins University.

Mathematica Policy Research, Inc. 2001. *Does Job Corps Work? Summary of the National Job Corps Study.* Princeton, NJ: Mathematica.

U.S. Department of Labor. 2001. *Job Corps FY 2000 Annual Report.* Washington, DC: U.S. Dept. of Labor.

Job Placement and Recruitment Firms

Job placement and recruitment firms, also known as employment agencies, perform a variety of staffing-related services that match jobseeker skills with specific positions of employment at a client company. These firms work to attract both new jobseekers and, in some cases, to lure existing employees from one company to another. In 1999, employment agencies generated approximately $91 billion in revenues (Staffing Industry Analysts 2000, 10). In 2000, the U.S. Bureau of Labor statistics estimated that there were an estimated 390,000 jobs arranged by approximately 18,000 employment agencies throughout the United States (U.S. Department of Labor 2002). With employment growth on the rise among these firms, job placement and recruiting companies comprise a vigorous portion of the U.S. workforce and economy.

There is significant diversity within the job placement and recruiting industry. Some firms specialize in placing candidates into jobs within a specific field, such as health care, whereas others specialize in filling jobs associated with a particular level of management. These firms should not be confused with other types of staffing agencies, such as temporary help firms and outsourcing firms, that engage in employee leasing. This term refers to a relationship wherein a jobseeker is hired by an agency and assigned to work at a client company location. Although the client often maintains some supervisory duties, the individual is employed by the staffing agency. Some companies, termed "full service" staffing agencies, perform both job placement and employee leasing functions. However, placement and recruiting activities foster a direct employment relationship between the jobseeker and an employer; employee leasing does not.

Most job placement and recruitment companies work on behalf of client companies to advertise, screen for, and fill open positions with applicants seeking new jobs. Generally, employers pay the firm a fee when they accept a candidate referred by the agency. Companies that use this method of job placement are often referred to as "contingency firms."

Many companies that specialize in full-time executive placement also work as "retained search firms," which generally refers to the process of locating a candidate for a specific position at a client company. In this case, the client pays a fee to the firm, regardless of whether a placement is made (Staffing Industry Analysts 2002). Retained searches generally focus on recruiting existing employees from other companies. Therefore, this service is sometimes derogatorily referred to as "headhunting" (Staffing Industry Analysts 2002).

Job placement firms can also be hired by client companies to deliver outplacement services to recently laid-off employees. These services help guide terminated workers into new jobs or careers through the provision of short- or long-term counseling and supportive services, such as resume writing assistance and interest and skill assessments (Staffing Industry Analysts 2002).

Many job placement firms also incorporate Internet-based recruiting strategies. Some of these Web-based approaches include posting positions on job boards, tracking applicant resumes, and screening candidates. This aspect of the recruiting industry eliminates many administrative inefficiencies and, consequently, results in lower client costs. As a result, Internet recruiting is becoming a more widely accepted alternative to traditional agency models (Lee 2002).

Because employers are becoming increasingly reliant on outside agencies to perform the preliminary screening of candidates, job growth is projected to increase among employment agencies between 2000 and 2010 (U.S. Department of Labor 2002). However, this growth is expected to be slower than that of other portions of the staffing industry because of the increased efficiencies associated with the use of Internet-based recruiting methods.

Jennifer Cleary

See also Contingent and Temporary Workers

References and further reading

Lee, Brian P. 2002. *Internet Recruiting 2002: State of the Industry Report.* Hunt-Scanlon Advisors. http://www.hunt-scanlon.com/research/esi_index.htm (cited October 2, 2002).

Staffing Industry Analysts. 2000. *Staffing Industry Report.* Vol. 11, no. 9. http://www.sireport.com/pdfs/indgrowth.pdf (cited October 10, 2002).

———. 2002. *The Staffing Industry Glossary of Terms.* http://www.sireport.com/resources/glossary.html (cited October 10, 2002).

U.S. Department of Labor, Bureau of Labor Statistics. 2002. "Personnel Supply Services." *Occupational Outlook Handbook 2002–2003.* http://www.bls.gov/oco/cg/cgs039.htm (cited October 2, 2002).

Job Security

Job security is the assurance workers have that they will not be released from their employment involuntarily, through discharge or layoff. In the United States, the default rule governing employment is known as employment at will, which essentially means that an employer has the absolute right to discharge or lay off an employee at any time. Therefore, employees do not have job security as a general rule. To get it, they must look to the law or to a contract.

The law in the United States does not provide a great deal of job security to employees. In fact, there is no law at either the state or federal level that provides complete job security to employees. There are a number of laws in the United States that make it illegal for employers to discharge employees for specific reasons (for example, a variety of laws prohibit discharge based on race, sex, religion, age, disability, etc.), but there is no law that prevents employers from discharging employees merely because they feel like it. Therefore, employees in the United States have job security from the law against certain types of discharges, but the law provides employees very limited job security in general.

Laws in the U. S. also provide employees very little job security against being laid off. The Worker Adjustment Retraining Notification Act of 1988 requires employers to provide employees with notice of layoffs in certain circumstances. Also, most employees who are laid off are entitled to unemployment insurance. No law limits employers' ability to lay off employees, however.

Employees also may acquire job security contractually. An employer and employee are free to enter into a contract that will provide job security to the employee, but the majority of employees do not have an individual employment contract. One sector of the workforce that does have a great deal of job security is the unionized sector. The vast majority of unionized employees are covered by a collective bargaining agreement, which is a contract between an employer and the union representing its employees that provides certain rights or benefits to the employees covered by the agreement. The vast majority of collective bargaining agreements in this country contain a just cause provision, meaning that an employee cannot be discharged without a good reason. Therefore, most unionized employees have job security that they will not be discharged at the whim of the employer..

It can be argued that the best way for U.S. employees to obtain job security is for them to provide it for themselves. According to this argument, an employer will not discharge an employee who is indispensable, therefore providing workers with job security. It is suggested that employees can do this by requiring unique skills and abilities that are needed by their employers.

In general, U.S. workers are extremely concerned about job security. A survey done by the John J. Heldrich Center for Workforce Development in 1998 revealed that 87 percent of Americans are concerned about job security for those currently employed and that 21 percent of U.S. workers believe that working hard will not guarantee them a job until retirement. It is interesting to note, however, that Americans are generally satisfied with their levels of job security. Despite employers' virtually unfettered ability to discharge or lay off employees at will, 86 percent are very or somewhat satisfied with their job security. This may be explained by the fact that most people are not aware of how little job security they have. A 1997 study by Pauline Kim showed that workers greatly overestimate the protections afforded by law, believing that they have far greater rights against unjust or arbitrary discharges than they in fact have under an at-will contract.

Steven E. Abraham

See also Collective Bargaining; Comparable Worth; Downsizing; Layoffs; Outplacement

References and further reading

Aaronson, Daniel, and Daniel G. Sullivan. 1998. "The Decline of Job Security in the 1990s: Displacement, Anxiety, and Their Effect on Wage Growth." Federal Reserve Bank of Chicago, *Economic Perspectives* 22, no. 1: 17–43.

Estlund, Cynthia L. 2002. "How Wrong Are Employees about Their Rights, and Why Does It Matter?" *New York University Law Review* 77, no. 1 (April): 6–35.

Foulkes, F. K. 1980. *Personnel Policies in Large Non-union Companies.* Englewood Cliffs, NJ: Prentice Hall.

Foulkes, F. K., and A. Whitman. 1985. "Marketing Strategies to Maintain Full Employment." *Harvard Business Review* (July/August): 30–32.

Freeman, R., and J. Medoff. 1984. *What Do Unions Do?* New York: Basic Books.

John J. Heldrich Center for Workplace Development. 1998. *Work Trends I: The Economy and Job Security.* September 3.

Kim, Pauline T. 1997. "Bargaining with Imperfect Information: A Study of Worker Perceptions of Legal Protection in an At-Will World." *Cornell Law Review* 83, no. 1: 105–160.

Schmidt, Stefanie, and Shirley V. Svorny. 1998. "Recent Trends in Job Security and Stability." *Journal of Labor Research* 19 (Fall): 647–668.

Valletta, Robert G. 1999. "Declining Job Security." *Journal of Labor Economics* 17, no. 4 (October): S170.

Veracierto, Marcello. 2002. "The Aggregate Effects of Advance Notice Requirements." *Economic Perspectives* 26, no. 1 (Spring): 19–30.

Job Skills

Throughout history, changes in technology, transportation, and communications have changed the ways in which U.S. companies conduct business. To remain competitive in the changing markets, these companies have required that their employees adapt to these new workplace advancements (Greenspan 2002, 1). As a result, U.S. workers need to update their skill sets so as to remain valuable as employees. Along the same lines, employers need to ensure that their employees are trained in the latest technologies so that they can remain competitive in the global economy (U.S. Department of Commerce 1999, 1).

The transition to a global economy has brought with it a change in the ways in which business is conducted in the U.S. workplace and in the skills needed for employment. A greater share of the workforce requires higher levels of computer and technological skills than ever before. Also, although many jobs once consisted of a small number of repetitive tasks, today's employees are expected to possess many skills that allow them to oversee several different tasks at the same time (U.S. Department of Commerce 1999, 2–3). It is not surprising then, that many employers now seek out employees with developed skill sets or the desire to improve their skills through continued education and training (U.S. Department of Commerce 1999, 4). In fact, many employers are willing to provide or even pay for this training for their employees. Lifelong learning has become the trend for the U.S. labor force, in which basic skills are no longer adequate and no longer ensure long-term employment (Greenspan 2000, 3). The following sections enumerate some of the laws and studies that have affected the delivery of and outlook on skills training in the United States.

Reports and Legislation Affecting Job Skills

Comprehensive Employment and Training Act of 1973

The Comprehensive Employment and Training Act (CETA) was enacted in 1973. The legislation effectively replaced the Manpower Development and Training Act of 1962, which provided funds to train employees who lacked the skills to keep up with current changes in workplace technologies (Gordon 1999, 70–72). CETA brought about significant changes in the relationship between training and state and federal entities, since, through CETA, states were provided more authority over training programs. Local and state governments were given discretion to establish how funds should be used and to determine how programs should be developed for their area (Gordon 1999, 74). Through funding for employment counseling, on-the-job training, and classroom training, CETA had marked impacts on the education of U.S. workers (Gordon 1999, 74).

Job Training Partnership Act of 1982

In 1982, CETA was replaced by the Job Training Partnership Act (JTPA), which was created to establish programs to assist unskilled adults and youth with entry into the workforce. The JTPA also focused on the economically disadvantaged by establishing job-training programs that would specifically help this population to obtain gainful employment (Gordon 1999, 76).

Private industries and state government were granted an increased role in the creation of training programs through the JTPA. However, they were also required to accept more responsibility for the success of these programs (Gordon 1999, 76). One goal of the JTPA was to promote a stronger connection between job-training programs and private businesses that might lend valuable expertise to the learning environment. Once these new links were established, the goals of the JTPA turned toward providing more training for individuals, particularly economically disadvantaged persons, who might be in need of employment training or retraining (Gordon 1999, 76–77).

A Nation at Risk: The Imperative for Education Reform

President Ronald Reagan's secretary of education, Terrell H. Bell, commissioned a report from the National Commission on Excellence in Education on the state of the educational system in the United States. The commission produced a report entitled *A Nation at Risk: The Imperative for Education Reform,* which sparked the nation's interest in U.S. education (Bell 1986, 3–4). The report detailed poor test scores, failing schools, and the reality that U.S. students could not compete with international students who excelled in the subjects of math and science (Levy 1996, 127).

This revival of attention to education policy motivated several new policies that attempted to improve the global competitiveness of U.S. students. As a result, new education policies emerged that focused on the enhancement of students' skill sets and abilities, particularly in the areas of science and mathematics (Thomas 2001; Reagan 1984). Thus a renewed focus on education opened new opportunities to link education with job training.

Carl D. Perkins Vocational Education Act of 1984

Although primarily a piece of legislation focused on improving the future of vocational education, the Carl D. Perkins Vocational Education Act of 1984 also had a distinct focus on job skills. The act amended the Vocational Education Act of 1963 and replaced the Vocational Education Act Amendments of 1968 and 1976. There were two primary objectives of the 1984 legislation. First, Perkins established programs that would serve to improve the job skills of those already participating in the labor force. Second, the legislation created opportunities for adults to enroll in vocational education initiatives. Through the Perkins Act, a link was created between vocational education and job readiness, job skills, and continuing education while ensuring that adults as well as students had access to these valuable programs (Gordon 1999, 77).

The Forgotten Half: Pathways to Success for America's Youth and Young Families

The Forgotten Half was a study of young American adults, published in 1988 by the William T. Grant Foundation. The report focused on young high school graduates who declined to attend college. According to the report, these young adults, particularly those aged twenty to twenty-four, had one of the highest unemployment rates in the country (William T. Grant 1988, 2). In determining the cause of this phenomenon, the report contended that the U.S. educational system neglected the needs of these students. School curricula focused on preparing college-bound students for their future while failing to supply non-college-bound youth with the necessary skills to hold gainful, long-term employment. In addition, *The Forgotten Half* argued that what little skill preparation these students did receive was severely outdated for the changing labor market. As a result, these young adults were forced to survive on low-paying jobs with little or no opportunities for advancement (William T. Grant 1988, 3).

Four proposals were made in *The Forgotten Half*, inspiring a new outlook on the preparation of non-college-bound students for graduation. First, the report advocated a more significant relationship between the adults and youth of the nation (William T. Grant 1988, 5–6). Second, the commission recommended the creation of more opportunities for community-based leadership for students. The idea was that students should be involved in the planning and implementation of the very programs that develop their futures (William T. Grant 1988, 6–8).

The report's third recommendation was centered on examples of "best practices" of existing community-based programs. An appeal was then made to government leaders at all levels to support the establishment of these community-based programs through new legislation and the encouragement of local business participation (William T. Grant 1988, 9). The fourth recommendation of the report came in the form of a legislative proposal, the Fair Chance: Youth Opportunities Demonstration Act. This legislation called for a national pilot program that would include high school graduates as candidates for admission to training and education programs (William T. Grant 1988, 10). This legislation established an opportunity for all students to obtain valuable training and the skills necessary to gain high-paying, long-term employment.

America's Choice: High Skills or Low Wages!

In June 1990, the Commission on the Skills of the American Workforce presented *America's Choice: High Skills or Low Wages!* The report detailed the fact that income levels were continually decreasing for those in the lowest wage brackets but were increasing for those in the highest wage brackets (Commission on the Skills of the American Workforce 1990). In addition, the commission noted that young adults were entering the workforce without the skills necessary to maintain gainful employment. To rectify this situation, the commission recommended a restructuring of the U.S. educational system. This new system would ensure that all students met certain skill standards upon graduation, thus leaving them more adequately prepared to enter the workforce (Commission on the Skills of the American Workforce 1990).

The Secretary's Commission on Achieving Necessary Skills (SCANS)

In June 1991, the Secretary's Commission on Achieving Necessary Skills (SCANS) published its original report, *What Work Requires of Schools.* The report discussed the most important skills that all U.S. students should know in order to be successful future employees. Through the report, the commission also described specific teaching strategies that might help teachers to foster these skills within the classroom. Extensive research allowed the secretary's commission to comment on the skills that employers most commonly classify as being important for a successful employee. The main point of this first report was to foster the academic programs that would create a more productive workplace and produce workers with higher skill levels and higher wages (SCANS 1991).

Another goal of the SCANS report was to emphasize not only the academic skills but also the interpersonal skills that employees need in order to be successful in the workplace. Public schools were seen again as a place in which these skills should be fostered and taught to all students. This focus on public education led the commission to establish a three-part academic foundation and a list of the five most vital competencies that all students should master in school. Students must learn these skills, the commission reiterated, in order to survive in the U.S. workforce (SCANS 1991).

Since publication of the SCANS report, curriculum developers have often used the commission's curriculum foundation and list of competencies as a blueprint for future change in academic programs. Subsequent reports from SCANS have further encouraged the adoption of the SCANS recommendations.

The School-to-Work Opportunities Act of 1994

The School-to-Work Opportunities Act of 1994 (STWOA) reinvented vocational education in the United States. Appropriations from the legislation allowed states to establish their own network of school-to-work programs. These plans served to link local businesses with high school youth interested in learning a specific trade (U.S. Senate 1993). The goal of the STWOA was to provide non-college-bound students with the opportunity to learn the skills that would provide them with high-paying, long-term employment.

National Skills Standards Act of 1994

The National Skills Standards Act of 1994 created the National Skills Standards Board, which encouraged the expansion of a national voluntary system of standards and assessments for skill attainment. The legislation was created to strengthen the skills of the U.S. workforce. The board was also set up to serve as an intermediary among employers, employees, and training providers. It would ensure that vital communication lines remained open so that the needs of each group were continually met. The act also aimed to foster a better connection among employers and training programs, ensuring that employers had a voice in the development of training programs and classes. Lastly, through the legislation, the National Skills Standards Board was charged with the responsibility of forging a smooth transition from the classroom to the workplace (Department of Education 2002).

The Workforce Investment Act of 1998

The Workforce Investment Act of 1998 (WIA) instituted a system of one-stop career centers throughout the nation. Each state is responsible for the establishment and maintenance of several one-stop centers, which are financed with federal funds. These centers provide employment counseling, resume assistance, job skills training, and information resources for all persons seeking employment or wishing to enhance their personal skills set (McNeil 1999, 1).

The WIA allows training providers to run their programs within these one-stop centers, but an accountability measure is imposed upon them. Training programs must demonstrate that they provide quality classes and obtain effective results for their patrons (McNeil 1999, 5). As one way of ensuring this quality, training providers are required to offer several specific services enumerated within the legislation (McNeil 1999, 3, 8).

Karin A. Garver

See also Earnings and Education; Education Reform and the Workforce; Lifelong Learning

References and further reading

Bell, Terrell H. 1986. "Education Policy: An Inside View of the Reagan Administration." *Education Digest* 52 (November): 2–6.

Commission on the Skills of the American Workforce. 1990. *America's Choice: High Skills or Low Wages!* Rochester: National Center on Education and the Economy.

Gordon, Howard R. D. 1999. *The History and Growth of Vocational Education in America.* Boston: Allyn and Bacon.

Greenspan, Alan. 2002. "The Evolving Demand for Skills." Speech delivered at the U.S. Department of Labor National Skills Summit, Washington, DC.

Levy, Peter B. 1996. *Encyclopedia of the Reagan-Bush Years.* Westport: Greenwood Press.

McNeil, Patricia W. 1999. *Program Memorandum: Responsibilities and Opportunities Created by Title I of the Workforce Investment Act of 1998.* Washington, DC: United States Department of Education. http://www.ed.gov (cited August 18, 2002).

SCANS (Secretary's Commission on Achieving Necessary Skills). 1991. *What Work Requires of Schools: A SCANS Report for America 2000.* Washington, DC: U.S. Department of Labor.

THOMAS: Legislative Information on the Internet. 1983. "H.R. 1310—Public Law: 98–377." http://thomas.loc.gov (cited April 11, 2001).

U.S. Department of Commerce, U.S. Department of Education, U.S. Department of Labor, National Institute of Literacy, and the Small Business Administration. 1999. "Twenty-First-Century Skills for Twenty-First-Century Jobs." A Report of the U.S. Department of Commerce, U.S. Department of Education, U.S. Department of Labor, National Institute of Literacy, and the Small Business Administration.

U.S. Department of Education. 2002. *National Skills Standards Act of 1994.* http://www.ed.gov/legislation/GOALS2000/TheAct/sec502.html (cited June 22, 2002).

U.S. Senate. 1993. *School-to-Work Opportunities Act of 1993 Report.* 103rd Congress, 1st session.

William T. Grant Foundation Commission on Work, Family, and Citizenship. 1988. *The Forgotten Half: Pathways to Success for America's Youth and Young Families.* Washington, DC: William T. Grant Foundation.

Job Training Partnership Act (JTPA) (1982)

On October 13, 1982, with the national unemployment rate at 10.1 percent, the federal Job Training

Partnership Act (JTPA) was signed into law. This legislation, which replaced the decade-old Comprehensive Employment and Training program (CETA), authorized funding for a year-round training program for disadvantaged adults and youth and for a summer youth program. For a program or organization to qualify for participation in most JTPA programs, at least 90 percent of the participants it served had to be economically disadvantaged. Welfare recipients and school dropouts aged sixteen to twenty-one were to be served in proportion to their incidence in the overall eligible population. Each service area was required to spend at least 40 percent of its JTPA funds on youth. Expenditures for a combination of administrative and other nontraining costs, such as supportive services for participants, were capped at 30 percent. Although the administration of President Ronald Reagan tried to eliminate the Job Corps program (a 1960s residential program that removed deeply economically disadvantaged youth from their home environments), it was continued under Title IV of JTPA.

Although criticized throughout its fifteen-year tenure for "creaming" (serving a largely job-ready and temporarily unemployed population), the JTPA program nevertheless had a lasting impact on the shape of employment and training service delivery in the United States. In keeping with President Reagan's philosophy of government downsizing and devolution (shifting service delivery from the federal to the state and local levels), JTPA shifted primary responsibility for employment and training program administration to states and localities. It also established a significant role for business and industry in planning and monitoring services and moved the focus away from public sector employment and toward training for unsubsidized jobs. Finally, JTPA introduced a strong emphasis on performance standards, such as increases in employment and earnings and a reduction in welfare dependency.

Under JTPA, state governors appointed and shared administrative authority with advisory job training coordinating councils. States were divided into service delivery areas (SDAs), the primary vehicles for providing training services. Each state and SDA prepared a two-year program plan, and each SDA established a private industry council (PIC), consisting of a majority of local business leaders, as well as representatives of educational and economic development agencies, community-based organizations, and the public employment service. PIC members were appointed by locally elected officials and provided overall policy guidance and oversight in partnership with local officials. In the early days, many public statements by Labor Secretary Raymond Donovan reflected the Reagan administration's belief that a strong reliance on the private sector would result in creation of more permanent jobs.

Criticism of JTPA programs emerged as early as 1984. The National Youth Employment Coalition surveyed 1,000 local groups involved with youth training and reported that losses of service for youth most seriously at risk and needing more lengthy and costly assistance had already occurred. An independent review of JTPA by Grinker, Walker Associates in 1984 acknowledged the positive involvement of the private sector in the development and implementation of local employment and training policies. However, the review also found that SDAs were oriented toward serving individuals needing minimal services and training.

This concern that restrictive provisions resulted in an emphasis on short-term training and employment placement and placed programs at risk of serving those less in need of services became a recurring theme in the JTPA program. Despite growing worries about this practice, only minor legislative changes were made in 1986, and two years later Congress expanded only the Title III program for dislocated workers. Although the Department of Labor prepared major amendments to Titles II-A and II-B, Congress took no action in either 1989 or 1990.

A 1989 General Accounting Office (GAO) report found that more employable JTPA program participants were receiving higher levels of service than dropouts, welfare recipients, and minorities. The most disadvantaged participants were also less likely to receive occupational training and to be trained in high-skilled occupations. In a 1991 analysis of data provided by 277 SDAs, a GAO report entitled *Job Training Partnership Act: Racial and Gender Disparities* found that black participants were more likely than white to receive only job search assistance and that women, although receiving more classroom training than men, received training for lower-wage occupations.

Congress was finally stimulated to act by these GAO reports and other JTPA program evaluations.

The Job Training Reform Amendments of 1992 took effect July 1, 1993. Employment and training services for economically disadvantaged out-of-school youth were separated from Title II-A and put into a new Title II-C. States were required to spend at least 40 percent of funds for adult training programs and 40 percent for youth, 65 percent of youth served had to be in identified "hard-to-serve" categories, and 50 percent had to be out-of-school youth. Concerns about creaming were addressed by targeting additional populations, such as individuals with basic skills deficiencies and those who were behind in grade level, pregnant or parenting, or homeless or runaways. These amendments required that shorter-term services such as job search assistance and job search skills training be accompanied by other educational or training services. Local programs were also mandated to assess participant skills and service needs and develop individual service plans.

In a 1995 review of JTPA evaluation studies, Norton Grubb found very modest earnings increases for adults who participated in JTPA programs, with women showing a greater impact than men. He concluded that the benefits to participants were too small to aid them in leaving the welfare rolls or escaping poverty. Furthermore, the impact for youth was zero or negative.

During the mid-1990s, the Clinton administration, now operating in a stronger economic climate, began to shape its own ideas about employment and training. On August 7, 1998, President Clinton signed the Workforce Investment Act of 1998 (WIA), comprehensive reform legislation that superseded the Job Training Partnership Act (JTPA) and had as its cornerstone the concept of one-stop service delivery.

Natalie Ammarell

See also Comprehensive Employment and Training Act; Employment and Training Administration; Welfare to Work; Workforce Investment Act

References and further reading

Bloom, Howard S., Larry L. Orr, George Cave, Stephen H. Bell, Fred Doolittle, and Winston Lin. 1994. *The National JTPA Study: Overview: Impacts, Benefits, and Costs of Title II-A*. Bethesda, MD: Abt Associates, March.

Grinker, Walker and Associates. 1984. *An Independent Sector Assessment of JTPA—Phase One: The Initial Transition.* New York: Grinker, Walker and Associates.

Grubb, W. N. 1995. *Evaluating Job Training Programs in the United States: Evidence and Explanations.* Technical Assistance Report MDS–1047. Berkeley: University of California, May.

Kogan, Deborah, et al. 1989. *Improving the Quality of Training under JTPA*. Berkeley: Berkeley Planning Associates and SRI International, for the U.S. Department of Labor.

U.S. Department of Labor. "Training and Employment Report of the Secretary of Labor." Reports for the periods July 1986–September 1987, July 1988–September 1990, July 1990–September 1991, July 1991–September 1992, July 1992–September 1993, and July 1995–September 1996 are all available at http://wdr.doleta.gov/opr/FULLTEXT/default.asp?titlesort=yes (cited June 15, 2002).

U.S. General Accounting Office. 1989. *Job Training Partnership Act: Services and Outcomes for Participants with Differing Needs.* June 9. Gaithersburg, MD: U.S. General Accounting Office.

Justice for Janitors

A nationwide campaign of the Service Employees International Union (SEIU), Justice for Janitors (JFJ) helps organize janitors by using direct action in their struggle for living wages, health benefits, and secure full-time jobs. JFJ is notable for its effort to broaden the U.S. labor movement to include immigrant and lower-skilled workers who have had little voice in the public arena. The JFJ campaign began in Denver in 1985, and by 2002 it represented 202,000 members nationwide. The organizing techniques employed by the SEIU are now used across the nation and the world in a number of industries. In 1995, SEIU president John Sweeney won the presidency of the AFL-CIO in its first contested election, and he set about implementing the organizing strategies used by the SEIU on a wider scale.

SEIU has a lengthy history, beginning as an association of apartment janitors in Chicago at the turn of the twentieth century. Since that time, SEIU has broadened its scope to become the largest union in the American Federation of Labor and Congress of Industrial Organizations (AFL-CIO), representing 1.5 million building service, health care, public service, and industrial service workers.

The JFJ campaign began at a particularly important time in SEIU's history. The 1970s and 1980s had seen an overall weakening of unions generally. Industrial and office janitors in particular were facing the growth of a phenomenon in urban economies called "outsourcing" or "contracting out": the use of private contractors to supply building services rather than the direct employment of workers covered by a city-wide master contract. Since labor makes up the bulk of costs in the service industry, contractors tend to cut workers' wages and benefits and to employ workers who do not have the protection of unions. In addition, the use of contractors tends to make owners less accountable and to result in both employers and employees being spread out over a city, making organization all the more difficult (Howley 1990; Williams 1999).

The SEIU has responded with its Justice for Janitors campaign to bring public awareness to the challenges facing workers, and it has successfully achieved living wages, health care benefits, and full-time employment in the cities in which it has organized. The campaign has used a variety of means, including rallies, press conferences, leafleting, and even civil disobedience (Howley 1990). The campaign began in 1985 with an effort to organize janitors in Denver. It was a significant turning point in the SEIU's efforts, for several reasons. The Denver effort marked the first JFJ campaign, bringing new attention to its agenda, but equally important, the Denver JFJ also accomplished two novel goals: it organized workers in a new area throughout the city, and it organized all workers, including undocumented immigrants.

The JFJ campaign has continued to bring public attention to issues of social justice facing janitors through the 1990s and into the present. In 1990, a Los Angeles rally was videotaped during which sixty demonstrators were beaten by police. The resulting publicity helped SEIU to win its strike and, more important, to capture the sympathy of an international public. In 1995, JFJ won public attention with a sit-in that blocked traffic on a busy bridge in Washington, D.C., leading to a successful citywide union contract. And in 2000, simultaneous JFJ campaigns won health care benefits and wage increases for workers in St. Louis, Chicago, and Los Angeles. This pattern of achievements typifies JFJ's strategy of organizing city by city to respond to the particular challenges of each area.

Since the beginning of the JFJ campaign in 1985, janitors' membership in SEIU has increased from 150,000 to 202,000 (Lerner 2002). SEIU and JFJ continue to work to increase full-time employment; secure health care and basic benefits, and expand the protection of immigrant workers.

Derek Barker

See also American Federation of Labor and Congress of Industrial Organizations; Health Insurance; Immigrants and Work; Living Wage; Sweeney, John J.

References and further reading

Howley, John. 1990. "Justice for Janitors: The Challenge of Organizing in the Contract Service." *Labor Research Review* 15 (Spring): 60–71.

Lerner, Stephen, director of SEIU Building Services Division. Telephone interview by Derek Barker, July 2002.

Services Employees International Union. 2002. http://www.seiu.org/ (cited July 12, 2002).

Williams, Jane. 1999. "Restructuring Labor's Identity: The Justice for Janitors Campaign in Washington, D.C." Pp. 203–217 in *The Transformation of U.S. Unions.* Edited by Ray M. Tillman and Michael S. Cummings. Boulder, CO: Lynne Rienner Publishers.

K

Knights of Labor

The Noble Order of the Knights of Labor was the most radical of the dominant U.S. labor organizations during the Gilded Age of the late nineteenth century. In an era of industrial expansion, speculation, and a widening gap between workers and financiers, the Knights of Labor was motivated by a radically inclusive vision of the solidarity of all labor. It was in the Knights of Labor that, for the first time, unskilled workers found a place within the U.S. labor movement.

The order was originally founded as a fraternal society with a distinct vision of community, in which workers would help each other to alleviate the toils of labor through education and cooperation. Unlike the trade unions at the time, the Knights of Labor refused to exclude unskilled workers or to be divided by particular crafts and industries. In the words of Terence Powderly, the organization's most important leader, "It was because the trade union failed to recognize the rights of man, and looked only to the rights of tradesmen, that the Knights of Labor became a possibility" (Powderly 1890/1967). Despite this vision of solidarity, the Knights of Labor attempted to distance itself from the label of "socialism," proclaiming "we mean no conflict with legitimate enterprise, no antagonism to necessary capital" (Commons 1918/1966, 198). The Knights of Labor rejected violence and revolution and often distanced itself from strikes. Instead, throughout its history the order was committed to the improvement of workers' lives by providing education about temperance, cooperation, fraternal values, and the implications of the wage system.

The Knights of Labor was established in 1869 by Uriah S. Stephens as a fraternal society for a small group of garment workers in Philadelphia. In reaction to the persecution of groups that openly advocated socialism and anarchism, the Knights of Labor originally shunned political action. Instead, the group began as a secret society in the style of the Freemasons, but specifically devoted itself to worker education and cooperatives. The worker-owned cooperatives sometimes (though not often) provided material benefits, but the rewards of membership during this period were largely cultural, including, for example, poetry, storytelling, sporting events, and, in the Masonic tradition, ritual. These cultural dimensions persisted in varying degrees throughout the Knights of Labor's history (Weir 1996).

The Knights of Labor's first step toward national prominence was to abandon the policy of secrecy in 1874. Following that decision, the organization gradually expanded its involvement in political action. In 1879, Stephens was replaced by Terence V. Powderly as general master workman, and it was under Powderly's leadership that the Knights of Labor would reach its peak of development. The order then established a new constitution that created a central infrastructure capable of building a national organization. Membership began to expand during this

Illustration from Frank Leslie's Illustrated *of the tenth annual convention of the Knights of Labor in 1886, with an African American delegate introducing Terence Powderly. (Library of Congress)*

period, from 9,000 in 1878 to 52,000 by 1883 (Commons 1918/1966, 339).

It was at this time that the Knights of Labor became more active in strikes and in political organizing, leading to its most important material successes. In 1883, the Knights of Labor supported a telegraph workers' strike against Western Union. Although the strike ultimately failed, it helped to mobilize the order for future organizing. The Knights of Labor engaged in its most important and successful strike against the Jay Gould railroad empire in 1885. During this period, the organization also participated in aggressive political action and achieved its most important legislative victories on such issues as child labor and shorter workdays. Perhaps most important, the Knights of Labor helped establish state and federal labor bureaus to further the public's awareness of workers' conditions. In 1886, the Knights of Labor reached its peak membership of 700,000 (Commons 1918/1966).

As the Knights of Labor expanded into national prominence, it also became more diverse. The order refused to exclude blacks, declaring that, "the (outside) color of a candidate shall not debar him from admission: rather let the coloring of his mind and heart be the test." (Kessler 1952, 249). Because trade unions emphasized only the interests of skilled workers, the Knights of Labor's inclusive vision of solidarity was friendlier to the interests of newly emancipated African Americans than were other parts of the U.S. labor movement. Although local prejudices sometimes kept individual chapters segregated, the district and state assemblies were all integrated. As a result, the multiracial Knights of Labor regularly faced intimidation from employers in the Jim Crow South. The race issue was regularly deployed to divide support for strikes, many locals were forced into secrecy, and one white organizer was lynched and shot. Nevertheless, African American membership reached a peak of 60,000 in 1886 (Kessler 1952).

Women were also a significant presence in the Knights of Labor, again through both mixed organizations and so-called ladies' locals, with female membership estimated at 65,000 in 1887 (Levine 1983). As women entered the factory workforce in greater numbers, they joined their male counterparts in seeking reform of the wage system and establishing cooperatives. The Knights of Labor tapped into this growing population by dedicating itself to women's suffrage, equal pay for equal work, and even the recognition of housework as productive labor. Women had often gained organizing experience in the suffrage and temperance movements and proved equally adept at organizing strikes and cooperatives. One labor newspaper exclaimed that "they are the best men in the Order" (Levine 1983).

The Knights of Labor experienced a rapid decline after reaching its peak in 1886. This decline may have been the inevitable result of its utopian ideology, but changing circumstances also played a role. Since the Knights of Labor had been formed as an alternative to the skilled workers' unions, the unions resisted the Knights of Labor's all-inclusive vision. The first sign of animosity between the two groups was the leaking of a top secret memo from Powderly ordering the Knights of Labor not to participate when the unions called for a general strike in support of the eight-hour work day. Competition with skilled workers came to a head with the formation of the American Federation of Labor in 1886. To compound matters, employer associations had been forming and organizing successful lockouts against the Knights of Labor. And finally, the order suffered from negative publicity when it was falsely associated with the Haymarket Square Incident. By 1890, membership was reduced to 100,000. With the dissolution of the Knights of Labor, Powderly and other former leaders went on to join forces with the Farmer's Alliance and the populist movement.

Derek Barker

See also American Federation of Labor and Congress of Industrial Organizations; Bureau of Labor Statistics; Haymarket Square Incident; Socialism; Strikes

References and further reading

Commons, John R., et al. 1918/1966. *History of Labor in the United States.* Vol. 2. New York: Macmillan.

Kessler, Sidney H. 1952. "The Organization of Negroes in the Knights of Labor." *Journal of Negro History* 37, no. 3: 248–276.

Levine, Susan. 1983. "Labor's True Woman: Domesticity and Equal Rights in the Knights of Labor." *Journal of American History* 70, no. 2: 323–339.

Phelan, Craig. 2000. *Grand Master Workman: Terence Powderly and the Knights of Labor.* Westport, CT: Greenwood Press.

Powderly, Terence V. 1890/1967. *Thirty Years of Labor, 1859 to 1889.* New York: Augustus M. Kelly.

Weir, Robert. 1996. *Beyond Labor's Veil: The Culture of the Knights of Labor.* University Park: Pennsylvania State University Press.

L

La Follette, Robert (1855–1925)

Born on June 14, 1855, in Primrose, Wisconsin, "Fighting Bob" La Follette served as a Republican in the House of Representatives from 1885 to 1891. Returning to civilian life as a lawyer, he became convinced that a wealthy lumber baron named Philetus Sawyer had tried to bribe him to fix a legal case, triggering a lifelong campaign against big business. He saw his main role as protecting the people against corporations and selfish interests.

A brilliant orator, he tapped into the farmers and small businesspeople's anger at eastern capitalists and the railroads and their control of the political process. In 1900, he was elected governor of Wisconsin and quickly initiated railroad reform. He pushed through a new tax on railroad property and set up a commission to regulate its activities. To combat the corruption of Wisconsin politics by big business, he championed the institution of direct primary elections and spending limits on campaigns. In 1905, toward the end of his term as governor, he recommended that his state adopt a graduated income tax to tax singles with incomes over $800 and married couples with incomes over $1,200. These reforms became part of what was known as "the Wisconsin idea."

In 1906, La Follette was elected to the U.S. Senate. He would remain in Washington until his death on June 18, 1925. For there, he continued his campaign against corporations and railroads. He believed that 100 industrialists controlled the

Robert La Follette, ca. 1901–1925 (Library of Congress)

nation's economy. He promoted the growth of trade unions as a check on big business and opposed the Payne-Aldrich tariff on a variety of imported goods, believing that monopolies would benefit from it more than the average working person.

While seeking the presidential nomination in 1908 and 1912, he founded *La Follette's Weekly*

Magazine (1909) and the National Progressive Republican League (1911) to promote his reform ideals. His identification with working people led him to oppose U.S. entry into World War I and to almost be expelled from the Senate for disloyalty in 1917.

In the last three years of his life, La Follette supported the Conference for Progressive Political Action (CPPA), which comprised the leaders of several machinists' unions and railway brotherhoods. The CPPA, adopting the moniker "Progressive Party," named La Follette as its presidential candidate in 1924, although he ran as an independent because he feared being linked to socialism and garnered 17 percent of the vote. He campaigned against child labor and the use of court injunctions to end labor disputes but supported the breakup of monopolies and near monopolies, public ownership of railroads and natural resources, farm relief measures, laws to aid the less privileged, and direct election of federal judges. After his death a year later, the Progressive Party crumbled as a national force. Yet his two sons, Robert and Philip, carried on his campaign and organized the Progressive Party in Wisconsin. Much of the reforms that he advocated throughout his life would become national policy after his death.

T. Jason Soderstrum

See also Communism in the U.S. Trade Union Movement; Democratic Socialism

References and further reading

Burgchardt, Carl R. 1992. *Robert M. La Follette, Sr.: The Voice of Conscience.* New York: Greenwood Press.

Greenbaum, Fred. 1975. *Robert Marion La Follette.* Boston: Twayne Publishers.

La Follette, Robert M. 1960. *La Follette's Autobiography.* Madison: University of Wisconsin Press.

Thelen, David P. 1966. *The Early Life of Robert M. La Follette, 1855–1884.* Chicago: Loyola University Press.

Thelen, David P. 1986. *Robert M. LaFollette and the Insurgent Spirit.* Madison: University of Wisconsin Press.

Unger, Nancy C. 2000. *Fighting Bob La Follette: The Righteous Reformer.* Chapel Hill: University of North Carolina Press.

Weisberger, Bernard A. 1994. *The La Follettes of Wisconsin: Love and Politics in Progressive America.* Madison: University of Wisconsin Press.

Labor Force

A nation's labor force is the total population of people looking for work or already working. Incorporated into the concept of the labor force are all of the historical, demographic, political, and social factors present in a society and how they affect the number of people working or looking for work. These factors have changed enormously throughout U.S. history, as different groups within the population enter and leave the workforce over time (Toossi 2002, 15). A closer look at some of these factors will help to decipher the nuances of what is called the "labor force."

Historical Changes in the Labor Force

The composition of the U.S. labor force has exhibited significant growth and change throughout history. Variation in participation rates and population growth are the two main elements that affect growth in the labor force (Toossi 2002, 16). Many factors have shaped labor force participation and growth over time and provide an important glance into the trends that continually determine the composition of the labor force.

Population and Birth Patterns

During the twentieth century, changing birth patterns have played a major role in the composition of the labor force. In the 1920s and 1930s, a period of time characterized as a "birth dearth," the number of births in the United States declined significantly. Consequently, as this generation of children entered and continued to participate in the workforce, they represented a blip in the labor force that was much smaller than the other age groups in the workforce. Similarly, the "baby bust" in the late 1960s and 1970s was characterized by a notable drop in the birth rate. This generation of citizens will affect the labor force in ways similar to the birth dearth generation (Toossi 2002, 16).

The "baby boom" from 1946 to 1964 represents another significant phenomenon that would later have enormous effects in the U.S. labor force. The large number of individuals from this generation entering the workforce has posed many different issues for the country's labor force (Toossi 2002, 16; Kutscher 1993, 3). Most recently, the question of adequate Social Security benefits has become a major concern for this unusually large section of the population as it begins to retire from the workforce. In addition, the baby boom generation has created a new generational phenomenon called the "baby boomlet," representing the children of the baby boomers, who will likewise flood the labor force in the coming years, resulting in labor situations similar to those faced by their parents (Toossi 2002, 16).

Gender and the Labor Force

One of the most significant factors affecting the growth and change of the U.S. labor force over time has been the increased labor force participation of women. In the decades following World War II, the United States experienced an expansion that resulted in marked economic growth. The demand for labor increased rapidly, creating opportunities for women to enter the workforce in record numbers (Toossi 2002, 16; Fullerton 1999, 3, 5; Kutscher 1993, 3). The civil rights movement, coupled with the women's movement, established a situation within the country in which it became more acceptable for women to hold gainful employment. Since this time, the participation rate of women in the workforce has increased with every passing decade (Toossi 2002, 16).

Race and Ethnicity in the Labor Force

Particularly since the 1950s, the U.S. population has become more ethnically and racially diverse. As a result, the U.S. labor force has also become much more diverse. Immigration is the major source of this population and diversity increase in the United States (Fullerton 1991, 6; Kutscher 1993, 4–5; Toossi 2002, 16, 20). Population data from 1980 reports that the United States' population consisted of 86 percent whites (including those of Hispanic origin), 11.8 percent blacks, 0.6 percent American Indians, and 1.6 percent Asians. Ten years later, blacks rose to 12.3 percent of the population, American Indians and Asians rose to 0.8 and 3 percent respectively, and whites fell to 84 percent of the population (Toossi 2002, 20; U.S. Census 2001). Similarly, the 2000 U.S. Census shows that whites continued to decline to 82 percent of the population, while blacks, American Indians, and Asians all rose to 12.8, 0.9, and 4.1 percent, respectively, of the population (U.S. Census 2001).

In future decades, projections show that non-Hispanic whites will continue to decline in number, perhaps falling to as low as 54 percent of the population by 2050. At the same time, Hispanics are expected to reach 23 percent of the population, blacks 15 percent of the population, and "others" 10 percent of the population during the same time period (Toossi 2002, 20, 23). Consequently, these population changes are expected to change dramatically the diversity of and the participation in the U.S. labor force (Toossi 2002, 23).

The Future of the U.S. Labor Force

One function of the Bureau of Labor Statistics is to examine labor force trends to predict how the labor force may grow and change in coming years. These forecasts then shape the future of workforce policy for the country. The forecasts, often stretching fifty years into the future, are based on two main indicators: the predicted trends of different populations in the labor force and the past size and growth of different populations (Toossi 2002, 16). One current prediction is that labor force growth will slow down in the coming decades. The U.S. labor force grew rapidly during the last fifty years of the twentieth century. In the future, this growth is expected to continue but at a much slower rate (Toossi 2002, 15; Fullerton 1999, 7).

The age and gender composition of the labor force is also expected to change in the coming decades. Although the increase of females in the workforce is not expected to stop entirely, it will likely slow in future decades, similar to the way in which overall labor force participation will continue to grow at a slower rate (Toossi 2002, 15; Fullerton 1999, 7). As the baby boomer and boomlet generations of workers mature, the overall age of the labor force will increase as well. For several decades, the United States will experience an overall age increase in the population of those in the workforce (Toossi 2002, 15; Fullerton 1999, 6).

In addition to these changing factors, the ethnic and racial composition of the U.S. labor force is also expected to change dramatically in the near future. Labor force projections indicate that the U.S. labor force will continue to become more diverse. The Bureau of Labor Statistics predicts that minorities will comprise a larger overall percentage of the labor force than whites in the future (Toossi 2002, 15–16; Fullerton 1999, 11–12).

Karin A. Garver

See also Careers; Labor Market; Occupations and Occupational Trends in the United States; Unemployment Rate

References and further reading

Fullerton, Howard N., Jr. 1999. "Labor Force Participation: 75 Years of Change, 1950–98 and 1998–2025." *Monthly Labor Review* 122, no. 12: 3–12.

Kutscher, Ronald E. 1993. "Historical Trends, 1950–92, and Current Uncertainties." *Monthly Labor Review* 116, no. 11: 3–10.

Toossi, Mitra. 2002. "A Century of Change: The U.S. Labor Force, 1950–2050." *Monthly Labor Review* 125, no. 5: 15–28.

U.S. Census Bureau. 2001. "Resident Population by Race, 1980 to 2000, and Projections, 2005 to 2050." *Statistical Abstract of the United States: 2001.* Washington, DC: U.S. Census Bureau.

Labor Market

Changes in employment and unemployment are widely regarded as the two most instructive labor market indicators for developed countries. These indicators provide information about both the overall economy and current labor market performance (Sorrentino and Moy 2002, 15). In general, the labor market of a particular country can tell a great deal about the strength of the economy, the power of the workers, and the degree to which the state is involved in labor relations (Gordon, Edwards, and Reich 1982, 21).

The Labor Market and Freedom

The establishment of labor markets in the United States created a newfound freedom for U.S. workers. Where once workers held a servantlike position with masters rather than bosses, now workers enjoyed the freedom of moving from one job to the next as they pleased. Employers quickly learned that if they treated their workers poorly, more often than not, there was another employer offering more benefits and better conditions waiting to hire their employees. Employers had come to rely on the institution of indentured servitude to provide dependable labor, so as this practice began to decline, the institution of slavery took its place in U.S. society (Jacoby 1998, 25).

At the same time that slavery bound workers to masters, the new U.S. labor market afforded others freedoms they had never before experienced. Workers were no longer forced into any particular line of work as determined by birth but rather became willing participants in the labor market. They entered into an agreement with an employer that they were free to terminate at any time. The active labor market afforded workers a set of choices. No longer did status, custom, or law determine the fate of a laborer, but rather the labor market and his or her own desires held this power (Jacoby 1998, 35). It is important to reiterate, however, that the exercise of slavery in the United States meant that not all Americans were afforded this power.

Slow Integration of the U.S. Labor Market

In the years following the Civil War, advancements in the areas of communications and transportation allowed U.S. business owners to expand their companies to a national level (Rosenbloom 1996a, 626; Rosenbloom 1990, 440). Communication and transportation are two important factors in the integration of labor markets. An "integrated" labor market is characterized as one in which there is a free and rapid exchange of information among labor market participants (Rosenbloom 1996b, 3). Thus, these improvements in transportation and communication allowed for a more integrated labor market in the United States.

However, research shows that the country's labor market integrated only regionally at first. The north central and northeastern regions of the United States produced a highly integrated labor market, whereas the southern region of the United States produced its own integrated labor market. These markets, however, initially failed to integrate with each other. It was not until after World War I that the U.S. labor market began to emerge as one entity, integrated throughout the entire country (Rosenbloom 1996, 627).

The Modern Labor Market

Early labor markets, in which employees switched from job to job frequently with little stability for either the employee or the employer, are thought to have given way to the modern labor market sometime in the 1940s and 1950s. The pre–World War II market is often characterized as chaotic. Within this labor market structure, workers had little job security, received few or menial wage increases over their lifetimes, held no rights as aging workers, and were often disciplined through fines or firing. In contrast, in the modern labor market, workers have obtained more long-terms contracts for work with their employers. In addition, they receive more substantial wage increases over time, have more job security, are afforded rights as they get older, enjoy benefits from their employers, and are more often disciplined through the awarding or withholding of incentives (Goldin 1994, 28).

The evolution of the U.S. labor market, or the change from a market in which job security was low to a market in which job security was high, is one that is difficult to define. Exploring different ideas on the subject will help to define the possibilities of what caused the change in the U.S. labor market system. One school of thought looks toward technology as the impetus for a more stable labor market. As new technologies were developed, employers were forced to spend time and resources training their employees to use them effectively. Once employers provided these resources, they had a higher incentive to retain the workers they trained. Thus, employers began to engage in tactics to hold on to their workers for longer periods of time (Goldin 1994, 29).

Along with this hypothesis goes the idea that an increase in the bureaucratic nature of business created a change in the structure of the labor market. As U.S. firms grew larger, the rules of foremen and supervisors gave way to the rules of upper-level management. Personnel offices were established to enforce the rules of the company, thus reducing the opportunity for lower-level supervisors to hire and fire at will. The emergence of personnel offices and specific company policies on employment led to a more stable employee base for many businesses that had been losing and gaining employees rapidly as a result of the whims of oppressive foremen (Goldin 1994, 29).

Comparisons with the European Labor Market

The U.S. labor market is different from those commonly seen in Europe. Although U.S. businesses normally resort to layoffs when faced with difficult times, European businesses more commonly rely on attrition and work sharing to get through financial crises (Houseman 1994, 1). Some of the differences in U.S. and European labor markets can be linked to differences in labor policy. Although layoffs are discouraged in Europe and notice must be given to employees before being fired, U.S. policies are quite different. U.S. companies are not required to give notice to employees when layoffs are a result of an unexpected financial downturn within the company or if the company has taken certain steps to avoid the layoffs. In addition, U.S. businesses are not required to provide any compensation to employees who are laid off (Houseman 1994, 1).

Karin Garver

See also Labor Force; Recession

References and further reading

Goldin, Claudia. 1994. "Labor Markets in the Twentieth Century." NBER Working Paper Series on Historical Factors in Long-Run Growth. Cambridge: National Bureau of Economic Research.

Gordon, David M., Richard Edwards, and Michael Reich. 1982. *Segmented Work, Divided Workers: The Historical Transformation of Labor in the United States.* Cambridge: Cambridge University Press.

Houseman, Susan N. 1994. "Job Security v. Labor Market Flexibility: Is There a Tradeoff?" Kalamazoo, MI: W. E. Upjohn Institute for Employment Research.

Jacoby, Daniel. 1998. *Laboring for Freedom: A New Look at the History of Labor in America.* Armonk: M. E. Sharpe.

Rosenbloom, Joshua. 1990. "Labor Market Institutions and the Geographic Integration of Labor Markets in the Late Nineteenth-Century United States." *Journal of Economic History* 50, no. 2: 440–441.

———. 1996a. "Was There a National Labor Market at the End of the Nineteenth Century? New Evidence on Earnings in Manufacturing." *Journal of Economic History* 56, no. 3: 626–656.

———. 1996b. "The Extent of the Labor Market in the United States, 1950–1914." NBER Historical Paper 78, 1–24.

Sorrentino, Constance, and Joyanna Moy. 2002. "U.S. Labor Market Performance in International Perspective." *Monthly Labor Review* 125, no. 6: 15–35.

Layoffs

Layoffs are generally the involuntary termination of employees that are not based on their wrongdoing. According to Organization for Economic Cooperation and Development (OECD), a person who is laid off is "a person whose contract of employment has been suspended for a specified or unspecified period at the end of which the person concerned has a recognized right to recover his employment" (OECD 1983, 13). The National Commission for Employment Policy defines layoffs as "a reduction of workers in a firm, lasting weeks, a few days, months or being permanent, in case the firm decides to close down any sector or even an entire production line." (National Commission for Employment Policy 1991, 1). In addition, this commission also defines the worker who has been permanently laid off or has no expectation to be recalled to work as a dislocated worker.

There is generally a cyclical trend to layoffs within an economy. For the most part, a rise in the gross domestic product (GDP) is linked to a reduction in the number of layoffs, as firms need to expand their workforces to keep up with consumer demand. During a recession, however, declining GDP tends to increase the rate of layoffs because firms must reduce their production in response to the fall in demand. A specific firm can initiate a lay-

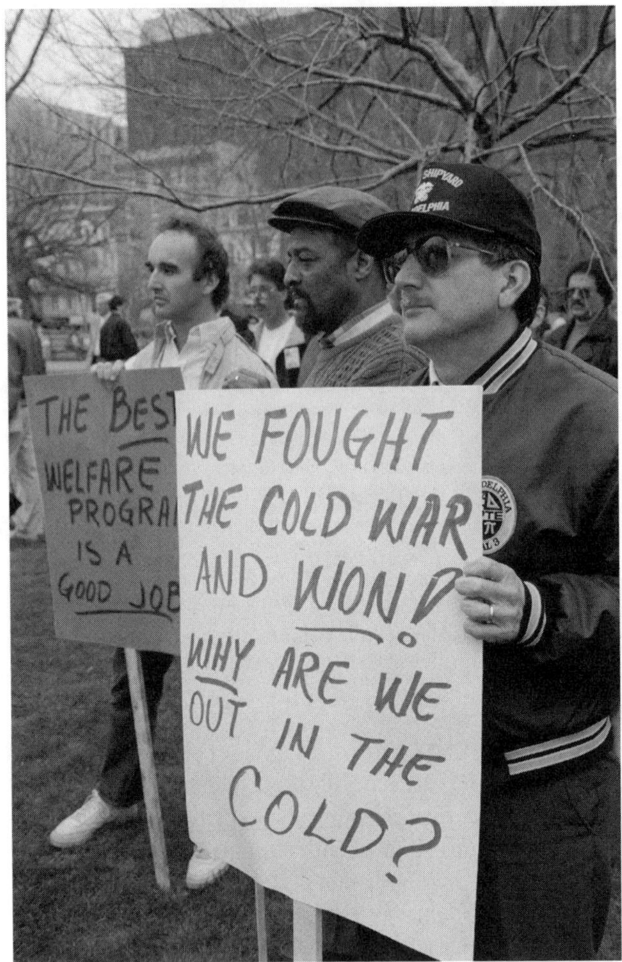

Unemployed defense industry workers protest job losses, Washington, D.C., April 1992 (Wally McNamee/Corbis)

off for many reasons. Most have to do with the firm's desire to reduce costs, improve efficiency, and so on.

It should be noted that there has been a change in the way employers have responded to recessionary periods over time. In the late nineteenth and early twentieth centuries, layoffs were not commonly used. Instead, employers resorted to devices such as work sharing and reducing wages in an effort to keep as many people employed as possible. These practices changed after the passage of the Social Security Act (that is, unemployment insurance) in 1935. A person must be totally out of work to collect unemployment insurance; benefits may not be collected if a person is working part-time. As a result, employers stopped using work sharing and similar arrangements and moved toward using layoffs. For example, layoffs were not very common during the major recessions of 1893, 1921, or 1929 but were very common in the early 1960s, 1970s, and 1980s.

Once a firm decides to lay off workers, there is very little to prevent it from doing so. The Worker Adjustment Retraining Notification Act of 1988 requires employers to provide employees with notice of layoffs in certain circumstances, but no law limits employers' ability to lay off employees. Employees who are laid off are entitled to unemployment insurance. There is a difference in how layoffs are carried out in unionized and nonunion firms, however. In nonunion firms, there are no restrictions on whom the firm decides to lay off, whether the employer is required to pay severance to the employees who are laid off or to implement other arrangements (for example, work sharing) to avoid having to lay off employees.

In the unionized sector, however, layoffs are often covered by the collective bargaining agreement between the employer and the union. Provisions may address issues such as whether seniority must be applied in decisions about who is laid off, whether advance notice of a layoff is required, what are the recall rights after the layoff, whether senior employees scheduled to be laid off may transfer to other jobs and "bump" less senior employees into being laid off, and whether the employer must provide alternatives to a layoff. In addition, if layoffs are not covered by a collective bargaining agreement, an employer in a unionized firm must bargain with any union that represents employees who are targeted to be laid off. Although the employer may or may not have to bargain with the union about the decision to implement the layoff in the first place, the employer clearly will have to bargain about all of the issues just mentioned (for example, seniority rights, recall rights, etc.). Thus, unionized employees have much greater protection from layoffs and their consequences than do nonunion employees.

A great deal of research has been done on the impacts of layoffs. Quite a few scholars have considered the impact of layoff announcements on firms' stock prices, using a methodology known as "event study." Briefly, event studies look at the movement of firms' stock prices in response to a particular event. If stock prices in a sample of firms fell in response to that event, it indicated that the event was detrimental to the firms' profitability. An increase in stock prices meant that the event was beneficial to the firms' profitability. Virtually all the researchers who evaluated the impact of layoff announcements with event study methodology found that firm stock prices decreased in response to such an announcement. In other words, even though layoffs might enable a firm to reduce labor costs and become more efficient, investors still felt that a layoff indicated something negative about a firm's financial state.

Another stream of research has examined the effects of layoffs on the employees who are not laid off. These scholars have found that workers who remain with a company after a layoff become less loyal to the firm, less motivated, and less productive following the downsizing.

Finally, as stated above, layoffs—especially temporary layoffs—tend to run in cycles. There was a great increase in the number of temporary layoffs in the early 1980s and the early 1990s, although there was a difference in the character of the layoffs associated with those two periods. Most of the layoffs that took place in the early 1980s were similar to previous rounds of layoffs in that they involved blue-collar employees, especially in manufacturing and mining. The 1990s saw a shift in the character of the layoff. For the first time, many firms began to lay off white-collar employees who had been employed in executive, administrative, or managerial capacities in an effort to become more efficient. And research lends support to the view that laying off white-collar employees may benefit firms. Richard Caves and Matthew Krepps analyzed the effects of layoff announcements occurring from 1987 to 1991 and found that layoff announcements in general decrease shareholder returns but that shareholder returns did not fall in response to the layoff of solely white-collar employees. In other words, laying off white-collar employees was not detrimental to firms' profitability, whereas laying off blue-collar employees was.

Steven E. Abraham

See also Downsizing; Job Security; Social Security Act; Unemployment Rate

References and further reading

Brockner, J., Steven Grover, Thomas F. Reed, Roy L. Dewitt, and M. O'Malley. 1987. "Survivors' Reaction to Layoffs: We Get by with a Little Help from Our Friends." *Administrative Science Quarterly* 32: 526–541.

Carroll, Glenn R. 1994. "Organizations . . . the Smaller They Get." *Management Review* 37, no. 1: 28–40.

Caves, Richard E., and Matthew B. Krepps. 1993. "Fat: The Displacements of Non-production Workers from U.S. Manufacturing Industries." Brookings Papers on Economic Activity, Microeconomics 2, Brookings Institution, Washington, D.C.

Costa, Patricia Lino. 1999. *Layoffs in the U.S.: Overviewing the American Experience.* Washington, DC: George Washington University, Institutio Cultural Minerva.

Hendricks, Charles F. 1992. *The Rightsizing Remedy.* Homewood, IL: Business One, Irwin.

Huberman, Michael. 1997. "An Economic and Business History of Worksharing: The Bell Canada and Volkswagen." *Business and Economic History* 26, no. 2: 404–415.

Nienstedt, Philip R. 1989. "Effectively Downsizing Management Structures." *Human Resource Planning* 12: 155–164.

Organisation for Economic Cooperation and Development. 1983. "Layoffs and Short Time Working in Selected Countries." Paris: OECD.

United States National Commission for Employment Policy. 1991. "Assisting Dislocated Workers: Alternatives to Layoffs and the Role of Employment Service under the Economic Dislocation and Worker Adjustment Assistance Act (EDWAA)." Special Report no. 30 (October). Washington, DC: National Commission on Employment Policy.

U.S. General Accounting Office. 1995. "Workplace Reductions: Downsizing Strategies Used in Selected Organizations." Chapter Report GAO/GGD-95-54. Gaithersburg, MD: U.S. General Accounting Office.

Worrell, Don L., Wallace N. Davidson, and Varinder Sharma. 1991. "Layoff Announcements and Stockholder Wealth." *Academy of Management Journal* 34, no. 3: 662–678.

Levittown

Levittown, a housing development constructed by real estate entrepreneur William Levitt outside New York City in 1947, was the most well-known of a growing number of suburban communities in the post–World War II United States to make homeownership broadly available to the nation's lower middle class. Built in response to the housing shortage of the immediate postwar years and marketed to returning veterans taking advantage of low-interest federal home loans, Levittown quickly assumed a place in American culture as the quintessential suburb.

An aerial view of Levittown, New York, 1953 (Library of Congress)

Levitt and Sons developed a method of onsite fabrication during World War II to meet the intense demand for housing for defense workers. Builders moved in teams from house to house, completing one stage of construction on a unit, and then went to the next site to complete the same stage again. Standardized components were purchased in bulk directly from manufacturers. Construction workers at Levittown were paid by the number of homes they completed, allowing Levitt to produce as many as 150 houses a week by July 1948 (Kelly 1993, 26). These factorylike methods enabled Levitt to build homes quickly and cheaply. By 1951, Levittown contained over 17,000 Cape Cod and ranch-style homes, as well as retail stores and recreation centers.

The initial units constructed in the 1947–1948 period were built in direct response to the postwar housing shortage and were rented or owned mainly by returning war veterans of working-class and lower-middle-class background. Although some African American families rented homes, racially restrictive covenants inserted into the property deeds by William Levitt prevented them from becoming owners until the *Shelley v. Kraemer* U.S. Supreme Court decision in May 1948. In this decision, the Court ruled racially restrictive orders were violations of the Equal Protection Clause of the

Fourteenth Amendment and therefore unconstitutional. Federal housing and veterans programs were critical to the viability of Levittown and similar postwar developments around the nation. The Federal Housing Administration, created in 1934, strongly encouraged the spread of homeownership, particularly of free-standing single-family homes in suburban areas, by underwriting mortgages. The Veterans Administration also insured mortgage loans after the war, and the Veterans Emergency Housing Program provided loans to the emerging factory-produced home construction industry in an effort to alleviate the postwar housing shortage. By 1949, veterans could buy a home in Levittown with no down payment and a $60-per-month mortgage.

As the most famous U.S. suburb in the postwar decades, Levittown was the frequent focus of both cultural criticism and scholarly inquiry. Some observers used Levittown to criticize the privatism and social and architectural sameness of similar communities around the nation. Others applauded the growth of suburban homeownership, viewing it as the ideal setting for family life and a bulwark against social instability and radicalism. "No man who owns his house and lot can be a Communist," William Levitt remarked in 1948. "He has too much to do." (Larrabee 1948, 84). Aided by federal programs, Levittown and similar developments played a key role in expanding and redefining the prerequisites for middle-class status in the United States, making homeownership a critical component of social citizenship.

Mark Santow

See also GI Bill; New Deal; Suburbanization and Work; Veterans; Worker Housing

References and further reading

Baxandall, Rosalyn, and Elizabeth Ewen. 2000. *Picture Windows: How the Suburbs Happened.* New York: Basic Books.

Gans, Herbert. 1967. *The Levittowners: Ways of Life and Politics in a New Suburban Community.* New York: Columbia University Press.

Jackson, Kenneth. 1987. *Crabgrass Frontier: The Suburbanization of the United States.* New York: Oxford University Press.

Kelly, Barbara. 1993. *Expanding the American Dream: Building and Rebuilding Levittown.* Albany: State University of New York Press.

Larrabee, Eric. 1948. "The Six Thousand Homes That Levitt Built." *Harpers* (September): 48.

"Up from the Potato Fields." *Time,* July 3, 1950, 68.

Weiss, Marc. 1987. *The Rise of the Community Builders: The American Real Estate Industry and Urban Land Planning.* New York: Columbia University Press.

Wright, Gwendolyn. 1981. *Building the Dream: A Social History of Housing in America.* New York: Pantheon Books.

Lewis, John L. (1880–1969)

John Llewellyn Lewis served as president of United Mine Workers of America (UMWA) from 1920 to 1960 and oversaw the largest period of growth and power for the UMWA. Born to Welsh parents on February 12, 1880, in Iowa, Lewis and his family moved from town to town throughout his childhood. He entered the mines in 1906, joined the UMWA, and served as the Lucas County, Iowa, delegate to the UMWA convention. By 1908, Lewis decided to fully pursue a career in the union and moved his family to Panama, Illinois.

Lewis spent three years in Panama controlling the local union hierarchy. His ambitions, however, prevented him from being complacent. In 1911, he left the coal mines to become a special agent for the American Federation of Labor (AFL) in New Mexico territory. The new job compensated Lewis much better than the mines could and allowed him to gain valuable experience and expertise in recruiting new members for organized labor. Throughout his tenure with the AFL, Lewis began to influence the national policy of the UMWA, until union president John White appointed him international statistician for the union in 1917. Lewis's influence within the union grew, and later in the year, the union elected him vice president.

In 1920, Lewis won the presidency of the UMWA, a position that he held for forty years. In 1921, he challenged Samuel Gompers for the presidency of the AFL, an election that he lost. Despite the setback, Lewis preserved the UMWA as the largest trade union in the nation and helped, in a national coal strike in 1922, to secure the high wages miners had won during World War I. Although it seemed that the UMWA was stronger than ever, the victory in the 1922 strike destabilized the union. Despite the problems, Lewis was in firm control of the UMWA by 1924.

As Lewis consolidated his control over the UMWA during the late 1920s, the union began to collapse under pressure from external forces. The bituminous coal industry suffered from a severe

John L. Lewis, meeting with Representative John Nolan, chairman of the Labor Committee of the House of Representatives, April 1933 (Library of Congress)

depression. Domestic output of bituminous coal fell in 1927 to nearly 60 million tons below the 1920 level. Employment fell during the same period from more than 700,000 coal miners nationwide to about 575,000 (Dubofsky and Van Tine 1977, 133). For the miners who kept their jobs, the economic conditions of the late 1920s and early 1930s required significant cuts in wages and working conditions. By 1932, the union was in disarray. Membership fell, and the UMWA ceased to be a functioning entity in the coalfields of central Appalachia and Alabama.

Although a lifelong Republican, Lewis supported Franklin Delano Roosevelt in the election of 1932 because he believed the federal government needed to intervene to stabilize industry in the United States. The passage of the National Industrial Recovery Act (NIRA) in 1933 guaranteed workers the right to bargain collectively with industry, leading to a rebirth of the UMWA. Wages and union membership increased, but whether because of increased labor costs or bad luck for the union, the passage of the NIRA led to increased mechanization in the coal industry and decreased employment throughout the 1940s and 1950s. Lewis believed that mechanization would help stabilize the industry and supported the operators' initiative.

During the 1930s, Lewis advocated the organization of workers in the mass production industries. This position put him at odds with the AFL leadership. In response to the opposition to industrial unionism within the AFL, Lewis and seven other union heads withdrew from the AFL and formed the Committee for Industrial Organization (CIO) in 1935, which changed its name to the Congress of Industrial Organizations in 1938. Lewis became president of the CIO and worked for the rest of the decade trying to organize workers in mass production industries. Although he supported Roosevelt and many of the New Deal programs, Lewis opposed Roosevelt in 1940 and threatened to resign as president of the CIO if Roosevelt was reelected. Roosevelt won, and Lewis resigned as president of the CIO. By 1942, increasing antagonism between Lewis and CIO president Phillip Murray led to the withdrawal of the UMWA from the organization.

During World War II, Lewis led many strikes that improved wages for miners. The success of the strikes during a "no-strike" period invoked the hostility of the War Labor Board and contributed to the passage of the Taft-Hartley Act in 1947, which placed significant restrictions on trade unions. During the 1950s, however, Lewis retreated from his aggressive tactics and became more conciliatory and accommodating toward the coal industry. He retired as president of the UMWA on January 14, 1960, because of his failing health. After serving as chairman of the UMWA's Welfare and Retirement Fund, Lewis died in Washington on June 11, 1969.

Mark Myers

See also Black Lung Disease; Federal Mine and Safety Act;/Mine Work; United Mine Workers of America

References and further reading

Brophy, John. 1964. *A Miner's Life: An Autobiography.* Madison: University of Wisconsin Press.

Dix, Keith. 1988. *What's a Coal Miner to Do? The Mechanization of Coal Mining.* Pittsburgh: University of Pittsburgh Press.

Dubofsky, Martin, and Warren Van Tine. 1977. *John L. Lewis: A Biography.* New York: Quadrangle/ New York Times Book Company.

Lewis, John L. 1925. *Miners' Fight for American Standards.* Indianapolis: Bell Publishing.

Wechsler, James. 1972. *Labor Baron: A Portrait of John L. Lewis.* Westport, CT: Greenwood Press.

Zieger, Robert H. 1986. *American Workers, American Unions: 1920–1985.* Baltimore: Johns Hopkins University Press.

Lewis, Sinclair (1885–1951)

Described as "the indelible voice of the raucous 1920s" Harry Sinclair Lewis was at the height of his writing career between 1920 and 1930, when his most important works were published (Lingeman 2002, xix). Lewis was a masterful satiricist, and his portrayals of the hypocrisies of American life resonated with the general disillusionment of post–World War I society. In Lewis's work, "America is not a functioning democracy but a dysfunctional sales convention where business, medicine, and religion are all a scam" (Di Renzo 1997, xxxiv–xxxv). His novels *Main Street* (1920) and *Babbitt* (1922) drew wide praise and attention for their satire of U.S. middle-class business mores and small-town America and influenced a generation of writers to

Sinclair Lewis , ca. 1900–1940 (Library of Congress)

question the work-hard, make-good American ethic. Lewis was the first U.S. writer to receive the Nobel Prize for literature (1930), and the first to refuse a Pulitzer Prize. In the course of his career, Lewis wrote twenty-three novels, four plays, and numerous short stories, many of which were published in the *Saturday Evening Post,* a journal that "single-handedly created the market for business fiction" (Di Renzo 1997, xx).

After graduating from Yale University in 1908, Lewis spent several years working as a copywriter and publicist in New York. These early experiences accorded him the insights he would use in crafting his novels. With the outbreak of World War I, and "as Wall Street profited from mutilation and murder and advertising became little more than state-sponsored propaganda," Lewis introduced U.S. readers to his form of "bare-knuckled satire" (Di Renzo 1997, xxvi). Lewis's seventh novel, *Main Street: The Story of Carol Kennicott* was received with critical acclaim. In *Main Street,* Lewis interrogated the provincialism and narrow self-assuredness of small-town America. In 1922 Lewis's satire was directed toward white-collar businessmen in the character of George Follansbee Babbitt, a real estate salesman. *Babbitt* examines the unimaginative aspirations of the U.S. middle class and the role work plays in defining white-collar worth and embodies the type of the U.S. businessman in literature. *Arrowsmith* (1925), considered Lewis's best work, portrays medical doctor Martin Arrowsmith's quest for pure science in the face of hostility and corruption. Lewis was awarded the Pulitzer Prize for *Arrowsmith* in 1930 but refused the award because he felt his characterization was antithetical to the Pulitzer criterion for "wholesomeness." *Elmer Gantry* (1927) satirized the corruptive qualities of charismatic evangelism and earned for Lewis inclusion in a cadre of writers critic Carl Van Doren called "The Revolt from the Village," which included Theodore Dreiser, H. L. Mencken, and Sherwood Anderson (quoted in Hutchisson 1996, 1). In 1930 Sinclair Lewis became the first American to win the Nobel Prize for literature. He continued to write, but his work lacked the edginess that gave it power: "Lewis simply lost touch with the times. He was a satirist with nothing left to satirize" (Hutchisson 1996, 2). Lewis died of heart disease in 1951, and his remains are buried in his hometown of Sauk Centre, Minnesota, the town he immortalized in *Main Street*'s fictional Gopher Prairie.

Sandra L. Dahlberg

See also Capitalism; Levittown; Professionals; Work in Literature

References and further reading

Di Renzo, Anthony, ed. 1997. "Introduction." Pp. xiii–xxxvii in *If I Were Boss: The Early Business Stories of Sinclair Lewis.* Carbondale: Southern Illinois University Press.

Gale Literary Databases. 2002. "(Harry) Sinclair Lewis." http://uhdfortis.dt.uh.edu:2055/servlet/GLD (cited November 27, 2002).

Harper and Row. 1987. "(Harry) Sinclair Lewis." *Benét's Reader's Encyclopedia,* 3d ed. New York: Harper and Row.

Hutchisson, James M. 1996. *The Rise of Sinclair Lewis, 1920–1930.* University Park: Pennsylvania State University Press.

Lingeman, Richard. 2002. *Sinclair Lewis: Rebel from Main Street.* New York: Random House.

Love, Glen A. 1993. *Babbitt: An American Life.* New York: Twayne Publishers.

Lifelong Learning

At the most basic level, lifelong learning refers to education throughout a lifetime, particularly as it relates to ensuring widespread access to the changing information, knowledge, and skills required for productive work. In this context, lifelong learning is primarily related to adult access to continuing education programs and the links between vocational or job-training programs and the formal education system. The term *lifelong learning,* however, has multiple interpretations. In many contexts, it has come to be understood in a much broader sense, referring to a more comprehensive set of processes in the workplace and society at large that shape the ability of individuals to continuously learn throughout a lifetime. In this context, lifelong learning goes beyond the formal education system to include both formal and informal organizational structures in the workplace, community, and society at large. Furthermore, in this broader context, lifelong learning frequently has an element of social empowerment and civic engagement rather than focusing simply on needs in the workplace.

Interest in lifelong learning, in both its specific and broader contexts, has increased in recent years for two major reasons. The first force that has helped create greater interest in lifelong learning is rooted in long-term demographic, lifestyle, and value system changes. Increased immigration, greater participation by women in the workforce, longer lifetimes, more leisure time, and the movement toward personal development or "self-fulfillment" have all increased the demand by adults for more learning opportunities at later points in life. The second is rooted in the economy, as the increasingly rapid pace of economic and technological change has led to increased demands for new skills. Faster rates of skills obsolescence and new occupational demands, combined with corporate restructuring that has reduced internal career paths within the same firm, has led adults to more frequently turn to learning activities at later points in their life to maintain or regain their competencies and earning potential. These two broad forces have helped to place lifelong learning and related concepts of a learning economy and learning society at the center of contemporary concerns about socioeconomic development.

The concept of lifelong learning itself is not new. Related concepts can be traced at least as far back as Plato in the fourth century B.C.E., and a fully articulated vision of the importance of lifelong education as a continuing aspect of everyday life can be found as early as the 1920s (Yeaxlee 1929). Nonetheless, until the 1970s, lifelong learning remained a marginal concern. The vast majority of education resources and policy attention was focused on the compulsory K-12 system and immediate postsecondary education. This education system was treated as the primary means by which people gained the skills, knowledge, and education they needed to be both productive workers and productive citizens in society for a lifetime. This role for education was underpinned by the relatively stable, large-firm-based economy that dominated the United States for much of the twentieth century. Most people entered the workforce after completing their education, and any additional skills they would need over the course of a career were expected to be learned on the job or provided by their employer. To the extent that adult education and job training programs for adults developed, such as those created through federal legislation like the Comprehensive Employment and Training Act (1973), the Job Training Partnership Act (1982), and the Workforce Investment Act (1998), they were seen as a "second chance" system relevant only to a minority of people who faced special barriers to effective employment (Grubb 1996).

In recent years, however, there has been a dramatic increase in demand by adults for educational opportunities at later points in their life. For example, although the number of full-time enrollments in U.S. higher education stayed relatively steady in the 1990s, rising from 14 million in 1991 to 15 million in 1999, the number of adults enrolled in educational institutions jumped from 58 million in 1991 to 90 million in 1999 (National Center for Education Statistics 2000). As a result, the distinction between education and training is increasingly breaking down and being replaced by various approaches to lifelong learning. Educational institutions are no longer limited to educating individuals before they enter the job market. Community colleges and university systems are taking a greater role in providing lifelong educational opportunities while offering more short-term certification courses and extension programs. They are developing more customized training and education programs, working in partnership with private sector firms to promote training in areas linked to employment opportunities. There has also been a rapid expansion in nontraditional, for-profit private universities catering specifically to adult learners and specializing in evening courses and distance education. Meanwhile, the public job training system is being restructured (for example, through the Workforce Investment Act) in an effort to make it more of a universal system that will have relevance for all job seekers, not simply those with special needs.

This increased demand for lifelong learning is driven in part simply by demographic and lifestyle changes in the population. Higher levels of immigration have increased the demand for classes in adult English as a second language and various adult basic education and credential programs. With more women now in the workforce, more are reentering after spending some time away raising their families, increasing demands for work-related courses. The workforce as a whole is aging, with more people working longer years, even past retirement age, leading to a higher level of job and career shifts over a lifetime and contributing to increased demand for work-related courses. Finally, an expanding interest in personal development has increased the demand for many "quality of life" or self-fulfillment courses.

The most significant force contributing to the rise in demand for lifelong learning, however, has to do with changes in the economy. Since the 1970s, rapid changes in technology, corporate structure, and economic activity have resulted in greater instability in work patterns. Few workers now can expect long-term stable employment with a single employer, and most workers instead hold many different jobs, working for a range of different employers, over their lifetimes. Rapidly changing technology and market conditions are leading to high levels of skill obsolescence. Without continual learning, employees become less valuable to their employers, becoming "obsolete" with successive waves of technological innovation. At the same time, however, corporations have restructured their operations, flattening corporate hierarchies, reducing the opportunities on internal career ladders, and cutting their expenditures on formal training programs. Thus, many more adult workers are required to go back to school to maintain their employment opportunities in the labor market.

The impact of economic changes on lifelong learning, however, goes beyond its simple impact on formal adult education and job training programs. Economic success for firms, regions, and nations is increasingly driven by their ability to effectively adapt to changing market conditions, identify and capitalize on new opportunities, and successfully respond to new challenges (Lundvall and Johnson 1994). Such economic learning is ultimately dependent on the ability of individuals to learn in an ongoing way in a social context. Lifelong learning is therefore about much more than access to formal education; it relates to the ways in which knowledge is acquired, developed, and applied through the interpretation of experience in work, family, and community settings as much as in educational settings. This change has led to a widespread interest in concepts such as the "learning organization" (Easterby-Smith, Araujo, and Burgoyne 1991), learning regions (Simmie 1997), and the learning society (Oliver 1999; Ranson 1999).

Finally, for some people, the term *lifelong learning* includes an aspect of social empowerment and civic engagement. This perspective has roots in the radical project of adult education of people like Paulo Freire (Freire 1970), in which adult education is based on dialogue, not mere transmission of knowledge and skill, and education is not only for personal development and advancement but also is integrally linked with social change. Lifelong learning, therefore, is a continuous social process, encompassing both individual and collective learning, rooted in the realities of community life and connected directly with the interests and aspirations of ordinary people. The concern here, therefore, is less about formal structures of state and educational institutions and more about the interests of civil society and social movements. The concept of lifelong learning includes notions of equitable access, democratic participation, and community capacity building (Longworth 1999; Martin 1999).

Chris Benner

See also Careers; Comprehensive Employment and Training Act; Earnings and Education; Education Reform and the Workforce; Job Skills; Job Training Partnership Act; On-the-Job Training; Workforce Investment Act

References and further reading

Easterby-Smith, Mark, Luis Araujo, and John Burgoyne, eds. 1991. *Organizational Learning and the Learning Organization: Developments in Theory and Practice.* Thousand Oaks, CA: Sage.

Freire, Paolo. 1970. *Pedagogy of the Oppressed.* New York: Herder and Herder.

Grubb, Norton. 1996. *Learning to Work: The Case for Reintegrating Job Training and Education.* New York: Russell Sage Foundation.

Longworth, Norman. 1999. *Making Lifelong Learning Work: Learning Cities for a Learning Century.* London: Kogan Page.

Lundvall, Bengt-Ake, and B. Johnson. 1994. "The Learning Economy." *Journal of Industrial Studies* 1/2: 23–42.

Martin, Ian. 1999. "Lifelong Learning: Stretching the Discourse." In *Lifelong and Continuing Education: What Is a Learning Society?* Edited by Paul Oliver. Aldershot, UK and Brookfield, VT: Ashgate.

National Center for Education Statistics. 2000. *National Household Education Survey (1991, 1995, 1999).* Washington, DC: The National Center for Education Statistics.

Oliver, Paul, ed. 1999. *Lifelong and Continuing Education: What Is a Learning Society?* Aldershot, UK and Brookfield, VT: Ashgate.

Ranson, Stewart, ed. 1999. *Inside the Learning Society.* London: Cassell.

Simmie, James, ed. 1997. *Innovation, Networks and Learning Regions.* London: Regional Studies Association.

Yeaxlee, Basil A. 1929. *Lifelong Education: A Sketch of the Range and Significance of the Adult Education Movement.* London: Cassell.

Literacy

The concept of literacy has undergone various transformations throughout the centuries; once those who could sign their names were considered literate, and then by the nineteenth century, those who had completed the third grade were literate. Then, in the mid–twentieth century, the terms *functional literacy* and *functional illiteracy* became catchwords, thereby changing the definition of literacy yet again. However, the idea that a well-educated society is also a stable society dates back to the time of Confucius, at least 2,500 years ago. From the sixteenth to the nineteenth centuries, organized religion throughout much of the world was responsible for establishing levels of literacy. It would be the early nineteenth century before society realized that education should be the responsibility of the state. Even in the writing of the Constitution in the United States in 1789, the framers said nothing about an unalienable right to read or write. In essence, literacy became a notable social issue, and one that promoted the public good over the next two centuries.

Literacy is not a clearly defined concept; it is impossible to easily define people as either literate or illiterate. The National Center for Education Statistics (NCES), which has conducted several surveys on literacy since 1985, has grouped the concept of literacy into five levels, and individuals fall into these categories according to their ability to complete certain tasks. Individuals who can read a magazine such as *Time* and comprehend the reading material are classified as a minimum of level three, whereas those who can relate the articles to their business or financial interests would fall into level four or five. Only 20 percent of adults fall into the latter two levels. A little over 20 percent of Americans over the age of sixteen have level one literacy skills, which categorizes the most basic literacy skills; however, one-quarter of this number are also recent immigrants, and one-third are elderly.

The various measurements of literacy have their limitations, but there are three main ways of measuring literacy: (1) self-assessments, in which individuals determine their own reading and writing capabilities; (2) surrogate measures, which imply completion of a certain grade level; and (3) direct measures, otherwise known as tests. Self-assessments have been recorded since the 1850 U.S. Census, but after World War I, analysts began to argue that the results from self-assessments were skewed since the respondents tended to exaggerate their personal literacy levels. Considering this difficulty, officials, and specifically the army, began to use completion of a certain grade level as a surrogate measure of literacy. However, the limitations of this approach, including that the number of years of schooling does not guarantee skill mastery, make this approach less than desirable. Of all the methods, direct testing may be preferable, but one of its drawbacks is the misconception of literacy as "English literacy." In "Measuring the Nation's Literacy" (1991), Terrence Wiley contends that even though English may be the dominant language of the United States, omitting languages other than English from literacy surveys exaggerates the perception of the so-called "literacy crisis."

In an attempt to combat the literacy crisis, one of the first organizations designed to enhance literacy in the United States, Literacy Volunteers of America, founded in 1962 in Syracuse, New York, by Ruth Colvin, tried to increase public recognition of the literacy problem. The movement spread to other communities in New York, and it became a tax-exempt nonprofit corporation with a volunteer board of directors in 1967. In 1972, Literacy Volunteers changed its name to Literacy Volunteers of America so that it could emphasize and "foster increased literacy in the United States" (Literacy Volunteers of America 1987). Its programs became more varied, including English as a second language, adult basic education, family literacy, and the creation of a student leadership institute to train students to serve as adult literacy spokespersons for the organization.

Most literacy programs place an emphasis on adult literacy. In 1990, the National Governors' Association identified adult literacy as one of the six key areas for improvement during the decade, and in 1991, Congress enacted the National Literacy Act, which was designed "to enhance the literacy and basic skills necessary to function effectively and achieve the greatest possible opportunity in their work and in their lives, and to strengthen and coordinate adult literacy programs" (Bowen 1998, 314). In 1993, the U.S. Department of Education released the results of the National Adult Literacy Survey, which focused on the number of adults with lower levels of literacy and the range of literacy levels from low to high. This survey has met with controversy, particularly since 5 percent of those taking the survey, or 10 million adults, were unable to complete the survey. However, despite these alarming statistics, government involvement in literacy programs equates to less than $400 per person, in a century in which annual per person enrollment expenditures can exceed $7,500 for the K-12 system and $16,000 for the higher education system.

Adults in need of literacy instruction do so for a variety of goals, including job advancement, success for their children in school, or the pleasure of reading and writing on their own. The National Adult Literacy Survey (NALS) defined literacy broadly, as the ability to "use printed and written information to function in society, to achieve one's goals, and to develop one's knowledge and potential" (Bowen 1998, 315). It assessed literacy on three scales: prose literacy, the ability to understand and use information from articles, fiction, or consumer information; document literacy, the ability to locate and use information from charts and forms; and quantitative literacy, the ability to solve basic arithmetic problems and apply those solutions to life. Critic David Berliner argued in a 1996 article that testing revealed only an individual's typical literary skills and that only tasks in which individuals work on what is important to them will reveal their true literacy level.

Literacy tests also raise questions of economic status and uneven spending on education. Schools in the wealthier districts provide a minimum of 36 percent more revenue for public education than do schools in the poorer districts. Even when cost-of-living differences are taken into account, the spending difference still remains 16 percent. Yet, adults with low literacy skills may be unfamiliar with more sophisticated skills, and increases in literacy can cause the learner to feel both estranged from his or her own community and not yet accepted into a larger, more literate society. Of those scoring in the level one range as determined by the National Center for Education Statistics, about 43 percent lived in poverty, whereas only 4–6 percent of those scoring in the level five range lived in poverty. Therefore, on average, all measurements of economic success, including full-time employment, weekly earnings, and interest on savings accounts, increased with a comparable increase in literacy skills. Those adults in the general population with level one prose literacy scores reported earning an average of $15,480 in 1991, whereas those who lived on food stamps and had the same literacy skills reported earning about $7,740, thereby demonstrating the relationship between literacy and economic status (Bowen 1998, 319). Since literate individuals often equate their literacy with the opening of doors in society and a subsequent change in social or economic status, they may feel that illiteracy is the cause of poverty and crime. As Betsy Bowen noted, "Low literacy skills are cited as a cause of both welfare dependency and the United States' problems competing in the global marketplace" (1998, 315).

Similarly, gender can be a part of the economic status and literacy debate. Men and women tended to score on the same level on prose literacy, whereas men tended to average higher scores for document literacy and quantitative literacy. With this in mind, much research has been done on the issues of family and gender literacy. The family literacy approach addresses the literacy skills of both parents and children, as well as the value of parental involvement in the experiences of children in school. Programs to improve family literacy address parents as the children's first teachers, but again, these programs face criticism for their avoidance of working with those of low literacy and low incomes. The other approach is woman-centered and typically covers the individual learner and the way gender shapes the woman's learning experience. The Laubach Literacy International's Women in Literacy/USA (WIL/USA), first launched overseas in 1990 and then in the United States in 1994, sought to empower women to take control of their own lives.

These campaigns represent a determined effort to eradicate "functional illiteracy." In April 2000, the U.S. Department of Education's Office of Educational Research and Improvements (OERI) published "Literacy in the Labor Force," and the Organization for Economic Cooperation and Development (OECD) published "Literacy in an Information Age," both of which deconstructed the concept of "functional literacy." Both reports used a scale of 0–500 to rate an individual's literacy but often collapsed this scale into five categories or levels. In the OECD document, literacy refers to "the ability to understand and employ printed information in daily activities; at home, at work, and in the community—to achieve one's goals and to develop one's knowledge and potential." In other words, reading for pleasure is not a part of the OECD definition. The three levels of literacy—prose, document, and quantitative—were used in both reports.

These reports centered on the concept of workplace literacy. Enhancing it is one of the goals of the National Workplace Literacy Program (NWLP) funded by the U.S. Department of Education, which provides educational enterprises and businesses with the opportunity to develop workplace literacy programs. Businesses have realized that they must improve workers' skills to meet the challenges of growing competition. Workers who participate in workplace literacy programs report improved literacy at home, including helping children with homework.

The empowerment of the workforce should be the most important goal of such programs, but the transfer of learning is just as important. Defined as the application of job skills and knowledge gained as the result of attending an educational program, transfer of learning is an effective method to determine workplace literacy. It can be positive when performance is facilitated, but it can also be negative when acquisition or performance has been impeded. The most significant barrier to transfer of learning is the lack of reinforcement from instructors and support for the application of training to their jobs. The instructor is required to identify the information being taught, but programmatic elements such as the length of the session, the size of the class, or location can affect the success of the transfer of learning.

The transfer of knowledge certainly has an

impact on the concept of literacy and adult literacy in particular. Literacy education cannot be separated from tensions in U.S. politics and society over the role of government in assisting lower-income poor, immigrant, and minority Americans. The essential question is whether literacy training programs prepare the poor and minorities for the workforce and society in general. Literacy training in the workforce can easily ignore the differences between people and communities and the reasons why people want to learn to read and write, yet these programs were initiated to better emphasize the importance of a qualified workforce. Author Jonathan Kozol has stressed that community-based and community-controlled programs can concentrate on both work opportunities and familial love. "Experts have some complicated theories about 'adult motivation.' I believe that love is the most potent motivation in our souls. Wise government policy, tending toward a family literacy concept, might enable us to draw upon the longing of the old to share their memories and heritage with those they love the most" (Kazemek 1991, 60).

Jennifer Harrison

See also Education Reform and the Workforce

References and further reading

Askov, Eunice. 2000. "Workplace Literacy: Evaluation of Three Model Programs." *Adult Basic Education* 10, no. 2 (Summer): 100–108.

Bowen, Betsy. 1998. "Four Puzzles in Adult Literacy: Reflection on the National Adult Literacy Survey." *Journal of Adolescent and Adult Literacy* 42, no. 4: 314–324.

Bracey, Gerald W. 2000. "Literacy in the Information Age." *Phi Delta Kappan* 82, no. 1: 91–93.

"Great Learning: Literacy and Education Have Set Twentieth-Century People Apart from All Others." 1999. *Economist* 353: 73–75.

"History of Literacy Volunteers of America, Inc." http://www.literacyvolunteers.org.

Kazemek, F. E. 1991. "'In Ignorance of It to View a Small Portion and Think That All': The False Promise of Job Literacy." *Journal of Education* 173, no. 1: 51–55.

Taylor, Maurice. 2000. "Transfer of Learning in Workplace Literacy Programs." *Adult Basic Education* 10, no. 1 (Spring): 3–21.

Wiley, Terrence. 1991. "Measuring the Nation's Literacy: Important Considerations." *ERIC Digest* ED334870.

Living Wage

The "living wage" campaign refers to a range of initiatives across the United States that have sought to raise employee wages in order to create economic security for low-income workers. These campaigns attempt to mandate that private businesses that benefit from public money pay a wage that allows workers and their families to live above the poverty level (this figure is calculated yearly, at the federal level). Initiatives are crafted to ensure that public contracts awarded to private providers are linked to the payment of a living wage; that tax assistance, economic development funds, or other forms of state aid go only to corporations that pay a living wage; that pay for contractual workers does not fall behind that of city employees; and/or that all employers within specific jurisdictions pay their employees a living wage (ACORN 2001).

In 1994, an alliance of labor and religious leaders in Baltimore, Maryland, successfully lobbied for legislation that required service contractors for the city to pay a living wage, calculated as a wage that allowed a family of four to live above the poverty level in that municipality (New Party 2000). Similar ordinances were subsequently passed in Boston, Detroit, Los Angeles, Milwaukee, Minneapolis, Oakland, Portland, San Jose, St. Louis, and Tucson. By, 2002 there were ninety-three national living wage ordinances on the books in cities across the nation (New Party 2000).

Living wage campaigns comprise members from community groups, labor unions, and religious organizations working together to develop living wage principles, affect wage-related legislation, and organize endorsements. The campaign's focus is most often on an increase in wages, but organizations have also addressed issues related to community standards, health benefits, family leave policies, vacation pay, community hiring goals, environmental standards, and support of union organizing (Pollin and Luce 1998, 63; ACORN 2001). In the process these coalitions develop community networks, build leadership skills among community members, and publicly highlight issues of economic justice (ACORN 2001).

The New Party, Association of Community Organizations for Reform Now (ACORN), and American Federation of Labor and Congress of Industrial Organizations have made living wage campaigns a centerpiece of their programs. ACORN is the nation's oldest and largest grassroots organization of low- and moderate-income people, with over 100,000 members in over thirty cities, and first began lobbying for a national living wage in 1992 (ACORN 2001).

All three organizations tie the living wage campaign to minimum wage activism and legislation, attempting to guarantee that full-time, minimum wage workers receive a salary that allows them to live above the poverty level. In 2002 a full-time, minimum wage worker in the United States earned $10,000 to $12,000 per year, an income well below the poverty line for a family of three (Mishel, Bernstein, and Boushen 2002, 9).

Living wage activists employ two distinct strategies when calculating living wage requirements. The first ensures that full-time, minimum wage workers earn salaries that allow them to support their families above the poverty level. The second methodology involves tying a living wage to a family self-sufficiency index, based on either "fair market rent" standards—reflecting shelter and utility costs in a given area—or the federal Housing and Urban Development (HUD) standard dictating that no more than 30 percent of a person's gross monthly income be spent on housing (New Party 2000).

Opponents to the campaign believe that living wage legislation will create a "hostile business climate," that it will place too great a burden on small businesses, and that ultimately it will hurt the population it was intended to assist by leading to job displacement and high rates of unemployment. Some have argued that for every 10 percent increase in the minimum wage, 100,000 jobs are lost (Brocht 2000).

Supporters of living wage legislation counter these arguments by pointing to Princeton economists David Card and Alan Krueger's study of minimum wage employees in New Jersey, which found little or no impact on employment from raising the minimum wage (Bernstein 2000, 3). Further, they argue that without living wage legislation, economic development subsidies will not be tied to job quality or economic security; that living wage ordinances do not represent a significant cost increase to cities; that these ordinances do not reduce the competitiveness of the contractual process; that firms can remain profitable while increasing their costs by paying a living wage to employees; and that the passage of living wage ordinances does not result in significant job loss (Bernstein 2000, 12). Rather, they argue that a national living wage would promote responsible economic development policies and encourage the creation of an economically secure and justly compensated low-income workforce in the United States.

Vivyan C. Adair

See also Minimum Wage; Unemployment Rate; Welfare-to-Work; Work First

References and further reading

ACORN (Association of Community Organizations for Reform Now). 2001. "Living Wage Resource Center." www.livingwagecampaign.org (cited October 8, 2002).

Bernstein, Jarred. 2000. "Higher Wages Lead to More Efficient Service Provisions: The Impact of Living Wage Ordinance on the Public Contract Process." Washington, DC: Economic Policy Institute.

Brocht, Chauna. 2000. "The Forgotten Workforce." Washington, DC: Economic Policy Institute.

Mishel, Lawrence, Jaren Bernstein, and Heather Boushen. 2002. *The State of Working America 2002–03.* Washington, DC: Economic Policy Institute.

New Party. 2000. "The Living Wage Campaign." www.newparty.org/livwag/livwag.html (cited October, 2000).

Pollin, Robert, and Stephanie Luce. 1998. *The Living Wage: Building a Fair Economy.* New York: New Press..

Local 1199 Health Care Workers

Local 1199 was formed in 1932 when two New York City pharmacy unions—the Pharmacists' Union of Greater New York and the New York Drug Clerks Association—merged under the direction of founding president Leon Davis. Although originally conceived as a union of pharmacists, Local 1199 left its mark on labor history in the second half of the twentieth century with its remarkable organizing and collective bargaining achievements in the previously unorganized arena of U.S. health care facilities. Significantly, Local 1199 promoted a broad social agenda beyond the realm of traditional trade unionism. Through militant action, keen coalition building, and political savvy, Local 1199 won major victories in a historically antiunion industry during some of the labor movement's darkest days.

In 1959, Local 1199 embarked on an organizing campaign aimed at one of New York City's most exploited workforces—the 35,000 employees who toiled in its voluntary hospitals that provided care to low-income and uninsured citizens. In the face of staunch hospital resistance, Local 1199 led hospital workers in a number of work stoppages throughout the 1960s. Pointing to a large contingent of minority hospital employees, Local 1199 framed the labor conflict as part of the broader struggle for social justice. The civil rights movement quickly adopted Local 1199's cause, creating a formidable coalition that would benefit Local 1199 for many years to come. By the end of the 1960s, Local 1199 claimed more than 30,000 members from dozens of health care institutions in the city. In spite of the large membership, Local 1199's success was severely hampered by the fact that New York State labor law specifically precluded hospital employees from its collective bargaining protections. In 1963, Local 1199 leveraged its political prowess to successfully lobby for the passage of legislation extending collective bargaining protections to hospital employees.

Using the strategies it honed in the New York City hospital campaigns, Local 1199 spread out to other areas of the country in the early 1970s. It won major organizing campaigns in cities as diverse as Charleston, South Carolina, and Philadelphia, Pennsylvania. By 1974, Local 1199 had over 80,000 members in fourteen states and the District of Columbia. However, a period of governmental cost control in health care in the 1970s soon slowed Local 1199's success. Indeed, this cost control, along with increased competition between rival health care unions and increasingly aggressive antiunion campaigns by the hospitals, combined to further curtail the union's ability to maintain the level of success in its organizing drives. In 1980, in an effort to regain some of its previous strength, Local 1199 began to contemplate a merger with the Service Employees Industrial Union (SEIU). Although bitter internal leadership struggles and mounting division between the New York base and the national outposts prevented advancement on the merger talks for several years, Local 1199 finally teamed up with SEIU in 1989 to form 1199/SEIU, the largest health care union in the country. Today, the union continues its mission to organize the unorganized and has most recently devoted its attention to the plight of the often unorganized home health care workforce.

Kerry Sheldon

See also Collective Bargaining; Solidarity

References and further reading

Dyer, James Metcalfe. 1971. *The Lawrence Hospital Strike: Civil Rights Influence in a Labor Union Dispute.* Ithaca: Cornell University Press.

Fink, Leon, and Greenberg, Brian. 1989. *Upheaval in the Quiet Zone: A History of Hospital Workers' Union, Local 1199.* Urbana: University of Illinois Press.

Lowell Strike

The first Lowell Strike of 1834 was a bellwether of change in U.S. industry's relations with labor. Though unsuccessful, it signaled the end of the labor relations ideal promoted in the "Lowell experiment." Lowell, Massachusetts, has been famous as a center of the U.S. textile industry for much of its history. It was first known for its important role in the transition from home manufacture of textiles to the birth of the organized textile industry via the "putting out" system, in which the process was divided between homework and in-factory work. By 1814, however, with the introduction of the power loom, textile manufacturing was increasingly transferred within the mills and performed by in-house millworkers.

It was Francis Cabot Lowell (for whom the mill town was named), however, who wrought a revolution (however short-lived) in the image of millwork by introducing the boardinghouses for the all-female operatives of his mill in 1821. Millwork, as it grew during the Industrial Revolution in England, developed a singularly unsavory image as a life of squalor and oppression and was considered especially unsuitable for young, unmarried women of Yankee background. Yet Lowell, in staffing his textile factories, succeeded not only in attracting a workforce of young U.S.-born women but in making it an attractive alternative for these women, whose other working options were limited to teaching, sewing, and domestic work, none of which paid as well as the Lowell Mills. Aside from offering better pay, the Lowell Mills boarded its workers in supervised boarding houses and required workers to conform to rules that included keeping rooms clean, observing curfews, and regularly attending church.

Although this paternalistic system did not appear to offer the "Lowell girls" much freedom after their long work hours, they found it attractive because it offered them the chance to live independently from their families while reassuring their families that this work was respectable for them. Living together in the boardinghouses, furthermore, created a sense of community among the millworkers, which they used at first to enhance their after-hours lives at Lowell. Their activities ranged from lending libraries and debating clubs to charitable projects, but the most famous of them was the *Lowell Offering,* a literary magazine that published

Young women, such as this Massachusetts "mill girl" found mill work attractive because it offered them the chance to live independently from their families in company boardinghouses and the opportunity of respectable work. (Library of Congress)

their writings, frequently in praise of life and work at the Lowell Mills. A few former millworkers, such as Lucy Larcom and Harriet Robinson, later published praiseworthy memoirs of their time in Lowell. It should be added, however, that none of the "mill girls" expected to work there all their lives. Most worked at the mills for a few years before marrying, making the Lowell system a success in that working there did not impair their "respectable" status and hence marriageability.

Where, then, did things start to go wrong with the Lowell system, ending the ideal of company paternalism and beginning the part of Lowell's history characterized by labor struggle? First and foremost, increased business demands resulted in speedups and wage cuts. In response to the early threat of wage cuts, workers organized a strike, or a "turnout" as it was then called in 1834, marching to other mills to encourage others to join their cause and petitioning potential supporters. The strike was over in a few days and failed to accomplish its objective of preventing wage cuts, but it was the first event that seriously challenged the idyllic picture of life and work in the Lowell Mills. If anything, the paternalistic system of the boardinghouses had backfired by creating solidarity among the young women who worked and lived together for significant periods of time. Mill owners viewed the strikers as unfeminine and lacking gratitude. The women struck, however, because they viewed the wage cuts as both an economic threat and as an affront to their sense of dignity and social equality, which they regarded as their birthright. In particular, the wage cuts were seen as the beginning of potential economic dependence and hence "enslavement" to their jobs.

Another turnout over wage cuts ensued in 1836, attracting more participants and lasting much longer than the first. The walkout cut into mill production, and fewer workers returned when it was over. Additionally, to better coordinate the second strike, the Lowell workers had founded the Factory Girls Association in 1834. This strike too ended in defeat, and during the subsequent economic depression from 1837 to 1843, workers made no effort to protest subsequent wage cuts. The return of prosperity in the 1840s, though, did not bring a return of turnouts. Instead, the female Lowell mill operatives, along with their male counterparts, turned to political action. They petitioned state legislators, no longer against wage cuts or the speedup of work but to limit the hours of work and improve other working conditions in the mills. This new approach in turn spurred the growth of the Lowell Female Labor Reform Association, which worked in tandem with the New England Workingmen's Association, as well as the ten-hour movement. The former organizations published *The Voice of Industry* to air worker grievances and in counterpoint to the company-sponsored *Lowell Offering*. Although women lacked the political clout of voting rights, their active participation in these organizations made them a highly visible presence in the struggle to improve working conditions during this period.

Although these forms of activism were built on the older model of preserving the dignity and independence of "daughters of freemen," they also signaled the origins of a working-class identity and a more overt rejection of the paternalism that ironically created the sense of solidarity and community that made these protests possible. The growing discontent, however, led the Lowell mill management to abandon any pretense of paternalism, as they increasingly hired Irish immigrants in place of Yankee women. Thus began the pattern of worker protest and new efforts at management control that would characterize the rest of Lowell's history as an industrial community.

Susan Roth Breitzer

See also Garment/Textile Industries; Manufacturing Jobs; Strikes; Women and Work; Worker Housing

References and further reading

Blewett, Mary H., ed. 1982. *Surviving Hard Times: The Working People of Lowell.* Lowell: Lowell Museum.

Dublin, Thomas. 1979. *Women at Work: The Transformation of Work and Community in Lowell, Massachusetts, 1826–1960.* New York: Columbia University Press.

Eno, Arthur L., Jr., ed. 1976. *Cotton Was King: A History of Lowell, Massachusetts.* Lowell: Lowell Historical Society.

Josephson, Hannah. 1949. *The Golden Threads: New England's Mill Girls and Magnates.* New York; Duell, Sloan, and Pearce.

Miller, Henry Adolphus. 1972. *Lowell, As It Was, and As It Is.* New York: Arno Press.

Robinson, Harriet. 1976. *Loom and Spindle, or Life among the Early Mill Girls, with a Sketch of "The Lowell Offering" and Some of Its Contributors.* Kailia, HI: Press Pacifica.

Weible, Robert, ed. 1991. *The Continuing Revolution: A History of Lowell, Massachusetts.* Lowell: Lowell Historical Society.

Woloch, Nancy. 1984. *Women and the American Experience.* New York: Alfred A. Knopf.

Manpower Inc.

Established in 1948, Manpower is currently the second-largest temporary employment company in the world. Principal operations include job placement in office, industrial, and professional positions; contract services; and training and testing of temporary and permanent workers. Manpower's success is partly due to the increased use of temporary workers at all levels of business in the United States and abroad. Employers typically use temporary workers during early periods of growth, after a recession, or for seasonal or unusual projects with the firm. But temporary hiring became more widespread in the 1990s, when many employers adopted temporary worker hiring as an ongoing workforce strategy for two reasons: the substantial cost savings from not providing guaranteed employee benefits and additional labor force flexibility. Manpower became an industry leader in this era by becoming the first such company to make substantial investments of time and money in training its workers for hire, instituting a computer-based training program in 1978 long before personal computers became a staple in the working world.

In 2000 Manpower was ranked 177 in the Fortune 500, with profits of $171.2 million (http://www.fortune.com 2001). Manpower maintains 400,000 customers in fifty-nine countries worldwide, including ninety-nine of the Fortune 100 companies in the United States as well as 95 percent of the Fortune 500 (http://www.manpower.com 2001). Currently, office and light industrial placements account for the company's highest sales, with professional placement as the fastest-growing division.

Elmer L. Winter and Aaron Scheinfeld formed Manpower in Milwaukee, Wisconsin, in 1948, in response to the labor shortage following World War II. The company established its first franchise in 1956, creating the first of many Manpower offices across the country. During the 1960s, the company expanded into Europe, and by the late 1970s, Chief Executive Officer (CEO) Mitchell S. Fromstein brought innovations to the temporary industry, including a new focus on office work and on assessing and accommodating client needs. Manpower dominated the temp industry primarily because of its unmatched commitment to training employees before placement. This was evidenced in 1978 when Manpower announced a $15 million investment in Skillware, an interactive, self-paced computer-training program that employees used to develop their proficiency at various tasks. As a result, Manpower employees were sought after more than other agencies because they required less training and were more productive in a shorter period of time.

According to the Bureau of Labor Statistics, the percentage of temporary jobs in the workforce doubled to 1 percent from 1980 to 1989. Throughout the 1980s, employee benefit costs exceeded wage increases, largely contributing to the growing importance of the temp industry in the United

States. Employers found that paying temporary employee wages and additional fees to their placement agencies was a cheaper option than recruiting and training workers and providing benefits in-house. Furthermore, employers were able to confidently hire the temps who succeeded during their placements as experienced full-time employees. Temporary work also became attractive to dual-income families because of the flexibility and rising cost of child care in the 1980s.

In the 1990s temporary employment services became one of the fastest-growing international industries. Many of Manpower's competitors grew by consolidating many firms into large conglomerates with many international offices. However, Manpower expanded its international business independently, without acquisition, resulting in the loss of its lead among the competition.

Adecco, formed in the 1997 merger of Switzerland's Adia and France's Ecco, replaced Manpower as the world leader in the industry. Even so, Manpower has consistently increased in revenue growth each year since its inception. In fact, in 1998, systemwide sales surpassed $10 billion, doubling the previous five years' revenue.

In the late 1990s, information technology became the fastest-growing sector of the staffing industry, growing at a rate of nearly 25 percent each year (Pederson 2000). Adecco was well equipped in this area, accounting for approximately 20 percent of total revenues. In comparison, information technology placements accounted for roughly 10 percent of Manpower revenue at this time. In 1999 longtime CEO Mitchell S. Fromstein retired and was replaced by Jeffrey Joerres. Under new direction, Manpower is striving to embrace the information technology market. By the close of 1999, over 200 Manpower offices were devoted solely to staffing needs in technical and information technology fields.

Elayne M. Marinos

See also Contingent and Temporary Workers; Job Placement and Recruitment Firms

References and further reading

Fortune. 2001. "Manpower, Inc." http://www.fortune.com (cited 2001).

Hoover's Online Business Network. 2001. "Manpower Inc." http://www.hoovers.com/co/capsule/9/0,2163,16919,00.html (cited September 30, 2001).

Manpower Inc. 2001. "Our Story." http://www.manpower.com (cited September 30, 2001).

Pederson, Jay P., ed. 2000. *International Directory of Company Histories,* Vol. 30. Detroit: St. James Press.

Schaffner, Herbert A., and Carl E. Van Horn. 2002. *A Nation at Work: The Heldrich Guide to the American Workforce.* New Brunswick: Rutgers University Press.

U.S. Department of Labor, Bureau of Labor Statistics. 1997. *Report on the American Workforce.* Washington, DC: U.S. Department of Labor, Bureau of Labor Statistics.

Van Horn, Carl E. 1996. *No One Left Behind.* New York: Twentieth Century Fund Press.

Working Today. http://www.workingtoday.org.

Manufacturing Jobs

Since the period of intense industrialization from the mid–nineteenth century onward, manufacturing jobs—those that require workers to create or assemble products from raw or component materials through mechanical, physical, or chemical processes—have held an important place in the U.S. economy. Replacing high-quality, low-volume craft production with tasks that used machine labor in mass production, manufacturing jobs in central sites, such as factories or mills, became the hallmark of the U.S. system by 1900. Manufacturing jobs change not only the nature of the workplace but U.S. society as well. Along with mass-production manufacturing jobs went the spread of wage labor, the rise of a professional industrial management cadre, and for many workers, membership in labor unions. Scholars have noted three distinct periods of industrialization in the twentieth-century United States, and some have even predicted the gradual demise of manufacturing jobs in a twenty-first-century, postindustrial economy based on service sector jobs.

In the early 1800s, the United States was still a rural society, and agricultural production expanded as new territories were opened for settlement. Although many families produced items for their own consumption, specialized craftspeople also made items such as clothing, shoes, and harnesses for the commercial market. These highly skilled artisans typically produced for a small local market; few manufactured items were sold as exports, a sector that was dominated by trade in raw materials such as wood, cotton, and foodstuffs. The rise of the mass-production manufacturing system in the United States dates from around 1820, when a group of investors called the Boston Associates decided to undercut the British sale of cotton cloth, which used U.S. cotton in British mills to create a finished product for the U.S. market. Essentially copying the manufacturing process and mill designs from their British competitors, the investors emphasized the de-skilling of labor throughout their operations. In contrast to cloth produced at home or by master weavers, machines were used at every step in the process of weaving the cloth. Centralizing the production of mass-produced, low-cost goods, the Boston Associates created the first U.S. factory city. By 1830 the former village of Chelmsford, Massachusetts—renamed Lowell—had a population of 7,000, a figure that tripled by 1840. By that time, other groups of investors had built cotton and woolen mills throughout New England, transforming places like Pawtucket and Woonsocket in Rhode Island, Lawrence and Chicopee in Massachusetts, and Manchester in New Hampshire into U.S. mill towns.

The status of the textile industry as the most dynamic sector of the U.S. economy did not last much beyond a generation; by 1860, a second wave of industrialization was led by the growth of railroads and associated industries such as steelmaking and railcar manufacturing. Spurred on by the need to transport goods over greater distances—a trend fostered by the search for new markets by textile producers—railroads completed a transportation revolution in the United States, while steelmaking transformed its economy. As in the industrialization of textile making, the steel industry eliminated as much skilled work as possible from the production process. Focusing on large-scale production of items for use by other industrial consumers, steelmaking depended on the widespread use of machine labor; in fact, the investment required for the machinery meant that industrial plants required a much larger capital investment than in earlier decades. A textile mill could be established with about a million-dollar investment, but a steel mill required about fifty times that amount. Production of steel accordingly took place on a significantly grander scale than the production of items for the consumer market. The first phase of industrialization was symbolized by the orderly mills and workers' houses of Lowell, whereas the second phase—lasting from about 1860 to 1910—was best represented by the seeming disorder and grime of Gary, Indiana, the site of U.S. Steel's massive works built after 1907. By 1940, Gary was a city of over 100,000 people, with steel mills and blast furnaces that dominated the skyline.

A third wave of industrialization after 1900 continued to emphasize machine production, technological advances, and unskilled labor in manufacturing goods, but manufacturing work increasingly focused on the creation of durable goods for the consumer market. The most dynamic manufacturing sector, the automobile industry, symbolized the changing nature of manufacturing jobs, particularly with innovations in assembly line production at Henry Ford's Highland Park plant, opened in 1909 to produce the Model T. Using the scientific management concepts developed by followers of Frederick Winslow Taylor, tasks were simplified, routinized, and de-skilled, while component parts were standardized and made interchangeable. Adding to the increases in worker productivity, Ford's system also increased the pace of the assembly line to new levels, causing many workers to flee the line. With employment turnover reaching 380 percent at Highland Park by 1913, Ford attempted to stabilize employment levels by offering a Five Dollar Day to workers—actually, a base rate with additional incentive pay. With other manufacturers in the automobile industry soon rivaling Ford's offer, manufacturing workers began to participate in the mass consumer economy of the 1920s.

The economic expansion of the 1920s briefly papered over the long-standing divisions between skilled and unskilled manufacturing workers. With specialized training, skilled workers earned higher wages and enjoyed greater job security, factors aided by membership in one of the trade unions organized under the American Federation of Labor (AFL) since 1886. Conservative in its approach to labor issues, the AFL typified "bread-and-butter" unionism that focused on higher wages for its members, not larger concerns such as control of the workplace. In contrast, unskilled manufacturing workers, a majority of whom were foreign-born by 1900, did not enjoy the higher wages or job security that skilled workers had achieved. They also were largely unorganized; the AFL refused to pursue the formation of industrial unions for unskilled workers, and other attempts at unionization were often brutally crushed from the 1890s onward. The Industrial Workers of the World, formed in 1905 as "one big union" that attempted to organize unskilled workers while calling for the overthrow of capitalism, was essentially defunct by 1919. Although it had successfully organized unskilled manufacturing

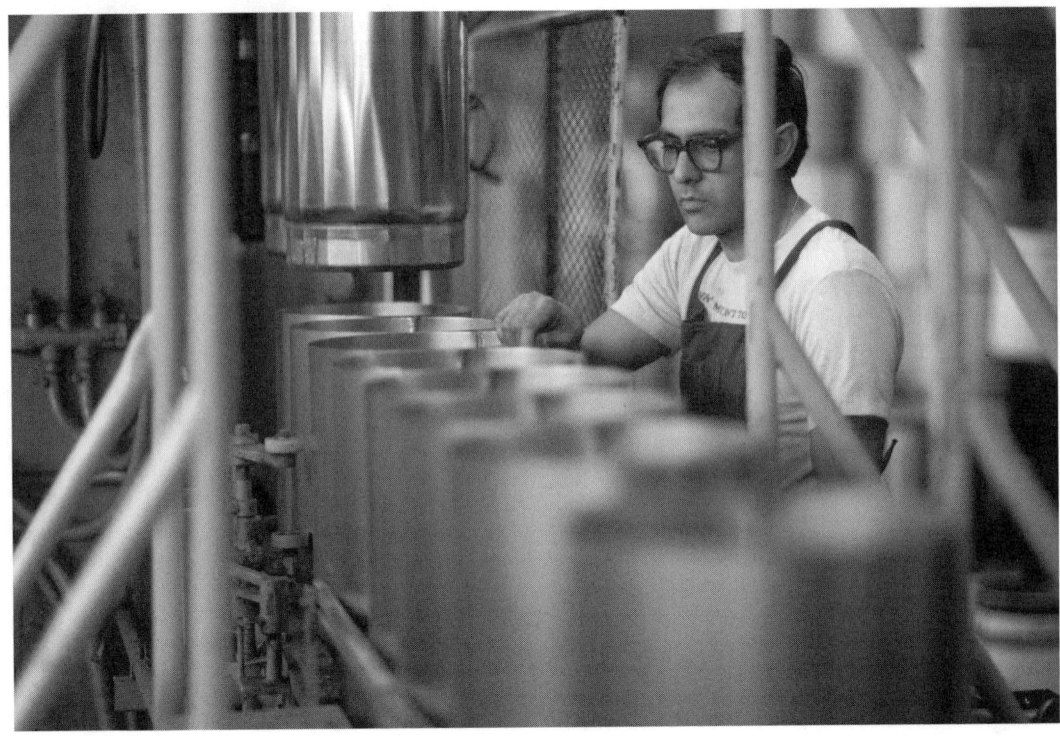

A worker assembling aluminum pipes. The Bureau of Labor Statistics predicts little growth in production/manufacturing jobs in the coming decade. (Vince Streano/Corbis)

workers in a number of industries, its radical stance had spurred responses by employers and government officials that sometimes turned violent.

With the onset of the Great Depression in 1929, unemployment climbed from its official rate of 3.2 percent to 25 percent in 1932. Manufacturing centers were hit particularly hard by the economic downturn. Unemployment in Detroit reached 50 percent in 1932 and U.S. Steel, which had retained about 225,000 workers in 1929, employed no full-time workers by 1933. Those who kept their manufacturing jobs found that employers often stretched out their jobs with additional tasks while speeding up the production pace. In response to growing unrest, the Roosevelt administration passed a series of New Deal measures to provide relief to workers, reform government, and promote economic recovery. In the manufacturing sector, the National Industrial Recovery Act of June 1933 seemed to promote the organization of workers into independent labor unions. It was only after a series of bitter strikes and the promulgation of the 1935 National Labor Relations Act (Wagner Act), however, that workers were secure in their legal right to join labor unions without fear of losing their jobs.

With the federal government acting as an arbitrator of labor disputes though agencies such as the National Labor Relations Board, workers in the heavy manufacturing industries such as steel, automobiles, and appliances were almost completely unionized by the end of World War II. By 1955, about 40 percent of U.S. workers belonged to a labor union. Some manufacturers resisted the trend toward unionization, however, and relocated their operations to regions in the South and West that had enacted "right-to-work" laws and other measures that discouraged labor union membership. Although unionized workers enjoyed higher wages, better benefits, and greater job security than their nonunionized colleagues, the general economic expansion after World War II increased most workers' ability to participate in the consumer boom of the postwar era. With generally stable labor-management relations and a growing economy, the period of the 1950s and 1960s was indeed something of a golden age for U.S. manufacturers, particularly those that produced consumer items and durable goods. Although recessions occurred in some years, they were typically mild and short-lived.

With European economies slowly recovering from the devastation of World War II and Asian economies just beginning to industrialize, the U.S. manufacturing sector was viewed by many as the most innovative and competitive in the world.

During the 1970s, several factors modified the status of manufacturing jobs in the United States. First, fiercer competition by foreign manufacturers increased the demands for cost cutting, efficiency, and productivity by U.S. manufacturers. Second, spikes in energy prices spurred on by the Organization of Petroleum Exporting Countries (OPEC) cartel after 1973 not only hiked manufacturing costs but inaugurated years of relatively high inflation rates as well. Manufacturers spent more on energy costs and in some cases on higher wages linked to cost-of-living adjustments; with interest rates increased to dampen inflation, they also found it more expensive to borrow money for investments in new technologies and modern physical plants. With profits falling and the manufacturing system facing apparent decline, corporations undertook numerous cost-cutting measures that put an end to the era of relative stability that manufacturing workers had enjoyed since the end of World War II.

Just as many manufacturers had moved their facilities to lower-wage sites in the South and West after World War II, many corporations now relocated their operations to overseas sites in developing nations that offered an even cheaper and more compliant pool of labor. Other companies outsourced more of their production for component parts to smaller, nonunion plants or by hiring more part-time workers and giving them few, if any, benefits. By the mid-1980s, about 17 percent of workers at major U.S. corporations worked only part-time. With the assistance of the Reagan administration, manufacturers also took a tougher stance at the collective bargaining table; by 1982, over 40 percent of union contracts agreed to wage reductions, and in other instances, manufacturers refused to negotiate with recognized bargaining agents at all. As a result of these upheavals, manufacturing workers' incomes failed to keep pace with inflation during the 1980s, experiencing an 8 percent relative decline during the decade.

Because of its emphasis on service sector jobs—often related to information technologies—after 1980, many observers described the U.S. economy as "postindustrial" and predicted an even lower profile for the manufacturing sector in the years to come. By 1997 just 16 percent of Americans worked in manufacturing jobs, a percentage that paled beside Germany's rate of around 30 percent. Although some foreign automobile manufacturers built new plants in the United States in the 1980s and 1990s, the trend toward globalization seemed to promise further declines in the prowess of U.S. manufacturing. With union membership also dropping to less than 16 percent of all U.S. workers in the 1980s, the promise of higher wages, improved benefits, and job security also vanished for those who retained their manufacturing jobs.

Timothy G. Borden

See also American Federation of Labor and Congress of Industrial Organizations; Automotive Industry; Blue Collar; Capitalism; Collective Bargaining; Ergonomics; Ford, Henry; General Motors; Globalization and Workers; Hawthorne Plant Experiments; Industrial Revolution and Assembly Line Work; *Maquiladora* Zone; National Labor Relations Act; North American Free Trade Agreement; Postindustrial Workforce; Productivity; Quality Circles; Reuther, Walter; Rust Belt; Strikes; Swing Shift; Taylor, Frederick Winslow; Time Cards; United Auto Workers; Working Class

References and further reading

Chandler, Alfred D., Jr. 1990. *Scale and Scope: The Dynamics of Industrial Capitalism.* Cambridge, MA: Harvard University Press.

Cowie, Jefferson R. 1999. *Capital Moves: RCA's Seventy-Year Quest for Cheap Labor.* Ithaca, NY: Cornell University Press.

Dudley, Kathryn. 1994. *The End of the Line: Lost Jobs, New Lives in Postindustrial America.* Chicago: University of Chicago Press.

Fingleton, Eamonn. 1999. *In Praise of Hard Industries: Why Manufacturing, Not the Information Economy, Is the Key to Future Prosperity.* Boston: Houghton Mifflin.

Graham, Laurie. 1995. *On the Line at Subaru-Isuzu: The Japanese Model and the American Worker.* Ithaca, NY: Cornell University Press.

Green, William C., and Ernest J. Yanarella, eds. 1996. *North American Auto Unions in Crisis: Lean Production as Contested Terrain.* Albany: State University of New York Press.

Gutman, Herbert G. 1977. *Work and Culture in Industrializing America: Essays on America's Working Class and Social History.* New York: Vintage Books.

Hamper, Ben. 1991. *Rivethead: Tales from the Assembly Line.* New York: Warner Books.

Hobsbawm, Eric. 1989. *The Age of Empire, 1875–1914.* New York: Vintage Books.

———. 1996. *The Age of Extremes: A History of the World, 1914–1991.* New York: Vintage Books.

Milkman, Ruth. 1997. *Farewell to the Factory: Auto Workers in the Late Twentieth Century.* Berkeley: University of California Press.

Nelson, Daniel. 1995. *Farm and Factory: Workers in the Midwest, 1880–1990.* Bloomington: Indiana University Press.

Sellers, Charles. 1991. *The Market Revolution: Jacksonian America, 1815–1846.* New York: Oxford University Press.

Sugrue, Thomas. 1996. *The Origins of the Urban Crisis: Race and Inequality in Postwar Detroit.* Princeton: Princeton University Press.

U.S. Department of the Census. 2001. "1997 Economic Census: Manufacturing." http://www.census.gov/epcd/www/97EC31.HTM (cited January 8, 2001).

Zieger, Robert. 1995. *The CIO, 1935–1955.* Chapel Hill: University of North Carolina Press.

Maquiladora Zone

Maquiladora zones are tax-free export zones (historically located just south of the U.S. border) that contain U.S.-controlled industrial plants (*maquiladoras*) employing low-wage Mexican workers. Spawned by Mexican government incentives, these plants import primary materials or components (tax-free), provide value-added labor-intensive improvements, and export intermediate or basic final products (taxed only on value added) back to the United States. In 1964, the U.S. eliminated its bracero program, which since 1942 had provided U.S. agricultural and construction jobs to hundreds of thousands of Mexican migrant workers. To create employment for this out-of-work population, Mexico implemented the Border Industrialization Program (BIP), establishing tax-free manufacturing zones in imitation of East Asian models. U.S. manufacturers flocked to Mexico for cheap labor, weak environmental regulations, and abolished taxes. U.S. labor unions protested the move; they labeled the potential loss of U.S. manufacturing jobs to low-skill, low-wage Mexican workers "the giant sucking sound." Precisely how many U.S. jobs were lost is unclear, but *maquiladora* employment reached over 1,000,000 by the year 2000 (INEGI 2000). By the 1990s, *maquiladoras* had become the largest source of foreign exchange for Mexico (Cravey 1998, 2).

Many are critical of the composition of the *maquiladora* workforce: most employees are young women who are thought to be conscientious and docile and are paid very low wages. Political economists suggest that *maquiladoras* are representative of wider structural processes that increasingly allow capital to bypass national authorities focused on the public interest. On the other end of the ideological spectrum, economists argue that Americans now consume cheaper goods and that Mexico has increased productivity because of the zones. In either case, recent studies show manufacturers leaving Mexico for even cheaper labor zones (as in Central America or Southeast Asia) or for locations with inexpensive, highly skilled labor (as in China). In addition, because of decreased demand for goods and production components in the United States, some *maquiladoras* have failed. The Mexican government now views *maquiladoras* as having few linkages to the economy and only limited potential to drive overall growth. As official support declines, the *maquiladora* zones are rapidly disappearing or converting into other, more sophisticated, manufacturing processes. Furthermore, in 2001, the BIP was subsumed under the auspices of the North American Free Trade Agreement (NAFTA): thus, *maquiladora* zones no longer officially exist.

The *maquiladora* zone has gone through four main phases. The first phase lasted from the 1960s to 1972, during which the Mexican government, under pressure to boost employment, implemented incentives to attract U.S. manufacturers below the 2000-mile-long U.S-Mexican border. The move contradicted the government's key economic development strategy at the time, called import-substitution industrialization (ISI). ISI was aimed at protecting the development of national industries and productive capacity until such time that the country could compete on an international basis. *Maquiladoras,* however, were export-focused, though their reach into the Mexican economy was limited (they created only "enclave," or noninterrelated economies). Most analyses agree that labor was heavily exploited during this period, suffering abysmal wages and poor living conditions. Women with only primary-level education comprised over 70 percent of the workforce (Iglesias Prieto 1997, xix; Cravey 1998, 13). This feminine labor focus not only diminished work opportunities for men in the *maquiladoras* but also reduced the viability of many rural areas, where women play a key role in local economies (Sassen 1998, 42).

During the second phase (1972–1983), labor strength advanced in the zone; unionization brought increases in worker benefits and living conditions. However, U.S. corporations, cutting back because of recession at home and now free to exploit other low-cost labor arenas, actually decreased *maquiladora* production and employment in the early period of this phase (1972–1976). In 1976, however, a massive devaluation of the Mexican currency made manufacturing there once again attractive, and employment grew at a rapid pace. Because capital interests had successfully threatened to move to other export-free zones, both labor and Mexican officials backed off from prior gains in labor and environmental protections.

Phase three lasted from 1983 until the North American Free Trade Agreement (NAFTA) was ratified by the United States, Canada, and Mexico and took effect in 1994. The Mexican government, under increased pressure from international development agencies such as the World Bank and viewing the success of the "Asian tiger" economies, shifted its economic strategy from ISI to export-led growth (along the lines of neoliberal economic models). The existing *maquiladora* sector, already employing some 200,000 Mexicans, became the rallying focus for future economic development. Mexico proposed to reduce trade deficits, maintain a devalued currency, decrease government expenditures, and open its borders to trade. In other words, the BIP approach to development would be nationalized. Although employment in the *maquiladora* sector continued along impressive growth lines (see Figure 5), wages dropped, and living standards for workers decreased.

Figure 5
Mexican *Maquiladora* Employment

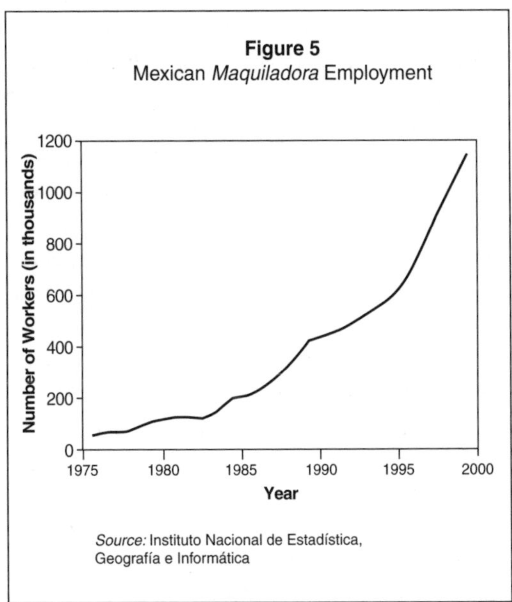

Source: Instituto Nacional de Estadística, Geografía e Informática

It can be argued that since 1994, when NAFTA took effect, the entire territory of Mexico has become a *maquiladora* zone (that is, with free trade everywhere), enabling U.S. firms to locate wherever natural resources, labor, trade routes or incentives might produce the highest profits. Technically, as of January 21, 2001, *maquiladora* zones no longer exist; the original incentives have been overridden by NAFTA (Gruben 2001, 12). Indeed, NAFTA can be considered the culmination of a set of policies put in place, beginning with the *maquiladora* zones, to open Mexico to the free market. Overall, the old *maquiladora* labor force has become more technical and administrative as well as more masculine, and producers have turned to higher-end manufacturing (such as electronics and car parts). In turn, traditional low-skill, very low-wage manufacturing, liberated by NAFTA, is increasingly located in poorer internal Mexican regions, marking a shift away from the border.

On the one hand, U.S. unions were opposed to NAFTA's tariff reductions, worrying that even more manufacturing jobs would be lost. On the other hand, governmental negotiators argued that Americans could consume cheaper Mexican-made goods and that Mexican productivity would increase. Both were right. Manufacturing jobs in the United States have steadily decreased since the 1970s, and at least some of the losses are due to *maquiladoras.* But products are less expensive for U.S. consumers, and productivity has increased in Mexico (if only slightly). The support for *maquiladora* zones is considered the policy precursor of a wider governmental move toward free trade and deregulation and is emblematic of the increasing globalization of manufacturing. However, the new Mexican government, led by the centrist National Action Party (PAN) believes that the original design of the *maquiladoras* provided few linkages with local Mexican businesses. As *maquiladoras* are shuttering and jobs are being lost, Mexicans are rethinking its export-led growth strategy. They look back at a history of poor labor conditions, increased exposure to environmental degradation, and few local benefits and question the wisdom of export-free zones.

Jesse Keyes

See also Capitalism; Contingent and Temporary Workers; Downsizing; Export-Processing Zones; Globalization and Workers; Immigrants and Work; North American

Free Trade Agreement; Trade Adjustment Assistance Program; Women and Work

References and further reading

Campbell, Bruce, Andrew Jackson, Mehren Larudee, and Teresa Gutierrez Haces. 1999. "Labour Market Effects under CUFTA/NAFTA." *Employment and Training Papers* 29. Employment and Training Department, International Labour Office, Geneva.

Cravey, Altha J. 1998. *Women and Work in Mexico's* Maquiladoras. Lanham, MD: Rowman and Littlefield.

Gruben, William C. 2001. "Was NAFTA behind Mexico's High *Maquiladora* Growth?" *Economic and Financial Review* (Third Quarter): 11–21.

Hanson, Gordon H. 1996. "Localization Economies, Vertical Organization, and Trade." *American Economic Review* 5 (December): 1266–1278.

Iglesias Prieto, Norma. 1997. *Beautiful Flowers of the Maquiladora.* Austin: University of Texas Press.

INEGI (Instituto Nacional de Estadística, Geografía, e Informática). 2000. "Industria *Maquiladora* de Exportación." Aguascalientes, Mexico. October.

Kopinak, Kathryn. 1996. *Desert Capitalism:* Maquiladoras *in North America's Western Industrial Corridor.* Tucson: University of Arizona Press.

Pena, Leticia. 2000. "Retaining a Mexican Labor Force." *Journal of Business Ethics* 2: 123–131.

Sassen, Saskia. 1998. *Globalization and Its Discontents: Essays on the New Mobility of People and Money.* New York: New Press.

Wilson, Patricia A. 1992. *Exports and Local Development: Mexico's New* Maquiladoras. Austin: University of Texas Press.

Maritime Trades and Work

Seafaring and longshoring (loading and unloading cargo, which is called "stevedoring" in most other English-speaking countries) are among the world's oldest occupations, dating from long before the founding of the United States. One of the earliest issues in U.S. foreign policy involved the treatment of U.S. seafarers by foreign vessels, in particular, British military vessels impressing (that is, kidnapping) U.S. seafarers into the British navy.

Seafaring has long been an occupation both dangerous and unpleasant. As Samuel Johnson said, "No man will be a sailor who has contrivance enough to get himself into jail; for being in a ship is being in a jail, with the chance of being drowned." Andrew Furuseth, the early giant of U.S. maritime unionism, commented this way on the prospect of imprisonment: "You can put me in jail, but you cannot give me narrower quarters than as a seaman I have always had. You cannot give me coarser food than I have always eaten. You cannot make me lonelier than I have always been" (Boswell 1791).

Because of the dangers of seafaring, to work onboard ship was to work in the ultimate of undemocratic, militaristic environments. Ships' masters (captains) long retained almost unlimited authority over the seafarers who worked on their vessels, including the right to inflict corporal punishment; seafarers who protested their treatment could be charged with mutiny. So complete was the subjection of seafarers that the Thirteenth Amendment to the U.S. Constitution prohibiting involuntary servitude (slavery) was held by courts not to apply to those who worked aboard ship. In this environment, seafaring clearly attracted mostly those with few or no other options.

An early attempt by U.S. seafarers to unionize that met with some significant success was the International Seamen's Union, founded in 1892. Andrew Furuseth was elected president of that organization in 1908 and became the voice of U.S. seafarers. Marine Engineers had already begun to unionize earlier when the Marine Engineers Beneficial Association was founded in 1875, and pilots began to organize in 1887.

Seafarers had little or no significant legal protection until the passage of the LaFollette Seamen's Act in 1915. That act, for which Furuseth had fought long and hard, was hailed as the Magna Carta of the sea. It sought to protect seafarers from a variety of abuses, including those aboard ship (requiring decent food and water, for example); those that involved their being expelled from their ships in distant, sometimes foreign, ports; and those that enabled ship owners to refuse to pay them agreed-upon wages or to meet other agreed and/or humane conditions.

The Depression of the 1930s initially decimated maritime unionism. However, legislative help was about to arrive. In addition to the earlier Jones Act (1920), which required vessels engaged in commerce between U.S. ports to fly the U.S. flag, and the passage of the National Labor Relations Act (Wagner Act) in 1935, the key piece of legislation was the Merchant Marine Act of 1936. That act recognized the value of a U.S.-flag-flying commercial fleet both for U.S. commerce and for national security and provided subsidies both to build ships for the U.S.-flag fleet and to operate those vessels. It continued the requirement that officers on such vessels be U.S. citizens and required that most nonofficer seafarers employed on those vessels also be citizens. The U.S. government was now committed to the promotion of the maritime industry and the people who worked aboard ship.

The result of all this legislation, together with the increased need for shipping created by World War II, was a dramatic increase in the fleet and in the number of seafarers working aboard the ships of that fleet. Those seafarers became almost completely unionized and were almost all covered by collective bargaining agreements. However, they belonged to a variety of different unions that were often the bitterest of rivals. Every category of maritime labor (deck and engine officers, unlicensed deck crew, unlicensed engine crew, the stewards' department, and radio officers) had and still has multiple unions competing for membership and allegiance. These unions formed shifting and uncertain alliances with each other and with the longshoring unions, and these alliances and rivalries survived long past the merger of the American Federation of Labor (AFL) and the Congress of Industrial Organizations (CIO) in 1955. The maritime unions had some of the most colorful and influential union officers in the nation, including Joe Curran (National Maritime Union), Paul Hall (Seafarers International Union), and Harry Lundeberg (Seamen's Union of the Pacific), but these men and their contemporaries often devoted themselves as much to their battles with each other as to those with the employers.

The postwar period was characterized by a dramatic long-term decline in employment on the U.S.-flag fleet. There were several causes of the decline. One major factor was that technological change aboard ship and in cargo handling (particularly the containerization of cargoes) allowed for larger ships to carry much more cargo with much smaller crews. Thus by the end of the twentieth century, vessels many times larger than those of 1950 were operating with crews of twenty or fewer, whereas the vessels of 1950 might have had crews of fifty or more. The number of nonofficer seafarers on each ship has declined the most.

In addition, high costs of operating U.S.-flag vessels stemming from high wage and benefit packages and strict regulatory rules caused the U.S.-flag fleet to lose out competitively to foreign-flag fleets. Often those foreign-flag vessels were owned by Americans but were operating under "flags of convenience." That is, they were operated under the auspices of nations that invited foreigners to register their vessels there and imposed low taxation and few regulations. By 2000, these flags of convenience led the world in vessel registration, with Panama and Liberia accounting for the most but with over twenty others available. Increasingly, only U.S.-flag vessels that were subsidized or were in protected market niches (for example, trading between U.S. ports and thus covered by the Jones Act) could survive. U.S.-owned flag-of-convenience vessels generally did not use U.S.-citizen crews or provide wages and working conditions comparable to those on the U.S.-flag fleet.

In the 1990s, it was clear that without subsidy, the U.S.-flag fleet would not survive. With subsidy contracts under the Merchant Marine Act of 1936 gradually expiring and the government refusing to enter into any more, it was clear that the U.S.-flag oceangoing fleet was on the edge of extinction. At least a small part of it was saved by the Maritime Security Program (1996), which provided more limited subsidies (compared to those that had been available under the Merchant Marine Act) to some forty vessels engaged in international trade. Even then, the U.S.-flag vessel operators forced the maritime unions to make major collective bargaining concessions before the operators would agree to participate in the Maritime Security Program, as opposed to registering their remaining vessels overseas.

By the year 2000, seafaring was no longer a major U.S. occupation, with only a few thousand jobs available. Most of the major maritime unions had a fraction of their former memberships, and others had to branch out of the maritime industry to survive.

In the last twenty years of the twentieth century, strikes virtually disappeared in the U.S.-flag maritime industry (strikes had been common in the 1940s and 1950s). The unions had been shrinking for the previous fifty years and spent much of their energy (the part that wasn't spent fighting each other) joining the employers in an effort to maintain and increase the direct and indirect subsidies to the industry on which the wages and working conditions of their members were based. At the same time, a series of internal financial and election scandals plagued several of the remaining significant unions in the industry (in particular, the National Maritime Union, the Marine Engineers Beneficial Association, and the Masters, Mates, and Pilots), sapping much of what remained of their vitality.

Longshore work also tended to attract workers

who were desperate and downtrodden. Workers were traditionally hired by the day and often had to pay bribes or kickbacks to get work. Unionization and collective bargaining ultimately brought about improved treatment and employment security.

Longshoring has also had more than one union, but the unions long ago stopped competing for members. The International Longshoremen's Association has dominated on the East and Gulf Coasts, and the International Longshoremen's and Warehousemen's Union has been the dominant influence on the West coast. The latter union also produced one of the most colorful union leaders in the United States, Harry Bridges. He emerged as a leader in the dramatic strikes of 1934 and remained president of the union for decades.

Foreign competition is not as serious an issue in longshoring as in seafaring. Ships of any flag that arrive in U.S. ports are loaded and unloaded by U.S. longshoremen. However, containerization of cargoes and related cargo-handling technologies have dramatically altered the process of loading and unloading and have led to large decreases in employment, although those who continue working earn high wages and receive excellent benefits. Strikes have largely disappeared (except as brief local phenomena) from this segment of the industry as well, with the lockout of 2002 the first such coastwide conflict in decades.

At the beginning of the twenty-first century, there remain a relatively small number of seafaring jobs in the U.S.-flag segment of the maritime industry and a shrinking number in longshoring. Those jobs that remain still provide good pay and working conditions, but it is hard for all but a small number of seafarers and an aging group of longshoremen to find regular enough work in the industry to support themselves. The bulk of the remaining seafaring jobs would disappear if direct subsidy and indirect subsidy (mostly in the form of various "cargo reservation" requirements) were eliminated.

Clifford B. Donn

See also American Federation of Labor and Congress of Industrial Organizations; Building Trades Unions; Globalization and Workers; Occupational Safety and Health Act

References and further reading

Boswell, James. 1971. *Life of Samuel Johnson.* London: Henry Baldwin.

Chapman, Paul K. 1992. *Trouble on Board: The Plight of International Seafarers.* Ithaca, NY: ILR Press.

Forsyth, Craig J. 1987. "The Creation of a Stigmatized Occupation: An Historical Analysis of the American Merchant Marine." *Maritime Policy and Management* 14, no. 2: 99–108.

Forsyth, Craig J., and Alexander Cullison. 1984. "Conflict in the U.S. Maritime Industry: An Account of Historical Cycles." *Maritime Policy and Management* 11, no. 4: 251–259.

Gibson, Andrew, and Arthur Donovan. 2000. *The Abandoned Ocean: A History of United States Maritime Policy.* Columbia: University of South Carolina Press.

Goldberg, Joseph P. 1971. "Modernization in the Maritime Industry: Labor Management Adjustments to Technological Change." Pp. 243–421 in *Collective Bargaining and Technological Change in American Transportation.* Edited by Harold M. Levinson et al. Evanston: Transportation Center at Northwestern University.

Kilgour, John G. 1975. *The United States' Merchant Marine: National Maritime Policy and Industrial Relations.* New York: Praeger.

Nelson, Bruce. 1988. *Workers on the Waterfront: Seamen, Longshoremen, and Unionism in the 1930s.* Urbana: University of Illinois Press.

Thoms, William E. 1996. "Labor Relations in the U.S. Merchant Marine." In *United States Shipping Policies and the World Market.* Edited by William A. Lovett. Westport, CT: Quorum Books.

Meany, George (1894–1980)

Meany served as the first president of the American Federation of Labor and Congress of Industrial Organizations (AFL-CIO), from the AFL's merger with the CIO in 1955 until 1979. Considered to be a quintessential business unionist, Meany was known for his defense of craft union privilege, his virulent anti-Communism, his support of U.S. foreign policy and U.S. involvement in the Vietnam War, and his opposition to the peace and feminist movements that emerged in the 1960s.

Meany was born on August 16, 1894, in Harlem. Although his father worked as a plumber, he did not want the young Meany to become active in the trade, hoping that his son would obtain a better position in life. After spending one year in high school, Meany took a job as a messenger at a Manhattan advertising agency in June 1909 and considered attending night school to earn a business degree. However, he began to work as a plumber in October 1910, achieving journeyman status in 1914 and full membership in the Plumbers Union in January 1917. Shortly thereafter, Meany began his rise through the union's hierarchy. In 1919, he won a seat

George Meany meeting with Jimmy Carter, January 1978 (Courtesy of the Jimmy Carter Library)

on Bronx Local 463's executive board, and in 1922, he was elected business agent in the local. The next year, Meany became the secretary of the AFL Building Trades Council in New York City.

After becoming vice president of the New York State Federation of Labor in August 1932 and elected to its presidency in August 1934, Meany successfully promoted the federation's agenda. Meany's work on behalf of the AFL helped to achieve the passage of many new laws in 1935, including state unemployment insurance and worker's compensation laws, as well as the formation of a state labor relations board. To ensure that Franklin Delano Roosevelt won New York State's electoral votes in the 1936 election, Meany helped to organize, campaign for, and served as an elector for the American Labor Party, which ran Roosevelt on its presidential line. Acknowledged as being a highly effective political lobbyist for the state federation in Albany, Meany was elected by acclamation to the position of AFL secretary-treasurer at the federation's national convention in October 1939.

Moving to the AFL headquarters in Washington, D.C., Secretary-Treasurer Meany spent the World War II years as an AFL representative sitting on the War Labor Board and sharpening his anti-Communist political orientation. Shortly after the conclusion of the war, in what Paul Buhle (1999, 127) characterizes as "one of the very rare courageous or militant moments of his life," Meany led the AFL opposition to the 1947 passage of the antilabor Taft-Hartley Act. However, within a short time, Meany relented and accepted the act's implementation. Around the same time, the 1947 AFL convention accepted Meany's recommendation for the creation of Labor's League for Political Education, a formal arm of the federation for promoting the AFL's interests within the political arena.

After AFL president William Green died from a heart attack on November 21, 1952, the AFL Executive Council elected Meany interim president, and his election was approved by acclamation at the 1953 AFL convention. To encourage the continuing movement toward unity between the AFL and the CIO, Meany hammered out a "no raiding" agreement that was accepted by virtually all CIO unions by the middle of June 1954 but by only 65 of the 111 AFL affiliated unions (Buhle 1999, 133). In spite of the AFL's mixed reaction to the "no raiding" pact, talks continued, and formal unity of the AFL-CIO was achieved in December 1955, with Meany elected president of the merged federation, a position he held until November 1979. He died two months later on January 10, 1980.

As AFL-CIO president for nearly a quarter century, Meany's record has been lauded by supporters and attacked by detractors. Supporters praised (and critics attacked) his consistent anti-Communism at home and abroad, his support for U.S. foreign policy and U.S. involvement in the Vietnam War, as well as his attacks on what he viewed as extremely liberal Democrats, peace activists, environmentalists, feminists, and gay activists. Even though Meany supported the bill that was to become the 1964 Civil Rights Act and insisted that Title VII be included, white, conservative craft unionists, many found in the building trades, appreciated Meany's defense of their race privilege in the workplace and his weak support for both civil rights and the integration of their virtually lily-white unions. Although the AFL-CIO traditionally supported the Democratic Party candidates in local and national elections, Meany refused to back the 1972 Democratic presidential candidate George McGovern, believing that he was soft on communism and that he advocated surrender in Vietnam. In spite of his initial support for Nixon's reelection in 1972, Meany never publicly called for a vote for Nixon.

Several years before the end of Meany's tenure, union density had fallen from a peak of 33.2 percent in 1955 at the time of the AFL-CIO merger to 27.4 percent in 1971 (Goulden 1972, 466). When asked in 1972 why union density was falling, Meany replied, "I don't know, I don't care" (Goulden 1972, 466). The failure to organize the unorganized was a real disappointment of the Meany administration, which had originally believed that the AFL-CIO merger would revitalize the U.S. trade union movement.

Victor G. Devinatz

See also American Federation of Labor and Congress of Industrial Organizations; Building Trades Unions; Sweeney, John J.

References and further reading

Buhle, Paul. 1999. *Taking Care of Business: Samuel Gompers, George Meany, Lane Kirkland, and the Tragedy of American Labor.* New York: Monthly Review Press.

Dubofsky, Melvyn. 1973. "George Meany: Perfect Bureaucrat." *New Politics* 10: 30–33.

Goulden, Joseph C. 1972. *Meany: The Unchallenged Strong Man of American Labor.* New York: Atheneum.

Robinson, Archie. 1981. *George Meany and His Times.* New York: Simon and Schuster.

Meatpacking Industry

The development of the meatpacking industry was at first a slow process. In Europe and in the United States during the pre–Civil War era, obtaining meats usually took one of two forms: either one was a farmer who raised livestock for his or her own purposes; or one went to local butchers, who might have raised the livestock they slaughtered themselves or purchased animals from farmers.

Some people slaughtered their own animals for distribution, but the major problem in doing so was in shipping, especially before the widespread construction of railroads or if one was not near a canal. Preserving meats for long-distance travel usually required smoking or salting the food. Many of the early meat distributors were also involved in other business ventures.

In the pre–Civil War era, pork tended to be the primary meat for packing, but most people preferred fresh beef. Before the advent of refrigeration, those involved in the early days of meatpacking preferred to do so in winter, using the cold weather to their advantage.

Two events helped spark the meatpacking industry—the Civil War and the growth of railroads. During the Civil War, the need was to mobilize resources, especially food. The railroads, as opposed to canals, made transporting meats over longer distances faster and easier. During the Civil War, Chicago began to emerge as the meatpacking center of the country, after innovators such as Philip Armour, Gustavus Swift, and Nelson Morris transformed meatpacking into a highly centralized business. The meatpacking industry experienced incredible growth after the Civil War, using the help of the railroads and the advent of the refrigerated railcar.

Despite gains made by unionization, workers in the meatpacking industry face long hours, low pay, and frequent injuries. (Peter Vadnai/Corbis)

The meatpacking industry also became a highly mechanized business, especially because it was the first to utilize what became known as the assembly line. In 1893, close to 14 million animals were processed (Miller 1996). It took less than ten minutes to kill, clean, cut, and refrigerate a hog. At this point, with pork, the meat then went through additional processing, whether it was smoked or made into ham. It was said of slaughtering animals in the packing houses that everything was used but the squeal. Beef animals tended to be sent straight out to a butcher or a railroad car for shipment.

Working in a meatpacking plant was extremely hazardous. Blood and animal parts would splatter the workers, often flying into their eyes. Injuries to workers were commonplace, whether from cutting implements, a running animal, or a slip on a blood-covered floor. At times, an animal might get loose and run amuck on the shop floor.

Sanitary conditions were deplorable. Many diseased animals were slaughtered, processed, and sent out. Rodents loose in the plant might be accidentally ground up into the other meats, and sick workers themselves might further pollute the product. Upton Sinclair's infamous 1906 book *The Jungle* is best known for its exposé of the conditions in the meatpacking industry, although his main point was to convert people to socialism. The outcry over this work resulted in the federal Meat Inspection Act of that same year, which called for sanitary conditions and the inspection of all meats intended for interstate commerce.

Meatpackers also subjugated the independent butchers, as smaller businesses went from handling their own animals to handling meats already processed by the plants. The meatpackers were also able to open their own butcher shops and sell meats at prices lower than those of the independent butchers. Many of these local butcher shops would go along with the meatpackers and sell only those meats processed by those plants. Meatpackers also combined to control the marketplace, resources, and the price of labor.

Along with the harsh working conditions, meatpacking workers were also subjected to frequent and seasonal unemployment. Their early attempts to unionize were met with resistance by the meatpackers. The Amalgamated Meat Cutters and Butcher Workmen's organization was created in 1897 and faced near decimation in the 1920s, only to find revival and nationwide legitimacy in the 1930s with the help of the newly formed Congress of Industrial Organizations (CIO) and the National Labor Relations Act (Wagner Act).

Health, labor, and injury problems are still prevalent in the industry in the twenty-first century. Major fast food chains have become somewhat involved, claiming that they will purchase only those meat products that have been processed in specific ways. Inspections have become stricter, and many companies market "organic" meats, that is, animals that were raised and fed without the use of hormone treatments or any other "unnatural" chemical processes. It is just assumed that government inspection is carried out on a diligent basis. On occasion, tainted meats have found their way into the marketplace and onto the national news. The two most infamous meatpacking scandals involve Europe's "mad cow" disease and the discovery of E. coli organisms in beef in the United States, both of which can result in illness or death.

Labor issues are still very important to those within the industry, depending upon the location. In some areas, such as at some Texas plants, cooperation between the unions and management have helped improve the lives of many meatpacking workers, who are over 90 percent Latino, by offering a fair contract with good benefits and even English classes. In other areas, like some plants in North Carolina, the workforce is not unified. The majority of supervisory jobs are still held by whites, whereas groups such as African Americans and Mexicans are still delegated the dirtier aspects of the job, such as doing the killing and cleaning. In places that are not unionized, the common complaints among workers are the long hours and low pay. Regardless of unionization, long hours, low pay, and frequent injuries produced frequent turnover.

Many workers report health issues, including muscle problems and the loss of the ability to use their arms in a normal manner, injuries that are common to meatpacking workers. These injuries are especially common among those who use heavy-duty equipment to cut carcasses or even smaller knifes to produce smaller cuts of meat.

Regardless of any problems still lurking in the industry, the media still continues to serve as a watchdog for meatpacking conditions. Recalls of meat products have been reported with more frequency in the past few years, along with increased reports of industry-related injuries and illnesses. But although this coverage has affected how some people conduct their dietary habits, the United States itself has hardly given up on its taste for meat.

Mitchell Newton-Matza

See also Occupational Safety and Health Act; Sinclair, Upton; Workplace Safety

References and further reading

Barrett, James R. 1987. *Work and Community in the Jungle: Chicago's Packinghouse Workers, 1894–1922.* Urbana: University of Illinois Press.

Green, James R. 1980. *The World of the Worker.* New York: Hill and Wang.

Jablonski, Thomas J. 1993. *Pride in the Jungle: Community and Everyday Life in Back of the Yards Chicago.* Baltimore: Johns Hopkins University Press.

Miller, Donald L. 1996. *City of the Century.* New York: Simon and Schuster.

Sinclair, Upton. 1960. *The Jungle.* Reprint, Signet Classics.

Slayton, Robert A. 1986. *Back of the Yards: The Making of a Local Democracy.* Chicago: University of Chicago Press.

Wade, Louise Carroll. 1987. *Chicago's Pride: The Stockyards, Packingtown, and Environs in the Nineteenth Century.* Urbana: University of Illinois Press.

Medicaid

Medicaid is a medical insurance program, jointly funded by the state and federal government, that covers the cost of care for targeted populations in the United States. The program generally serves low-income adults and children (74 percent of those enrolled, using 29 percent of the services budget); the elderly (10 percent of those enrolled, using 30 percent of the services budget); and the disabled, blind, and chronically ill (16 percent of the Medicaid population, using 40 percent of the budget) (Legal Information Institute 2000). In 2000, more than 40 million Americans were covered by Medicaid, at an annual cost to the federal government of more than $200 billion dollars, with an equal dollar match at the state level (Wattenberg 2002, 1). At the end of the 1990s and in the early 2000s, Medicaid began a process of evolving from a poverty-based program to a more traditional health insurance program, serving working and working poor populations. In national surveys, most respondent-recipients expressed satisfaction with the Medicaid system, and as a result of this program, supporters claim that the United States has seen a dramatic drop in the number of medically uninsured low-income adults and children since the program's inception in 1965 (Centers for Medicare and Medicaid Services 2001, 3). However, critics of the Medicaid system cite as problems the limited choice of providers offered to recipients; lower reimbursement rates, which sometimes make it difficult for Medicaid patients to secure medical care; bureaucratic delays; and skyrocketing costs at the state and federal levels.

The History of Medicaid

The Medicaid program was developed as a result of a 1965 amendment (Title XIX) to the Social Security Act of 1935. This amendment required states to provide health care to all children in families receiving cash assistance under the Aid to Families with Dependent Children (AFDC) program. With passage of the act, the federal government allowed states to establish their own eligibility standards, determine the scope of services offered, set the payment rates for services, and administer their own programs. As a result, the Medicaid program varies from state to state, as well as changing over time in any given state.

States retain some discretion in deciding which groups will be eligible for Medicaid coverage and in determining the financial criteria for such eligibility. However, to receive matching federal funds, states must provide Medicaid coverage for most individuals who receive federally assisted income-maintenance payments; low-income children; infants born to Medicaid-eligible pregnant women; children under the age of nineteen whose families or who themselves are income eligible; recipients of adoption assistance and foster care under Title IV-E of the Social Security Act; and other "categorically needy" groups. Many states additionally cover income-eligible institutionalized patients, those who are cared for at home, recipients of state supplementary payments, persons infected with tuberculosis and acquired immunodeficiency syndrome (AIDS), and specific uninsured women with breast and cervical cancer.

For states to receive federal matching funds, they must offer certain basic services to categorically needy populations, including inpatient and outpatient hospital services; laboratory and X-ray services; the services of skilled nursing home professionals, physical therapists, nurses, and physicians; hospice care and rehabilitative services; medical and surgical dental services; rural health clinic services; nurse-midwife services (if authorized under state law); and early and periodic screening, diagnosis, and treatment (EPSDT) for individuals under the age of twenty-one.

Medicaid does not provide medical coverage for every poor person because income eligibility is just one facet of threshold criteria. Assets and resources can also disqualify individuals from the program, although medically needy persons in target groups can be deemed eligible solely because of excessive medical expenses. States can additionally exercise a degree of flexibility when determining how applicants are judged as medically and financially needy, and some states allow recipients to "spend down" to Medicaid eligibility, by paying monthly premiums incurred for medical care until they meet the asset eligibility standards.

Medicaid is a vendor payment program, with providers paid directly for the services they perform. Providers must accept the Medicaid reimbursement offered as payment in full. For the most part, states determine the reimbursement methodology and rate of service, and providers accept reimbursement at rates generally lower than the standard. Medicaid patients may also be asked to pay minimal deductibles, coinsurance, or copayments for certain services, and providers cannot be required to accept patients with Medicaid insurance. Rather, states set reimbursement rates that are high enough to attract and enlist "sufficient" providers in a given area.

The federal payment to the Medicaid program, known as the federal medical assistance percentage (FMAP), is determined for each state by a formula comparing the state's average per capita income level with that of the nation. The FMAP must not be lower than 50 percent or greater than 83 percent of Medicaid expenses for the state (Fein 1986, 12). As a result, states with a higher per capita income pay a larger share of their Medicaid costs and receive a smaller share of federal reimbursement. The federal government also pays between 50 percent and 100 percent (depending on the functions and activities provided) of the costs of administering state Medicaid programs (Fein 1986, 134).

Much Medicaid-related legislation enacted between 1984 and 1990 expanded the programs' mandate to cover low-income children. Originally, eligibility for children was tied to state welfare rules; in incremental steps, legislation broke this link, eventually establishing a minimum of at least 100 percent of the federal poverty level to cover a broader range of children under the age of nineteen. At the federal level, the Deficit Reduction Act of 1984, Omnibus Budget Reconciliation Act of 1987, Medicare Catastrophic Coverage Act of 1988, Omnibus Budget Reconciliation Act of 1989, and Omnibus Budget Reconciliation Act of 1990 each mandated that states make a broader range of patients eligible for Medicaid services. In 2000, the federal guarantee of Medicaid eligibility for most poor children, coupled with the optional expansions implemented by many states to extend Medicaid coverage (Children's Health Insurance Program [CHIPS]) to low-income children above the poverty level, extended basic health insurance coverage to nearly 24 million children in the United States (Mishel, Bernstein, and Boushen 2002, 6). However, about 11 percent or 8.4 million children under the age of eighteen remained uninsured in 2000.

Medicaid also addresses the unmet health insurance needs of elderly individuals. Indeed, Medicaid was the primary source of funds for nursing home care in the United States in 2000 (Wattenberg 2002, 38). Some older individuals are able to use coverage from both Medicaid and Medicare services. These "dual eligibles" are entitled to payments from both programs up to the state's payment limit, additional services, and help with monthly health insurance premiums.

Medicaid can also be an important resource in allowing disabled individuals to secure the health care they need to become financially secure and independent workers. In 1997, section 4733 of the Balanced Budget Act required that states provide Medicaid coverage to working individuals with disabilities who could not qualify for the program under statutory provisions because of their earnings. States provided Medicaid coverage to these workers by creating a new optional "categorically needy" eligibility group. Then, with passage of the Ticket to Work and Work Incentives Improvement Act of 1999, two new optional categories of "needy Medicaid eligibility groups" were created for disabled workers who might not otherwise qualify for this coverage. Again in 1999, the Supreme Court issued the *Olmstead v. L. C.* decision, mandating that federal, state, and local governments develop more opportunities for individuals with disabilities through more accessible systems of cost-effective community-based services, such as Medicaid.

In 2001, the Center for Medical Services estimated that 218,000 persons living with AIDS were also served by the Medicaid program. The cost of this coverage is estimated at $7.7 billion. States must provide a full range of Medicaid services to eligible AIDS patients, including case management, prevention services, hospice care, and pharmaceutical therapy.

Welfare Reform and Medicaid

Prior to the 1996 reform law, Medicaid eligibility was linked to AFDC, the federal welfare program. In essence, this linkage determined that families eligible for cash assistance through AFDC were automatically eligible for Medicaid and those who lost eligibility because of increased income could continue to cover their children on Medicaid for an additional period of time. When the central act of welfare reform, the Personal Responsibility and Work Opportunities Reconciliation Act (PRWORA) was passed in 1996, the link between welfare assistance and eligibility for Medicaid was severed. As a result, although states are still mandated to serve some welfare-eligible populations (specifically pregnant women and children), under this new legislation they are permitted to deny benefits to others, particularly those heads of household who lose welfare benefits because of their "refusal to work."

PRWORA also established greater welfare eligibility for the working poor. Under the 1996 rules, low-income working families, workers who are additionally in treatment facilities, former welfare recipients who work, and some student workers are eligible for continued Medicaid coverage under work incentive programs. Specifically, those eligible for Social Security or Supplemental Security Disability Income (SSDI) and Supplemental Security Income (SSI) benefits may remain eligible for this publicly financed health insurance program.

Transitional medical assistance (TMA) was designed to strengthen incentives for welfare recipients to go to work and remain employed without losing health insurance coverage. Nevertheless, the percentage of low-income working parents who were insured by Medicaid fell by almost one-quarter from 1995 to 2000, according to census data, whereas the share who are uninsured rose by 7 percent (U.S. Census Bureau 2000a, 2000b, 2000c). Income eligibility limits for working parents in most states remain well below the poverty line, and about one-third of low-income working parents remain uninsured (U.S. Census Bureau 2000a).

Welfare reform additionally affected the Medicaid eligibility of disabled children. Prior to enactment of the reform law, the definition of childhood disability was linked to the parents' income eligibility. Again, section 211 of PRWORA broke this link by redefining the term *disability.* As a result, in states called "1634 states," where eligibility had been tied to Supplemental Security Income, children who had been determined to be disabled but no longer met the new criteria were terminated from the program. The new definitions forwarded under welfare reform additionally threatened Medicaid eligibility of disabled children in "criteria states"; in other words, children were disqualified not because of a change in their disability or income but because of a change in Medicaid definitions.

Passage of PRWORA also changed eligibility requirements for legal immigrants deemed "noncitizens" for the Medicaid program. In the past, legal immigrants were eligible for the full range of Medicaid benefits. In contrast, "undocumented aliens" were eligible only for emergency medical benefits. Under the new welfare reform law, with certain exceptions, noncitizen legal immigrants were barred from Medicaid, although they might still be covered for emergency services. Generally, only "qualified aliens" are eligible for coverage, and some of them may not be qualified until they fulfill lengthy duration-of-residency requirements. Additionally, the income of the immigrant's sponsor is newly counted in determining income eligibility as a result of welfare reform in the United States.

Although PRWORA transformed Medicaid into a more punitive and restrictive program, it did aid the states financially. The legislation had an impact on federal financial participation (FFP) rates, national limitations on total funding, time limitations, and eligibility restrictions. Section 114 of the law provides for a fund of $500 million to enhance the federal matching fund for state expenditures attributable to administrative costs of determining who is eligible for Medicaid. Normally, these rates are 50 percent, but under this new law, the FFP rate can move above 50 percent, yielding a more profitable process but one that has no direct benefit to those insured under this program. In 1999, in the Balanced Budget Refinement Act, Congress removed national and state-specific expiration dates for this $500 million fund.

Despite increased restrictions, the rate of Medicaid enrollment in the United States doubled during 2001. This growth has been dramatic for uninsured working poor families, children and pregnant women, working disabled populations, and the aged. The program continues to serve uninsured, low-income, working populations, providing a much-needed health insurance safety net for those increasingly at risk in the United States.

Vivyan C. Adair

See also Elder Care; Health Insurance; Living Wage; Minimum Wage; Unemployment Rate; Women and Work; Work First

References and further reading

Alexander, Raymond, and Simon Podair. 1968. *Medicaid: The People's Health Plan.* New York: Public Affairs Committee.

Bovbjerg, Randall. 1982. *Medicaid in the Reagan Era: Federal Policy and State Choices.* Washington, DC: Urban Institute Press.

Centers for Medicare and Medicaid Services. 2001. "Medicaid Information." http://cms.hhs.gov/medicaid (cited December 10, 2002).

Fein, Rashi. 1986. *Medical Care: Medical Costs: The Search for a Health Insurance Policy.* Cambridge MA: Harvard University Press.

Legal Information Institute. 2000. "Medicaid Law: An Overview." Ithaca, NY: Legal Information Institute, Cornell Law School. http://lii.law.cornell.edu.

Mishel, Lawrence, Jared Bernstein, and Heather Boushen. 2002. *The State of Working America 2002–03.* Washington, DC: Economic Policy Institute.

National Conference of State Legislatures. 2001. "Medicaid Survival Kit: Executive Summary." Washington, DC: National Conference of State Legislatures.

U.S. Census Bureau. 2000a. "Money Matters: Money Income, 1999." In *Population Profile of the United States: 1999.* Washington, DC: U.S. Census Bureau.

———. 2000b. "Disability and Income." In *Population Profile of the United States: 1999.* Washington, DC: U.S. Census Bureau.

———. 2000c. "Annual Demographic Survey." In *Current Population Series.* Washington, DC: U.S. Census Bureau.

Wattenberg, Ben. 2002. "The First Measured Century." New York: Public Broadcasting System.

Middle Management

During most of the twentieth century, middle management was the linchpin of the modern U.S. enterprise. Middle management is a group of employees located between the first level of supervision and the top executives. Middle managers have a double function. First, they must implement the long-range plans and schemes devised by top executives. It is they who translate such plans into concrete projects for production workers and their supervisors. Second, they must provide top executives with information about the production process so they can devise long-term strategies. In the last thirty years, however, middle managers have been criticized for their inefficiency. Overall, their fate has risen and fallen with that of modern U.S. management.

Until the late nineteenth century, most U.S. enterprises were still small concerns run by independent entrepreneurs and their families. Typically, firms were single-unit enterprises that performed only one activity (transportation or selling, for example) in a limited geographical area. Because the volume of daily production was rather small, it could easily be supervised by the owners of the companies or their families. The centerpiece of the production process was the foreman, who was entrusted with the task of hiring workers, setting wage rates, and determining the pace of production. In the late nineteenth century, however, the U.S. economy was transformed by a great improvement in communication and transportation capacity. Faced with the need to produce ever greater volumes of goods for a national market, U.S. entrepreneurs resorted to mergers to create bigger companies and started combining mass production with mass distribution. U.S. enterprises thus became complex, integrated organizations that carried on every task that was necessary to transform raw material into a product and send it to the consumer. Such enterprises were characterized by their multiple units—they were composed of several departments that carried the tasks previously performed by different businesses. Not only were such departments administratively distinct, but they could be located in different areas of the country. As these enterprises developed, it became impossible for the entrepreneurs to oversee by themselves the workings of their company. On the contrary, they relied upon salaried employees whose task was to ensure that all the units would work congruently. Because their role was to coordinate production and distribution along principles of efficiency, middle managers were the fulcrum upon which the modern U.S. enterprise was built.

To carry out their task of coordination, middle managers ran their divisions and departments to the last detail, thereby depriving foremen of most of their responsibilities. They improved storage methods, refined accounting techniques, and oversaw the acquisition of materials. Middle managers evinced the same commitment to efficiency in their management of the production process—they endorsed scientific management methods to increase the productivity of the workforce. Overall, middle managers were essential to U.S. firms because they found ways of reducing costs and increasing output. Indeed, some took such an important role in the success of their firm that their names are still remembered: Bill Jones, a middle manager for Carnegie Edgar Thomson works, established world production records while at Ford Motor Company; and Russell McCarroll's unusual inventive skills earned him the moniker of Ford's "in-house Edison."

Since the 1970s, however, three economic and technological developments have led many to question the U.S. managerial structure in general and the function and status of middle managers in particular. First, the advent of computerization has reduced the need for middle management. Top executives no longer need to rely on them to gather the data they need to plan ahead. Second, work has undergone a transformation from a labor-intensive process to a knowledge-intensive one. The economy has shifted from manufacturing to services, and even in the manufacturing sector, automation has enhanced the need to rely on workers' knowledge at the expense of their muscles. These changes profoundly altered the nature of management, for any employee that exercises expertise or judgment on the job needs autonomy. Such employees cannot be managed as the production workers that stood at the core of the Taylorist system.

Third, by the early 1970s, the globalization of the market was well underway, and by 1980, 70 percent of the goods produced in the United States competed with foreign goods. Such competition threw many U.S. corporate giants off balance—particularly in the steel, automobile, and textile sectors, where U.S. industries were no longer competitive. Such setbacks resulted in a thorough questioning of U.S. managerial practices, while the organizational principles of Japan—whose economy was booming—were extolled. In Japanese enterprises, hierarchy was de-emphasized, and management was left to the lowest level. In every division and department, Japanese employees were encouraged to work in teams to analyze their problems and devise solutions. Compounding the effect of foreign competition were the recessions that hit the United States in the 1970s and early 1980s. In those times of austerity, many top executives sought to reduce costs and improve the productivity of their enterprises.

In the 1980s and 1990s, these three factors combined to convey the idea that the middle management ranks of U.S. enterprises were wastefully overstaffed with employees whose morale and motivation were low and whose overall contribution was questionable. As a result, many enterprises downsized their workforce, and the middle management ranks were cut to the bone. Feeling that they were the forgotten people in the middle, middle managers voiced their anxiety and sometimes contemplated creating unions. Doing so, however, further deteriorated their image, for they now appeared to be mediocre employees who were resistant to change.

Recently, however, middle managers have experienced somewhat of a rebirth in managerial theory. Reducing middle management ranks, some specialists argue, was a mistake because they remain a company's best source of entrepreneurial ideas and are best suited to solve problems that arise when companies try to implement changes. Most importantly, it is now apparent that companies that have adopted new managerial structures have fared no better than those that have kept traditional forms of organization. The classical hierarchical structure might be making a comeback.

Jean-Christian Vinel

See also Baldrige Awards; Corporate Consolidation and Reengineering; Downsizing; Postindustrial Workforce

References and further reading

Chandler, Alfred. 1977. *The Visible Hand: The Managerial Revolution in American Business.* Cambridge, MA: Belknap.

Hearn, Frank. 1988. *The Transformation of Industrial Organization: Management, Labor, and Society in the United States.* Belmont, CA: Wadsworth.

Skrabek, Quentin R., Jr. 2001. "The Lost Grail of Middle Management." *Industrial Management* (May–June).

"Special Report on Middle Management." *Business Week,* April 25, 1983.

Military Jobs and Careers

In the first decade of the twenty-first century, the U.S. military remains a central element of U.S. foreign policy, with more than 1.3 million personnel, including 253,000 deployed across the globe in 151 foreign countries. Although many talked of a "peace dividend" in the post-1989 collapse of the Soviet bloc, U.S. leaders concluded that the benefits from being the world's only superpower were more than worth the price in continued high military expenditures. Thus, the fiscal year 2002 U.S. military budget was $343 billion dollars—accounting for 36 percent of the world's total military expenditures and greater than the total combined spending of the next fifteen largest national military budgets (Center for Defense Information 2002). Although the U.S. military has a long and deeply rooted tradition of subservience to civilian authority, its sheer mass makes it an influential force in U.S. society. Since the elimination of the draft in 1973, the United States has relied on a large force of long-serving volunteers. The disappearance of the national consensus supporting military service as an obligation of citizenship has altered the tenor of military recruiting, as recruiters now rely heavily on "selling" the service to potential enlistees.

The All-Volunteer Force: A Brief History

Since the abandonment of the draft in 1973, the U.S. military has become an all-volunteer force (AVF). Initially, making the AVF work required major shifts in military policy. With the disappearance of draftees and draft-motivated volunteers, all four armed services had to redouble their recruiting efforts. Pay and benefits for enlisted soldiers rose dramatically with the end of the draft, as the services now had to make at least some effort to compete with jobs potential recruits might secure in the civilian economy. The fact that military personnel budgets were finite and manpower demands large helped keep military wages below those of the civilian sector, but the services sought to make up the difference by providing benefits such as housing allowances, medical care, and child care. Recruiters for all four services found that although higher pay, fringe benefits, bonuses, and college money were important in attracting recruits, recruits' perceptions that military life offered a unique personal experience proved vital. That being said, however, the services find recruiting much easier during periods of economic recession, when civilian jobs are harder to obtain (Ricks 1996).

One consequence of the military services'

recruiting struggles during the 1970s was a dramatic increase in the recruitment of women and a commensurate expansion of opportunities for women in the military. During a period when the services were struggling to recruit even low-quality male recruits, they concluded that they could no longer afford to turn away educated, intelligent, would-be female recruits. Women had formerly been restricted to acceptably "female" positions such as clerks, nurses, and the like; the AVF era saw virtually all military jobs opened to women—although women were prohibited from serving in combat units and on Navy ships. Although the traditional male-dominated culture of the military continues to struggle with integrating women, women now make up 14 percent of military personnel strength. The combination of the performance of women service members during the 1991 Persian Gulf War and evolving U.S. social and political attitudes regarding women has resulted in the erosion of the limitations on women in combat. Although women in the army and marine corps are still prohibited from serving in units likely to engage in "close combat" with the enemy on the ground, women crew combat aircraft in all four services and now go to sea aboard navy ships (see Francke 1997).

The armed services' difficulty in integrating women is indicative of a deeper tension both within the military and between the military and society over the continued relevance of the military's traditional "warrior culture." The increasing emphasis on technology creates demand for technical experts over combat leaders within the military ranks, and the "information warfare" paradigm touted by military planners as the means to perpetuate U.S. military dominance in the twenty-first century further emphasizes decentralized decision making and delegation of authority, which to some observers suggests a need to reinterpret the traditional hierarchical model of military institutions. At the same time, the fundamentally conservative ethos of the military, always at odds with that of an individualistic American society, is further alienated from the American mainstream by the decreasing numbers of military veterans among civilian elites—a direct consequence of the elimination of the draft—and by the increasing willingness of officers to take sides in partisan politics. Military officers, who tend to be the primary repositories of military values and culture because of their longer tenure in the service, feel that any effort to "civilianize" the military or employ it for "social experiments" is damaging to its warfighting ability. They point to the military's effectiveness and argue that the culture is an integral part in its success. This argument was deployed shrilly in response to the Clinton administration's 1993 proposal to overturn the military's ban on homosexual activity, a move that military traditionalists claimed would cause chaos in the ranks and induce many potential recruits to avoid the service. The fact that the officer corps has abandoned its traditional apoliticism and developed a partisan identification with the Republican Party further complicates relations between the military and civilian society (see Kohn 1994; and Feaver and Kohn 2001).

Despite these tensions, however, the military's place in American society is secure. Scattered concerns over the long-term vitality of the AVF reemerged during the 1990s because of recruiting difficulties in a post–Cold War era and a booming economy, but the system has not really been in crisis since the early 1980s. Given that political realities make a return to the draft extremely unlikely, any future recruiting shortfalls will likely be made up by a combination of measures, such as lowering standards for enlistment (the fact that the plentiful supply of recruits since the mid-1980s has permitted the services to insist that every recruit possess a high school diploma has led many military and civilian leaders to forget that it was not always thus), reducing the length of enlistment, or increasing compensation.

Military Life: An Overview

Rank and the Enlisted/Officer Distinction

The U.S. military is divided into two main categories of personnel: enlisted personnel and officers. To perform effectively under the trying conditions of combat, the military has a highly formal hierarchical structure of authority. The system is designed so that if a unit's leader is killed, injured, or otherwise unavailable in the chaos of combat, the integrity of the organization is maintained and it can continue to function. Accordingly, with the exception of a small number of dentists, lawyers, and physicians and a handful of other personnel, there is no such thing as "lateral entry" into the military. Individuals start at the bottom and work their way up, initially mostly through seniority, but with an ever-increasing focus on performance at higher ranks. There are ten officer ranks (designated O-1 to O-10) and nine enlisted ranks (E-1 through E-9). The lowest-ranking officer in the service formally outranks the highest-ranking enlisted man or woman. Higher-ranking enlisted personnel (grades E-4 and above) are classified as "noncommissioned officers" (NCOs) and exercise increased supervision responsibilities over their fellow enlisted personnel. Essentially, however, officers issue orders, and NCOs are responsible for direct supervision of enlisted troops in the execution of those orders. The relationship is in some way analogous to the management-foreman/supervisor-worker relationship in the civilian economy. In terms of numbers, the military had 1,157,947 enlisted personnel and 216,715 officers as of October 2001 (see Department of Defense 2002; Office of the Assistant Secretary of Defense 1999, chaps. 3, 4).

Officers are distinguished from enlisted personnel by the fact that they receive a "commission," granting them greater authority and demanding greater responsibility. There are three sources for officers: the service academies; collegiate Reserve Officer Training Corps (ROTC) programs; and officer candidate schools (OCS), a compressed program through which college graduates without prior ROTC training and a small number of exceptional enlisted personnel can gain a commission. Most of the officers in the four services gain their commissions through graduation from an ROTC program. Academy graduates and a select group of ROTC and OCS graduates are classified as "regular" officers upon their commissioning, but the bulk of ROTC and OCS officers are classified as "reserve" officers. Regular officers enjoy greater job security than reserve officers, who may or may not serve on active duty. All officers who either reach their eleventh year of active duty or are promoted to O-4 rank are offered regular status (most by their fifth year of active duty, in fact).

Age

The military is a relatively youthful institution compared to most large civilian organizations. Forty-six percent of military personnel are under twenty-five years of age. Most enlisted military personnel enter the service in their late teens or early twenties, usually right after graduation from high school. Most officers enter the service in their early to midtwenties, following graduation from college. About one-quarter of enlisted personnel reenlist after their initial term of service (generally a two- to six-year commitment, depending on the popularity of their chosen specialty). Recent statistics showed that the average active-duty military officer was 34.3 years old, whereas the average active-duty enlisted person was 27.3 (Office of the Assistant Secretary of Defense 1999, chaps. 2, 3, 4).

Social Background

When the all-volunteer force was instituted, one of the fears was that the military ranks would be filled overwhelmingly by unskilled, unqualified individuals. This did not come to pass in the dramatic fashion predicted by some—the services' recruiting success has allowed them to set fairly high standards that act as a barrier to undereducated individuals. However, the enlisted ranks in particular are skewed toward recruits from middle- and lower-middle class background, whereas few children of wealthy families choose a military career. African Americans are overrepresented in the enlisted ranks of the military and underrepresented in the officer ranks, a source of recurring distress for both military and civilian leaders. Despite this situation, a substantial number of African American enlisted personnel choose to pursue an extended career in the service—as a consequence, there are large numbers of African Americans in the senior enlisted grades. Hispanics are underrepresented in both the officer and enlisted ranks. Military personnel are more likely to hail from the South, West, and Midwest—the Northeast and Great Lakes regions are underrepresented in the military (Office of the Assistant Secretary of Defense 1999, chaps. 2, 3, 4). These characteristics may result in part from the large military presence in the South and West, which creates a positive relationship between citizens and the military—and not simply some sort of cultural divide.

Education

The military does not *require* a high school diploma for enlisted personnel but greatly prefers high school graduates because it feels that the diploma represents not only a level of intellectual ability but also an ability to persevere to accomplish a goal—making the holder more likely to adjust successfully to military life. The positive recruiting situation since the 1970s has seen a dramatic shift in the educational achievements of enlisted troops: 99.3 percent of enlisted personnel were high school graduates or general equivalency diploma (GED) holders in 1999, and 27.8 percent have at least some college experience. Among officers, 97 percent are graduates of a four-year college or university—even enlisted personnel who gain commissions through officer candidate schools usually obtain a college degree while on active duty following their commissioning (Office of the Assistant Secretary of Defense 1999, chaps. 2, 3, 4).

While in the service, both enlisted and officer personnel receive a great deal of training and education. In addition to field exercises and technical training for their particular military specialties, enlisted personnel receive training in subjects such as leadership and human relations. In a move that has upset some traditionalists, promotion for more senior noncommissioned officers is now contingent on meeting increasingly strict academic standards. Officers follow a similar range of educational pursuits but at a more advanced level. As officers rise in rank, their military education focuses more on larger issues of military operations and strategy. Officers who reach the rank of O-6 are usually graduates of one of the nation's "war colleges," where issues involved in integrating military force into national grand strategy are considered during a year-long course. Forty-five percent of officers also obtain graduate degrees, many of them from elite civilian universities (Office of the Assistant Secretary of Defense 1999, Executive Summary).

Promotion

Military personnel strength is set by Congress; officer strength usually varies year to year, according to a ratio of the strength of the enlisted forces. Military personnel are only promoted as vacancies occur in the ranks above them. Among officers, these vacancies result from promotion, retirement, or separation from service. Among enlisted personnel, the relatively large number of one-term enlistees—one-third of whom do not even successfully complete their initial obligated service—ensures rapid turnover in the E-1 to E-4 ranks, after which limited annual promotions and a system of competitive examinations thin the ranks.

To keep the system flowing, the laws governing personnel management impose an "up or out" policy. It is true with enlisted personnel but is most acutely felt among officers: whereas only a minority of enlisted personnel are inclined to stay in the military for the twenty-year period required to qualify for retirement, the majority of officers hope to make a career of military service. Most officers are promoted to O-3 rank, but after that the competition for promotion becomes increasingly intense. Officers who are twice passed over for promotion while in a given rank are subject to involuntarily separation from the service, although officers with eighteen or more years service are permitted to serve through the end of their twentieth year to vest their retirement. Although the other compulsory retirement provisions make it a rarity, officers may also be retired for age at sixty-two years—with the exception of O-9 or O-10 officers, who receive a special deferment from the president and must retire at sixty-four.

To manage the flow of officer personnel according to the shifting needs of their services, the service secretaries set "promotion zones" for officers, which may be longer than the period stipulated by law. Promotion boards exercising authority delegated by Congress and the president evaluate officers for selection for promotion as they "enter the zone" by having served in their current rank for the specified length of time. A small number of exceptional officers may be promoted from "below the zone," a mark of significant distinction.

Compensation

Military compensation is a constant source of controversy. Certainly pay has increased substantially since the institution of the AVF, but military members and advocates frequently complain that it remains insufficient. Claims that low military pay leads to loss of military personnel to the civilian sector are a recurrent theme. Although it is true that military pay often lags behind that in the civilian sector, the inclusion of various nonmonetary benefits evens up the discrepancy substantially. Pay increases with rank and tenure of service—thus, an E-1 enlisted soldier with less than one year's service makes just over $12,000 per year, whereas an E-7 enlisted person with ten years' service makes around $30,000 per year. Officer pay is higher: an O-1 officer with less than two years' service makes around $25,000 per year, whereas an O-4 officer with ten years' service makes over $56,000 per year.

One major problem in military pay has resulted from the services' efforts to attract new recruits over the years: pay for junior enlisted personnel has been substantially increased over the years, but increases for middle and senior enlisted personnel have been much smaller. As a consequence of this "pay compression" phenomenon, many enlisted personnel become increasingly disappointed with their compensation at midcareer, leading them to leave the service for civilian employment (Defense Finance and Accounting Service 2002).

Families

Since the institution of the all-volunteer force, the number of servicemen and women with spouses and/or children has risen dramatically. Today, over 50 percent of enlisted personnel are married (over 65 percent of officers are married). The services have attempted to respond by greatly increasing the amount of on-base family housing available, but many enlisted families in particular must employ a housing allowance to defray the cost of off-post housing (Office of the Assistant Secretary of Defense 1999, chaps. 2, 3, 4). Junior enlisted pay is often stretched very thin in these instances, leading some military families to apply for food stamps—occurrences of this phenomenon have been repeatedly cited by military supporters throughout the thirty years of the AVF era, but the reality is that it is more of a dramatic departure than a widespread problem.

One complication for military families is frequent moves—typically, one-third of the military population makes a "permanent change of station" (PCS) move each year, and each military family can expect to move approximately every two years. Although service members are compensated by the government for PCS moving expenses, the amount allotted is often insufficient. In addition, service members are often deployed overseas for extended periods of time to areas where families may not accompany them. This has long been problematic for naval personnel because of their extended time at sea but has become increasingly difficult for the other services, given the burgeoning number of overseas deployments in the post–Cold War era. Approximately 14 percent of military members with spouses and/or children were deployed in so-called hardship tour deployments during 1999. An added complication is the increasing number of single-parent or dual-military-parent households (General Accounting Office 2001, 23).

Retirement

The basic military retirement system is fairly unique, both because of the services' emphasis on youth and because only a small percentage of military personnel serve long enough to qualify for retirement. Career service members who serve twenty years on active duty are permitted to retire, drawing lifetime retirement pay equal to 50 percent of their highest active duty pay (with periodic adjustments for inflation). Given that most service members retiring after twenty years are in their forties (in 1990, the average retiring officer retired at forty-six, after twenty-four years of service), they typically rely on this fairly generous sum to supplement income from a second career. Service members may elect to remain on active duty, accruing an additional 2.5 percent retirement benefit per year of additional service until they reach mandatory retirement and a 75 percent pension at thirty years of service. This system has been much criticized. Some observers argue that the system is unfair to the majority of military personnel, given that only 30–40 percent of officer personnel and 10–15 percent of enlisted personnel survive the "up or out" system for twenty years. Others suggest that those who do qualify for retirement are allowed to retire too early, depriving the government of the well-honed skills and long experience developed at government expense while they are still very productive—after which the government is obliged to pay their retirement for decades (Rostker et al. 1993, 96; Asch, Johnson, and Warner 1998, 1–3).

Erik Blaine Riker-Coleman

See also Defense Industry; Gays at Work; GI Bill; Rosie the Riveter; Sexual Harassment; Veterans; Wartime and Work

References and further reading

Asch, Beth J., Richard Johnson, and John T. Warner. 1998. "Reforming the Military Retirement System." RAND Corporation. http://www.rand.org/publications/MR/MR748 (cited January 15, 2002).

Center for Defense Information. 2002. "World Military Expenditures." Washington, DC: Center for Defense Information. http://www.cdi.org/issues/wme (cited January 15, 2002).

"Citizens, Soldiers, and Service to the Nation." 2001. *Parameters: Journal of the U.S. Army War College* 31, no. 2 (Summer): 18–73. Available online at:

http://carlisle-www.army.mil/usawc/Parameters/01summer/contents.htm (cited January 15, 2002).

Defense Finance and Accounting Service. 2002. "2002 Military Pay Rates." http://www.dfas.mil/money/milpay/pay (cited January 15, 2002).

Department of Defense, Statistical Information and Analysis Division. 2002. "Military Personnel Statistics." http://web1.whs.osd.mil/mmid/military/miltop.htm (cited January 15, 2002).

Feaver, Peter D., and Richard H. Kohn, eds. 2001. *Soldiers and Civilians: The Civil-Military Gap and American National Security.* Cambridge, MA: MIT Press.

Francke, Linda Bird. 1997. *Ground Zero: The Gender Wars in the Military.* New York: Simon and Schuster.

General Accounting Office. 2001. "Military Personnel: Longer Time between Moves Related to Higher Satisfaction and Retention." Washington, DC: Government Printing Office. http://www.hhgfaa.org/ltbmove.pdf (cited January 15, 2002).

Huntington, Samuel. 1957. *The Soldier and the State: The Theory and Politics of Civil-Military Relations.* Cambridge, MA: Belknap Press of Harvard University Press.

Janowitz, Morris. 1960. *The Professional Soldier: A Social and Political Portrait.* New York: Free Press.

Kohn, Richard H. 1994. "Out of Control: The Crisis in U.S. Civil-Military Relations." *National Interest* 35 (Spring): 3–17.

Moskos, Charles C., and John S. Butler. 1996. *All That We Can Be: Black Leadership and Racial Integration the Army Way.* New York: Basic Books.

Office of the Assistant Secretary of Defense, Force Management Policy. 2002. "Population Representation 1999." http://www.dod.mil/prhome/poprep99/ (cited January 15, 2002).

Rhem, Sgt. 1st Class Kathleen T. 2001. "Twenty-Year-High Military Pay Raise Averages 6.9 Percent." American Forces Information Service. January 7. http://www.defenselink.mil/news/Jan2002/n01072002_200201072.html (cited January 15, 2002).

Ricks, Thomas E. 1996. "The Great Society in Camouflage." *Atlantic Monthly* 276, no. 6 (December): 24–38. Available online at: http://www.theatlantic.com/issues/96dec/military/military.htm (cited January 15, 2002).

———. 1997. *Making the Corps.* New York: Scribner's.

Rostker, Bernard, Harry Thie, James L. Lacy, Jennifer H. Kawata, and S. W. Purnell. 1993. *The Defense Officer Personnel Manpower Act of 1980: A Retrospective Assessment.* RAND Corporation. http://www.rand.org/publications/R/R4246.pdf/R4246.appa.pdf (cited January 15, 2002).

Minimum Wage

The U.S. federal minimum wage established a wage floor (or a baseline wage) for compensation that increased cash flow to workers at the low end of the wage scale. The introduction of federal minimum wage legislation in the 1930s redefined relationships among labor, business, and government. Minimum wage laws moved the United States from a feudalistic system consistent with an agrarian-based economy (and employer-based control) into a wage labor market in which government regulated some aspects of the work environment, such as wages, work hours, and working conditions (Levin-Waldman 2001, 82–83). Franklin Delano Roosevelt's intention in devising the minimum wage component of the Fair Labor Standards Act of 1938 (FLSA) was to stimulate U.S. business in the wake of the Great Depression. Roosevelt believed a minimum wage would stabilize the labor market, increase consumer spending, and ameliorate regional wage disparities. Since its inception, the effectiveness of the minimum wage and even its intent has been the subject of much debate. Unlike federal benefit programs like Social Security, the minimum wage has never been indexed for inflation but remains subject to political processes for increases.

Massachusetts passed the first U.S. minimum wage law in 1912, followed by fourteen other states and the District of Columbia within six years. Most of these early minimum wage laws were directed toward women and/or children. Vigorously challenged by business interests and unions, most of these laws were deemed unconstitutional in state and federal courts on the grounds that minimum wage requirements "violated both the employer's and employee's 'liberty of contract'" (Waltman 2000, 29). Passage of constitutionally viable minimum wage legislation came after the Supreme Court struck down previous federal efforts, including the National Industrial Recovery Act of 1933 (NIRA). As a component of Roosevelt's New Deal progressivism, the 1938 FLSA established minimum wage levels, maximum work hours, and some workplace oversight provisions. The FLSA was successful because of the ways in which the minimum wage applied to labor. The FLSA's regulations covered workers engaged in the production goods sold through interstate commerce, over which Congress had constitutionally mandated control. Employees working in fields associated with transportation, communication, trade, or commerce (products and services that crossed state lines) were covered under the FLSA. Employees classified as professional, executive, or administrative were exempted from the FLSA. More importantly, FLSA exempted workers considered uninvolved with interstate commerce, including those employed in agriculture, retail, external sales, apprenticeships, and those working for small employers.

Passage of the FLSA occurred in spite of the resistance offered by business and industrial groups, unions, and the southern politicians. Unions objected to a minimum wage because of concerns that an established minimum wage would become a wage ceiling and fears that legislated wages would undermine collective bargaining. The South, as a region, had the lowest wages in the country and argued for exemptions based on industrial variance (agriculture) and for subminimum wages for black workers (Levin-Waldman 2001, 88). Roosevelt, however, saw the minimum wage as an opportunity to "modernize" the South "and to correct the existing economic imbalance" that resulted from the South's low wage rates (Levin-Waldman 2001, 85). Roosevelt felt a uniform wage was needed to increase and stabilize consumer spending on a national basis. When enacted, the FLSA instituted a minimum wage of twenty-five cents an hour in 1938, with increases until 1945, when the rate reached forty cents an hour. No rate-based subminimum was included in the bill, although agricultural workers were exempted.

Under the Truman administration, the minimum wage increased in 1949 to seventy-five cents an hour, but the legislation reduced the covered worker categories of the FLSA to only those whose jobs were deemed integral to interstate commerce, rather than workers whose jobs were "'closely related . . . or necessary'" to interstate commerce (Waltman 2000, 35). By 1961, Congress raised the minimum wage to $1.25 an hour, and retail workers employed by businesses grossing $1 million became subject to the minimum wage. At the same time, exemptions were extended to "laundries, automobile and farm equipment dealerships, and cotton gins" (Waltman 2000, 39). Over the next twelve years, changes in the legislation encompassing increased numbers of retail workers by lowering the gross exemption level of their employers (the lowest level was set in 1966 at $250,000; today's limit is $500,000) and the concept of a subminimum wage for youth, including its terms, length of effectiveness, and the actual reduction percentage, were introduced, enacted, repealed, and reinstituted in the process of continued legislative action. Over time, worker categories affected by the minimum wage expanded to include agricultural workers, state and civic workers, laundry workers, and to a lesser level, tipped employees. In the case of tipped employees—wait-staff, for instance—minimum wage provisions now require employers pay a wage that is 50 percent of minimum wage, with the rest made up in tips. Prior to this 50 percent provision, many employers paid no hourly wage to tipped employees, and tips comprised the only source of income for these workers (Waltman 2000, 41). The last increase of the minimum wage occurred in 1996 during the Clinton administration and brought the hourly federal minimum wage to $5.15. (An effort in 2000 to increase the minimum wage by one dollar was unsuccessful.)

The rationale for the minimum wage in 1938 shows little resemblance to that expressed today. In 1938, the FLSA was designed to improve the faltering condition of U.S. commerce. Because of high unemployment during the Great Depression, wages were suppressed, thereby creating an "unhealthy" economic environment (Krumm 1981, 1). The FLSA sought to restrict unfair labor competition, stabilize declining wages, and stimulate consumer purchasing (Waltman 2000, 32; Krumm 1981, 1). Today, the issues surrounding the minimum wage focus on the effectiveness of minimum wages: that is, who benefits from minimum wage mandates and to what degree. Over time, unions became ardent supporters of the minimum wage, once it was evident that minimum wages provided a wage floor and not a wage ceiling and when collective bargaining did not suffer (Levin-Waldman 2001, 78, 90).

At present, two primary economic philosophies underpin the minimum wage debate. The neoclassical, or standard, model based on the law of supply and demand is represented by George Stigler's assertion that increases in minimum wage rates will cause job reductions, resulting in net losses for the minimum wage constituency (Card and Krueger 1995, 1). The standard model relies on time-series data and deductive reasoning to demonstrate the resultant levels of disemployment. The most commonly cited study was conducted in 1982 by Charles Brown, Curtis Gilroy, and Andrew Kohen and concluded that a 10 percent increase in the minimum wage results in a 1–3 percent disemployment rate (Krueger 2001, 245; Brown 1996, 88). Further analy-

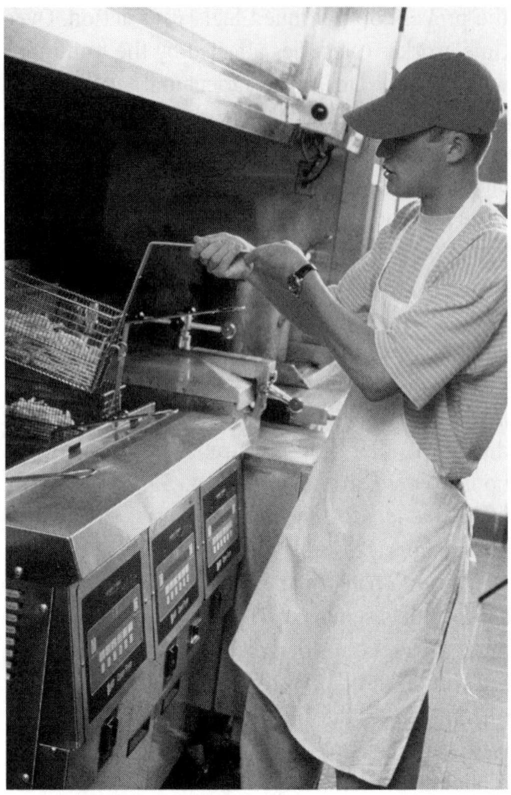

Measuring the effects of minimum wages on poverty in the United States has been complicated because most studies focus on teens who earn minimum wage, like this fast food worker, and not on poor families or low-wage work patterns. (Ariel Skelley/Corbis)

sis, however, by Brown, Gilroy, and Kohen in 1983 indicated that a 1 percent disemployment rate was most supportable by the data (Brown 1996, 88). Proponents of this model usually contend that the standard model is always correct and that increases in the minimum wage will always result in employment reductions (Card and Krueger 1995, 383; Deere, Murphy, and Welch 1996, 26). Critics suggest that the model is incomplete and that data do not support a level of disemployment sufficiently significant to impact the low-wage labor market, but rather a level so statistically insignificant as to render no effect. Critics of the standard model as it is commonly implemented also charge that traditional time-series studies focus too narrowly on teenage workers, who constitute only one-third of the 5 percent of workers earning the minimum wage (Card and Krueger 1995, 3). At the same time, critics also reinforce the standard model by acknowledging that it would be accurate if the minimum wage were increased too precipitously.

Proponents of the other perspective, identified as social economics revisionism, conduct empirical studies or natural experiments combined with inductive reasoning. These studies, the best known of which was administered in 1995 by David Card and Alan B. Krueger and focused on New Jersey and Pennsylvania fast food workers, advanced analyses that demonstrated no statistically definable disemployment rate but instead a slight (but also statistically negligible) increase in employment due to minimum wage increases. It is important to note that the intent of revisionists is to empirically test the validity of theoretical models and time-series data. Another aspect of this debate is to reframe the discussion regarding the minimum wage from teen labor to focus more on adult minimum wage earners and the effects that minimum wage increases have on poverty (Carrington and Fallick 2001; Neumark and Wascher 2002). These studies have addressed questions about the effectiveness of the minimum wage as a poverty policy and raise concerns about the ability to recognize its effectiveness, if teen workers rather than adults are primarily examined (Sobel 1999, 773).

Poverty is an integral component of the current minimum wage debate, as scholars analyze the demographics of the low-wage workforce and the ways in which a minimum wage influences conditions for low-wage workers. The positions expressed by the neoclassicists and revisionists represent the opposing poles of the debate. The first is associated with free market advocates who contend that a governmentally imposed wage floor inhibits the economy by interfering with the free exchange of labor and should, therefore, be repealed. On the other side are individuals who see the minimum wage as a tool for reducing poverty, with government as a needed oversight agent. Both sides view the minimum wage as a $5.5 billion cash transfer program (one that does not raise taxes), but they differ greatly on their analyses of the efficiency of that cash transfer. David Neumark and Williams Wascher argue that the disemployment associated with minimum wage increases "could result in net income losses for poor families" and reduce other previously nonpoor families to poverty, even as the income levels of poor families still below the poverty level increase (Neumark and Wascher 2002, 332). By extension, if no benefit can be established, then there would appear to be no justification for legislating minimum wages.

Measuring the effects of minimum wages on poverty is complicated in part because studies have had a tendency to focus on teens and not poor families or low-wage work patterns. That tendency appears to be changing. In an effort to determine if "long-term minimum wage employment is rare," as was presumed, William J. Carrington and Bruce C. Fallick found that "more than 8 percent of workers spend at least 50 percent of their first 10 years in jobs paying minimum wage plus $1.00" (2001, 17). In addition, they contend that a "nontrivial fraction" of adults are minimum wage or near minimum wage workers. They found that 2.5 percent of adult workers earned the minimum wage plus twenty-five cents and that 8 percent of adults earned just $1.00 above the minimum wage, even during the midlife years when earnings usually peak (Carrington and Fallick 2001, 18).

Although studies provide conflicting data regarding the changes in poverty levels associated with increases in the minimum wage, when polled, the American public has consistently and overwhelmingly supported increases to the minimum wage. Gender, ethnicity, and income do affect the magnitude of support for the minimum wage, but fully 89 percent of Americans supported the minimum wage increase in 1996. The lowest levels of support were expressed by individuals earning over $75,000 a year (62 percent), those identifying themselves as conservative (61 percent) or as Republicans (61 percent) (Waltman 2000, 52). Women, blacks, and Hispanics tend to offer stronger support for the minimum wage than do men, whites, and Asian Americans (Waltman 2000, 51). As a whole, the American public views the minimum wage as a way to relieve poverty and ensure fair compensation. At the same time, this support is passive—the public displays little initiative to prompt legislative action.

Politically, the minimum wage is controversial. Republicans (and business) tend to embrace the standard model, whereas the Democrats (and labor unions) are aligned with revisionist models, thus sharply polarizing the debates. In recent years, increases to the minimum wage have occurred in conjunction with election-year initiatives, as both parties tried to invigorate public involvement and garner votes. The increase in 1996 came only after intense efforts by some Senate Democrats and the American Federation of Labor and Congress of Industrial Organizations (AFL-CIO) to address the drop in real wages and buying power caused by inflation. The 1996 increase to $5.15 still represents a 30 percent decrease in actual value, when adjusted for inflation, from the 1968 minimum wage levels.

Currently, the minimum wage differs from other federal income-benefit programs because it is not indexed to allow for regular or consistent increases. Instead, all increases are implemented through congressional action. Three indexing options have been proposed for the minimum wage: (1) indexing the minimum wage to the inflation rate, (2) indexing the minimum wage to the Consumer Price Index (CPI), and (3) indexing the minimum wage to a percentile of the wage distribution (Card and Krueger 1995, 395). There has been no action toward indexing in part because there is no consensus for an indexing method. Economic and political controversies, coupled with a passive public, inhibit regular reviews of the minimum wage.

Sandra L. Dahlberg

See also Compensation; Equal Pay Act; Fair Labor Standards Act; Living Wage; Pay Equity; Prevailing Wage Laws; Unemployment Rate; Wage Gap; Welfare to Work; Work First

References and further reading

Brown, Charles C. 1996. "The Old Minimum-Wage Literature and Its Lesson for the New." Pp. 87–98 in *The Effects of the Minimum Wage on Employment*. Edited by Marvin H. Kosters. Washington, DC: American Enterprise Institute Press.

Brown, Charles, Curtis Gilroy, and Andrew Kohen. 1982. "The Effect of the Minimum Wage on Employment and Unemployment." *Journal of Economic Literature* 20: 487–528.

Card, David, and Alan B. Krueger. 1995. *Myth and Measurement: The New Economics of the Minimum Wage*. Princeton: Princeton University Press.

Carrington, William J., and Bruce C. Fallick. 2001. "Do Some Workers Have Minimum Wage Careers?" *Monthly Labor Review* (May): 17–27.

Deere, Donald R., Kevin M. Murphy, and Finis R. Welch. 1996. "Examining the Evidence on Minimum Wages and Employment." Pp. 26–54 in *The Effects of the Minimum Wage on Employment*. Edited by Marvin H. Kosters. Washington, DC: American Enterprise Institute Press.

Krueger, Alan B. 2001. "Teaching the Minimum Wage in Econ 101 in Light of the New Economics of the Minimum Wage." *Journal of Economic Education* 32, no. 3: 243–258.

Krumm, Ronald J. 1981. *The Impact of the Minimum Wage on Regional Labor Markets.* Washington, DC: American Enterprise Institute for Public Policy Research.
Levin-Waldman, Oren W. 2001. *The Case of the Minimum Wage: Competing Policy Models.* Albany: State University of New York Press.
Neumark, David, and William Wascher. 2002. "Do Minimum Wages Fight Poverty?" *Economic Inquiry* 40, no. 3: 315–333.
Sobel, Russell. 1999. "Theory and Evidence on the Political Economy of the Minimum Wage." *Journal of Political Economy* 107, no. 4: 761–785.
Waltman, Jerold. 2000. *The Politics of the Minimum Wage.* Urbana: University of Illinois Press.

Mommy Track

The term *mommy track* was coined in the late 1980s to describe the organizational phenomenon in which working women are shunted to lower-paying positions if they are anticipated or perceived to need flexible schedules in order to care for their families. This issue has been widely analyzed and discussed because of its implications for women, who are often the primary caregivers for children in American society. This perception prevents many women—even those who don't have children or who have made arrangements for child care—from reaching top company positions because employers fear that they will leave the workforce at some point to have children. Employers worry that they will lose their investment in such women, who may not return to the workforce or may do so only part-time. To avoid the expense of lost resources, companies pass over women for promotions and high-paying positions and disproportionately promote male workers, whom they perceive to be more committed to the workforce.

The debate began after publication of a controversial article in the *Harvard Business Review* in 1989. Felice Schwartz, president and founder of Catalyst, an organization that works to foster the career and leadership development of women, wrote in her article "Management Women and the New Facts of Life," that the cost of employing women in managerial positions is higher than that of employing men. But since global competition is increasing for managerial talent, firms need to search for and employ women in top positions or risk losing this competition. Then she argued that there are two types of women employees: career-primary and career-and-family. Career-primary women are willing to put their careers first and make the tradeoffs (such as spending less time with their children or hiring someone else to raise them) traditionally expected of men who seek leadership positions. Schwartz advised companies to recognize these women early and to remove any artificial barriers to their success in the firm. Career-and-family women, however, want to pursue careers but also want to participate actively in the care of their children. These women, she argued, are willing to trade some career growth and higher wages for flexible schedules, shorter hours, and freedom from working weekends.

The debate that followed this article was heated and continues today. Feminists charged Schwartz with reinforcing the idea that women must become like men to compete in the work world and that a women cannot have both a career and a family. Others argued that Schwartz's advice would encourage companies to reduce pay and withhold promotions in exchange for family-friendly practices like parental leave, flextime, and child care. Schwartz's rebuttal argued that the career path for career-and-family women was not a dead end but an alternative track for any committed professional who wanted to devote time to her family yet advance in her career.

The mommy track debate continues as more women enter the workforce. Nearly sixty percent of all U.S. women participated in the labor force in 2002 (Bureau of Labor Statistics 2003), and women comprise 46 percent of the labor force today (U.S. Department of Labor 2000). Opponents of the mommy track point to the lack of women in leadership positions (497 of Fortune 500 chief executive officers are male) to argue that women are still trapped in this dead-end track (Ezzard 2001). One study found that women with M.B.A.'s who took nine months or less off after the birth of a child were still earning 17 percent less ten years later than similarly qualified employees without such an employment gap (Kagan, Gall 1998).

At the same time, in response to the growing number of female workers and dual-earner families (60 percent of married couples were dual-career couples in 1995), many employers are offering flexible work arrangements (Catalyst 2001). More than 60 percent of Fortune 500 companies offer some kind of flexible options at work, including flextime, telecommuting, and job sharing (Schwartz 1999). As women are becoming more committed to the workforce, companies may increasingly find that these flexible arrangements are also sought by men who wish to devote time to their families.

Denise A. Pierson-Balik

See also Glass Ceiling; Pay Equity; Pink Collar; Steinem, Gloria; Women and Work

References and further reading

Bureau of Labor Statistics. 2003. "Employment Status of the Civilian Population by Age and Sex." http://www.bls.gov/news.release/empsit.to1.htm (cited June 9, 2003).

Catalyst. 2001. "Flexible Work Arrangements III: A Ten-Year Retrospective of Part-Time Arrangements for Managers and Professionals." http://www.catalystwomen.org (cited September 18, 2001).

Ezzard, Martha. 2001. "Get Off the Mommy Track." *Denver Post,* May 15, B-7.

Kagan, Jerome, and Susan B. Gall, eds. "The Mommy Track." 1998. In *Gale Encyclopedia of Childhood and Adolescence.* Detroit: Gale.

Schwartz, Felice N. 1989. "Management Women and the New Facts of Life." *Harvard Business Review* 67 (January–February): 65–76.

Schwartz, Tony. "While the Balance of Power Has Already Begun to Shift, Most Male CEOs Still Don't Fully Get It." http://www.fastcompany.com/online/30/tschwartz.html (cited September 18, 2001).

Shaw, William, and Vincent Barry. 1995. *Moral Issues in Business.* 6th ed. Belmont, CA: Wadsworth Publishing, 332–334.

Snell, M. B. 1990. "Careerus Interruptus." *New Perspectives Quarterly* 7 (Winter): 16–19.

U.S. Department of Labor, Women's Bureau. 2000. "Twenty Facts on Working Women." March. http://www.dol.gov/dol/wb/public/wb_pubs/20fact00.htm (cited September 17, 2001).

Mother Jones (1837?–1930)

Mother Jones was a union organizer and early activist in the vanguard of the U.S. labor movement. Her reform efforts were credited by the U.S. Department of Labor as ultimately leading to the abolition of child labor, acceptance of the eight-hour workday, and implementation of Social Security and the minimum wage. In 1992, she was inducted into the department's Labor Hall of Fame.

Born in Cork, Ireland, as Mary Harris, many details of Mother Jones's life are disputed, including her birth year, which is considered to be 1837 based on a parish baptismal notice. It is probable that the Great Famine propelled her father and then the rest of the family to emigrate to the United States. His work as a railway construction laborer took him to Canada, where Mary Harris received her educational preparation for teaching.

After an early stint of teaching in Monroe, Michigan, and then dressmaking in Chicago, she relocated to Memphis, Tennessee, where she met and married her husband. George Jones was a skilled foundry worker and member of the International Iron Moulders Union, an early trade organization. Most especially through her husband, Jones came to know the abuses of low wages, long hours, unsafe working conditions, and the ever-present threat of blacklisting for workers who complained. In 1867, yellow fever swept through Memphis, and Mary Harris Jones's husband and four young children succumbed to the epidemic. This personal tragedy changed the course of her life.

Widowed and alone, she returned to dressmaking for the wealthy in Chicago. The social inequities and class disparities that she observed weighed on her mind. When the Chicago Fire of 1871 struck, she lost all. Turning for assistance to the Knights of Labor, then the largest union in the country, she began attending their meetings and allied herself with efforts to alleviate the misery of working people. Free of the responsibilities of family and home, Mary Harris Jones found her calling and devoted her energies for some sixty years to visiting the coal mines, railroad yards, factories, and mills across the country. She observed conditions, raised funds, and exhorted collective action among workers to effect a political solution to their difficulties. Jones's petite appearance and demure attire in bonnets and lace-accessorized clothing belied the influence of her fiery oratory. That she was not intimidated by the threat of imprisonment or violence inspired the workers, who came to respect her and see her as a blend of stern matriarch and loving mother.

Jones is said to have stood with the railroad workers in Pittsburgh as they staged the first national strike in 1877. She traveled the country, educating laborers about the working-class movement; worked with Eugene V. Debs in the 1890s in organizing the Socialist Party; and built the readership of the leading political weekly newspaper *Appeal to Reason,* a vehicle used to expose the difficulties of workers. Using the moniker "Mother Jones," she also wrote for the influential *International Socialist Review.* Exposure to the mills of Cottondale and Tuscaloosa, Alabama, sensitized her to child labor abuses. She additionally organized Penn-

Mother Jones, meeting with President Calvin Coolidge, September 26, 1924 (Library of Congress)

sylvania miners and used a broom-and-mop brigade of striker's wives to rout potential strikebreakers. This ploy brought the attention of religious leaders, educators, and the press to the anthracite coal strikes of 1900 and 1902. When the Pennsylvania situation was settled, the bituminous coal regions of West Virginia were not part of the agreement. Mother Jones staged a strike there that the United Mine Workers did not support. Breaking with the union, Jones turned her attentions to the striking machinists of the Southern Pacific Railroad, the Western Federation of Miners' concerns about the closing of copper pits in Arizona, and she even raised funds for the legal defense of imprisoned Mexican revolutionaries who took refuge in the United States. In 1903, Jones led a march of striking textile mill children walking from Kensington, Pennsylvania, to the home of Theodore Roosevelt at Oyster Bay, New York. Although the marchers did not get to speak to the president, nevertheless the march itself brought national attention to the abuses of child labor and paved the way for federal legislation that limited child labor (1938) and finally outlawed it (1949).

Mother Jones's work in the West Virginia miners' strike of 1912–1913 turned violent, and after the state declared martial law, she was sentenced to a twenty-year term of imprisonment. Amid widespread national public censure, a state commission intervened and abrogated her sentence. By the end of the decade, nearly half of the mines in West Virginia were unionized, largely because of Jones's work. Another bitter dispute in which Mother Jones participated was the 1913–1915 strike against Rockefeller-controlled mines in Colorado. She was again imprisoned but was released through the intercession of Mexican revolutionary Pancho Villa who offered to exchange a prisoner requested by Woodrow Wilson in her stead. (A grateful Villa remembered Jones's earlier support of his fellow revolutionaries and her later discussion with Mexican president Francisco Madero about unionizing miners.) While Mother Jones gave testimony about the strike before the House Mines and Mining Committee, the Colorado militia killed twenty men, women, and children from the striker's tent colony. This extreme act assured national attention on the underlying issues of the strike, which was finally settled through federal mediation.

A charismatic speaker and self described "hell-raiser," Mother Jones had the intelligence, wit, energy, and even rage to motivate workers. Once dubbed "the most dangerous woman in America," she knew how to shape public opinion and make the country aware of the exploitation of its workers by industry. Her deep commitment to labor forged an identity for oppressed workers, lifted their morale, and mobilized them to improve their lot through unionization. As she requested, Mother Jones was buried upon her death in the Union Miners' Cemetery in Mount Olive, Illinois.

Janet Butler Munch

See also United Mine Workers of America

References and further reading

Gorn, Elliott J. 2002. *Mother Jones: The Most Dangerous Woman in America.* New York: Hill and Wang.

"Labor Hall of Fame." 1992. *Monthly Labor Review* 115, no. 11 (November): 2.

Mother Jones. 1990. *Autobiography of Mother Jones.* 4th ed. Chicago: Charles H. Kerr.

Steel, Edward M., ed. 1985. *The Correspondence of Mother Jones.* Pittsburgh: University of Pittsburgh Press.

———. 1988. *The Speeches and Writings of Mother Jones.* Pittsburgh: University of Pittsburgh Press.

Tonn, Mari Boor. 1996. "Militant Motherhood: Labor's Mary Harris 'Mother Jones.'" *Quarterly Journal of Speech* 82 (February): 1–21.

Wake, Dorothy. 2001. *Mother Jones: Revolutionary Leader of Labor and Social Reform.* Philadelphia: Xlibris Corp.